ETHNICITY, NATIONALISM AND CONFLICT IN AND AFTER THE SOVIET UNION

🏛 PRIO

International Peace Research Institute, Oslo
Fuglehauggata 11, N-0260 Oslo, Norway
Telephone: (47) 22 54 77 00
Telefax: (47) 22 54 77 01
Cable address: PEACERESEARCH OSLO
E-mail: info@prio.no

The International Peace Research Institute, Oslo (PRIO) is an independent international institute of peace and conflict research, founded in 1959. It is governed by an international Governing Board of seven individuals, and its main source of income is the Norwegian Research Council. The results of all PRIO research are available to the public.

PRIO's publications include the quarterlies *Journal of Peace Research* (1964–) and *Security Dialogue* (formerly *Bulletin of Peace Proposals*) (1969–) and a series of books.

The United Nations Research Institute for Social Development (UNRISD) is an autonomous agency engaging in multi-disciplinary research on the social dimensions of contemporary development problems. Its work is guided by the conviction that, for effective development policies to be formulated, an understanding of the social and political context is crucial. The Institute attempts to provide governments, development agencies, grassroots organisations and scholars with a better understanding of how development policies and processes of economic, social and environmental change affect different social groups. Working through an extensive network of national research centres, UNRISD aims to promote original research and strengthen research capacity in developing countries.

Its research themes include The Challenge of Rebuilding War-torn Societies; Integrating Gender into Development Policy; Environment, Sustainable Development and Social Change; Crisis, Adjustment and Social Change; Participation and Changes in Property Relations in Communist and Post-Communist Societies; Ethnic Conflict and Development; Political Violence and Social Movements; and Socio-Economic and Political Consequences of the International Trade in Illicit Drugs. UNRISD research projects focused on the 1995 World Summit for Social Development included Rethinking Social Development in the 1990s; Economic Restructuring and Social Policy; Ethnic Diversity and Public Policies; and Social Integration at the Grassroots: The Urban Dimension. A list of the Institute's free and priced publications can be obtained by writing: UNRISD, Reference Centre, Palais des Nations, CH-1211, Geneva 10, Switzerland.

ETHNICITY, NATIONALISM AND CONFLICT IN AND AFTER THE SOVIET UNION

The Mind Aflame

VALERY TISHKOV

International Peace Research Institute, Oslo

United Nations Research Institute for Social Development

SAGE Publications

London • Thousand Oaks • New Delhi

© United Nations Research Institute for Social Development, 1997

First published 1997

SAGE Publications Ltd
6 Bonhill Street
London EC2A 4PU

SAGE Publications Inc
2455 Teller Road
Thousand Oaks, CA 91320

SAGE Publications India Pvt Ltd
32, M-Block Market
Greater Kailash – I
New Delhi 110 048

British Library Cataloguing in Publication data

A catalogue record for this book is available from the British Library.

ISBN 0 7619 5184 9
      0 7619 5185 7 (pbk)

Library of Congress catalog record available

Typeset by M Rules
Printed in Great Britain by The Cromwell Press Ltd,
Broughton Gifford, Melksham, Wiltshire

Contents

Acknowledgements

Many people and institutions have been involved in making this study possible and in enabling this book to be published. The research staff of the Institute of Ethnology and Anthropology (IEA), Russian Academy of Sciences, shared with me their field experience and research results, of which, unfortunately, I was able to use only a tiny portion. Mikhail Guboglo and Leokadia Drobizheva let me include my questions and also use some results of the sociological surveys they carried out in the republics of Russia as a part of international research projects. Sergei Savoskul and Alla Ginzburg's sociological survey in Central Asia provided a main source for writing Chapter 6. Anatoly Yamskov, who assisted with preparing Chapters 4 and 5, was also a most useful reader of the manuscript. Sergei Sokolovsky and Abilabek Asankanov helped with preparing Chapter 7. Many other people provided advice and references. Several distinguished colleagues read or critiqued the manuscript, foremost among whom I wish to mention Ernest Gellner, Bohdan Nahajlo, Donald Horowitz, Gail Lapidus, Dan Smith and Rodolfo Stavenhagen. To all my colleagues I express my deep gratitude.

Local experts, politicians, and activists provided help and advice during my extensive travels to Armenia, Estonia, Georgia, Kazakhstan, Kirgizia and to republics of the Russian Federation: Bashkiria, Chechnya, Chuvashia, Kabardino-Balkaria, Kalmykia, North Ossetia, Tatarstan, Yakutia. The Network of Ethnological Monitoring and Early Warning (EAWARN), which I founded in 1993 as part of an international project on Management of Ethnic Conflicts in post-Soviet States, has since evolved into a mutually enriching dialogue of leading experts on ethno-political issues in their countries and regions. This book has also benefited from the insights of all these people.

The hardest task was to write the text in a language which is not my native tongue. Only Chapters 9 and 10 were translated professionally by Stephen and Ethel Dunn, and a shorter version of Chapter 6 was originally translated as a conference paper in a book edited by Yaacov Ro'i (1995). The rest is the result of my own writing in imperfect English, greatly improved by two language editors, Susan Høivik and Lynn Parker; the former, with her broad knowledge and competence, did more than language editing. Jan Tore Knutsen helped significantly at the final stage of organizing the text prior to publication.

Several institutions provided support for research and writing. The United Nations Research Institute for Social Development (UNRISD) initially contracted me for this study, expecting from me a sooner return but demonstrating patience and understanding with this late submission. A grant from the Harry Frank Guggenheim Foundation made possible my research on ethnic violence and conflict, especially enabling travels, the getting of materials and commissioning of assistance. Since 1994, I have enjoyed the privilege of being a part-time senior research consultant at the International Peace Research Institute, Oslo (PRIO), where I have been able to use its facilities and support for completing this monograph. Two earlier versions of Chapters 7 and 12 were published in PRIO's periodicals *Journal of Peace Research* (1995, vol. 32, no. 2) and *Security Dialogue* (1995, vol. 26, no. 1). A shorter version of Chapter 11 was published in *The*

New Europe's Nationalism edited by Richard Caplan and John Pfeffer (1996, London: Oxford University Press). Chapter 13 includes borrowings from *The Kona Statement* – a result of a meeting organized by the Project on Ethnic Relations when Donald Horowitz, William Pfaff, and myself provided main contributions for writing this report on conflict resolution.

To all these various institutions and individuals, I express my gratitude.

On the Use of Titles, Names, and Categories

Naming is a most important part of language discourse. Through naming, we convey a meaning and a message reflecting identification and the changing dispositions of power. Not by accident, the deep societal and geopolitical transformations of recent years have given rise to an unprecedented process of renaming, from the global to the local and even personal levels. Most of these renamings, especially the official titles of states, the names of capitals, and other changes crucial for legitimization and recognition, have already been included in international protocols, diplomatic instructions, maps and atlases, and the basic reference literature. But these titles and names are not a *fait accompli*. Time is needed to introduce a new vocabluary into the mass mentality, political jargon, and academic texts. Many definitions are still searching to become a precise reflection of new realities, undergoing the test of time and a process of selection. Some definitions are still to be subjected to ideological manipulation and in-fighting. This process is far from being over, and new names are still cropping up in post-Soviet political and cultural geography. The most recent change took place on the very day I wrote this introductory note: on 23 April 1996, the City Council of the western Ukrainian city of Lviv approved a proposal by the nationalist Ukrainian Assembly to rename a street after the Chechen leader Dzhokhar Dudayev. The street in question had previously been named after the Russian poet Mikhail Lermontov. Insofar as naming and labeling come as the result of someone's initiative and decision, I feel it appropriate to make my own choices as to terms and names in transition, and to provide my own explanations.

I have chosen not to use the term 'post-Soviet space', because to me it sounds like something vague, lacking structure or personification. Instead, I write of the *former Soviet Union* (FSU) as a more proper, albeit time-limited category. Obviously, this cannot be used in a more distant historical perspective, just as one cannot today rationally speak of the 'former Austro-Hungarian Empire' or the 'former Carolingian Empire'. I use this term to encompass all parts of what was the Soviet Union, including the Baltics, well aware that Baltic politicians and intellectuals are opposed to such usage. Interestingly, international protocol seems to have capitulated on this point and has excluded the Baltics as a category of the former Soviet Union's territory. Moreover, in 1992 the US State Department decided to avoid an official use of *the Commonwealth of Independent States (CIS)* as the title of an interstate coalition, thus implicitly questioning (or at least not assisting) the reintegration of post-Soviet states. Instead, *the Newly Independent States (NIS)* was suggested as an appropriate term. I also feel uncomfortable with this category, for a non-political reason: it simply does not fit the cultural and conflict areas which I cover in this book. For me a more appealing term could be *Eurasia* (all FSU but the Baltics), but unfortunately, I find myself among the few experts who see this term as promising and politically/culturally acceptable for labeling most of the territory of what used to be the Soviet Union.

Other verbal inventions have been invoked to grapple with new geopolitical realities, not all of which I find successful. For example, the term *near-abroad* has been widely used in the political and academic language of Russia. Actually, this phrase – *blizhnee zarubezhie* – emerged spontaneously, not through any politically motivated decree. Only more recently has it become laden with revenge ideology and reactive suspicions towards those who view the area around Russia as something different from what is usually understood as *abroad*. Another reason for not using this term is because of its contextual incorrectness (China and Norway are also *near-abroad* for Russia). It might be more precise to name this reality as *recent* or *new abroad*, but again (as in the case with FSU) this would be a short-lived category: how long can it continue to be called new?

Another problem involves how to categorize that part of the population of new states around Russia who are mainly non-titular Russian speakers. They are still called the Russian-speaking (*russkoyazychnoie*) population or ethnic Rossians (*etnicheskie rossiyane*), which I find inaccurate: after all, a considerable proportion of the titulars in new states are also Russian-speakers, while *Rossian* is a civic category perceived in citizenship terms. The less politically sensitive and more precise categories *new diaspora* and *new minorities* have been used here, despite my reservations concerning the use of a minority concept for post-Soviet states where many large, well-established ethnic communities do not fit this category and its axiological context. It is especially true of Russians in Estonia, Kazakhstan, Latvia, and Ukraine.

Concerning the new titles of some new states and internal autonomies, the easiest way could be to use the terms that have been officially constituted and internationally recognized. But there are at least two difficulties. First, much of narration and empirical data goes back to the time before the change took place; thus, it is ahistorical to write of *Turkmenia* as *Turkmenistan,* when such a name never existed. It is like writing a history of Bessarabia before World War II and calling it Moldavia or Moldova. Second, some renamings have not been linguistically and politically successful enterprises; they are still not accepted by those on behalf of whom renamings were done. In this situation, I have decided to exercise the prerogative to make my own choices. Thus, I have opted for the old spelling in a few cases – for Belorussia, Kirgizia, Moldavia, and Turkmenia. This book is not the text of a diplomatic document, and I prefer to reflect the ongoing terminological process in a way closer to the everyday language of the lay public and politicians. And, as I am informed, some new titles are in use exclusively among the elite; in some states a big split exists on this issue. For instance, most intellectuals and ordinary people keep the title *Kirgizia* and the name *Kirgiz,* in explicit opposition to less-modernized nationalists who managed to impose a more 'correct' spelling with the wave of radical changes that came in the early 1990s. Moreover, some changes were against established Russian linguistic norms; for many Russian speakers in the new states it is difficult to adjust to such new language. On the other hand, I am sure that some changes are irreversible, needing only time to become rooted in mass mentality and language. *Moldova* and *Belarus* are words that sound better in native languages and are also fully acceptable in Russian as well. *Turkmenistan* and *Kyrgyzstan* may gain wide use from continuing political and intellectual efforts, or perhaps a compromise version like *Kirgizstan* will establish itself in the end.

One remarkable example of a speedy shift to a new title is the case of *Tataria,* when intensive public debates on the sovereignty issue brought wide circulation of the new name for this republic: *Tatarstan.* That is why this term is used here, but at the same time I have preferred to keep *Bashkiria* (rather than *Bashkortostan*), because the ethnic elite of this republic replaced the old title with one that sounds quite awkward in Russian – the language spoken by the overwhelming majority of the population there. The same argument could be cited for using Tuva (not *Tyva*), Mari (not *Mari-El)*, and Yakutia (not *Sakha*) as names of republics.

At the same time, I have wished to introduce a linguistic neologism of major significance: a more correct spelling of the title of the state *Russia* as *Rossia*. Despite the long tradition of writing the word with 'u', as for the ethnic term 'Russian', it has always been a reason for profound distortion that these two words are perceived as deriving from the same stem. In reality, two distinct words exist in the Russian language: one is *Rossia* as the name of a state, the other is *russkii* (Russian) as the name of the people, their language and culture. This ambigious language use has caused – and is still causing – widespread misperceptions and wrong meanings. For the outside world, ethnic non-Russians from Rossia may be termed *Russians* – however, they do not identify themselves as such, but rather as *Rossians (rossiyane)*. Calling the federal troops in Chechnya the *Russian* army or *Russian* military, or just *Russians*, involves direct ethnic projections – in fact, there are many different nationalities among the military recruits. The *Russian* general Lev Rokhlin who destroyed Grozny could just as well have been a Jew as an ethnic Russian. This is a sensitive issue because when the expression *Russian fascism* (that is, fascism in Russia) is translated as *russkii fascism,* it is strongly rejected by ethnic Russians – even though they may provide the main source for ultra-rightists in this country. Thus, the term *Rossia* is used in this book starting with Chapter 12, where I deal specifically with this issue as being one of more precise spelling, not a change in Russian writing per se. This spelling is then used for all derivatives (*Rossian Federation, authorities, army, mafia,* etc.), except of course for direct quotations from English.

Ethnic categories and names (ethnonyms) may be the subject of endless debates, including those motivated by recent political transformations and by changing academic perceptions. I prefer to use internationally accepted terminology within the discipline of social and cultural anthropology. The basic category of *ethnic group* is used irrespective of status and size of ethno-cultural entities which have already undergone scholastic and ideological taxonomy in Soviet and post-Soviet political and academic language. My sole concession to Soviet legacies concerns the term *nationalities* (in the plural) as equal to *ethnic groups*, as this has found wide use in everyday language as well as in scholarly texts, including Western literature on this part of the world. The term *nationalities* provides me with a legitimate basis for using political categories like *nationalities policy* or *nationalities issues*. I avoid using the terms *national question* or *national policy* primarily because I am trying to dismantle, from the academic and official language, the term *nation* as an ethnic category, as an ethnonation.

All ethnic names have here been put in their contemporary widely used spellings (in tables in the singular) despite naive rhetoric and efforts to return to 'real', 'authentic' names, rather than those imposed by 'outsiders': anthropologists know that most names are in fact exoethnonyms. In a few cases the process of group retitling may yield unexpected results for the initiators. If the shift from *Yakut* to *Sakha* succeeds as name of the people, while the republic keeps its previous title Yakutia, this will bring a certain dissociation between ethnic group and territory. This may be useful for building a civic society, but will surely not be welcomed by those who initiated this change. Meanwhile, I encourage naming multi-ethnic political entities with titles not fully coinciding with the name of the dominant group. This can provide a chance for constructing a common name for all people living in and loyal to a state, as distinct from ethnic labels. Thus, we may speak of Rossia with Rossians and Russians, Kazakhstan with Kazakhstani and Kazakhs, Moldova with Moldovs (*moldovzy*) and Moldavians, Latvia with Latvians (*latviitzy*) and Letts or Latviesh, etc. The first two cases already exist in practice; the last two are as yet more hypothetical. And this only serves to illustrate a primary characteristic of language: its innate flexibility.

INTRODUCTION
THE FEEL OF THE GAME

Dubrovnik, Yugoslavia, June 1991. It was to be the last peaceful summer for this ancient Adriatic city and for the country as a whole. None of the experts, not even the local ones, who were gathered at the International Working Seminar on Ethnic Conflict and Development organized by the United Nations Research Institute for Social Development (UNRISD) could have predicted the dawn of ethnic war and destruction. Nevertheless, among the specialists at the seminar there was serious concern about the growing challenge of extreme ethnonationalism and ethnic conflicts, not least in former Communist countries. On the basis of this growing anxiety, it was agreed that a series of monographs on ethnic conflict should be prepared. I was assigned the task of writing a book on the Soviet Union. Who could have predicted that this country had only a few months left to exist! The challenging research agenda agreed upon in Dubrovnik was to provide a rare opportunity to study complex social phenomena as they unfolded.

It is no easy task to analyze volatile and uncertain social realities from a contemporary vantage point. The method of 'participant observation' embraced by social anthropologists can prove to be a fragile foundation for analysis – especially if the author happens to be in the midst of events and also carries a position of political responsibility influencing the course of those events. This was the case when I served as Minister of Nationalities in the Government of the Russian Federation from February to October 1992. Even after that time I remained involved in policy-making, inter alia, participating in the first round of negotiations with the Chechens in December 1994, and contributing to the search for a way out of this conflict in spring 1996 as a member of the Chernomyrdin Commission on Chechnya. These political assignments served to enrich my general knowledge and deepen my understanding of ethnic conflict.

Rodolfo Stavenhagen, coordinator of the project on Ethnic Conflict and Development, asked me in Dubrovnik what type of methodology I planned to apply in my study. 'Methodological individualism,' was my reply. The complexity of the subject invites the use of an interdisciplinary approach. Moreover, for a post-Soviet scholar who has been through the period of prescribed Marxist–Leninist methodology, it is only natural to want to avoid a rigid determinism and a positivistic belief in the ability of 'scientific knowledge' to adequately reflect 'social realities' and 'manage society'.

In this book I do not subscribe to one single exclusive concept or cultural theory. To be sure, some sets of ideas have influenced my thinking more than others. The subtitle 'The Mind Aflame' was inspired by Russian literary theorist and philosopher Mikhail Bakhtin, with his emphasis on the 'dialogue' or a 'discourse' between 'mentalities' and 'realities', and between 'the sacred' and 'the profane' in culture. A further influence has been the French philosopher Pierre Bourdieu, who writes:

> Constructing the notion of habitus as a system of acquired dispositions functioning on the practical level as categories of perception and assessment or as classificatory principles as well as being the organizing principles of action meant constituting the social

agent in his true role as the practical operator of the construction of the objects (Bourdieu, 1990, p. 13).

What this formulation means is that in societies individuals (or social agents) are not 'automatically regulated like clocks, in accordance with laws which they do not understand' (Bourdieu, 1990, p. 9). There also exists what Bourdieu calls a 'feel of the game', enabling an infinite number of 'moves' adapted to the infinite number of possible situations which no rule can ever foresee.

Bourdieu's emphasis on the creative and innovative capacity for acting agents to behave according to their position in social space, as well as the mental structures through which they perceive this space, can help us to understand both individual and collective strategies in post-Soviet societies. Guided by the feel of the game, both leaders and the rank-and-file act in ways that may appear rational, yet their actions are not based on reason alone. Many actions are based on impulse because 'conditions of rational calculation are rarely given in practice: time is limited, information is restricted, etc.'. And yet, continues Bourdieu, agents do perform expected actions ('the only thing to do') much more often than would be the case if they were acting randomly. He goes on to explain that 'this is because, following the intuitions of a "logic of practice" which is the product of a lasting exposure to conditions similar to those in which they are placed, they anticipate the necessity immanent in the way of the world' (Bourdieu, 1990, p. 11).

Let us take an example that illustrates the relevance of this theory for my study. Many partial and impartial observers have produced seemingly rational interpretations of the causes of the Chechen War; but I remember my first encounter with the rebel leaders with whom we negotiated on 12–14 December 1994. Routine polite inquiries such as 'How are you?', or to translate the Russian literally, 'How is your mood?' were asked. 'Our mood is a revolutionary one', and 'We had been taught these things for a long period of time'[1] were the replies of Teimaz Abubakarov, head of Dudayev's delegation. Similar statements, repeated many times later, are examples of the mental structures through which the Chechen leaders viewed the situation. What kind of private strategy would Chechen Minister of Oil and Finance Teimaz Abubakarov have pursued if he had just returned from a trip to Western Europe? This is also a question for analysis. But the revolutionary mood, whether rational or irrational, of the activists in social space served as a powerful element in constructing the mentality of the Chechens.

Representing the opposition, President Boris Yeltsin, who is widely thought to possess 'great political intuition', acted impulsively and showed little control when he decided to wage war in Chechnya. His advisers had assured him that it was impossible to reach an agreement with Dudayev, and that this rebel leader would bring humiliation to the President of Russia: 'it was improper for the President to talk with Dudayev; now, it is possible', as Yeltsin publicly explained his decision to meet a new Chechen leader Yandarbiev (after Dudayev's death) on 27 May 1996). I myself feel quite sure that if Yeltsin had called Dudayev and invited him to the Kremlin for a talk, the war could have been prevented. Rationalizations about the 'only thing to do' came later for Yeltsin. These rationalizations were concocted by his associates who were assigned to write reports on the issue for the Russian Parliament and the Constitutional Court. Thus, the Chechen conflict cannot be explained solely by the materialistic theory of 'reflection'. 'Active subjectivity' is equally important to the explanatory model.

Such an approach differs radically from those of Soviet and post-Soviet social science research as well as public mentality. A monistic ideology and a totalitarian way of thinking presupposed the existence of a formula for 'the scientific management of society'. Society was viewed as a system governed by primordial (historical) laws. Those who held positions of power – members of the Party, the state *nomenklatura,* and the intellectual propagandists – were given their mandate under the assumption that they held the knowledge for predicting the future pattern of social development. The ruling elite received prescriptions from scholars who were supposedly able to penetrate and reflect on the 'objective realities', mainly because they were equipped with the 'right scientific teaching' – that is, the theory of Marxism-Leninism. This also included an important ingredient called 'the Marxist-Leninist theory of nation and the national question', which has already been reviewed by such influential critics as Walker Connor (1984) and Ernest Gellner (1988).

Although the old system and its ideology have collapsed, the old mentality and patterns of behavior of ordinary people as well as the professional producers of 'scientific knowledge' remain basically unchanged. This mentality has produced an intolerance toward vicissitudes in politics and in the academic community. This can be demonstrated by preserving 'hostility towards deviation from approved theory' (Plotkin, 1990, p. 7), even though the theory itself has been challenged to the point of collapse.

Along with the repressive party-state apparatus, one important power factor for the high priests of the Communist Party was their role in formulating programmatic postulates and then passing them down through the ranks. The same basis of prestige was enjoyed by Soviet social scientists who supplied the ideology which legitimized the System. With regard to the 'national question', this was the exclusive preserve of theoreticians of the Party's Central Committees, who were occasionally consulted by Moscow-based academics. Innovations in theory and terminology were 'worked out', 'matched by practice' and 'implemented' through propaganda. The concept of 'ethnic conflict' was not allowed in official discourse; it was euphemized into 'contradictions', 'difficulties', or the like.

Little has changed in the methodological horizons of academics and in the minds of policy practitioners in Russia. A search for the causes of disorders, crises, and conflicts continued to be pursued in the absence of a 'scientific concept' and of a 'correct nationalities policy'. At Mikhail Gorbachev's request, a decision was made at the February 1991 session of the USSR Supreme Soviet to develop a 'general concept of the mechanisms for overcoming inter-ethnic conflicts'. Later, the Council of Nationalities of Russia's Supreme Soviet approved a State Program of National Rebirth for the Peoples of Russia. On 30 July 1992, I initiated Cabinet discussions on a document entitled 'The Concept of Nationalities Policy in the Russian Federation', in response to public demands, as well as because of a desire to strengthen my own political position and the status of the Ministry of Nationalities.[2] Three years later, in May 1995, I was invited to a government meeting to comment on a draft law on national-cultural autonomy. Interestingly, I could now hear similar arguments put forth by my former colleagues who were also calling for a 'unified concept of nationalities policy before the approval of any draft laws'.[3] Finally, on 11 April 1996, a new document – a White Paper – was approved by the federal government. Acting Minister of Nationalities Vyacheslav Mikhailov, with whom I personally spent several late evenings formulating the final text, was very proud of this accomplishment. For the public the concept was presented as a major political event.

It is important to realize that when a society is accustomed to a one-dimensional symbolic system, it cannot become a multidimensional space over night. It is difficult for such a society to abandon the absolutism surrounding political power, state institutions and academic formulae. Submissive belief in the formulae supplied by intellectual and political elites has become almost a generic characteristic of the Soviet people.

In a situation of radical societal transformation, such terminology and labels as 'ethnos', 'nation', 'self-determination', 'sovereignty' and the like can become powerful political instruments. The function of producing and explaining 'the symbolic' is assigned to literary writers, historians, and artists, as well as to professionals – be they film-makers, mass-media barons, or indeed leaders of ethnic movements. To achieve recognition and a mandate to exercise power, they employ a language which may carry a special meaning for a group and can re-animate mythical arguments. This may be a reaction to past traumas or glories experienced by previous generations, or an expectation to meet contemporary challenges with appealing political promises. Totalitarian inertia has facil-itated the replacement of a tyranny of party programs by a no less rigid tyranny of group thinking and myths. Although Russia has been liberated from Communist rule, a new form of dictatorship is evolving. Today, no single Armenian can oppose a policy of the Karabakh movement, and no single Ingush can stand against unification of the foothill region of North Ossetia within the Ingush Republic. The late Georgian philosopher Merab Mamardashvili was unique in his disapproval of the mass euphoria which brought to power the ultra-nationalist leader Zviad Gamsakhurdia in 1991. Mamardashvili clearly rejected this special brand of totalitarian collective thinking as shown in his state-ment: 'For the truth's sake I will go against my own people.'

Another striking feature of post-Soviet societies is the disproportionately high presence and extremely influential role of intellectual elites in positions previously held by the now demoralized and ousted old guard. A struggle for power by means of knowledge has become a sign of post-Communism. The old system may have crumbled, but the knowl-edge and dogmas of social scientists as well as the presentation skills of other intellectuals have remained in demand. This gave them the opportunity to achieve political mobiliza-tion. The horrendous devastation caused by the conflicts in Nagorno Karabakh, South and North Ossetia, Abkhazia, Moldavia, as well as through the Chechen War, should compel politically active intellectuals to assume responsibility for the situation. With the collapse of the USSR, new leaders who had previously staged admirable Shakespearean tragedies and held academic battles with the written word are now find-ing it all too simple to arm their subjects, issue orders to kill, and fight wars with sophisticated weapons, left behind in poorly controlled military arsenals.

In this situation of over-educated and emotionally overloaded societies, the struggle for knowledge as a shared belief and for prescribed conceptual terms gets combined and abused to produce mass violence and vast destruction. Through the use of designated ideas, damage has been inflicted upon the very people on whose behalf the national leaders pretend to speak. The President of Armenia, Levon Ter-Petrosyan, a former pro-fessor of social science and a leader of the Karabakh movement, has stated: 'the right of a nation to self-determination is an absolute. . . . Once people have decided to take their fate into their own hands, no one can reverse this process, except by force' (*Komsomol'skaya pravda*, 6 June 1991). Such a thesis lacks any scientific foundation, but is nevertheless pronounced as an official prescription for a society that enjoys the world's highest education level and currently finds itself in a state of political exaltation.

Throughout the former Soviet Union, leaders, ethnic activists, journalists and intel-lectuals alike make abundant use of strikingly similar declarations. Galina Starovoitova, who is considered to be an authority on ethnic issues and was an adviser to President Yeltsin on nationalities issues in 1991–92, reported her recent research findings on nine or ten stages through which every struggle for self-determination in its secessionist form is destined to proceed, up to open war. Accused of provocative statements and actions during the escalation of Nagorno Karabakh and other ongoing conflicts, she defended herself with the naïve argument, 'Can anybody believe that the people are just waiting for some stupid woman to prompt them about how to exterminate their children in a war in a more rapid way?' (Starovoitova, 1994, p. 5). In this self-defensive reflection we can read implicit recognition of the major role which elitist prescription and provocation as social phenomena are playing in ethno-politics today.

This is not to say that I condemn political participation by social scientists, or the recruitment of academics to government and ethnic movements. I do not even doubt the sincerity and good intentions of those who have acquired power. Nor do I question the usefulness and perhaps even necessity of such a course of action. My evaluation of their activity is not a criticism of individuals, who in most cases deserve respect and sympathy; the fate of present-day intellectuals in ethnic politics is often dramatic and tragic. This book is, however, intended inter alia as a critical analysis of the overly exclusive role played by post-Soviet intellectuals and political actors who are overloaded with the legacy of obsolete knowledge and who frequently lack the ability of self-reflection.

If my politically active colleagues were not so burdened with the Marxist tendency to stress ontological substance – that is, on 'real' groups, including ethnic groups, and their membership, boundaries, rights, and so forth – to the detriment of relationships in social space and private strategies, they might rid themselves of the intellectual illusion of viewing theoretically and politically constructed definitions and classifications as if they were groups of people acting in real life, or laws of social evolution. They could then display greater sensitivity and understanding in research and politics, and would not be in such a hurry to translate the symbolic struggle into the language of state decrees, administrative borders, or military orders.

A deeper understanding of how social experience and historical data combine to produce a personal and collective version of the 'ideal present' would prevent adherence to the simplistic Wilson-cum-Lenin formula of self-determination in its narrowest ethnic variant. There would be less of a basis for conclusions such as, 'after the conflicts in Yugoslavia, Czechoslovakia, South Ossetia, Nagorno Karabakh, and the Trans-Dniestria area: in the 21st century this problem of self-determination will arise in its full magnitude for the people of Africa, where postcolonial boundaries have artificially divided ethnic territories' (see the dialogue between Starovoitova and Kedrov in *Izvestia*, 10 August 1992). Moreover, experts and politicians may begin to share the opinion that 'in the world system as it has been formed, formulae of sovereignty dating from the time of Suarez, Bodin, or even Rousseau are simply absurd. . . . It is primarily the elites of the new political formations that determine themselves and redetermine each other' (Filippov, 1992, p. 112).[4] It is necessary for the scholar-turned-politician who acts within the sphere of everyday dogmatism and drama to distinguish between mythopoetic rhetoric and real interests. To sound a personal note here: I submitted my letter of resignation to President Boris Yeltsin after I experienced this drama. And that gave me the chance to complete this study for the reader.

Notes

1   Personal notes, 12 December 1994, Vladikavkaz, North Ossetia.

2   This document was not made public, but all major ideas and recommendations were elaborated later in several publications. (See, e.g., Tishkov, ed. 1993; Tishkov, 1994b.)

3   Personal notes from the meeting of the Government of the Russian Federation, 11 May 1995, Moscow.

4   Strong support for this oberservation has come recently from an expert on post-Soviet studies, Rogers Brubaker. He refers to a theory on 'new institutionalism' (also built partly on Bourdieu's ideas), and concludes that 'Soviet and post-Soviet "national struggles" were and are not the struggles of nations, but the struggles of institutionally constituted national elites – that is elites institutionally defined *as national* – and aspiring counter-elites' (Brubaker, 1994, p. 48).

PART ONE
GENERAL APPROACHES AND ISSUES

1

Ethnicity in the Soviet and Post-Soviet Context

1.1 The Power of Primordialism

The Russian social science tradition, especially with respect to interpreting ethnicity, is heavily dominated by the primordial approach. Its adherents see ethnicity as an objective 'given', a sort of primordial characteristic of humanity. For primordialists there exist objective entities with inherent features such as territory, language, recognizable membership, and even a common mentality. In its extreme form, this approach sees ethnicity in sociobiological categories as a 'comprehensive form of natural selection and kinship connections', as a primordial instinctive impulse (Van den Berghe, 1981). Some hold that a recognition of group affiliation is included in the genetic code and is the product of early human evolution, when an ability to recognize the members of one's family group was necessary for survival (Shaw & Wong, 1989).

The term 'primordialism' was coined by Shils (1957) and further developed by Geertz, who explained it as follows:

> By primordial attachment is meant one that stems from the 'givens' – or, more precisely, as culture is inevitably involved in such matters, the assumed 'givens' – of social existence: immediate contiguity and kin connection mainly, but beyond them the givenness that stems from being born into a particular religious community, speaking a particular language, or even a dialect of a language, and following particular social practices. These congruities of blood, speech, custom and so on, are seen to have an ineffable, and at times overpowering coerciveness in and of themselves (Geertz, 1973, p. 259).

Primordialism has received severe criticism. For instance: 'primordialism presents us with a picture of underived and socially-unconstructed emotions that are unanalyzable, overpowering and coercive yet varying. A more unintelligible and unsociological concept would be hard to imagine. Furthermore, a variety of sources from sociology, anthropology, and psychology have emerged in recent years which render the concept theoretically vacuous and empirically indefensible' (Eller & Coughlan, 1993, p. 187).

Today, primordialism has been definitively discarded in the West – but not in post-Soviet social science. The Russian tradition of interpretation of ethnicity stems from 19th-century ethnography, with its emphasis on the Russian 'folk' (*narod*). Slavophile romanticism and pro-Western self-criticism have since competed to discover the 'true features' of the peasantry (see Balzer, 1995; Greenfeld, 1992; Slezkine, 1994b). Many earlier texts have reemerged during the post-perestroika publishing renaissance, and the painful search for new identities. These texts strengthened rather than challenged the dominating theories. In the 1920s Sergei Shirokogorov used ethnographic materials on the Tungus peoples of Siberia to help formulate a general model and 'classification of ethnoses'. According to Shirokogorov, various elements of the 'ethnographic complex' exist and develop unequally, with some mutual dependence and ties 'which are impossible to destroy and the magnitude of which could be changed only with the retention of balance and buoyancy' (1922, p. 8). In order to exist, people attempt to maintain such a balance, which can be reached only when some elements develop at the expense of other, weaker ones. As an example of this 'law of balance', Shirokogorov cited the USA (he considered the US population to be an 'American ethnos') which 'exhibits immense development of technology, but an embryonic state in the arts of painting, music, literature, etc.' (1922, p. 21).

Shirokogorov proposed the following definition of ethnos: 'a group of people, speaking the same language, who recognize their shared heritage, and have a shared complex of social mores, mode of life, retained and sanctified traditions which differentiate them from other groups' (1922, p. 4). This definition is notable in many respects. It provides an early sociobiological view of ethnos that does see it exclusively as a biological class – an analogue, perhaps, to classification in zoology. In his *Ethnos*, Shirokogorov writes that 'for ethnos any form of existence is acceptable if it sustains its being, that is the goal of its life as a species. The more complex the organization and the higher the form of specialized adaptation, the shorter the existence of the species (that is of the ethnos); the less developed ethnoses survive longer' (1923, pp. 100, 118-119).

So superficial were these observations that even though his book was published in French (Shirokogorov emigrated to China) it was largely ignored in ethnological circles, which were dominated by British and North American evolutionists. However, Shirokogorov's constructions were to find a following in post-Stalinist Soviet ethnography. Two well-known scholars, Lev Gumilev and Yulian Bromley, together with an army of domestic experts from 1960 to throughout the 1980s, made major contributions to what was called the 'Soviet theory of ethnos', and which has remained a dominant theoretical paradigm for the study of ethnicity in Russia. Lev Gumilev – whose writings are compelling in their literary form, problematic approaches, and factual material – has gained enormous popularity, especially in recent years. To the Russian people, Gumilev's name is shrouded in the nimbus surrounding his parents, the two great Russian poets Anna Akhmatova and Nikolai Gumilev. Gumilev's personal life included incarceration in Stalinist camps and a ban on the publication of some of his highly controversial works until the late 1980s.[1] Before he died in 1992, his last two monographs on the geography of ethnos and ethnogenesis became bestsellers when they were finally published in 1989 and 1990 in the former Soviet Union. Although these texts are basically polemics against official academic scholarship, they nevertheless revive and strengthen the existing primordialist treatment of ethnicity.

For Gumilev, 'ethnos' is a form of existence for *Homo sapiens* as a species (a complete repetition of Shirokogorov), but it is also something greater – 'a phenomenon on the border of biosphere and sociosphere which has a highly special function in the formation of the biospheres of the earth' (1989, p. 24). Gumilev uncritically included in his category of ethnos practically all historically known cultural, political, religious and other formations, groupings and polities, dividing them into categories of 'super-ethnos', 'ethnos', 'sub-ethnos', 'ethnic relicts', etc. Depending on landscape, energy resources, and particularly internal 'passionarism', ethnoses as described by Gumilev live their own lives (of about 1200–1500 years) passing through the various stages or 'phases' of ethnogenesis, rise, breakdown, inertia, and finally death.

Gumilev's works are ridden with construed pseudo-scholarly terms and categories which could never be placed in any disciplinary discourse or tested seriously. And yet, there were no serious criticisms of Gumilev's works in Russian literature, apart from a handful of articles written by Bromley and Kozlov (1989) and by Kozlov (1990). Nor – strangely enough – has any Western expert on Russian ethnology and anthropology ever undertaken a critical review of Gumilev's writings.

At the same time it would be wrong not to acknowledge certain positive aspects of Gumilev's work, the same aspects that explain his popularity among non-Russian audiences in particular. He was one of few to draw attention to previously ignored factual materials regarding the role of other cultures and peoples in Russia's past, as well as mutually enriching cultural interactions and cooperation. This represented a step away from the traditional myth of a national history full of 'invaders', 'the yoke', 'patriotic wars' and other clichés of official Russo-centric Soviet historiography. Thus, Gumilev's popularity is a kind of 'logical backlash that whatever was outlawed by the Soviets must be worth reading' (Balzer's note to Tishkov, 1994–95, p. 91). And this can probably explain why Western experts motivated by political correctness also spare this author from any serious criticism.

Academician Yulian Bromley – the second well-known influential author – was another established authority in Soviet ethnic studies whose works were central in practically all research texts of the 1970s and 1980s. Former Director of the Institute of Ethnography, USSR Academy of Sciences, Bromley has published a series of standard monographs (1973, 1981, 1983, 1987), largely theoretical in character, which greatly influenced generations of Soviet social scientists. For Bromley, 'ethnos is a historically stable entity of people developed on a certain territory and possessing common, relatively stable features of culture (including language) and psyche as well as a consciousness of their unity and of their difference from other similar entities (self-awareness) fixed in a self-name (ethnonym)' (1981, p. 27).

This definition does not differ significantly from that given in 1922 by Shirokogorov, being based primarily on the assumption that ethnoses are ancient, self-contained bodies making their own journey through history. In this case, ethnicity is natural, innate and inescapable: 'ethnos' as an 'ethno-social organism, ESO' is the basic category and archetype, with its highest manifestation expressed through being a nation. A special taxonomy of ethnoses was invented, including a notion of 'ethnikos' or 'ethnos in its narrow sense' – meaning all people of the same ethnic origin. For example, Ukrainians in the Ukraine, or Tatars in the Tatarstan republic, or Armenians in Armenia were ESO; but Ukrainians, Tatars or Armenians in Moscow, Georgia – or in the USA or Canada – were members of 'ethnikoses'. Even people of the same ethnicity living in neighboring villages, but divided by administrative borders, were thereby assumed to belong to different types of ethnic entities.

Despite its greater sensitivity towards aspects of identity and self-awareness, Bromley's ethnos theory was mainly based on such key factors as exclusive group membership and status reflected in titular statehoods granted to the major non-Russian nationalities in the Soviet Union. Those who had their 'own' union or autonomous republics were considered 'socialist nations', the highest type of ethnos. Those with a lower status of administrative autonomy (like the Northern indigenous peoples), or who did not have any status at all (like Volga Germans, Gagauz, Poles, Jews, and others) were dismissed as *narodnost* – an untranslatable term indicating something between a tribe and a nation – not even *ethnikoses,* because many of them did not have their own 'ESO'. Thus, according to Bromley and his followers, 'nation' is not an ethnic group with a titular statehood – it is exclusively that part of the group which resides on its 'own' national territory. To more adequately address Soviet realities and ideological innovation on a 'new entity of people – the Soviet people' (*sovetskii narod*) – ethnographers had to invent a notion of 'meta-ethnic community' (Bromley, 1987, p. 37) echoing Gumilev's rhetoric on 'super-ethnoses', such as Eastern Slavs or Turks.

Post-Soviet scholars have remained strongly attached to a primordial vision of ethnicity. Only one university textbook on ethnology exists in the whole country; recently it has been revised and published as a 'new generation' of textbook for democratic Russia. This text informs students and the public that 'ethnoses emerge through human evolution, being one of the forms of group integration . . . With full assurance that it is possible to tell that ethnoses have existed since the upper-paleolithic times when Homo sapiens erectus appeared' (Markov & Pimenov, 1994, pp. 5-6). Warning against attempts to consider nations or nationalities (i.e. ethnoses) as being based on feelings of identity, and against viewing ethnoses as intellectual or social constructs, the authors of this textbook reach an arrogantly intolerant conclusion:

> None of these conceptions will be recognized by the scholarly community because their theoretical essence is based on negation and abolishing the science per se . . . In Russian social science, views of ethnic communities as existing in reality as objects which emerge by historical law for a certain functioning, evolution, and interactions have always existed. This approach will still be a strong part of domestic ethnology (Markov & Pimenov, 1994, pp. 5–6).

To disperse any doubts as to what ethnicity means in post-Soviet academic discourse and in curriculum texts, I provide one more quotation from the concluding chapter of the same textbook:

> Human history is not only a history of states, of outstanding personalities, and of ideas, it is also a history of the peoples-ethnoses who make states, delegate from their milieu outstanding figures, construct cultures and languages. It is a history of ethnoses who work together during peace and fight during war, who make inventions, heroic achievements, and tragic mistakes (1994, p. 361).

Thus, ethnoses are a *sine qua non* of all human evolution, of all existing political and cultural structures, of contemporary collective and individual strategies.

Recently, Soviet ethnic studies have become a subject of serious criticism in world ethnological literature (see Chichlo, 1990; Gellner, 1980; Khazanov, 1990; Plotkin, 1990; Skalnik, 1988) and in a few domestic publications. Sometimes this critique has also been politically motivated – e.g., accusing Bromley and the Institute of Ethnography of devilishly setting out to destroy ethnic cultures, plotting with the USSR State Committee for Statistics to minimize the 'number of the peoples' in the country, and being the main culprits behind conflicts of nationalities (Ochirova, 1990; Tenishev & Bystrov, 1989). Interestingly enough, the opposite criticism has also been directed at the Institute for 'spreading the metastasis of ethnicity' in Soviet society; this came from the leading experts at the Institute of Marxism–Leninism in the Central Committee of the CPSU.[2]

Serious debates on 'the crisis in Soviet ethnography' took place after the publication of my article under the same title (Tishkov, 1992a), but I found the results of this discussion as well as real changes in the field of ethnic studies disheartening. Ontologizing scholarly definitions and ascribing them an existential essence remains a major weakness of Russian social sciences. Very few of my colleagues (see, e.g., Kon, 1993; Sokolovsky, 1994) could recognize the primarily heuristic value of definitions that help give meaning to and organize one's life experience and research materials. In contemporary Russian ethnology, a conservative orthodoxy still dominates. It is represented mainly by members of older generations who deeply believe that 'a spirit of materialistic theory of reflection, a theory of reproduction of an objective world in a man's consciousness, is a non-dismantleable one in social science. Any attempts to substitute it with another theory of cognition, irrespective of its name – neo-Kantianism, relativism, or post-modernism – are doomed to failure' (Semenov, 1993, p. 19).

In ethnic studies, the post-Soviet academic tradition continues its vigorous rejection of any steps away from the long-shared approved methodology. As Yuri Semenov, a well-known Russian scholar, has explained, 'although there exists a notion of "bread", there also exists real bread which is eaten. And although there exists a notion of "chair," real chairs on which people sit also exist. Applied scholarship, this means that although there exists . . . a notion of "ethnos", there are also real ethnoses, and the peoples exist, like Russians, English, Serbs, and Abkhazians' (Semenov, 1993, p. 4).

Reviewing my analysis of the state of affairs in post-Soviet ethnography, especially with respect to the immense amount of what purports to be scholarly publication, I have come to the conclusion that it is *not* a crisis. No, it is something more serious: a failure of the discipline to meet the challenges of today (Tishkov, 1994-95).

Meanwhile, many ethnographic texts were not so overloaded with ideology and scholasticism. They were and are heavily empirical and based on serious field research intended to distinguish cultural differences and to map an ethnic mosaic, especially in the

Table 1.1   *Ethnic Background of PhD Candidates Enrolled at IEA, 1990–1995*

Ethnic group	1990	1991	1992	1993	1994	1995
Russian	6	5	10	9	9	4
Non-Russian	9	6	2	1	10	4
Abkhazian			1			
Adygei					1	
Altai		2				
Armenian						1
Azerbaijani					1	
Balkar	1					
Bashkir	1					
Belorussian		1			1	
Buryat	1					1
Crimean Tatar					1	
Evenk	1					
Iranian		1				
Jew	1	1		1		
Kabardin					1	
Karachai	1					
Kazakh	1					
Kumyk					1	
Laks					1	
Nogai						1
Osset					2	
Tat	1					
Tatar			1			
Ukrainian	1	1			1	1

Source: IEA administration files

Table 1.2   *Ethnic Background of Advanced Degree Recipients at IEA, 1990–1995*

Ethnic group	Doctorate recipients	Post-doctorate recipients
Russian	33	19
Non-Russian	31	16
Abkhazian	1	1
Armenian	-	1
Azerbaijani	1	-
Buryat	2	1
Chechen	1	1
Cherkess	1	–
Chuvash	–	1
Dargin	1	–
Dungan	1	–
Georgian	1	1
Jew	2	1
Kabardin	–	2
Kalmyk	–	1
Karachai	1	1
Kazakh	2	1
Kirgiz	1	1
Laks	1	–
Moldavian	–	1
Mordva	2	–
Osset	1	–
Tajik	1	–
Tatar	1	1
Turkmen	1	–
Ukrainian	6	–
Uzbek	2	1
Yakut	1	–
Others	8	–

Source: IEA administration files

field of so-called 'material culture'. Immense efforts were put into detailed descriptions of ethnic histories, traditional ways of subsistence, patterns of dwellings, food, costumes, folklore, rituals and ceremonies, ethnic demography and cartography. This discipline, because of what appeared to be its archaic and non-ideological character, had managed to preserve rather high academic standards in Soviet times. As a result, ethnographic writings were not so disastrously devalued with the coming of liberalization as were works within many other social science disciplines. Furthermore, the ethnic cultural and political revival has drawn its arguments and recruits in many respects from existing ethnographic literature and from a pool of professional ethnographers trained mainly at the Center and, specifically, at the Institute of Ethnography in Moscow. Many ideological and political leaders of ethnic movements in the former Soviet Union and now in the republics of Russia received their PhDs from this Institute. Many arguments and postulates for political platforms and for cultural programs have been borrowed from academic publications.

The situation has not changed significantly since the emergence of new states, and since Russia's ethnic periphery has begun to reassert its political and cultural autonomy. At least, with regard to ethnic studies and the role of Moscow-based scholarship, the Russian Academy of Sciences still exercises a combination of old-style empirical ethnography with traditionalist sociology. It coexists peacefully with all kinds of nationalistic rhetoric; even more, it remains a main producer of 'national cadres' of ethnographers and a chief referee of scholarly debates. The data on teaching and degree-granting activities of the Institute of Ethnology and Anthropology (IEA) for 1990–95 tell their own story (Tables 1.1 and 1.2).

It was quite embarrassing then to read a statement by a US 'specialist on the Soviet nationality problem, not on Soviet ethnic problems' (an explicit self-definition of Martha Olcott, 1995b, p. 137) that delegitimized the research involvement of 'imperial' central scholars with their former Soviet colleagues or even colleagues outside Moscow:

> We should take particular caution that lack of funding or lack of desire to face field conditions not allow a new form of Russian 'gate keeping' to replace the Soviet closed countryside of the past. There are already far too many joint Russo-American projects under way, purporting to study situations in one or another of the new republics through projects funded by Americans but designed and conducted by Russians rather than by scholars indigenous to the republic of study. Too many of the Russian scholars who are now working on 'nationality' themes still suffer from 'great power chauvinism,' believing that local scholars cannot function without Russian direction and support (Olcott, 1995b, p. 144).

Although inaccurate, the statement demonstrates another serious challenge for post-Soviet ethnology. In addition to its internal inability to reconsider basic theoretical paradigms and vocabulary in the short run, the discipline faces outside pressures of political correctness on the part of ideological warriors and watchdogs of academic 'purity'. Thus the discipline of studying ethnicity in what was the Soviet Union finds itself squeezed between the primordialism of theory and the politics of academia. The time to write a requiem for ethnos has not yet come.

1.2 Use and Abuse of Theory

With the emergence of ethnic politics in the former Soviet Union, ethnographic primordialism ceased to be merely a marginal and empirical approach and suddenly revealed its potential for being enthusiastically applied in the quest for new identities, as well as in nationalist political discourse. The term 'ethnos' became a central one in intellectual and political debates of the late 1980s and early 1990s. Many aspects of ethnos theory, posing as pure scholarly exercises, were made part of painful public displays, led to conflict-generating political projects and, finally, violent manifestations of ethnic entrepreneurs. Practically all leaders and proponents of ethnonationalism use these categories and logic very extensively in their language. Raphael Khakimov, political adviser to the President of the Tatarstan republic and one of the ideological leaders of the local nationalist movement, writes in his pamphlet 'The Twilight of Empire: About a Nation and a State':

> Ethnos is a biosocial phenomenon, combining nature and society. Ethnos carries in itself a biological energy and is subject to other laws than those for social processes. Sometimes one can hear appeals to forget about ethnic origin and not to divide people according to this category. These appeals are derived from the misunderstanding of

the nature of the phenomenon. Ethnic features are not just wishful thinking, nor a devil's plot on the part of 'separatists'; they are destined from birth (Khakimov, 1993, p. 19).

A representative of the Yakut 'ethnos', Dr Uliyana Vinokurova, a professional ethnosociologist with a Moscow PhD, writes about the necessity of the Yakuts establishing their 'own scientific interdisciplinary approach to ethnogenesis of the people of Sakha (Yakuts)', as opposed to the 'old superpower ethnography' (Vinokurova, 1994, p. 27). Referring to archeological materials, she postulates that it was on the vast territory of the middle Lena river – home of today's Yakut ethnos, – that the Yakut *narodnost* was formed prior to the 16th century. She concludes:

> Thus, the Yakuts are a very young ethnos formed from Mongol- and Turko-linguistic components and, probably, influenced by the Samoyed indigenous population of Siberia and the North. According to Gumilev's theory, the energetic potential of ethnos lasts for approximately 1200–1500 years. At that point, ethnos becomes a component of a continuous network of ethnic varieties of humanity. . . . Even hypothetically, it is a pity to feel that you belong to a disappearing ethnos' (Vinokurova, 1994, p. 27).

The use and abuse of a 'theoretical' construct of ethnoses as living bodies embodies a double-edged paradox. On the one hand, it is nicer to feel young, dynamic and with good prospects for a future; on the other hand, age can testify to the ancient roots of an ethnos and its exclusive indigenousness to a particular territory (in the lexicon of Soviet ethnography – 'ethnic territories'). So, for one proponent of ethnos, a few centuries can suffice to declare that 'the people of Sakha are an indigenous people of Yakutia, formed as a unified ethnos on the middle Lena' and 'Yakutia is a historical motherland of the people of Sakha' (Vinokurova, 1994, pp. 30–31). For another, however, a different political implication is more important: 'History knows cases of existing empires which incorporated hostile ethnoses, not forming one nation. Such forceful conglomerates are possible, but they are temporal phenomena compared with the lives of ethnoses (according to Gumilev, ca. 1200 years)', writes Khakimov (1993, p. 21). Thus, ethnoses are seen as formations with deep roots in a specific territory, to which only one ethnos may lay claim, the so-called indigenous ethnos: 'The indigenous people are an ethnos, formed on this very territory and preserved in its ethnic features' (Khakimov, 1993, p. 26).

The most alarmist debates in ethnic discourse revolve around topics like the 'dying out' or 'disappearing' of ethnoses – which is taken not as a scholarly concept that gradually fell out of fashion, but rather to mean the actual physical death of great numbers of people. Such debates only add fuel to the fire in a situation of real socio-economic crises and relatively low living standards – both of which existed long before the ongoing transformations. Concerns about the 'death of ethnos' are expressed by experts writing not only about small, vanishing cultures, but also about large dominant groups, like the Russians.

> The growing process of uncompromisable reorientations of economic and social relations has put the Russian ethnos to a test of survival (and not for the first time!). At historical turning points, like the present, not only ethnoses but whole civilizations disappear. The question, 'what will happen to the Russians?' has not been properly asked yet (Bagramov et al., 1993, p. 63).

Professor Victor Kozlov, of the Institute of Ethnology and Anthropology, has concluded, on the basis of recent demographic tendencies, that 'the Russian nation is dying out'. In his recent text, *The Russian Question: A History of the Tragedy of a Great People*, he ignores Gumilev's thesis on the predetermined 'life of ethnos', according to which the fate of Russian ethnos is prescribed by 'laws of Nature' and should thus be accepted. 'To avoid the death of Russian ethnos,' Victor Kozlov proposes purely political measures:

> There are many difficulties in this issue, the main one being how, under conditions of social degradation, to awaken Russian consciousness and ethnically oriented mass activities. It is a question of how, under presidential rule, to democratically elect a President who can realize his historical responsibility and who is capable of changing a traditionally Russophobic nationalities policy. Of course, the character of a President and his 'team' should not be limited by Russophobia only, . . . but a moderate Russophilia is a prerequisite in this situation (Kozlov, 1995, p. 329).

The pro-Russian nationalistic strain is clear – as is the implicit anti-reformist message.

In recent years, debates on the concept of ethnos have reached a wider audience, with elements of racism and intolerance. In an academic context, Bromley, among others, elaborated a thesis on 'ethnic functions of endogamy', meaning that for an ethnos to survive as a 'stable entity', certain mechanisms are needed to provide this stability and 'a reproduction of ethnos'. One of these mechanisms is endogamy, the tendency to marry within one's own group. Bromley is speaking not of primitive tribes or isolated communities, but of a 'large ethnosocial organism, like, for example, contemporary nations' (1983, pp. 200–211). Even more controversial is the argument presented by Gumilev, who sees ethnically mixed marriages as 'anomalies' and 'chimeras'. According to Gumilev, 'Bromley's view on the stabilizing role of endogamy as a barrier against incorporation is undebatable' (1989, p. 90).

Finally, Professor Vladimir Pimenov, head of the Ethnology Department at Moscow State University and principal author of the standard textbook, has employed quantitative calculations to ascertain a critical level of endogamy: 'A proportion of ethnically mixed marriages exceeding 12–15% of all marriages can cause an irreversible trend towards the disappearance of an ethnos' (Markov & Pimenov, 1994, pp. 368–369).

Here I do not intend to debate what is considered in Russian anthropology to be 'undebatable'. Let me merely point out how this theme is echoed in popular literary texts. In 1993 Aidar Khalim, editor of the Russian-language journal *Argamak*, published in Kazan (Tatarstan), wrote an article, 'Contemporary Mixed Marriages, or a Ring of Irresponsibility', which was reprinted in other widely circulated periodicals. Khalim inveighed against Tatar-Russian marriages, which in his opinion had acquired the scale of a 'cholera epidemic' and should be branded 'immoral and destructive to national culture and language'.

> In old times, Tatars were constantly entering into marriages with representatives of other ethnoses. Such marriages, being based, as a rule, on real love, improved the gene-fund and refreshed the blood of the nation. That kind of marriage differs from current inter-ethnic marriages as day differs from night. In those times, they were like '*tein* in tea', a microscopic ingredient in a body of ethnos not destroying its essence, and existed as an isolated phenomenon. What do we see now? Mixed families, encouraged by the state policy of nation-merging, serve now to deprive the people of their national features, to impose impersonality, and to cause genetic decline (Khalim, 1993, pp. 4–5).

The essentially racist notion of the 'purity' of an ethnos or nation, with the accompanying idea of dangerous miscegenation, was implicitly incorporated into official demographic policies of states like Estonia and Latvia, and into public attitudes. On a train from Moscow to Tallinn in June 1995, I asked my companion, an Estonian businessman of Russian origin, about the issue of ethnic intermarriage in the country. 'No, they [ethnic Estonians] hardly ever marry others because of the fear that their people may disappear', he replied. Thus, while in small or low birth-rate societies intermarriage may be considered a means of maintaining the populace, at least in demographic terms, in post-Soviet societies another logic would seem to prevail. There is not even a social category for people of mixed ethnic origin: not in censuses and other official statistics, not in public policy, and not in social sciences or opinion polls. And this is in an area with one of the highest levels of intermarriage in the world: 13.5% of all Soviet families were ethnically mixed in 1979 (see Susokolov, 1987).

'Organic' visions of ethnos have generated a lot of pseudo-scholarly speculation on a specific ethnocentric character. One's own ethnos is described in most complimentary terms, in distinction to 'others'. According to Vinokurova, there exists a

> . . . Yakutian way of thinking by scholars of different scientific disciplines and by philosophers. . . . Comparing neighbouring and kin ethnoses, the people of Sakha are marked by especially careful attitudes towards traditional sources of their own culture . . . The Yakuts as an ethnos tend to be more Asiatic than European people and they are exhausting their tolerance to European influence (1994, pp. 52–56).

And finally, a startling discovery: 'the Yakuts have special predisposition for long-distance running' (1994, p. 54) – because several local athletes achieved good results in international sports competitions!

The ethnos theory appeals not only to experts and activists from non-Russian segments of the country's population. It is also used (or rather *ab*used) enthusiastically by those who pretend to represent ethnic Russians as well as other dominant groups of post-Soviet states. Pamphlets and articles are circulated in millions of copies, disseminating obscure pseudo-theoretical constructions with explicit ethnocentric, exclusivist, and hatred-oriented views. One example is an article by Igor Shishkin published in the right-wing newspaper *Zavtra* (Tomorrow), which changed its title from *Den'* (Today) after being banished for explicit support of the pro-Communist coup in August 1991. The paper is a kind of a popular guide on Gumilev's writings for a wider audience. In this recent article, the reader learns that there are over one hundred ethnoses living in the territory of Russia. These may be subsumed into seven super-ethnoses, which 'were formed in their regions as a result of a passionate push (*tolchka*)' (Shishkin, 1995, p. 4). These seven super-ethnoses are Great Russians (*Velikorossi*), which include Ukrainians, Belorussians and even Tatars; Western Europeans (the Balts and Western Ukrainians); Muslims (Turkmens, Uzbeks, Crimean Tatars, etc.); 'remnants' of the Byzantine super-ethnos (Georgians, Armenians); steppes people (Kazakhs, Buryats, Kalmyks, etc.); 'relics' of Siberian circumpolar super-ethnoses (small peoples of the North); and a 'floating' super-ethnos – the Jews. According to Gumilev, explains Shishkin, there are three different forms of contacts between ethnoses: *symbiosis*, *xenia*, and *chimera*. Symbiosis is a situation when each ethnos occupies its own ecological niche, its own landscape, and fully preserves its 'national pecularity'. 'It is the most optimal form of a contact,' argues Shishkin. Xenia is when one ethnos is a 'guest', an ingredient (*vkraplenie*) in a body of another ethnos, harmless to the recipient ethnos. But when the 'guest' starts to break out of its isolated position, it may transform itself into chimera. Chimera is when two ethnoses belonging to super-ethnoses with a 'negative mutual complementarity' live together and intermingle. Blood, devastation and even the death of one or of both ethnoses are unavoidable.

These arguments are employed to legitimize and propagate various programmatic postulates of Russian nationalism. First, says Shishkin, 'as proved by Gumilev, the coexistence of a number of the peoples on the territory of Russia for centuries has become possible because of a positive complementarity and natural compatibility of the Russians and of the Siberia and Great Steppe ethnoses'. For many centuries the Russian government built its policy on recognizing the right of all the peoples to independence, which allowed Russia to remain a strong and solid state. In the 19th century 'we refused to live separately but as friends, and moved towards the European norms of trying to make everyone similar . . . and as a result, we have now the widespread phenomenon of chimera'. Danger arises when there is an ethnic chimera between ethnoses with 'negative mutual complementarity'. Shishkin (1995, p. 4) goes on to say:

An incoming ethnos with an absolutely different life history and different energetics [!] does not live isolated but mingles and at the same time does not assimilate into a 'ghost' ethnos. As a result, we observe a situation where representatives of ethnoses with different patterns of behavior and with incompatible systems of values are studying at the same school or working at the same institution. Speaking of chimera, one should recognize that its devastating effects are caused by natural laws, not by the very fact that some people are good and others are bad. They are just different to the point of incompatibility.

The intriguing question, of course, is just who these ethnoses are that are causing such dangerous chimeras for Russia. Before providing an answer, Shishkin adds a few more dramatic statements:

Chimera contacts are extremely dangerous in a situation of changing phases of ethnogenesis (through which we are currently passing), that is, when an ethnos is sick. As L.N. Gumilev writes, during these historically short time periods, systemic links inside an ethnos are being restructured, the behavioral stereotype is changing. In this situation, under chimera contact, a stereotype behavior of an indigenous ethnos could be completely destroyed, its ethnic system could fall apart, and that means death of an ethnos. Unfortunately, these zones of chimera contact are currently widely spread throughout the territory of Russia.

Shishkin offers only one illustrative case of 'incompatibility of ethnoses': the Jews. Here the main characteristic feature is that 'contacts between the Jews and other ethnoses always went along a line of chimera'. This – argues Shishkin – is because the Jewish super-ethnos has never occupied its own landscape or ecological niche. Their settlement in urban landscapes and the break with the natural environment of any country has allowed the Jews to 'conserve their passionarism [Gumilev's term defining the highest level of energy manifestation on the part of an ethnos – VT] at a rather high level and maintain their longevity'. At the same time, this made it impossible to establish contacts with indigenous ethnoses not only in a form of symbiosis, but even in a form of xenia (isolation). What this 'floating' or 'guest' ethnos of the Jews has sought is to adapt the system of a 'ghost' ethnos to its own needs. That is why most actions deemed 'anti-Semitic', especially those relating to 'state anti-Semitism', represent a defensive reaction of indigenous ethnos, he maintains.

Shishkin quite explicitly pays tribute to Gumilev's theory for explaining the 'Jewish question' on a 'solid scientific basis' and for explaining the character of contact (chimera) of the Jews with other ethnoses 'by natural laws exclusively, by the power of things'. In addition to propagating anti-Semitism, this use of 'theory' proceeds along exclusivist lines, where any 'external' influences or modifications of 'accumulated experience' are considered dangerous. 'If we change our super-ethnos' affiliation by entering the European Community, then we can expect to share the fate of the Arab khalifat: it was once a powerful state but at a stage of breakdown chimeras consumed its body . . .' (1995, p. 4).

Surely this is indeed a mind aflame! Unbelievably pseudo-scholastic, hate-oriented speech, translated into terms to feed the mass mentality. While attending a conference in Orenburg in September 1994, I received the following note from the audience after my presentation: 'Professor Tishkov! Why not build our entire nationalities policy according to Gumilev's theory, assigning each ethnos a special program reflecting the nature and stage of its evolution?'[3]

I have quoted only a few examples from a vast amount of similar literature that has been produced about the former Soviet territories. The material quoted here should suffice to show that in the post-Soviet context the 'poverty of primordialism' coexists with the power of primordialism, influencing not only intellectual debates, but also political inspirations and the behavior of social actors. It should also be clear that I prefer to look for other approaches for interpreting ethnicity, approaches more likely to yield increasing understanding of this important subject.

1.3 Constructive Ethnicity

In recent decades, scholars throughout the world have began to focus more attention on ethnicity as a means – an instrument – employed by a collectivity in its efforts to gain material or political advantages in the social arena. This *instrumentalist* approach sees a collectivity's claims to ethnicity and to ethnic status as being based on academic and political myths that are created, propagated, and often manipulated by elites seeking recognition and power.

Ethnicity is also increasingly seen as a part of the repertoire that is calculated and chosen consciously by an individual or a group in order to satisfy certain interests and to achieve certain goals. Such an approach resembles what is called the *constructivist* view of ethnicity, which also regards ethnicity as a modern phenomenon. It posits a process of identity formation in which cultural elites play a significant, but not necessarily manipulative, role. Ethnic identities frequently develop out of the recognition and articulation of a shared experience of discrimination and subordination. They can emerge or re-emerge as a result of changing power structures. At the same time, such powerful forms of social groupings, like states, create loyalties and cultural systems through their institutions which transform these loyalties and cultures or assert them as ethnic identities. A complex dialogue takes place between the cultural mosaic and power structures, 'producing' ethnic groups by defining their boundaries. Otherwise, however, culture as such remains silent. Both the constructivist and instrumentalist approaches tend to see ethnic boundaries as constantly appropriating and eliminating elements, that is, as permeable and relatively fluid (Barth, 1969; Eriksen, 1993; Handler, 1988; Verdery, 1991).

The constructivist approach views ethnic sentiment, which is created through historical differences in culture, as well as the myths, conceptions, and doctrines that are formed in its context, as an intellectual and social construct. As such, ethnic sentiment is seen as the result of purposeful efforts of elites who are 'professional producers of subjective visions of the social world' (Bourdieu, 1984, p. 6). These 'professionals' include writers, scholars, and politicians, whose intellectual production became transmittable on a mass level with the spread of the printed word and education. The very idea of nation and so-called national awareness (or self-awareness), the intellectual product of Western elites, thus spread around the world simultaneously with the process of modernization (Gellner, 1983; Greenfeld, 1992; Hobsbawm, 1990). In the second half of the 19th century and the beginning of the 20th, this idea found support in Eastern Europe and Russia, especially among leaders of the peripheral nationalities of the former Ottoman, Austro-Hungarian and Russian empires. Later – particularly because of the increasing availability of education and the creation of intellectual elites among the nationalities of the former Soviet Union (as in the countries of Eastern Europe) – the idea and doctrine of nationalism acquired deep emotional legimacy. Today these elites are promoting attempts to convert such myths and emotions into socio-political engineering (Roeder, 1991, 1993; Tishkov, 1992b).

The constructivist approach pays special attention to mentalities and language as key symbols around which a perception of ethnic distinctiveness crystallizes. For example, written texts and speeches contain historical reconstructions which are used to justify the authenticity and the continuity of one or another ethnic identity. Soviet and post-Soviet historiography, archeology, and ethnography often reduce the past to the present, and represent a look back into history viewed as 'gradualness' and 'homogeneity'.

Every contemporary reading of past cultures draws upon history as a resource for addressing the political tasks of today. Political and heavily ideological archeology and ethnography have flourished for decades in the academies – central and peripheral – of the former Soviet Union. What is new is that unprecedented battles to 'reconcile the past' with new political agendas are taking place with far greater ferocity and insulting language than during times of censorship and limited publishing opportunities (see Shnirelman, 1996). To achieve immediate political effects, established scholars prefer to publish widely circulated pamphlets and brochures, rather than solid academic monographs. Here let me note only a few examples of this 'struggle for the past' which deserve analysis beyond the conclusion that 'competition and conflicts between scholars of various ethnic origins were a result of a general growth in ethnic self-consciousness and inter-ethnic tensions' (Shnirelman, 1993, p. 7).

While visiting Tbilisi in summer 1992, only one month before major war broke out between the Georgians and Abkhazians, I picked up a small brochure entitled 'Abkhazians and Abkhazia' (printed in Georgian, Russian, and English) written by the well-known Georgian archeologist and medieval historian Mariam Lordkipanidze. Describing the events in the 19th and 20th centuries, she concluded:

> The Kingdom of Abkhazia was a Georgian (Western Georgian) state. A vast majority of its population were Georgians: Karts, Egris, Svans, and part were Abkhazians proper. . . . Had the kingdom of the Abkhazia not been a Georgian state its capital would not have been Kutaisi, center of ancient Georgian statehood and culture, in the heartland of Georgian population (Lordkipanidze, 1990, p. 65).

She goes on to say that 'the Abkhazian Principality of the late feudal period was culturally and politically the same "Georgia" as were the other "Georgias"' and that 'the Abkhazians did not live in cities and strongholds . . . and they were never molested by others, but they attacked and plundered one another' (p. 67). And finally, when an independent Abkhazian republic was proclaimed in 1922,

> Georgian Bolsheviks were neither interested in nor worried about the fact that by this concession they were compromising Georgia's unity – her historical borders in defense

of which the Georgian people had fought over the centuries. They ignored and violated the legitimate rights of the Georgian people, in particular of that part of the
Georgian people which had for centuries lived on their own land, and would now have
to live in the Abkhazian state . . . The so-called independent Abkhazian SSR was an
artificially created entity, whose existence in isolation from Georgia was absolutely
unnatural and untenable historically and culturally. The existence of Abkhazian
autonomy in any form within the boundaries in which it took shape under Soviet rule
is absolutely unjustified (Lordkipanidze, 1990, p. 74).

This short text was written at the time Zviad Gamsakhurdia came to power and Georgia
was proclaiming its independence. These words were widely read in a society with one of
the highest proportions of PhDs and professional intellectuals in the world. Evidently the
brochure was intended as more than an academic argument in a long-standing debate
between Georgians and Abkhazians. These words were meant as a vindication and moral
order to start putting into political practice the slogan 'Georgia for the Georgians!',
under which philologist Gamsakhurdia and other local academics had attained power.
This tragic step was first taken not in Abkhazia, but in the South Ossetia autonomy
which Georgian intellectuals hurried to rename 'Shida Kartli' or 'Samachablo', both
meaning belonging to Georgia. An attempt to abolish this autonomy by force caused a
three-year war; the conflict is still not over.

In practical terms, little has changed in Georgia with the rise to power of native son
Eduard Shevardnadze, who formed a government of 28 people including 11 philologists,
historians and philosophers, seven artists and journalists and only three lawyers and one
economist. His War Minister, Tengiz Kitovani, a former artist, initiated military operations against Abkhazia, involving the state and the people in an ongoing and devastating
ethnic conflict. During my personal meeting with Shevardnadze in June 1992 in Tbilisi,
he pointed out that 'not one politician can speak now of restoring South Ossetia's status
without committing political suicide'.[4] Ethnocentric declarations and political strategy
based on intellectual myths about the Georgian ethnonation as a historical and monolithic entity overwhelmed their authors. The irony is that 'Georgian' as a group identity
is in fact a recent construct, initiated by late 19th-century intellectuals and finalized during the Soviet period when the borders of the republic configured an ethnically complex
territory with a dominant Kartli cultural component (see Suny, 1988). Several groups
among the Georgians still speak different languages (Svans, Megrels).

General similarities could be observed for practically all other conflicting areas in the
former Soviet Union. Azerbaijani historians had for decades been promoting the controversial concept of Caucasus Albania, including ancient Albania, as the
'grandfatherland of Azeris', territories which Armenians view as 'historical Armenia'.
This conception of a 'rich' and 'ancient' history of the Azerbaijani people includes, as a
necessary component, a description of the Karabakh territory as the 'heart of
Azerbaijan'. In response, Armenian intellectuals produced fiery propaganda about the
'barbarian', 'bloodthirsty' Turks from whom the Azeris trace their origin and who constantly carried out a policy of genocide against Armenians. In October 1987, the Institute
of Ethnography, along with Armenian and US colleagues, convened a seminar on ethnic
issues in Dilijan, Armenia, where the participants enjoyed the privilege of having as a
guide the distinguished Armenian academician Babken Arakelyan (who died shortly
afterwards). Standing in the ruins of an ancient Armenian temple or by the monument to
the victims of Armenian genocide, the academician Arakelyan delivered heart-rending
stories of the atrocities committed against the Armenians by the Turks, instinctively
directing his face and even his gestures to the East – the territory of the neighboring
Azerbaijan republic.

Ingush leaders consider the village of Angusht, located in a disputed area, to be the 'grandfatherland of the Ingush'; and Ossetian intellectuals have developed a thesis about the Alans, the cultural predecessors of the Ossetians, whose 'bones are scattered throughout the Northern Caucasus'.[5] Little is known about the Alan archeological cultural complex, and its legacies could be shared by many local indigenous groups. Even a traditional Russian physical anthropological effort to link archeological cultures and cranial materials with contemporary populations of the area has been inconclusive; the historical roots of the Ossets are debatable, and their cultural (quite heterogeneous) profile seems to have developed as the result of fairly recent migrations and interactions (Alexeev, 1974; Gerasimova, 1994; Volkova, 1974). This, however, has not prevented Ossetian intellectuals from inventing an elaborate myth about 'their ancient predecessors', nor local authorities from adding a new word to the title of the North Ossetia republic – 'Alania'. For the first national holiday (after the new Constitution was ratified), local choreographers designed women's costumes and staged dances of the mythical 'Amazons' who were to have lived in ancient Alania.

In December 1994, during my stay in Vladikavkaz for negotiations with the Chechens, I visited a few local booksellers and was amazed to see how powerfully and attractively a fresh version of the history of the Ossetian nation was presented. A massive volume entitled *Ossetia and Ossetians,* with an introduction written by the local President Galazov, began with a chapter on Scythian, Sarmatian, and Alanian cultures and concluded with a chapter entitled 'The Ingush Aggression against Ossetia' (Chelekhsaty, 1994). Also on sale were more popular brochures written for the general public, presenting the Ossetian background of Jesus and of the Emperor Frederick Barbarossa. It is not megalomaniacs who write these texts: they were by local intellectuals with scholarly degrees (Khamitsev and Balayev, 1992).

1.4 Ethnographic Processing

Most of the national histories, encyclopedias, and cultural research churned out during recent decades reflect little of the people's actual history and ethnography. These texts and beliefs have been intended mainly to legitimize politically constructed ethnonations and their 'own' states. Even the very nomenclature of the peoples (or ethnoses) is the result of the prescriptions of outsiders – whether by long-dead writers and travellers, or contemporary scholars and politicians – and differs quite significantly from that set out, for example, in the Imperial census of 1897. The lists of ethnic groups registered by the last Russian Imperial census and by Soviet censuses, as well as the principle of registration, show dramatic differences: even major ethnic groups re-acquired new 'ethnonyms'. For instance, Turks (or Tatars) in Azerbaijan became Azerbaijanis, Kirgiz became Kazakhs, Kara-Kirgiz became Kirgiz. 'Smaller' identities were aggregated into larger categories: in the census of 1926, from 530 into 194; in 1937, from 769 into 168; in 1989, from 823 into 128 (see Table 1.3). Closer analysis shows that during the time of the Soviet Union, the nomenclature of the various groups was determined by scholarly and political decisions or by rational choices made by ethnic leaders.

Let me provide a few illustrations of 20th-century ethnic engineering, some of them successful, some not. A modern list of indigenous peoples of Siberia and the North was drawn up on the basis of categorizations suggested by leading academic authorities, like Patkanov (1923); Bogoraz (1934-39; 1991), Levin and Potapov (1956; 1961), and Dolgikh (1960), who seriously influenced the political process of establishing ethno-territorial autonomies for these groups in the pre-war period. The simple fact that indigenous

Table 1.3   *Ethnographic processing of the peoples of the USSR (main groups only)*

Official names	Non-registered names included into official category		
	Census 1926	Census 1937	Census 1989
Armenian	*zoki*	*akuliscy, gajkane, zoki, somyekhi, tumbul'cy, khaj, yermeni, yermiloj, bosha, armyanskie zygane, gnchu, karachi, lom, khemshiny*	*khaj(gaj), cherkesogaji, ermeni, ermely, yermeni, frank, karabakhskie armyane, somekhi, khamsheny, khemshil, khamshecy, shirakcy, aparancy, polsocy, lorijcy, zangezurcy, donskie armyane*
Azerbaijani	Were included in the wider category of Turks (see below)	Were included in the wider category of Turks (see below)	*azerbajdzhanly, azerbajdzhan lylar, tyurk, padary, karapapakhi, shakhseveny, ajrymy, ajrumy*
Belorussian			*belarus, pinchuki, breshchuki, poleshukii, poleshchuki, litvin, litvyak, tutejshie*
Estonian	*yestoncy, kurlyandcy, liflyandcy, poluvercy, setukezy*	*viro, virolajset, poluvercy, setukezy, yestlazed, yestlanye, yestoncy*	*yesty, yeyestlane, yeyesti setu, chukhoncy*
Georgian	*kartvely, gurijcy, dzhavakhcy, imeretiny, imery, ingiloi, kartlancy, kortlely, kakhetincy, kakhi, klardzhijcy, lechkhumcy, makhovcy, meskhijcy, mokhevcy, mtiulety, pshavy, rachincy, somkhitcy, taojcy, khevsury, khevcy*	*gurijcy, gyurzhi, dzhavakhcy, engilojcy, imeretiny, imery, ingiloi, jerli, kartalincy, kartvely, kartlely, kakhetincy, kakhi, klardzhijcy, kobuletcy, lechkhumcy, makhovcy, mered, meskhi, misliman, mokhevcy, mtiulety, pshavy, rachincy, somkhity, taojcy, tiul'cy, tushiny, khat, khevsury, khiu, bacbii, bacav, bacy, cova-tushiny, lazy, arkhavcy, atincy, akhvarcy, viccy, joi, khopcy, chany, chkhal'cy, megrely, margali, mingrel'cy, svany, lakhamul'cy, lashkhcy, lentekhcy, mushvan, svanety, cholurcy, shvanar, shon*	*kartveli, adzharcy, adzhareli, kartalincy, kartlijcy, gudamakarcy, gurijcy, dzhavakhi, imeretiny, kakhetincy, lechkhumcy, meskhijcy, mokhevcy, mtiuly, pshavy, rachincy, tushiny, khevsury, vraci, ingilojcy, gyurdzhi, lazy, chany, megrely, mingrely, margali, svany, cova-tushiny, bacbijcy, bacav*
Kazakh	*kirgiz-kazaki, kirgiz-kajsaki*	*adban, alimuly, argyn, bajuly, girgizoj, dzheti-urug, dzhityru, dulat, kazakh-kirgizy, kirgiz-*	*kazak, adaj, alban, argyn, bersh, beskalmak, dulat, zhagalbajly, zhalair, zhappas, kerej, kongrat,*

Table 1.3 *(cont.)*

Official names	Non-registered names included into official category		
	Census 1926	Census 1937	Census 1989
		kazakhi, kirej, kishidzhyuz, ulu-dzhyuz, chala-kazakhi, chaprashty	*kypchak, najman, nogyj, oshakty, sary-ujsun, srgejli, suan, tabyn, tama, tortkara, uak, sherkesh, shekty, ysty*
Kirgiz	*kirgizy, buruty, karakirgizy, kyrgyz-kypchaki*	*asyk, bagysh, bugu, buruty, ichkilik, kamennye kirgizy, karakirgizy, kushchu, munduz, on, sarybagysh, sayak, sol, soru, sultu, khadyrsha*	*kyrgyz*
Latvian	*kurish-kenigi*	*kurish-kenigi, latvieshi, latvijcy*	*latvietis, latvieshi, latgal'cy, latgalietis, latvis*
Lithuanian		*litvaki, litviny, l'etuvej, l'etuvis, zhmud'*	*letuvyaj, letuvis, litvin i litvyak, lituvnik, tutejshie, aukshtajtn, zhemajty, dzuki, zanaviki, zanavikaj, zhagunas, girgitunas, letuveshi, lietuvietis, lietuvieshi, lejshi, lejtis*
Moldavian		*moldoven, moldovyan*	*moldoven', volokh'*
Russian	*velikorussy, molokane*	*velikorossy, velikorussy, gazki, moskali, rossiyane, urusy*	*kazaki, kamchadaly, kerzhaki, kolymchane, kolymskie, pokhoshchane, pashennye, yamskie, markovcy, pomory, semejskie, kamenshchiki*
Tajik	*aratorcy, gornye Tajiki, gorogcy, Tajiki gornye*	*aratorcy, gal'cha, gornye Tajiki, gorogcy, pamircy, todzhik vakhancy, vakhi, vukh, khajbari, khik, ishkashimcy, ishkoshumi, sredneaziatskie zygane, dzhugi, kashkari, lyuli, mazang, moltani, shugnancy, baredzh, bartangcy, mundzhancy, oroshorcy, rushancy, rushni, khugnoni, khufcy, shugni, yagnobcy, yazgulyamcy, zgamit, yuzdom*	*todzhik, chagataj, kharduri, kardiri, darvozi, vanchi, vandzh, goroncy, pamirskie Tajiki, pripamirskie Tajiki, badzhuvcy, badzhujcy, badzhavidzh, badzhuvedzh, barvozcy, barvozidzh, bartangcy, bartangidzh, bartangi, vakhancy, khik, vakhi, vakhidzh, gundcy, gundedzh, gundi, ishkashimcy, shikoshumi, ishkoshumi, mundzhoni, oroshorcy, roshorvidzh, rushancy, rushchoni, rykhen, sarykol'cy, sarikuli, khufcy, khufidzh, shakhdarincy,*

Table 1.3 *(cont.)*

Official names	Non-registered names included into official category		
	Census 1926	Census 1937	Census 1989
			shakhdarachi, shokhdaragi, shugnancy, khugnoni, khugni, shugnoni, shugni, yagnobcy, yagnobi, yazgulyamcy, yazgulomi, zgamik
Tatar	*abincy, agrzhancy, akhatleli, borchaloeli, kryimcy, chulyimcy; meshcheryaki, meshchera*	*abalar, abincy, agrzhancy, akhatleli, borchaloeli, geziloj, kazanskie tatary, karagachi, kryimskie tatary, kryimcy, povolzhskie tatary, stepnyie tatary, yuzhnoberezhnyie (kryimskie) tatary; mishari= meshchera, meshcheryaki, mizher*	*tatar, barabincy, baraba, paraba, karagasy tomskie, karinskie (nukratskie) tatary, kryashenyi, astrakhanskie tataryi, karagashi (kundrovskie tatary), meshcheriaki, mishari, misher, mizher, nagaibaki, tarlik, teptyari, teptyari-tatary, tobolik, turamincy, chulyimskie tatary, chulyimskie tyurki, chaty, chulyimcy, yeushtincyi, yaushta*
Turk	*karapapakhi*	*abugachi, azerbajdzhancy, azeri-tyurk, ajrum, akkoyunlu, bayat, davichi, dzhalair, kadzhary, karakoyunlu, kengerly, motory, mugaly, naurusovcy, padar, tangut, khaladzh, shakhseveny; budukhi, budad; dzheki, dzhejly; karapapakhi, tarakama, terekeme; kryzy, kryzly, rutuly, mykhabur, mykhadar, mykhady, mykhashura, khaputlincy, gaputlincy, khaputcy, kherad, khinalugi, kettidu, kettitturdur, cakhury, zagurcy, jikby, cakhby, cakhij-galij*	
Turkmen	*ilieli, arabachi, ata, goklany, igdyr, iomudy, karadashly, murcha, nukhur, salory, saryki, seidy, teke, tekincy, trukhmeny, trukhmyane, khodzha, chaudor, shikh, yemreli, yersari*	*alieli, arsari, ata, goklany, igdyr, jomudy, karadashly, murcha, nukhur, salory, saryki, seidy, teke, tekincy, trukhmeny, khodzha, chaudory, shikh, yemreli, yersari*	*alili (ala-yeli), anevli, ata, gandyry, gokleny, emreli (imrili), jomudy (emuty), karadashly, mukry, nokhurli, salory, saryki, sakary, surkhy, teke (tekincy), tyurk, chovdury, govdury, yersari, trukhmeny, shikh*

Table 1.3   *(cont.)*

Official names	Non-registered names included into official category		
	Census 1926	Census 1937	Census 1989
Ukrainian	*galichane, malorusy, rusiny,* *ugrorusy*	*alichane, malorossy,* *malorussy, rusiny*	*bukovincy, verkhovincy,* *guculy, gajnaly, kazaki,* *pinchuki, poleshchuki,* *rusiny, rus'kij, bojki, lemki*
Uzbek	*sarty, uzbek-kypchaki*	*durmen, katagan, kenegez,* *kongrad, ktaj, kyrk, lokajcy,* *mangyt, ming, najman,* *nuratincy, ozbak, saraj,* *sarty, kipchaki,* *karakipchaki, kurama,* *kuramincy, ujsyn,* *samarkandskie i* *ferganskie tyurki,* *sredneaziatskie zygane,* *dzhugi, kashkari, lyuli,* *mazang, moltani*	*ozbak, ozbek, chagataj,* *kangly, lakaj,* *lakajcy,kongrat, mangyt,* *kuramincy, kurama,* *kypchak, tyurk, yuz, kirk,* *najman, saraj, katagan,* *karluk, durmen,barlas,* *mugul, musobozori, turkman*

Source: Sokolovsky, ed., 1994, pp. 117-154

groups of the Far East (or Amur area) had not at that time been 'ethnographically processed' in the way that Arctic and southern Siberia groups had been, resulted in denying them local administrative power. Subsequently, commenting on the system of 'dual' ethnic autonomies in Western Siberia (Khanty-Mansi, Dolgano-Nenetz, etc.), Vladimir Dolgikh mentioned in a private conversation that most likely he was wrong in creating these 'pairs' and there were equally good arguments for qualifying these groups as different 'ethnoses'.[6] Meanwhile, lack of ethnographic data on the sparsely settled Evenki (Tungus) people has allowed their categorization as a single group, thus defining a separate Evenki autonomy. Only later was it discovered that the Evenki exhibited great internal cultural diversity, also in language: this gave rise to a number of angry questions directed at politicians and scholars by indigenous activists from this and other groups.

A striking example of construction is seen in the history of the term 'Khakas', borrowed by intellectuals from medieval Chinese and Mongol chronicles that recounted the process of assembling several local indigenous groups to create an autonomy. Before this process, members of these groups had never heard such a word. Intra-tribal power politics of traditional leaders together with expectations of material rewards facilitated the creation of a new people, the 'Altai', comprising about a dozen small indigenous groups in southern Siberia with autonomous status.[7] This ethnonym gained wide acceptance; only recently has it been challenged by native ethnographers and activists, especially after the draft Law on Small Numerous Peoples was discussed in the Russian Parliament in 1992. Various special rights and privileges inscribed under this draft law instigated an upsurge of micro-nationalism among small indigenous groups.

Ethnic constructivism was not limited to indigenous groups who had lacked their own 'voice'. During the Soviet era, many larger groups ('nations') had also acquired new labels and unified membership with ethnographically designed 'cultural types'. This is how the USSR's ethnic identities pool became filled with Azerbaijanis, Tajiks, Kazakhs, Ukrainians, Russians and many other new all-inclusive labels. Belonging to an 'indigenous nation' named after the title of the republic became more prestigious – indeed, and even safer – in a tumultuous Soviet period than previously ascribed non-political identities. Thus the 'Tatars' or 'Turks' in Azerbaijan started calling themselves 'Azerbaijani'; 'Cossacks' and 'Pomors' in the Russian Federation (RSFSR) re-baptized themselves 'Russians' (*russkie*). A new structure of ethnic identities began to be imposed in Central Asia after the 'national-territorial delimitation' of the early 1930s, when a new political-administrative map of the region was drawn up for local 'socialist nations'. Large-scale membership recruitment into ethnonations began throughout the country, gradually replacing regional, religious, clan and other group identities.

There is a scene in Sergei Eisenstein's movie *Battleship Potemkin* when a terrified Russian soldier sitting on the ground with bombs exploding all around him prays for safety by repeating the words, *'Mi pskovskiie, Mi pskovskiie . . .'* ('We are Pskovitians, from the area of Pskov, we are Pskovitians . . .'). For Russian peasants – and they comprised the overwhelming majority of the population – that kind of affinity was the most important, probably the only form of identity which could serve as a shield or refuge in huge national, civic and political battles. It was the culture workers, the census takers, local administrators, and intellectuals who established the notion of 'real' ethnic affiliation or 'corrected' a 'wrong' one. A famous ethnographer Yelena Peschereva, who was active in establishing ethnic and republican borders in Central Asia, confessed at the end of her career that during the first Soviet census she 'had given birth to thousands of Tajiks' by simply registering them as such, so as to suit the purposes of the Committee on national-territorial delimitation.[8] Even more Tajiks were registered as Uzbeks.

Many Soviet citizens showed only vague feelings of ethnonational belonging at a time when it looked as if the process of the 'formation of socialist nations' had been successfully completed. My mother, a primary school teacher in a small town in the Urals, used to visit every family in her school district to register prospective new pupils. Back in the late 1950s I can remember she was always complaining of families who would not identify their name and nationality, who just said that they 'belonged to God' (*Mi bogovi*). These were the descendants of the Old Believers, and their identities were still shaped primarily by religious loyalties despite years of anti-religious Soviet propaganda and suppression. My colleagues from the Institute carrying out field research in the Ukrainian–Russian bi-cultural belt cited several examples where local people described their ethnicity thus: 'under one regime we were Ukrainians, under another – Russians, but frankly speaking we do not know who we are' (see Chizhikova, 1988).

During the Soviet period there were plenty of opportunities to design ethnicity, or to construct 'ethnoses', and there will be certainly no fewer opportunities in the future. What is clear is that a crucial factor in this process has *not* been the existence of a shared name held in common by a group of people and thereby signifying the primordial existence of a collective entity – an 'ethnos' which should now be properly rediscovered through 'correct' census procedure and scholarly investigation (Kryukov, 1989). No, the crucial factor has always been the political will of 'outsiders' or group elites, and intellectual/academic exercises. In 1978, I visited the city of Kazan, the capital of Tataria. The local party chief, Fikrat Tabeev, in unofficial conversation complained that 'a big mistake was made in the 1920s. We should have named our new republic "Boulgar" and its people "Boulgars" to avoid unpleasant associations with the epoch of Tatar–Mongol rule of Russia'.[9]

Tabeev was in all likelihood correct: 'Tatars' remained a very loosely defined term (synonymous with 'Muslim' or even 'non-Orthodox') in the country until the 1920s, and the Kazan group of Tatars could easily choose a new label. Without difficulties it could be legitimized by any political regime as well as by historical-cultural arguments. These are an indigenous people who can trace their history to pre-Mongolian times, when an ancient polity of Boulgars existed in the area. Until the mid-1980s, a time of Tatar nationalist revival, local archeologists, historians, and ethnographers expended tremendous efforts in tracing the roots of the Boulgars and propagating these cultural legacies, which distanced contemporary Tatars from those who arrived with Genghis Khan in the 13th century. Only recently have Tatar intellectuals started reconsidering the legacies of the 'Golden Horde', seeking to broaden the Tatar identity – a kind of pan-Tatarness which strives to include quite distinct groups, like the linguistically different Siberian Tatars. On the other hand, previous constructivism did not prove totally fruitless. As Director of the Institute, I received an appeal from the Chairman of the Boulgar National Community to the President of the Russian Academy of Sciences to provide 'an interpretation of the constitutional right to individual identification' and to assist in official recognition of their namè as a people, 'Boulgars', with its inclusion in a list of nationalities and languages.[10]

1.5   Ethnicity as a Tool for Solidarity and Mobilization

These observations on the role of intellectual constructions do not deny the reality of the cultural/ethnic mosaic per se, nor existing collectivistic identities. But defining 'a people' in the sense of an ethnic community needs serious reconsideration. 'People' is most often understood in contemporary scholarship as a group whose members share a common name and common elements of culture, who possess a myth of common origin and a common historical memory, who associate themselves with a particular territory and who share a feeling of solidarity. Shared beliefs and feelings of solidarity are key elements of this definition because they are the results of specific efforts and the nation-building process. They are the result of family socialization and education. In the same way, nations are, according to Benedict Anderson's widely accepted definition, 'imagined communities' (Anderson, 1983).

It is difficult to overcome the dogmatism that derives from Stalin's definition of a nation as a community of people with objective characteristics (territory, common form of economy, language, mentality). But it is no less imperative to perceive the nature of ethnic phenomena and their projection onto sociopolitical life in a more nuanced manner. Nationality in the sense of ethnic identity is not an innate human trait, although it is most frequently perceived as such. Nations are constructs, created by people, by the efforts of intellectuals and by the political will of the state. 'Nation' is an in-group definition: it is not possible to assign to it strictly scientific or legal formulae. As to the category of 'ethnos', this is an artificial construct which should be removed from public and, probably, academic discourse. Unfortunately, both primordial definitions (nations as ethnonations and ethnos) are widely and carelessly used in contemporary political language, as well as in normative and legal texts. I recall an interesting dialogue between Deputy Prime Minister Sergei Shakhrai and myself on the Cossacks as an 'ethno-cultural entity'. Shakhrai responded, 'Yes, I know that they are not a separate people but a social stratum; however, it may be useful for the state to support this mass movement.'[11]

I replied, 'No, it is not a social stratum but a mobilized memory about a past social stratum, and this mobilization pursues certain goals, mainly on the part of a limited number of activists.'

At that point in 1992 there were various options for the emerging Cossack movement: to keep it at the level of cultural and public group activities directed towards re-establishing their historical roots and memories, which had been severely suppressed by the Bolsheviks in the early Soviet period; or to legitimize the movement as one of the forms of 'national rebirth' among the Russian people with subsequent rights for self-government, special status, and property rights. Three years later, when dozen of books had been published on the Cossacks, including a detailed register of the various groupings (Tabolina, 1994) (some of them in fact a camouflage for criminal activities), when bureaucratic structures were constituted in federal and regional authorities dealing with 'a Cossack problem', and when the Cossacks' organizations and atamans had established themselves as parallel power structures in several regions – by then, it was already too late to handle this challenge within the limits of amateur cultural activities. Re-published ethnographic writings on the Cossacks in the late 1980s were transfomed into a powerful political tool and into costly, widely publicized state-sponsored programs.

Although the concept of ethnonational communities may be an imagined one, this does not keep it from becoming a powerful reality and a vital basis for collective action. In the contemporary world, ethno-cultural diversity does not remain simply a result of historical evolution: increasingly, it is moving from the domain of material culture and 'silent ethnicity' to the sphere of consciousness and practical values. We exercise ethnic identity and affiliation as a means of adapting and orienting in a challenging and complex modern world, and as a mechanism for achieving certain social goals. In Russia, the people are regaining lost feelings of personal worth and collective pride through ethnicity, while leaders often achieve social control and political mobilization by invoking ethnic reasoning or coalitions. Thus, this ethnic construct becomes directly projected onto the exercise of power.

Soviet intellectuals who have in many ways constructed the subject of their studies and concerns without being aware of their own 'co-creation' of a rebellious reality, are limiting their own opportunities to influence and participate in the process of change and innovation. Understanding that ethnicity is a social construction will, as M.P. Smith argues,

> bring greater capacity to mediate politically and socioculturally modify social relations within and among ethnic groups by creative symbolic action than is acknowledged by those who conceive ethnicity either in naturalistic terms, regarding 'ethnos' like 'eros' and 'thanatos' as a deep structural dimension of consciousness, or in essentialistic terms as a component of personal identity so rooted in past historical memory that little can be done by human agency in the present to shape its character or temper the antagonistic posture of ethnic groups toward ethnic otherness and difference (1992, p. 526).

Such a methodological approach could constitute a genuine breakthrough for the study of ethnic issues and conflicts in the territory of the former Soviet Union. This approach has never been seriously attempted, notwithstanding a recent book by Ronald Suny (1993), and a few articles (Brubaker, 1994; Comaroff, 1991; Sokolovsky, 1994), and even though many of its intellectual roots can be found in the Russian tradition of social thought. Ethnicity is constructed and reconstructed by specific verbal and political actions that reflect contemporary conditions, including power relations among social groups, and the meanings that people give to these conditions. We must recognize this, and refrain from regarding ethnicity as some kind of extratemporal and primordial feature of human existence. If only we could do this, then the activity of leaders from the political and cultural elites and social activists, as well as the everyday interventions of rank-and-file citizens in ethnic discourse, would take on new significance and a new awareness.

Notes

1 It was an interesting paradox of Soviet times that strictly controlled publishing processes banned not only ideologically 'deviant' printed words but also pseudo-scholarly and megalomaniac texts. Negative reviews of Gumilev's theoretical exercises written by Bromley and other established scholars were enough to get Gumilev's name included on the black list of Soviet publishing houses. However, several of his books on the history of the Turkic peoples and on the role of the Steppe culture in Russia were published and widely read.

2 In 1988, Mikhail Kulichenko, a leading party authority on the 'theory of the national question' wrote a letter to the Politburo of the CPSU accusing the Institute of 'idelogical diversion', but by this time, the climate had changed with respect to undertaking any 'measures' against academia. An odd answer was forwarded from the Institute without further reaction.

3 A note of 9 September 1994, signed by Dr Petrov, Orenburg. Personal files.

4 Notes from a meeting with Eduard Shevardnadze, 19 June 1992, Tbilisi. Personal files.

5 A quote from Akhsarbek Galazov, President of North Ossetia, Pyatigorsk-Vladikavkaz, 9 October 1992. Personal files.

6 Personal communication from Professor Zoya Sokolova.

7 Personal communication from Dr Dmitri Funk.

8 Personal communication from Professor Balkis Karmysheva.

9 Notes from a meeting with Fikrat Tabeev, 15 March 1978, Kazan, Tataria.

10 Institute of Ethnology and Anthropology, Director's files.

11 Conversation with Sergei Shakhrai, 5 June 1992, Moscow. Personal files.

2

Soviet Ethnic Engineering:
Success and Failure

2.1 Introduction

Various interpretations have been offered of the history of inter-ethnic relations and causes of ethnic conflict in the former Soviet Union. The dominant paradigm is that of the 'disintegration of an empire' combined with the 'national revival' of the peoples of the former USSR. Such a concept presupposes that the major reason behind the disintegration of the USSR as a multi-ethnic state was the diminished status of and discrimination against the non-Russian peoples whose cultures and identities were forcibly suppressed to conform to the official concept of the 'merging of nations' and the creation of a single 'Soviet people'.

The main conclusion drawn by the supporters of such an approach is that the Soviet Union was the last empire of the late 20th century, and that like all empires in the past it was doomed to vanish, according to the laws of history. As historian Yuri Afanasyev has put it, 'the USSR is neither a country nor a state. The Eurasian territory thus mapped is a world of worlds comprising different cultures and civilization, . . . and the USSR as a country has no future' (1990, p. 35). The main factor behind this disintegration is usually described as the inexorable urge of these peoples to attain national sovereignty and self-determination. The latter is seen as a historical regularity realized in all the other regions of the world but not in the territory of the USSR because of its totalitarian regime. 'The Soviet Union is the last empire going through the world process of decolonization which began with the end of the Second World War . . . Our state developed artificially and it was based on violence' (Starovoitova, 1992, pp. 119-121).

On the whole, this theory of disintegration is built on serious arguments. In many aspects the USSR was indeed an empire-type polity whose history was marked by territorial expansion, colonial methods of rule, and the cultural assimilation of ethnic groups by more dominant languages and cultures. Moreover, the Communist regime had a long record of crimes and conscious acts of violence committed against the Soviet nationalities, particularly during the Stalinist period. Among these crimes were mass deportations and repressions, annexation and liquidation of sovereign state entities, the disastrous destruction of the environment, and the undermining of traditional subsistence systems of many ethnic groups through an inefficient and militarized economy. Third, the Soviet State pursued a semi-official Russian-language policy through its 'international' Communist ideology, suppressing attempts to establish political cultural autonomy for ethnic minorities unless these attempts were sanctioned by central or peripheral elites. Finally, the ruling Communist bureaucracy strictly regulated the daily lives of the citizenry, violating their rights and freedoms and ignoring the interests connected with ethnic culture and values.

There was no lack of arguments in favor of the disintegration of the USSR, or reasons to explain the ensuing ethnic crisis. But for me, these arguments and reasonings are no more or less convincing than arguments in favor of improving the governance and maintaining the political and cultural cohesion of the USSR on a new, democratic, basis. It is like the case of Yugoslavia: although no less legitimate and culturally tolerant than most other states, it followed the scenario of disintegration as one of the possibilities realized through particular power dispositions and mobilized mass sentiments.

Only by avoiding the narrowness of inevitability can more sophisticated questions be asked in the research agenda. Why is it that after disintegration the ethnic crisis has continued, and is even growing? And why is it that the most discriminated groups have not been the ones to initiate the various ethnonational movements or the disintegration of the Soviet Union – as might have been expected? Why is it that ethnic conflicts, wars, and cleansing have taken place not between the dominant people – Russians – and those who are obtaining their 'national independence', but mostly between or towards small and non-status minorities? And, finally, why is it that the processes of 'national revival' have turned so soon from being allies of democracy, to being its opponents, and have taken on the mantle of narrow ethnic nationalism and of post-totalitarian xenophobia and violence? No answers to these questions are supplied either by the 'fallen empire' model (or, *l'empire éclaté*, to use the label pioneered by Hélène Carrère d'Encausse, 1978) or by its later modifications that seek to explain current conflicts by a conspiracy of pro-imperial conservative forces and by the agony of a disintegrating monster-state (see Chervonnaya, 1994; Goldenberg, 1994).

Among Russia's social scientists we may also note another trend in explaining the history of the so-called national question in Russia, and today's ethnic problems. I call this approach 'protective-conservative', because it consists essentially in finding distortions or faults admitted in the domain of nationalities politics, in the departure from some 'ideal' principles or in the irresponsible political improvisations of recent years by neophyte politicians (Bagramov et al., 1993; Cheshko, 1993; Kozlov, 1995; Semenov, 1995). The weak point of such arguments is that same kind of over-simplification used in approaching the phenomenon of ethnicity, and the ubiquitous positivism that remains characteristic of the Marxist–Leninist theory of nations. Returning to the past, or imposing a new holism on behalf of the people (usually ethnic Russians) or of the state as a sacred cow and overruling value – these are the prevailing motives of this type of discourse.

Western, mainly US, scholarship in the field of Soviet and post-Soviet studies has contributed significantly to the research agenda on ethnic problems. About two dozen solid monographs and over one hundred scholarly articles on ethnic issues have appeared in the West since 1988, when 'the national question' began to dominate the public life of the Soviet Union. The leading approach was shaped mainly by political scientists and historians who, probably more than representatives of any other discipline, were influenced by the inertia of the Cold War and by the victory of liberalism. Most of these authors have propagated the illegitimacy and repressive nature of the Soviet system, as well as the imperial character of its nationalities policy.

The main question in the Western mind is why Soviet studies failed to predict the end of the USSR, and why so many gifted scholars chose to write on the 'unresolved' national question while overlooking the main issue. A feeling of professional guilt has spread over Western Sovietology; mutual accusations have intensified. The very few scholars lucky enough to have displayed penetrating intuition, predictive power, and uncompromised honesty have been hailed as celebrities. Even editors of the most serious collections of essays have adopted an apologetic tone and written prefaces like:

> While a vanguard of scholars – Amalrik, Brzezinski, Conquest – had insisted collapse would come, the scenario of a reform-minded Communist Party General Secretary

producing a series of unintended consequences that led inexorably to regime change still seemed implausible in March 1985 when Gorbachev succeeded Chernenko. Understandably, therefore, at the outset of the six-year Gorbachev era specialists were preoccupied with the agenda of *reform* of the Soviet political and economic system (Bremmer & Taras, 1993, p. xix).

Those who happened to be among this 'vanguard' are now being asked to write forewords for scholarly publications to display their superior foresight. Robert Conquest, for example, writes with disarming simplicity and hidden arrogance:

> Anyone who has even a moderate knowledge of Soviet nationality problems has long known that a 'democratic Soviet Union' would be a contradiction in terms. For it was plain that nationality problems in the USSR had not been solved; that feelings repressed, rather than satisfied, over several generations would re-emerge if and when any civil liberty was restored; and that given freedom to do so citizens of the peripheral nationalities would vote against the system (Bremmer & Taras, 1993, p. xvii).

That kind of hindsight among Western academics demonstrates the same methodological weaknesses I wrote about with respect to the Soviet interpretation of ethnicity. Deterministic treatment of the breakup of the USSR as inevitable, and accusing specialists of failing to understand the 'tectonics' of the system merely serves to demonstrate scholarly provincialism.

The bulk of retrospective interpretations of events and societal changes in the USSR and post-USSR would seem to fall into one of two extreme categories: either they focus on the Kremlin's chess game, or they concern themselves with collective bodies called 'nations' or 'nationalities'. There is still no room for other actors of social space, for rationality and irrationality in private and group stategies, for any power dispositions and cultural choices in all their varieties. Nor is there any opportunity for granting recognition to any good intentions and moral motivations in a political domain of the 'devil's empire'. Liberals loathed Communism with a hatred so deeply embedded that their practitioners still consider everything connected with this system – be it ordinary human beings or a professional colleague – as something inherently damaged and not fully legitimate. While extensively using research results of many Soviet specialists as reference literature and a source of information, some US scholars question whether relations ought even to be maintained with 'tainted colleagues . . . whose careers had been made during the last decades of the Soviet regime' (Orlovsky, 1995, p. 5; see especially Olcott, 1995b, pp. 141–143).

In the meantime, more and more experts have borrowed enrichening approaches from contemporary socio-cultural anthropology and sociology and have now started to view the situation in less static and less essentialist ways (e.g., Brubaker, Dallin, Laitin, Lapidus, Roeder, Slezkine, Suny, Zaslavsky). But even these cases sometimes show unconvincing attempts to distinguish between the totalizing negation of the Soviet/Russian state and its policy (at least, on the 'intentional' level) and some fleeting images labeled 'unintended consequences'. Fighting the constraints of political correctness, researchers may point out that 'seldom have intentions and consequences diverged as spectacularly as they did in this case' (Brubaker, 1994, p. 49). In other words, it was the 'intentions' (systemic, political, cultural, group, individual) that were basically wrong, illegitimate, and immoral; the 'consequences' could be positive, relevant, and even 'successful'.

For me, the failure of Western Soviet studies lies not in their inability to predict, but in their ideologically motivated exclusion of more sophisticated social science analysis – that may include elements of 'good intentions', rational choices, altruism, human creativity, and irrationality as opposed to 'tectonic' determinism and totalizing illegitimacy – for this part of the world. The real failure lies in the creation of a new mythology, and the current inability to discard Cold War influences and to minimize the ideological component of research. In other words, Western scholars are facing exactly the same kind of problem as are their colleagues in the former Soviet Union.

2.2 The Bolshevik Experiment

By the end of the 19th century, Russia spanned 22.5 million km^2 of territory, peopled by 128.2 million inhabitants with an extremely rich cultural mosaic, and with ethnic Russians comprising less than a half of the population (Table 2.1). The multi-ethnic composition of the state's population had evolved over the course of centuries of territorial expansion in the form of military conquests, colonization and the development of new lands carried out by the state – first in the form of the Moscow Principality and later the so-called Russian Centralized State. But the major agents of colonization were those who sought to escape this state with its serfdom, tyranny, and life-long military service – peasants, religious dissidents, individual entrepreneurs, etc.

Table 2.1   *Major Ethnic Groups of the Russian Empire, 1897*

Ethnic group[1]	Number (thousands)	% of total
Russian	55,670	43.4
Ukrainian	22,380	17.5
Pole	7,930	6.2
Belorussian	5,890	4.6
Jew	5,060	3.9
Kazakh	3,800	3.0
Finn	2,660	2.1
Tatar	2,230	1.7
German	1,790	1.4
Uzbek	1,700	1.3
Lithuanian	1,660	1.3
Azerbaijani	1,480	1.2
Latvian	1,435	1.1
Georgian	1,350	1.1
Bashkir	1,320	1.0
Moldavian	1,120	0.9
Mordva	1,025	0.8
Estonian	1,000	0.8
Chuvash	845	0.7
Kirgiz	600	0.5
Udmurt	420	0.3
Tajik	350	0.2
Others	6,485	5.0
Total	128,200	100%

[1]This list of modern names was projected on tribal, cultural and religious groups and regional identities that existed in 1897.

Source: Compiled by Solomon I. Brook (Tishkov, ed., 1994, p. 25)

The dominant ethnic component of the state was Eastern Slavs, whose cultures were to give rise to the ethnic identities of Russians, Ukrainians and Belorussians. However, from the earliest stages of its formation, the population of Russia also included Finns, Balts, Turkic and other non-Slavic groups. The ethnic mosaic grew particularly complex after the 16th-century annexation of the Volga area and the colonization of Siberia. In the 17th century the state added the Ukraine, West Siberia and a part of the Caucasus; in the 18th–19th centuries East Siberia, Caucasus and Central Asia were included either by force or by treaty.

With respect to *inorodtsy* (literally 'non-Orthodox') the policy of the Russian monarchy was that of social oppression and cultural assimilation. Widely practised was appropriation of lands inhabited by indigenous peoples; such land went to the state, to landlords and monasteries, the latter being the main means of spreading Orthodoxy. A system of various taxes and levies was applied to this category of the population, as well as the practice of non-equivalent goods exchanges: in other words, the well-known forms of colonial policies long employed by the states of the Old and New Worlds. Unlike the classic colonial empires, however, Russia's metropolis was not so geographically distant from the colonized peripheries. Moreover, the population of the ethnic periphery was extremely diverse with respect to levels of modernization and political consolidation. Siberia and the Far East were inhabited mostly by small, unrelated groups of hunters and gatherers, but the same territory was used to form the early states of a number of Turkic and Mongolian peoples (Siberian Tatars, Yakuts, Buryats). By the time they became a part of the Russian Empire, Central Asia and Transcaucasus had a long tradition of statehood, with cultural and political communities based on dynastic, religious or regional principles.

The so-called 'indirect rule' method was applied rather widely in the Russian Empire: many of the areas and cultural communities in the territory were granted differing degrees of autonomy and self-government. Serfdom and compulsory military service applied mainly to the ethnic Russian population. Some centuries of inter-ethnic communication and contacts resulted in a high degree of mutual cultural influence and integration, especially between the Slavic and Turkic peoples. Many representatives from the periphery became incorporated into the social elite of Russia. Local nobility, political and religious leaders retained social control over their group members and enjoyed a special alliance with the All-Russian ruling elite. In the second half of the 19th century, the periphery of the Empire saw the growth of nationalist movements echoing in spirit the East European social democratic movements which embraced the peoples within the range of the three major imperial entities: the Austro-Hungarian, Ottoman and Russian (see Gellner, 1983; Hobsbawm, 1990; Hroch, 1985; Seton-Watson, 1967).

World War I and the Versailles Treaty put an end to two empires which were then supplanted by a scattering of new 'national' states. A similar process began in Russia as well, where political tendencies towards decentralization and regional autonomization had been growing under the tsarist regime, imposing on the population state unitarism and cultural assimilation. After the overthrow of the monarchy in February 1917, Finland and Poland acquired their political independence from Russia. In the early years of the Bolshevik rise to power, independence was proclaimed by the Ukraine, the Transcaucasian republics (Georgia, Armenia, Azerbaijan, Abkhazia) and the Baltic countries (Lithuania, Latvia, Estonia). Movements for autonomy sprang up among major regions of Russia, most of which had a distinct ethnic make-up – like the Bashkirs and the Tatars.

The initiators and ideologists of nationalism behind these movements were the local intelligentsia, who had been educated in St Petersburg, Moscow, or at some secular or religious centers abroad. The social democratic programs and ideas of Austrian Marxism concerning the question of nations and national self-determination gained currency among that segment of the population, and in Russian social democratic circles. As early as 1913 Stalin wrote his work 'Marxism and the Question of Nationalities', defining a nation as 'a historically developed and stable community of people that has emerged on the basis of the commonality of their language, territory, economic life and psychological make-up as manifest in the community of culture . . . Absence of at least one of these traits is enough for a nation not to be a nation' (Stalin, 1951–52, pp. 296–297).

In contrast to their political opponents who advocated 'one and indivisible Russia', the Bolsheviks supported political movements among the non-Russian peoples, viewing them as allies in the struggle against absolutism. The very first document adopted at the Second All-Russia Congress of Soviets, 25 October 1917, declared that the Soviet power 'shall provide all the nations that inhabit Russia with the genuine right to self-determination' (Lenin, 1962, vol. 35, p. 11). On 2 November 1917 the 'Declaration of Rights of the Peoples of Russia' was proclaimed; it included the following basic provisions.

1 Equality and sovereignty of the peoples of Russia.
2 The right of the peoples of Russia to free self-determination up to separation and the formation of independent states.
3 Abolition of every and any national and national-religious privilege or restriction.
4 Free development of national minorities and ethnographical groups inhabiting the territory of Russia.

Immediately after the Declaration the government issued a statement, 'To all the Working Moslems of Russia and of the East' promising Moslem peoples respect for their religion and rights, and calling upon them to support the socialist revolution (*Dekrety*, 1957, p. 40). The first Soviet government established a special body, the People's Commissariat for the Affairs of Nationalities (*Narkomnatz*), which was headed by Stalin and remained in existence until 1924.

The Bolsheviks' declarations received an enthusiastic response from nationalist activists in the periphery and provided the new power with much-needed support from the non-Russian population. At this point, in declaring itself to be an internationalist movement, Marxism in Russia actually included in its program the doctrine of ethnic nationalism. This doctrine can explain the rather easy rise to power experienced by the Bolsheviks all over the country and their victories in the Civil War. Two main postulates were particularly attractive to the multi-ethnic country: first, the doctrine recognized that a nation as an ethnic group has a set of inalienable characteristics, including its own territory, commonality of economic ties, common language, and a distinct sociopsychological mentality. Although Lenin used the terms 'nation', 'nationality', and '*narodnost*' almost interchangeably, Stalin later moulded a definition of 'nation' that has remained predominant in public ideology and political practice even to this day. Secondly, the doctrine established that a necessary condition for the existence and development of a nation was the existence of an ethnic group declared to be an 'indigenous nation' (*korennaya natsia*) within their 'own' statehood.

This doctrine enabled representatives of some periphery groups (or, more correctly, their elites) to formulate the right to secession or to an exclusive status within 'their own' state. Such challenges to the Bolsheviks were soon formulated within the framework of their own doctrine and thrown at them by the nationalist parties in Armenia, the Baltic area, Georgia, the Ukraine, and in other regions of the country.

Once they had consolidated their power, the Bolsheviks then proceeded to eliminate the right to secession from their practice, labeling supporters of the idea of independent national states as 'bourgeois nationalists'. To 'bourgeois nationalism', Soviet ideology suggested the counter-formula of 'proletarian internationalism' – which meant essentially that the solidarity of the toiling people of Russia, in the name of the common revolutionary cause, required that they be united within a single state. Lenin wrote,

> We want the largest state possible, the closest union possible and the greatest possible number of nations living next to the Great Russians (*velikorossy*): we want this in the interests of democracy and socialism, in the interests of drawing into the struggle of the proletariat the greatest possible number of toiling people of different nations (Lenin, 1962, vol. 34, p. 379).

The Bolsheviks decided to realize the right to national self-determination within the borders of a single state. Such a state was to be built on the principles of 'socialist federalism' as opposed to 'bourgeois federalism', in that the internal division of the state was to be based not on the principle of administrative territories, but on the principle of 'national statehoods'. In January 1918 the Third All-Russia Congress of Soviets announced that 'the Soviet Russian Republic was established on the basis of free nations as a federation of Soviet national republics' (Chugaev, 1968, vol. 1, p. 94).

But the principles and norms of federalization were not defined, or at least not publically proclaimed at that time. Fighting for influence in ethnic regions, the Soviet government supported the idea of buffer republics in the periphery, as well as in areas of active military activity during the Civil War. At the same time, the Soviet government, including Lenin himself, was not an enthusiastic supporter of ethnic federalism, copious political rhetoric notwithstanding. The real challenge came not from 'national', but from regional (so-called 'autonomist') movements, which only in a few cases had developed ethnic manifestations. That is why many of the territorial autonomies formed during the first years of Soviet rule – like Stavropol, Donetzk, Don, Kuban, Tersk, North Caucasus, and the Black Sea Republics – did not have an ethnic character. As Stalin described it, the 'absurdity of federalism' ('as many republics as there are Soviets') began to disconcert the Soviet government and pushed them toward a decision to constitute 'national republics' only (Nenarokov, 1995, pp. 138-139). Thus, ethnic federalism in its explicit form can be traced back no earlier than 1923, when the so-called Soviet nationalities policy finally took on its ethnonationalist form, and when its critics had been chastised as 'great-power chauvinists' (see Nenarokov, 1991). This policy became a 'missionary project after the Soviets strengthened their power and Stalin became the true "father of nations" (albeit not all nations and not all the time)' (Slezkine, 1994c, p. 414).

In other words, the ethnic policy of the Soviet Union was designed on an improvised basis partly to meet the serious challenges issuing from the regions and ethnic peripheries of the Russian Empire, and partly to meet doctrinal aspirations. Regardless of the precise reasons, however, this ideology of ethnonations necessitated social engineering to put the idea into practice – or, more precisely, to construct realities that could correspond to political myths and intellectual exercises.

The first task of this social engineering was an inventory of ethnonations – which meant inventing nations where necessary. After all, in many Soviet regions the cultural mosaic did not conform to strict boundaries, and ethnicity was overshadowed by other forms of identity. The census of 1897 (the first properly organized population census in Russia) had registered 146 languages and dialects in the country. Religion and language, not ethnicity, were regarded as the principles for group belonging. But the state proclaimed the right of self-determination for 'formerly oppressed nations' (in Lenin's words) and introduced ethnic federalism; thus it became crucial to count not languages, but ethnic groups per se. For that purpose the first Soviet census of 1926 asked citizens to indicate their *narodnost* ('nationality'). This experiment produced the spectacular result of some 190 different identities displaying varying sorts of particularism, from locality to clan affiliation.

It was a crucial step on the part of a state to institutionalize ethnicity as 'nationality', pushing aside any opportunity to link this definition with citizenship. Seventy years later, citizens of post-Soviet states still encounter difficulties in filling visa applications and other documents with a category – 'nationality'. A Tatar or a Ukrainian living in Russia cannot understand that he is being asked about citizenship and not about ethnic affiliation.

Thus, this list of 190 different 'national' identities immediately became the subject of scholarly ethnographic processing and political manipulations that have continued to this day. Ethnographers, linguists, and historians went to work to redefine the list by declaring some identities dialectal, sub-ethnic, or local variants of larger *ethnoses*. Many new names were given; many groups were renamed. In the end, scholars labeled all Soviet nations and *narodnosti* ('peoples') and created a hierarchy of ethnic groups. Ethnic engineers in academia elaborated later on a notion of 'ethnic processes' such as 'consolidation' and 'integration' in order to minimize the number of potential claimants for further, more advanced territorial recognition. In part, this reflected a process of vanishing tribal and local identities under the rapid industrialization and 'socialization' of the country. Here we should note the census of 1939, before which (in November 1936) Stalin used the phrase 'about 60 nations, national groups and *narodnosti* comprise the multinational Soviet State' (Stalin, 1947, p. 513). This was enough to reduce the number of ethnic groups in the next census to 99!

From its very inception the national state-building project encountered a central obstacle: the impossibility of drawing internal 'national state' boundaries along ethnic lines. The country's population in many areas was ethnically mixed and the boundaries of ethnicity itself were extremely shifting, making it impossible to determine distinctly even the very names of Soviet nationalities, worse still to outline their 'own' territories. Having been called upon to fix 'national' boundaries, ethnographers and other experts attempted to territorialize ethnicity, thereby providing a powerful impetus to the development of ethnic cartography in Russian ethnography. The following two advantages were emphasized in the effort: the creation of its 'own' statehood for each nation, and the economic development of national republics under formation. That was why territories with predominantly non-titular ethnicities were included in the boundaries of many of the republics and other autonomies that were formed. No less important in this process were political and personal factors, such as the sympathies and aversions of the Kremlin's leaders and Stalin himself, as well as possibilities for lobbying and pressure from below on the part of local elites.

2.3 Lobbying for Borders and Status

The early history of Soviet ethnic autonomies shows a dramatic mixture of missionary projects and local rivalries, with results reflecting momentous power dispositions. Let us look at a few instances of building nationhoods.

A group of Bashkir leaders disagreed with a decision taken by an all-Muslim congress in Moscow in spring 1917 to form a Muslim republic in Russia, and proclaimed Bashkir autonomy in November 1917. Powerful Tatar politicians who did not consider Bashkirs as a separate group (just a part of Turko-Tatars) proposed the Idel-Ural state as a wider form of territorial autonomy for the indigenous peoples of the Volga-Ural area. In March 1918, this proposal was transformed into the Kremlin decision to constitute the Tatar-Bashkir republic. In March 1919, when the militant Bashkir leader Zaki Validov gathered his own army, exercising control of a territory peopled with a predominantly Bashkir population, central Soviet authorities reached an agreement on establishing the autonomous republic of Bashkiria, which was essentially the same as the controlled area (the so-called Malaya Bashkiria/Bashkiria Minor area).

Once the military situation had improved for the Bolsheviks, the government severely restricted the status of this autonomy, and Lenin told Validov that the previous agreement was just 'a piece of paper' (Valeev, 1994, p. 64). Local uprisings against Soviet power in 1920–21 and later appeals by Bashkir authorities to include the Ufa region with its sub-stantial portion of Bashkirs into the republic's territory brought about a new decision to expand the borders of Bashkiria. Within these new borders, which included all of the more or less significantly Bashkir populated areas, the Bashkirs themselves became a minority numerically inferior to the Russians and Tatars. Through the logic of prestige and elite motivation, the city of Ufa, which had practically no Bashkir inhabitants at the time, was established as the capital of the republic.

This gave Bashkiria access to the Trans-Siberian railway and a major industrial center. It was a reasonable step towards strengthening this territorial autonomy and there is no historical evidence available to judge it otherwise, as was done by a contemporary local historian:

> No doubt, there was a ground for formation of Bolshaya Bashkiria (Great Bashkiria) because there were historical Bashkir territories there. But Soviet leaders took this step not by motivations to return these lands to Bashkirs. It was done to pursue a goal to disperse Bashkirs in a multi-national environment where non-Bashkirs dominated (Valeev, 1994, p. 72).

Motives behind major decisions on granting autonomy and establishing republics were determined by political raison d'être rather than by any conscious 'nation killing' strategy. That is why this policy seemed to have so many inconsistencies and appeared so impulsive. With respect to moral aspects, there was a combination of aspirations to reward 'oppressed nations' and to keep one state under Soviet rule. In 1919 a represen-tative of the Party Central Committee, Alexander Ioffe, stated to the Belorussian Bolsheviks that the formation of Belorussian and Lithuanian republics was presupposed by a 'desire . . . to avoid direct impact of imperialism on Russia' and 'to build between imperialism and Russia a number of buffer republics' (Nenarokov, 1995, p. 139). Soon the attitude to the Belorussian republic had changed; to strengthen the territorial/regional, and not purely ethnic principles, it was transformed into the Lithuanian-Belorussian republic. Probably the same motives lay behind the unification of Armenia, Georgia and Azerbaijan into the Transcaucasian Federation in 1922 after they were 'sovietized' in 1920–21.

A no less interesting situation developed in the case of the Armenian enclave in Azerbaijan – Nagorno Karabakh. Long and heated debates about its affiliation were resolved by the Caucasian Bureau of the Central Committee of the Russian Communist Party of Bolsheviks in 1920 after the head of the government of Azerbaijan, Nariman Narimanov, threatened to stop the deliveries of kerosene from Baku. A certain role was also played by the position of Turkey's leader, Kemal Ataturk, who was bent on achiev-ing rapprochement with the Bolshevik regime.

Because the number of claimants to 'their own' statehood proved to be much greater than the Bolsheviks had probably supposed, one more innovation of the 'socialist federalism' was born – a kind of hierarchy of ethnonational units of the Russian *matrushka-doll* type. In order to legitimate this practice later, a special theory was formulated about different types of developmental levels in the ethnic communities. Groups that were larger (numbering more than 100,000 members) and more modernized were labeled 'nations'; the smaller ones became '*narodnost(i)*' (a derivative of the Russian word '*narod*' meaning a nationality or a people). The former had the right to their own statehood in the form of a union or an autonomous republic, while the others were entitled only to a lower national-administrative status. However, even in this case, much depended on the spatial homogeneity of a given group, the degree of its political consolidation, and on some other factors. Moreover, in some areas the ethnic principle could not be strictly observed, particularly where the more powerful basis for a collective identity was religion, dynastic or regional belonging, or where the ethnic mosaic was too complex to draw up administrative lines. Such was the situation in Central Asia and the Caucasus where the new republics often received names with no specific ethnic connotations.

In 1918 the Turkestan autonomous republic was set up within the RSFSR. Its borders corresponded to the former Turkestan territory, which was inhabited by numerous ethnic groups with complex tribal structures. The Kirgiz (later called Kazakh) autonomous republic was established within the RSFSR in 1920. The same year, after the defeat of the Khan of Khiva and of the Emir of Bukhara, the Khorezmian and Bukhara republics were proclaimed, initially recognized by the RSFSR government as sovereign states.

In 1918 in the North Caucasus, the Soviet Terskaya *oblast* (Tersk region) was established with territories inhabited by the Tersk Cossacks, Kabardin, Ingush, Chechen and others. It was followed in 1920 by the Kalmyk autonomous *oblast*. In 1921 the so-called *raskazachivanie* (the dispossession of the Cossacks allegedly unloyal to the new regime) caused new reorganization; the Terskaya *oblast* was reorganized into the Gorskaya autonomous republic from which separate autonomous *oblast*s were detached almost immediately: the Kabardino-Balkarian and Chechen *oblast*s. In 1924 the Gorskaya republic was dissolved and its remaining territory was divided into the North Ossetian and Ingush autonomous *oblast*s and Sunzhenskii *okrug* (territory) with one administrative center – the city of Vladikavkaz. In 1928, within the limits of Stavropol *krai* (territory), the Cherkess autonomous *oblast* was set up. In Transcaucasus the Abkhazian autonomous republic joined Georgia under the Treaty of 1921. Two more autonomies emerged within Georgia: the southern Ossets and the islamized Georgians (Adjars).

The establishment of Soviet power in Central Asia and in North Caucasus was accompanied by cruel repressions and mass migrations of the indigenous population. Several hundred thousand people, mostly representatives of the aboriginal elites and ordinary participants of the resistance *basmatch* and *mokhadjir* movements, were forced to leave their homelands. These numerous diasporas remained completely isolated for many decades; through the process of recent liberalization their representatives have now begun to play an important and shifting role prone to radical scenarios and vengeful motivations.

In the early Bolshevik years in the Volga and Urals areas, some autonomies of different levels were formed for the Bashkirs, Chuvash, Germans, Komi, Mari, and Mordva. In 1921 the Crimean autonomous republic was established on the territory of the Crimea, supposedly to institutionalize the Crimean Tatars' nationhood. In the North and in Siberia a dozen ethno-territorial units of different levels emerged: the Buryat autonomous *oblast*, the Karel autonomy (first, as a Labor Commune, then as a republic), the Khanty-Mansi and Nenetz national *okrug*s, the Oirat autonomous *oblast*, the Yakut autonomous republic, and others.

In December 1922 the Union of Soviet Socialist Republics (USSR) took shape; and in

1924 the first Soviet constitution was adopted. However, the process of territorialization of ethnicity in the form of titular statehoods was not finished. The 1920s saw the continued imposition of ethno-territorial borders in Central Asia. Based on the non-ethnic republics of Turkestan, Khorezmian and Bukhara, new republics with redefined borders drawn closer to ethnic lines were formed for the Kazakhs, Kirgiz, Tajiks, Turkmen, and Uzbeks. Up to 1936 their status and territories changed several times, especially in the Fergana Valley. However, attempts to achieve ethnic homogeneity failed. A significant portion of the Uzbeks remained in Kirgizia and Tajikistan, and the Uzbek-populated rural regions around the predominantly Tajik cities of Bukhara and Samarkand were included in the Uzbek Republic. Because of economic considerations, vast territories with a predominantly Russian population were included in the Kazakh Republic when its status was elevated to a constituent union republic in 1936. This whole process – accompanied by zealous activity on the part of many economists, geographers, and ethnographers – was to go down in history as nation-state delimitation (*natsional'no-gosudarstvennoe razmezhevanie*) among the peoples of Central Asia (see Zhdanko, 1972).

The Soviet Constitution of 1936 registered the state's structure as consisting of 11 union republics and 20 autonomous republics. The 1939 Molotov–Ribbentrop Pact enabled Stalin to annex western Belarus and western Ukraine, as well as Bessarabia. This last territory, which along with the Moldavian autonomous republic (now the self-proclaimed Trans-Dniestrian Republic) had once formed part of the Ukraine, constituted a new union republic. In 1940 the three Baltic states were annexed to the USSR and in 1944 Tuva, by the headwaters of the Yenitsei River in southern Siberia. By the time of its demise, the USSR included 53 national-state entities: 15 union and 20 autonomous republics, 8 autonomous *oblast*s and 10 autonomous *okrug*s. These were peopled by representatives of 128 ethnic groups, numbering from a few hundred to several million, some densely settled, others widely dispersed.

The history of nation-building in the USSR has imprinted on the memories of its people numerous traumas and conflict-generating issues which were to manifest themselves during the years of perestroika and afterwards. It became an academic and political truism to explain ethnic conflicts and tensions as a backlash of the previous Communist 'divide and rule' policy towards nationalities. The literature abounds with references to how 'artificial borders' were deliberately designed by the 'Soviet axe' (Masov, 1991; Valeev, 1994). However, from the positions of today, it is far from easy to evaluate such a massive project – not least its territorial aspects – which had aimed at realizing the doctrine of ethnic nationalism. For one thing, it is hard to find any reliable historical evidence to show that Soviet authorities deliberately planted 'ethnic time-bombs' or exercised some kind of diabolic plot in the ethnic peripheries. What is available are rich archival materials produced by the Commission on Economic Development and Productive Forces, which operated under the auspices of the State Planning Committee (GOSPLAN) and which had among its priorities to study and develop suggestions on the administrative division of the territory, including the borders of ethno-territorial formations. Hundreds of experts, among them professional ethnographers, were involved in the search for the most appropriate and acceptable borders, not only from an ethno-cultural point of view, but also in terms of economics and geography (Zhdanko, 1972).

Especially in the North Caucasus, several nationhoods acquired a 'dual' character, combining in one polity sometimes quite different cultural groups – like Kabardin and Balkar, Karachai and Cherkess. This approach has now come under strong criticism. In reality, a prevailing motive behind this was to establish economically viable republics, with mountain and foothill resources and with natural communications and appropriate geographies – not to implement the 'divide and rule' principle. Some ethno-historians have argued that creating ethnic autonomies ('nation-states') for major groups in the region helped to prevent the outbreak of long-standing and bloody feuds among these groups and to provide better conditions for 'nation-building' (Volkova & Lavrov, 1968). Surely these arguments are more convincing than the purely politicized view that the Center undertook the division of the Gorskaya republic into new national republican formations so as to split up the historically rebellious North Caucasian groups (Conquest, 1960; Uralov (Avtorkhanov), 1952; Wixman, 1980).

2.4 The Policy of Repressions

Large-scale ethnic engineering within a single state proved possible only because of its totalitarian regime. Stalinism was ruthless, showing no mercy to any manifestations of initiative not sanctioned from above and to any displays of local nationalism. Soviet nationalities policy was characterized by its dual nature and inner contradictions, with gaps between idea and implementation, between expectations and practical results. This contradictory duality made itself felt as early as the first years of Bolshevik rule.

In June 1923, the Central Committee of the RCP(b) called a conference of representatives from all national republics and *oblasts*. On Stalin's initiative, the conference agenda included the question of Sultan-Galiyev, Chairman of the Federal Lands Committee and a prominent Tatar political leader. By that time, some republics had already begun taking certain steps to affirm their real sovereignty, particularly in economic affairs. Bashkiria, Tataria, Chuvashia, and Turkestan demanded more freedom to manage their agricultural lands according to local conditions and traditions. The central government was unwilling to share power with the republics, and those who supported their demands were accused of nationalism. Included in this category was Sultan-Galiyev, who was falsely accused of maintaining ties with the 'enemies of Soviet power'. Sultan-Galiyev became the first well-known victim of Stalinist purges; after his dismissal he was arrested and later shot.

The June 1923 conference put an end to any discussion of nationalities in the country and ushered in a long period of ruthless repression against leaders in the republics. Victims of those repressions included many outstanding political figures and cultural workers of the Ukraine, Caucasus and Central Asia. The same conference adopted a program of measures to develop the economy and culture in the national republics, and to expand the political representation of non-Russian nationalities, as well as making several other useful and positive decisions (*Tainy*, 1992). That was especially true with relation to the so-called *korenizatsiia* (nativization) policy, which remained for many years one of the priorities of the Kremlin rulers, and has been quite extensively recorded in historical literature (see, e.g., Carrère d'Encausse, 1991; Dahshleiger, 1965; Lieber, 1992; Yakubovskaya, 1966).

The nativization policy along with further related programs provided resources and guarantees for educational development and for training managerial workers, civil servants, and intelligentsia from the ranks of the 'native nationalities'. Beyond doubt, this policy gave an enormous boost to modernization and social improvements. But the same policy served as a tool for the system of indirect governance and for imposing Communist indoctrination under strict control from the Center. Thus, through this dual use of repressions and privileges the regime was able to exercise control over the periphery for many decades. As Rogers Brubaker has pointed out,

> Those policies . . . were intended to do two things: first, to harness, contain, channel, and control the potentially disruptive political expression of nationality by creating national-territorial administrative structures and by cultivating, co-opting, and (when

they threatened to get out of line) repressing national elites; and second, to drain nationality of its content even while legitimating it as a form, and thereby to promote the long-term withering away of nationality as a vital component of social life (1994, p. 49).

This last statement nevertheless overestimates the existing political architecture, including a strategy of promoting the slow death of nationality. Brubaker also makes the common mistake of overlooking the roles of momentum, improvised reactive acts, a search for immediate responses to challenges (everyday 'political opportunism' in Lenin's favorite words), and finally, power dispositions in the Soviet state. It is misleading to consider the nationalities policy as divorced from the general context of the constant struggles for power in the Kremlin. As can be seen from the materials of the 1923 Conference, in the first years of Bolshevik rule Stalin was in favor of creating state forms for smaller ethnic groups so as to weaken the positions of representatives of the larger ones – who could emerge as serious contenders in the struggle for control over the Center. The fight against 'Sultan-Galiyevism' was spearheaded in fact not so much against the Turkic peoples as against the growing tension between the representatives of Moscow and Kiev, as well as against Stalin's opponents in the central leadership. The analogy drawn by Stalin in 1923 between the Mensheviks and the 'nationalism of the country's periphery' (*Tainy*, 1992, p. 84), and the appeal to fight the latter, were meant to help him and his supporters consolidate their authority within the party and the country – and in this, Stalin succeeded.

For a long period Soviet nationalities policy remained subordinate to the basic ideological doctrine of creating socially homogeneous 'nations' of toiling people – nations which would, according to this theory, embody no internal strife but would, on the contrary, begin the process of rapprochement. 'Homogeneity' was to be achieved by building 'harmonious social structures' of nations, including not only efforts to construct a class of industrial workers among all nations but also severe repression of any 'bourgeois elements'. During the years of the Civil War and immediately after, among the first to be branded as such bourgeois elements were the Cossacks – a distinct socio-cultural stratum of the population mostly of Russo-Ukrainian ethnic origin in southern regions of Russia. (On the Cossacks in the Civil War, see Averyanov, 1993; Lazarev, 1995).

Repressions against the Cossacks started in 1919, and approximately 1,250,000 people suffered. In April 1921 alone, 70,000 Cossacks were forcefully deported from the North Caucasus to Kazakhstan and Siberia. That was the first major act of genocide based on group affinity. It had an extremely negative effect on Soviet inter-ethnic relations for many decades, as did other brutal acts against social, religious, and ethnic groups. With cynical simplicity Stalin himself explained the situation in his speech at the Congress of the peoples of Terskaya *oblast* on 17 November 1920:

> Soviet power has tried to protect the interests of the Cossacks from any violations . . . But the Cossacks behaved themselves more than suspiciously. They were always looking elsewhere and wouldn't trust Soviet power . . . Soviet power was patient for a long time but any patience has its limits . . . There was no way but to take some severe measures against them. Several guilty Cossack settlements had been deported and repeopled by the Chechens. The mountain people have understood it that now the Tersk Cossacks could be offended with impunity . . . If the mountain people do not stop these excesses the Soviet authorities will punish them with all the strictness of the revolutionary power (Stalin, 1947, vol. 4, pp. 399–400).

The most terrible acts of genocide were committed in the form of deportations and organized hunger in the campaign against the *kulaks* and to effect mass collectivization (Conquest, 1986). Realized in the late 1920s and early 1930s, this policy mostly affected the regions of the Ukraine, southern Russia and Kazakhstan. In 1932–33 two million people were deported from the Kuban area alone, with its relatively prosperous rural population. During the period of forced collectivization of 1931–32 in Kazakhstan, over two million Kazakhs died of hunger or left their homeplaces because of the destruction of the traditional nomadic economy and social order. Many of them migrated to China (Olcott, 1987). Victims of collectivization were primarily representatives of the larger groups – Ukrainians, Russians, Kazakhs – but the anti-*kulak* struggle and repressions took place all over the country and severely hurt many communities, including small indigenous groups in Siberia. Quotas for 'disclosing' *kulaks* and other 'enemies' were proclaimed for even the most distant areas of the country and 'distributed' among all localities 'for immediate execution'. Professor Leonid Potapov, one of the grand old men of Russian ethnography who carried out field research in the Altai region in the late 1920s and 1930s, reported to me that his first work on shamanism among Altaic indigenous people was ordered by local commissars to be published within the course of one week.[1] Field ethnography on the shamans and their social role, written from the Marxist 'class approach', was employed intentionally for ideological and political goals. It was used to prove the fact of an existing class society among Siberian natives; shamans were represented as 'exploiters' of ordinary people. As a result, severe repressions were exercised against traditional leaders, especially religious figures. Hundreds of Siberian shamans were sent to prison, their sacred objects destroyed, and their practices were forbidden.

Immediately after the 'total victory' of collectivization from the mid-1930s, purely ethnic deportations began. On many occasions the aims could hardly be explained by anything else but paranoic geopolitical fantasies of the 'Father of the peoples' and his maniacal distrust. An undeclared but highly probable aim in deporting several nationalities was to simplify the internal ethnic mosaic of the country, which did not fit into the scheme of forming 'socialist nations' on the basis of national state formations. Sometimes deportations or mass resettlements were implemented in order to repopulate places left desolate as the result of earlier repressions. Behind some of the deportations, especially in the case of smaller ethnic groups from national republics, stood the initiative of local authorities who willingly subscribed to the policy of ethnic cleansing.

Literature on the Stalinist deportations and their effects is rich in detail and replete with painful descriptions of the history of events (see Conquest, 1960; Critchlov, 1991; Nekrich, 1978; Uralov, 1952). However, it fails to take up questions which do not fit the contemporary political agenda and could even be viewed as a kind of vindication for repression. First, there is the question of adaptation (sometimes quite successful, as in the cases of Koreans and Germans) of deported people to new territories and what makes their post-Soviet resettlement 'back to historical motherlands', advocated by leaders and activists, a new variant of imposed will. Second, there is the question of the socio-cultural role of deported or relocated people in areas where, for the indigenous population, their first massive historical contacts with people of other, mainly more European, culture occurred. Nor has anyone yet studied how ethnic deportations influenced and strengthened identity formation. Carrying a passport with the special mark of deported person was, on an everyday level, a highly significant reminder of being an Ingush, a Chechen, etc. 'Punished peoples' identities, as a combination of fatality, resistance, and accommodation, are a complex social psychological problem, one which could not be solved solely by new legislation or new migration scenarios.

The first purely ethnic deportation was carried out against the sizeable Korean minority of the Far East, who were moved to Kazakhstan in 1935. In 1937, the remaining

Koreans along with the Chinese were forcibly moved to various areas of Siberia and Central Asia under the pretext of the need to 'strengthen the border'. The then-secret decision of the Soviet government 'On the resettlement of the Koreans' (taken on 8 September 1937) stated that 'the resettled Koreans are to be transported by train as economically formed collectivities, taking agricultural equipment and fishing tools with them [!]'(*Deportazii narodov*, 1992, p. 32). No explanation was provided as to how maritime Korean fishermen were going to engage in fishing in the desert and steppe areas of Uzbekistan and Kazakhstan. In 1937 many Kurds and Turks were deported from the Transcaucasian republics; and in 1939–40 mass deportations began from the newly annexed areas of Bessarabia, West Ukraine, West Belarus, and the Baltics.

The outbreak of war with Nazi Germany served as the excuse to deport the Germans living in the Volga region and other areas. A decree of the Presidium of the Supreme Soviet of the USSR of 28 August 1941 offered the following explanation, which only underlines the irrationality of Stalin's act:

> According to reliable data obtained by the military authorities, among the German population residing in the areas of the Volga River, there are thousands and dozens of thousands of saboteurs and spies ready to detonate explosives upon a signal from Germany in the areas populated by the Volga Germans. None of the Germans living in the Volga area have reported to the Soviet authorities about the presence of such a great number of saboteurs and spies among the Volga Germans – it follows then that the German population of the Volga areas hides in its midst enemies of the Soviet People and Soviet Power (*Deportazii narodov*, 1992, p. 34).

Similar variants of 'collaborationism' were also used for further deportations during the 1941–45 war. Completely deported from the North Caucasus were the Karachai people (December 1943), the Ingush and Chechens (February 1944), and the Balkars (March 1944). In December 1943, the Kalmyks were deported, in May 1944 the Crimean Tatars, in November 1944 the Meskhetian Turks and Khemshins from Georgia, and in June 1944 the Greeks from the Crimea. The territorial autonomies of 'punished' peoples were abolished; their land was divided among other republics and *oblast*s, or new administrative units were established. Repressions and deportations continued even after the end of the war.

By the time of Stalin's death in 1953, the total number of deportees with the status of so-called 'special settlers' (*spezposelentsy*) constituted 2,753,356 people, including 1.2 million Germans, 316,000 Chechens, 84,000 Ingush, 165,000 Crimean Tatars, 100,000 Lithuanians, 81,000 Kalmyks, 63,000 Karachai, 52,000 Greeks, 50,000 Meskhetian Turks, 45,000 Moldavians, 40,000 Letts, and 20,000 Estonians (Bugai, 1989). These figures do not include those imprisoned or shot, or those who died of hunger or disease. Other sources indicate that 3.5 million people were forcefully removed from their homelands between 1936 and 1956.

The living conditions of these 'special settlers' were hard and humiliating. They had to perform physical labor, they were granted only limited civil rights and were denied the possibility to practice their cultural and religious customs and traditions, to teach their children in their native languages, and to be engaged in managerial or pedagogical work. Their young people had restricted access to higher education. The most severe restriction that survived up to 1957, and for some peoples (Crimean Tatars, Ingush) up until very recently, was that they were forbidden to return to their former homeplaces. Most other deportees were allowed to return to their native places soon after 1956, following a series of governmental decisions to remove restrictions on 'special settlers'. The Checheno-Ingush, Karachai-Cherkess, Kabardino-Balkar, and Kalmyk autonomous republics were reinstituted, although not with their previous borders. Part of the Kalmyk territory remained within the limits of the Astrakhan *oblast,* and part of the Ingush territory within North Ossetia.

During the Stalinist period, the repressed peoples had to experience a tremendous physical and emotional trauma – the trauma of humiliation and loss of their collective dignity, which, along with some territorial problems, has carried directly over into the political situation of today, serving as a major cause of inter-ethnic tension and conflict. The problem of these peoples was aggravated by slow and limited rehabilitation measures, and, in some instances, because of counteraction against these measures on the part of authorities and the local population. It was not until 14 November 1989 that the Supreme Soviet of the USSR adopted the Declaration 'On Recognizing as Unlawful and Criminal the Repressive Acts Against the Peoples Subjected to Forced Resettlement'; on 22 April 1991 the Supreme Soviet of the Russian Federation adopted the law 'On Rehabilitation of the Repressed Peoples'. Both acts were important steps towards democratization, but ironically, the latter law has caused more problems than it resolved because it legitimized local territorial claims, demands for exclusive state support, and material compensation for members of deported groups.

2.5   The Policy of Prestige

Before trying to analyze recent developments in the ethno-political situation in Russia, however, let us consider the second major aspect of the ideology and implementation of Soviet nationalities policy. I have already mentioned the deep contradictions within Bolshevik aims in the 'national question': on the one hand, they pursued a harsh policy of repression and hyper-centralized power; on the other, they carried out a policy of ethnonational state-building, accompanied by support for prestigious institutions and elites as a means to preserve the integrity of the state and exercise totalitarian rule.

Although guided by motives of prestige and propaganda, the Soviet regime invested a great deal of effort and resources in substantiating its declaration about 'complete solution of the national question'. In the republics and among the smaller indigenous peoples, the development of education was strongly encouraged (written languages and textbooks were developed for about 50 ethnic groups). Culture in its professional forms (music, theater, literature, cinema) as well as other attributes of national statehood (academies of sciences, professional unions of creative workers, mass information, media and publishing, university education) were developed, supported, and paraded to demonstrate the success of the system. Local intelligentsia and managerial personnel, as well as influential bureaucracy, were formed already in the pre-war period through the nativization policy amongst Soviet nationalities (Bromley, 1977; Dahshleiger, 1985; Simon, 1991).

The 1960s–80s were an important period in the history of Soviet nationalities. The gap that had existed in social structures of main ethnic groups was practically eliminated as a result of social mobility, together with quotas and preferences in the sphere of education. Average educational standards in the ethnic republics – in particular, the percentage of those holding university diplomas and scholarly degrees – grew considerably higher than the average national indices, outstripping the corresponding figures for the Russian majority (Arutunyan & Bromley, 1986; Drobizheva, 1981; Simon, 1991).

Rising social expectations and the growing power of the peripheral elites were accompanied in some cases by serious demographic shifts; the numerical growth among non-Russians (or, more exactly, non-Slavic and non-Baltic peoples) was much higher than that of the Russians, Ukrainians, Belorussians and the Balts (Tables 2.2 and 2.3).

Table 2.2   *Ethnic Composition and Demographic Growth of the USSR's Population,
1959–1989*

Main ethnic group	Number (thousands)			% increase from 1959–1989	% of total	
	1959	1979	1989		1959	1989
Russian	114,114	137,397	145,155	127.2	54.6	50.8
Ukrainian	37,253	42,347	44,186	118.6	17.8	15.5
Uzbek	6,015	12,456	16,698	277.6	2.9	5.8
Belorussian	7,913	9,463	10,036	126.8	3.8	3.5
Kazakh	3,622	6,556	8,136	224.6	1.7	2.8
Azerbaijani	2,940	5,477	6,770	332.3	1.4	2.4
Tatar	4,918	6,185	6,649	135.2	2.4	2.3
Armenian	2,787	4,151	4,623	165.9	1.3	1.6
Tajik	1,397	2,898	4,215	301.7	0.7	1.5
Georgian	2,692	3,571	3,981	147.9	1.3	1.4
Moldavian	2,214	2,968	3,352	151.4	1.1	1.2
Lithuanian	2,326	2,851	3,067	131.9	1.1	1.1
Turkmen	1,002	2,028	2,729	272.4	0.5	1.0
Kirgiz	969	1,906	2,529	261.0	0.5	0.9
German	1,620	1,936	2,039	125.9	0.8	0.7
Polish	1,380	1,151	1,126	81.6	0.7	0.7
Chuvash	1,470	1,751	1,842	125.3	0.7	0.6
Latvian	1,400	1,439	1,459	104.2	0.7	0.5
Bashkir	989	1,371	1,449	146.5	0.5	0.5
Jew	2,177	1,762	1,378	63.3	1.0	0.5
Mordva	1,285	1,192	1,154	89.8	0.6	0.4
Estonian	989	1,020	1,027	103.8	0.5	0.4
Chechen	419	756	957	228.4	0.2	0.3
Udmurt	625	714	747	119.5	0.3	0.3
Mari	504	622	671	113.1	0.2	0.2
Avar	270	483	601	124.5	0.1	0.2
Osset	413	542	598	114.9	0.2	0.2

Source: Tishkov, ed., 1994, p. 30

From 1979 to 1989, the Russian population in the USSR increased by 5.6%, Ukrainians by 4.2% and Belorussians by 6%. During the same period, population growth among the Azerbaijanis was 24%, Uzbeks and Turkmens 24%, Kirgiz 32%, and Tajiks 45%. In contrast, the natural growth among Latvians and Estonians was the lowest in the country (1.4 and 2.4% respectively) – which subsequently provided a powerful argument for exclusive local nationalism to 'restore the demographic balance'.

In most republics the 1970s were marked by the emerging process of ethnic homogenization in favor of the titular nationalities. The main reason for this development was the migration of the Russians from areas of Central Asia and the Transcaucasus. Meanwhile, in such republics as the Ukraine, Kazakhstan, Belarus, Latvia and Estonia, the proportion of Russians increased (Table 2.4).

In the case of Central Asia and the Transcaucasus, it came as no surprise to see increasing claims and competitiveness by the titular groups to control the institutions of power and distribution of resources. In Estonia and Kazakhstan, however, the changing demography resulted in growing anxiety among the titulars about losing the dominant

Table 2.3 *Population Growth in Union Republics of the USSR, 1969–1989 (%)*

Republic	1969–79	1980–89
Armenia	17.4	15.6
Azerbaijan	18.2	20.0
Belorussia	6.1	4.9
Estonia	2.8	3.7
Georgia	9.1	8.1
Kazakhstan	15.9	15.4
Kirgizia	21.1	23.2
Latvia	1.4	2.4
Lithuania	4.6	4.8
Moldavia	9.7	9.7
Russia	4.9	3.9
Tajikistan	28.9	32.2
Turkmenia	26.0	27.3
Ukraine	3.5	1.7
Uzbekistan	26.4	27.0
USSR	8.0	7.6

Source: Narodnoe khozyaistvo SSSR v 1989 g. Statisticheski sbornik [National Economy of the USSR. Statistical Survey]. Moscow: Statistika, 1990, p. 38

Table 2.4. *Population of the USSR in 1989*

Republic	Population (thousands)	% of total	Titular nationality in USSR (thousands)	%	Titular nationality in republic (%)	Russians in republic (%)
Russia	147,386	51.4	145,072	50.6	–	82
Armenia	3,283	1.1	4,627	1.6	93	2
Azerbaijan	7,029	2.5	6,791	2.4	83	6
Belorussia	10,200	3.6	10,030	3.5	78	13
Estonia	1,573	0.5	1,029	0.4	62	30
Georgia	5,449	1.9	3,983	1.4	70	6
Kazakhstan	16,538	5.8	8,138	2.8	40	38
Kirgizia	4,291	1.5	2,531	0.9	52	21
Latvia	2,681	0.9	1,459	0.5	52	34
Lithuania	3,690	1.3	3,068	1.1	80	9
Moldavia	4,341	1.5	3,355	1.2	64	13
Tajikistan	5,112	1.8	4,217	1.5	62	8
Turkmenia	3,534	1.2	2,718	0.9	72	9
Ukraine	51,704	18.0	44,136	15.5	73	22
Uzbekistan	19,906	6.9	16,686	5.8	71	8
USSR	286,717	100.0				

Source: Compiled from 1989 census data

majority in their 'own' republics and becoming subject to an even greater degree of acculturation towards Russian culture.

The economic policy of the Soviet state exerted a contradictory influence on the ethnic situation. From the very first years of Bolshevik government there was an officially proclaimed goal to eliminate the economic backwardness of the national republics. In the predominantly rural areas, industrial enterprises were built specifically for the purpose of ensuring the growth of the working class, which the regime saw as its main stronghold, and to improve social conditions. After World War II, modern industrial enterprises were established in the republics to help accelerate the urbanization of the population. However, such measures did not prevent the introduction in some republics of a mono-cultural agrarian economy, with grave repercussions on natural environments and health conditions. (A specific case in point was the massive cotton-growing economy of Central Asia.) In total, Soviet economic policy led to a high degree of economic interdependence between all union republics, with the Russian Republic providing large subsidies to other republics, supplying cheap energy and raw materials. In 1989, the Russian Republic provided nearly 67 billion roubles in subsidies to other republics, while Russia was the least dependent on trade with other republics.

The unitary strategy of development and the imposition of Russian-language ideo-logical presentations from the Center resulted in the formation of similar socio-professional structures and many common cultural and value orientations among the various Soviet nationalities (Arutunyan & Bromley, 1986). The emergence of the 'one community of Soviet people' doctrine in the country was no accident: the over-whelming majority of Soviet citizens shared the same (or very similar) social, political, and even cultural values. On the other hand, differences in cultural traditions, industrial development, demographic behavior and political culture managed to survive all through the Soviet period:

> the attempt to introduce a monolithic and homogeneous super-structure into an extremely diverse mosaic of cultures met with a considerable opposition and in many regions of the country yielded but very modest results. What is very important is that the Soviet politics preserved and enlarged the gap in the development levels between the Union republics (Lapidus & Zaslavsky, 1992, p. 3).

This statement is probably too strong and polemical. Socio-economic indices and statistics on living standards show that only Central Asian republics experienced serious developmental gaps compared with other republics. These republics were followed by Russia and Moldavia, with the Baltic, Armenian, and Georgian republics representing the highest standards. Thus, the model that seeks to explain disintegration by reference to developmental levels and by the 'winners and losers' dichotomy fails to explain the situation that existed, and contradicts the fact that it was the most advantaged and well-off republics that finally initiated the disintegration of the USSR. Even more difficult to accept is the thesis that cultural differences between republics stem from the very nature of their civilizational character, and that such differences could never coexist in the bosom of a single state (see Prazauskas, 1991).

While the Soviet central power was strong enough to control the local administrations, and at the same time suppress any attempts at organized nationalist movements, it was also in a position to secure the tolerance and consent of key social actors through the notion of a single multi-ethnic state. But as soon as the power and unified ideology weakened, the very foundation of the nationalities policy lost its hold. Ethnicity as a basis of group solidarity, and ethnic nationalism as a political doctrine, challenged the status quo. It was a kind of 'national answer' to the national question, the cumulative result of the previous social engineering and at the same time a major innovation on the part of people and politicians in the course of their multi-variant history. Nothing was predetermined or unavoidable; neither the demise of the Soviet state, nor the conflicts and wars. Contemporary as well as past scenarios are largely the result of emancipatory political projects rationally (or irrationally) planned and implemented by powerholders through chaotic forms of competition within and between different networks. As one of these networks, ethnicity played a vital role in shaping and re-shaping the 'state versus society' dichotomy during the Soviet period. But, as Chris Hann noted, 'most of the time, most "ordinary people" simply took the system for granted, accommodated to it and got on with their lives . . . "muddling through", just as people do in other kinds of society' (1993, pp. 11–12). The events of the Gorbachev–Yeltsin era support this type of observation, and not an evasive approach based on 'essentialist' and 'historical law' arguments of evolutionary and positivist frameworks.

Notes

1   See my interview with Leonid Potapov in *Etnograficheskoie obozrenie*, 1993, no. 1, pp. 31–45.

3

Ethno-politics in a Time of Transition

3.1 Introduction

The 'triumph of nations' is indeed a beguiling phrase – coined by Hélène Carrère d'Encausse (1993) – to signify the dissolution of the Soviet Union. It is now commonplace in literature on the perestroika era to argue that Mikhail Gorbachev committed a serious error of judgement in underestimating the national question and initiating his liberal reforms without foreseeing the explosion of ethnic problems that was to follow.

In considering the 'triumph of nations' notion in my own research analysis and participatory experience, however, I have encountered serious difficulties. The first problem concerns defining 'nations' as real groups or even (relational) communicative systems. Drawing on the immensely rich discourse on 'the wrath of nations' (to use another journalistic phrase by William Pfaff) during the Gorbachev–Yeltsin era and applying it to political and personal interactions, we find nation neither as a discrete social actor nor as a type of social interaction which can be labeled 'inter-national relations' (*mezhnatsional'nye otnosheniia*). For me, Oleg Glebov and John Crowfoot's presentation of 'nations speak out' (1989) in a published collection of statements from speakers at the First Congress of the Peoples Deputies in May–June 1989, or my colleague Mikhail Guboglo's project on 'national movements' in the former Soviet Union in over 30 volumes of published documents, should be seen in terms of expressions of particularist perspectives and individual interests or of injecting a meaning into a sphere of social discourse – but not exclusively in terms of the collective actions, 'movements', or interactions of real groups.

Said in another way: if Gorbachev and his associates were so blind in their interpretation of the situation as to overlook the aspect of 'hidden nations' in their political scenario, why then did an entire legion of Soviet and Western experts fail to monitor this situation more sensitively and suggest appropriate action? This question has been asked many times: it is, however, the wrong question, asked by persons on the borderlines of recognized social science. Behind the powerful, emotionally legitimate but allegorical and academically empty word 'nation', we are losing something much more important and 'real' in the multifaceted roles that ethnicity and nationalist rhetoric play in individual and group action. We are probably introducing into the research agenda a phenomenon that is simply not there and passing judgement on political actors and their accomplishments on the basis of false criteria and mythopoetic definitions.

In 1992 during my only personal encounter with Mikhail Gorbachev, he asked me what should have been done during his time with respect to the nationalities policy. This was an interesting question to be posed by the former leader of a former country, not least as it indicated how he has been convinced by prevailing opinion of his failure in this regard. My answer to Gorbachev was that he should have abolished *Vyezdnaya komissia* (a special Department of the Communist Party's Central Committee which granted permission for trips abroad) and should have allowed republican leaders to have personal jets for business flights. This was in fact a serious answer, motivated by my observation of the summit of CIS leaders held one day earlier, in June in the Presidential Hotel in Moscow.

I had met the President of the Moldovan Republic, Mr Mircea Snegur, at the airport and escorted him to a special residence normally occupied by heads of state visiting the USSR. 'Before, we were not allowed even to be behind these gates,' remarked President Snegur. 'Now we are treated like people.' This desire 'to be treated like people' carries more explanatory weight than many oft-cited arguments on 'national independence'. It touches on the issue of how wide the circle of the 'we' is for a leader of a nation – and it is also rather evident that an unexpected challenge to Gorbachev's perestroika came not so much from 'hidden nations' but from elite elements who empowered themselves through a new set of arguments and group mobilization.

In this book, I wish to challenge the widespread notion of 'fighting nations' as homogeneous entities capable of speaking with one voice and acting with one will. In Soviet and post-Soviet contexts, this notion negates a perspective recognized in the analysis of other societies – that is, the role of actors exercising individual strategies, the acknowledgement that individuals may have 'an enormous variety of viewpoints, which they often are prepared to defend with violence' (Stokes, 1995, p. 150). Again, from my personal experience, it has been important to observe what may qualify as the Tatar nation ('a nation without a state' by common ideological definition – Bremmer & Taras, 1993, p. 419) struggling against the Russians for sovereignty – especially during the tense situation from 1992 until agreement was reached in February 1994. First, during negotiations between delegations of Tatarstan and Russia – headed by the republic's Vice President Vasilii Likhachev and by Russian State Secretary Gennadi Burbulis – there were no fewer ethnic Russians in the Tatarstan delegation than among the Russian delegation. Second, behind the nationalist rhetoric, there was a legitimate desire to devolve power and the right to control resources and taxation in favor of the local elite who wanted more personal benefits, room to exercise individual freedom, and upward social mobility. Vasilii Likhachev, for example, asked me in private to approach Gennadi Burbulis and inquire about an opportunity for him to get a Russian ambassadorial post in 'one of the European countries'. Incidentally, three years later he achieved his major aspiration of being elected Deputy Head of the Council of the Federation, the upper chamber of the Russian parliament.

For me, the turning point in the difficult Russia–Tatarstan dialogue was not the signing of the treaty on the delimitation of power, which was a more or less symbolic act. No, the decisive point was reached when President Shaimiev had accumulated enough authority and resources to manage an intercontinental flight in his private plane to deliver a lecture at Harvard University and introduce Tatarstan's businessmen and politicians to useful and enjoyable outside world contacts. The importance of this hedonistic struggle for power through collective, including ethnic, mobilization has been totally overlooked by most scholars and writers on the Soviet collapse, because it contradicts the politically correct and predominant notion of Soviet nations aspiring to their own statehoods.

We need a more sophisticated and unbiased analysis of the events since the late 1980s. It is important to study the surging tide of ethnic declarations at top political levels and to read how and for what purposes and rewards these declarations were translated into mass sentiments and expectations. 'We had learned the technology of how to call up national forces, how to organize and to direct them. Now we control the nationals (*nationaly*) because we had achieved a lot and have another agenda,'[1] acknowledged Raphael Khakimov, political adviser to the Tatarstan President Shaimiev, in October 1995.

How wide was the circle of 'we' for Raphael Khakimov at this time? Doubtless its content had changed since local intellectuals and politicans in this republic, after proclaiming sovereignty, started to implement the doctrine of building a civic, multi-ethnic Tatarstan nation including ethnic Russians and other groups living in this republic. Raphael

Khakimov's personal political strategy had also changed, gradually including the formation of an alliance with the most powerful Russian nationalist movement, the Congress of Russian Communities (KRO) headed by Yuri Skokov and General Alexander Lebed. Behind these interactions and coalitions how many things had changed for the members of that club called 'a nation'? I have come to the conclusion that rank-and-file members of 'we' are blocked from receiving many of the rewards that proponents of changes, including in Moscow, are trying to introduce through market reforms and civic freedoms. And who is blocking them? Those who usurp the power to speak out on behalf of the 'we' – the Tatar, the Bashkir, the Chechen and other 'nations'. Thus it would be more appropriate to qualify accomplished and ongoing events in the former Soviet Union as a triumph of the allegory of the 'triumph of nations'. And scholars are among those who have contributed to this process by constructing these powerful allegories.

3.2 Sovereignty as Allegory

Reading narrations of ethnic manifestation since Gorbachev's ascent to power is an intriguing task for a revisionist social science analysis. Many well-written and balanced reports have already been produced, full of data and interesting interpretations. But something is missing – most of all, the direct voices of the actors and some basic understanding of the society. With regard to the latter we should reckon the behavioral/moral patterns of Soviet people as well as the role of the institutions and networks, like the mass media, international public opinion, and diasporas, which have never been put under serious scrutiny before. In his book *Will the Non-Russians Rebel?* Alexander Motyl had specified some structural grounds for opposition and latent conflict tendencies embedded in the ethnic pattern of domination of the Soviet Russian state. As he noted:

> At some point, non-Russians may massively want to rebel. But will they? As long as the public sphere is occupied and, more important, as long as the KGB remains intact, the de-privatization of anti-state attitudes will be problematic, anti-state collectivities and elites will be unlikely to mobilize, alliances between workers and intellectuals will not materialize, and rebellion, revolt, and insurrection will be well-nigh impossible. Because they cannot rebel, non-Russians will not rebel (Motyl, 1987, p. 170).

This was a correct conclusion in many aspects. Civic apathy, along with the collectivistic egalitarianism strongly associated with the distributive state, were (and remain) major characteristics of former Soviet compatriots. There were no worker–intelligentsia alliances, nor any need for such alliances, because a disproportionate number of Soviet intellectuals who were indoctrinated to play a messianic role ('engineers of human souls' in Stalin's words) managed to define a profile of political process and a course of events without recourse to 'strategic allies'. There was no explicit revolt or insurrection on the part of non-Russians. Mass rallies and demonstrations were full of praise – for Leninist nationalities policy, for perestroika, for Mikhail Gorbachev personally or in combination with particular demands like keeping a long-time party boss in office (Kazakhstan, December 1986), annexation of a territory (Armenia, January–February 1988), and environmental and cultural demands (Baltic republics, Moldavia, Georgia in 1988–89). In March 1989, a demonstration in Riga gathered 20,000 people against the Latvian Party Central Committee's condemnation of 'anti-Soviet and separatist' currents in the republic.

What was really taking place was a grandiose learning curve in free individual manifestation in the Soviet tradition – a form of mass demonstration. According to the definition of Armenian scholar Levon Abramyan, it was a phenomenon of 'demonstration as folk festival' (Abramyan & Borodatova, 1992). In many aspects this was a reassertion of individual and collective dignity, irrespective of ethnic meaning. Ethnic revolt as a stand was to be learned later; it could be traced as such only in the Baltic republics and in exclusively peaceful forms. In 1988, the Institute of Ethnology and Anthropology organized a round-table discussion on 'What is the future of the Union?' The result was an open discussion of liberal-minded experts but in our Baltic colleagues' presentations not a word was said about scenarios of political independence. I had asked future political celebrity Viktor Gryazin, whose paper contained sociological survey data on pro-independence attitudes among a certain portion of the Estonian population, the question, 'Why are there no reflections on this perspective in political strategy designs?' The answer was quite astonishing, from the perspective of today: 'We have considered this factor but do not need full independence, despite the strong push from abroad, especially from our diaspora.'[2]

In a situation of political liberalization, weakening state institutions, and the rising role of local initiatives, ethnic unrest in the USSR started not as a major political cleavage but as inter-ethnic riots and communal clashes directed mainly towards vulnerable 'double minorities' in national republics. Here we should note the anti-Armenian pogrom in Sumgait, Azerbaijan, in February 1988; the expulsion of Meskhetian Turks from the Fergana region of Uzbekistan in June 1989; anti-minorities riots in the Tajik capital of Dushanbe in February 1990 and other similar events. Not all major cases of conflicting ethnicity were directed at the Russian imperial center, not even in the Baltic, where there were far greater reasons and legitimacy for political upheaval. Only later did there arise the feeling that this was all a big game – and then it took on a spontaneous, explosive form, demonstrating that major events would be undetermined and unexpected. Probably the most important influence in this course of events was to be found behind Kremlin walls, where the most massive demonstration of growing sentiments of free expression was broadcast all over the country.

The first Congress of People's Deputies elected in 1989 could boast a remarkable representation of major Soviet nationalities. The most eloquent and flamboyant figures were sent first to the all-union Parliament to speak out on the country's problems as well as on the concerns of the republics and regions. Judging by its behavior and topics of discussion, this Congress was not so much a federal parliament as an 'assembly of nations' each trying to attain their own goals and objectives (see Tishkov, 1990a). A symbol of the fatal weakness of the state doctrine became just one letter, 's', added to the text of the Presidential oath after a discussion in the Parliament. The first (and the last) President of the USSR, Mikhail Gorbachev, had to pledge his allegiance not 'to the people of the Soviet Union' but 'to the peoples of the Soviet Union,' as proposed by the poet Evgeni Yevtushenko, and decreed by the Congress of People's Deputies.

The first serious challenge to Gorbachev's gradual top-down liberalization and gradual economic reforms came from the Baltic republics – where the need for socio-cultural improvements was in fact less urgent than elsewhere in the USSR. But the Baltic republics were smaller polities with articulate Westernized elites quick to grasp the opportunities of the opening society. There were well-established cultural profiles and strong communicative systems reaching local communities. The Balts enjoyed also relatively higher standards of living – and these they wanted to keep and to strengthen, rather than lose them through the slow movement of the larger Soviet society. Along with this reassertion came the image of the 'occupied nation', which became the core of the re-emerging Baltic political identity.

The Baltic example was followed by growing public articulations in the form of 'national rebirth' projects in Georgia, Azerbaijan, and Moldavia. These, mainly verbal and mutually misinterpreted, dialogues between Center and Periphery were basically of a vertical, political character, but they were directed also against local rulers and 'aliens'. They first presented 'denationalized' Communist *nomenklatura* as 'enemies of the nation.' The 'aliens' were easy to identify: they were the non-titular part of the local population (Russian military and managerial personnel, small, non-status minorities, ethnic enclaves of neighboring peoples).

The programmatic context of so-called 'national movements' in the USSR was diffuse and rapidly changing. It was a mixture of romantic nationalism from the late 19th century and cold-blooded calculations of political activists who were bent on gaining power. Few of the leaders of the Periphery (Ukrainian Vladimir Ivashko, Georgian Eduard Shevardnadze, Uzbek Rafik Nishanov, and others) linked their position with Gorbachev and his program. Many more switched loyalties and doctrinal baggage to become nationalists. As Gale Stokes has noted, 'Ethnic nationalism is attractive to former communists because its vision of a uniform and disciplined society in which leaders define what constitutes the popular will mimics the totalitarian pretensions of Stalinism' (1995, p. 151).

Formerly deported ethnic groups who had lost their political status in Stalin's time – or, rather, the activists of their movements – began formulating programs to restore 'their own' statehoods. Leaders of autonomous republics started to campaign to get their status raised to the level of union republics, and thus avoid 'double' subordination and 'double' acculturation pressure not only from Moscow, but also from republican centers. That is how a bloc of people's deputies from the Parliament, and the leader of this group, Vladislav Ardzinba from Abkhazia, put forward radical demands – majority quotas in autonomies' legislatures, a flow of subsidies between Moscow and autonomies, and signing of the new Union Treaty on equal terms with the union republics.

The Center proved ill-prepared to undertake serious steps, conduct negotiations or make the concessions necessary to meet these challenges. Its reaction was mainly impulsive, directed primarily at the policy of force and punishment. While some Communist Party leaders and academic experts were trying to transform the official policy towards ethnic issues and to revise political platforms and legal documents, adherents of force were suppressing the rising local opposition in Tbilisi (April 1989), Baku (January 1990) and Vilnius (January 1991). Even the local actions of minorities (as in Nagorno Karabakh) were sometimes used to manipulate the regional situation. Often, the same people in power, including Gorbachev himself, demonstrated impulsive, contradictory behavior in the multifaceted and previously unheard-of tumult of public life. There was a strikingly limited arsenal of arguments and appeals that central authorities could use to confront the newly permitted expressions of long-accumulated complaints and expectations. On the declarative level, one 'sacred cow' of nationalities policy – the appeal 'to keep and strengthen friendships of the peoples' – simply stopped functioning. At the top levels there was programmatic poverty, with chaotic fluctuations between conciliatory and coercive measures. In September 1989, the Party's Central Committee plenum on nationalities issues took place. It was quite astonishing to note the absence of constructive, innovative approaches at this impressive forum of central *apparatchiks*, 'national' Communists and intellectuals. The following year, in July 1990, the 28th Congress of the CPSU discussed the same problems at a special one-day session where I participated as a delegate and made my only speech at any top communist forum. On 5 July, we spent the evening prior to the final day of the conference with Estonian academician Viktor Palme in the office of Vyacheslav Mikhailov, then head of the Nationalities Department at the

Central Committee of the CPSU, drafting from scratch a resolution which was passed the next day as a major party document on nationalities policy. As my main contribution, I reformulated the goal of the nationalities policy to read: 'to safeguard appropriate conditions and guarantees for all Soviet citizens to exercise their rights and aspirations based on their nationality affiliation and for the peoples of the Soviet Union to preserve and develop their distinctiveness and integrity, and to determine their way of life'. This was a decisive substitute for the old cliché of 'strengthening friendship and unity of the peoples'. It was also the first formulation of state ethnic policy based on the primacy of individual rights – but it meant nothing for concrete political moves. Some of those who voted in favor of this resolution were to issue the order to use military force in one of the republics shortly thereafter. Such an inconsistent and unclear policy served merely to provoke greater dissatisfaction, destroying illusions about the ability of the Center to provide more responsible governance and freedoms to the 'non-dominant' nationalities and peripheral territories.

3.3 Sovereignty as a Clash of Powers

The ethnic policy of the perestroika period proved a failure, exploited by Gorbachev's opponents in Moscow and by opponents of Moscow in the Periphery as the main argument to abolish the Soviet Union. The demise of the state could at the same time be considered a great achievement of the leaders of the main non-Russian groups who were able to realize their not clearly articulated but extremely appealing aspirations peacefully. The irony of the situation is that the initiator of this disintegration was in fact the Russian Federation and its leader, Boris Yeltsin, who was brought to power by radical democratic groups and could register significant victories in the Russian republican elections of 4 March 1990. On 12 June 1990, the Russian Congress of People's Deputies adopted the Declaration of Sovereignty for this largest and most powerful of the Soviet republics. The legal status of this document was unclear, but its political meaning was explicitly directed against Gorbachev and the Union's power structure, and towards more revolutionary changes in the country. Congress then passed the proposal 'On Delimitation of Power Authorities on the Territory of RSFSR' as the point of departure for a new Union Treaty. This document incorporated a provision on the transfer of major power, including finance, defense, the KGB and foreign policy, to the Russian authorities. It proposed making direct treaties in all spheres of relations with other union republics 'on an equal and voluntary basis'. In July 1990, a law was passed granting the Russian authorities full control over all resources, economy, and wealth. October 1990 saw the passage of a law setting the economic foundation for the sovereignty of Russia, which provided a practical scenario for the peaceful dissolution of the union state and the disintegration of the central government.

From a holistic point of view, this could be interpreted as a clash of two strategies and of two political blocs on the question of how to proceed with reforms and democratization. But it was also a fight for power in a situation where political opponents were not held back by respect for the law or by responsible civic institutions. As described by one scholar, after the fall of 1990 'Yeltsin and Gorbachev were locked in a power struggle'; Yeltsin undertook a series of radical steps to expel Gorbachev and his other former Politburo compatriots from the Kremlin (Garthoff, 1994, p. 439). Yeltsin rejected the compromise economic reform plan adopted by the Supreme Soviet in October 1990, and announced a more radical 500-day economic plan for the Russian Republic alone. Russia's Supreme Soviet also reaffirmed the primacy of its own legislative acts for the territory of this republic. The leadership of the Russian Republic blocked all efforts of the Union Center to reorganize the structure of the entire country.

Other republics followed suit. On 16 July 1990, the Supreme Soviet of Ukraine passed its Declaration of Sovereignty which called not only for full autonomy but for a separate national army. Declarations of sovereignty and the supremacy of the authorities of the various republics were announced and actually established throughout much of the Union. Periphery leaders urged scepticism and disregard for the efforts of Gorbachev and the All-Union Supreme Soviet to work out a new Union Treaty. I myself participated as an expert in one of the meetings of the Chamber of Nationalities' committee on the preparation of the draft Union Treaty in October 1990. There was a quite amazing discussion among influential Moscow politicians, mainly of non-Russian ethnic background, about how to counter Boris Yeltsin's efforts to eliminate the Union Center. Discussants included an Uzbek (Rafik Nishanov), Ukrainians (Nikolai Revenko and Vladimir Girenko), a Belorussian (Georgii Tarasevich), and a Tatar (Gumer Usmanov) among others.

On 23 November, Gorbachev presented to the Supreme Soviet the draft Union Treaty, which granted considerably more power to the republics and established the central Federation Council as a policy-making body made up of leaders from each republic. Despite some serious reservations, it was accepted by eleven republics (minus the Baltics and Georgia) but the future of the new Union Treaty was seriously undermined by the signing of a bilateral treaty between Russia and Ukraine after Yeltsin's visit to Kiev. The text of this document was designed as an agreement between two sovereign states, omitting any mention of the USSR or other political supra-structures. In December 1990, at the session of the Congress of People's Deputies, Gorbachev proposed calling popular referenda in all the republics on the new Union Treaty, to neutralize the 'dark forces' of nationalism and to preserve a union of those republics where the majority would support it. An attempt to relegitimize the authority of the Soviet Union was made through a referendum on 17 March 1991 with the question: 'Do you consider it necessary to preserve the Union of Soviet Socialist Republics as a renewed federation of equal sovereign republics, in which the rights and freedom of the individual of any nationality will be fully guaranteed?' Six republics (Armenia, Georgia, Moldavia, and the three Baltic republics) boycotted the referendum openly; there was no way to control the situation. Leaders of the three largest republics decided to follow a 'words only' policy, suggesting a slightly modified formulation of the question but with different meaning. Nursultan Nazarbaev in Kazakhstan used the question 'Do you regard it as necessary to preserve the USSR as a Union of equal and sovereign states?' Leonid Kravchuk in Ukraine reformulated the question so that Ukrainian membership could be based on its own declaration of state sovereignty. In Russia another question was added – about introducing a presidency in the republic.

On the same day that Gorbachev made a television appeal to his 'dear fellow citizens to say "yes" to the integrity of the state with a millennium history' (*Pravda*, 16 March 1991), Boris Yeltsin decried the referendum as 'an attempt to get support for the country's leadership in order to pursue further politics of preservation of the imperial essence of the Union' (*Nezavisimaya gazeta*, 16 March 1991). The people were confused, unsure as to what they were being asked about. In fact, the results astonished many who had expected the referendum on the preservation of the Soviet Union to fail. With an 80% turnout (148.5 million voted) a 'yes' answer was given by 113.5 million people (76.4%). Highest support came from the Central Asian republics and the lowest – from Russia. Among Russia's autonomies the lowest turnout (58.8%) and the lowest support (75.9%) were observed in the Checheno-Ingush Republic (Table 3.1).

Table 3.1 *Results of 17 March 1991 Referendum on Preservation of the Soviet Union*

Republic	Voted (*N*)	Turnout (%)	'Yes' (*N*)	'Yes" (%)	'No' (*N*)	'No' (%)
Russia	79,701,169	75.4	56,860,783	71.3	21,030,753	26.4
Bashkiria	2,719,637	81.7	1,908,875	85.9	269,007	12.1
Buryatia	535,802	80.2	447,438	83.5	78,167	14.6
Checheno-						
Ingushetia	419,012	58.8	318,059	75.9	94,737	22.6
Chuvashia	748,420	83.1	616,387	82.4	113,249	15.1
Daghestan	812,009	80.5	670,488	82.6	131,522	16.2
Kabardino-						
Balkaria	372,607	76.1	290,380	77.9	77,399	20.8
Kalmykia	169,124	82.8	148,462	87.8	17,833	10.5
Karelia	418,101	75.8	317,854	76.0	92,703	22.2
Komi	543,403	62.8	412,842	76.0	119,678	22.0
Mari	418,599	79.6	333,319	79.6	77,239	18.5
Mordovia	571,631	84.3	459,021	80.3	101,886	17.8
North Ossetia	367,858	85.9	331,823	90.2	32,786	8.9
Tataria	1,951,768	77.1	1,708,193	87.5	211,516	10.8
Tuva	138,496	80.6	126,598	91.4	9,404	6.8
Udmurtia	819,140	74.3	622,714	76.0	180,289	22.0
Yakutia	541,993	78.7	415,712	76.7	116,798	21.6
Azerbaijan	2,903,797	75.1	2,709,246	93.3	169,225	5.8
Belorussia	6.126,983	83.3	5,069,313	82.7	986,079	16.1
Georgia (only						
Abkhazia)	166,544	52.3	164,231	98.6	1,566	0.9
Kazakhstan	8,816,543	88.2	8,295,519	94.1	436,560	5.0
Kirgizia	2,174,593	92.9	2,057,971	94.6	86,245	4.0
Tajikistan	2,407,552	94.2	2,315,755	96.2	75,300	3.1
Turkmenia	1,847,310	97.7	1,804,138	97.9	31,203	1.7
Ukraine	31,514,244	83.5	22,110,899	70.2	8,820,089	28.0
Uzbekistan	9,816,333	95.4	9,196,848	93.7	511,373	5.2
Kara-						
Kalpakia	577,717	98.9	563,916	97.6	10,133	1.8

Source: *Pravda*, 27 March 1991

In the spring of 1991, Gorbachev initiated the Novo-Ogarevo process to keep together at least those parts of the country where leaders were ready to negotiate a new and looser formula for the Union. Nine leaders met with Gorbachev and issued a statement 'on measures of stabilization and overcoming crisis in the country'. Three meetings were held in Novo-Ogarevo (near Moscow) in May, June, and July, at which republican leaders and leaders of ethno-territorial autonomies (like Abkhazia in Georgia, Tatarstan and Bashkiria in Russia) bargained fiercely for their own interests amidst efforts to work out the text of the new treaty. This was a dramatic period; debates of the highest political priority and historical significance were conducted without any proper expertise, publicity, or indeed feelings of personal responsibility. Everyone was referring to 'the will' of their 'own' peoples or parliaments, pursuing their own personal visions of the situation and their own verbal formulae. It was a demonstration of a striking feature of Soviet political culture – the lack of legal constraint and civic consensus.

At the second meeting on 3 June, Gorbachev complained desperately: 'If such sharing (*delezh*) takes place, that means the end: we will not be able to stop ourselves. If disintegration proceeds at such a tempo, we will put all the peoples in a state of turmoil and invite complete chaos' (*Soiuz*, 1995, p. 157). After these words, Nazarbaev remarked gloomily (when Boris Yeltsin had left the meeting room), addressing Gorbachev: 'The time has arrived to use force at least once,' Luk'yanov responded immediately to Nazarbaev with a question: 'Are you ready to assign that kind of right to the President?' The answer was silence, as registered in the notes taken by Yuri Baturin, Mikhail Gorbachev's adviser on legal questions (*Soiuz*, 1995, p. 161). Yuri Baturin published an intriguing report of the last meeting in Novo-Ogarevo on 23 July, calling it 'a chess diplomacy': 'the disputes which took place there sometimes were, in reality, a rather subtle game – sometimes improvisations, sometimes flagrant setups. That is, a kind of political chess game' (Baturin, 1994, p. 212). It was a giant improvisation of powerful actors motivated by emotions, personal interests, and political concerns. The dialogue resulted in the agreed text of a new Union Treaty – which, however, did not prevent the Russian Republic from recognizing the independence of Lithuania one week later. Ratification was set for 20 August 1991.

The August coup is usually presented as a clash of ideologies and as an attempt to re-establish Communist rule in the country. In fact, internal political strategy was not the main issue. It was more a question of the ongoing disintegration of the country, viewed by conservative, non-reformist forces as a catastrophe and as an unacceptable price for liberalization. Thus we can say that the territorial integrity of the Soviet state was actually the main issue of the coup. This was to become a painful reality after Russia took the lead in the process of dissolving the Soviet Union. After that time, the political focus shifted from the nearly accomplished Baltic secession to the complete breakup of the Soviet polity. Upon being elected President of the Russian Republic on 12 June 1991, Yeltsin stressed the sovereignty of the RSFSR, not simply as a part of the USSR but as a fully sovereign state. By that time, republics like Lithuania had already proclaimed their complete independence. This provided arguments for the conservative forces – in the form of an 'appeal to the people' (*slovo k nrodu*) – to speak of the 'enormous, unprecedented misfortune that has befallen us . . .', and of 'sly and pompous rulers... carving the country up into parts . . . our differences are nothing in the face of the common love for the homeland, which we see as a single, indivisible entity that has united fraternal peoples in a mighty state, without which we would have no existence' (*Sovetskaya Rossia*, 23 July 1991).

The coup failed, leaving in its wake a high degree of political enthusiasm among the winning Russian democracy. After the coup, radical democrats led by Yeltsin seized a number of powers and assets of the central regime, which induced the other republics to follow suit. Soon afterwards I talked to Sergei Stankevich, at that time one of Yeltsin's close associates, who told me 'it is more interesting to follow the line of making 15 independent states'. Pursuing 'interesting' options is probably one of the most underestimated features of both individual and collective strategies – especially when a person or group has the power to carry out such a strategy. The slogan 'We are building a new Russia' immediately replaced the old one, 'We are building Communism!' As Raymond Garthoff remarks:

> Yeltsin, indeed, not only played the central political role in defeating the coup, but used the opportunity in effect to mount a counter-coup, usurping the powers of the union president and other central institutions. Although the coup leaders had acted illegally in confining Gorbachev and attempting to exercise his emergency powers, they did not challenge the institutions of the central government, and one of their main aims was to reinforce the existing structure. Yeltsin, in contrast, tore down the

whole existing constitutional structure. And many of Yeltsin's actions were no more legal in constitutional terms than those of the coupmakers. It was Yeltsin's counter-coup, far more than the inept coup itself, that undercut Gorbachev's efforts to restabilize the status quo of controlled change under perestroika and to legitimize a renewed union (1994, p. 479).

Thus it was Russia, not the other republics, that was the key actor in the demise of the USSR. Its Declaration of Sovereignty, followed by similar documents in other republics, cleared the way for eliminating the federal Union with its strong Center. 'The logic of the struggle against Gorbachev's equivocations and the dangers of a conservative backlash at the union level drove the motor of destruction,' Richard Sakwa has pointed out (1993, p. 37). Even Baltic independence could have been questionable without the explicit support it got from the Russian democratic movement and from an appeal of the Russian Supreme Soviet to Russian soldiers not to participate in military actions against the republics. The demise of the Soviet Union was a political improvisation not preceded by any assessment of the decision and its possible consequences. Boris Yeltsin and his close advisors were prisoners of the same Marxist–Leninist theory of nationalities which knows only one solution to the problems of multi-ethnic societies: national self-determination up to and including the right to secession. The new leaders of Russia have inherited the deeply contradictory views of their predecessors, and have already repeated much of the same contradictory policy.

What is important in assessing the results of this policy is not to admit even the thought that the division of the territory of the USSR into nation-states is a mistake and instead to accept that it was 'definitely to the good' (see Simon, 1995). These are political rather than scholarly questions. What *is* significant for a better understanding of 'big events' is to recognize the possibility that these 'tectonic shifts' may be unpredictable. Not only leaders but ordinary people and collectivities may undertake a near-infinite number of 'moves' adapted to the infinite number of unforeseeable situations and influenced by rapidly changing, and unclearly perceived motivations. About five years after the event, in February 1996, the President of Kazakhstan Nursultan Nazarbaev made an interesting observation:

It was a serious game. As many, I had a feeling that at the beginning of breakup and chaos something should happen and everything will return back. But it turned out in another way. This is a big issue. I have some thoughts on the breakup of the Soviet Union: not only 'agents of influence', not only devil's design; but we all, Soviet people, and our leaders first of all, made it happen (*Eurasiiskii soiuz*, 1996, p. 19).

It may appear as mysterious only to hard practitioners of political science and sociology that over one hundred million people could vote for the Soviet Union in March 1991 and yet vote or peacefully accept the opposite scenario only nine months later. That kind of 'mysterious' change of sympathies has happened in the USSR during transition periods and will continue to happen in the future.

There are at least two reasons for this. First, emotional mobilization and an appealing sense of change may play a significant role even in better structured and civically more mature societies. A French-Canadian anthropologist colleague wrote to me from Montreal with her comments on the Quebec referendum in November 1995: 'The whole issue is so grounded in emotions rather than rational factors like economics and building a peaceful better life . . . Too many people voted against the federals by despair and disgust of politics. They thought, "what the hell, a little change cannot hurt," as if it was a matter of changing hair style or diet habits.'[3] This observation is relevant for our analysis too; it may even represent 'a rule' for 'defrosted' societies where most identities are in transition. Second, the apathy and subordination of rank-and-file social actors makes them manipulable, as well as vulnerable to outside forces. In this situation 'the will of the people' is but one of the allegories and a political tool. And it appears to be the norm rather than an anomaly.

3.4   Sovereignty as Declaration

Ethnic collisions have not disappeared with the disintegration of the Soviet Union. There has been no 'resolution' of ethnic problems, as expected by radical democrats and nationalists. Many points of tension have evolved into violent conflicts. Furthermore, 25 million Russians now find themselves 'new minorities' within the newly independent countries. Their dissatisfaction, and Russia's awkward policy towards this issue, has caused inter-state tensions. Yeltsin's team has erred in some major issues. Dimitri Simes explains this in the following way:

> . . . when the Soviet Union took the path of disintegration, the attitude to the 'nearest foreign countries' was based on desired expectations and considerations: because all the post-Soviet nations had been in their time victims to the Communist regime they would be able to cooperate harmoniously with due attention for each other's interests. Moreover, there was an obvious hope that Russia, as the far more powerful among the new independent states, will be readily accepted as the first among the equals (1994, p. 78).

But reality soon proved different. Departure from the Soviet legacy for successor states often meant political distancing from Russia and cultural de-russification. Rapid political reintegration did not occur, nor was there a speedy arrival of democracy and social improvements in the new countries. In Russia, there was growing disillusionment as well as feelings of betrayal on the part of those to whom Russian democrats had 'granted' freedom. The most alarming factor for the reformers was, however, the possibility that the Russian Federation itself might face disintegration. Many of its 20 constituent ethnic autonomies elected to exploit the paralysis of the central authorities in Moscow and take their own path. In his struggle for the presidency, Boris Yeltsin made outspoken promises to the ethnic territories of Russia: 'as much sovereignty as you can swallow' and the restoration of all the abolished ethnic autonomies in their pre-deportation configurations. This statement was taken seriously by Russia's Periphery. From August 1990 to May 1991, 16 autonomous republics of Russia passed their own declarations of state sovereignty. This process (a 'parade of sovereignties') was provoked first by political clashes between the Union and Russian leaderships. In order to limit the political space of Yeltsin's leadership, Gorbachev had opted to support 'second echelon' nationalisms within Russia proper. This was a kind of warning to Yeltsin and could serve as a potential ceiling for Russia's radical democrats in their plans to 'abolish the empire'. Gorbachev supported the ambitions of leaders from Russian ethnic autonomies and autonomies of other Union republics (Abkhazia and South Ossetia in Georgia) to achieve participation as equals in a new Union Treaty. It could weaken the exclusive rights of Union republic leaders to define a new state structure for the country. For Gorbachev to maintain the Center's leading role via a formula of '15 + 1', it was important to destroy the monolithic positions of the republics and restrain his most powerful opponent – Boris Yeltsin.

Including the leaders of the autonomies into the Novo-Ogarevo process meant they urgently needed to constitute their own political platforms as self-determined, sovereign state formations – as had already been done by the Union republics. However, it became common for radical democrats and nationalists to criticize the hierarchy of nation-state formations existing in the USSR. In all its political naïveté, abolishing of this hierarchy had been suggested two years earlier by academician Andrei Sakharov in his draft 'Constitution of the United States of Europe and Asia', which had called for the creation of 53 sovereign nation-states on the basis of existing administrative-territorial divisions (*New Times*, no. 52, 1989, pp. 26-28).

In *Realpolitik* this plan was enthusiastically seized upon by leaders of most large autonomies – Tatarstan, Bashkiria, Yakutia, Checheno-Ingushetia – whose dimished political status did not correspond to their economic potential, or the sizes of their population and territory. Under an ethnic federalism system, differences in status and parameters of constituting units are usually perceived not as results of historical, geographical, or political factors but as a purposeful ranking of ethnonations by more or less privileged categories. The logic of ethnic federalists perceives the multilevel administrative subordination of territories within federal states in the exercise of governance as a form of administering one nation over another, as an infringement of the right of self-determination. While widely accepted in world practice, the term 'autonomy' was rejected under post-Soviet nationalism. In the text of their declarations, Russia's republics announced their refusal of the 'autonomous' status because, as explained in the Yakut declaration, the notion of 'autonomy' simply means local self-government and locally run economies, and this is incompatible with the notion of 'republic' (Abdulatipov et al., 1993, p. 42).

In turn, because of political and doctrinal considerations, the Russian leadership also supported sovereignization of Russia's republics, even constituting several more on a basis of former autonomous *oblast*s. In July 1991, the Supreme Soviet of the Russian Federation passed laws establishing the new republics of Adygei, Gorni Altai, Khakass, and Karachai-Cherkessia. Like Gorbachev, Yeltsin also saw the 'parade of sovereignties' as an instrument for widening his electorate and political coalitions. That is why the most risky of his statements in favor of local claims were made in Tatarstan and Checheno-Ingushetia during the presidential election campaign. In the meantime, Russian federal authorities met, without enthusiasm, the new participants of the Novo-Ogarevo negotiations and insisted on *not* granting them equal status. The same position was shared by other leaders of Union republics with existing or potential autonomies (see Baturin, 1994). Leaders of the 'first order' had no desire to expand the membership of the 'founding fathers' club.

Along with the Union republics that became new independent states, former Russia's autonomies encountered the even more difficult dilemma of ethnic self-determination because of their multi-ethnic character. The long-cherished doctrine had allowed and even demanded self-determination for ethnonations which were minorities in most autonomies. To avoid immediate internal clashes, local nationalist leaders understood that sovereignty could be proclaimed only on behalf of all citizens living in a republic – that is why an ambivalent political formula was invented for the texts of declaration and, later, for the constitutions of the various republics. On the one hand, independence and state sovereignty were proclaimed on behalf of a people (sometimes an additional word 'multi-national' – *mnogonatsional'ni* – was used) as a territorial entity. On the other hand, the same statehoods were announced as a form of self-determination for ethnic entities, like the Udmurt, Chuvash, or Khakass nations.

In the case of Russia itself, political language and structure encouraged peripheral nationalism. The federal structure included ethno-territorial as well as purely administrative formations; there was no official titular Russian ethnonation doctrine like that of the other former Union republics. It was for this reason that state sovereignty was announced on behalf of the 'multi-national people of Russia' – the same formula subsequently included in the text of the Constitution. With respect to the right to self-determination, Russia's Declaration on State Sovereignty of 12 June 1990 delegated this right to each people (a nation) 'in freely chosen nation-state forms'. This was a tribute not only to political realities, but to a doctrine of ethnonationalism which was a programmatic element throughout the political spectrum – from radical democrats to ultra-nationalists (Russian and non-Russian). According to the logic of this doctrine, Russia could not be considered a national state (or a nation-state). Once the Russian Federation was proclaimed as a state of many nations, the logic of ethnic self-determination demanded first that these nations be constituted in the form of republics, including a national Russian (*Russkaya*) republic, and only afterwards that there be established a federation of these republics. Thus, the generally accepted principle of a people – 'demos' – as the source of sovereignty and the delegation of authority on behalf of territorial civic entities was decisively interpreted in the ethnographic sense of the people as 'ethnos' – and its highest incarnation, 'nation', as the sole legitimate source of authority.

Ethnonational self-determination became a political project that was even more difficult to realize as an explanatory formula, which in reality explained a rather simple and natural phenomenon – the drive for further decentralization of power. The formula of 'national statehood' for Russia's republics was seriously questioned by the emergent democracy based on the principle 'one man – one vote'. In this situation, republics could establish themselves as sovereign entities and could bargain for power only if there was proper internal support on the part of non-titulars who comprised the demographic majority in 15 out of 21 republics. Russia's ethnic periphery found it necessary to behave in a less threatening way than the former Union republics. Moreover, unilateral secession was practically impossible; by now neither Russian authorities nor the international community seemed willing to accept a new round of disintegration.

Only a few republican leaders opted for a rather radical scenario of sovereignization and copied the political language of Union republics. This was especially true when declarations of sovereignty were issued while the USSR still existed and there was a chance for the autonomies to become founders of a new Union. The most radical texts were passed by authorities of Checheno-Ingushetia and Tatarstan. In the text of the Checheno-Ingushetia declaration, passed on 27 November 1990 under the leadership of Doka Zavgayev (predecessor to Dzhokhar Dudayev) there was no mention of the USSR or the Russian Federation at all; the whole doctrine was based on the principle that the republic is a 'sovereign state constituted as a result of the self-determination of the Chechen and Ingush peoples' (Article 1). It was their 'own' statehood because 'others' were defined as citizens living 'outside their own nation-state formations' (Article 5). These 'others' comprised about one-third of the population, including the majority in the capital city, Grozny. The declaration proclaimed land and all resources to be the exclusive property of 'the people of Checheno-Ingushetia' (an interesting mixture of civic and ethnic formulae in one and the same text!).

In the Tatarstan declaration, passed on 30 August 1990, the two reasons given for self-determination seemed even more contradictory. State sovereignty was declared as the 'realization of the inalienable right of the Tatar nation, of all people of the republic to self-determination'. However, the notion of 'multi-national people of the republic' was also present in the text. Later I spoke with all the key figures behind the Tatarstan movement for sovereignty, including President Mintimer Shaimiev, Chairman of the Supreme Soviet Farid Mukhamedshin, and Raphael Khakimov. My conclusion was that they were well aware of these doctrinal inconsistencies and had tried to find a creative approach to the text that would allow them to satisfy all major public forces and at the same time exploit ethnonationalism as the major argument to provide bargaining power with the Center.

A similar approach was followed by other autonomies where the titular group enjoyed a significant demographic and political presence and where other groups were not sufficiently mobilized to challenge a radical nationalist strategy. The contradictory, but politically acceptable, formula of 'nation – multi-national people' was used in other declarations. The preamble of the Kalmyk declaration states that it is 'based on the right of the Kalmyk people to free self-determination and taking into consideration the desire of the people of Kalmykia', but Article 1 constitutes the Kalmyk Republic 'on the basis of implementing, by the Kalmyk nation and the people of Kalmykia, their inalienable right of self-determination'. Despite these minor differences, the basic assumption is the same for most of the texts: a 'right' belongs to a nation, that is, to an ethnic entity; 'people of a republic', that is, civic communities, have only 'a desire'. It was an explicit message that a republic came into being and its sovereignty was achieved on the basis of the rights of a particular ethnonation. Thus, for example, the Udmurt Republic was declared 'a sovereign state historically established on the basis of the implemention, by the Udmurt nation, of the inalienable right of self-determination'. However, this was followed by other statements expressing rather different sentiments: 'the development of the Udmurt Republic within the existing borders is exercised in all spheres of state, and is built with the equal participation of all nations and *narodnost*s of the republic', and 'citizens of the republic of all nationalitites make the people of Udmurtia'; furthermore, they are 'the only source of state power'.

There is one interesting element in the text of the Chuvash declaration – this issuing from a republic with a significant titular majority and also with a sizeable diaspora: 'The Chuvash Soviet Socialist Republic is a sovereign state, the only nation-state formation of the Chuvash nation.' The term *only* reflects another fundamental postulate of Soviet self-determination doctrine: each ethnonation can and must realize this right only once and only in one place, on 'its own' territory. Thus it is considered an anomaly when members of one ethnic group do not have their own state, or have several ethno-territorial autonomies. For this reason, leaders of Volga Germans, Greeks, Karaims, Crimean Tatars, and other 'non-status' groups living in post-Soviet states have expressed dissatisfaction over their non-self-determined nations. And for the same reason, Buryat radical-nationalists are angrily demanding to know why their nation is divided into three autonomies, and why it would not be better to demand one greater Buryatia.

It is precisely this logic of 'anomaly' that kept Buryat political activists from two autonomous *okrug*s (Aginsky and Ust'-Ordynsky) from demanding that their status be elevated to the rank of autonomous republic. Within other (non-doctrinal) parameters – such as size of territory and population, cultural distinctiveness and economic potential – these two formations had no less reason for pursuing self-determination than Adygei, Khakassia, and Gornyi Altai. But initiators of this project could assuredly expect the reply that one Buryat national statehood already existed, and there could be no more than this one.

Reflecting local specificity and political mentalities, several declarations avoided manifest nationalist ideology and were based more on the civic principle of self-determination as expressed in the notion of 'the people of the republic'. This is how sovereignty was declared in the republics of North Ossetia, Tuva, Karelia, and Komi. In Buryatia, only the expression 'multi-national people of Buryatia' was used. In Yakutia, the formulation was: 'the bearer of sovereignty and the source of state power in the Yakut–Sakha SSR is its people consisting of all citizens of all nationalities'. Motivations behind this civic formulation might not signify a break with ethnonationalism. In Tuva and North Ossetia, where ethnonationalism is strong, the titular groups enjoy such a dominant status that there was no need to provide additional safeguards through provocative statements. In Karelia, Komi, Yakutia, and Buryatia, however, the titulars comprise less than one-third of the population; here it seemed too risky to inscribe into official text that which was elsewhere seen as a 'normal' formulation. Thus, the language of ethnonationalism proved to be an instrumentalist tool used mainly in highly competitive situations when the proportion of titulars to the rest of the population lay around 40/60, and where power dispositions made it possible to impose political ethnonationalism through formal legal procedures.

Declarations reflected specific local concerns as well. For republics rich in resources it was a priority to announce their exclusive right to land, mineral, water and other resources, and even the air and continental shelf areas. Gold and diamond producing Yakutia established its right to a fair share of export profits. The same was done in the gas and oil producing Komi Republic. All segments of local societies irrespective of ethnicity felt united on this issue.

Most republics with administrative borders that had been established in the past on the basis of rural titular preferences hurried to declare their territorial integrity and the possibility of making border changes with their own consent only. This was especially crucial for North Ossetia and the other North Caucasian republics with their mutual territorial disputes and irredentist movements, as in Daghestan. Meanwhile, in Kabardino-Balkaria's declaration, the 'inalienable right to self-determination up to secession and formation of an independent state' was inscribed for the Kabardin and Balkar nations. This was designed to pacify Balkar radical nationalists who were then demanding their 'own' republic. The Balkar leader, Temir Ul'bashev, visited my ministerial office in the summer of 1992 lobbying for a separate republic. When I asked him if there would be enough taxpayers among the Balkars to support a costly republican administration and how it was possible to define a territory for the 'Balkar national state' with ethnically mixed Balkar–Kabardin mountainous villages, his answer was disarmingly naïve: 'It is exactly how it was done in other cases and we don't want to be looked upon as a "half-nation". We want to have a normal national statehood without Kabardins.'[4] It was the end of the working day and we left the Ministry together. I saw at the entrance of the building a huge Lincoln sedan which had brought Mr Ul'bashev to the meeting. One of my associates told me that the Balkar leader, before coming to Moscow, had collected money from his ethnic compatriots for the 'independence struggle'. For him the circle of 'we' clearly needed to be rather wide to enable him to live lavishly in the country's capital.

In cases where the territorial aspect of self-determination was viewed by local leaders and intellectual activists as unfavorable, they tried to incorporate hidden or open claims into the text of their declarations. This was particularly true for republics reconstituted after a period of deportation. For example, the Kabardino-Balkaria declaration mentioned the necessity of 're-establishing the administrative *raion*s of Kabardino-Balkaria that existed before March 1944'. This had a clear territorial address to Georgia. In Kalmykia, the declaration stated that the 'Kalmyk SSR is a legal successor to the Kalmyk ASSR and has the right to take measures towards the unconditional restoration of the Kalmyk people's rights according to the USSR Supreme Soviet's Declaration which recognizes all repressive acts and forceful relocations as illegal'. Behind this lay the desire to take over a part of a territory of the Astrakhan *oblast* and to access the Volga Delta with its rich fish resources. As the head of Kalmykia's government, Batyr Mikhailov, told me in a private conversation during my visit to Kalmykia with President Yeltsin in July 1992, 'We need black caviar, not a territory with Russian people living on it.'[5]

Territorial claim to neighboring land was expressed most explicitly by the Checheno-Ingush Republic with respect to North Ossetia:

> The Checheno-Ingush republic confirms the just demand of the Ingush people to re-establish their national statehood and to return to territories that previously belonged to the Ingush people and were alienated as a result of Stalin's repressions. These territories are: the Prigorodny *raion*, part of the Malgobekskii *raion* in its former borders, and the left-bank part of Ordzhonikidze (Vladikavkaz) (Abdulatipov et al., 1993, p. 49).

This republic set the resolution of this territorial issue as a condition for signing the new Union Treaty. A couple of years later, I asked Doka Zavgayev, who was the First Secretary of the Communist Party and Chairman of the Checheno-Ingush Supreme Soviet when the declaration was passed, how it had happened that the language of the document was so radical. Zavgayev, by then dismissed by Dzhokhar Dudayev (in October 1995 he was to head the pro-federal government in Chechnya again), told me that 'a radical nationalist mood prevailed in the newly elected Supreme Soviet and it was hard to resist, especially with respect to the territorial issue, so as not to lose control of the situation. Besides, we felt that taking an extreme position would force the Center to make decisions in our favor.'[6] Again, a 'feeling of playing a game' in a situation of rapid changes and uncertainties was there. There was a powerful but publicly undeclared psychological climate of making 'new' Center–Periphery relations.

While the territorial aspect of sovereignization ideology had a rather rational and even utilitarian meaning, the language, culture, and religion aspects were more significant on the symbolic and mobilization level. Here, enthusiasts of 'national statehood' encountered the fundamental incompatibility between the idea and praxis. In contrast to former Union republics, the ethnic cultures of Russia's autonomies had undergone much stronger assimilation towards Russian culture and language. The overwhelming majority of non-Russians in the Russian Federation use Russian as the language spoken at home and at work. In many cases, especially in the Volga and Siberia regions, language assimilation took place several generations ago as a result of close contacts between local cultures and the Russian culture. The doctrine of ethnonationalism interprets this situation exclusively as an act of violence and as an anomaly which is to be 'corrected' by a return to a lost 'normality'. National statehoods, even if they are internal autonomies, must speak their 'own' languages: this is made a requirement not only for the bureaucracy, but for the population at large, especially for members of the self-determined nation.

How was this collision resolved in the texts of declarations and, later, in the constitutions of these new republics? In two extreme cases this issue was not addressed at all. One situation was when the level of native language retention among the titulars with majority status was already so high that declaring this language the official (or state) language could not be expected to yield much in the way of political dividends. Nor could it be used to limit access to power for Russian-speakers who boasted a knowledge of the native language. This is what occurred in Tuva and in Checheno-Ingushetia. The converse situation is the virtually complete loss of the native langue by the titulars and their demographic minority, making it quite meaningless to declare any official status for this language. This was the case in the Karel Republic. In all other situations, official bilingualism or trilingualism was declared. The latter was declared in republics with two 'self-determined nations' (Kabardino-Balkaria) or with strong intra-ethnic languages (so-called 'sub-ethnic groups' with their own 'dialects') like the Mordva (Erzya and Moksha languages) and Mari (mountain and plains dialects) Republics. Among Ossets, the question of internal language differences was not addressed by local intellectuals when the declaration was passed. The Digor and Iron dialects of the Osset language were established as official (together with the Russian language) in the republic's constitution two years afterwards. Only one republic could not find a proper response to the existing language situation without departing from titular nationalism. In Bashkiria, it was politically risky to declare official Bashkir–Russian bilingualism because of the significant presence of ethnic Tatars. At the same time, ethnic Bashkirs enjoying political leadership could not accept the Tatar language as an official one, fearing the loss of their domination under demographic minority status. Neither was the solution to be found in the text of the constitution, where this question was completely avoided.

'The parade of sovereignties' in Russia strengthens political ethnonationalism and its doctrinal context through new creative experiences in the elaboration and formulation of its stands. A new generation of Periphery experts, political thinkers, and international lawyers has emerged as a result of the public debates and the drafting of texts of declarations, constitutions, local legislation, etc. The language of top Periphery leaders has been noticeably enriched by new vocabulary and new arguments. Many useful norms have been borrowed from the rich experience of international debates on collective rights, self-determination, indigenous peoples, and minorities problems, and have been put to use. Dialogue between federal and republican elites has at times been tense and painful. Political ethnicity has proven to be a powerful instrument in hard bargaining with the unitarianism of federal authorities.

3.5   Quest for a New Treaty

Starting in 1992, Russia's federal authorities began taking serious steps to tackle the critical situation associated with the new challenges presented by its many ethnic regions. Devolving some of the power concentrated in the new Center which had taken over the same offices and the same distributive functions previously belonging to the Union authorities became unavoidable. There is evidence that it was President Yeltsin who formulated the idea of preparing a new Federal Treaty with all constituent parts of the Federation. And yet, it was members of his team who had been opposed to this process up to the moment when the Treaty was signed (Abdulatipov, 1995, p. 14). In any case, it was a legislative body – the Supreme Soviet headed by Ruslan Khasbulatov and its Chamber of Nationalities headed by Ramazan Abdulatipov – who worked hard to find a solution for the growing problems of disintegration and demands from the periphery. The reason lay not in the non-Russian ethnic backgrounds of these two leaders[7] – who without any doubt were more sensitive towards these issues – but rather it lay in the character of representative power as such. The Supreme Soviet of the Russian Federation was the only central authority to have many strong and eloquent leaders delegated from the non-Russian electorate and representing the regional and cultural mosaic of Russia. (On the ethnic composition of the Supreme Soviet see Tishkov, 1990b.) The Supreme Soviet's committees and subcommittees as well as the routine work of its apparatus were greatly influenced by rapidly growing ethnic and regional lobbies. There were also a number of liberal-minded experts from Moscow academies to provide the necessary expertise based on proper legal language and on the democratic assumption of decentralization as a common good.

Drafts of the Federal Treaty were sent to the authorities of republics, and of each *krai* and *oblast*, and autonomous *okrug* several times for critical review and suggestions. Local experts could participate in the Moscow-based working group as well. Over 300 serious amendments and new formulae were suggested during the difficult process of finalizing the text. These suggestions were systematized, made public, and many of them were incorporated into the text of the Treaty (for a list of suggestions and amendments see Abdulatipov et al., 1993, pp. 140–171). In April and March of 1992 I participated in working discussions and meetings of all local leaders and the Supreme Soviet's leadership to ratify the Treaty. Major disagreements centered around:

1 Taxation and budget issues – the republics did not want to have direct, multi-channel federal taxation; the Center did not want to allocate more subsidies and to increase tax and budget revenues for the republics.
2 Control of resources and state industrial assets – republics and regions demanded a larger share in production, export and their own state industrial properties; the Center wanted to control industry and foreign trade and did not want to transfer huge industrial assets into the hands of a regional bureaucracy instead of privatizing them or exercising control as before.
3 Judicial and police systems – the republics wanted to have locally controlled courts, prosecution officers, and police; the Center insisted on the absolute necessity of preserving 'unified legal space' (*edinoe pravovoe prostranstvo*).

Interestingly enough, the arguments used in those heated debates more often referred to outside world experience or pre-Soviet history than to the will of the taxpayers or the decisions of local legislatures. This occurred after practically all republics had already declared their sovereignty. These supposedly legitimate grounds for negotiating were out of debates making the whole issue of the Federal Treaty important but basically an elitist enterprise. For example, one of the arguments I advanced to support a demand for legal plurality and regional police was a reference to an American film shown on Russian TV where criminals could cross borders between two states but the police could not; I also mentioned that Native American reservations in North America have their own local police. These arguments did not persuade federal experts to surrender their positions at that time. Uneasy compromises on major political issues were achieved through a rather symbolic form of sharing power – defining a large amount of authority as the domain of joint responsibility and competence (*sovmestnoe pol'zovanie*). Hidden gestures were made by federal authorities to persuade local leaders to support the final draft. I heard two short but meaningful remarks in this respect: first, Yuri Voronin, Deputy Chairman of the Supreme Soviet, mentioned privately after all the debates had finished that the agreement to sign the document had cost as many cars as there were people sitting at the table; second, Murtaza Rakhimov, the President of Bashkiria, mentioned that during a tense talk in the Kremlin with Gennadi Burbulis, Burbulis had said that if the Treaty wasn't signed, Rakhimov might not leave the Kremlin without trouble. However, this argument did not work; Bashkiria's leader agreed to sign the document only after signing a separate protocol with the Center on additional concessions to the republic on taxation, economic and legal issues.

On 31 March 1992 all constituent members of the Federation, except the Chechen and Tatar republics, signed the Federal Treaty on the delimitation of powers of authority. This was presented as the major success of Yeltsin's nationalities policy, a measure which would prevent the disintegration of Russia and usher in the beginning of true federalism. No doubt it was a promising document – allowing the leaders of the republics to continue building their nation statehoods and to bargain with the Center for more privileges and favorable budget redistributions. In reality, however, the Federal Treaty revealed once again the symbolic meaning of official declarations and the dual character of policy: to agree in declaring the republics 'sovereign states' but to block their aspirations through the bureaucracy of the Center and financial control. Because the mechanisms for distributing authority and for implementation were not defined in the Treaty or in other legal documents, many things did not change. As in the past, the Moscow bureaucracy allocated resources and defined key elements of development for the republics, most of which were economically non-sustainable. The whole issue of the Federal Treaty as a provisional compromise was shoved aside under the pressure of growing feelings in the Center that the Russian federal state should be based not on treaties but a constitution. These concerns were strengthened by the fact that new constitutions passed in some republics, especially in Tatarstan, Yakutia, and Tuva, contradicted the acting Federal Constitution.

The Supreme Soviet of the Russian Federation undertook serious efforts to prepare and pass various laws regulating the domain of ethnic issues. Several committees and expert groups began preparing bills of rights for small indigenous peoples, on Cossacks' status and rights, the rights of minorities, traditional subsistence communities, etc. All of them failed to become laws, but not because of the political profile of the Parliament: Khasbulatov's Supreme Soviet was not an anti-minority or pro-chauvinistic body as its successor, the State Duma, was to be. The major reasons for the failure were the lack of competence, as well as internal rivalries between those hungering for the prestigious authorship of a national law.

A draft Law on Minorities prepared by the Supreme Soviet's Committee on Inter-ethnic Relations headed by the ambitious but poorly educated Nikolai Medvedev was written in such a way as to define and defend the rights of any group, including ethnic Russians, in republic territories, but not the titular population considered 'nations'. And yet it was precisely these groups like the Mordva (a native group for Medvedev himself), Komi, Karels, Khakass, or Chukchi who needed legal protection, even on their 'own' territories. A draft Law on Small Indigenous Peoples prepared by the Committee on Indigenous Peoples of the North and Siberia headed by Aleksei Aipin repeated the provocative rhetoric borrowed from political statements of international indigenous movements claiming exclusive control of lands comprising over half of the country's territory. This met strong resistance from regional administrators, economic barons, and the military. In addition, rights and privileges were defined not for those with a way of life based on traditional subsistence economy but on nationality and demographic figures (less than fifty thousand people). It immediately provoked a strong lobbying effort on the part of small ethnic groups of the North Caucasus (Daghestan) who wanted to see themselves as subjects of this legislation. The draft Law included an official list of prospective clients, which began to grow longer and longer. Supporting this draft as a major legal act, I asked Ramazan Abdulatipov not to include this list in the text, lest he destroy his own Avar nation – a nation of Soviet ethnic construction incorporating, in addition to Avars proper, about a dozen small linguistically and culturally different communities who had recently developed a pan-Avar identity but could easily reactivate their lower-level identities for utilitarian, political purpose. As Director of the Institute of Ethnology and Anthropology, I very soon received appeals from several other groups who wanted to be qualified as separate 'small ethnoses'. The legislators should have known that the cultural mosaic of Russia could provide many more new clients of this law in future – which at the same time should not be considered as an argument against it. This draft Law passed two readings in the Supreme Soviet; unfortunately it never received final approval because of the October 1993 crisis. Thus, the record of the Russian legislative body before it was dis-

solved was not very impressive, nor was the record of the 1994–95 State Duma which succeeded it.

3.6 Search for New Approaches

The Russian executive government headed by Boris Yeltsin and Yegor Gaidar was under
great pressure from the many competing priorities and had rather uncertain views of the
state-building doctrine and how to manage ethnic issues in a time of transition.
Economic reforms and social problems headed the government's agenda at that time. In
the meantime, the President and the government were quite concerned about the need to
build a structure and expertise on the federal level to deal with nationalities issues. Since
the end of 1991, a special inter-ministerial committee headed by Gennadi Burbulis and
Sergei Shakhrai has been functioning, and representatives of various governmental bodies have had the opportunity to discuss complex situations and coordinate joint efforts
and approaches. Among his first advisers, Boris Yeltsin appointed a professional ethnologist, Galina Starovoitova, former researcher at the Institute of Ethnology and
Anthropology, who held this position till the end of 1992. Constituted in 1991, the State
Committee on Nationalities Policy (*Goskomnats*) was considered the principal agency for
providing other sectors of the government with expertise and information on ethnic
matters and for coordinating major activities. Its chairman was granted the status of a
federal minister.

In February 1992 I assumed this position, still retaining my post as Director of the
Institute. In my first meeting with the President he raised several questions, among which
one was quite symbolic of the Russian top political mentality: 'Should we allocate more
resources and support for any one of the republics in North Caucasus, say, Daghestan, so
as to make it a kind of stronghold in the region?'.[8] This was, of course, a manipulation
syndrome inherited from the Soviet political tradition; it could also be a result of the
influence of several top federal politicians originally from this region (Vice Prime
Minister Valery Makharadze and Ramazan Abdulatipov). Yeltsin also repeated the same
argument about the absence of 'new theory' as a major reason for the continuation of
ethnic clashes and for the failures of government: 'We need a scientific basis for our
nationalities policy; you as a scholar taking this post of Minister can contribute to this
task.' Later, the President proved to be more of a 'Realpolitiker' than a 'scientist' in dealing with nationalities issues.

I myself harbored certain reservations concerning this whole issue of 'conceptualizing'
politics, especially in a time of transition that was fraught with complex doctrinal and
emotional legacies. But in this particular context I had agreed to produce a conceptual
platform for the Russian government and the public. Preparatory work was carried out
in the spring of 1992, and the document was presented to the Cabinet at a meeting on 30
July. Various interpretations of this initiative have been given by observers of Russian politics (see, e.g., Kremenyuk, 1994), not all of them accurate.

First, the language of the document, including basic definitions, was deliberately
meant to be less challenging, without repeating confrontational terms like 'nations' or
'national states' in an ethnic sense. I found it perfectly appropriate to express everything
in categories like 'the peoples' and 'nationalities' which were also widely used and no less
legitimate. At that time, even the term 'minority' I found to be politically and emotionally unacceptable because it had been rejected by social scientists as 'politically incorrect'
and completely excluded from the Soviet public discourse during the postwar period.

Second, taking into consideration the demographic factor (only 47% of non-Russians live in the territories of their 'own' republics, and all regions have multi-ethnic populations), I suggested making all territories subject to state nationalities policy, rather than limiting this to relations between the federal Center and the republics. Large urban centers like Moscow and others belong within the purview of nationalities policy as well. 'Non-status' groups, ethnic enclaves, indigenous communities all deserve equal priorities in state legislations and governmental programs.

Third, because of the high level of cultural integration of non-Russian groups into the state of Russia, I suggested a formula for a new Russia as a multi-ethnic state pursuing the politics of cultural pluralism. Russia cannot be a national state of ethnic Russians: likewise, republics are not the exclusive property of one titular group. Russia would keep its referent cultural component expressing the Russian language and culture, representative of the overwhelming majority of the population. The republics would keep and strengthen their own cultural profiles, represented by the cultures of their titular nationalities.

Fourth, I suggested a formula of new federalism for Russia based on further decentralization of power and strong local self-government, preserving different types of federal units, and expanding the rights of territorial units to the level of republics. At the same time it did not question the existing ethno-territorial autonomies and their status within the Federation, seeing this as a potent political legacy of the past and an instrument which had played and can still play a constructive role in safeguarding the interests, rights, and integrity of non-dominant groups. On this point, several writers have wrongly ascribed to me an 'abolition' position (see, e.g. Hill, 1995, p. 33; Lapidus, 1995, p. 111).

Fifth, the concept suggested strategies and mechanisms for governing a multi-ethnic society and preventing ethnic conflict, such as: ensuring a multi-ethnic character for the Center, including representation in cultural, educational, and mass communications domains as well as politics; encouraging and building inter-ethnic coalitions and cooperation; reducing ethnic disparities and unequal distribution of resources, wealth, and rank among groups, and introducing extra-territorial cultural autonomy.

Finally, there were separate recommendations for dealing with ethnic violence and conflicts. These included analyses of the claims, grievances, and demands of conflicting parties; the role of elites and ethnic movements; the historical and religious/cultural backgrounds; measures for controlling the access to arms and paramilitary activities; special efforts in the case of major instigators of violence; and therapy among victims of conflicts.

The ensuing discussion was mainly confined to my answering questions posed by the President and members of the Cabinet. Questions focused on the timeliness of that kind of document and how the republics might react to this new platform. I was convinced that Boris Yeltsin had been deliberately misinformed on the context of the Concept. Like many other members of the government, he was not ready to discuss the issue in the suggested categories. This was partly because of a trivial fact: two key figures in this field (Starovoitova and Abdulatipov), who had not been involved directly in the preparation of the document (no doubt a major mistake on my part), expressed their doubts about it to the President just before the Cabinet meeting. This was the main reason why the session was closed to the press, and the document not made public. A few days later, Abdulatipov published in the newspaper *Federatsia* the text of what purported to be an alternative platform prepared by the Supreme Soviet of Russia.

It is impossible to say whether, if the government had approved the Concept of a nationalities policy, Russia would have gone through the bloody conflict in North Ossetia in the fall of 1992 and the destructive war in Chechnya since December 1994. Changing political strategy does not always yield immediate results, but it can influence the chain of events when viewed in perspective as well as formulating the long-term approaches needed to influence political strategy. That is what we can observe in the case of Russia.

In December 1993 a new Constitution, fashioned at Yeltsin's behest, was approved by a general referendum. It confirmed the existing structure of the state as consisting of 89 federal units: 57 administrative territories (i.e. of 55 *krai*s and *oblast*s, and two federal cities) and 32 ethno-territorial entities (21 republics, one autonomous *oblast*, and ten autonomous *okrug*s). The Constitution expanded the power and prerogatives of ethnic autonomies and safeguarded their statehood, but it did not qualify republics as 'sovereign national states' although this had been a major source of conflict between federal state authorities and republican leaders. The latter have agreed therefore to exchange a divisive declaration in favor of unrestrained power for greater economic and cultural control as well as the capacity to constitute their own prestigious status. The most significant departure from the doctrine of ethnonationalism at the level of Russian governmental policy came on 24 February 1994, when President Yeltsin addressed the newly elected Russian Parliament. For the first time in Soviet and post-Soviet history the country's leader spoke about great contradictions in the previous nationalities policy:

> A great number of national [one should read: ethnic] problems are caused by the contradiction between two principles underlying the basis of the state system of the Russian Federation: i.e. between the national-territorial and administrative-territorial systems. Today, when the distribution of powers between the federal government and the subjects of the federation is being decided, this contradiction has become absolutely clear. In the contemporary situation there is a historical necessity to combine the two principles. At the same time this contradiction will lessen due to the new meaning of nation as co-citizenship, as set out in the Constitution (*Rossiiskaya gazeta*, 25 February 1994).

The mention of 'co-citizenship' (*sograzhdanstvo*) in this statement did not please the Periphery leaders who did not want to abandon the possibility of creating ethnonations in the future, but at least they could understand what the President was talking about. Those who rejected doctrinal innovation were mainly 'central figures' with long-time ambitions to act as theoretical 'fathers' of the nationalities policy. I discuss one of these negative reactions in Chapter 12 as a part of conceptual debates. For this chapter where I analyze current political process, it is important to stress that the most persistent proponents of ethnonations are to be found in Moscow now, not in the republics. In April 1995, Deputy Chairman of the Federation Council Ramazan Abdulatipov wrote a public letter to President Yeltsin accusing 'politicians without nationality from the Center' of 'successfully burying' his own conception of the nationalities policy.

> It was blocked by bureaucratic structures which, I have no doubt, feel a kind of 'allergy' toward everything concerning nations, national relations, and national policy. What is ideal for them is unitarianism, unification, and co-citizenship. By the way, the last idea was 'implanted' in your last year's annual message. Speeding up the process of building co-citizenship means behaving like the Bolsheviks who were in a hurry to merge the peoples (1995, p. 20).

This influential politician, whom I hold in very high regard, appealed to the President not with arguments (they are mostly contradictory and self-exclusive) but with emotions, fears, and 'warnings' to prove his point. Most of his concerns were about ethnic Russians, or the Russian ethnos, which he qualified as a 'state-formative nation' (*gosudarstvo-obzazuiuschaya natsia*) and whose interests and feelings have been ignored by politicians, experts, and journalists still pursuing the goal of 'Westernizing' Russia. As

Abdulatipov writes:

> The Western experience of state-building based on assimilation, including forceful assimilation, is imposed on us. Our uniqueness is preserved in the ethnic distinctiveness, cultures, and languages of the 150 peoples who live in Russia. This is a spectacular manifestation of humanity on the part of the Russian nation [*Russkaya natsia*] . . .Today, collective ethnic rights for the peoples of Russia have not less but probably more meaning than individual rights, although the priority of the latter could be recognized in the future. At least in Russia individual rights will not become an absolute value as in the West, where this was achieved through the elimination of whole peoples and tribes notwithstanding 'sacred devotion' to humanistic values. Thank God that the Russian nation has historically been lacking that kind of hypocrisy (Abdulatipov, 1995, p. 19).

It would be inaccurate to describe Abdulatipov's position in primordial terms; and surely, he is not a Russian, or even a non-Russian, nationalist. His position is a reflection of many things at once: the painful and sincere search for an appropriate explanatory model after many years of spouting old theory; a political stand oriented towards a certain part of the electorate; a personal struggle for prescriptive superiority. He cannot accept 'co-citizenship' because it is not his invention. He would prefer a superficial elaboration of 'a unique phenomenon in the history of human civilization as Russian (*Rossiisky*) super-ethnos', or suggest his own definition for the country's civic community – 'compatriots' (*sootechestvenniky*).

From all these chaotic and infinite 'moves' of political actors toward nationalities issues in Russia, we may distinguish at least three main tendencies today. Two of them are at the extreme of the political spectrum, both playing the same game of ethnic nationalism, but with one big difference – one appeals to non-Russian nationalism, another calls for ethnic Russian mobilization. The first one has practically disappeared at the federal political level, following a spectacular demonstration of Russian nationalist and statist rhetoric in December 1993 elections. After the beginning of the Chechen War and after bargaining and agreements by periphery ethnic leaders resulted in real rewards, this tendency lost its demonstrative and challenging character in the republics of Russia also. But it is still there, learning how to be more responsible and respectful and how to coexist with other political programs in a larger state. In January 1995, Mintimer Shaimiev, addressing a group of leaders from breakaway regions of the former Soviet Union, said that he personally never used the word 'independence' because he knew 'nobody would recognize us'; at the same time he could not abandon the idea of self-determination because 'our people would not understand us'. That is why in their positions and declarations there were many contradictory elements but this 'reflected a compromise we had reached peacefully'.[9]

The second tendency is growing in the political life of Russia and it has never been lacking intellectual arguments. In recent years all that major authors had written in the past on 'the Russian idea' gained an immense audience, and new prophets of Russian nationalism appeared. Politicians of ultra-patriotic and liberal democratic orientation are strangely similar in their ignorance of the non-Russian factor. Some, like two political antipodes, Vladimir Zhirinovsky and Gavriil Popov, here formulated proposals to dismantle ethnic autonomies in Russia and to return to the pre-revolutionary system of administrative division by provinces (*gubernii*). Sometimes the same position has been erroneously attributed to the former Minister of Nationalities Sergei Shakhrai (1992–94) who called for administrative division reform in the country, not dismantling ethnic republics. Moderate Russian nationalism has been demonstrated by the State Duma

(Parliament) of the Russian Federation. In two years (1994–95), it did not pass a single law on nationalities issues. The December 1995 election brought even more Russian nationalists and 'statists' (*derzhavniki*) into the Federal Parliament.

The third tendency is that responsible governance in a multi-ethnic country built on a basic democratic structure and values is weak in contemporary Russia. The devastating adventure of the President and the Government of Russia in Chechnya initiated by proponents of force, including Minister of Nationalities Nikolai Yegorov (brought in to succeed the moderate Sergei Shakhrai), has precipitated a major crisis in the country, seriously damaging many positive tendencies observed in relations with the republics. Since August 1995, Viktor Chernomyrdin's Cabinet together with the Prime Minister himself, as well as the Minister of Nationalities and Regional Policy Vyacheslav Mikhailov, has been trying to work out new approaches and demonstrate its allegiance to non-violent methods of conflict resolution, respect and support of the country's ethnic mosaic. On 11 April 1996, the government of Russia adopted 'The Concept of the State Nationalities Policy' worked out by the Ministry of Nationalities and the Institute of Ethnology and Anthropology. This document reflected not only Moscow's visions and concerns, but also major criticisms and suggestions on behalf of all subjects of the Russian Federation. It was a document of basic principles for political management of ethnic issues in a framework of emerging post-Soviet democracy (see Vyacheslav Mikhailov's interview in *Nezavisimaya gazeta*, 4 June 1996, and my article 'Plach po konzeptsii [Lament for a Concept]' in *Moskovskie Novosti*, N23, 9–16 June 1996). Not enough time has elapsed to be able to evaluate this approach. Again, too many actors are operating in the political arena in a situation of poorly functioning structures and poorly qualified leadership. Any reservoir for responsible creativity and for enriching new ideas remains more an idea than reality. Learning quick lessons but at a high price would seem to be the political formula for a new Russia.

Notes

1   Statement by Raphael Khakimov at the annual Seminar of the Network of Ethnological Monitoring and Early Warning, 16 October 1995, Limassol, Cyprus.

2   Personal notes, 18 July 1988, Moscow.

3   Catherine Lussier, communication, 10 November 1995, Montreal.

4   Personal notes, 30 July 1992, Moscow.

5   Personal notes, 23 July 1992, Elista, Kalmykia.

6   Personal notes, 2 September 1992, Moscow.

7   Ruslan Khasbulatov is a Chechen, Ramazan Abdulatipov is an Avar (Daghestan).

8   Personal notes, 23 February 1992, Moscow.

9   Statement by Mintimer Shaimiev at a round-table meeting: personal notes, 14 January 1995, The Hague.

4

Territories, Resources, and Power

4.1 Introduction

Previous chapters have discussed how ethnicity operates both in general and in the specific case of the Soviet and post-Soviet context. We have seen how it was socially engineered and institutionalized, and how it found its main doctrinal and practical expression in various forms of ethno-politics. I do not deny the significance of what may be called 'objective realities' or 'fundamental factors' – by which I mean both social conditions such as basic human resources and distribution of material wealth, as well as the equally important access to power to achieve material and social objectives. The materialistic tradition of presupposing that economic and social factors have primacy in societal life is also relevant in studying ethnicity. A number of illuminating studies have been published recently, establishing a direct correlation between developmental and economic dependence problems and conflict manifestations (see Adekanye, 1995; Gurr, 1993; Gurr & Harff, 1994; Samarisinghe & Coughlan, 1991; D. Smith, 1994b; Stavenhagen, 1990.)

I agree with Peter Worsley that 'cultural traits are not absolutes or simply intellectual categories, but are invoked to provide identities which legitimize claims to rights. They are strategies or weapons in competitions over scarce social goods' (1984, p. 249). Even more compelling is Nash's view of ethnicity as 'a reservoir for unrest in a world where power, prosperity and rank are distributed in an unequal and illegal way between and within nations' (1989, p. 127). The concept of 'social goods' is not universal: rather it is an important parameter of analysis which it would be erroneous to exclude, as would be drawing a rigid line between so-called 'fundamental' and 'subjective' factors. These factors not only interact, but are often inseparable. I also share Michel Foucault's sentiment that 'nothing is fundamental . . . in the analysis of society' (1993, p. 164); the foundations of power in a society or the self-institution of a society are not a self-evident phenomenon. 'There are only reciprocal relations, and the perpetual gaps between intentions in relations to one another' (p. 164). This is why I have chosen to break away from the long-standing tradition in Soviet social science following the sequence from the economic level of analysis to the social and politico/ideological issues. This book does not lend itself to this type of approach also because the very character of societies is under question. What is now called 'post-Soviet' space, where conflicts have evolved and keep evolving, is not made up of impoverished societies with marked social stratifications. It is composed of basically egalitarian polities, despite the rapidly growing gap between the winners and the losers of ongoing reforms.

Although my research has focused primarily on the ideological aspects of Soviet ethnic legacies, this chapter deals with socio-economic and other 'basic' factors. Recent scholarship motivated by materialistic determinism has produced a lot of useful, but often simplistic, interpretations of ethnic issues. During the perestroika years, the 'politically correct' and widely shared academic view was that ethnically based movements and political manifestations were motivated by the struggle for economic control (*khozraschet*) in the union and autonomous republics where the 'reproduction of ethnoses is taking place' (Perepelkin & Shkaratan, 1989, p. 39). More recently, practitioners of hard sociology have put forward their arguments explaining ethnic politics and crises in terms of social stratification along ethnic lines (Ivanov & Smolaynsky, 1994). Other works of interest include Feshbach and Friendly's (1992) painstaking report on 'ecocide' in the USSR and how it has affected different ethnic and regional communities (see also Feshbach, 1995).

While all these works have their merits, only some aspects are relevant for this study. First, what is of interest here is how the 'basic issues' evolved during the recent transformations and how they were included in the public discourse. Second, I consider how the 'reality' of 'basic needs' may differ from how they are perceived; and how 'needs' may be explained and taught. Finally, I look at the implications of the deep societal transformations that have taken place in post-Soviet social life.

Especially relevant is what I call a 'rhetoric of grievances' (or complaints). This is a crucial but poorly understood phenomenon that can be illustrated by the story of Samuel Gellis, my longtime neighbor in our Moscow apartment building and a retired military researcher. Despite his relatively well-off status and liberal mentality, he is constantly complaining of the 'bad life that came with reforms' and the 'danger of Russian fascism'. At the same time, his son has achieved remarkable success with a semi-private computer enterprise. Within two or three years the young man was able to buy a country house, a good car, and large appliances like a Japanese TV set and a German refrigerator, as well as spend vacations abroad with his family. Although my neighbor appeared ready to return to the 'good old days', surely he would want to leave his son in the present!

4.2 Debating the Environment and Resources

With no demonstrable accomplishments in the field of economy, the Soviet society and state were fairly harsh and careless about managing environmental and resource issues. With a territory spanning one-fifth of the globe, and no system of individual property rights, Soviet citizens felt alienated from any sense of individual and collective responsibility for environmental protection and resource use. It was the exclusive responsibility of the state – highly politicized, militarized, and bureaucratic though it was – to implement any environmental policy. The Communist regime controlled all domains of public life; the economy, especially heavy and military industries, was carefully guarded by the Center. Huge but poorly managed industrial projects with wasteful and inefficient technologies were established throughout the country, their placement determined primarily by the availability of natural and human resources. Some economic developments were based on strategic/geopolitical interests – like the cotton-producing monoculture imposed in Central Asia (cotton was considered a strategic product for the military) or building the Baikal–Amur railway far to the north of the southern border with China. Immense territories were isolated for the needs of the military complex (nuclear production and testing sites, military installations and garrisons, etc.). Some of these projects were accompanied by population resettlements or by the elimination of traditional local economies. The damage to the social and cultural conditions of several regions and ethnic groups was severe, even irreversible in many aspects. The term 'ecocide' has been used to describe this situation (see Feshbach & Friendly, 1992). A lot of dramatic texts and political statements were produced by experts and activists, especially during the period of struggle for sovereignty and independence.

Two hypotheses dominate these writings. First, it is argued that the central government uses economic/resource issues to exploit the Periphery in favor of the dominant Russian population – or for the 'divide and rule' policy. The second contention is that this ecocide and socio-cultural degradation of non-Russian nationalities was brought about solely by the Soviet regime. However, a more balanced analysis does not show support for such an extremist view. Any measurement of ecological and cultural damage in former Soviet territories should be seen in relation to development, and be compared with other regions of the world where large-scale development projects initiated by multinational corporations and national governments have destroyed dozens of indigenous cultures, as well as their environments and resources. There is no doubt, however, that in the former Soviet Union, control of the environment was largely concentrated in the central political institutions. On regional and local levels, major development activities were proclaimed and promoted as successful results of Soviet economic planning. Republican and regional politicians and management (or economic) barons strove to include as many as possible of their local enterprises under 'Union subordination' (*soiuznoe podchineniie*) status, which promised better salaries, supplies, and social funding. Likewise, there was a greater chance of getting a better qualified labor force through all-Union recruitment procedures (*orgnabory*). Also, in the Baltic republics leaders begged for mainly Russian/Belorussian labor to be sent to their republics to work at modern construction projects and factories (Kozlov, 1995, p. 220).

In the public mind, however, central decisions and control were viewed as forceful impositions, quite often associated with the interests of 'outsiders', or of other nationalities. Thus, problems of resource wastage and deteriorating environmental conditions entered the domain of inter-ethnic relations, generating inter-ethnic tensions. The increasingly vocal dissatisfaction of local actors since early glasnost times usually took the form of demands for redistribution of access to resources in favor of their own group advantages or their own personal interests – camouflaged by a rhetoric of 'the nation's interests' and 'imperial exploitation'. For example, in Checheno-Ingushetia after Dzhokhar Dudayev came to power, a substantial amount of propaganda was generated about how the immensely rich resources of this republic had been stolen by the imperial regime of Russia. The anticipated and later proclaimed state independence of the republic was intended to put local resources under the control of the Chechen 'national' government and to bring prosperity to the Chechens. However, as one field commander commented, 'we could have a republic as rich as Kuwait and live lavishly, but all these people at the top, including Dudayev, sold out our resources for their own private interests.'[1]

Heated political debates and conflicts over environmental and economic issues initiated by non-Russian activists preceded cultural and political nationalism. Even those whom I call 'double minorities' ('non-status' groups or groups with autonomies within republics) accused the Center and the republican/regional authorities of 'nation-destroying', and began to demand radical improvements of their environmental and social conditions. That was the beginning of political manifestations on the part of Karabakh Armenians, Abkhazians, and the Arctic and Siberian peoples. Behind this drive there was a goal of self-reliance, i.e. freedom to exercise one's own power over resources and territories, including those mutually used and long disputed among different ethnic communities. This struggle promised rich rewards for those who were involved. Many leaders reiterated the argument that, without a proper material basis, no nationality could attain prosperity. My own content analyses of speeches at the first Congress of the People's Deputies in 1988–89 have shown that among the issues raised, the questions of environmental conditions, economic sustainability, and local economic control outranked issues of political sovereignty, democratization, and human rights.

Only a few years later, the problems of natural resource use and ecological issues had moved far from the focus of public debates and political concerns. In several cases it was clear from the very beginning that environmental and resource-use concerns had never been essential. The very process of conflict evolution eliminated or transformed these issues into political ones or into disputes of general property rights.

The situation in Estonia can be taken as an example. Edgar Savesaar, then leader of the ethnonational Estonian movement, announced in 1988 that 'our nation received its first experience of mass organization in the action aimed against the mining of phosphates' (*Narodnyi Kongress*, 1989, p. 20). This action took the form of challenging plans from central Soviet ministries to carry out phosphorus mining in significant areas of Estonia. The issue was to lead to the formulation of other demands: at the political level (whether the right to manage the territory and natural resources of Estonia belonged to the Center or to republican government), at the economic level (whether phosphate mining was in the economic interests of the Estonian republic) and at the demographic level (whether the largely Russian composition of the new labor force needed for phosphate mining was in the best interests of the Estonians and their republic). Thus, the original environmental issue yielded priority to the emerging conflict between the Estonian ethnonational movement and the Soviet government, and began to be perceived in primarily political terms.

The events around the plans to mine phosphates in the Rakvere region, where the Russian population has dominated the industrial centers, had a wide resonance on Estonia but did not cause immediate public protest. However, a similar situation arose in the ethnically homogeneous region of Estonia near the town of Volga, where not the Centre, but republican authorities initiated the construction of a large oil producing repository. An accident here could have led to large-scale pollution of the Byaik-Emajogi rivers and Vortsjärv lake, located in the very heart of Estonia. It provoked strong public outcry. In the words of Tijta Vjaxi, 'the battle against the repository laid the ground for the Valgask National Front. In the course of a few days several thousand people rallied around the idea of a protest' (*Narodnyi Kongress*, 1989, p. 144). In this manner, the fight for the environmental interests of the local Estonian population became a stand in defense of ethnic/national interests. This provided experience in mass mobilization which took on the character of ethnonational movements even in situations when the government of Estonia stood on the opposite side. In this case, the latter was perceived as a conductor and defender of the plans of the central government, especially when it became known that the project to build the oil repository had been finally negotiated and approved in Moscow.

4.3 Shared and Disputed Habitats

Ethnic problems take on an entirely different character, however, when they concern the territorial borders of a habitat and when the power institutions of a modern industrial state are set up against ethnic movements among groups with a traditional way of life, a kind of pre-agrarian subsistence system. In this case, environmental factors not only generate the conflict situation, but they determine the whole programmatic context. Such situations occurred in areas inhabited by the indigenous peoples of the North and Siberia, as well as among larger nationalities (like the Yakuts and the Buryats) and the Russian old settlers of Siberia, whose economy is partly based on reindeer husbandry, fishing and hunting. Industrial development of mineral deposits, and the construction of hydro-electric dams, oil and gas pipelines, railways and highways, have meant that hunting and fishing grounds and reindeer grazing lands have been confiscated from the local population (on damage to the reindeer economy, see Tishkov, 1991b). Not only does this restrict traditional economic activities, it makes the very preservation of basic systems of subsistence and transmission of cultures impossible. Entire ethnic groups and communities are placed in danger of social and cultural degradation and assimilation into the new industrial settlements and new towns on what had always been their territory.

Colliding relations on this ground have generated conflict also in situations where ethnic movements of the indigenous locals joined with non-indigenous old settlers in opposing central governmental structures as well as the immigration of newcomers who usually take better jobs and show less respect for local nature and traditions. For example, 200,000 people live in the Vilui region of Yakutia, among whom 47% are Yakuts, 39% are Russian old settlers and 4% are Evens. The development of hydro-power projects and mineral extraction in the 1960s–1980s undermined fishing in the Vilui River and its major tributaries and severely curtailed hunting possibilities. The rising movement for protection of the local environment against the negative consequences of industrial development acquired the character of a conflict between the autochthons and the newcomers. In a 1991 sociological survey, 25% of the Russians, 27% of the Yakuts, and 16% of the Evens named ecological deterioration as the major cause of the inter-ethnic tensions (Maksimov, 1991, p. 93). Similar situations have developed elsewhere in Yakutia as well. Thus, protecting resources and environmental concerns may serve as one of the main reasons for the fomenting of ethnonationalist sentiments in this republic and in other areas of the North and Siberia. In fact it would be more correct to describe these sentiments and their political expressions as ethno-regionalism or environmental nationalism based on the interests of the local populations, irrespective of ethnic affiliation.

In the summer of 1995 I talked with the Deputy Head of the Yakutia government Vasilii Vlasov and the President of the Republic of Yakutia Mikhail Nikolaev about how they assessed the ethnic situation in the republic and their relations with the federal authorities. Both politicians were born in rural areas of Yakutia: one is an ethnic Russian, the other is an ethnic Yakut. Their perceptions were strikingly similar – not because they now belonged to the top political establishment, but because of this deep attachment to this territory and their common interests. 'Local Russians are more like Yakuts here and they always can come to agreement with their long-time neighbors, especially in villages and small settlements. What had happened in Yakutsk in 1988 [student demonstrations] was more the university teachers' manipulations of "hot headed" youngsters than Yakut nationalism as claimed by the Center,'[2] said the Deputy Head. The President expressed concern that 'outside emissaries are trying to find inter-ethnic conflict in the republic instead of understanding that we are one people – the Yakutians (*Yakutyane*) – who live here. We possess an immensely rich country and want to use it for our own benefit and for our future generations. That is why we have proclaimed our sovereignty and are demanding more control and a share of our resources.'[3]

Deeply felt environmentalist sentiments have emerged within indigenous movements of small Arctic and Siberian groups. Their cultures are more vulnerable, and social conditions are much worse than among larger groups like the Yakuts or the Buryats. The 'Appeal of Native Inhabitants to the Session of the All-Union Congress of People's Deputies' serves as a good illustration of this situation. The Appeal was written by the Association of Nationalities of the North Kamchatka Region, which led a successful drive to gather signatures to the Appeal. It reads:

We, the native peoples of Kamchatka: Koryaks, Evens, Chukchis, Itel'men, Kamchadals [Russian-speaking descendants of mixed marriages of Russians with Itel'men and Koryaks in the 18th century – V.T.], strongly oppose the development of a gold-mining industry in our region. The mining of gold and other raw materials will render our region uninhabitable. Reindeer grazing land, spawning rivers, and hunting grounds will all be destroyed. And this means that the traditional economic livelihood of the native population will fall into decline. With the disappearance of our traditional livelihood, our national cultures and native tongues will disappear. Without our traditional livelihoods the indigenous nationalities of Kamchatka will disappear (Murashko, 1991, p. 5).

Ethnic conflicts related to territory and resources acquire a special character in those regions where the early 1930s witnessed forced collectivization and where propagandist projects were undertaken to make nomadic groups adopt a sedentary way of life. Among these projects were resettlement plans whereby the mountain peoples were to move down to the plains to better their social conditions. Programs of that kind were being implemented until rather recently, in the 1950s and 1960s in areas of the North Caucasus. These social transformations, managed from above, were motivated basically by positive goals and aspirations; and in many cases they resulted in real improvements. However, they have also brought about serious complications and conflict because of the erosion of traditional social structures, economic activities and communal exchanges. These are complex and contradictory influences of modernization projects that can be observed elsewhere around the world as well.

Significant in the context of these changes was that in some areas – like the Caucasus, Central Asia, and southern Siberia regions – two or more ethnic groups with quite different traditional economies and social structures had historically shared the same relatively small territories. They made use of different natural resources and geographical zones of one region: sedentary cultivators would occupy one niche and pastoral nomads another. This is a phenomenon known in social anthropology as 'economic complementarity', and has been widely observed all over the world (Eriksen, 1993, pp. 40-41; Haaland, 1969, pp. 59-65). To return to the territory of the former USSR: in the Central Asian–Kazakhstan region, the seasonal routes of nomadic Kirgiz and Kazakhs went from the plains to the mountains through the foothills and river valleys settled by agricultural people (Uzbeks, Sartams, and from the end of the 19th century – Uigurs, Russians, Dungans). Thus, in these areas amidst the arable lands of the farmers were the grazing lands and watering-places essential for the herders. In such conditions, one region was essential to the existence of both the agriculturalists and the nomads. Members of both groups recognized this reality and considered such territories – with their mixture of agricultural fields, grazing land, and water sources – a kind of shared property. This did not avoid recurrent disputes and clashes, but in most respects the traditional system of coexisting cultures remained rather stable for a long time.

The 'nation-state' demarcations introduced by the Soviets in order to create 'national republics' could not reflect the complex local systems of land- and water-use. The creation of republican borders rigidly divided territories and groups which may have had different cultural practices but were undivided. Leading Russian ethnologist Sergei Arutiunov described these instances as cases of 'cultural symbiosis', or 'associated ethnoses' (Arutiunov, 1989, pp. 89–91). Serious grounds for new rivalries, now on a more institutionalized level, were established long before the realization of Soviet industrial programs in Central Asia. Today these conflict grounds manifest themselves in a dual manner. First, in some places where there have been historical contacts between agrarian and nomadic herding groups, direct conflicts over specific plots of land and water sources have continued. Recent years have seen serious land disputes between the Tajiks of the Isfarinskii region of Tajikistan (old agricultural settlers of this part of the Fergana Valley) and the Kirgiz (formerly nomadic herders) of the Batken region of Osh *oblast*. There is still no mutually agreed border between these regions, which now means potential inter-state conflict between Tajikistan and Kirgizia. In 1989 this conflict led to direct clashes with loss of human life, but martial law was effectively implemented and order was restored. In order to resolve the situation, along with hopes of achieving an understand-ing on the demarcation of the border, representatives of Tajikistan at the 28th Communist Party Congress in 1990 proposed the creation of a special economic zone and joint agri-cultural and industrial ventures in the disputed area and bordering regions of both republics. After the breakup of the USSR, this issue was shelved, however.

This Tajik–Kirgiz land-use dispute has flared up several times in recent years: in 1982, 1988, 1989 (when events received the greatest attention) and in 1991 (Abashin & Bushkov, 1991, p. 2; Bushkov, 1990, p. 1). The valley of the Isfara River serves as an epicenter of the arguments over land and water. A large part of this valley was included in the Tajik Republic as an enclave around the ancient settlement of Vorux, surrounded by the terri-tory of Kirgizia. Here the waters of the Isfara have long been considered as belonging to the Tajiks, because they had cultivated and irrigated this part of the river valley in the 19th century and long before. However, in the Isfara Valley there was also much fallow land on which, also according to tradition, the nomadic Kirgiz wintered with their herds. In this area of regular winter pastures and stopovers, permanent Kirgiz settlements appeared in the middle of the 19th century; the local Kirgiz also turned to agriculture, channeling water from the river to their fields. Today Kirgiz settlers justifiably consider these as their own lands, which they began to use not only for herding but also for agri-culture – especially since the area is now under the administrative control of independent Kirgizia. This attitude is hard to reconcile with the traditional views of the Tajiks that all cultivated land or indeed all potentially arable land, as well as the waters of the Isfara, are historically 'their' territory and – most important – 'their' water.

The intensification of inter-ethnic tensions over land and water issues is exacerbated by a very high population growth and by obvious rural overpopulation, particularly in Tajikistan. The population of the Isfara district of Tajikistan, where 75% are Tajik and 6% Kirgiz, has increased 4.7 times between 1970 and 1990. In the neighboring Batken region of Kirgizia, where ethnic Kirgiz dominate, the population has increased only 2.5 times from 1964 to 1990 (Bushkov, 1990, pp. 4–5, 7–9).

Group competition for resources and territories is also taking place in western regions of Tajikistan along the Fergana Valley and its foothills. There the competitors for land and water resources are traditional Tajik farmers living within the borders of Tajikistan, and the descendants of nomadic and semi-nomadic Turkic tribal-clan groups living in the bordering area of Uzbekistan (Abashin & Bushkov, 1991, pp. 8–9, 11–12). To date, there have been no mass violent manifestations, but in a situation of political instability and growing social deprivations, the Fergana Valley area with its high population density (308.2 people per km^2) could well experience open conflicts.

Elsewhere in the former Soviet Union as well, environment/resource issues are often linked with ethnic conflicts. Within the Russian Federation itself, it is primarily the North Caucasus that, with its scarce land resources, high population density, tumultuous polit-ical history, and cultural complexity (Table 4.1), became one of the regions most troubled with such conflicts. The situations in the East Transcaucasus region (the Armenian–Azerbaijan conflict in Nagorno Karabakh) as well as in the Fergana Valley (the Uzbek–Kirgiz conflict in the Osh *oblast*) illustrate this phenomenon also. In Transcaucasus the borders of republics and of internal autonomies cut across the ancient routes of the Azeri nomadic herders between winter grazing plains (*kishlags*) and summer mountain pastures (*yailogs*). The summer mountain pastures of the Karabakh mountain plateaus and the Karabakh and Murovdag ranges were traditionally used by Azeri

Table 4.1 *Population Density in Successor States and in Republics of Russia, 1989 (per km²)*

USSR	13.0
Russia	8.7
Adygei	53.3
Altai	2.1
Bashkiria	27.6
Buryatia	3.0
Checheno-Ingushetia	66.8
Chuvashia	73.2
Daghestan	36.2
Kabardino-Balkaria	61.2
Kalmykia	4.3
Karachai-Cherkessia	29.9
Karelia	4.6
Khakassia	9.3
Komi	3.0
Mari	32.5
Mordovia	36.8
North Ossetia	79.7
Tatarstan	53.8
Tuva	1.8
Udmurtia	38.5
Yakutia	0.4
Armenia	110.5
Azerbaijan	82.3
Nagorno Karabakh	43.7
Belorussia	49.4
Estonia	35.1
Georgia	78.1
Abkhazia	62.5
South Ossetia	25.4
Kazakhstan	6.1
Kirgizia	22.0
Osh *oblast*	26.6
Latvia	41.7
Lithuania	57.1
Moldavia	129.4
Tajikistan	36.7
Turkmenia	7.4
Ukraine	85.9
Crimea	92.6
Uzbekistan	45.4
Fergana *oblast*	308.2
Kara-Kalpakia	7.5

Source: *Narodnoe khozyaistvo SSSR v 1989 g. Statisticheski sbornik* [National Economy of the USSR. Statistical Survey]. Moscow: Statistika, 1990, pp. 19–24

herders, migrating in the winter to the Mil'sko-Karabakh steppe between Nagorno Karabakh, and the Kura and Araks rivers. Almost all of these nomadic routes transversed the territory of the modern-day Nagorno Karabakh autonomous region, and some Azeri herders spent the warm seasons in the mountainous zones of what is now Nagorno Karabakh. The transition of the Azeris to a settled life on the plains regions of the Mil'sko-Karabakh steppe in the early 1930s did not change the character of their animal husbandry; it remained primarily based on the year-round herding of livestock.

Until the beginning of armed conflict in Nagorno Karabakh, Azerbaijani shepherds (*chabans*), according to tradition, crossed the territory of Nagorno Karabakh with the *kolkhoz* herds every spring and fall accompanied by their families. Some of them spent all summer in the high mountains of the autonomous region. These *chabans*, like their fellow villagers, tended their own family livestock in addition to the collective herds. Access to the mountainous summer pastures, including those in the administrative territory of Nagorno Karabakh, and use of the traditional herding routes throughout this region, meant for them the possibility to continue their accustomed way of life (for a more detailed analysis of the resource backgrounds for the Nagorno Karabakh conflict see Yamskov, 1991). Therefore, boundary questions were central in the formation of the position of Azerbaijanis coming from the border regions between Azerbaijan and Nagorno Karabakh. It was this group who spoke out most strongly against having this autonomous region joined to Armenia.

In the Osh region of Kirgizia, the borders of the republics were patterned differently, with most of the territory of both summer mountain and winter plains/foothills pastures of Kirgiz nomads falling under the authority of Kirgizia. However, some Kirgiz settled in the region of winter plains pastures, which ended up being on the territory of the neighboring Andizhan region of Uzbekistan. The main problem, however, lay not in this territorial demarcation, but in a similar decision which led to considerable foothill regions being included in the Osh region of Kirgizia, which had historically been populated by Uzbeks as well. Animal husbandry with year-round rotation of livestock to summer mountain and winter plains/foothills pastures has also been maintained. As throughout the ages, it comprises the economic foundation of many, if not the majority of local Kirgiz. Even the first uncertain attempts to establish a movement for territorial autonomy for Uzbek areas of Osh *oblast* were met with scorn by the Kirgiz. It was viewed as a threat to complicate, or even block, their access to winter pastures located in historically Uzbek settlements or where the route passed through Uzbek regions. As in the Karabakh case, the territorial-resource factor as a question of spatial habitat frontiers also played a role in the formation of the Uzbek–Kirgiz ethnic conflict – although it was further complicated by socio-economic, psychological, and political factors.

A final example of a territorial-resource conflict can be found in the steppe plains of the North Caucasus between the Terek and Kura rivers. Here Nogai nomadic herders have lived ever since the 15th century. Under the Russian Empire this territory constituted a separate administrative unit – the 'Nogai Steppe'. Later, in Soviet times, this territory continued to be treated as a separate administrative unit, under larger governance. In 1957, after the re-establishment of the Checheno-Ingush Republic and the return of Ingush and Chechens from exile in Kazakhstan, the Nogai Steppe, along with the Terek River Valley, which was settled by descendants of Russian Cossacks, was divided into three. The smallest part was included in the Stavropol *krai*, the other two into Checheno–Ingushetia and Daghestan. A major reason behind this decision was the desire to improve conditions for the development of traditional semi-nomadic stockbreeding in the region, particularly in connection with the return of the Chechens to their native areas and the necessity of revitalizing their economy. Even before the 1917 revolution, the

Nogais had regularly allocated some of their land to their neighbors (Russian peasants and Cossacks, Chechens and Daghestan mountain dwellers like the Avars and Dargins) for winter grazing land. In the summer the mountain shepherds kept their livestock in the mountain pastures of the Great Caucasus Range and its spurs. The *kolkhozy* continued this tradition during the Soviet period, all the more so since the forced sedentarization of the Nogais during collectivization considerably reduced the dimensions of their stock-breeding economy and, consequently, their need for pastures.

New arrivals used the pasture lands of the Nogai steppe aggressively, resulting in erosion which could be observed as early as the beginning of this century (Yamskov, 1986, pp. 27–29). During the Soviet period the overuse of pasture lands increased still further, and the desertification of the Nogai Steppe acquired particularly worrying dimensions. Recent decades saw the resettling of mountain peoples and Russians in the Nogai Steppe, and in many places the Nogai became a minority. Futhermore, mountain herders, particularly the Dargins, gradually began to squeeze the Nogai out of the stockbreeding on state collective farms (*sovkhozes*) and *kolkhozy* of the Nogai Steppe (Kalinovskaya & Markov, 1990 pp. 10–11). These developments were, naturally, distressing to the Nogai and caused them to protest. Nogai poet K. Kumratova gave voice to the sentiments of his people: 'Steppe singers sing of the desecrated steppe. Bureaucracy renamed the Nogai Steppe the Kizlyar pastures. There are no people here, and the land is used for livestock . . .' (*Polovetskaya Luna*, 1991, pp. 15-16).

Thus, a main reason for the development of the Nogai ethnonational movement was the partition of 'their' land among three different administrative territories. Two of these were 'national states' – Checheno-Ingushetia and Daghestan – where local titular groups began to populate and exploit what had been Nogai lands. The political and intellectual elite of these republics also sought to develop an ideology of belonging there as a 'historical right'. Subsequent political demands for a separate territorial autonomy for the Nogai proved a source of great concern to local and federal authorities. During the Chechen War, provocative statements on the part of local Cossacks to redraw the boundaries of the Chechen Republic to pre-deportation status, together with provocative activities of Nogai leaders, caused the Daghestan authorities to start feeling quite nervous. At one meeting of experts at the State Duma in February 1995, the Daghestan Minister of Nationalities, Magomed Gusayev stated, 'There are no Chechens from Daghestan participating in Dudayev's forces. This is proved by the fact that we did not have funerals for men who were killed [local tradition dictates that people be buried in their native land], but we will fight for the Kizlyar: it is our land!'[4]

Thus, the territorial and resource aspects of conflicting ethnicity can feed into existing political tensions, generating causes around which it is easy to mobilize, because these are issues that touch ordinary people in direct ways, threatening their land or their water sources. Also in cases where the autochthons still live and use their accustomed territory which now falls under the administrative authority of another group, they are inclined to perceive themselves as being alienated from 'their' land. Perceptions and complaints of that kind have been expressed by the Ingush who lived in the disputed region of North Ossetia and who had their own land and houses, using other arable lands as a basis of collective farming before their expulsion in the fall of 1992.

4.4 Environmental Disaster and Conflict

The over-exploitation of natural resources, technological catastrophes, large-scale pollution and military projects affected not only small indigenous groups but also large territories with multi-million populations. The environmental damage from the Chernobyl incident tragically affected a large nationality like the Belorussians, in an area that will have to be abandoned for centuries. Another major ecological disaster concerns the region of the Aral Sea, with waste territory of the Kara-Kalpak autonomy in Uzbekistan becoming uninhabitable. Such large-scale disasters often mean that serious damage is transmitted from the territory of one state to that of another, or from a region peopled by other nationalities. Sometimes outside agents are responsible. The accident at Chernobyl occurred on Ukrainian territory, the major responsibility was ascribed to Moscow experts and decision-makers, and yet it was primarily the Belorussians who suffered. Environmental disaster causes great human suffering, material and emotional, and may spur people to extreme forms of behavior. Chernobyl was one of the driving forces behind sovereignty movements in Belorussia and Ukraine, at least in the initial stage and at the level of mass mobilization.

The ethnonationalist movement in Belorussia gained strength and received mass support in the struggle against the ramifications of the Chernobyl catastrophe, and against plans to construct a hydro-electric dam at Daugavpils in the bordering region of Latvia (which could cause flooding in Belorussian territory). These events moved local activists to announce themselves as a serious public force influencing the political process. The Belorussian movement was at its most influential in 1989, when Chernobyl was the main priority. Especially important were demands for accurate and full information and the rehabilitation of contaminated territories (Tereshkovich, 1991, pp. 157, 160).

A similar situation could be observed in Ukraine as well. In both Belorussia and Ukraine, the Union Center was seen as the instigator of dangerous projects, and guilty of withholding information. At least up until 1991, mass public movements in these republics were not distinctly anti-Russian in character, partly because of the active participation of local ethnic Russians in protest activities against the cover-up actions of the central and republican authorities, as well as the leading role played by Russian scientists, engineers, military and medical personnel in clean-up work at Chernobyl.

Environmental issues have been a driving force behind the emergent mass movements in other republics as well, such as Armenia, Georgia, and Azerbaijan, where the ecological situation (except in the capital city of Yerevan), although not so disastrous, was exaggerated to the level of hysteria by local activists (Abramyan & Marutyan, 1991, p. 37). In some cases, public outcries led to self-destructive decisions such as the closure of the nuclear power plant in Armenia, which had been the main supplier of electricity to the local population. In 1995 work on re-starting the plant began, but re-activating it will require major new investments and re-training the personnel.

Although environmental issues may have acted as thinly disguised excuses for demanding sovereignty and self-governance, the central government could hardly deny their validity. Thus, environmental issues, along with language and culture issues, helped legitimate ethno-political movements in the USSR. The ecological factors themselves could not be described as direct causes of ethnic conflict; rather, they were seized upon by activists in their efforts at mass mobilization. Although environmental degradation in some other regions was much worse, it was not projected into the political discourse.

This is illustrated by the case of Central Asia where the environmental disaster in Kara-Kalpakia was not in itself enough to generate conflict. Natural resource depletion due to over-exploitation by 'outsiders' or by neighboring nationalities is a major problem in the Kara-Kalpakia and Arals regions of Kazakhstan, particularly with respect to water (the lower reaches of the Amu-Dariya in Kara-Kalpakia) and air pollution (the regions of the Fergana Valley of Uzbekistan located northeast of the Isfarin aluminum plant in Tajikistan). Potentially dangerous events of the first half of 1989 in the Fergana regions bordering Tajikistan were partly caused by growing awareness of air-borne pollutants. The rural Uzbek population attempted to organize protest marches and demonstrations in neighboring Tajikistan, with the demand to stop the emissions from the Isfarin plant. The Uzbek activists accused the Tajik government and the plant managers of releasing pollutants into the water and soil of nearby Uzbek villages, leading to an increase in infant mortality and birth defects as well as higher morbidity and mortality rates among the general population. Although the situation became tense, the authorities were able to maintain control, and the opposition was unable to organize a collective protest.

The most tragic example of the effects an ecological crisis can have on an ethnic situation is found in the Aral Sea region. The development of irrigation farming for cotton-growing in the Amu-Dariya (Uzbekistan and Turkmenia) and Syr-Dariya (Kazakhstan and Uzbekistan) river basins led to a situation where very little water was flowing into the lower basins of these rivers at their entry into the Aral Sea. This reduced flow has meant far higher concentrations of dangerous chemical substances (pesticides, defoliants, artificial fertilizers) in this area. The population of the lower reaches of these rivers is forced to use the polluted water for drinking and irrigating their fields and gardens. This ecological catastrophe received great public attention, and leaders of the Central Asian and Kazakhstan republics promised jointly to undertake measures to improve the situation (*Zayavlenie*, Statement 1990, p. 57).

A serious situation developed in the Kara-Kalpak autonomous republic, located on the delta of the Amu-Dariya River and on the southern littoral of the rapidly evaporating Aral Sea, where only 30% of the original volume of water remains. In 1989, 1.2 million people lived there, of whom 32% were ethnic Kara-Kalpaks, 33% Uzbeks, and 26% Kazakhs (*Natsional'ny sostav*, 1991, p. 92). About 70% of the adult population and 60% of the children in this republic were unwell; infant mortality here was 53 per thousand, as compared to an average in Uzbekistan of 38, and 31 in the Tashkent region (not including the city of Tashkent) (*Demograficheskii ezhegodnik*, 1990, p. 135).

The tragedy of the health situation is reflected in the age structure of the population: people over 60 comprise only 3.3% of the population of Kara-Kalpakia. In 1970 the all-Union figure was 11.9%, and 8.7% in Uzbekistan as a whole. This discrepancy cannot be explained by a difference in birthrates, as Kara-Kalpakia and the rest of Uzbekistan have very similar birthrates, 35% and 33% respectively (*Demograficheskii ezhegodnik*, 1990, p. 11, 135). And yet, such an obvious ecological precondition for serious political conflict has not led to mass public action nor to protests by the local population, much less to the appearance of inter-ethnic tensions. One likely explanation is the multi-ethnic composition of the Kara-Kalpakia population, making it difficult to channel discontent and despair against one specific ethnic enemy. When the Kara-Kalpak movement did emerge as a vocal political actor, this was not at a time when similar movements were flourishing. A weak protest was spearheaded only by a few local writers and journalists publishing on ecological and historical-cultural problems. One explanation for this was suggested by a well-known Kara-Kalpak writer, Tulepbergen Kaipbergenov: 'All the efforts of our nation are focused on one thing now, and that is physical survival as such. We aren't capable of anything more: not anger, not the search for culprits. We think only of one thing: to survive, to save ourselves' (*Sovetskaya kul'tura*, 31 March 1990).

4.5 The Impact of Recent Transformations

Dissolution of the USSR has seriously challenged the national economies of new states as well as the economies of internal autonomies of Russia. Economic improvements have top priority for the various governments of the region. Success or failure will have an immediate impact on interstate and inter-ethnic relations alike.

The relative success of the Baltic economies and active participation in local commercial activities by the non-titular population, which is largely excluded from the political process, has kept the Russians of Estonia and Latvia from aggressive political action and from a painful mass exodus, as has been the case in some other regions. The slow move towards reform without economic collapse in Belorussia, Ukraine, and Moldavia does not influence ethnic issues there, but in conflict areas economic issues are very much at stake. Trans-Dniestrian separatism slowed down partly because of bad economic performance, even though some 40% of Moldavia's industrial potential is concentrated in this region. A similar situation could be observed in Crimea, where the population and leaders are losing belief in the economic prosperity of the peninsula despite its rich recreational resources. In the Transcaucasus region, conflicts and war have devastated local economies; only Azerbaijan, with its rich oil and agricultural resources, has good prospects for economic sustainability. All these states still face major dilemmas over how to map an economic strategy that can provide political stability. The growing realization that Russia, Ukraine and other post-Soviet states will remain major markets has, at least, in Armenia and Georgia, given rise to tendencies towards reintegration without sacrificing political independence.

Irrespective of heated political debates on integration into regional or world economies, legions of young entrepreneurs from Georgia, Armenia, and Azerbaijan are still doing an increasingly successful business in Russian towns and cities. Much of the fruit, vegetable and flower trade as well as small street trade is in their hands. It is estimated that about one-third of the working male population from the Caucasus is making a living in Russia. Many have acquired property and invested money outside their homelands. This individual rational behavior stands in contradiction to political and elitist rhetoric. If the local authorities in Russia were to impose strict borders, tax and customs regulations, together with other measures against the 'southerners', that could block a major source of family income in the Transcaucasus and make the social situation there even more desperate. My colleague-ethnographer Yuri Mkrtumyan, acting Armenian ambassador in Russia, told me that it is crucial for many Armenians to have jobs in Russia now because this allows them to support their families, who lack even basic necessities in their country. 'Thanks to my ambassador's salary I can support three families at home.'[5]

For many decades, scarcity of resources and economic opportunity in the Caucasus forced local male labor to migrate for seasonal work and entrepreneurial activities all over the Soviet Union, especially to central and eastern parts of Russia. The construction of a great number of local roads, office buildings, and agricultural works in rural areas was carried out by seasonal brigades from Armenia, Azerbaijan, Checheno-Ingushetia, and elsewhere. An entire cultural and social network has emerged around these activities. In the summer of 1995 I discovered in Yakutia that the local Armenian community of about 1500 people controls all the construction business in the republic, calling upon their ethnic compatriots for contract work. 'There was a time when the government could not transfer money for us so we paid a few months' salaries from our personal assets to people we invited from Armenia. We do all the construction here while the Yakuts and Jews control diamond and gold production with Russian managerial and working personnel', the leader of the Armenian community in Yakutsk told me.[6]

In the North Caucasus, all five republics remain heavily subsidized by the federal budget (from 85% in Ingushetia and Daghestan to 65% in North Ossetia). The economies of Chechnya and Ingushetia have been devastated after the division of the republic followed the Ingush-Ossetian conflict in 1992 and the war in 1994–1996. This area is not rich in resources, nor as climatically favorable as Transcaucasus. It has never had the heavy and military industries so vital to the Volga republics of Russia. The question of land, jobs, and housing is especially acute throughout the area. Land is at a premium in the mountainous Caucasus, and the area has historically suffered from land scarcity (Arutiunov et al., 1994, pp. 2–3). This factor lies behind many of the conflicts, from the interpersonal to the territorial claims between ethnic communities and republics.

The current transition to privatization and a market economy with loose and unclear rules stimulates old and new rivalries in these poorly modernized societies, often along ethnic, clan, and family lines. Struggles concern not only plots of land, but factories and mines, shops, hotels and health resorts, as people calculate their future earning potential. In the long run, the formation of a class of private owners and investors will improve the social climate, producing more responsible citizens. But at this stage, a Wild West mentality prevails, severely damaging local societies with hatred and intolerance. 'Until Khubiev [Chairman of the Karachai-Cherkessia's Supreme Soviet, ethnic Karachai] and his people finish dividing state properties among themselves there will be no democracy or even real elections', noted Azamat Dzhendubaev, my assistant in the Ministry, who is an ethnic Cherkessian.[7]

No serious land reforms have yet been proposed by federal or local authorities. Something must be done to work out a plan of land reform tailor-made for this area, where a general transition from the Soviet collective farm system to individual farming may well cause endless and bloody disputes. Such a plan should focus not so much on the preservation of ethnic cultures and languages, as on access to resources and properties formerly controlled by the state, or more specifically, by local bureaucrats and underground entrepreneurs (tshekhoviki). In May 1992 when Gaidar's government started its program of privatization through a voucher system, Deputy Prime Minister Anatoli Chubais asked my advice about how to go about 'denationalizing' state properties in this region. I warned him that centrally planned approaches could face serious difficulties and opposition there because many industrial and real estate properties belong to the state only nominally, whereas behind the scenes there are individuals who regard these assets as their private property. Distribution of vouchers among all citizens might prove to be a second 'nationalizing': this is a situation that should be managed from local perspectives first.

Economic transformation in multi-ethnic regions involves previously unobserved social parameters of ethnicity. The Soviet Union never experienced spatial segregation of urban settings along ethnic lines, mainly because of the housing shortage and lack of a housing market. People lived where they were lucky enough to get state apartments or to build their own condominiums in strictly designated areas. The same rule governed the process of getting countryside plots for building dachas. Now, new opportunities allow greater individual choice as well as activities based on ethnic networks. In and around the cities of greater Russia, 'ethnic quarters' and concentrations of ostentatious mansions belonging to people of the same ethnic stock are slowly beginning to appear. In other states as well similar tendencies are emerging. Individual competition for acquiring properties becomes transformed into inter-group rivalries, allowing them to present the matter as a correction of 'ethnic injustices' previously committed by one group against another.

Seizing the properties of ethnic aliens through collectively executed violence became a feature of conflicts and riots in former Soviet territory. This could be observed in the ethnic pogroms of the late 1980s against the Armenians in Sumgait and against the Meskhetian Turks in Uzbekistan. Stereotypes about 'the fancy homes occupied by outsiders on our land' usually precede violent acts as well as individual expectations to improve the living conditions or job opportunities. In ethnic wars it has long been a rule for paramilitary warriors to confiscate properties and personal belongings as a reward for the risky profession of killing. This is a huge problem which the authorities and leaders cannot or do not want to cope with properly. Concessions and encouragement are meted out more often than legal prosecutions and punishments.

A typical example could be cited for Kirgizia, where the authorities of the republic failed to manage mass illegal seizures of land around the capital city of Frunze (after 1990, Bishkek) by young Kirgiz students living in shabby dormitories. Most of these students came from rural areas or other towns of the republic and were socially deprived compared to capital dwellers, the majority of whom were ethnic Russians. The authorities turned a blind eye to squatting; since 1989, Bishkek has been surrounded by temporary settlements equal in size to the territory of the city itself. Of the 40,000 young squatters, 98% were ethnic Kirgiz and 90% were without permanent jobs (Nazarov & Nikolaev, 1995, p. 18). This radically changed the established multi-ethnic character of the city, with its traditional high level of inter-ethnic cooperation and tolerance. Many of the formerly rural Kirgiz found it hard to adjust to the competitive capital environment and rushed into illegal and criminal activities. These new urban migrants became a main recruiting pool for nationalist extremists and a social basis for the nationalist political parties 'Asaba' and 'ERK'. In 1989–90, these new ethno-social dispositions and a changed political climate caused the first serious tensions between two major ethnic communities – the Kirgiz and the Russians. Russians constituted the overwhelming majority of the local industrial labor force; many of them who had poor apartments and could not afford to build their own homes started to complain and to worry about their future. These events signaled the first serious ethnic watershed, which culminated in the mass exodus of Russians from the republic: in 1990, about 42,000 left Kirgizia, and in 1993 the number of emigrants reached 120,000 (Nazarov & Nikolaev, 1995, pp. 15, 20)

A similar chain of events occurred in the city of Grozny under Dudayev's government. After 1991, many Chechens – most of them from mountainous rural areas – moved to the capital to 'make a national revolution'. In the prevailing legal disorder, many of them were transformed into hoodlums, seizing cars and apartments from local Russians, and less from Chechens who could rely on collective response measures better than Russians. Some 100,000 Russians left Grozny under Dudayev's government, moving to other places with feelings of anger and despair. This led many Russians to form an image of the Dudayev regime as a criminal one, and seriously undermined the hopes of Chechen leaders to attain economic prosperity. As Professor Djabrail Gakkayev, one of the authors of the Chechen Constitution, confessed in a private conversation, 'Our major mistake was to allow Chechen marginals to assault Russians and to force them to leave the republic.'[8]

Much remains to be done in analyzing the role of expected material rewards for proponents of extreme nationalism and for those who perpetrated ethnic violence, but what is clear is that this is a serious driving force of personal motivation. It is not enough to study ethno-social and economic disparities on the sociological macrolevel. Ethnic inequalities along social (or class) cleavages – in other words, 'indirect violence' – make negative perceptions of others or of the existing status quo practically unavoidable, and may provoke outright violence. But when and how this line is crossed between dissent and action for change cannot be understood without considering the broader political and cultural context and the psychological motivations of the actors.

Notes

1 Interview with Ballaudi Movsaev, 23 February 1995, between Nazran and Samashky, Ingushetia.
2 Personal notes, 21 June 1995, Yakutsk.
3 Personal notes, 23 June 1995, Yakutsk.
4 Personal notes, 17 February 1995, Moscow.
5 Personal conversation, 18 June 1995, Moscow.
6 Personal conversation with Pavel Kazaryan, 23 June, 1995, Yakutsk.
7 Personal notes, 9 October 1992, Pyatigorsk.
8 Personal conversation, 9 October 1995, Grozny, Chechnya.

5

Cultures and Languages in Conflict

5.1 Introduction

By the mid-1980s a complex situation had developed in the sphere of the social functions of languages and cultures of Soviet nationalities. Along with developing and supporting non-Russian languages and cultures, the Russian language received further dissemination into daily urban culture, becoming the language of work and of governance and services throughout the country. In homes all over the Soviet Union, the mass media – especially television – broadcast predominantly in Russian.

Scholars, including ethnologists and sociolinguists, have undertaken many detailed investigations of the language situation in the USSR (Arutunyan and Bromley, 1986; Bromley, 1977; Guboglo, 1984) as well as of post-Soviet mobilized linguicism (Guboglo, 1993, 1994a; Laitin et al., 1992; Neroznak, 1994) – without, however, coming to any far-reaching conclusions. The basic weakness of these studies has been their uncritical belief in the misleading results of Soviet census data concerning language behavior and language status. The most recent works are greatly influenced by politics, deep emotional involvement in intellectual debates, and are occasionally lacking in professionalism. One example is an Estonian sociolinguist's argument against Estonian-Russian bilingualism, especially in childhood, 'because it slows down intellectual development, . . . as a result dangerous speech distortions may appear' (Hint, 1988, p. 105).

The dominant explanatory model since the late 1980s derived its theoretical and ideological background from the widely acclaimed notion of 'structural violence' (Galtung, 1969) and cultural discrimination and assimilation discourse – concepts very popular with the anti-colonial movements of the 1960s–1970s, and among the political lobby movements for minorities and indigenous peoples in the 1980s and early 1990s. Many leading experts have been fond of citing the 'destruction of minority cultures' thesis as a major cause of ethnic conflict and political disintegration. But this thesis has seen little empirical testing; nor has it been removed from the political context and studied in a broader comparative perspective. This approach dismisses as politically incorrect the difficult question of the cultural and language mosaic which was preserved, and in many aspects indeed flourishing, during the Soviet period. It also exaggerates cultural cleavages to the level of irreconcilable 'civilizational clashes' rejecting the significance of cultural dialogue and individual strategies as something impossible under totalitarianism. It delegitimizes and dehumanizes the Soviet cultural legacy as evil or even criminal. Finally, this approach can produce facile policy-oriented conclusions like those drawn by Martha Olcott: 'specifically, Russians should not be allowed to continue the privileges they once enjoyed as colonizers but rather be encouraged to assume their new position as minority members of new states' (1995, p. 142). Its inherent weaknesses are revealed as soon as it is tested against analyses of similar language and cultural situations in regions and countries less targeted by the mind-sets and geopolitical rivalries of the Cold War. I do not know of any serious scholar who would demand that the Scots in Great Britain, or the French Canadians in Canada, or the white South Africans should assume the status and behavior of a minority group. For these societies, the starting assumption is a privilege of partnership – whether this is to be equal or unequal is another question.

5.2 Politics of Language and Culture

The history of Russian Soviet culture(s), including the so-called 'cultural revolution' of the 1930s, has been interpreted by many scholars. (See e.g., the works of such Western scholars as Brooks, 1985; Guenther, 1990; Simon, 1991; Slezkine, 1994a; Starr, 1983; Stites, 1992.) Detailed ethnographic descriptions of all major groups have been prepared through the joint efforts of national and republican research teams (see *Narody mira*, 1954–66; Tishkov, ed., 1994). In-depth analyses of socio-cultural and language situations carried out by Soviet scholars of previous decades have been widely acknowledged despite recent re-evaluations of the methodological background. My point is that some important aspects of language and culture politics have not been studied – whether on the level of individual and elite aspirations and choices, or with respect to disparities between wishful, declarative statements and everyday reality.

In the face of growing political and socio-cultural demands for increased social mobility among all nationalities, especially in the 1960s–1980s, the cultural landscape of the country changed, together with the instrumental functions of the cultural components and dispositions of different cultural systems in the larger national culture.[1] The major shift to take place in recent decades concerned the Russian language: with the process of urbanization, it became a powerful tool of individual choices for better career opportunities, as well as a means of communication – in Soviet society at large, and in ethnically mixed regions specifically, like the North Caucasus or Volga regions. Individual choice or strategy, irrespective of politics, has always influenced language behavior and preferences. However, state politics also play a crucial role in defining the status of languages. Professor Solomon Brook, long-time Deputy Director of the IEA, told me a story of his youth in the small town of Rogachev, Belorussia, where there was a significant Jewish minority. There were two Belorussian high schools, one Russian high school, and one Jewish high school, with corresponding languages of instruction up to the tenth and final year. Born to a poor Jewish family of seven children, Brook told me: 'One thing was sure – I did not want to go to the Jewish school. I wanted to go only to the Russian school but at that time, in 1927–28, Russian schools in Belorussia were open, apart from ethnic Russians, exclusively to the children of the *nomenklatura*. Even we children understood that only the children of those who worked in the government could get into this school; it was for 'reliable' (*proverennie*) Belorussians. "Second-class" children went to the Belorussian school.'[2] This could be interpreted as a kind of discrimination; however, it also attests to the efforts of the Soviet authorities to maintain full higher education also in non-Russian languages, as well as to the non-Russians' aspirations to a more prestigious education and integration into the larger culture. Thus, the real tyranny in this case was not in 'nation-destroying', but in imposing from above a language not spoken by most of the population.

Massive dissemination of the Russian language began during and after World War II, when major relocations of people took place and the official propaganda of Soviet patriotism and glory reached the most remote areas. And yet, the census of 1970 revealed that there were 57 from 112 million non-Russians in the country who could not speak fluent Russian. It became a new drive and an important component in creating a single 'Soviet people' for all citizens to learn and to speak Russian. There were, however, no top-level decisions made against non-Russian languages in the Khrushchev and Brezhnev periods.

Research and education institutes in Moscow and Leningrad continued to develop literary languages for small indigenous groups and curricula for 'national schools', and to print textbooks for republics and autonomies which lacked such facilities. Introducing about 50 written languages, the Soviet government could be proud of this cultural accomplishment. It is hard to agree with Hélène Carrère d'Encausse who describes it as 'ridiculous' that 'prominent scholars were called in to transform dialects spoken by groups of a few hundred people into languages for literary use' (1995, p. 22). But the idea of everyone speaking one language was probably no less appealing to non-Russian bureaucracies and managerial personnel. In the 1960s–1970s local authorities implemented drastic cuts in native language education in, for example, North Caucasus. In North Ossetia, where the level of Russification had been relatively higher, the entire education system became Russian-speaking by the late 1970s. Kabardino-Balkaria, Checheno-Ingushetia, Karachaevo-Cherkessia, Adygei and Kalmykia followed the same pattern: the language of instruction in all schools became Russian (Bromley, 1977, p. 273). In the 1970s there were only two autonomous republics in Russia (Tataria and Bashkiria) where several schools kept native language instruction from the first to the tenth grades. But at the time of my visit to Kazan in 1978, there was only one (!) 'national Tatar' high school for all children in Tataria's capital – a city with a population of about 993,000, of which 38% were ethnic Tatars, according to the census of 1979.

This situation was not seriously challenged after the beginning of perestroika. In the Political Statement of the CPSU presented at the 27th Party Congress in 1986, Mikhail Gorbachev stressed that it had been a primary aim of the nationalities policy of the preceding period to form a 'new social and multi-national community – the Soviet people' and their 'Soviet multi-national socialist culture'. Strengthening and further developing what had been achieved in this sphere was formulated as a goal for the future as well (*Materialy*, 1986, p. 53). This doctrine presupposed that 'the Soviet people' as the bearer of 'Soviet culture' should share, in addition to other features, one common language. Thus, the goal of 'mastering Russian (as well as one's native language) voluntarily accepted by the Soviet people as a means of international communication' occupied an important place in the new version of the Communist Party Program at the 27th Congress. Simultaneously this Program guaranteed 'in the future to protect the free development and equal rights to use native languages for all citizens of the Soviet Union' (1986, p. 157).

In contrast to the predominant interpretation of the 'Soviet man' doctrine, I do not see this as a basic fallacy from a socio-cultural point of view. The similar concept of 'one Canadian people' as put forward by Pierre Trudeau in the late 1960s (see Tishkov & Koshelev, 1982), as well as dozens of 'one people' doctrines formulated and imposed by multi-ethnic states, from the USA and Jamaica to India and Singapore, have not been questioned with such vigor. The problem with the 'Soviet man' doctrine was not so much the absence of socio-cultural commonality as it was the presence of the totalitarian framework and strongly ideological context for implementing this basically legitimate idea.

Thus – and quite understandably for such a large and diverse country – state priorities in cultural-linguistic politics, together with the ideological thesis of the 'further blossoming and rapprochement' of Soviet nationalities, served to push the authorities to even more enthusiastic dissemination of the Russian language and cultural-ideological indoctrination among the non-Russian populations of the Soviet Union, through the mass media, educational system, and industrial and military collectives. The Central television and the press used only one language, except for regular 30-minute educational programs in English, French, and Spanish. Today, after ten years of liberalization, there is still not one word in Tatar, Bashkir, Chuvash, Chechen or any other major non-Russian language spoken on Moscow-based TV broadcasts. When I proposed making national broadcasting more multilingual at the Russian government's meeting presided over by Boris Yeltsin in July 1992, the Deputy Prime Minister (in charge of mass media) Mikhail Poltoranin reacted gloomily, 'It will blow up the whole country. Russians will not stand for it.'[3]

In this book I do not evaluate the extent to which the dissemination of the Russian language and of common Soviet cultural values was introduced forcefully, and to what extent it was a 'natural' process in a country with ethnic Russians both as an ethnic majority and as a kind of 'state-bearing nationality'. The fact that this country went through industrialization and rapid urbanization in the 20th century could not but lead to a certain cultural unification. Whatever the relative importance of these factors (political efforts and the modernization process), the results of their combined influences were perceived by the contemporary non-Russian intelligentsia and political activists as the result of deliberate efforts at Russifying minority languages and cultures through state policy. Ironically, this very process of disseminating 'socialist Soviet culture' also produced dissatisfaction amongst ethnic Russians themselves, on the part of the intelligentsia – primarily writers. To many of them, it signified a 'loss of one's roots' and abandoning the traditions of Russian folk (primarily peasant) culture. What was considered Russification by the non-Russian intellectuals meant 'Sovietization' for Russian nationalists. This dissent served as a major cause behind the emergence of the Russian national-patriotic movement, which in many aspects was the political analogue of ethnonationalist movements among other nationalities of the Soviet Union.

In 1990–91, widespread appeals to revive Russian cultural, religious, and national traditions (including such nostalgic symbolism as the doubleheaded eagle, tsarist flag, Orthodox crest) played an important role in mobilizing the masses in support of the opposition who challenged the Union Center. The Center was viewed as a stronghold of the Communists – supporters of 'denationalized' or even 'anti-national' culture. As a backlash, such Russian nationalist rhetoric caused resentment among the non-Russian population. Thus, a painful and emotional discourse has developed around language and culture issues since the beginning of perestroika. Belorussian writer Vasil Bykov publicly proclaimed, 'I would prefer to die than to witness the disappearance of my language.' All the same, this had never prevented him from writing and publishing in Russian throughout his previous professional career, nor had it been an impediment to the many other writers who had reached national and worldwide audiences through the Russian language. I remember my conversation with Estonian academician Yukhan Kahk who published his historical monograph in Russian: 'My book in Russian about Estonia will be read by a hundred times more people in the country and abroad than it would have been if I had written it in Estonian,'[4] he said.

5.3 Measuring Language Data and Orientations

In the Soviet censuses, the ambiguous question, 'What is your native language?' followed the question, 'What is your nationality?'.[5] This resulted in data not on the language situation but on the issue of identity. The overwhelming majority of Soviet citizens of non-Russian origin answered the question on language the same way as they had answered the previous one on 'nationality'. In most cases, at least within Russia, their mother tongue and everyday spoken language was in fact Russian, but they opted to indicate the language of their nationality as their 'native' (*rodnoi*) language because for a Soviet citizen it was 'natural' and 'proper' for ethnic origin and native language to correspond.

In the summer of 1990 I was doing field research in the Ust'-Ordynsky Buryat autonomous *okrug* (Irkutsk *oblast*, West Siberia) where Buryats comprise about 36% of the population (with the rest predominantly Russian) and where they enjoy the status of titular group for which this autonomy was constituted. This group of western Buryats had a long history of contact with Russians; they had converted to the Russian Orthodox religion and had become strongly acculturated into Russian culture. All the local people speak Russian at home and only a few can speak the native language. At the same time, Buryats have preserved a strong ethnic identity and a feeling of group solidarity; the educated Buryat elite controls local political and intellectual life as well as dominating professional services, like education and health. I did not hear the Buryat language at all during my two-week stay there, and yet according to the 1989 census data, Buryat is the native tongue of 90% of the local Buryats (*Natsional'ny sostav* 1991, p. 47). In one family of local school teachers (school education is in Russian there) the mother explained to me why she had registered Buryat as the native language of all family members including the children, who did not know a word of the language: 'I do not feel it is proper to show Russian as our native language when we are Buryats. We will never be Russians because we look different.'[6]

Thus, the author of the no. 1 US bestseller *Polar Star* was far off the mark when one of his heroes, Arkadi Renko, fled to the northern city of Norilsk where he 'worked with two Buryats. Neither of them understood Russian' (Smith, 1990, p. 19). In the late 1980s it was impossible to find a working male Buryat who could not speak Russian!

The real situation was quite the opposite: there were more non-Russians who could not speak the language of their nationality than those who could not speak Russian. Thus, in 1989, 99% of the Kazakhs living in Kazakhstan identified Kazakh as their native tongue (*Natsional'ny sostav*, 1991, p.102). However, according to expert estimates, about one-third of the Kazakhs in the republic spoke Kazakh either poorly or not at all. The Kazakh language was actively used in only 10 out of 50 functioning sectors of social life (Kuanyshev, 1991, p. 40). Even more striking disparities between census data and the real language situation could be demonstrated in Belarus. In the Grodnen *oblast* of Belarus, located in the northwestern part of the republic bordering Poland and Lithuania, the population consists of 60% Belorussians, 26% Poles, and 11% Russians. In the 1989 census, 68% of the population identified Belorussian as their native tongue (this figure includes 85% of the Belorussians and 62% of the Poles). Another 12% of the population claimed fluency in Belorussian as a second language. A total of 27% of the population of the Grodnen *oblast* considered Russian as their native language, and another 46% said they were fluent in Russian as a second language (*Natsional'ny sostav*, 1991, pp. 90–91). However, sociological research disclosed quite a different language situation: 91% of those studied have a fluent command of Russian, 38% of Belorussian, and 3% of Polish. The language spoken at home, at work and in public places was, respectively: Belorussian 9%, 3%, 3%; Polish 3%, 0.4%, 0.5%; and Russian 67%, 78% and 81% (Bogush, 1991, p. 29).

Or take the Ukraine, where 1989 census data show that 12.2% of the Ukrainians regarded the Russian language as their 'native language' and 59.5% reported knowing Russian. The real level of language acculturation, however, was considerably higher. A 1988 survey of parents of first-grade pupils in Kiev found that only 16.5% of the respondents used Ukrainian in the home, and only 4.7% used the language at work (Bremmer & Taras, 1993, p. 85). In several regions of this country, the Russian language fully dominates all spheres of public life. One such region is the Crimea peninsula, with its Russian majority population. Another is the south-eastern part of Ukraine called Donbas, where 6 out of 11 million Ukrainian Russians live, comprising 44% of the Donbas population.

This region, historically poised between Ukraine and Russia, is still the subject of bitter disagreement between the two states (Wilson, 1995). A major goal for Ukrainian radical nationalists became the 'de-Russification' of the region and 're-Ukrainization' of those local Ukrainians (51% of the Donbas population) who consider their native language to be Russian (38% in 1989). As a member of the Ukrainian Parliament told me, state authorities and intellectuals are working now to correct the 'false consciousness' of those who lost their Ukrainian-ness. 'I personally already made two dozen Ukrainian kids when I established a Ukrainian-speaking kindergarten in Kharkiv' (the main city of Donbas).[7] However, the language situation in this area posed no easy task for the politics of Ukrainian nationalism, which was based largely on wishful thinking and rules imposed from above. Until recently, the Donbas region was predominantly Russian-speaking, including most of the Ukrainians there. Prior to Ukrainian independence, no more than 3% of the local children received their schooling in the Ukrainian language.

Thus, the Soviet census data on the number of persons who indicate the language of their nationality as their 'native' tongue do not reflect the number of those for whom it is actually the main spoken language. Nor can changes thus recorded from census to census and presented in scholarly texts (see e.g. Carrère d'Encausse, 1978; Karklins, 1986; Simon, 1991) be regarded as reflecting the true situation. This in turn means that such inaccurate data cannot serve as the basis for conclusions about the language situation in the former Soviet Union. On the other hand, neither can data on the proportion of the population who profess a good command of Russian as a second language (Bromley, 1977, pp. 301–302, 310) reflect the actual dissemination of Russian in the former Soviet republics and autonomous *oblasts*. Frequently 10–20% and even up to 40% of the population, particularly those of the titular nationalities of Russia's autonomies (Chuvash, Karel, Komi, Mordva, Osset, Udmurt etc.), claim Russian as their native language, which means in reality that they are predominantly Russian-speakers.

The 1989 census data compiled by Anatoly Yamskov (1994) provide more help here (see Tables 5.1–5.3). The category 'persons with knowledge of Russian' combines those non-Russian titulars (a) who named Russian as their native language even though this was not congruent with nationality and (b) who claimed fluency in Russian (if it was not claimed as a native tongue) as a second language. These figures include all Russian-speakers of that nationality living in the republics or autonomous *oblasts*. In other words, this indicator more adequately reflects the proportion among major ethnic groups who indicated Russian or the titular language as one of their first two languages.

For example, in Belarus the proportion of Belorussians 'fluent in Russian' includes those who named Russian as their native language (20%), and those who considered either Belorussian or another language as native, but indicated fluency in Russian as a second language (another 60%). In reality, 80% of all Belorussians know, i.e. speak, Russian. Likewise, in Belorussia, the category for Russians 'fluent in the language of the titular nationality' (in this case Belorussian), combines those who named Belorussian as their native language (2%), and those who considered Russian as their native language but indicated fluency in Belorussian as a second language (another 25%). This means that 27% of the Russians in Belarus know and can speak Belorussian. From the data of the Soviet population censuses, it is impossible to establish what percentage of, for example, Belorussians actually know Belorussian. As indicated above, information about native language, when it corresponds with the respondent's ethnic background, frequently fails to reflect actual knowledge or use of this language. But such data can reflect at least two important things: first, that the main spoken language in this republic (now, a state) is Russian; second, that a high level of bilingualism exists not only among ethnic Belorussians but among ethnic Russians as well.

Table 5.1 *Language Situation in the USSR, 1989. I: Ethnic Composition of Population and Knowledge of Russian Language and Language of the Titular Nationality in the Union Republics*

Republic	Main group (%)	% with Knowledge of	
		Russian language	Titular language
Armenia	Armenian (93)	45	–
	Azerbaijani (3)	19	7
	Kurd (2)	7	75
	Russian (2)	–	33
Azerbaijan	Azerbaijani (83)	32	–
	Russian (6)	–	15
	Armenian (6)	69	7
	Lezgin (2)	29	54
	Avar (1)	9	70
Belorussia	Belorussian (78)	80	–
	Russian (13)	–	27
	Pole (4)	82	67
Estonia	Estonian (62)	35	–
	Russian (30)	–	15
	Ukrainian (3)	94	8
Georgia	Georgian (70)	32	–
	Armenian (8)	52	26
	Russian (6)	–	24
	Azerbaijani (6)	35	10
	Osset (3)	39	54
	Greek (2)	80	20
	Abkhazian (2)	82	3
Kazakhstan	Kazakh (40)	64	–
	Russian (38)	–	9
	German (6)	96	7
	Ukrainian (5)	96	6
	Uzbek (2)	55	10
	Tatar (2)	92	7
Kirgizia	Kirgiz (52)	37	–
	Russian (22)	–	12
	Uzbek (13)	39	4
	Ukrainian (3)	94	2
	German (2)	95	0.3
Latvia	Latvian (52)	68	–
	Russian (34)	–	22
	Belorussian (5)	86	18
Lithuania	Lithuanian (80)	38	–
	Russian (9)	–	38
	Pole (7)	67	21
	Belorussian (2)	89	21

Table 5.1   *(Cont.)*

Republic	Main group (%)	% with Knowledge of	
		Russian language	Titular language
Moldavia	Moldavian (65)	58	–
	Ukrainian (14)	80	14
	Russian (13)	–	12
	Gagauz (4)	80	6
Tajikistan	Tajik (62)	31	–
	Uzbek (24)	22	17
	Russian (8)	–	4
	Tatar (1)	88	3
	Kirgiz (1)	19	13
Turkmenia	Turkmen (72)	28	–
	Russian (10)	–	2
	Uzbeks (9)	29	16
	Kazakhs (3)	41	18
	Tatar (1)	87	8
	Ukrainian (1)	92	2
Ukraine	Ukrainian (73)	72	–
	Russian (22)	–	34
	Jew (1)	98	49
Uzbekistan	Uzbek (71)	27	–
	Russian (8)	–	5
	Tajik (5)	18	42
	Kazakh (4)	31	15
	Tatar (2)	81	12
	Karakalpak (2)	20	6

Source: SSSR. Etnicheskii sostav naseleniia SSSR [USSR. Ethnic Composition of the USSR Population], 1991, Moscow: Finansy i Statistika.

A few more points should be noted with respect to Tables 5.1–5.3 and the accuracy of Soviet language data. First, up until January 1989, when the last Soviet census was taken, ethnic tensions had led to clashes and pogroms only in the Transcaucasus region. Elsewhere, ethnonational movements were still in their infancy, if they existed at all. This means that, besides its major discrepancy, the information on native-language retention among Soviet nationalities can be assumed to be not distorted by excessive politicization. The same could be expected of the data on command of Russian among the titular populations of the republics and autonomies. However, the ambivalences are significant. By early 1989, many titular nationalities of union republics had already started to reject the official Soviet culture and ideology, and the Russian language began to be considered a symbol of oppression. This undoubtedly influenced how people responded in the census. Moreover, in recent decades Ukrainians and Belorussians have in fact under-reported their command of Russian. Because these mutually understandable languages are so close, they believe that what they can speak is only a 'Russian-Ukrainian (or Belorussian) blend' and not 'real' Russian (i.e., the classical literary form).

Also, data on the non-titular Turkic-speaking nationalities' command of the republic's official language was obviously understated when the titular language is another Turkic language. As is the case with the Slavic nationalities, the respondents answered

Table 5.2　*Language Situation in the USSR, 1989. II: Ethnic Composition of Population and Knowledge of Languages (Russian, Titular Nationality of Union Republic, Titular Nationality of the Autonomy) in Autonomous Provinces outside of Russia, 1989*

Republic and autonomy	Main group (%)	% with Knowledge of		
		Russian language	Language of republic	Titular language
Ukraine			(Ukrainian)	(none)
Crimea	Russian (67)	–	10.0	
	Ukrainian (26)	90	–	
	Belorussian (2)	94	0.6	
	Crimean Tatar (2)	87	0.5	
Azerbaijan			(Azerbaijanian)	(Armenian)
Nagorno	Armenian (77)	57	0.3	–
Karabakh	Azerbaijani (22)	22	–	2
Nakhichevan	Azerbaijani (96)	20	–	(none)
	Russian (1)	–	10.0	
Georgia			(Georgian)	(Abkhazian)
Abkhazia	Abkhazian (18)	84	2.0	–
	Georgian (46)	65	–	0.4
	Armenian (15)	82	1.0	0
	Russian (14)	–	3.3	1.0
	Greek (3)	88	2.4	0.3
Adjaria	Georgian (83)	42	–	(none)
	Russian (8)	–	20.0	
	Armenian (4)	75	19.0	
	Greek (2)	80	18.0	
				(Ossetian)
South	Osset (68)	68	15.0	–
Ossetia	Georgian (30)	28	–	7.0
Tajikistan			(Tajik)	(none)
Gorno-	Tajik (89)	39	–	
Badakhshan	Kirgiz (7)	0	36.0	
Uzbekistan			(Uzbek)	(Karakalpak)
Karakalpakia	Karakalpak (32)	20	4.0	–
	Uzbek (33)	16	–	9.0
	Kazakh (26)	21	7.0	23.0
	Turkmen (5)	8	18.0	5.0

Source: As for Table 5.1

Table 5.3 *Language Situation in the USSR, 1989. III: Ethnic Composition of Population and Knowledge of Languages (Russian, Titular Nationality of Autonomous Republic and Okrug) in Russia*

Autonomous republic and *okrug*		% with knowledge of Russian, including reported Russian as native (in parentheses)		% with knowledge of language of titular nationality
European region and the Urals				
Karelia	Karel (10%)	98	(48.0)	64.0
	Russian (74%)	–	–	0.3
	Belorussian (7%)	90	(71.0)	0.3
Komi	Komi (23%)	91	(26.0)	80.0
	Russian (58%)	–	–	1.0
	Ukrainian (8%)	97	(53.0)	0.7
Komi-Permyak *okrug*	Komi-Permiak (60%)	87	(17.0)	87.0
	Russian (36%)	–	–	4.0
Udmurtia	Udmurt (31%)	92	(24.0)	80.0
	Russian (59%)	–	–	2.0
	Tatar (7%)	92	(18.0)	1.0
Mordovia	Mordva (33%)	92	(12.0)	92.0
	Russian (61%)	–	–	0.8
	Tatars (5%)	92	(6.0)	0.1
Mari	Mari (43%)	87	(12.0)	90.0
	Russian (48%)	–	–	1.0
	Tatar (6%)	88	(12.0)	1.0
Chuvashia	Chuvash (68%)	84	(15.0)	88.0
	Russian (27%)	–	–	3.0
	Tatar (3%)	71	(9.0)	8.0
Tataria	Tatar (49%)	81	(3.0)	97.0
	Russian (43%)		–	1.0
	Chuvash (4%)	82	(12.0)	4.0
Bashkiria	Bashkir (22%)	79	(5.0)	76.0
	Russian (39%)	–	–	0.3
	Tatar (28%)	83	(7.0)	0.7
	Chuvash (3%)	87	(16.0)	0.8
	Mari (3%)	77	(8.0)	0.2
Kalmykia	Kalmyk (45%)	94	(4.0)	97.0
	Russian (48%)	–	–	0.2
	Dargin (4%)	79	(0.5)	0.0
	Chechen (3%)	83	(2.0)	0.0
Siberia				
Gornyi Altai	Altai (30%)	78	(10.0)	91.0
	Russian (60%)	–	–	0.7
	Kazakh (6%)	71	(4.0)	3.0

Table 5.3   *(Cont.)*

Autonomous republic and *okrug*		% with knowledge of Russian, including reported Russian as native (in parentheses)		% with knowledge of language of titular nationality
Tuva	Tuvin (64%)	59	(0.9)	99.0
	Russian (32%)	–	–	0.6
Khakassia	Khakass (11%)	89	(17.0)	85.0
	Russian (80%)	–	–	0.1
	Ukrainian (2%)	95	(54.0)	0.1
	German (2%)	97	(62.0)	0.3
Buryatia	Buryat (24%)	84	(11.0)	91.0
	Russian (70%)	–	–	0.3
	Ukrainian (2%)	93	(50.0)	0.1
Aginsky	Buryat (55%)	75	(2.0)	98.0
Buryat *okrug*	Russian (41%)	–	–	2.0
Ust'-Ordynsky	Buryat (55%)	90	(10.0)	92.0
Buryat *okrug*	Russian (57%)	–	–	0.8
	Tatar (3%)	91	(23.0)	4.0
Yakutia	Yakut (33%)	70	(5.0)	96.0
	Russian (50%)	–	–	2.0
	Ukrainian (7%)	97	(50.0)	0.3
	Tatar (2%)	97	(44.0)	1.0
Jewish	Jew (4%)	90	(88.0)	18.0
autonomous	Russian (83%)	–	–	0.0
oblast	Ukrainian (7%)	94	(63.0)	0.0
North Caucasus				
Adygei	Adygei (22%)	85	(2.0)	–
	Russian (69%)	–	–	0.2
	Ukrainian (3%)	96	(52.0)	0.1
	Armenian (2%)	92	(22.0)	0.2
Karachai-	Karachai (31%)	80	(0.7)	–
Cherkessia	Cherkess (10%)	80	(2.0)	–
	Russian (42%)	–	–	0.3
	Abazin (7%)	81	(2.0)	5.0
	Nogai (3%)	87	(2.0)	2.0
Kabardino-	Kabardin (48%)	80	(1.0)	–
Balkaria	Balkar (9%)	84	(1.0)	–
	Russian (32%)	–	–	0.6
	Ukrainian (2%)	94	(44.0)	0.5
North Ossetia	Osset (53%)	89	(2.0)	–
	Russian (30%)	–	–	2.0
	Ingush (5%)	86	(0.8)	0.3
	Armenian (2%)	95	(26.0)	1.0
	Georgian (2%)	92	(11.0)	4.0

Table 5.3 *(Cont.)*

Autonomous republic and *okrug*		% with knowledge of Russian, including reported Russian as native (in parentheses)		% with knowledge of language of titular nationality
Checheno-	Chechen (58%)	74	(0.2)	–
Ingushetia	Ingush (13%)	80	(0.3)	–
	Russian (23%)	–	–	0.4
	Armenian (1%)	94	(27.0)	0.1
	Ukrainian (1%)	93	(41.0)	0.5
	Kumyk (0.8%)	78	(1.0)	6.0
	Nogai (0.5%)	81	(0.7)	0.1
Daghestan	Avar (28%)	63	(0.7)	–
	Dargin (16%)	67	(0.7)	–
	Kumyk (13%)	75	(0.8)	–
	Lezgin (11%)	70	(0.9)	–
	Laks (5%)	80	(2.0)	–
	Tabasaran (4%)	61	(0.7)	–
	Nogai (2%)	78	(0.5)	–
	Rutul (0.8%)	63	(0.8)	–
	Agul (0.8%)	70	(0.9)	–
	Tsakhur (0.3%)	53	(0.7)	–
	Russian (9%)	–	–	1.0
	Azerbaijani (4%)	74	(2.0)	1.0
	Chechen (3%)	74	(0.4)	3.0
	Tat (0.7%)	91	(7.0)	0.9

Source: As for Table 5.1.

the census question in terms of the 'high' literary form of the titular language. In reality, the various Turkic languages are so close that their native speakers can easily learn to communicate with each other on a basic level. This primarily concerns the Bashkir language in Tataria, and Tatar in Bashkiria. Thus, relatively low census figures hide the much higher actual level of language communication among non-Russian Turkic-language speakers.

The Baltic nationalities understated their knowledge of Russian as well, probably due more to the prevalent emotional and political climate in that region. That in 1989 half as many Estonians (35%) as Latvians (68%) admitted to speaking Russian, reflects the level of political mobilization and the effect of the Estonian nationalist movement. It is difficult to imagine that so many Estonians could lose their command of the Russian language during the period between the two censuses; in 1979 the same figure had stood at 44%. My most recent observations in Estonia (June 1995) confirmed the very wide knowledge of Russian among Estonians. A local taxi driver told me that he 'did not know anybody in Tallinn who could not speak Russian'.[8]

By contrast, in Central Asia and the Caucasus, it was highly prestigious to have a command of Russian. In these regions responses concerning the spread of Russian may frequently be exaggerated. In the Volga area and the Siberian autonomies of Russia, information about non-Russians' knowledge of Russian is more reliable. The prestige involved in knowing Russian, together with a lower degree of ideological engagement, did not distort the picture to such an extent as in the Union republics.

The data in Tables 5.1–5.3 show two important results of language processes in the Soviet Union, results which could not be changed overnight after the USSR had split up into 15 new states. First, there is a very significant spread of the Russian language among other nationalities. In Latvia and Kazakhstan, the proportion of Russian-speakers is particularly high: 68% of the Latvians and 64% of the Kazakhs report that they can speak Russian. Actually, about half of the Kazakhs use only Russian in practice, starting from President Nazarbaev's home and office. Due to historical ties and the similarity of East-Slavic languages, this indicator increases to 72% and 80% in Ukraine and Belarus. In the republics of the Russian Federation an even greater segment of the titular population reports knowing Russian: 70–95% (only in Tuva is the figure as low as 60%). Even among Chechens, who showed the highest level of native language retention among non-Russians, Russian is the main language of public communications and of politics. It was the language of the Chechen Constitution, of Dudayev's decrees and of guerrilla commanders. It was the language of communication between members of the Chechen delegation when I met them in Vladikavkaz in December 1994 at the first round of negotiations.

Recent ethno-linguistic research in several of Russia's republics has demonstrated the strong dominance of Russian language in major spheres of competence. In Kalmykia, for example, ethnic Kalmyks had experienced a process of acculturation since the 1920s which accelerated during the period of deportations and in the 1960s–1980s. As of 1985, 93% of the urban Kalmyks and 87.2% of the rural Kalmyks could speak, read, and write Russian; the same level of competence for the Kalmyk language was found in only 27.3% of the urban and 45.8% of the rural Kalmyk population. Even those who knew their 'native' language preferred to speak Russian both at home and work. In Elista, the capital, 50% of the Kalmyks spoke only Russian at home and 81% at work (Dambinova & Korostelev, 1993, pp. 94–104). The explanation of this striking example of 'Russification' is not simple. This group has never had a written language nor a literary tradition. Three centuries of close contact with Russians started the spread of the Russian language among this group in the 17th century. In recent years, the remarkable increase in the level of educational and social mobility has influenced many people's choices, especially parents' strategies, in favor of a more powerful and promising language; thus, while maintaining spoken bilingualism, Kalmyks started to read literature written mainly in Russian.

It is also common that among 'non-status' minorities of the former Union and autonomous republics (neither titular nor Russian) the majority speak Russian as a main language and not the language of the dominant local group. In Lithuania, 67% of the Poles reported a knowledge of Russian whereas only 21% know Lithuanian; in Moldavia 80% of the Gagauz speak Russian and only 6% Moldavian; in Azerbaijan 69% of the Armenians know Russian and only 7% the Azerbaijani language; in Kazakhstan 96% of the Germans and 92% of the Tatars speak Russian and only 7% speak Kazakh. Also in the autonomies of Georgia and Azerbaijan the language situation could be characterized by Russian-language domination. Here, however, census results should be viewed even more critically because these areas have already been seriously touched by the political climate and conflict, especially in Nagorno Karabakh. For example, according to census data, only 0.3% of the Armenians in Nagorno Karabakh said they knew the Azerbaijani language, and only 2% of the Azerbaijanis in Nagorno Karabakh admitted to knowing Armenian. Census data from Abkhazia demonstrate a similar tendency: only 2% of the Abkhazians said that they spoke Georgian. In South Ossetia, 60% of the Ossets and 15% of the Georgians stated that they knew Russian.

Field research carried out by the Institute of Ethnology and Anthropology and my own observations in Abkhazia in 1985 and in South Ossetia in 1992 revealed an extremely high level of bi- and trilingualism among the people of these autonomies. The field research does not show a demonstrative ignorance of the Azerbaijani language among Karabakh Armenians (Yamskov, 1991). But at the peak of the Karabakh nationalist movement and after the Sumgait pogrom, only one in 300 Armenians was willing to admit to knowing the 'enemy' language. Fifteen years ago, language disposition among Armenians and Azeris was quite different, at least among intellectuals of both groups. In 1975, at the 14th International Congress of Historical Sciences, there were two well-known scholars, Azerbaijani academician Ali Sumbatzade and Armenian academician Zhatur Agayan. Long-time friends, they preferred to speak together with each using the language of the other. 'You can imagine what a great meaning it has for our two peoples to be able to speak this way,' they told me.[9] Both men died before the bloody conflict erupted.

Also evident is the tendency for local Russians not to know the language of the titular nationality. Excluding Belorussia and Ukraine, where the figures are 27% and 34%, and Lithuania, where the figure is 38%, knowledge of the language of the titular nationality by Russians ranges between 5 and 25%. In the republics of the Russian Federation, only 1–3% of the Russians know the languages of the titular nationalities.

This indicates how the former Soviet Union was formed and developed as a state in which the ethnic majority of the population was Russian: therefore the Russian language dominated – although to varying degrees. In most cases, the non-Russian population was oriented to learning Russian before any other language, including the language of their own nationality. There were only a few cases where an ethnic 'double' minority knew the 'republic' language better than Russian: among the Kurds in Armenia, Lezgins and Avars in Azerbaijan, Ossets of the inner regions of Georgia (not in South Ossetia), Tajiks of Uzbekistan, and Badakhshan Kirgiz of Tajikistan.

Practically all non-Russian nationalities found themselves to be cultural-linguistic minorities of the Russian-speaking USSR. This also applies to most of the administrative regions of Russia with ethnically-mixed populations. Under these conditions, contacting ethnic groups adapted (mastered the language and social norms) not so much to each other, but to the Russian-speaking majority of the country's population.

The example of Nagorno Karabakh demonstrates this situation clearly. The local Armenians did not consider themselves (and rightly so) a minority in the cultural-linguistic sense in Azerbaijan, to which the Nagorno Karabakh autonomous *oblast* belongs. They behaved as a minority in the Soviet Union as a whole and therefore preferred to learn Russian (57% know Russian), rather than Azerbaijani. But the Azerbaijanis of Nagorno Karabakh did not become a cultural-linguistic minority of this Armenian autonomy in the full sense: 22% of the Azerbaijanis of Nagorno Karabakh knew Russian; even less (but more than 2%!) knew Armenian. Thus, the ethnic groups of this region had rather a weak mutual cultural-linguistic interface. Interaction with (or rather adaptation to) the common Soviet Russian-speaking environment had primary significance for inter-group alienation, whereas the formal status of the 'titular' or 'non-titular' nationality played a minimal role. There was no particular sense in establishing which language was 'more important' in the territory of Nagorno Karabakh: Armenian (the language of the titular nationality of that autonomy) or Azerbaijani (the language of the titular nationality of the republic). In the everyday life of the people of Nagorno Karabakh, the Russian language played the leading role. A knowledge of Russian was essential for Armenians and Azerbaijanis to communicate with each other and to exercise social mobility in a wider Soviet space. Looking backwards, official tri-lingualism could be the best strategy for those kinds of complex communities.

The demise of the Soviet Union has radically changed the ideological and political conditions of linguistic problems. Millions of Russians and representatives of other non-titular nationalities have suddenly found themselves in an ascribed position of being ethnic minorities, whereas they used to consider themselves part of the dominant Russian-speaking cultural-linguistic milieu of the Soviet Union. Thus, for most successor states the main task is seen as not protecting the rights of ethnic minorities, but transforming the local Russian and Russian-speaking population – previously oriented primarily toward the Russian language and Soviet culture – into an ethnic minority oriented to learning the official languages and absorbing cultural values and norms of the titular nationalities of these new states. Accomplishing this goal will often demand radical changes in the cultural-linguistic patterns developed over the past 70 years or even over centuries. Comparisons with other regions that have gone through a similar process show that the language legacies of former metropolises tend to survive and can become an important cultural element of the new states.

5.4   Language Nationalism and Responses

So far, the formation of new states and the rising status of internal autonomies (or the struggle for this status) has taken place within a doctrine of ethnic nationalism which has demanded the strengthening of the position of 'national' languages. To a large extent, the militancy concerning language has been motivated not so much by a wish to preserve and strengthen native identities, as by the desire to take a strong anti-Russian political stand. The same phenomenon has been observed in many other cases of language nationalism – such as with Québecois (French Canadians) towards the English, or with the Bretons towards the French. As Thomas Hylland Eriksen has pointed out:

> Since the French state chose the French language as the foremost symbol of its nationalism, the most efficient and visible kind of resistance against that nationalism may be a rejection of that language . . . By using Breton in public context, Bretons signal that they do not acquiesce in French domination. A notion of cultural roots alone would not have been enough: roots were never sufficient to revive a vanishing identity (1993, p. 110).

The major difference between this reference and the Soviet experience is that the 14 non-Russian languages rebelling against the dominance of Russian could not be described as dying or even endangered languages. These are languages that have been strong enough to oust Russian from many spheres of public life, in Union republics and later in sovereign states. Before the breakup of the USSR, the languages of the titular groups acquired exclusive official status through legislation enacted by the local authorities. In several cases, the issue has acquired a deeply emotional and political character. In August 1989, Moldavians rallied to make Moldavian (Romanian) the official language of the republic. The driving force behind language nationalism was the faculty and students of local universities who were predominantly recruited from 'national cadres'. Only Belarus and Kirgizia have elected to have official bilingualism; Kazakhstan almost chose this option, but Nursultan Nazarbaev's promises to introduce Russian as a second official language were not realized. A main requirement of these new official language laws has been the translation (within a period of two to four years) of all documentation in state institutions and enterprises into the language of the titular nationality, and the introduction of qualifying language examinations for government employees and managerial personnel.

For the majority of the non-titulars, this has meant not only the necessity of learning the official language in a very short period of time, but also a serious change in social status and career possibilities. Previously, the Russian-speaking population – including the substantial number of titulars (or their predecessors) who had shifted to the Russian language – had enjoyed certain advantages: in getting better education and professional training in Russian, and in being promoted to high positions in many institutions. With the enactment of official language laws, the situation for the non-titular population changed radically. The only way to maintain their status or to be promoted to prestigious positions was to learn the official language, or to put forward political counter-demands. Another possibility, of course, was to leave the 'unfriendly' environment.

By the late 1980s, in almost all regions of the former Soviet Union, there were cases where language issues intensified or even generated open violent conflicts. In Moldavia, for example, the conflict of the Gagauz and predominantly Russian-Ukrainian population of the Trans-Dniestrian region with the central government evolved into a mass political movement after the decision was made in Kishinev to quickly organize language certification of managerial personnel. This could have led to massive dismissals of local non-titulars and their replacement by ethnic Moldavians (Kul'chik & Rumyantsev, 1991, p. 9). The President of the self-proclaimed Trans-Dniestrian Republic, Igor Smirnov, confessed in conversation with me that directors of local enterprises had called for him to organize a resistance movement in this region: 'They told me that they do not want to be Romanianized or to lose their positions, and decided to delegate me into politics.'[10] The first steps undertaken by breakaway leaders and self-proclaimed republics in the Gagauz and Trans-Dniestrian areas were local decrees on official trilingualism (Gagauz–Moldavian–Russian and Moldavian–Russian–Ukrainian). Military clashes followed later.

In Kazakhstan the 'State Program for Development of the Kazakh Language', approved in 1990, required the translation of the entire body of office regulations and documentation into the Kazakh language by 1994. This caused a great deal of dissatisfaction among Russian and other non-Kazakh groups, particularly in the northern and northeastern parts of Kazakhstan where Kazakhs are a minority. It fueled the growing tensions between Russian and Kazakh ethnonational movements in the city of Uralsk where Kazakhs comprised only 23% of the population. In September 1994 I visited Orenburg *oblast*, including the area bordering the northern Aktubunskaya *oblast* of Kazakhstan. The chairman of a local collective farm told me a story about his long-time colleague across the border ('we do not know where the border line goes exactly, as we often do not know where the borders are between our *kolkhozy*: only arable lands are divided by collective owners')[11] who recently was dismissed because he could not 'read instructions or communicate with Kazakh supervisors, which had to be done in the official language, while between themselves the Kazakhs speak in Russian'.[12] Later on, practically all new states revised or abolished militant stands concerning exclusive language usage, but the damage to inter-ethnic relations had already been done. For example, the government of Moldavia's decisions to liberalize language policy caused militant student demonstrations under nationalist slogans in Kishinev in spring 1995, and considerable effort was needed to manage this crisis.

In the republics of the Transcaucasus region, the languages of the titular nationalities were the official languages according to the Constitutions of the Union republics since the 1970s. This constitutional status of local languages distinguished Azerbaijan, Armenia, and Georgia from other Union republics but did not in any real sense influence the spread of Russian or the languages of the titular nationalities in the Transcaucasus republics. Both local and Russian languages enjoyed strong positions, coexisting in a mutually enriching bilingual framework. Ethnonationalism, however, demanded a more militant attitude toward 'outside' cultural components. Therefore, in Georgia, for example, a 'State Program for Development of the Georgian Language' was announced in 1988, changing the official language of all office work and documentation in the republic (including the South Ossetian and Abkhazian autonomies) from Russian to Georgian. In response, the governments of Abkhazia and South Ossetia announced official trilingualism (Georgian–Abkhazian–Russian and Georgian–Ossetian–Russian) and refused to obey Tbilisi. Leaders of the South Ossetian ethnonational movement saw this language program as the turning point in Georgian–Ossetian tensions, which soon developed into armed confrontation (Kulumbegov, 1991, pp. 3-4).

The translation of official documentation from Russian and Ossetian into Georgian could create conditions for a drastic change of the cultural environment in South Ossetia and require replacements in many positions. Not by coincidence, the most outspoken and militant activists of the secessionist movement in South Ossetia were recruited from local educational and managerial personnel – such as the Head of the Supreme Soviet of South Ossetia, Tores Kulumbegov, and the main ideologist of 'national self-determination', Alan Chochiev, both secondary school teachers in Zhinvali. During my visits to this conflict area in 1992, it was mainly teachers and other intellectuals from Zhinvali who were still painting a picture of irreconcilable differences after three years of exhausting military clashes.

Also, in many other regions of the former Soviet Union the language factor generated or at least shaped the ideology of ethnic conflicts. Initially, many of these conflicts were provoked by attempts by titular activists to escape the status of cultural-linguistic minority within the Russian-speaking Soviet Union. After such goals had been achieved in new states and, partly, in Russia's republics, conflicts of the non-titular groups and 'third-language minorities' with the titular nationalities have begun to arise more frequently over emerging or perceived language discrimination against Russian and other non-titular language speakers. For the past few years, the languages of the titular nationalities have become not only formally, but actually, a sign of privileged positions. In this case, the problem is no longer how to escape the situation of a cultural-linguistic minority by declaring their 'own' independent state or sovereign republic. The problem is more complex now: it concerns whether numerous and still culturally powerful Russian-speakers will recognize their transformation into a linguistic minority in the new states and the possibility of acculturation, or whether they will refuse to learn the languages of the titular nationalities in short time-spans and will opt instead for strategies within the framework of what used to be the dominant cultural system.

The demise of the Soviet Union has not brought about dramatic changes in the real language situation. It is a well-established phenomenon in sociolinguistics that language disparities and unequal statuses are not solely the result of politics and elitist efforts: they are also the results of the total numbers of speakers and of language communication dispositions at the regional, national and global levels (Laitin et al., 1992). English, French, Russian, or Chinese will always be a more privileged reference component and a more appealing choice in contacts with other 'smaller' languages, or in a situation of a multilingual milieu. In the Soviet Union, the Russian language has served as a vehicle for inter-ethnic and 'outside world' communications. And there are no rational reasons for this to change as a result of new inflammatory propaganda. Nor are there any real competitors capable of replacing the Russian language in this role.

Even in the Baltic states, where prospects for dismantling Russian in favor of English looked more promising, this process has not yet reached further than a small group of social scientists and politicians in the capital cities. *Izvestia* columnist Leonid Mlechin reports from his trip to this region: 'as in Russia, it is the former *nomenklatura* who adjusted to a new life first. While in the past, everybody spoke Russian in the Party's Central Committee, now the same people speak exclusively in English' (*Neatkariga Cina*, 16 August 1995, p. 3). Most Lithuanians, Latvians, and Estonians have used Russian in the past and will probably continue using it in the future, as a second language in intra-Baltic communications and in contacts with people in Russia and Belarus and in other post-Soviet states. Even the heads of state during the Baltic assemblies and other top politicians in their regional or bilateral contacts have had to use the Russian language in times of less public but more precise communication. Generational changes may bring English to the Baltic states as a substitute for Russian on a limited elite level, but there are no grounds to predict that English or German will have the same chances as Russian with respect to grass-roots local use.

Penalizing the Russian language served for Baltic nationalism as a major instrument for changing the demographic situation in favor of 'indigenous nations' and strengthening cultural isolationism for purposes of mobilization. Both strategies have played important political roles and served individual interests, without realistic prospects of their ever being accomplished. The Russians have tended to stay on in the Baltic states (Tishkov, 1992c); local titular populations, especially their socially active sectors, are searching for wider language spaces to break the bonds of the limited nature of their own 'small' languages and broaden their social and information mobility. Because the Russian language is the most readily available tool for interpersonal communication, it has maintained its chances of keeping this status, irrespective of the political and emotional orientations of the activists. In June 1995, at the central railway station in Tallinn, I observed four Estonian policemen happily conversing in Russian. As one of them explained to me, 'Among us Lieutenant Alexeev does not speak Estonian and we always use Russian at work; anyhow, it is more convenient because everybody we have to address understands this language.'[13] This occurred right after I had left a scholarly conference where many of my Baltic colleagues had been unwilling to speak Russian or, even more striking, to discuss the prospects of the Russian language in their states.

Among local Russian-speakers there is an expectation and trend to learn official languages, but progress is slow. At the Tallinn railway station I could not find any Estonian–Russian dictionaries or instruction manuals and the saleswoman told me that such books are very difficult to obtain, especially outside the capital. Although it may seem unlikely, establishing official bilingualism in Latvia and Estonia could be a constructive political step, not only towards stabilizing the situation but also towards granting language rights to other groups.

Dismantling the Russian language in Belarus and Ukraine was no longer part of the political agenda after radical ethnonationalism cooled down its aggressive rhetoric and all necessary language symbolism had been enshrined in official texts and ceremonies. Belarus peacefully introduced official bilingualism, satisfying the overwhelming majority of the population and provoking scant reaction from the radical nationalists. In Ukraine, the state and the public have accepted the dominance of the Russian language in areas like Donbas and Crimea, and have not attempted to enforce official language legislation or legalize its de facto status. Moldavia has reconsidered its language legislation, and has not attempted to force Gagauz or Trans-Dniestrian residents to stop using Russian and shift to the Moldavian language.

It is not difficult to conclude that cultural-linguistic factors as such were recognized and influential only in the first stages of the development of ethnic conflicts. Many of these factors quickly took on political significance involving questions of power: who can and should define the grounds of ethno-cultural and linguistic politics, and to what extent? The Soviet Union's history of nation-building has deeply ingrained in the public mind the idea that it is the mission of the state to determine cultural-linguistic politics. The question being debated now is to what extent the state can in fact exercise this power. For all post-Soviet politicians, it is axiomatic that a state has the right to demand that all citizens speak an official language, even if this demand may contradict basic human rights and has been borrowed from some states where the naturalization procedures are quite different from local realities. The dissolution of the Union meant that no such power could be exercised at one centre only, so the question today revolves around the new states' national governments and the political institutions, as well as the leaders of the autonomous formations constituted within them for non-titular groups. Between these levels of power, new contradictions arise on the language issue.

We must stress that the political institutions of the internal autonomies (republics), like Gagauz and Trans-Dniestria, have insisted on granting the status of state language not only to their 'own' languages, but also to Russian, as a counterbalance to the governments of the previous Union republics, now sovereign states. This is precisely what has led to heated debates, because retaining Russian as one of the official languages has undermined the primary goal of linguistic nationalism: the construction of national states of the titular nationalities 'where the language of the republic' serves all the main functions of life in society. According to this doctrine, Russian should be retained only as the language of one of the many ethnic minorities, used in 'Russian' schools and in the home life of local Russian populations.

After 1991, problems of that kind began to arise in several republics of the Russian Federation. While formally maintaining the equal status of Russian and the 'titular' languages, the local governments undertook concerted efforts to change their actual functions. They sought to widen the spheres of use of the 'republic' languages, while narrowing social functions of Russian. Such a language policy may well result in a situation similar to that in the former Union republics. Intensification of ethnic feelings and even the outbreak of ethnic conflict between the titular and non-titular population are quite possible. In some cases, this may lead to secession demands from compact settlements of the non-titular nationalities. For example, the reason Bashkiria did not define any official language was the fear of negative reactions from local Tatars as well as the resistance of the nationalist leadership to granting equal status to the Bashkir, Russian, and Tatar languages because such a step would undermine the very idea of a Bashkir 'national state' and break the constitutionally established rule that only those who spoke Bashkir could run for the Presidency of the republic. In this case, language has been an instrument for attaining to or being excluded from power positions. Pursuant to this rule, the highest power position in Bashkiria is safely reserved for a small minority of local citizens. On the other hand, a serious sociolinguistic study carried out in Bashkiria in 1993 showed a very high level of inter-ethnic tolerance concerning the language issue: 90% of ethnic Bashkir citizens do not agree that non-Bashkir residents of the republic should have to learn the Bashkir language, and are ready to accept different models of educational practice based on bilingualism or trilingualism principles (Guboglo, 1994b, p. 110).

The transformation of cultural-linguistic aspects of ethnic relations into conflict brings politics to the forefront of public life. In times of conflict, culture gets forgotten. But ethnic culture and language continue to play an important role in the political confrontation on behalf of nationalities. Such a situation will clearly continue in the foreseeable future. The multi-ethnic population may well adapt to the transformation in the cultural-linguistic environment in the former Union and some autonomous republics, but this is certain to require many years, even decades.

5.5   The Ideology of Return

French scholar Michel Foucault, when asked about the importance of historical reference and language in the modern episteme, replied:

> I think that there is a widespread and facile tendency, which one should combat, to designate that which has just occurred as the primary enemy, as if this were always the principal form of oppression from which one had to liberate oneself. Now this simple attitude entails a number of dangerous consequences: first, an inclination to seek out some cheap form of archaism or some imaginary past forms of happiness that people did not, in fact, have at all . . . There is in this hatred of the present or the immediate past a dangerous tendency to invoke a completely mythical past (Foucault, 1993, pp. 164–5).

This 'ideology of return' is found extensively in post-Soviet society. It begins with elitist academic debates and goes down to grass-roots discourse.

Discovering 'forgotten names', the 'neglected past' and fully rejecting the recent experience has become a major theme for intellectuals of varying methodological and political orientations. For many reasons, but primarily due to lack of professionalism and civic responsibility, social scientists and enlightened journalists have not followed the strategy recommended by Foucault. He writes that when 'society is being modernized and rationalized by managers and experts, (social scientists) are to remain critics of nostalgic, Utopian and overly abstract thought' (Foucault, 1993, p. 161). The leading academic journals found themselves full of back-to-the-19th-century rhetoric about 'Eurasianism', 'Russian idea', and 'Russian destiny'. Some experts on medieval Russia have been spreading gloomy views of the current situation as a return of medieval barbarism – a period known in the country's history as the 'time of troubles' (*smuta*) (Sakharov, 1995). In non-Russian republics it has become a major concern for local intellectuals to establish and document an external cause of contemporary problems and to glorify an invented past (for the Volga area, see Shnirelman, 1996). Thus, in Tatarstan a widespread image of the pre-Mongol invasion, prosperous national Tatar state of the 13th century had become so politicized that during my 1992 visit to the headquarters of the radical nationalist organization – the Tatar Public Center – one of its leaders announced that 'we want to restore the peaceful and militarily strong Boulgar state, and this is probably our last chance'.[14]

The most important element of this drive has been the return of cultural and political symbols of the formerly existing polities in the territory of the Soviet Union. Thus, in the Baltic republics the Estonian, Latvian, and Lithuanian state flags and other symbols of the 1920s and 1930s were restored, along with enthusiastic glorification of these short-lived and non-democratic regimes. The same process has taken place in Moldavia, Transcaucasus and practically all the former Union republics. In Russia, for example, the democratic opposition revived the white-blue-and-red flag (now the national flag of Russia), while the national-patriotic movement began to use the black-yellow-and-white flag, which can also trace its origin to the period of the Russian Empire.

In contrast, political movements defending the interests of the non-titular, 'russophone' population in the Baltics and Moldavia refused to recognize the attempts to change the state (republic) symbols, leading their mass meetings and demonstrations under the flags of the Soviet state, or the official flags of the corresponding Soviet republics. That is why, observing the hammer and sickle emblem or the red star symbol, many experts have been inclined to interpret this as a demonstration of loyalty to Communism or Sovietism, and have deemed some public forces and regions as strongholds of the old regime. In reality, far more complex feelings and messages underlie this stand. Important here was the fear (sometimes an overreaction) of becoming the object of political and cultural discrimination. As noted ironically by Igor Smirnov, leader of the 'pro-Communist' Trans-Dniestrian region, 'it was Mr Lutchinsky, former Communist party leader and now Head of the Moldavia Parliament, who barred me from Party membership because I was a "bad Communist"'.[15]

Besides state symbols, the next important cultural issue has involved such symbolic aspects of language as alphabet. Breaking away from the USSR or Russia meant for many intellectual and political radicals a change from Cyrillic script to the Latin or Arabic scripts, which were viewed as more 'normal' and 'anti-colonial'. The Moldavian nationalist movement's demand and the governmental decision to convert to the Latin script used in linguistically identical Romania, in addition to the choice of Romanian state colors, became the major excuse for the secessionist movement and then for a violent conflict in Trans-Dniestria where the local population strongly opposed 'Romanianization' (Kul'chik & Rumyantsev, 1991, p.4).

Ethnonyms and toponyms – the names of nationalities, countries, cities, and towns – became a part of the political battle to establish the status and prestige of a group. The right to name things became a crucial point. A move for 'returning' historical or traditional names and for linguistic 'corrections' of Russian-language transliteration according to the 'true meaning' swept the territory from Moscow to the most distant corners of the country. This process still continues in new states. Moldavia has become 'Moldova', Yakutia is 'Sakha', Kirgiz 'Kyrgyz', and Belorussia 'Belarus'. The Turkic-speaking states acquired the ending '-stan': Bashkiria has become 'Bashkortostan', Tataria 'Tatarstan', and Kirgizia has ended up as 'Kyrgyzstan'. This change has had special appeal because 'stan' means 'a state'.

This was not simply a farewell to Soviet symbolism and Bolshevik heroes, and not simply a return to pre-Soviet names. The status of the titular nationalities is confirmed, in symbolic forms, through the language of the names. Thus, for example, the capital of Kirgizia, Frunze, was renamed 'Bishkek' (the Kirgiz name of an old settlement whose etymology is not clear even to the Kirgiz themselves). However, the capital of Kazakhstan remains 'Alma-Ata' (or rather, 'Almaty') because its pre-Soviet (until 1921) name, 'Vernyi' (Russian meaning 'true, faithful'), was too blatantly associated with Russian colonization.

After the August 1991 coup, the renaming of cities, streets, rivers and other topographical sites swept through the territory of the Russian Federation. This process became an expression of an 'internal self-defining' in the system of cultural symbols, and is clearly far from complete today. Recently leaders of some ethnic groups have proposed changing the ethnonyms themselves, considering them 'humiliating' or too closely tied to colonization. Not realizing that almost all the world's ethnic names are exoethnonyms (that is, given by outsiders during inter-ethnic contacts), they are formulating demands to change the existing group names ('Tatars' to 'Boulgars', Siberian 'Eskimos' to 'Yupiks', 'Yakuts' to 'Sakha', etc.). This kind of ethno-politics also finds support among some academics who believe that somewhere in a native language and on the level of everyday social communication there exists a 'natural' name for the ethnos (contrary to 'artificial' names sanctioned by the state). It is thus the task for scholars to develop a scientific inventory of all ethnic entities (Kryukov, 1989).

As a rule, conflicts arise when the titular groups in new states try to limit the rights of minorities or to do away with existing territorial autonomies by using mobilized linguicism to achieve political goals. For example, Georgia rejected the name 'South Ossetia' in favor of the Georgian word 'Shida Kartli' (Inner Kartlia) or 'Samachablo', the name of an ancient royal estate which was declared to be the 'heart of Georgia'. In response, the southern Ossets changed the name of their administrative center from 'Tzhinvali' to

'Tzhinval', and the Abkhazians began to call 'Sukhumi' 'Sukhum' to sound less Georgian. This debate over the letter 'i' blew up into a harsh political debate, and then military clash. For the Armenians there is no 'Karabakh' anymore, but there is 'Artzakh'; for Azerbaijanis, it remains 'Karabakh'. For the Azerbaijanis there is no Stepanokert (capital city of Karabakh) anymore, but there is Khankendy.

5.6   Religious Labeling of Culture

In recent years, religion has been revived as a cultural symbol, with a growing role in social life. This has contributed to the construction of politically significant cultural differences and new group boundaries along primarily ethnic lines. But bringing religion into ethnic discourse does not necessarily mean a 'return of religion', nor does it mean the institutionalization of churches or mosques into Soviet and post-Soviet life. In scholarly and journalistic texts, the religious labels used to distinguish ethnic groups in multi-ethnic Russia and other new states refer more to differences of the past, not the present. Anthropologists have already pointed out this phenomenon of using vanishing or revived religious legacies for ethnic boundary maintenance (Eriksen, 1993, p. 39). The most comparable case here is ex-Yugoslavia, where Bosnian Muslim, Serb, and Croat identifications carry the implication of having been Muslim, Orthodox, or Roman Catholic in the past, not now.

Religious labels have been introduced to justify political divisiveness and an invented image of these groups as irreconcilable and culturally incompatible. This is used to legitimize geopolitical changes as well as war and committed atrocities. Rare cases of *sancta simplicitas*, like the remark of the Norwegian diplomat Stoltenberg 'they are all Serbs' are immediately branded as politically incorrect because they undermine the politically and ideologically loaded paradigm. And yet, in anthropological terms, Stoltenberg was not so far from the truth – if any such thing exists in scholarship. At least, he could be perfectly right in calling the fighting parties 'Yugoslavs' and even 'Serbo-Croats' in a cultural sense because the cultural differences between these groups are minimal compared to what they have in common.

A similar situation can be observed in and after the USSR. The dominant view has been that religious beliefs and practices were always present, and that fundamental cleavages along religious and ethnic lines have simply been permitted freer expression with political liberalization and disintegration. As Martha Olcott writes,

> among the surprises brought by independence in Central Asia was the discovery that Islam proved to have been much more pervasive in Soviet times than was previously imagined . . . Independence has made it plain that during the seven decades of Soviet domination most of the people of Central Asia continued to observe important Islamic holidays and rites of passage . . . (Olcott, 1995a, p. 21).

To confirm this thesis, she mentions the practice of celebrating festivals like Qurban-Bairam and other Islamic rituals like circumcision, marriage, and mourning. Some writers consider social organizations like neighborhood (*mahallas*) in Uzbekistan and kinship groups (*elats*) in Turkmenia as signs of a thriving Islamic culture (Polyakov, 1992, pp. 53–94). According to this logic, practically the whole cultural complex, except for the economy and language, is considered Islamic and interpreted as the presence of religion in a society. But this can scarcely be said to be sufficient evidence; using this criterion one should view St Patrick's Day, which has become a national holiday for all Americans, as a symbol of conversion to Roman Catholicism or assimilation into Irish culture. Holidays, festivities, and rituals, even when they can be interpreted as religiously derived and originally prescribed by a certain faith, cannot be taken as a serious measurement of religious presence. In my hometown near Sverdlovsk, where a sizeable minority of Tatars live, one of the most popular summer festivals is *Sabantui*, celebrated by all locals including my parents – ethnic Russian schoolteachers with a firm atheist background. No one at that time saw *Sabantui* as a 'national' Tatar or 'Islamic' holiday, although we knew that the holiday stemmed from the Tatar culture.

The political actualization of religion and its linkage with an ethnic context deserve a more balanced interpretation. Despite the official tsarist Orthodoxy, Russia used to be a multi-denominational state, where religious affiliations have rarely corresponded with ethnic boundaries. Nevertheless, some forms of religion were a kind of ethnicity – or at least they produced ethnically defined identities. Until the 18th century 'Orthodoxy' could be viewed as a kind of ethnic label because the words 'Russian' (*russkii*) and 'Orthodox' (*pravoslavny*) were perceived as synonymous. 'Ethnographic processing' of peoples by customs and culture was to appear considerably later in the Russian Empire (Slezkine, 1994b). Orthodoxy is practiced by some members of many ethnic groups in Russia and other post-Soviet states, including Chuvash, Mordva, Udmurts, Mari, some Tatars and Kalmyks in the Volga area, Ossets and some Kabardins and Georgians in the Caucasus, Karels, Komi, Nenetz, Mansi, Yakuts, Khakas and some Buryats in Siberia, most Ukrainians, Belorussians, Moldavians, Gagauz, etc. without conflicting or being congruent with ethnicity.

Many of the non-Russian titular nationalities were historically Islamic. In Central Asia and Kazakhstan this includes Uzbeks, Tajiks, Turkmen, Kirgiz, Kazakhs, and Karakalpaks; in the Transcaucasus this applies to Azerbaijanis and Adjars (Muslim Georgians) of the Adjar Autonomous Republic of Georgia; in the North Caucasus region, this refers to Adygeis, Karachais, Cherkess, Kabardins and Balkars, and some Ossets (the Digors minority), Chechens and Ingush, the nationalities of Daghestan; in the Volga–Urals region this includes Tatars and Bashkirs; in the Crimea region, Crimean Tatars. Furthermore, Buryats, Tuvins, and Kalmyks are Buddhists, although some Kalmyks and Buryats have converted to Orthodox Christianity.

The religious revival began in the late 1980s (see, e.g., Balzer, 1993; Olcott, 1995a). Basically a cultural phenomenon, it has also acquired characteristics of political symbolism and associated itself with existing or emerging state structures. One almost immediate effect was changes in the official calendars of the republics. Formerly secular states started to mobilize this potent cultural institution for political needs. Each republic (and later new states) as well as the internal autonomies chose one religion as a kind of official, titular religion. The Russian authorities responded enthusiastically to the long-cherished hope of having the Russian Orthodox church made an official church; in republics with other religious traditions among titular groups, other institutions were established. Boris Yeltsin took his Presidential oath in the presence of the Russian Orthodox Patriarch Alexii II; Dzhokhar Dudayev followed by taking his Presidential oath on the Koran. But at the grass-roots level, religious cleavages have not had much impact. In September 1994, I heard presentations made by leaders of the Muslim and Russian Orthodox faiths in Tatarstan. Both seemed optimistic and pleased with the situation in this republic, and their main concerns were a lack of active believers.

In a country where religious practice was banned for many decades it is not easy to reintroduce religion without allying it with the state. Earlier in the Soviet Union, all official holidays had a strictly secular character, which meant that they were impartially perceived by all, regardless of religious belief. Today, in all new states and republics, religious holidays have become official non-working days. This means that, for example,

Russians, Ukrainians, and other 'Europeans' living in 'Islamic' and 'Buddhist' republics get time off on Islamic and Buddhist holidays – but not on Christian ones. And the converse: Muslims and Buddhists in many parts of Russia get days off for Christmas, but must go to work on their main religious holidays. Although not the most significant point of contention, this practice certainly plays a role in the formation of inter-ethnic tensions. Most important here is the huge symbolic role of the new holidays, which indicate clearly who are seen as the 'insiders' and who are the 'outsiders' in the different territories of the former Soviet Union. Thus, religion has not returned to society playing its expected role of moral and social control. Rather it has become an additional marker of intergroup differences and hierarchies.

In many cases religion has become an element in the ethno-politics of mobilization, division, and exclusion. Referring to religion as a cleavage in and after the Soviet Union has become an academic and journalistic truism. Many scholarly texts present maps of Muslim areas and data on the number of Muslims living in Russia, etc. The areas usually highlighted for this purpose are the Volga and North Caucasus regions and their populations. There are at least two simplifications involved here. First, the demographic majority in both regions is enjoyed by Russians and Ukrainians, who are generally Christian Orthodox. A considerable number of those groups among whom Islam had been spread in the past converted to Russian Orthodoxy during tsarist times. Second, 70 years of anti-religious propaganda and suppression have made atheists of practically all new generations of the Soviet populace. The recent interest shown by young people in religious rituals and ceremonies like marriage and baptism is rather an expression of a new fashion, and of adding significance and pageantry to such important social events. Only in a few areas – the Baltic, Western Ukraine, and Armenia regions – have the Church and religion kept their social and even political role, first under the Soviet regime and now since the time of perestroika. But even in these areas the number of believers – including regular church-goers – declined between the 1960s and the 1980s, comprising, according to my estimates, no more than 35% of the population in contemporary Russia.

The Ichmiadzin is the center of the Armenian Church and the residence of the Patriarch, near the capital city of Yerevan. In October 1987 I observed there activities associated with major religious holidays. There were services, marriage ceremonies, animal sacrifices, etc. A lot of people visited a cemetery. But none of the Armenians I spoke with had any religious texts at home nor knew any of the basic prayers by heart. The situation had not changed significantly almost ten years later when I interviewed three young Armenians, none of whom could cite even one prayer. 'But we all love very much our *Catholikos* [Patriarch] who has a great reputation and serves as a symbol for our nation,' remarked Knarik Kamalyan.[16] In the case of Armenians and the Armenian Church, ethnic and religious boundaries correspond to a great degree. Here religion is a decisive differentiating marker that serves to strengthen ethnic cohesion. This is why the Armenian–Azerbaijani conflict is frequently cited as an example of a clash along religious/civilizational lines. On the other hand, religion appears to be irrelevant to the emergence of the recent war around Nagorno Karabakh (see Yamskov, 1991).

With respect to Islam, the role of this religion as an opposition to Russian Orthodoxy is combined with cross-ethnic appeals concerning regional level, as in Central Asia. Practitioners of Islam in this area tend to view the local population of five states as one people, and religion does not play a divisive role when it does not affect the non-titular population who are mostly Christian (if they profess any creed). In 1991 I had a conversation with Central Asian Muslim leader Muhhammed Sadyq Mama Yusupov, who told me that he does not divide people who believe in Allah by state or by nationality: 'We used to be one people and we will be one people in the future, I hope. Common religion will help us to resolve disputes and conflicts.'[17] Mama Yusupov also noted the same major problem which was mentioned during my visit to a new mosque in Kazan: 'Very few people know and believe the teaching of our Prophet and practically nobody can read the Koran.'[18] In Kazan, in September 1994, a new mosque stood empty at a time of daily prayer, and the mullah was having a private conversation with three young people who had come for advice and a blessing. The mosque is now regaining its status in Tatarstan, but the 'northernmost Islamic republic' is still basically secular. However, religion is used as a point of reference with respect to outside occurrences – such as to express solidarity with the Chechens.

The revival of Islam in secular post-Soviet societies has sparked off discussion in the mass media and even in the parliaments of several Central Asian states (for example in Kirgizia in early 1992) regarding the possible legalization of some traditional practices, including polygamy. Although such proposals have not been passed in any state legislation, they have greatly contributed to alienating the 'European' Russian-speaking population from the native inhabitants, and have caused heated debates and concerns among many titular activists, especially those who have studied in Moscow and hold rather modernized Western values and orientations. In some areas, including the Russian Federation, polygamy is practiced by some in a semi-official manner. One flamboyant Chechen soldier, Ruslan Labazanov, admitted openly to having three wives. In Ingushetia, President Ruslan Aushev abolished all old Soviet legislation forbidding and punishing polygamy, which was interpreted as an implicit message allowing this practice. During Dudayev's rule in Chechnya, there were attempts to introduce separate education for girls and boys, but this was not realized because of parental resistance and the general collapse of the education system in the republic.

The real growth in true believers or those who regularly go to church or the mosque is very small. Young and middle-aged urban dwellers, even in Central Asia, are practically still all non-believers. Any attempts on the part of 'traditionalists' to enforce strict religious norms and rituals meet strong resistance, and are perceived in such modernized republics as Kazakhstan and Kirgizia as a threat to democratization and personal freedom. In 1991 I interviewed female Kirgiz intellectuals who demonstrated their resolute opposition to 'bringing fundamentalism to our republic where the status of women was traditionally very high in nomadic cultures. Kirgiz and Kazakh women never wore the veil and it is ridiculous to think about it now.'[19] According to my observations, even among the most fundamentalist members of the Tajik opposition no women wear the veil and Islam is just a political symbol.

In central parts of Russia, despite the rapid restoration of many abandoned churches (mainly with state assistance) and a return of monasteries to the Orthodox Church, religious feelings and popular support of the church are still minimal. The same is true for the Volga area concerning Islam, and for Buryatia and Kalmykia concerning Buddhism. The church and the mosque as public institutions are trying to acquire something like official (or state) status, while remaining tolerant of other religions and often playing a pacifying role. But the opportunities for religious leaders are obviously limited, and many initiatives taken by them to prevent or resolve conflicting situations have proven ineffective. For example, since the beginning of serious internal rivalries and up to major war, religious leaders and elders in Chechnya have had no influence at all on the course of events. Ruslan Labazanov, in a television interview made soon after the terrorist incident at Budennovsk, stated explicitly that during his three years of activity in Chechnya – which included raids, fighting against Dudayev's forces, full control of one region of the republic, and finally cooperation with the federal regime in Grozny – he cannot remember one case where religious leaders or elders contributed to decision-making. 'They do what I tell them to do,' said Labazanov. 'Tell them to kill a man or to punish anybody and it will be done' (NTV News program, Moscow, 24 June 1995).

The romantic image of Chechen freedom fighters as well as the dehumanizing anti-Islamic propaganda presented by journalists cannot account for simple but profound things: Islam is used by secessionist leaders not only to better define the enemy but also to attract sympathy and support through pan-Islamic solidarity. As individuals, the same leaders behave no differently from the rest of Russia's population. Most members of Dudayev's delegation during the December 1994 negotiations in Vladikavkaz were drinking alcohol, eating pork and smoking tobacco, as do many other Chechens I know personally. No signs of religious ceremonies were observed among our partners during the three days of meetings and social interaction. Vyacheslav Mikhailov, who headed the second round of negotiation in Grozny, confirmed in July 1995 that the only demonstration of Islam by the Chechens during the one-month negotiations was the cry of 'Allah, akhbar!' shouted by Usman Imaev among supportive demonstrators.

Nationalist activists have used religion as a symbol quite successfully. First, previous suppressions of religion, destruction of churches, mosques, dazans, etc., as well as persecution of the clergy, were explicitly interpreted and translated in political debates as the 'destruction of national culture', and ' killing the soul of a nation' by outsiders. Second, in a situation of collapsed Soviet symbolism, the new leaders desperately needed not so much legal, as more sacred forms of legitimization – which could be and were provided by the clergy. Third, ethno-religious coalitions proved to be more coherent and militant forms of mobilization; no leader could avoid the temptation of using religion as an additional argument in fomenting ethnic fever.

5.7   Ethnic Incorporation and Transcendence

Much has been written about the deeply rooted cultural differences and civilizational cleavages among citizens of the former USSR. Any cultural similarities are usually dismissed as something abnormal, even evil. Any forms of assimilation, including linguistic acculturation and asymmetric bilingualism in favor of the dominant Russian language, are viewed as a type of oppression and political crime. The prevailing opinion supports eliminating imperial influences and returning to the roots of 'their own' cultures. For Russian nationalists, the rhetoric of rejection contains Western cultural influences as well as anti-minority stereotyping.

What is probably less obvious in such a politicized environment is the high degree to which the various cultures of former Soviet nationalities contain common features. The boundaries of institutionalized ethnicity are very strong, supporting the hypothesis that 'groups may actually become culturally more similar at the same time that boundaries are strengthened' (Eriksen, 1993, p. 38). Don Handelman (1977) suggested a typology of degrees of ethnic incorporation – from the very loose and socially insignificant ethnic category, to the ethnic network, the ethnic association and then to the ethnic community. Thomas Hylland Eriksen sees this typology as a developmental framework, a typology of ethnic organization and as a model of aspects of inter-ethnic processes (Eriksen, 1993, p. 43). In the Soviet Union, ethnic incorporation reached its last stage from the viewpoint of contemporary 'ethno-genesis' because all major non-Russian groups had been territorialized and linked to an assigned statehood. There were also all four forms of ethnic organization: more or less arbitrary ethnic labels, such as 'Armenian' or 'Tatar' for Muscovites with Armenian and Tatar family names; ethnic forms of solidarity for numerous internal diasporas and migrants; non-political and later politicized ethnic associations for 'non-status' groups; and finally, 'nations and *narodnosti*' in territorial autonomies representing rigidly defined ethnic communities.

It is an accepted view that cultures in constituted communities (in national republics) were stronger and healthier than non-status groups; this remains one of the most powerful arguments in favor of ethnonational self-determination in territorial form. But the production of ethnic cultures and a cultural dialogue was more contrived and complex. At least, ethnonational cultural expression at the professional 'high culture' level was to a considerable extent trained, staged, composed and published in or from Moscow. Many of these 'ethnics', although geographically far removed from their 'native' regions, made a greater contribution to their 'national' cultures than those living within the territory. In many ways, their ethnicity became just a label or identification tag, as demonstrated by Soviet encyclopedias which used such descriptions as 'Soviet Armenian composer' or 'Soviet Russian writer'. It was the Moscow-based intellectuals, professional translators, ballet and opera schools who literally generated much of the 'ethnic' or 'national' culture. While I was in Yakutia in June 1995 I was invited to see performed in the local national theatre the first Yakutian ballet, *'Curumchuku'* – which had been choreographed and staged in 1964 by a member of our Institute, Dr Maria Zhornitzkaya, former professional ballet dancer who lived in Yakutia and later wrote a book on traditional dance choreography of the Northern Peoples (Zhornitskaya, 1983).

Although until the late 1980s the state and official ideology followed a dual strategy of enforcing 'national' and 'Soviet' cultural components, the new political situation gave primacy to the demonstration of cultural uniqueness of titular groups and the rejection of any commonalities with Soviet/Russian cultural legacies. Politically motivated cultural isolationism took extreme forms in newly emergent states with the drive to reintegrate national cultures into other world language and information systems: from Russian to Western English-speaking in the Baltics and Transcaucasus, to Turkic-speaking in Central Asia. Some of these recent transformations have already considerably changed the character of the cultural dialogue, resulting in lower status for the Russian language and the increased presence of official languages of new states. As one of my informants reported in Armenia, after 1995 Russian became only one of the many foreign languages taught in the schools, and 'now all have started to study English'. 'My son is in the sixth grade and he hardly knows any Russian, while when I was at his age I had already read a lot of Russian literature and wrote compositions in Russian.'[20]

Despite mixed feelings and reactions among former compatriots with respect to these rapid and sometimes painful transformations, the growing cultural distances between new sovereign nations cannot be quantified by simplistic measurements. This is a process of gains and losses motivated not only by elites but also by individual choice. What can be tested is the widely circulated thesis that the collapse of Communism and totalitarianism has unleashed deep-rooted and previously suppressed cultural incompatibilities and ethnic hatreds. This thesis reflects Samuel Huntington's idea that

> ... The most important conflicts of the future will occur along the cultural fault lines separating (. . .) civilizations . . . [because] . . . cultural characteristics and differences are less mutable and hence less easily compromised and resolved than political and economic ones. In the former Soviet Union, communists can become democrats, the rich can become poor and the poor rich, but Russians cannot become Estonians and Azeris cannot become Armenians. . . . The people of Russia are as divided as the elite (Huntington, 1993, pp. 25, 27, 44).

Here I am not addressing the vagueness of the concept of civilization as such. Rather, I want to express the view that Huntington's interpretations of ethnicity and culture are not supported by any serious study carried out in recent decades. It is precisely in order to become rich, or at least better off, and to provide better social well-being for their children, that individuals in the former Soviet Union are opting to identify themselves as 'Germans' to be able to emigrate to Germany, or as 'Jews' to leave the country for the USA or Israel. Culturally they are Russian, but contemporary descendants of 18th-century colonists from the area which is now called Germany purposefully cultivate their German roots and identity, which until now were painful reminders of deportation. Hundreds of thousands of Jews and millions of other ethnic origins, especially those brought up in ethnically mixed families, declared themselves Russians in the former Soviet Union because of the existing political and cultural environment. As a result of intensive intercultural contacts, movements of people, and intermarriage, thousands of Azeris became Armenians or Russians, and Armenians became Azeris, Georgians, or Russians. Even after the Sumgait pogrom in Azerbaijan only about 18,000 Armenians stayed in Baku and preferred to become Azeris, changing their family names and adopting local cultures.

After the Cold War, changes in ethnic identity have become no less frequent and fluid, while in some cases group boundaries have become even more rigid. In post-Soviet states, including Russia, ethnic and cultural boundaries have become both loose and rigid at the same time, depending on social perspectives, the political situation, and the functional roles which identity can play in human behavior. In the past few years, according to my estimates, millions of people have changed their ethnic affiliation to achieve social or political aspirations or to meet new challenges brought by deep societal transformations. I expect much more dramatic changes in the near future: at the time of the next census in 1999, experts and politicians may discover the 'loss' of millions of ethnic Russians who prefer to cross 'fault lines' of civilizations on an individual basis, becoming Tatars, Ukrainians or Latvians in the territories of Tatarstan, Ukraine, and Latvia.

The heavily politicized notion of primordial ethnic animosities finds its 'proof' in the ongoing ethnic clashes and atrocities on the territory of the former Soviet Union. However, even in Stalin's time, Soviet citizens could marry freely: in fact, the level of ethnically mixed marriages was one of the highest in the world. From the 1950s to the 1970s, the number of mixed families in the country doubled from 5.2 (1959) to 9.9 (1979) million. This proportion has since increased from 10 to 15% (Susokolov, 1987, p. 40). In 1989, every seventh family in the Soviet Union was ethnically mixed; in the Latvian capital, Riga, it was every fourth. Through mixed marriages, people were crossing not only ethnic, but also religious (civilizational) lines. It was much harder to become a Communist (or Democrat) or to become rich than for a young non-Russian to marry a Russian girl – the most common form of inter-ethnic marriage that provided better opportunities for integration into the dominant social and cultural milieu. Thus, Samuel Huntington's thesis does not work for the interpretation of cultural cleavages, at least on the territory of the former USSR.

This is not to say that there are no problems of cultural distance, attitudes, and prejudices. But these need to be studied in a serious and less politically motivated manner. As mentioned in Chapter 1, cultural differences may always precipitate elements of inequality, competition, and domination. The crucial point is how people perceive their status and react to existing or prospective domination by others. The most recent sociological survey (March–August 1994) done by the Institute of Ethnology and Anthropology, in three Russian republics, revealed that an extremely low segment of the population said that they had 'often' experienced violations of their rights because of ethnic affiliation: 3.5% of the Tatars, 3.2% of the Ossets, and 5.3% of the Yakuts; and among local Russians, 1.7% in Tatarstan, 4.6% in North Ossetia, and 4.6% in Yakutia. Answering 'no,

Table 5.4   *Perceptions of Ethnic Discrimination in Republics of Russia, (%)*

Q: Have you experienced violation of your rights because of your nationality?	Tatarstan		North Ossetia		Yakutia	
	Tatar	Russian	Osset	Russian	Yakut	Russian
Yes, often	3.5	1.7	3.2	4.6	5.3	4.6
Sometimes, yes	18.0	16.9	8.8	25.2	32.4	21.9
No, not at all	68.8	77.2	83.2	61.9	50.7	63.3
No answer	9.7	4.2	4.8	8.3	11.6	10.2

Source: Survey carried out in March-August 1994 under the research project 'National Consciousness, Nationalism and Conflict Resolution in the Russian Federation' (coordinator Leokadia Drobizheva, IEA)

Table 5.5   *Ethnic Attitudes in Republics of Russia (%)*[1]

Q.: Are you willing to accept a person of another nationality as:	Tatarstan		North Ossetia		Yakutia	
	Tatar	Russian	Osset	Russian	Yakut	Russian
Citizen of your republic	77.0	83.7	90.4	93.3	68.7	71.4
Partner in common enterprise	61.0	74.1	68.8	65.4	57.5	53.8
Your boss	46.0	59.0	41.3	57.1	30.4	39.0
Neighbor	68.7	80.2	80.5	85.8	61.9	64.7
Friend in common leisure and entertainment	56.4	71.1	52.8	59.5	43.1	50.6
Mother (father) of your children	31.8	54.3	29.6	45.8	29.5	45.7
Spouse	25.7	47.7	23.5	39.7	21.5	30.6
Other	7.0	10.5	2.1	13.1	3.8	4.3

[1]Totals exceed 100% because respondents could give more than one answer.

Source: Compiled from Leokadia Drobizheva's survey carried out in March–August 1994

not at all' were 68.8% of the Tatars, 83.2% of the Ossets, and 50.7% of the Yakuts. Among local Russians, the percentage answering likewise was higher in Tatarstan (77.2%) and Yakutia (63.3%) and considerably lower in North Ossetia (61.9%) (Table 5.4).

A more sophisticated measurement of ethnic attitudes was carried out in the same republics with a question about the respondent's readiness to accept a person of another nationality as a social partner. The overwhelming majority of respondents (from 70 to 90%) of titular and Russian nationalities were ready to accept 'others' as citizens of their republic (the lowest figure was 68.7% for Yakuts). A majority in all groups expressed readiness to have 'others' as neighbors, as friends on the social level, and as business partners (again, the lowest figures are for Yakuts: 61.9%, 43.1%, and 57.5% respectively). More than 30–40% of the titulars expressed readiness to have a person of

Table 5.6   *Estimates of Inter-ethnic Relations in Republics of Russia (%)*

Q: How do you estimate relations in your republic?	Tatarstan		North Ossetia		Yakutia	
	Tatar	Russian	Osset	Russian	Yakut	Russian
Favorable	15.1	11.0	6.4	4.8	9.5	5.2
Calm	65.4	62.0	7.2	8.1	66.9	57.3
Tense	7.6	15.1	68.8	67.8	10.6	26.1
Critical, explosive	0.5	0.3	15.2	13.8	1.2	0.9
No answer	11.4	11.6	2.4	6.0	11.8	10.5

Source: Compiled from Leokadia Drobizheva's survey carried out in March–August 1994

another nationality as their supervisor or boss, but only 20–30% of the titulars were ready to accept 'others' as spouses or as mother/father of their children (Table 5.5).

It is important to note that in such sensitive issues of ethnic interactions as the choice of friends and marital partners, 'Muslim' and politicized Tatars nevertheless expressed a more tolerant attitude than the 'Christian' Yakuts. This may be because the Yakuts are one of the few ethnicities with non-Caucasian phenotypical characteristics; their physical appearance makes it much harder for them to cross ethnic boundaries or 'pass' in another culture. Thus, they themselves may place more importance on internal group cohesion and the correlation between phenotype and ethnicity.[21]

Finally, respondents were asked how they judged the situation of inter-ethnic relations in their republic. Not having heard of 'the Clash of Civilizations', they gave positive answers ('favorable' or 'calm') in most cases in Tatarstan and Yakutia (75–80%); only about 1% considered the situation in their republic 'critical' or 'explosive'. A quite different picture emerged in North Ossetia, where an open violent conflict between the Ossets and the Ingush had taken place in the fall of 1992, and the problem is yet to be resolved (Table 5.6).

Thus, I reject the thesis about the 'dividedness' of the peoples of Russia and about deep-rooted animosities based on 'we' and 'they' opposition. On the other hand, I see the rapid reshaping of former cultural systems and interactions as a serious problem. Here let me stress that it is not the *nature* of the change that creates the conflicts, but the *pace* and *perception* of the change. What is important here is not the number of 'nationalities' and cultures, nor the relative strength or weakness of their statuses: it is the availability of choices for groups and individuals, and their ability to adjust to rapid change. When choice and adjustment come too quickly and 'overload' a society, or are not allowed at all, cultural challenges can provoke dissent and protest – also in violent forms.

Notes

1   Here I use the term 'national culture' in the same sense as it is used with respect to 'British', 'American', 'Spanish', 'Mexican', etc. national cultures: to denote the entire complex of civic/ethnic cultural features and values actively present within the limits of a single state.

2   See my interview with Solomon Brook in *Etnograficheskoe obozrenie*, 1995, no. 1, January–February, p. 90.

3   Personal notes from the meeting of the government of the Russian Federation, 30 July 1992, Moscow.

4   Conversation with Yukhan Kahk, August 1981, Tallinn.

5   Instructions to census takers regarding this question were unclear and constantly revised. For example, in the 1929 census, 'native language' was described as that 'which a person is most familiar with and speaks at home'. In 1939, it was described as 'the language which a person regards as native. For children who do not speak yet, it is the language spoken at home.' In 1959 and 1970, if a person had difficulties indicating one language in particular, the native language was considered to be the one the individual knew best and usually used at home, or, the language the person regarded as his or her native tongue, which may or may not correspond to nationality. In 1979 and 1989, the instructions were the same except that for children who did not speak yet, the parents were to indicate native language. It is clear that the general intention was to register the number of people who spoke each 'main language', or 'mother tongue', or 'first spoken language', as is the case in the censuses in other countries. But the term 'native' (*rodnoi*) was confusing to those who lived with a rigidly institutionalized ethnic identity as a 'nationality'. To complicate matters further, the local ethnic bureaucracies and intellectuals who organized the census imposed their own subjective viewpoints on responses.

6   Personal notes, July 1990, Ust'-Orda, Irkutsk *oblast*. The Buryats are one of the few groups with a predominantly Mongoloid phenotype.

7   Personal notes, May 1993, Moscow.

8   Personal notes, 29 June 1995, Tallinn.

9   Personal notes, 1 September 1975, San Francisco, California.

10   Conversation with Igor Smirnov, 15 January 1995, The Hague.

11   Conversation with Vasilii Shegurov, 10 September 1994, Orenburg *oblast*.

12   Ibid.

13   Personal notes, 29 June 1995, Tallinn.

14   Notes from the meeting with VTOZ's leaders, 6 May 1992, Kazan, Tatarstan.

15   Conversation with Igor Smirnov, 15 January 1995, The Hague.

16   Interview with Knarik Kamalyan, 25 July 1995, Oslo.

17   Personal notes, September 1991, Alma-Ata, Kazakhstan.

18   Personal notes, 13 September 1994, Kazan, Tatarstan.

19   Conversation with Inura Elebaeva, 13 September 1991, Bishkek, Kirgizia.

20   Interview with Knarik Kamalyan, 25 July 1995, Oslo.

21   Here is a striking confession on the part of the ethnically mixed Russian-Kazakh Aman Tuleev, one of the most powerful regional leaders, member of the Federation Council from Kemerovskaya *oblast*, and one of the candidates in Russia's 1991 and 1996 presidential elections during an interview with Alexander Prokhanov for a right-wing Russian nationalist newspaper: 'Let us talk in this way: who am I – with such a face as mine and taking into consideration the current sensitivity of many, alas, to nationality? . . . I cannot shout at every corner that from kindergarten until the Academy of Social Sciences, I have been living like a Russian. And it is not known yet who is more Russian: Tuleev or those who announce it loudly' (*Den*, December 1995, no. 51 (56)).

PART TWO

CASE STUDIES

6

The Russians are Leaving: Central Asia and Kazakhstan

6.1 Introduction

After acquiring their independence unexpectedly and with little, if any, preparation, the states of the Central Asian region have entered a transitional period in their histories. All these states are now searching for new formulae and sociopolitical foundations of national development, hoping to find their own niche in the new geopolitical space. Inasmuch as the disintegration of the USSR took place under the banner of ethnic nationalism, it is only natural that the proclamation of so-called 'national states' within the borders of the former union republics should be made on behalf of the titular ethno-nations: the Kazakhs, Kirgiz, Tajiks, Turkmens, and Uzbeks.

Over the past 70 years, these formerly diverse cultural realms underwent ethnographic processing, followed by an extremely intensive process of 'nation-building'. The regional, religious, and dynastic-clan identities of the past gave way to a new ethnicity based on the concept of the 'socialist nation'. This new ethnicity was closely linked to the 'national-state delimitation' that was determined from above, and to the protracted sway of the Communist Party elite through which the Union center could exercise its rigidly central-ized rule in Central Asia and Kazakhstan. Radical changes attended the nation-building process: economic modernization, mass education, prestigious institutions of 'national statehood' based on a new powerful stratum – the administrative, creative, and scientific-technical intelligentsia. Finally, the 1960s–1980s saw a noticeable shift of the demographic balance in favor of the titular nations. By the late 1980s they comprised the majority in all states except Kazakhstan. By the mid-1990s, according to my estimates, ethnic Kazakhs comprised about half of the population in Kazakhstan.

The very contradictions of Soviet nationalities policy – which could sponsor awk-ward industrialization and cultural support at the same time as persistent centralization and political persecutions – were to make possible the growing thrust of the Central Asian periphery toward independence. Here I will not discuss economic performances nor the political process in these five states, as well as their relations with Russia and the rest of the world. Recent years have seen a number of serious studies of the region by Western experts (Akiner, 1991; Bremmer & Taras, 1993; Critchlov, 1992; Fierman, 1991; Lubin, 1984; Olcott, 1987; Ro'i, 1995; Rywkin, 1982) which provide background infor-mation and in-depth analyses. A virtually new generation of Central Asian studies has emerged in Russia and in Central Asia proper which, through their 'inside' view, has greatly contributed to our understanding the region in all its socio-cultural complexity. Research has been done on the question of inter-ethnic relations and conflicts, including the major issue of the status and fate of non-titular populations, first of all ethnic Russians (Ginzburg, 1995; Kolstoe, 1995; Lebedeva, 1996; Savoskul, 1993). Extensive ethno-sociological surveys have been conducted in Uzbekistan (1991), Kirgizia (1992), and Kazakhstan (1994) by members of the Institute of Ethnology and Anthropology in collaboration with Western and Central Asian colleagues. In this chapter, as the case study of conflicting ethnicity in the territory of the former Soviet Union, I consider the situation of what has become known as the 'new Russian diaspora'. When the USSR broke up, about 25 million Russians and several million other former Soviet citizens suddenly found themselves outside of their 'own' states. The most painful manifestations of this problem have occurred in Central Asia, where internal instability and greater cultural distances have caused a massive exodus of Russians. As yet, this problem has not found a solution and it is hard to predict how the situation will evolve in the future.

6.2   Demographic Background

According to the 1989 USSR census, the Russian population in the region numbered 9,500,000 and constituted 19.3% of the overall population. Russians accounted for 21.5% of the population in Kirgizia, 7.6% in Tajikistan, 8.4% in Uzbekistan, 37.8% in Kazakhstan, and 9.5% in Turkmenia (Table 6.1). Many of the Russians who settled here were old-timers, their origins dating back to the 17th–18th centuries when Russian peasants fled religious persecution and feudal rule. Later on they came to comprise a major pool for the Russian government's colonization projects, especially under Stolypin's reforms of the late 19th to early 20th centuries. Back in 1917 there were 1,500,000 Russians in the region, almost one-tenth of the population of the Turkestan administrative area which, at that time, included all territories in this region. Slightly less than half of these Russians had settled in rural areas; the rest were town dwellers. The newcomers from Russia had played a major part in the development of agricultural production, in irrigation, and the expansion of arable land, in building railroads and towns, and in the emergence of heavy and mining industries. This was especially the case in northeastern Kazakhstan, which formed part of the Orenburg *oblast* and afterwards, part of the RSFSR until 1936 when all of Kazakhstan became a constituent republic of the Soviet Union.

Under Soviet rule, the influx of migrants from Russia increased. The main reason was the Soviet doctrine of accelerated industrialization, in which the new arrivals – specialists and workers – were largely instrumental. Engineers and technicians, scientific and medical personnel, professionals in education and the arts arrived in the towns and cities of Central Asia and Kazakhstan. Then, in the 1930s, settlements of deported populations from Russia and Ukraine were formed in different regions, mainly in Kazakhstan. In 1949, there were about 800,000 'special settlers' (*spezposelentzy*) in the region, many of whom stayed on after the death of Stalin and the end of the deportation regime in the late 1950s. During the war of 1941–45 a great many factories, complete with personnel, were evacuated to Central Asia: 90 large factories with some 1,000,000 people were moved to Uzbekistan alone. Many of those people stayed on after the war was over. Thus, these war-related transfers of material and human resources became important building-blocks of the local societies.

The stream of immigrants continued throughout the postwar decades. In Uzbekistan, for instance, they accounted annually for 8–9% of the urban population growth (Maksakova, 1986, p. 53). In large measure the influx to the cities and industrial regions was generated by extensive industrial development and housing construction (especially

Table 6.1 *Russians in the USSR, 1989*

Republic	No. (thous.)	%	Urban %	Rural %	Age Distribution %			Education level of the working population (per 1000 persons)			
					Under working age	Working age[a]	Above working age	University	College	High school	Incompl. high school
Russian Federation	119,866	81.5	76.7	23.9	24.9	56.1	18.9	162	249	328	178
Armenia	52	1.6	85.3	14.7	19.4	62.6	18.0	391	278	314	92
Azerbaijan	392	5.6	95.0	5.0	20.7	55.2	24.1	238	269	328	123
Belorussia	1,342	13.2	86.7	13.3	25.0	59.6	15.4	294	253	329	86
Estonia	475	30.3	92.0	8.0	25.8	58.1	16.1	169	262	336	153
Georgia	341	6.3	86.2	13.8	20.5	55.3	24.2	239	248	346	115
Kazakhstan	6,228	37.8	77.5	22.5	30.5	55.6	13.8	153	268	350	158
Kirgizia	917	21.5	69.9	30.1	28.9	54.6	16.4	179	268	336	149
Latvia	906	34.0	85.0	15.0	24.5	57.4	18.1	194	212	367	158
Lithuania	344	9.4	89.8	10.2	24.1	59.1	16.8	223	272	326	120
Moldavia	562	13.0	86.1	13.9	29.6	54.3	16.1	241	274	327	117
Tajikistan	388	7.6	93.8	6.2	27.3	56.5	16.2	220	301	281	146
Turkmenia	334	9.5	97.0	3.0	26.6	57.6	15.8	220	326	250	154
Ukraine	11,356	22.1	87.6	12.4	24.0	57.5	18.5	216	266	355	114
Uzbekistan	1,653	8.4	94.8	5.2	27.2	56.8	16.0	231	308	283	136
Total	145,156	50.8	78.2	21.8							

[a]males: 16–59; females: 16–54 years of age.
Source: Compiled from USSR 1989 census data

Table 6.2   *Balance of migration*

	1961–70 (thousands)	1979–89 (thousands)
Kazakhstan	431	–789
Kirgizia	126	–157
Tajikistan	70	–102
Turkmenia	457	–850
Uzbekistan	257	–507

Source: Compiled from USSR census data

after the devastating earthquake in Tashkent) and the workforce recruiting campaign for the new industries. The 1950s also saw the mass resettlement of people from Russian rural areas (the Volga, Central Russia, Western Siberia) in Kazakhstan's 'virgin lands'. General demographic estimates of this large-scale state-sponsored program indicate around 1.8 million 'newlanders' (*tselinniki*) settled in Kazakhstan in the course of a mere decade – bringing the proportion of Kazakhs to 30% and Russians to 42%.

Not until the 1970s did the Russian population stop growing. The past two decades have seen a steady decrease in the absolute number of Russians and their share in the overall population in Uzbekistan, Tajikistan, and Turkmenia; in Kazakhstan and Kirgizia they increased only slightly in absolute terms. Compared with the 1960s, the

Figure 6.1   *Russians in Kazakhstan, 1989*

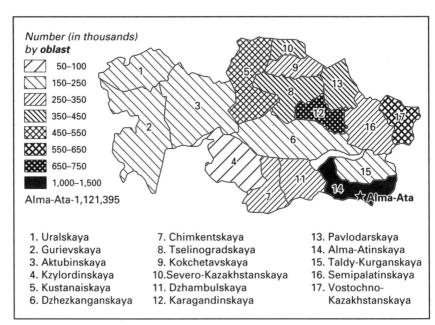

Number (in thousands) by **oblast**

- 50–100
- 150–250
- 250–350
- 350–450
- 450–550
- 550–650
- 650–750
- 1,000–1,500

Alma-Ata-1,121,395

1. Uralskaya
2. Gurievskaya
3. Aktubinskaya
4. Kzylordinskaya
5. Kustanaiskaya
6. Dzhezkanganskaya
7. Chimkentskaya
8. Tselinogradskaya
9. Kokchetavskaya
10. Severo-Kazakhstanskaya
11. Dzhambulskaya
12. Karagandinskaya
13. Pavlodarskaya
14. Alma-Atinskaya
15. Taldy-Kurganskaya
16. Semipalatinskaya
17. Vostochno-Kazakhstanskaya

Figure 6.2   *Russians in Uzbekistan, 1989*

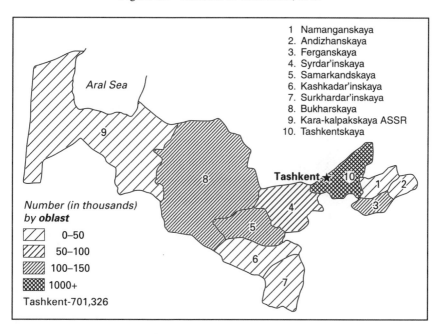

Figure 6.3   *Russians in Kirgizia, 1989*

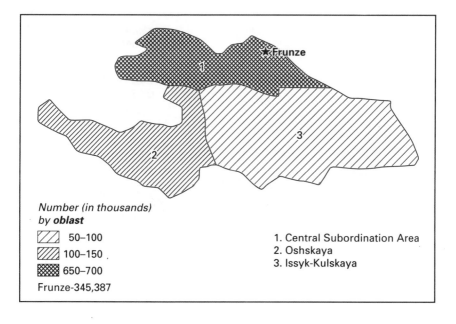

Figure 6.4   *Russians in Tajikistan, 1989*

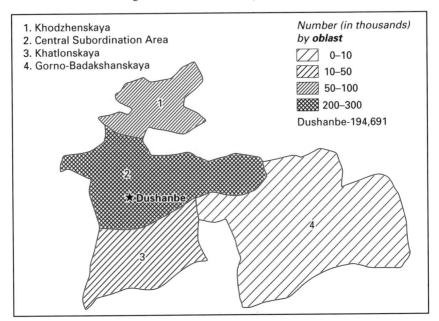

Figure 6.5   *Russians in Turkmenia, 1989*

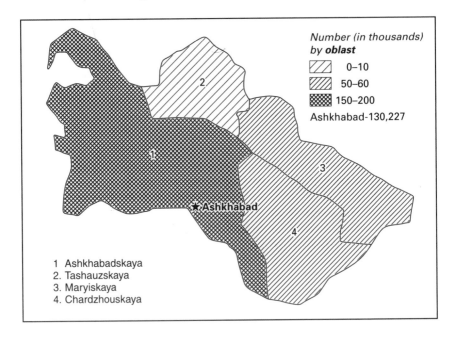

migration balance for the five republics was clearly negative in the 1980s (Table 6.2). According to 1989 data, slightly less than half the Russians living in the region had been born there (from 43.3% to 48.3%, depending on the republic), and about 30% of the new-comers had lived there for more than ten years (Arutunyan, 1992, p. 52).

Changes in population patterns since the 1970s were primarily the result of the high birth rate among the titular population, particularly in Uzbekistan and Tajikistan (where crisis symptoms generated by the runaway population growth were discernible), the increasing migration of people of local nationalities from the countryside to the cities, and the outflow of the Russian-speaking population from the region. Here it was the rural population that was dwindling the fastest, leaving for other parts of the USSR and for industrial centers in the region. Today, Russians and people of other European nation-alities are to be found mainly in the urban areas. From the distribution maps of Russians by administrative *oblast* of five republics (Figures 6.1–6.5) we see that Russians were con-centrated mainly in the capital city areas and in most industrially developed parts, like northeastern *oblast*s of Kazakhstan, Tashkentskaya and Bukharskaya *oblast*s of Uzbekistan. The proportion of Russians who are urban dwellers varies – from 70% in Kirgizia and 77% in Kazakhstan, to 94–97% in Tajikistan, Uzbekistan, and Turkmenia (as against 20.5%, 38.5%, 26.5%, 28%, and 34% of the titular population, respectively). Only in Kazakhstan and Kirgizia is there still a considerable proportion of Russians liv-ing in the countryside: approximately 22% and 30% in 1989. When compared with the bulk of the Russian population in Russia proper, this segment of the populace differs in its higher educational level and an age-distribution skewed in favor of younger genera-tions (Table 6.1). However, it still has a lower education level and growth rate than non-Russian populations in the same area, where there has been an education boom among the titulars during the past two or three decades.

6.3 Socio-Economic Situation

While the USSR existed, Russians in Central Asia and Kazakhstan were employed pri-marily in the development of industry, transportation, and urban construction. The basic social and professional pattern of Central Asia's Russians is different from the employ-ment pattern of the local nationalities, with a share that exceeded their proportion in the working population many times over (Table 6.3). Among the intelligentsia Russians com-prise the majority of specialists in technical fields and in the hard sciences (Arutunyan, 1992, p. 52). Only in Kazakhstan and Kirgizia has the percentage of Russians employed in agriculture remained high. Here they work mainly as machine operators and agricul-tural and animal husbandry specialists, however: people of the titular nationalities are predominantly employed in farming. In the cities, Russians work mostly in trade and the services; among white-collar workers they comprise the majority of managerial person-nel, cultural workers, and the professional intelligentsia. According to 1979 data, the share of Russians employed in industry ranged from 22.4% to 32.6% of the entire work-ing population in Uzbekistan, Kirgizia, Tajikistan, and Turkmenia; and in construction, from 12.2% to 18.2%. For the titular nationalities the figures were from 9.2% to 11.1% in industry and from 4.8% to 8.4% in construction. The proportion of Russians working in farming was 10.2% in Kirgizia, and between 2.7% and 3.4% in the other republics; the figures for the titular nationalities ranged from 52.6% to 56.9% (Narzikulov, 1991, p. 125). According to 1989 data, 22.4% of the Kazakh population and 52.6% of the Russian population of Kazakhstan were employed in industry. The share of Russians engaged in agriculture was steadily decreasing; in 1989 it stood at 17.7% in Kazakhstan, 6.8% in

Table 6.3   *Participation Index[1] for Urban Russians in Higher Positions, 1979–1989*

Republic	Specialists and senior managers		Highly skilled workers	
	1979	1989	1979	1989
Kazakhstan	98	99	107	105
Kirgizia	107	106	100	99
Tajikistan	125	122	108	107
Turkmenia	128	129	101	101
Uzbekistan	128	121	115	113

[1]The participation index is calculated by the formula: % of Russians in this category of manpower/% of Russians in the gainfully employed population x 100. The higher the participation index, the greater the Russian representation in the given category. A value of the index below 100 shows that Russian representation in the given category is lower than in the gainfully employed population.

Source: Sociological survey carried out by Alla Ginzburg and Sergei Savoskul (IEA), 1992

Kirgizia, 0.6% in Uzbekistan, and 0.7% in Turkmenia and Tajikistan. On the other hand, Russians accounted for 20.4%, 13.9%, 4.2%, 5.9%, 3.9% of farm managers and agricultural specialists and 26.8%, 17.5%, 1.3%, 2.1%, and 2.2% of machine operators in these republics, respectively (Arutunyan, 1992, p. 113).

Social and professional differentiation along ethnic lines was and has remained greater in Central Asia and Kazakhstan than elsewhere in the former USSR. The local population stays within its traditional village-farming economy niche, although in recent decades it has made a dramatic breakthrough into the more prestigious spheres of management, public education, public health and law, and now also into trade and commerce, light industry, and urban services. Central Asia's Russians have not expanded their social and professional profile in the 1990s but they have increased their share in the heavy industry workforce and in the industrial and technical intelligentsia. There are also a very few cases of successful entrepreneurial activities, to the extent they are allowed by local reform climate and ethnocratic regimes.

Even before the dramatic changes of the perestroika era began, the employment pattern of the Central Asian republics was marked by undercurrents of ethnic tension. The 'Russian problem' existed, although it had not actually surfaced. It was reflected in the inadequate representation of Russians both in the service sector (teachers, doctors, lawyers, the non-scientific intelligentsia) and in the power structure, especially in the courts of law, the militia, and administration. In recent years, the peculiar social and professional composition of the Russian population – which previously made for their comparatively high standard of living – has become a definitely negative factor. The reason has been the economic-sectoral and production reorientation: a reduction in heavy industrial enterprises, including the military–industrial complex, a general crisis in government-subsidized spheres, and an upsurge of commercial, brokering, and financial activity.

The Russian population in these republics has been faced with the serious problem of finding a new niche in the changing economic and socio-cultural situation. A sociological survey conducted in 1992 in Kirgizia by staff of the Institute of Ethnology and Anthropology (see Ginzburg, 1995; Savoskul, 1993) indicates that Russians are positive to the prospect of reorientation towards employment in the food and light industries, in agriculture, trade, and the services. However, for them actually to implement this

Table 6.4   *Urban Russians and Kirgiz by Employment Branch: Real and Preferred[1] (%)*

Industry	Russian		Kirgiz	
	Real	Preferred	Real	Preferred
Heavy industry	34.0	12.9	20.1	9.3
Light and food industries	8.9	12.5	9.8	16.2
Construction, transport, communications	20.5	9.5	22.6	12.3
Public health, education, science, culture, the arts	16.9	14.1	20.9	11.6
Trade, services, brokering, finance	10.5	32.0	14.2	36.0
Agriculture	2.1	12.9	8.1	13.9

[1]The real branch breakdown was calculated on the basis of the 1989 USSR census. The preferred breakdown was calculated on the basis of answers to the question: 'In what branch of the economy would you wish to be employed?'

Source: Sociological survey carried out by Alla Ginzburg and Sergei Savoskul (IEA), 1992

reorientation – to change professions, their sphere of activity and even forms of property (from state and cooperative to private) – is no simple matter in this region of tenacious labor traditions. The Russians in Kirgizia who wish to work in trade and the services, as middlemen or in finance, are three times as numerous as those already employed in these fields. Their prospects of ousting representatives of the titular nationality, who are even now predominant in these occupations and who desire to increase their representation in them in the future (Table 6.4), are dim indeed.

A partial solution to the problems could be for Russians to become more actively involved in free enterprise. However, the prospects here are limited as a result of insufficiently developed market relations and shortage of initial capital – which as a rule is accumulated illegally or in trade – coupled with misgivings regarding the status of Russians in the newly emergent states. According to the above-mentioned 1992 survey, only 16% of Russian urban dwellers in Kirgizia would like to become owners of private enterprises, whereas the number of such people among the Kirgiz is twice as high. Many Russians are pessimistic about their chances of acquiring property in Kirgizia (land or an enterprise in the sphere of production or in the service sector, a house, or an apartment); nearly a quarter think that, given the future process of privatization, their chances are worse than those of the Kirgiz.

The situation is especially complicated for those of the Russian intelligentsia whose work involves contacts with the local population and use of the language of the titular nationality. Insufficient language knowledge is a formidable obstacle for Russians working in public health, education, culture, and administrative work, often cited as a principal argument in favor of their dismissal. Such a state of affairs may further reduce the already insignificant number of Russian teachers, doctors, lawyers, writers, and journalists, which would be detrimental to the entire Russian-speaking population, including people of the titular nationalities close to Russian culture. Some local intellectuals have already expressed serious concerns about the retreating Russian culture. Professor Nurbulat Masanov wrote on the prospective situation in Kazakhstan where 400,000 left the country in 1994 alone, 60% of whom were Russians:

With the exodus of the Russians, the whole society is becoming more primitive. More specifically, the Kazakh language – which is currently serving as a tool to force the Russians out – is leading to the deterioration of the education system. Major scholarly works and textbooks in different disciplines have not been translated into Kazakh – nor will they be any time in the foreseeable future with such limited resources. The change of the education system over to the Kazakh language means the loss of accumulated knowledge, and this loss of intellectual potential cannot be measured in millions of dollars, which is what the local authorities expect to save by taking over the 300,000 apartments abandoned by the Russians over the last three or four years (*Pravda*, 31 May 1995, p. 3).

Recently, a resurgent wave of Muslim tradition has been sweeping some of the Central Asian countries. Especially the younger generation are proving receptive to its message of cultural traditions which are far removed from European canons. This will only complicate the activities of Russian educationalists and cultural workers. The spread of Islam may also affect the attitude of the population to female labor. To Russians it is normal for women to work as managers or practice technical professions. This may evoke negative reactions on the part of zealous Muslims and adversely affect job opportunities for Russian women. The problem of employment is already very acute for Russian women. In all the republics they are the first to be fired. Russian women living in an alien ethnic environment constitute the most vulnerable stratum because they are widely employed in face-to-face sectors like public health, education, office work, and in general as white-collar workers; there are few skilled blue-collar workers among them. Russian women, moreover, are even less familiar than Russian men with the language of the titular nationality. The problem of employment, education, and professional training is no less acute for young Russians living in the former Soviet non-Russian republics. Starting with the 1960s and up to the end of the 1980s, the number of Russian university and college students declined steadily in all the republics. The curtailment in the past few years of Russian-language instruction in technical schools and institutes of higher learning, can be expected to exacerbate this trend.

What solutions can be offered? What are the employment prospects for Russians who suddenly find themselves living in a new state? Much will depend on the economic situation and political orientation of new independent states, on how quickly market relations can develop within these countries, and on what steps are taken to solve the problems of the non-titular population and to improve inter-ethnic relations. During the years 1991–94 this situation deteriorated seriously, if not dramatically, in the states where there was still a significant presence of Russians. In Kirgizia, the unemployment rate among Russians soared, encompassing one-third of the available manpower. In Uzbekistan, over 37% of Russians of working age do not have permanent jobs now. In Turkmenia, the situation is somewhat better because of the small size of the Russian workforce, employed mainly in the gas industry. In Tajikistan, it is too late to speak of any future for local Russians: most of them have left; there are only a few thousand in Dushanbe and a few dozen families in the area of the Nurek hydroelectric complex. As for Kazakhstan, the Russian presence there is too big to talk about a full exodus. What surprised the experts, however, was the massive emigration of Russians from the southern regions – like Chimkentskaya *oblast* and the Alma-Ata area – where the concentration of Russians was the highest (see Figure 6.1).

Judging by the results of the ethno-sociological survey in Kirgizia in the summer of 1992, the majority of the local Russian population is now at a parting of the ways, as yet unwilling to take any decisive steps to change jobs, profession, or place of residence. And this is probably the case in the other Central Asian states as well. One solution may be gleaned from how respondents answered the question, 'How would you advise young Russians to make their way in life?' Significantly, only 13.2% of the Russians said they would advise them to leave Kirgizia, while a much larger proportion (30%) suggested that young Russians should study Kirgiz and Kirgiz culture and become fully fledged citizens of the country with equal opportunities for social advancement. Very significantly, 60% of the Kirgiz chose the latter variant for young Russians and only 12% suggested that they should leave the republic (Ginzburg, 1995, pp. 122–125).

On the whole, the Russians of Central Asia and Kazakhstan are highly qualified, possess organizational potential, technical skills, and extensive professional contacts in various regions of the Soviet Union and beyond its borders. Their chances to reconstruct their lives and find suitable jobs both inside and outside their republic are still quite good. The most favorable situation seems to pertain today in Kazakhstan and Kirgizia, where the influence of Islam is weaker, economic reorganization is more intensive, and skilled Russian workers, who constitute a considerable portion of the Russian population, are already widely employed both in those branches of heavy industry that are changing their profile and in other spheres of the economy. In Uzbekistan, Tajikistan, and Turkmenia, the development of market relations has been marking time, for various reasons. The signs are that the going will be harder for the local Russian population in these republics: most of them are white-collar workers or employed in heavy industry, and as such have experienced a greater psychological shock from the loss of their former social status, in addition to differing more sharply from the titular nationality regarding their spheres of employment. Precisely these fields of employment where Russians are typically found have been subject to the greatest depression or strongest competition.

6.4   The Ethno-Cultural Situation

In the former USSR, Russians enjoyed for decades the comfortable status of a people dominating all the major areas of socio-cultural life. Russian language and culture were reference points for national (state) culture that was transmitted from the center to the periphery via the educational system, the mass media, party and government structures – especially through the system of training managerial and intellectual elites – and military service. Under such circumstances, Russians residing in the Union republics had no overwhelming motivation to learn the languages of the titular nationalities or become integrated into the non-Russian ethno-cultural environment. The lowest motivation and real knowledge of titular language existed among Russians in those regions where they comprised the majority – as in city capitals – or a sizeable presence in administrative *oblasts*.

Moreover, local Russians generally enjoyed good possibilities for meeting their wider cultural requirements in Central Asia and Kazakhstan up until the disintegration of the USSR. Education at all levels was available in Russian, and the media and cultural activities (cinema, theater, libraries, etc.) were predominantly Russian. Russian was the language of office work and the social services. As a result, in Central Asia and Kazakhstan, Russians (about half of whom were first-generation settlers) basically retained their cultural profile, even though it was influenced to a certain extent by some of the local population's values. As far back as the 1970s, for instance, analysts noted that Russians in Central Asia tended to marry at an earlier age than in other regions, especially as compared with the Baltic republics. This undoubtedly was influenced by the traditions of the local nationalities (Bromley, 1977, pp. 493–497). Central Asian Russians, especially old settlers, had long since absorbed some local work traditions and living customs, including preferences in food and clothing (see Brusina, 1992).

Although there were, in all former Soviet republics, intensive inter-ethnic contacts and a high level of linguistic Russification, in this region the Russians and the titular population kept a cultural distance from one another. In effect, they were separate communities, with their own social niches and circles of everyday contacts. Mixed marriages between Russians and people of the local nationalities were and remain rare (Arutunyan, 1992, pp. 195-196). Marriages between Russians and Ukrainians, Germans, Tatars, and Koreans have been much more frequent. The percentage of Russians fluent in the language of the titular nationality is insignificant – from 4.5% in Uzbekistan to 0.9% in Kazakhstan, as compared with 38% and 34%, respectively, in Lithuania and Armenia.

Russians have preserved their traditional culture in everyday life, rites, and behavior (especially in rural areas). The Orthodox churches that exist in the towns and some villages are an important rallying factor for the Russian population. Most Russian folk traditions and rites are performed strictly within the closed Russian community, and Muslim neighbors often do not even know of their existence. On the other hand, especially in areas where Russians comprise only a small percentage of the overall population, many traditions connected with popular holidays have disappeared, and many religious festivals are on the way to oblivion (Brusina, 1992, p. 84). However, among the Russian population, some of the descendants of those who came to live in the region before the Revolution or before the war are a group unto themselves. They are better acquainted with the language, culture, and everyday life of the indigenous peoples, and are less condescending in their attitude. More often than not they see Central Asia or Kazakhstan, where they – and perhaps their parents and even grandparents – were born, and many of their relatives are buried, as their 'little homeland'. Yet both Russian old-timers and recent migrants feel an increasingly keen ethnic awareness; they are worried by the disregard of the new state authorities for their cultural and religious requirements, and by growing islamicization and traditionalism in official circles.

Language has proved an especially sensitive issue for local Russians. Vigorous manifestations of sovereignty in the realm of language have served as a major instrument in the titular group's assertion of its dominant political and socio-cultural status. In reply to the question concerning the law on the state language, the overwhelming majority of Russians in Tashkent (79%) said they would prefer to have two state languages: Uzbek and Russian. The Russian population was deeply worried at the speed with which the new law has been implemented – signboards with public transport timetables, street signs, and office work in public institutions (the medical, educational, and industrial establishments) are now only in Uzbek (see Fierman, 1995).

In Kirgizia, as well, the Russian population is greatly concerned over the status of the Russian language following the adoption of the language law. Over two-thirds of the Russians polled (68%) said the law had changed the position of the Russians. Just one-fifth said the law had not in fact changed anything, and the rest were either undecided or did not answer. Most of those polled said the law had first and foremost had an adverse effect on the social status of Russians, that is, it made it more difficult for them to enter institutions of higher education (24%), it limited job and promotion opportunities (17% and 16% respectively), and increased the chances of being fired (12%). Moreover, 16% said the law had created difficulties in everyday communication with the Kirgiz. Only 7% said that making Kirgiz the state language had diminished the quantity of information available in Russian. Fifteen per cent of the Russian respondents found positive aspects in the law: namely, that it made Russians realize the need to study Kirgiz.

The survey of the Russian urban population in Kirgizia indicates their concern lest there no longer be full use of the Russian language in education, culture, and the media. Over 80% of the respondents favored the preservation of higher and specialized secondary

Table 6.5 *Attitudes to the Kirgiz Language among Local Russians*

Without knowing Kirgiz it is difficult to:	%
Keep one's job	27
Get an education	15
Communicate in public transport, shops, market, etc.	27
Become integrated into the local culture	27

Source: Sociological survey carried out by Alla Ginzburg and Sergei Savoskul (IEA), 1992

educational establishments in Russian, 80% were for the preservation of the Russian theater, and 90% for television broadcasting in Russian. Over a quarter of those polled in Tashkent (27%) said it was necessary to have more Russian-language theaters; one-third believed that opportunities for receiving higher education in Russian must be augmented; more than two-thirds (68%) said that television broadcasting time in Russian should be increased. A vast majority (92%) favored resuming broadcasts of the Russian TV channel, which had been discontinued in August 1991.

On the other hand, concern over the fall in status of the Russian language and Russian culture does not mean that the Russian population of Central Asia is unwilling to master the languages of the titular groups. There is, indeed, a growing awareness among Russians that, if they want to stay in the newly emergent states of Central Asia, they must know the local languages much better than they do now. This is corroborated by the answers given by Russians living in Tashkent to the question: what is the best way of improving inter-ethnic relations in Uzbekistan today – that Russians learn Uzbek, or that Uzbeks learn Russian better? Thirty-six per cent favored the first as opposed to only half as many who favored the second. However, more than one-third of the respondents were unable to decide one way or the other.

Most of the Russians in Tashkent, as well as the Russian urban dwellers in Kirgizia, are realistic in assessing the negative consequences of their inadequate knowledge of the language of the titular nationality. Only slightly more than a quarter of the respondents found it difficult to answer as to what negative consequences their inadequate knowledge of Uzbek or Kirgiz might have, or said they personally did not see why they should learn these languages. The rest of the Russians polled in Tashkent said not knowing the local language complicated communication in the social sphere and in everyday life (54%), created career difficulties (26%), or limited their opportunities of receiving higher education (8%). Asked 'Do Russians need the Kirgiz language?', difficulties identified by respondents in not knowing Kirgiz are shown in Table 6.5. The most weighty argument cited in favor of knowing the language of the titular nationality is the threat of loss in social status, on the one hand, and the difficulties encountered in adapting to cultural and everyday life, on the other.

All this demonstrates a test of the theory that the practical behavior of individuals may be quite different from the inflamed pronouncements of political rhetoric, and that cultural differences and distances are more often actualized and dramatized for specific purposes. Intercultural predispositions between major groups are still quite high, as demonstrated by Russians and Kazakhs during a sociological survey taken in Kazakhstan in December 1994: both groups want to learn the language and culture of the other, and to live in a cooperative, peaceful way. The majority of Russians asked (63.5%) agree to see Kazakh language as a compulsory subject in all schools; 80.6% of the Kazakhs have the same attitude toward the Russian language. What is probably most important is that only 10.7% of Kazakhs and 7.2% of Russians consider all non-titular groups, including Russians, as minorities; 51.4% of the Kazakhs and 53% of the Russians surveyed consider as minorities all groups but Kazakhs and Russians (Guboglo, 1995, p. 237). These grass-roots attitudes that see Kazakhstan as a 'two-community' state with two 'peoples-partners' strikingly contradict efforts on the part of some experts and politicians to categorize large and old-settled communities of ethnic Russians as a minority in Kazakhstan.

6.5   Political Status and Inter-Ethnic Relations

Inter-ethnic relations in Central Asia and Kazakhstan have clearly deteriorated in recent years. The main cause is the upsurge in ethnic nationalism among the representatives of the titular groups, and the various inter-clan and inter-regional disputes that climaxed in a series of ethnic conflicts – even, in the case of Tajikistan, in a devastating civil war. Ethnic minorities deported to the region in earlier periods (such as the Meskhetian Turks in Uzbekistan) and groups of the autochthonous population living outside their 'own' republics (like the Uzbeks in Osh *oblast* in Kirgizia) were the main victims of this violence. Even the civil strife in Tajikistan has clear ethnic overtones, in that the hardest hit are the indigenous small groups of Gorno-Badakhshan.

Except for the summer 1990 events in Dushanbe, violence has not been targeted at Russians. However, today's social climate is marked by anti-Russian projections of blame for past injustices and crimes committed by the Center. Even after independence, the worsening economic situation and political instability are often blamed on the pernicious legacy of the Kremlin and Russia's current actions, which serves to keep anti-Russian sentiments alive. These sentiments are often fanned by politicians and ethnic activists in order to rally and consolidate the 'indigenous nations', torn as they are by internal dissension.

How, then, do the resident Russians view the situation? The social transformations taking place in the region are accompanied by economic crisis, unemployment, and inflation, all of which affect primarily the Russian urban population. To the Russians, it seems as if they are being 'ousted' from prestigious jobs and 'forced' out of the republics in which they live. The enactment of the laws on language and citizenship, the dwindling of opportunities for children to get schooling in their mother tongue, anti-Russian nationalistic rhetoric and actions of local radicals and fundamentalists evoke painful psychological reactions among the Russians. The situation is further aggravated by increasingly frequent threats against 'Europeans'. The alarmist rhetoric of the media in the Russian Federation and the official orientation of some government departments – like the Federal Migration Service – concerning the inevitable 'exodus' of Russians from Central Asia also have a negative impact on how the Russians living in these new states feel and act.

In my personal files I keep a note that had been attached to a memorandum I wrote to President Yeltsin on the situation in Kazakhstan. The memorandum – sent to Yeltsin for his meeting with President Nursultan Nazarbaev in August 1992 – was returned to me with a note attached from Ludmila Pikhoya, the President's speechwriter, who was preparing the background information for the meeting. The note was addressed to Viktor Iliushin, the President's First Aide:

Viktor Vasilievich,
This document, as it stands now, does not reflect the seriousness of the President's concerns about the situation of the Russians in Kazakhstan. It should not be forwarded to Yeltsin. It seems that the Goskomnatz [State Committee for Nationalities] does not possess proper information on this issue.

Thus, the memorandum was shelved because of its balanced, non-provocative character; those in the Presidential inner-circle preferred a more dramatic presentation that would influence the emotions of Yeltsin, and shape his arguments in his meeting with Nursultan Nazarbaev.

Recent ethno-sociological research in Uzbekistan and Kirgizia has confirmed that the situation surrounding the Russian community in Central Asia has serious potential for conflict. Deep divisions exist between the two sides. The Russians and the titular population are divided, for instance, in how they assess the role which Russians played in the life of the peoples of the USSR. The greater part of the Russian urban population in Kirgizia (78%) believe that Russians always played a progressive role in relations between the two peoples, and in general helped other peoples. Only one-third of the Kirgiz respondents from among the urban population share this opinion. On the other hand, the view that Russians have always been bent on dominating other peoples is held by a mere 3% of the Russians, but by more than a quarter (29%) of the Kirgiz surveyed. The view that Russians have not played any significant role in the life of the other peoples of the USSR is supported by 17% of the Kirgiz, as against only 7% of the Russians. Also notable is the discrepancy, although less marked than in the previous case, between Russians and Kirgiz regarding whether a policy of Russification was carried out in Kirgizia: 31% of the Russians but nearly half (49%) of the Kirgiz answering in the affirmative, and 43% of the Russians and 17% of the Kirgiz in the negative (Savoskul, 1993, p. 132).

There have been numerous – but in the eyes of the Russians, fundamentally negative – changes in the situation of the Russian population in the countries bordering on Russia, as a result of the disintegration of the USSR and the independence of the former Union republics. This has led to significant shifts in attitude towards that population – on the part of both the titular nationality and the ruling institutions of the new states. The IEA survey of the Russian population of the Central Asian republics leaves no doubt as to the Russian opinion on that score. In Tashkent, for instance, more than two-thirds of the Russians believe that over the past few years the attitude of the local authorities to them has changed for the worse. Only 7% are of the opinion that it has improved, while 12% see no change. In Kirgizia's urban centers the corresponding figures are, respectively, 48%, 11%, and 33% of the Russians. This clear divergence of views between Russians in Uzbekistan and in Kirgizia stems from the essentially differing overall policies pursued by these countries, and towards the local Russian population in particular. Approximately the same correlation exists among Russians in Tashkent and in Kirgizia's urban centers in their assessment of the change in inter-ethnic relations on the everyday life level. Here, the only difference is that the proportion of those who said these relations had improved or that there was no change was smaller than in the assessment of the situation on the official level.

A concrete manifestation of the negative turn in inter-ethnic relations is that people feel that their collective worth, or 'national pride', is under attack. Over half of the Russians in Tashkent said that they had experienced this recently and only about one-third said that they had not felt this. The respective figures for the Russians in Kirgizia's urban centers were 27% and 42%. The proportion of respondents who could cite specific circumstances, instances, etc., that aroused such a feeling (in comparison with those who said they felt their national dignity was being trampled upon in general) was somewhat lower. Some of the respondents (38% in Tashkent and 13% in Kirgizia's urban centers) linked such situations mainly to depersonalized episodes in commercial enterprises, at the market, in public transportation (so-called 'bus nationalism'), etc. Comparatively few people said they had experienced such affronts on the part of colleagues at work or university or in contacts with state institutions.

Table 6.6   *Defensive Attitudes among Russians in Kirgizia*

Q.: Who must defend the interests of Russians in Kirgizia?[1]	%
Supreme Soviet and government of Kirgizia	56
Supreme Soviet and government of Russia	31
World community, the UN	15
Russian troops	9
Orthodox Church	8
Russian public movement in Kirgizia	17
Russian public movement in Russia	13
Mass media	11

[1]Totals exceed 100% because respondents could give more than one answer.

Source: Sociological survey carried out by Alla Ginzburg and Sergei Savoskul (IEA), 1992

Table 6.7   *Perceptions of Russia's Policy Towards Russians in Kirgizia*

What action can Russia take to protect Russians in Kirgizia?[1]	%
Protection through bilateral agreements with Kirgizia	47
Economic and political sanctions	22
Help those wishing to leave Kirgizia	24
Support the public movement among Russian population	12

[1]Totals exceed 100% because respondents could give more than one answer.

Source: Sociological survey carried out by Alla Ginzburg and Sergei Savoskul (IEA), 1992

Significantly, only a small proportion of Russians – 1% in Tashkent and 17% in Kirgizia – expect inter-ethnic relations in their respective republics to get better, while more than half (56% in Tashkent and 52% in Kirgiz urban centers) believe they will get worse. In such a situation, it is only natural that the Russian population should feel defenseless. As many as 72% of the Russians living in Kirgizia's urban centers said that the Russians in the republic needed to be protected. Over half of the respondents thought that this should be the responsibility of Kirgizia's organs of power. Less than a third said that the responsibility lay with Russia. A far smaller percentage of those polled mentioned other states or international institutions and public movements as the bodies that should take responsibility for protecting the interests of the new Russian diaspora (Table 6.6.).

The assessment of the role of the Russian army as a potential protector of the local Russian population – 9% saw it in this role – was considerably lower than in response to the question: 'Will the position of the Russians in Kirgizia change if Russian troops pull out?' Two per cent of the respondents said that it would get a little worse and 17% that it would get much worse. Assessment of the perceived role for Russia in protecting Russians in Kirgizia revealed that Russia is expected to uphold the interests of Russians primarily in political, legal, and economic matters (Table 6.7.).

The appraisal of Russian policy on the part of the new Russian diaspora with respect to Russians in the new states, including those of Central Asia, is influenced by several factors, a vital one being Russia's stand on the ultimate destiny of the USSR. A sizeable percentage of the Russians in the new states disapprove of the Belovezhskaya Pushcha

Table 6.8   *Attitudes to Leaders Among Russians in Kirgizia*

Leaders	Trust		Mistrust	Undecided
	Fully	Partly		
Akaev	33	40	18	8
Karimov	9	22	21	48
Kravchuk	7	21	47	23
Nazarbaev	48	21	5	11
Yeltsin	19	34	32	13

Source: Sociological survey carried out by Alla Ginzburg and Sergei Savoskul (IEA), 1992

agreement to dissolve the USSR and create the Commonwealth of Independent States (CIS). The ethnocratic trends in the policies of these states serve to strengthen the negative view held by their Russian inhabitants as to the USSR's disintegration, and their opinion that the leadership of the new Russia is mainly responsible for this. Russia's inability, in view of its own economic difficulties, to absorb those of its nationals who want to leave the former constituent republics also serves to reinforce in the mass consciousness the notion that Russia does not need them, indeed, that Russia has betrayed them. These sentiments presumably explain why Yeltsin has had such a low rating as against other CIS leaders, shown by polls of Russian urban dwellers in Uzbekistan and Kirgizia. Only 14% of the Russians in Tashkent said they fully trusted Yeltsin – in contrast to Karimov and Nazarbaev, who each received 26%. Yeltsin is mistrusted by 33%, Karimov by 16%, and Nazarbaev by 8%. Table 6.8. shows how urban Russians living in Kirgizia rank various CIS leaders.

6.6   Prospects for Russia's Policy

Given the tense geopolitical and ethno-political situation after the demise of the USSR, it would be short-sighted indeed for the Russian leadership to ignore the problems of the Russian population and the rest of the so-called 'Russian-speaking population' in the 'new abroad'. A balanced policy towards these groups requires at least an idea of what measure of support they are likely to give it. Specifically, our recent survey information on the ethno-political orientation of the Russian population of Uzbekistan and Kirgizia indicates that there would be support for the preservation of ties among the former union republics – multilateral, within the framework of the CIS, and bilateral, between Russia and the other sovereign successor states. The same tendency among Russians was observed by scholars in Estonia (Kirch & Kirch, 1995).

The overwhelming majority of the Russians polled in Tashkent (96%) favored Uzbekistan's joining the CIS (the poll was taken when the CIS was under formation). They linked the preservation of the CIS with the stability of their own position. One-third of the respondents believed that the situation of the Russian population would improve if Uzbekistan joined the CIS, and more than half of them hoped it would at least remain as it was. Moreover, 76% of the respondents said that if Uzbekistan stayed out of the CIS, the situation of the Russians would worsen, while 18% believed there would be no appreciable change. Opinion samples taken among Kirgizia's urban dwellers revealed a similar ethno-political orientation. About half of those polled (44%) favored developing Kirgizia's foreign ties primarily within the CIS, 20% came out for a principally Russia-oriented policy, and 14% preferred a trilateral alliance involving Kirgizia, Russia and Kazakhstan.

Dual citizenship – that of their country of residence, and Russian – is seen by many Russians as a way to stabilize their status. As many as 74% of Russians in Tashkent said they would like to have dual citizenship, when asked what citizenship – Uzbekistan, Russian or dual – they would prefer. Sole Russian citizenship was chosen by 10% and sole Uzbek citizenship by 5%. The rest were undecided, providing a good pool for political manipulations. Opinion was almost equally divided in answering the question that followed: 'What citizenship would you prefer if you cannot get dual citizenship?' Here, 42% favored Russian citizenship and 41% Uzbek. In Kirgizia the picture was somewhat different. Dual citizenship was also favored by a majority, although a considerably smaller one than in Uzbekistan – 58%. Fifteen per cent opted for Russian citizenship, exactly the same percentage as those who said they would choose that of Kirgizia.

What, then, is their 'homeland'? Is it the former USSR as a whole, the republic in which they live, or Russia? Answers to this question can provide an indication of the ethno-political orientation of the Central Asian Russian population. The response of those polled in Tashkent was 50%, 20% and 15 %, respectively, and in Kirgizia's urban centers 52%, 28%, and 12%. The rest gave no answer or were undecided. All this shows that the overwhelming majority of the Russian population in the Central Asian republics, where opinion samples were taken, identify themselves with the USSR – an entity which has now become past history. Such a confused ethno-political orientation cannot but breed situations of conflict.

The new socio-cultural and political status of the Russians in the former Central Asian republics has led many of them to adopt ethno-political positions significantly at variance with those of the local leadership and by a large proportion of the titular nationalities. The overwhelming majority of the Russians living in these newly emergent independent countries seem unprepared and unwilling to accept the status of an ethnic minority. It would seem that the Russian population, hoping that their position will stabilize and reluctant to exacerbate their relations with the local authorities and populations, is willing to adapt to the new socio-cultural and ethno-political conditions – up to a certain point. But who can say just where this point lies? The steadfastly negative attitude of most Russians in the former constituent republics (apart from Russia) to the Russian leadership further complicates their ethno-political situation. The only way to dispel such sentiments lies in a resolute, unambiguous, and basically consistent policy, comprehensible to Russians living in the territory of new neighboring states.

The position of the Russians largely depends on the policies of these new states – policies which in turn are affected by the situation in Russia. The governments of Kazakhstan, Turkmenia, Kirgizia and lately Uzbekistan realize full well that an exodus of Russians would spell disaster for their manufacturing and extraction industries. Thus they have taken several steps to quell the fears of their Russian population, to ensure its safety and raise obstacles in the path of Russian emigration. In Kirgizia, for instance, a Slav University was opened in 1992. Moreover, in the summer of 1991 President Askar Akaev vetoed the article in the Land Law which proclaimed that the land was the 'property of the Kirgiz people', replacing it with a statement that the land was the property of all the citizens of the republic. Any organized activity of the Russians in Central Asia in defense of their rights and safety is weak, which reflects the generally quiescent behavior of the Russian population in most of the non-Russian regions of the former Soviet Union.

Two, relatively minor, sociopolitical movements among the Russian and other Russian-speaking (primarily non-titular) populations in the region are the Social Democratic

Party and the Unity Movement (*Edinstvo*) in Kazakhstan, both of which champion civil equality and democratic reforms. In recent years, the political and cultural organization '*Lad*' has acquired a high profile and wide recognition as a defender of the rights of Slavic peoples in Kazakhstan The Russian population of Uzbekistan has no organization of its own and has shown scant interest in the Uzbek opposition. However, in 1989, a numerically small *Intersoiuz* organization was formed, as a reaction of the Russian-speaking population to the growth of Uzbek radical nationalistic party, *Birlik*. The creation of *Intersoiuz* was in a way initiated by the authorities in Moscow and Tashkent, and was oriented towards the preservation of the Union. Yet, in early 1990, these same authorities took repressive actions against it; its activity then declined dramatically, and by 1992 it no longer existed (*Sredniia Aziia*, 1992, p. 18).

There are also other local movements among ethnic Russians which, with varying degrees of emphasis, have propounded the Russian nationalist idea, but they do not enjoy any appreciable support. Movements of this kind are the *Vozrozhdenie* (Rebirth) association and the Ural Cossack Host in Kazakhstan. The principal goal of the latter is the preservation of their own ethnic group identity and the struggle for Cossack autonomy. In Kirgizia, a Slav Foundation has been officially registered. Initially, in 1990, its main concern was the status of the Russian language, and it emphasized its non-political character. There is also a *Landsmannschaft* of Kirgizia Cossacks which, in 1992, had just a few dozen members. This is a conservative group which supported the State Emergency Committee (GKChP) during the abortive Moscow coup of August 1991.

In May 1992, an attempt was made to set up a 'Russian Community' in Turkmenia, but this was blocked by the authorities as unconstitutional (Kadyrov, 1992). Such a 'Russian Community' in fact exists in Tajikistan. Its program and main goals are typical of most of the organizations of the Russian-speaking population: they orient themselves towards the Russian government (previously, they tended to support the All-Union

Table 6.9 *Migrants between Russia and Other States, 1989–1993*

State	1989	1990	1991	1992	1993	1994	1995
Armenia	8,603	1,371	4,064	11,994	27,853	44,574	31,272
Azerbaijan	37,693	52,026	20,736	50,769	43,141	43,371	37,828
Belorussia	−4,565	23,320	−4,654	−21,308	−11,388	16,632	10,108
Estonia	582	3,251	4,164	21,839	12,758	10,192	7,714
Georgia	10,802	14,503	28,748	46,226	65,012	62,176	47,303
Kazakhstan	43,930	54,749	29,526	96,619	126,969	304,499	191,039
Kirgizia	4,958	21,212	17,745	49,773	86,672	56,542	18,250
Latvia	2,546	3,902	5,838	23,176	23,668	25,031	13,692
Lithuania	1,136	5,008	4,379	11,686	17,038	6,931	2,759
Moldavia	1,951	1,227	2,502	9,921	4,463	11,978	10,451
Tajikistan	6,698	40,284	17,559	66,670	62,863	41,969	38,509
Turkmenia	4,631	5,130	4,501	11,996	6,865	17,369	17,195
Ukraine	2,053	−4,124	−66,075	−109,981	17,276	138,981	89,021
Uzbekistan	41,602	65,862	35,873	86,357	70,619	135,352	97,077
(Other)	259,629	163,577	171,577	17,597	−9,620)	−68,865	−92,699
Total	162,620	287,721	104,906	355,737	553,809	845,732	519,519

Source: The Russian Federal Migration Service (FMS) and the State Statistics Committee's data

government), calling upon it to protect all Russians in the newly emergent states, promote the introduction of dual citizenship, maintain economic ties with the region, support industrial enterprises where the workforce is predominantly Russian, and declare its responsibility for the fate of the Russians of Central Asia.

The political inertia of the Russians of Central Asia is largely a result of their low hopes of being able to stay on in the region. Emigration sentiments are preponderant everywhere, except among the Russian-speaking inhabitants of most of Kazakhstan. In the past few years, emigration has increased sharply (Table 6.9.). The overwhelming majority of Russians have already left Tajikistan. In 1989–91, some 145,000 Europeans moved from Kirgizia, although a third have since returned (*Sovremennaya*, no. 50, 1993). In Turkmenia, the negative migration balance is growing despite an agreement signed with Russia after Yeltsin's visit in 1993, and when President Niyazov granted his 'friend' Boris dual citizenship.

Russians prefer to go to those Russian industrial or agricultural regions where it is relatively easy to get a job and housing, or where they have relatives. Their main destinations are the southern regions of European Russia, Krasnodar and Stavropol *krais*; and, to a lesser extent, Central Russia, especially Voronezh and Belgorod *oblasts*. Many move to southern Siberia, the Ural region and the Altai *krai*. Considerable numbers of emigrants have encountered formidable difficulties in their new places of residence, and not a few have returned – especially to Kirgizia, where there are still many Russians and living standards remain tolerable despite the economic crisis.

The Russian government has taken a passive stand with respect to these Russian migrants. Only those who have the status of 'refugees' or 'forced migrants' receive help or support. In some places, however, local authorities, interested in attracting a labor force, have given them credits and land to build settlements (on Russian migration policy see Tishkov, ed., 1996, pp. 11–54).

The most dynamic people of working age, young persons with specialized training who find it hard to get jobs, and parents concerned about their children's education – they are in the forefront of those who are leaving Central Asia. This distorts the natural age balance of the local Russian population, with the proportion of older people increasing and the birth rate decreasing. Moreover, the general potential of those remaining is in decline. Those 'Europeans' with good prospects of settling outside Central Asia have already departed: in the ten years between the 1979 and 1989 censuses the net outflow amounted to 850,000. Estimated emigration for the 1990s is one million people, most of whom will move to Russia (Perevedentsev, 1993, p. 155). Much will depend on the policies of the Central Asian governments. On the one hand, they are interested in retaining skilled personnel who are indispensable for the national economy; on the other, they know that they must provide jobs for today's unemployed and for the expanding workforce – whose members come primarily from the indigenous, not the Russian population. As to Russia's policy, it should abandon simplistic and provocative projects, like improvising with dual citizenship. Russia must adopt a long-term and consistent policy of supporting and defending ethnic compatriots abroad on a basis of inter-state cooperation within a framework of internationally recognized norms and practices.

7

The Culture of Ethnic Violence:
the Osh Conflict

7.1 Introduction

In studying ethnic conflict and violence in the former Soviet Union we have discovered certain incompatibilities between our own observations and the dominant model of conflict interpretation – the so-called 'human needs theory'. This approach claims that members of racial, religious, and ethnic groups share feelings of deep-rooted alienation and hostility towards 'others' or 'out-groups'. The source of this hostility and violence is an absence or rejection of a group's 'developmental requirements' which comprise absolutely essential needs (Azar, 1990; Burton & Dukes 1990; Sandole, 1992). This approach originates in part from the 'frustration–aggression theory' (Dollard et al., 1939) and its later modifications that suggest violence is produced 'when certain innate needs or demands are deeply frustrated' (Davies, 1973, p. 251). This view is also influenced by the human rights and peace and security studies that flourished in the 1970s and 1980s, and especially by the idea of 'structural violence' (Galtung, 1969).

One of the proponents of the 'human needs' approach, John Burton, argues that basic needs include the need for identity and security:

> Human needs theory argues . . . that there are certain ontological and genetic needs that will be pursued, and that the socialization process, if not compatible with such human needs, far from socializing, will lead to frustrations, and to disturbed and anti-social personal and group behaviors. Individuals cannot be socialized into behaviors that destroy their identity and other need goals and, therefore, must react against environments that do this (Burton & Dukes, 1990, pp. 33–34).

Denying a group basic needs causes a 'fear of group extinction' and this fear reflects a kind of 'biological element', making ethnic and cultural conflicts a constant and unavoidable component of sociopolitical systems: 'No matter what barriers they may encounter, people will aspire to meet their needs, one way or another, even to the extent that they may be defined by others as "deviant" even as "criminal" (e.g. terrorist)' (Sandole, 1992, p. 13).

These methodological assumptions provided the basis for a list of 233 'minorities at risk' published in a recent influential study. The author writes, 'these are groups whose members either have experienced systematic discrimination or have taken political action to assert their collective interests against the states that claim to govern them' (Gurr, 1993, p. 315).

The incompatibilities between this model and empirical observations can be seen in at least four areas. First, ethnic groups are not so coherent as to display constant stridency in a struggle for identity; most of these identities have very fluid boundaries and multiple elements. Within ethnic groups, sociopolitical and cultural statuses may differ dramatically and not necessarily correlate directly with expressions of 'needs' – which should first be explained, taught and molded into demands or a struggle. Intragroup contradictions and rivalries are no less devastating than intergroup collisions, as is demonstrated by the war in Tajikistan. Second, it is not the most deprived groups in terms of 'basic needs' who initiate violence; it is groups (to be precise, their elite elements) with titular status and with well-established cultural institutions who initiate the suppression of 'others' (Uzbeks towards Meskhetian Turks; Kirgiz towards Uzbeks; Azeris towards Armenians; Moldavians towards Gagauz and Russians; Georgians towards Abkhazians and Ossets; Ossets towards Ingush, etc.). Third, field studies and other data on conflicting ethnicity do not prove the thesis about deep-rooted and protracted interethnic hatred and alienation. Even in the Nagorno Karabakh region, Armenian–Azerbaijani intergroup relations, as well as Georgian–Abkhazian relations and other situations where conflict was later to erupt, had been characterized by a high level of tolerance and cooperation, prior to the time when open violence erupted (Arutunyan & Bromley, 1986; Drobizheva, 1981; Yamskov, 1991). Finally, it is quite dangerous to accept a thesis that grants legitimacy to the notion of 'violence because of group needs' while practically excluding from the analysis individual interests and motivations for exercising deviant or criminal behavior. At the risk of overgeneralization, any group violence is the sum of individual violent acts which are in most cases contrary to law and order.

7.2   Background to Osh Ethnic Conflict

The Osh ethnic conflict of summer 1990 was one of the most violent in the territory of the former USSR. It involved members of two Central Asian ethnic groups – Uzbeks and Kirgiz – both titular nationalities of the former Soviet Union. The conflict – categorized as a 'riot-type conflict'[1] – broke out in the Osh *oblast* in the Republic of Kirgizia, whose western region borders on Uzbekistan. Osh *oblast* is characterized by a multi-ethnic population: of 1.3 million inhabitants, ethnic Kirgiz comprise 60%, Uzbeks 26% and Russians 6%, in addition to many smaller minority groups (Tajiks, Tatars, Ukrainians, Volga Germans, Uigurs, Turks, Azeris and others). Settlement patterns of the main groups reflect differences in the traditional economic orientations of Kirgiz and Uzbeks: the former dwell mostly in the mountains and foothills, the latter in the plains. Uzbeks and Russians are more often urban dwellers than are Kirgiz; Uzbeks comprise 46%, Kirgiz 24% and Russians comprise about 20% in the administrative center of Osh (pop. 211,000). Uzbeks are also a majority in the regional center, the town of Uzgen: of its population of 34,167, Uzbeks number 27,525, Kirgiz 4,244, and Russians and Ukrainians 1,440. The rural population of the Uzgen administrative region (117,639 people) is made up of 86.9% Kirgiz, 6.5% Uzbeks, and 2.6% Russians and Ukrainians.

Industry is quite well developed in Osh *oblast*: all oil and almost all gas extraction (95%) in Kirgizia is carried out there. Metallurgical, machine-building, and construction industry enterprises are located in the area. Osh *oblast* accounts for about one-third of all industrial production of the republic. Rapidly growing urban centers are surrounded by fertile lands on which cotton, rice, tobacco, wheat, fruits and mulberry trees for silkworm production are cultivated. Osh *oblast* is the only region of Kirgizia where cotton is grown and silk is produced. The area produces 85% of the walnut yield of the CIS. Russians occupy leading positions in industry, whereas Uzbeks are mainly engaged in agriculture. Kirgiz dominate in cattle-, horse-, and sheep-breeding, as well as in the breeding of goats for their fine wool, the latter being practically unknown in the rest of Kirgizia.

Under conditions of low living standards, socio-economic crisis and political destabilization, inter-ethnic tension erupted. The immediate causes included increasing intergroup competition over resources (plots of land), the struggle for control over power structures, social differentiation along 'city–village' lines, unemployment, and lack of housing. Before the conflict, there were 40,000 people registered as waiting for state apartments to improve their living conditions in Osh *oblast* (Amelin, 1993, p. 100). In 1990, among 25 Communist party leaders in *raion*s and towns of Osh *oblast*, there was only one representative from the 0.5 million Uzbek minority. The apparatus of the Osh Soviet administration was dominated by ethnic Kirgiz (66.6% Kirgiz, 13.7% Russians, 5.8% Uzbeks) who practically usurped the most prestigious positions in local government (among heads of departments and committees there were 18 Kirgiz, but only 2 Russians and 1 Uzbek). Also in the city administration, Kirgiz took leading positons (70.8%), with 12% Russians and 10.8% Uzbeks. The Uzbeks could be found in less prestigious but materially rewarding positions in trade and services: in the town of Osh 79% of all taxi drivers and 71.4% of state trade employees were Uzbeks (Amelin, 1993, p. 51). Some scholars believe the incompetence of the *oblast* administration as well as the activities of nationalist groups among both the Kirgiz and the Uzbeks were significant factors in fomenting ethnic unrest and violence (Asankanov, 1996; Brusina, 1990; Elebaeva et al., 1991).

The conflict may have been related to the activities of an economic 'mafia' and the situation in the high-ranking power structures of the republic. As a result of political changes brought about by perestroika, a balance was violated in Kirgizia with respect to the distribution of higher-ranking and prestigious positions between the leading regional clans. This was a balance that had been in effect for decades and to some extent reflected former tribal distinctions as well as culturally specific groupings within the Kirgiz. The former First Secretary of the Kirgiz Communist Party, Jumgalbek Amanbaev, underscored this in conversation with me: 'In the past we had tried to keep track of how our three major groups divided high positions between themselves. The new leaders started to forget about that. It was a signal for them . . .'[2]

Open conflict in the form of mass riots and intercommunal clashes broke out on 4 June 1990 in the town of Osh and spread to Uzgen and other areas the next day. In addition, there were disturbances in several surrounding Kirgiz villages, with violence directed against Uzbeks. Groups of Kirgiz attempted to get to Uzgen under the pretence of defending their fellow Kirgiz and with the intention of expelling the Uzbeks from the city.

The outcome of the conflict was devastating: during the week of 4–10 June, 120 Uzbeks, 50 Kirgiz and one Russian were killed. According to the report of the investigating commission, more than 5,000 crimes were committed (murder, rape, assault and pillage). Violence was stopped by imposing a state of emergency and by sending army troops into the conflict zone. A sociological survey conducted by Kirgiz scholars one year after the conflict showed that inter-ethnic tension and the probability of new violence remained very high because the underlying problems had not been resolved; they were even exacerbated by growing unemployment and inflation as well as by geopolitical instability after the breakup of the USSR (Omuraliev & Elebaeva, 1993, p. 106).

7.3 Research Methods and Sources

The texts of court rulings provide the data used here. Definitions of ethnic violence (EV) vary within differing scholarly traditions. I choose here to consider EV as a subculture of violence in general with its own subjectivity and axiology, i.e. a system of values (or rather, anti-values) and evaluations. It is a form of violence carried out by a group or on behalf of a group against representatives of an 'alien' group (or groups), i.e. outsiders. Ethnic violence in the context of intergroup conflict takes the form of illegal acts (in contrast to violence on the part of the state); it is a kind of 'counter-power' by the representatives of the social periphery (i.e. those beyond the purview of official power) against 'alien' marginals, ethnic minorities, or low-status groups. In this conceptualization, EV is the violence of 'social marginals' against 'ethnic' or 'racial' marginals. Ethnic conflict as an intergroup interaction has EV as one of its components or 'levels', which gravitates towards an intermediate type of conflict situation (group aggression against the individual). The 'perpetrator' (the group committing violence) and the 'victim' have asymmetrical roles in EV, whereas in non-violent ethnic conflict the subjects and objects of contention may change places more than once or act in both roles at the same time.

In this connection the genre of micro-analysis used here may be more fruitful in studying ethnic violence as opposed to mass group conflicts. Micro-analysis is concerned with the 'local' context of the conflict behavior, in contrast to 'global' sociological analyses. Previous studies have thematized the Osh conflict in a macro-approach as the conflict of the two peoples, but to me it represents a series of specific 'local' episodes of EV, with the locally dominant group perpetrating violence against representatives of a local minority group.

So far, the Osh conflict has remained the only one in the territory of the former Soviet Union to be followed by an immediate court investigation. Several active participants were identified and sentences were passed on those convicted of criminal actions. This was possible owing in part to President Akayev's stand as well as to the efficiency of the law-enforcement bodies of Kirgizia, even though these bodies had been paralyzed during the conflict itself.

To conduct this research I used data from ten closed court trials held in 1991 before the panel of judges on criminal cases of the Supreme Court of the Kirgiz Republic and at Osh City Court. Forty-eight participants in the conflict were involved in the trials: 46 were sentenced and two were found not guilty. The courts passed sentences of varying degrees of severity, ranging from suspended sentences to up to 18 years of maximum-security prison. Texts of rulings which I used as the main source appear to contain routine data written in the standardized language of court documents, with the numerous repetitions and attributes typical of such texts. Certainly the materials of the investigation itself, especially the testimonies of the defendants and the witnesses, may be assumed to contain even richer information, but this huge amount of data (more than 300 volumes) could not be consulted, primarily because of the secrecy of the court cases. Nevertheless, the data available do merit the attention of conflict researchers and anthropologists.

Here I have limited myself almost exclusively to the court texts. These clearly bear the imprint of the dramatic character of the court investigation itself, of the mentality and orientation of the court and the prosecutors, as well as of the professional level and legal culture of the society in general. Since almost all defendants were ethnic Kirgiz, i.e. members of the titular nationality, the very fact of these trials, in conditions of an ethnically divided society, high group solidarity and low civic and legal culture, could indicate one of two possibilities: either a well-devised camouflage with respect to justice, or a true breakthrough towards creating a civic society with less ethnic nationalism. The latter, more positive, interpretation seems more likely in this case.

The judges and almost all lawyers were Kirgiz, whereas Russians and Ukrainians prevailed among the members of the jury (two of whom make up a court, together with a judge), or 'people's representatives' to use the Soviet terminology. Sessions were held in Russian, with translation into the Kirgiz language. The texts of sentences analyzed here were written in Russian, reflecting a high level of language russification, especially in an ethnically mixed region like this.

7.4   The Space Factor

Actors in the 'peripheral' events in and around the Uzgen region villages of Kyzyl-Oktyabr, Mirza-Aki, Dzhylsandy, and Boru were the only ones subject to the court investigations considered here. In contrast to the towns of Osh and Uzgen, no large-scale clashes occurred, though the nature and form of inter-ethnic conflict were similar. For example, in the village of Mirza-Aki, 19 people were assaulted on 5–7 June, 10 women were raped and 188 houses were destroyed and property looted.

These villages in the outlying districts of Uzgen have a predominantly Kirgiz population. Uzbeks are in a minority: 5.4% in Mirza-Aki, 2% in Kyzyl-Oktyabr, 3–4% in Dzhylsandy. These are quite large settlements engaged in the cultivation of rice as well as cattle-breeding, with populations varying from 3,000–5,000 to 12,000. Infrastructure is poorly developed, but includes public clubs, schools, first-aid stations, tea houses and village councils. Villages are connected by roads, and there is also a system of irrigation ditches and water reservoirs. Beehives and cattlegrounds are located outside the villages.

The landscape – flat terrain with open fields granting sparse shelter – may play a certain role in the evolution and configuration of the conflict. The victims had practically no opportunity to hide from their attackers by using natural shelter such as forests or canyons. They tried to hide in reeds, wheatfields and mulberry trees that grow along the roads; only the distant mountains could be used as better shelter. Entry to the town of Uzgen was blocked by rural Kirgiz, and 'self-defence posts' refused to admit the Uzbeks fleeing from the surrounding territory.

This lack of natural barriers contributed to diffusing mass confrontations. This is a consequence of the geography of the densely populated oases of Central Asia, surrounded as they are by sparsely inhabited open territory where people can be separated only with difficulty. The spatial overview of treeless plains and foothills increases the visual impact. In several cases it was exactly 'what was seen from the distance' ('a group of guys at the water reservoir', 'Uzbeks working in the field', 'a crowd at the end of the street', etc.) that contributed to the eruption of violence.

Apparently, then, densely populated flat territory with no natural barriers or shelters lends itself to immediate, mass outbursts of intercommunal violence to a much greater extent than mountainous and forested areas. On the other hand, precisely this type of landscape cannot sustain long-term ethnic violence with organized positions developing around geographical landmarks and a frontline. Elsewhere in the former USSR, mountains, rivers, or seashore prevented many mass clashes, but also contributed to the duration of any confrontation and its transformation into protracted civil war. This has been the case in Georgia, Armenia, Tajikistan, and Chechnya.

Let us take a look at the geography of mass EV zones in other countries. In India, South Africa, Sri Lanka, and Yugoslavia explosive clashes (usually of a pogrom character) took place in urban areas or in flat rural territory, while protracted conflicts leading to civil war were found in mountainous regions. Thus, the social geography of EV would seem to play an important role in shaping the character of violence.

Why do violence and intercommunal conflict under crisis conditions – or prior to them – spring up in one place and not in another? The collective portrait of the residential areas surrounding the towns of Osh and Uzgen may throw light on the matter, especially as to social institutions, cultural characteristics, and living conditions.

What do the texts of court documents tell with respect to the social content of EV space? Local toponyms, being a mix of Soviet ideological and semi-official and traditional Kirgiz names, are quite characteristic in themselves. Offenses investigated by the court were committed in the villages of Kyzyl-Oktyabr (Red October), Krasny Mayak (Red Lighthouse), Kirov (from the name of a Bolshevik leader), Komsomol, etc. Criminal acts occurred in the streets, almost all of which have names carrying ideological content which would mean nothing to local residents. For instance, one defendant convicted of murder, rape and pillage in the village of Mirza-Aki lived on Lenin Street, his sister lived on Soviet Street, and the assaults were committed on Moscow and Kirov streets. It is clear that the street names fail to provide any kind of value orientations or normative marker. The fact that in the former USSR no one ever paid attention to how the places where they lived were named was an implicit form of social disorientation.

The social space of Kirgiz villages appears to be poorly organized. In only one case was the central square mentioned, where residents gathered to learn what was going on in neighboring Uzgen and to make arrangements for joint actions. In other cases, the areas outside the local department store, club, garage, premises of the rural soviet (council) or the street itself, usually close to the main road, served as sites for meetings that led to collective actions. Not a single case of preparation or discussion of proposed actions took place indoors. The street and outdoor areas were the main space components for plotting and preparing for violent acts.

Both cars and horses were used – which also reflects the cultural mixture of modernization and traditionalism. In most cases groups were organized around vehicles which had been stolen or taken. This provided faster movement, both in search of potential victims and in transporting them to more convenient places where assaults were carried out. This pattern was especially common where Uzbek women were abducted and raped.

The use of a prestigious make of car was the mark of higher status amongst the main instigators, and it lent an aura of some authority. One of the court sentences gives the following detail:

> Further, he explains that when they were beaten a Volga car [the most expensive domestically made vehicle used by officials] and a truck came by. A man with a red band got out of the car saying: 'That's enough, guys, finish up with them, save your people.' The car and the truck took off and the beatings continued (Case no. 1–30, p. 11).

Private cars were generally not used since Kirgiz youth simply did not own them; in the Caucasus region, by contrast, many young people have their own cars, and these have been actively used for criminal purposes and in group conflict situations. Interestingly, no mention is made of motorcycles – the most common means of transportation amongst Soviet rural youth.

Horseback riding is commonplace in Kirgiz cultural tradition as well as in some professional activities in rural Kirgizia. The Kirgiz are held to be skilled riders, and many cultural values and merits are connected with the horse. This cultural component has distinguished them from the Uzbeks, who have traditionally been engaged in land cultivation and commerce. It was precisely the horse that was used in committing the most brutal murders of Uzbeks involved in agricultural work in remote and secluded places.

Four young Kirgiz shepherds rode on horseback to the foothills of Bak-Archa to kill the family of the bee-keeper Umurzakov, who had set up a private apiary in the spring of 1990 approximately three kilometers from the *koshara* (cattle ranch) of Kyiazov, one of the murderers. The text of the court ruling mentions an episode when the herdsmen's team leader from the *sovkhoz* had visited the apiary at the end of May, demanding it be removed on the grounds that 'the bees may sting horses'. The four assassins riding horses drove three Uzbek teenagers tied with a rope to the top of Tosmo peak (their father was not at the apiary then) and threw them down into the abyss from a height of about 100 meters.

By that time defendant Kalykov brought the rest of the horses and, as defendant Kalmatov has testified, defendant Matiev took a rope from the saddle of his horse, tied the hands of the Uzbeks with a square knot and at Kalmatov's suggestion took the other end of the rope and mounted a horse. He was the first to take off for the peak along the pass to the top of Tosmo which was approximately 800 meters away from the apiary site. The children followed Matiev in single line tied to a rope, they were apparently barefoot since afterwards only one shoe was found on Khalim Alimov's foot. The children were followed by Kalmatov, Kyiazov and Kalykov riding horses, urging the children on . . . (Sentence of the Supreme Court of 25 August 1991, p. 4).

According to Kalykov's story, Kalmatov drove the children on like sheep with a *kamchma* (a whip). In Kalmatov's story it was mostly Kalykov and Matiev who assaulted the children when they were climbing up the mountain. Defendant Kyiazov testified that when going up the mountain, Kalmatov beat the children with the *kamchma* when they fell on the ground. At the same interrogation he gave evidence that it was he who had proposed obtaining revenge for the Kirgiz and that he and Kalmatov took a rifle from Saipov to 'chase Uzbeks'.

Clearly, for young Kirgiz males the horse has a symbolic value as well as being a real means of asserting their superiority over members of another ethnic group, for it allowed them to chase Uzbeks 'like sheep'. Two more Kirgiz riding horses attacked Uzbeks on 7 July. They found the tent of an Uzbek family in the rice fields where Uzbek tenants had been working. They killed the owner and raped his wife (Supreme Court Sentence of 11 January 1991). Three teenage minors involved rode horses to the tent.

Mass movements and quick raids by Kirgiz riders on Uzbek homes were among the most common forms of Kirgiz participation in ethnic violence. On horseback, Kirgiz mobs from outlying territories made attempts to break through to the town of Uzgen, but were stopped by the opposing side and later by law-enforcement troops. From my informants in Kirgizia I got the impression that raiding a town seen as the stronghold of aliens was a way of punishing urban dwellers; the conflict had a strong rural–urban dimension.

7.5 The Time Factor

Mass ethnic violence seems to build up towards explosive but short-lived manifestations if it does not evolve into planned military actions with established front lines and organized paramilitary or military units. At any given place the duration of mass disturbances and violence is as a rule limited to two or three days, rarely a week or longer. Examples of this can be found in the large-scale intercommunal clashes in South Africa, India, Liberia, and Germany as well as in several Western cities (see Bjørgo & Witte, 1993). The pogroms against Armenians in Sumgait (Azerbaijan), Meskhetian Turks in the Fergana Valley (Uzbekistan) and several other cases within the former Soviet Union show similar characteristics and time-spans.

Various factors determine the time parameters of mass EV. First of all, the perpetrators of the violence find themselves in a state of social 'psychosis' and extreme aggressiveness with complete involvement in the actions that they commit (often without sleep and under the influence of alcohol and drugs). In the present case, not a single example of mass action by the defendants went on for more than two days and one night. After that a state of anxiety about the crimes committed develops, as well as the fear of possible revenge; family members and other pacifying factors make their influence felt as well. Participants often leave their homes, trying to hide evidence of the crimes they have committed or organizing an alibi. For instance, two of the Kirgiz men in the incident cited above returned to the foothills the next day to bury the corpses of the murdered teenagers.

Secondly, the purpose of violent action in ethnic clashes is not immediately related to the realization of long-term goals and strategies. Rather, it follows a simple formula – 'to punish', 'to take revenge', and so on. This purpose is accomplished in the short time needed to search for the victim(s) and carry out the violent act. Practically all participants in the cases considered here went looking for victims – Uzbeks in this case. At times the search was limited to a moment of accidental encounter ('Tutashev and an unidentified person of Kirgiz nationality noticed A. Siradzhinov, an ethnic Uzbek, who was passing by, and decided to finish him off . . .' (Case no. 1–29). Sometimes the search might take more time: '"Oh, bastards, we have been looking for you for so long!" cried Usenov to some Uzbek girls whom he found at a tea house; the girls had come from Uzgen with a group of students to work in the fields.' According to the testimony of the plaintiff Dzhorobayeva, Usenov told her when she was taken out of the room: 'I have been looking for you for three hours already' (Case no. 1–57).

The duration of violence itself depends upon the type of action. Attacks on houses, plundering property, and assault, including murder, usually took several hours in the Uzgen region. Rapes, often involving moving from one place to another a number of times and a peculiar form of imprisonment, sometimes lasted for more than 24 hours. Ten Kirgiz youngsters sentenced for raping two Uzbek girls drove them in a truck for a whole night, moving them from the tea house to a *koshara*, then to a water reservoir and eventually to the village of Yukos, where they left their victims.

Finally, the duration of mass unrest is limited by the forces of social control and public order, primarily the agencies of state power. The Uzbek–Kirgiz clashes were to a large extent halted by the armed forces. Local law-enforcement bodies were initially paralyzed and even partly involved in the events or inhibited because of their ethnic allegiance.

The time needed for sluggish state structures with a vertical hierarchy to initiate necessary responses and effect practical measures to separate the conflicting parties most frequently determines the duration of mass EV. Delayed responses are often interpreted by the participants as intentional encouragement to violence, as a positive sanction for committing criminal acts against fellow citizens of another ethnic background. Data on the conflict in Osh do not provide enough confirmation for such a plot, but it would be a mistake to exclude it as a possibility.

7.6   The Perpetrators

Gender

Certain generalized characteristics may be useful for analyzing the described social action. Among 48 defendants involved in the ten cases, there was only one female. This was a retired resident of Mirza-Aki village, who was sentenced to eight years imprisonment for active complicity (instigating and organizing violent acts) in the collective assault on two Uzbeks (one of whom was killed). A witness stated at the court:

At this time he saw four women standing beside him among whom there was defendant Kakieva. She was standing five meters away from him and shouted together with U. Kamchibekova: 'Kill them, or else they will get here in the evening and kill us.' They then began beating them again and he fell into the canal. After that Nazarov and Ermekbayev seized him, dragged him out of the canal and held him while the others, including teenagers, started beating him. Women did not beat him, but they shouted, demanding that they kill them (Case no. 1–30, pp. 10–11).

Our data for other conflict cases show that women did not take part in executing violent acts directly, but they proved to be quite active participants at the level of mobilizing the men. Women can become extremely active after human losses take place, as was the case in South Ossetia and Chechnya. The texts of court documents bear repeated witness to the provocative and inflammatory statements and acts on the part of local Kirgiz women:

Defendant Kyiazov provided evidence that when he and Kalmatov ran into the refugees, Kirgiz women were saying reproachfully: 'Why are you here? Uzbek kill Kirgiz in Osh, they throw them off the balconies, impale them on stakes.' The defendants found the weapons . . . (Supreme Court Sentence of 26 August 1991, p. 8).

A sociological survey among leaders and activists in Osh *oblast* in April 1991 confirms the same observation: 12.3% pointed to women's direct involvement in inter-ethnic conflicts (Elebaeva et al., 1991, p. 74).

Age

The predominance of young men and the active involvement of teenagers is a conspicuous phenomenon. Analysis of the responses to the aforementioned poll proves this as well: 79% pointed to young people and 23% to teenagers as those playing the most destructive role in inter-ethnic clashes (Elebaeva et al., 1991, p. 74).

In the cases studied, defendants fell into the following age-groups: 29 people were born in the 1960s, i.e. they were 25–30 years old. This is the most representative cohort of EV perpetrators. Eight of the defendants were born in the 1970s, and the same number in the 1950s. Men older than 40 proved to be a rare exception among those who actively participated in the EV. There was a separate legal procedure for the case of Ataman Tashaliev, born in 1940, and organizer of disturbances in the outskirts of Uzgen. Osman Suleymenov, born in 1924, was the most elderly participant of the conflict and the main organizer of an assault on two Uzbeks in Mirza-Aki village.

Marital status

Twenty-eight perpetrators were married, 17 were single and information on the other three does not include data regarding their marital status. Virtually all the married men had children – in all they were the fathers of 79 children. Apparently, fatherhood – presumably implying a higher level of social responsibility in one's behavior – did not serve as a restraining factor. Possibly, the defendants were certain of their impunity with respect to the crimes committed.

Level of education

The educational level of EV participants presents a striking feature: 40 defendants had completed high school or technical college, four had an incomplete secondary education and only Suleymenov, who was retired, had no higher than a 5th grade education; the only woman – there are no data on the other two participants – was the only one with no formal schooling. In other words, virtually all Kirgiz rural dwellers taking part in criminal acts were literate people with at least eight years of schooling. Practically all of them had jobs. Fourteen were tractor drivers and truck drivers; six were shepherds. Only four of the defendants had no jobs. Thus, there was no confirmation of the everyday myth that either certain mafia dealers (only two defendants had jobs related to commerce, and none of them was engaged in business) or declassé *lumpenproletariat* are the primary participants in disturbances and unrest. In this case, the social-professional status of EV participants looks fairly respectable by rural standards – almost a 'rural elite' – though there was a notable lack of local intelligentsia and managerial personnel among the defendants. Participants fit perfectly within the social category of rural working class – they should certainly not be indiscriminately regarded as 'criminal elements'. Five participants did have previous criminal records – but this had not prevented Tashaliev, for instance, from becoming a deputy of the USSR Supreme Soviet.

Nevertheless, formal data on social status may need to be adjusted to take into account the distortions of Soviet social reality. The universal compulsory secondary education practiced for a long time in the territories of the former Soviet Union became a hidden form of delayed start to employment, fostering dependency and a low level of social responsibility among the younger generation.

Prior to the army draft at 18 years of age, it was the accepted norm throughout the country to attend school and not to take up employment. As for the quality of secondary education, it has remained extremely poor, especially in the Central Asian villages.

Character of work

Although most of the young males seemed to have mastered professions and only four of those in the present sample were unskilled workers, in practice all of them were engaged in unqualified and fairly hard labor. For tractor drivers and shepherds, most of the working day (which is not fixed) is monotonous and isolated (they do not work in groups). One of the defendants denied guilt, referring to the fact that:

> On 5 June and on 6 June 1990 from morning until 3 p.m. he was working in the field, at 'Bavyr plot'. He worked alone on the tractor, there were no other tractor drivers in the field. During his working hours he had not seen and had not met with anybody. After lunch he saw some Kirgiz running past the field shouting to him that it was necessary to hide from Uzbeks who had attacked Kirgiz. However, he did not understand anything and because of that got in his tractor and went home to Mirza-Aki village. On Communist Street, where he was living, there was panic and people were running away to the mountains (Case no. 1–53, p. 5).

The court did not consider this testimony to be true, whereas my interpretation – which places greater emphasis on the feelings indicated by words like 'alone', 'the whole day', 'on the tractor' – would be much more inclined to see the testimony as authentic. In psychological terms, isolation stimulates an individual's attraction to extraordinary external circumstances, intensifying his striving for 'escape' through group excitement. The kind of work most EV participants performed allowed them to drop work and go, since their occupations were not tied to any kind of technological process which might have prevented their leaving at a moment's notice.

Alcohol/drug use

Alcohol or drug intoxication is an important element of the conditions under which EV erupts. Incidentally, this point is seldom referred to in the court documents (in contrast to the practice of other regions of the former USSR). Undoubtedly, intoxication and violence are related in intercommunal conflicts. An overwhelming majority of the defendants were either intoxicated at the start of the clashes or consumed alcohol once having embarked upon criminal acts. This can be ascertained from the documents, as the following examples illustrate:

> At this moment they were approached by defendant Zhokobayev, who felt hatred towards Uzbek after he had consumed liquor on that day in the center of Mirza-Aki. He intentionally hit M. Ibragimov with a stick on his back and his arm and then took off alone along Moscow Street (Case no. 1–53, p. 3).

> Zhokobayev himself testified that early in the morning on 6 June 1990, he went to the office of *sovkhoz* 'Alcha' because the car that takes tractor drivers to their workplace had not arrived to pick him up. He joined a group of Kirgiz men who were drinking alcohol near 'Galantereya' shop on Soviet Street and drank 150 grams of vodka together with them. Then he found a stick in the road to fight off Uzbeks should they attack him (p. 7).

The relationship between alcohol consumption and violence is very strong in all observed cases of violent conflicts in the former Soviet Union – a country with an extremely high rate of alcoholism (see Feshbach & Friendly, 1992). Among the Russians there is a cultural tradition of considering alcohol as the proper accompaniment to social situations where violence is present or is to be expected. This tradition of alcohol and violence has greatly influenced other cultural groups, even the 'Islamic' ones.

Leadership

Participants in EV did not have a rigid internal hierarchy or leadership determined by any official status. Only in one case can we speak of an obvious organizer. Since this person was well known and could be easily recognized as a deputy of the USSR Supreme Soviet, he succeeded in organizing a mob to carry out attacks in his village of Gulistan, leading that group to the outskirts of Uzgen, where they committed arson, assault and one murder. He issued commands that were followed with complete obedience: 'open fire at Sarts', 'set on fire', 'beat, kill Sarts', etc. (Supreme Court Sentence of 15 March 1991).[3]

In committing violence, rank-and-file participants of EV were constantly asking for permission before executing a decisive act.

> Then one of the participants in the attacks who burst into the room and was armed with a gun, asked Ataman [Tashaliev's name], 'Should we kill him?' Ataman replied that since he had children he may live. Then they asked him whether they could set the house on fire, but Ataman answered that should his [the victim's] house be set on fire, the neighboring houses where Kirgiz lived would also start burning. So he pointed out the houses of Kasimzhan-Ala and Vakhapzhan Sabirov. Then the pogrom participants poured gasoline over firewood near the houses and set them on fire (Supreme Court Sentence of 15 March 1991, p. 6).

Some individuals who did not participate in violent acts in a direct way, but who were empowered to give commands because of their status, may also be classified as leaders.

There were no local bosses among the defendants, but one of them, Eshiev, gave the following testimony:

> Early in the morning the next day [6 June] [he] drove a GAZ-53 truck #48-00 OShL to Uzgen state collective farm garage where he worked as a driver. He was called by the chairman of Dzhalandin rural Soviet, who said that a red Niva car with Uzbeks had gone in the direction of the village of Krasny Mayak and he ordered him to drive them back. About 15-20 people got into his truck, among them were all the defendants . . . (Case no. 1–56, p. 7).

It is quite clear that the word 'ordered' more than adequately reflects the situation. Local bosses were most likely indirect participants or witnesses of EV; they gave initial blessings and instructions, and secured the sense of permission among the activists and rank-and-file perpetrators. At any rate, our documents do not contain any evidence of peace-making or responsible activities among them.

7.7 The Victims

The question of the targets of EV represents a special theme for a researcher, but one common feature in open ethnic conflicts can easily be ascertained: conflicting sides tend to kill males and rape females. The former tactic is intended to weaken the adversary and suppress possible actions on his part (men being the principal danger); the latter is to humiliate the opposing group, demonstrate the 'superiority' of the perpetrator and gain satisfaction, both physical and moral.

In the cases considered, Uzbek men from outside the area and Uzbek women from Uzgen were the 'preferred' victims. The search for such 'double' aliens went on with special intensity, and it was against them that the most brutal forms of violence were applied. But local community members also suffered ethnic violence. In Mirza-Aki on 5 June:

> It was already after lunch that Kirgiz families dissociated themselves from their Uzbek neighbors and did not permit the latter to seek haven in their houses. Uzbek families that are in a minority in this village started to hide within the walls of their households or in the houses of Kirgiz neighbors who had abandoned their places for these days (Case no. 1–54, p. 2).

In fact, on the morning of 5 June, several Kirgiz, frightened by the news from Uzgen and by rumors of possible attacks on Uzbeks, started to send their families to the mountains. This vital detail demonstrates the presence of fear on both sides.

Children and female teenagers (boys could be assaulted) and elderly Uzbeks ('do not touch the elders' said one of the leaders to his assistants) did not generally become victims, though there were exceptions, particularly in the latter category. There were several assaults on and even murders of elderly Uzbeks, especially where the latter offered resistance and sought to defend their property.

How is identification achieved at the moment when EV erupts? Or, to be more precise, how are 'we' and 'they' distinguished? The issue of recognition becomes less problematic in interracial clashes or in cases where ethnic opponents have distinctive phenotypic features, especially skin color. Language may also serve as a powerful marker, particularly when deep language differences exist between the groups and bilingualism or language assimilation are not present. In the Kirgiz–Uzbek case the situation is somewhat more complicated.

A paradoxical element in the court texts is the often-repeated phrase 'unidentified individuals (or individual) of Uzbek (or Kirgiz) nationality'. While on the one hand this is nothing more than court style, it also reflects the in-depth system of distinguishing characteristics that enabled the participants of EV to identify 'their own' and 'the aliens'. In the first place there are certain possible distinctive features of physical appearance (anthropologically Uzbek and Kirgiz belong to different racial subtypes) and local residents can recognize 'typical' Uzbeks and Kirgiz. Secondly, the *tjubeteika* (a skullcap), the traditional Uzbek headdress, presents an important distinguishing element in dress. Finally, there is knowledge of each other's languages. In many instances, however, local Uzbeks express themselves in Kirgiz; it was exactly this circumstance that saved the life of one of the victims.

Thus, in the majority of cases, participants in the pogroms were well aware of who belonged to which group and what his or her place of residence was, at least with respect to their own village. Many had close contacts and could even have been friends before the violence. Mixed marriages are not infrequent in Kirgiz–Uzbek villages. The offspring of these unions now find themselves in a delicate position under the conditions of a deeply divided community.

The documents show that it proved more difficult to identify an 'alien' woman. In many cases rapists conducted a sort of interrogation to learn the ethnic membership of the chosen victim:

On arrival, defendants Mamatliev, Usenov, Chintayev, Amirov, Karabayev, Ergeshov, Alimbekov and Shaydullayev (the latter was armed with a knife and an axe) burst into the tea house, stirring up ethnic hatred, and began to identify individuals of Uzbek nationality among those who were in the building. They humiliated victims D. K. Dzhorobayeva, A. A. Abduraimova, E. R. Ergeshova, N. T. Ergeshov [there is here an absolute coincidence of Uzbek and Kirgiz surnames, thus excluding one of the markers from the situation - V.T.] and S. Mamatukhanov, having insulted their national esteem and dignity. Defendant Shaydullayev then threatened Dzhorobayeva, Abduraimova, Ergeshova and Satimova with a knife, having learned what their nationality was (Case no. 1–57, p. 2).

There is one more interesting detail in the way the aggrieved A. Abduraimova explains the same episode:

At the same moment defendant Shaydullayev came up to Dzhorobayeva, put a knife against her throat and started interrogating her about her nationality, threatening her with the knife . . . then she said 'Don't kill me, I'm a Kirgiz,' and Shaydullayev replied that 'she does not look like one' (p. 8).

The last phrase (in many cases the conversation was apparently conducted in Russian, as it is the general lingua franca) bears witness to the existence of a certain stereotype among the Kirgiz – the notion that particular physical characteristics are found among one's own group members. For those who found themselves in the epicenter of violence and whose appearance did not correspond to this stereotype, the situation might well have ended in tragedy:

Later Usenov, without having said anything, started beating up Nomonzhan Ergeshov, who was standing next to him. Usenov beat him with hands and feet, chasing him all over the tea house. Nomonzhan cried that he was Kirgiz and not an Uzbek, but Usenov replied that he was not a Kirgiz at all and continued beating him up (p. 10).

In another case, one of the pogrom participants explained why he had taken a gun and fired: 'to prove that I am a Kirgiz for I was aware that I do not look like one'.

7.8 Motives and Mechanisms of Violence

When interpreting an ethnic conflict, researchers usually focus on identifying its causes. Here we are concerned with the issue of motives and incentives of EV participants as well as the explanations for the behavior which ensued after the violence had been committed. Almost all participants come up with one common version: they were induced to act by events going on in Uzgen – the violence against their compatriots on the part of Uzbeks that had occurred the day before. This explanation is equally applicable to all the episodes considered here.

Rape

In the text of sentences at the Bishkek City Court (the trial was held in the town of Osh) in the case of seven defendants convicted for raping two Uzbek women it is noted:

> Having been interrogated a number of times in the course of preliminary investigations the defendants said 'no' to the investigator's question: 'Would you have committed rape had the victims been Kirgiz?' Makombayev explained his answer to this question: 'A fight between Kirgiz and Uzbeks is to blame for everything. Had there been no fight, I would not have been that mad at Uzbeks.' Temirkulov was angry with Uzbeks because his friend had been beaten up in Uzgen. Mamtumarov thought that his sister might have been raped by Uzbeks in Uzgen. All acts of the defendants against the victims originated from inter-ethnic conflict between Kirgiz and Uzbeks (Case no. 1–005, p. 17).

The latter statement certainly should not be regarded as a scholarly hypothesis. The rape of women, including by a group, is a more general socio-cultural phenomenon and occurs well beyond the limits of EV. At the same time it becomes an almost 'necessary' and stable component of EV, irrespective of region or culture. Here two main factors seem to be in force. First, the removal of taboos or social norms which occurs during mass violence and unrest. Second, as noted earlier, the demonstrative form of gaining revenge and humiliating the opposing group.

And, while clearly secondary to the factors listed above, it would be remiss not to acknowledge the role played by sexual frustration; for many of the young perpetrators, the frustration arising from living in a traditional, sexually repressed society found expression in their targeting of women. Under conditions of EV there emerges a desire to contravene the norm whereby women, especially Uzbek women, should keep their bodies covered. During the night of 6 June, Uzbek women who had come to take part in haymaking were abducted by Kirgiz men from a tea house. Undressing and showing off naked Uzbek women were the initial violent acts in virtually all the cases: 'Why do you stand on ceremony with her?', said Usenov; and 'then everybody started tearing off her clothes', testified Dzhorobayeva (Case no. 1–57, p. 4). At times, showing off of naked women occurred after performing sexual acts, thus demonstrating the desire to further humiliate rather than to satisfy sexual drives as such. Having killed Saliev and raped his wife in a tent 'M. K. Bekeiv tore off the rest of her clothes and offered everybody present the opportunity to take a look at a naked Uzbek woman and started exhibiting her genitals' (Supreme Court Sentence of 11 January 1991, p. 7).

Although the raping of these women took place primarily out of a need to demonstrate power and cause humiliation rather than to satisfy sexual needs, the actual completion of the sexual act was neverthess important to the individual perpetrators with respect to their own feelings of 'success' or 'failure'. Several participants denied their participation in the rapes with excuses like 'I failed, since my penis had not stiffened and I stood up and went to have a smoke. Having spent some time near a car I again experienced a desire to perform the sexual act . . .' (Karabayev, Case no. 1-57, p. 4). One of the defendants 'had pain in his scrotum' for he had caught it getting out of the car and this prevented him from having sex.

Dynamics of mobilization

What is it that leads to a breaking point in the mentality and behavior of a group and its representatives? When does open violence against ethnic aliens come into being? I should like to formulate this more precisely: in which situation and within which socio-cultural coordinates does ethnic identification become a sufficient justification for committing criminal acts in the form of physical violence? I shall here try to consider the individual and personality aspects of social behavior as a starting point in analyzing group behavior. Just as an ethnic conflict in its overt form consists of separate episodes of EV, the latter itself is nothing other than the totality of violent individual actions that are committed by a specific individual and that can be subjected to analysis and qualification. Let us look into the mobilization that led up to EV in the Osh conflict. In modern societies, the mass media are usually the most important means of mobilization. Television, radio, and the press constitute a wide-ranging component of the cultural space for all participants in a conflict. Every family in Osh *oblast*, including the villages of the Uzgen area, had a television or radio. Quite a few subscribed to periodicals. And yet, there was a striking and total lack of any reference to the mass media in the court sentences.

Here we might forward various hypotheses. First, that participants in EV belonged to that category of citizens that does not read newspapers, listen to the radio, or watch TV. Second, that no information came out via mass media – either because of censorship or because of the inefficiency of journalists and editors. Third, that the official accounts, imposed from above, were rejected or the participants in EV mistrusted them. Participants did not 'hear' them psychologically. Finally, it could be assumed that other means of communication and mobilization were so powerful as to render any mass media influence quite negligible.

The following is a generalized picture of the dynamics of mobilization preceding the crimes, drawn from the court version rather than from that of the defendants:

Village of Dzhylsandy, 6 June: The local population of individuals of Kirgiz nationality . . . being stirred up by rumors that Uzbeks had massacred all Kirgiz in the town of Uzgen and were going now to kill them, gathered beside [the Executive Committee building] for self-defense and to execute the instructions of local authorities in case there were attacks on their villages (Case No.1–52).

Village of Mirza-Aki, 5 June: In the territories of Uzgen and Sovietsky regions, rumors had spread about Uzbek attacks and atrocities against the Kirgiz population in the towns of Osh and Uzgen . . . Starting from the morning of 5 June about five thousand local Kirgiz got together in the center of the village to discuss the situation. Many went to the town of Uzgen, others started to send their families to seek safety in the mountains (Case No. 1–54).

Village of Boru, 5 June: In the morning of 5 June 1990, defendant Kyiazov, having come down from the pasture in Bak-Archa to his parents' house in the village of

Boru, 50 kilometers away from the town of Osh, learned about the events that had taken place there. He became aware that Uzbeks had driven Kirgiz out of the town and that bloody clashes had occurred there . . . Kirgiz refugees from Osh [said] that Uzbeks were killing Kirgiz, and they were reproached in their turn for not going to Osh to help their people (Court Sentence of 26 August 1991, p. 2).

These court statements may be supplemented by details provided by the EV actors themselves. Such details are valuable for the analysis even though the actors have undoubtedly subjected themselves to self-justification and often presented false information regarding their own actions. All accounts of the general situation and its personal perception by the defendants seem to me to be of importance. It is in these perceptions that we find the same consistent account of Uzbek killing of Kirgiz, and it is precisely here that new aspects of a psychological nature appear, which can aid our understanding of the motives and the condition which lead to EV.

Bakirov testified that since morning he had worked all alone on his tractor and 'after lunch saw Kirgiz running along the road by the field shouting to him that he should save himself from Uzbeks who had attacked Kirgiz'. Having got back home to Mirza-Aki village he saw 'panic and the people were fleeing to the mountains' (Case No.1–53, p.6).

Sultanov: 'After lunch at about 3 p.m. panic started in the street, people saying that in Mirza-Aki village Uzbeks had attacked Kirgiz. Being scared of attack, his mother and brother went to their relatives on Communist Street and he himself went to the nearby mountains' (Case No.1–53, p.6).

Zhokobayev: 'In the center of Mirza-Aki there were crowds of people of Kirgiz nationality, all of whom were excited and saying that Uzbeks in Uzgen had frightened Kirgiz and were now about to kill them' (Case No.1–53, p.7).

Kyiazov: When he 'heard about the conflict between Kirgiz and Uzbeks and told Kalmatov and then Matiev, they decided to go to the apiary and disarm Uzbeks so as to make shepherds' and herdsmen's encampments in the natural barrier secure against possible attack by Uzbeks'. Kyiazov pleaded together with his accomplice that 'the reason for attacking the apiary was the information that they got from Kirgiz women who fled Osh that Uzbeks are killing Kirgiz, throwing them off the balconies, impaling them on stakes' (Court Sentence of 26 August 1991, pp. 5–8).

Bakiev met Nurmatov in the center of Kirov village and learned from him about mass unrest in the town of Uzgen 'where his brother's friend had been killed' (Court case, 11 January 1991, p.4).

Eshiev: 'I have heard from the people that Kirgiz were being massacred in Uzgen, their houses were being set on fire.' Having returned home, he took a 28 caliber gun, went to the rural council office, spent some time there with the people who were very much concerned with the fate of Kirgiz and went back home. There was nobody there; everybody had escaped to the mountains (Case no. 1–56, p. 8).

From this we note the rather clearly formulated rumor or myth of mass murders of Kirgiz by Uzbeks in the towns of Osh and Uzgen, spread widely by word of mouth. Though Uzgen is located not far from the zone of EV, not a single source of information in this zone had been a first-hand witness to the supposed events. The myth was in fact created at the future scene of violence and it was there that it was consumed. It may appear as if the collective co-authorship was strictly confined within the framework of one group, the Kirgiz, but the other side of the conflict no doubt had similar, Uzbek, versions.

Rumors formulated in terms of this myth proved the main factor in provoking intergroup aggression. As is well known, tension with another group tends to promote the growth of unity and conformism within a group. It is in this atmosphere that the phenomenon of group thinking emerges, presenting ideal soil for the creation of myths. As Knud S. Larsen notes, '"group think" puts priority on consensus as the overriding motivation; groups in this cognitive frame fail to evaluate decisions accurately or realistically' (Larsen, 1993, p. xii).

The degree of 'group thinking' among EV participants was extremely high. Expressions like 'I thought', 'I decided', and the like were notably absent from the documents – in contrast to 'I was told by them', 'he told me', 'they were saying'. Individual critical thinking was supplanted by group thinking in the heat of conflict; group thinking lowered the threshold of comprehending reality, distorting moral perceptions and behavior of the participants. Experts on 'group think' tend to agree that it leads to 'irrational and dehumanizing actions against individuals that do not belong to the groups ("aliens", "opponents") as well as nourishing over-optimism, lack of vigilance with respect of one's own behavior, slogan mentality, etc.' (Janis, 1972, p. 29).

'Hit, kill Sarts!' or 'Death to Uzbeks, safety for the Kirgiz!' – these were the only slogans under which EV was committed. No other calls or demands or even explanations were formulated – except for explanations of revenge. And yet this sufficed. The initial myth was enough to motivate the conflict and the ensuing violent group behavior. More than that, it served to keep the aggression going:

> . . . during the pogroms in the outskirts of Uzgen, A. Iminov, an ethnic Uzbek who personally knew the leader of the pogrom group, A. Tashaliev, told the latter that 'Uzbeks and Kirgiz have made peace'. After that, six people with guns approached Iminov and said that should this not be true they would kill him, and they led him along the streets. While he was being led, Tashaliev was walking behind him, and the crowd followed, breaking in and damaging the houses of Uzbeks and setting them on fire (Supreme Court Sentence of 15 March 1991, p. 8).

The myth played a significant role in securing in-group mobilization and in escalating the conflict up to the level of EV itself. Moreover, communication between the conflicting sides was destroyed, information becoming much less meaningful and unreliable. Simplified, indisputable mythologems encouraged the replacement of individual reflection and assessment with unreflected group solidarity, built upon hostility towards the other group. Irrational responses to the ongoing events seem to lend their own logic (and logistics) to the conflict and foster its evolutionary spiral. The inertia inherent in conflict dynamics rapidly destroys dependence upon initial causes. EV actors are generally unable to give rational explanations for their actions. 'Why he took up a stick, went to the crowd and started beating up Baratbayev, an ethnic Uzbek, he cannot explain' (defendant Nazarov, Case no. 1–30, p. 8).

A suitable myth and the group solidarity built upon it can serve both to mobilize a group and to unleash internal constraints on aggressive behavior. 'At this moment an unknown man of Kirgiz nationality said to him: "Why are you just standing there? Come on, hit him!" and he, being frightened, kicked Baratbayev, who was lying on the ground, two times,' explained Ermekbayev, one of the defendants, to the court. 'He beat the aggrieved Baratbayev because an unknown man told him that in Uzgen Uzbeks are raping and beating Kirgiz, but he won't be able to identify the man, since he does not remember' (p. 8).

Social paranoia

This identification of the motives and mechanisms that led to EV in the Osh conflict would not be complete without referring to the theory of social paranoia. Some experts (see, e.g. Dobrovich, 1991) believe that social paranoia is related to a dogmatic consensus regarding social reality. In its extreme form, social paranoia implies the loss of individual identity and its replacement by identification with a mythological figure or idea. While individual paranoia has as its basis a defective perception of the world, social paranoia is based upon fear. Three aspects are of interest in this conception: (a) the particular psychological state of the group as a result of social realities or of indoctrination; (b) the role of paranoid individuals in the emergence of EV; and (c) the role of fear. I would argue that the circumstances of EV in the Osh conflict, particularly with respect to social psychological factors and the state of mass consciousness, bore quite distinct features of social paranoia – features that both the court and the specialists failed to take any note of.

We must recall that post-Soviet mentality has retained much of the one-dimensional perception of reality which, as a rule, is formulated by politically imposed prescriptions. Large masses of people had grown accustomed to believing in unified official doctrine as formulated at the center of the Soviet state. Since the fall of Communism, the ideology of ethnic nationalism that had previously served the interests of high-ranking individuals has invaded the ideological vacuum that has emerged. The long-term indoctrination of the past and the present-day propaganda for titular ethnonationalism have given rise to an apparently indestructible belief in postulates of the following nature amongst former Soviet citizens – in this case amongst the Kirgiz – both at the individual and at the collective level:

1   There exists an ancient and glorious Kirgiz nation to which the indigenous population of Kirgizia belongs;
2   Kirgiz, as representatives of the indigenous nation, live on the territory of their national state;
3   the republic, its resources, the state, and other institutions are the sole property of the Kirgiz nation.

Each of these emotionally powerful mythologems and unrealistic political declarations is apparently being introjected from the collective to the individual level of perception. Any discrepancies in this exclusive shared world picture (demographic or political preponderance on the part of 'others', cultural assimilation, social differences not in favor of one's own group, etc.) are dismissed as absurd contradictions to the truth, a conspiracy by the enemies, and so forth. This mass-level reading of the situation is characteristic of all the former 'Soviet nations and nationalities' under the conditions of crisis development in the post-Soviet sphere. One of the psychological roots of social paranoia is to be found here.

Group social paranoia is characterized by the feeling of one's own great significance, accompanied by suspiciousness, anxiety, fear, and hatred. Only minimal outside challenge is needed to elicit feelings of infringed esteem, vindictive sentiments and even the readiness for self-sacrifice in an effort to disgrace or kill the challenger. On a subjective level it is experienced as the struggle of the oppressed against the oppressor.

Signs of such conditions can be found in the Osh conflict. States of anxiety and fear, even panic, were present in almost all episodes of EV. The Kirgiz feared Uzbeks to the same extent that Uzbeks were frightened of the Kirgiz. Vengeance was the dominant reaction and the motive for action. The text of one of the sentences gives the following account:

Unidentified participants in mass riots . . . shouted that Uzbek women should be led naked along the street, in the same manner as Uzbeks were treating Kirgiz in Uzgen. Then defendant Bakirov together with Sultanov and other participants of mass riots tore the dresses off Makhturat, Khabibe and Khafize Yusupov (Case no. 1–53, p. 5).

Paranoid individuals play a special role in the state of social paranoia, especially in the rise of totalitarian regimes, despotism and, quite possibly, in such phenomena as EV. They are not necessarily the leaders of groups (in the episodes we consider, only Ataman Tashaliev may be qualified as such to a full extent). In communities with strong elements of social and cultural degradation there may be more than enough individuals displaying these clinical or subclinical symptoms. According to some psychologists, there exists a continuum from well to ill in every society and culture: 'impairment in life functioning may depend on types of disease and quantity of impairment in each cultural group'. Marvin Opler in his article (1964) on socio-cultural roots of emotional illness pointed out that people in pre-literate cultures suffering from hysterias are helped by the shaman and by community support in times of emotional crisis. Modern man is vulnerable to psychosomatic disorders, deep-set schizophrenias with paranoid reactions, or equally devastating affective disorders. Marvin Opler rephrased Freud's 'thrust into conflict' into the question:

What are the conditions for being thrust into conflict, or how does personality impairment and disintegration occur? We are today closer to the answer. Obviously, what Freud phrased as the 'condition for conflict', we must, in social psychiatry, rephrase as the social conditions for conflict, for impairment, or for personality disintegration (1964, p. 58).

A certain critical number of not only social marginals but also psychologically damaged personalities must be present when violence occurs outside 'normal' causality (or causal 'normality'). And in many areas of the former Soviet Union (Central Asia is the clearest case) widespread alcoholism, poor living and health conditions, and crumbling traditional structures of social control and therapy fuel the development of paranoid situations.

7.9 Conclusion

Analyses of ethnic violence engage two different domains of research: the phenomenon of ethnic conflict and the anthropology of violence. For both of these fields this study can be mutually enriching. In the introductory section to this chapter I argued in favor of a less monolithic approach than that usually suggested by political scientists and by sociologists. For a number of cases at least – like the Sumgait events in Azerbaijan in 1988, the pogrom of Meskhetian Turks by Uzbeks in Fergana in 1989, the Osh conflict of 1990, and the Osset–Ingush clash in 1992 – the usual interpretations have not managed to produce convincing answers. The micro-level, bottom-up observation of violent ethnic manifestations presented here can provide additional illumination, without denying the contribution of other approaches. It should be clear that important psychological determinants, the social environment and the communal culture can all contribute to precipitating the forces of violence and producing fear, aggressive distortions, dehumanization and paranoia. Otherwise it would be impossible to understand why hundreds (indeed thousands) of people are moved to violence and to kill others merely in order to implement the will and orders of someone else. To avoid future violence, it may well be that post-Soviet societies need more routine and intensive social therapy and psychiatric counselling on the individual and the group level, as well as to develop effective programs for preventing drug and alcohol abuse, and raising anti-violence awareness among youth. This approach may be more appropriate than limiting the perspective to that of hypothesized 'ethnic group needs'.

The anthropology of violence, in turn, needs a cross-cultural perspective. Even the notion of 'violence' as used in the literature is mainly a product of Western culture and social norms (see Riches, 1986). Major differences in understanding what is 'violent' exist between the Tajik, Ukrainian, and Estonian cultures – especially among those who display violent behavior. Cultural differences in the type of violent expression preferred are also apparent. Why in the situation analyzed in this chapter did stones and wooden sticks serve as major instruments of assault and killing, whereas in the Caucasus it was knives (*kinzhal*), and among the Russians it was axes? No relevant studies have appeared in anthropological literature on this issue. Because I do not subscribe to the view that violence has a strongly innate component with some kind of genetic basis, it is especially interesting to see how cultural factors produce and shape this behavior. Besides ethnic differences, the Soviet 'folk' culture in general was a submissive one in terms of individual expression – but it was violent in terms of the low value assigned to human life. It was a militant (and thus violent) culture praising force and will through many channels: from teaching 'historical epics' to parading highly sophisticated weapons on national holidays. One of my informants in Kirgizia told me the following story from the conflict: young Kirgiz on horseback were trying to demonstrate their strength and superiority by lifting up an opponent by his legs and smashing him down on the ground – exactly in the way the legendary Kirgiz heroes supposedly overpowered their enemies. 'We have read about it a lot, but this is the first time we've had the chance to try it out for ourselves!', they said. Some may call this a 'non-rational human need' for ethnic dignity or for self-esteem: I prefer to maintain my reservations on the issue.

Notes

1   Here I define riot- or pogrom-type conflicts as those with no far-reaching programmatic context, or structured armed forces or organized long-term fighting with explicit front lines.

2   Conversation with Jumgalbek Amanbaev, 27 May 1991, Bishkek, Kirgizia.

3   The term 'Sarts' is of ancient origin but has become a derogatory appellation for contemporary Uzbeks.

8

The Anatomy of Ethnic Cleansing: the Ingush–Ossetian Conflict

8.1 Introduction

The first openly violent ethnic conflict in the territory of the Russian Federation involved two peoples of the North Caucasus region, the Ossets and the Ingush, in late October 1992. This can be considered a deep-rooted conflict – a category to which specialists assign inter-ethnic and other types of group clashes that are difficult to settle owing to the far-reaching claims and demands of the conflicting parties (Burton, 1987, p. 3). As a rule, so many factors are at work in such conflicts – including deep-rooted sentiments, values, and aspirations – and so great is the level of mutual estrangement, that the usual ways of resolving conflict through legal mediation, negotiations or involving a higher or foreign power fail. Frequently, methods of sociopolitical or military deterrence, or of a legal punitive nature in combination with therapeutical work, will be applied. Even these steps rarely bring about resolution and may even have the opposite effect. The situation is often so volatile that the ego of one man with vested interests and high authority can overpower all efforts at conflict prevention or resolution.

The mentality of politicians and publicists is inclined toward a simplistic perception of these conflicts. Their explanations seek to pinpoint either some generic intergroup hostility (where ethnic identity supposedly forms around a simple structuralist scheme of 'us versus them') or malicious intentions on the part of other forces – usually represented by 'out-groups' or by higher authority. These forces are accused of either weakness and connivance, or abuse of power. To these arguments come sociobiological and historical naïveté; the result is then used in explanatory texts written about the conflict.

Three years after the Ingush–Ossetian conflict, not one scholarly study had been undertaken; I am aware of only two serious analyses, carried out not by professional scholars, but in one case by journalist Irina Dementieva (1993) who published a series of articles in *Izvestia*, and in the other by Oleg Orlov, who wrote a report based on the investigations of the Moscow-based human rights organization 'Memorial' (1994). The only works by professional scholars have been non-neutral analyses written by experts of Ossetian ethnic background who seek explanations rooted in history and social psychology which tend to support the Ossetian side (Soldatova, 1994; Zuziev, 1994).

The Ingush–Ossetian conflict is extremely interesting from the perspective of analyzing the role of elite elements capable of manipulating malleable masses in post-totalitarian societies to ethno-violence. Rank-and-file participants in the drama tended to follow a logic of collective behavior rather than rational individual strategy. This logic presupposes that elitist or collectively defined goals, fortune and disgrace, do not as such constitute a sufficient basis for each individual member of a group to participate in common actions to achieve these goals or change an unacceptable status quo. Selective incentives are needed for an individual to act in the interests of the group. These incentives could be of a positive as well as negative character – like a promise of a prestigious position and material rewards, or a threat of punishment. It is like paying taxes for a collective good: although this may be in the best interests of all, nobody would do it voluntarily, and so a system of inducements becomes necessary. The larger the group, the less the incentive for each individual member to cooperate because the expected share of the reward is correspondingly small, although the risk remains equally great for everyone.[1]

This distorted incentive structure applies when issues like independence/secession or territorial integrity/changes are involved. The changes are perceived by a group as a possible collective good, but this does not mean that every individual is ready to act rationally for the sake of this goal. The initiators of these collective actions are usually those who can expect to reap the greatest rewards: politicians, ethnic activists, managerial personnel, some intellectuals. For example, the Ingush conflicting party demanded the 'return' of the territory on which many Ingush lived at that moment and owned plots of land and houses. The real issue at stake was authority over the disputed territory; transferring the right to Ingush politicians and activists would strengthen their material resources and status. Meanwhile, the Ossetian paramilitary and mob participants were putting themselves in a situation of high risk, exposing themselves to future acts of revenge, without being able to expect any individual reward. And yet this did not prevent them from committing collective atrocities. Who or what played the role of selective incentives in this case? Perhaps the Presidential jet now owned by Akhsarbek Galazov, leader of North Ossetia, who rose to the very top soon after the conflict, played a role. Or perhaps there were other actors with vested interests in bringing the situation to a violent and tragic stage. Could these two ethnic groups have resolved their differences peacefully? Or were there systemic conditions and a primordial antagonism that precluded any peaceful settlement?

The Ingush–Ossetian conflict is heavily laden with emotionally charged factors – 'historical injustices', 'territorial affiliation', 'national government', 'border inviolability' and similar ideological constructs of nationalism – repeatedly cited as reasons for bloody conflicts and even major wars in the past. However, behind such so-called 'first-order' reasons, factors with social and political elements are usually also involved, although they may not be as obvious in ethnic conflict. These may include the just distribution of resources, access to power, and the status of group representatives in the surrounding political and cultural circles. In the Ingush–Ossetian case, ethnicity appears solely as a 'reservoir for agitation' in a society where power and well-being are allocated unjustly among different groups.

This study is meant as a first step towards a more comprehensive analysis of the Ingush–Ossetian conflict. However, I must admit that I find it difficult to write objectively about these events, having had a direct connection to them and feeling a certain sense of responsibility for what happened.

8.2 Warring Parties

The Ingush–Ossetian conflict involves two peoples living in the central part of the North Caucasus region, in territory made up of two administrative districts of the former USSR and the present Russian Federation: the North Ossetia Republic and the Checheno-Ingush Republic. Ossets form the majority of the population in North Ossetia (53%) where 335,000 of the 598,000 Ossets of the former USSR continue to live (as of 1 January 1989). The Ingush, who numbered about 215,000 for the entire USSR in 1989, lived for the most part in the Checheno-Ingush Republic (where they number 164,000 and make up 13% of the republic's population) and in North Ossetia (33,000 people or 6% of the population) (Figure 8.1). Ingush settlement is concentrated in three western *raion*s of

Figure 8.1 *Ethnic composition of North Ossetia, 1989*

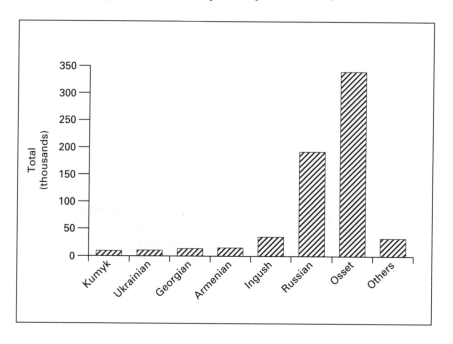

Figure 8.2 *Administrative division of North Ossetia (raion)*

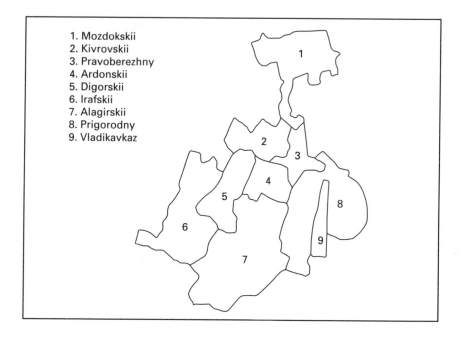

Figure 8.3   *Distribution of Ossets in North Ossetia, 1989*

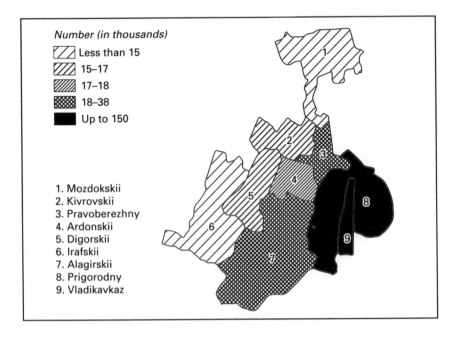

Figure 8.4   *Distribution of Ingush in North Ossetia, 1989*

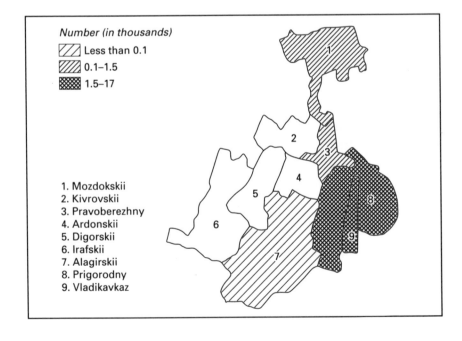

former Checheno-Ingushetia (Nazranovskii, Malgobekskii, and Sunzhenskii) where 140,000 Ingush have been living, comprising about 75% of the population of this region, as well as the Prigorodny *raion* of North Ossetia, where the official number of Ingush stood at around 18,000, but in reality was approximately twice that figure. In several villages in this region (Chermen, Dachnoe, Kurtat, Maiskoe, and Tarskoe), Ingush comprised from 50% to 80% of the entire population. Significant numbers of Ingush have also settled in the capitals of both republics, Grozny and Vladikavkaz. Vladikavkaz and the surrounding Prigorodny *raion* (Figure 8.2) were the most densely populated part of North Ossetia where live the majority of the population (Figures 8.3–8.5).

The doctrine of ethnonationalism, set in a system of so-called national state government and in an ideology of 'socialist federalism', envisions the presence of a titular nation. It is from this titular nation that the proposal of national autonomy is seen as having originated, and it is this group who consider the resulting autonomy 'their own' state – thus bringing inequality to the formal and real status of the titular and the non-titular groups. In Ossetia, the Ingush were considered a minority without status, that is, they had not gained any form of territorial autonomy (in the autonomous republics they were not authorized after the abolition of a system of small 'national *raions*' in the 1930s). This issue could not be raised even in Checheno-Ingushetia because officially the republic had been created as a form of national self-determination for two culturally similar peoples – as reflected in its very title. This practice of dual formation, widespread in the Soviet Union, has been preserved to this day. In the North Caucasus region, for example, we find Kabardino-Balkaria and Karachai-Cherkessia, although Balkar and Karachai activists have urged division on the basis of ethnicity – they almost succeeded when the President of the Russian Federation introduced a draft law on the division of

Figure 8.5   *Ethnic composition of Prigorodny raion, 1989*

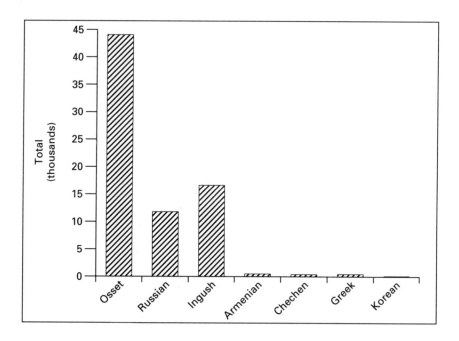

Karachai-Cherkessia early in 1992. Nationalist radicals among Ingush activists have also supported this course, especially after they succeeded in sending representatives to the Supreme Soviet of the Russian Federation and established a lobby in Moscow.

In both republics, the Ingush – constituting an ethnic minority and the third largest group by number (Russians total 30% of the population of North Ossetia and 23% of the population in Checheno-Ingushetia) – have lived with a humble status in the political and socio-economic spheres. The predominant majority (Chechens and Ossets) has controlled the power structures. In 1992 there were only seven Ingush in the Supreme Soviet of North Ossetia, and not one was among the members of the Presidium or the government of the republic. Ingush have been barred from prestigious and influential positions in public office and elsewhere, and Ingush youth have experienced various obstacles with respect to enrollment in institutions of higher education. Ingush activists delivered complaints to the Russian government in which they claimed that young Ingush found it impossible to enroll at the universities in Vladikavkaz and Grozny. In the Prigorodny *raion* of North Ossetia, a total of only five Ingush were to be found among the 53 leading positions in party and soviet organizations, and the economic and socio-cultural institutions (as of 12 October 1989).

In Checheno-Ingushetia, access to power positions was totally controlled by Chechens and Russians in a similar manner. In January 1990, there were only four Ingush out of 73 persons of authority working on the Republic Committee of the CPSU, only five Ingush Secretaries among the 19 City and Regional Committees of the CPSU, four Ingush among the 56 leading officials in the State apparatus; and only three Ingush of the 21 Ministers and Chairmen on the Government Committee. On the other hand, until 1990 the highest position in the Republic's Supreme Soviet was occupied for 17 years by an ethnic Ingush. This was Khazbikar Bokov, who left Grozny for Moscow to work as a Deputy-Minister of Nationalities in 1991. According to Bokov's assessment, real political power in the republic was concentrated more and more among the ethnic Chechens, with Ingush representation increasingly symbolic.[2]

Underrepresented in the power structure at the republic level, and with no possibility of gaining a 'voice' within the existing political system, many militant Ingush activists opted for a way out of the existing system ('voice or exit' being one of the rules of political behavior). What they sought was the creation of a polity where their representatives could dominate. This new polity, in accordance with the decades-long propagation of the postulates of the Marxist–Leninist theory of nations, should be a national (meaning ethnonational) autonomy: priority status for titular groups.

It might seem straightforward enough to divide the territory in question along lines of demographic predominance. However, in many cases – especially with small and dispersed groups – this option is simply not feasible. This then is what prompts activists to call for a 'historical homeland', or 'ethnic territory' and so forth. With this doctrine in hand, a group, even if it is a minority, can attempt to realize its right to command dominance by claiming 'personal' territory. Thus, for example, the Sunzhenskii *raion* of former Checheno-Ingushetia is considered 'Ingush territory': the Ingush managed to secure such a status at the expense of other ethnic groups. In 1989, 62,000 people lived in this region: 26,552 Ingush, 19,245 Russians, 13,247 Chechens and some 3,000 persons of other ethnic groups. Yet, in the 1989 elections, out of the 59 deputies elected to the Regional Council, 37 were Ingush, 14 were Russian and 8 Chechen; in the Executive Committee 10 were Ingush, 2 were Russian and none was of Chechen nationality. This exclusion of Chechens is especially noteworthy; apparently a kind of unspoken compromise was functioning in the republic which allowed the Ingush to control local power structures in the three western 'Ingush' administrative regions.

This compromise, however, was a forced one – at least on the part of the Ingush who were kept away from the republic's Center. Under conditions of non-democratic governance and strict, centralized distribution of vital resources through government channels, the possession of as much power as possible, and at as high a level as possible, in a multi-ethnic community allows representatives of the prevailing group to redistribute resources to their own advantage, at the expense of others. Resources from the 'main' Center, allocated from Moscow to the periphery Center, may get redistributed for various reasons – ranging from geopolitical to personal sympathy, for the benefit of one region or ethnic group. This practice flourished under the Soviet regime, but in recent years it has taken on even more blatant forms. With regard to North Ossetia and Checheno–Ingushetia, for a long time the latter received less than its due share from the Center in comparison with other regions. The Checheno-Ingush Republic produced noticeably more goods, placing them at the disposal of the Center. A comparison of the basic indicators of development and standards of living for the population of the two republics as of the late 1980s clearly favors North Ossetia; for a population half the size, there was a higher proportional volume of capital investment in non-productive spheres, monetary income per capita, expenditure on housing construction, market turnover/commodity circulation in trade per capita, doctors per person, schools, and so forth.

Among the Ingush there was the firm conviction that historically North Ossetia was in a more privileged position because 'Stalin was an Osset by nationality [his father had an Ossetian last name, Dzhugashvili (Dzugayev), and his mother was a Georgian], and having unlimited power, he naturally suppported all measures directed at the eminence of the Ossetian people over other peoples' (Mutaliev et al., 1992, p. 51). The Ingush saw this as 'a planned program of Stalin, together with cohorts among the leadership of North Ossetia' (p. 55).

The Ossets also have their own myths about the incapability of the Chechens and Ingush to establish a good life in their own republic and their excessive passion for 'seasonal work' outside Checheno-Ingushetia. Actually, seasonal labor migration and individual enterprise among the inhabitants of this republic were indeed comparatively higher, which makes any comparison of the two republics by official economic and social indicators alone incorrect. However, there has been an indisputable lag in the social development of the Ingush regions of the former Checheno-Ingush Republic and the Ingush settlements of the Prigorodny *raion* of North Ossetia. On the eve of open conflict, one of the most pressing problems was the extraordinarily high unemployment rate. As of 20 August 1992, in the territory of the newly created Ingush Republic (Nazranovskii, Malgobekskii, and the Sunzhenskii *raion*s minus three predominantly Chechen villages), 204,036 residents were registered, of whom 50,577 were unemployed – about half the entire adult population. It was precisely jobless young men who constituted the most explosive material for the provocations and criminal actions that ensued. Older Ingush leaders repeatedly expressed alarm and concern or employed pressure through authorities and village elders in an attempt to restrain the Ingush youth from extremism.

The radical removal of the Ingush minority from the wider political process in the Checheno-Ingush Republic occurred through a coup by General Dzhokhar Dudayev, supported by radical-nationalist forces of ethnic Chechens. In November 1991, a separate Chechen Republic was declared – without Ingush participation. The three administrative regions densely populated by Ingush remained beyond the borders of this self-proclaimed state. The Chechen leadership sought to treat the issue of territorial demarcation as if it were open, but in fact discontinued financial allocations and resource distribution and curtailed political ties with Ingushetia.

It is still not totally clear why the Chechen nationalist movement and its leaders expelled a people with a related language and culture along with part of the former territory of their republic, preferring to create an independent Chechnya instead of a separate Vaynakh state (Vaynakh is the common name for Chechens and Ingush). The most reasonable explanation is that this was a response to an earlier decision made by a radical segment of the Ingush nationalist movement about creating a separate Ingush republic within the borders of Russia, expressed in September 1989 at the Ingush People's Congress in Grozny. This impressive gathering of one thousand Ingush activists passed a resolution defining as negative the Ingush historical experience of living like 'guests' in others' homes (Karpov, 1990, pp. 31–32). Another possible interpretation is that geopolitical calculations by Chechen leaders led them to place the Ingush segment of the population in the desperate situation of having to create an autonomous republic in the backward western region (Grozny maintained control over the predominantly Chechen portion of Sunzhenskii *raion*) and fight for the restoration of the former Ingush Autonomous Oblast which includes a part of the Prigorodny *raion* of North Ossetia.

The actions of Chechen leaders clearly show that they were pushing the Ingush toward an uncompromising position on the territorial issue. In the summer of 1992, the Chechen Parliament adopted a special resolution which declared areas of the Ingush regions populated by Chechens to be under Chechen jurisdiction. Dudayev's guards expelled the local authorities by force and placed their own administrators in the Chechen villages. Dudayev repeatedly stated that 'there is nothing for Russia to help the Ingush with', and 'Russia can't return their territory to them'. The law adopted by the Supreme Soviet of the Russian Federation on 4 June 1992, 'On the Formation of the Ingush Republic within the Russian Federation' was received skeptically by Chechen leaders as well.

Some of my informants in those days averred that Chechnya was pursuing the policy goal of reunification with Ingushetia once Ingushetia managed to annex the disputed territory of the Prigorodny *raion*. My observations, however, call into question the thesis of two 'fraternal nations'. It is true that the cultural distance between the two ethnic groups is not really so great; the opportunities for constructing a common Vaynakh identity, at least in the Soviet period, were just as good as the opportunities for forming two 'socialist nations'. But cultural similarity is no guarantee against inter-ethnic tensions and conflicts: the example of the Serbs and Croats has shown this. The diminished status of the Ingush in Chechnya provided sufficient grounds for anti-Chechen sentiments, as well as the backwardness of the Ingush regions which was used to justify the policy of 'excluding' them from aspiring to independence. During the division of former Czechoslovakia, the Czechs behaved in the same manner towards the Slovaks. There are indications that the levels of inter-ethnic contacts – above all, of mixed marriages between Chechens and Ingush – were lower than with other nearby ethnic groups, like Russians. A study undertaken in 1983 showed that young Ingush (18–23 years old) identified more with Russians than with Chechens; this allowed Galina Soldatova (1994, p. 159) to conclude that there was little ethnic integration between these two groups, which had been living in the same republic since 1934, and that alienation was increasing. Some ethnographers hold that the Ingush cultural complex resembles the Ossetian cultural complex more closely than the Chechen (Kaloev, 1989, p. 144). It is possible to conclude from historical data also, that it was the inter-clan fighting between Vaynakhs that compelled the tsarist administration in the mid-19th century to take measures to divide and isolate the warring groups; after this more rigid ethnic boundaries started to form and a stronger feeling of belonging to either a Chechen or Ingush group appeared (Martirosyan, 1933; Tkachev, 1911).

On the whole, the diminished status of the Ingush in the former Checheno-Ingushetia seems to have created the fundamental reason for an ethno-political movement which advocated administrative separation so as to acquire the right to direct the distribution of resources from the Center and to establish its own ethnic administration. The reluctance of the dominant group of Chechens to ensure an appropriate and acceptable status for the Ingush minority strengthened the Ingush resolve. The movement was supported by leaders of the Ingush minority in North Ossetia, where political discrimination supplemented a policy of cultural oppression. Here let me add that I consider the high level of dominance of Russian culture and language acculturation in that republic as a kind of covert or indirect discrimination. Of all the republics of the North Caucasus, that kind of acculturation was probably the highest in North Ossetia. The Ossets are the only large indigenous group in the region who were deeply influenced by the Russian Orthodox Church in the past and in the Soviet period an influential Communist *nomenklatura* intensively cultivated Russian-speaking officialdom. In recent decades, largely through the efforts of the local elite, the Russian language almost totally replaced Ossetian and other languages in all public spheres, from government and mass media to the educational and service structures.

Russification of the republic appeared as a much greater and unwelcome challenge to the Ingush than to the Ossets because the former remained more traditional in cultural orientation and less urbanized. The census data on native versus Russian languages among the three ethnic groups, as noted in Chapter 5, cannot give an adequate reflection of the language situation because the survey question on language was unclearly formulated. In fact, the true native language (that spoken at home and at work) for the overwhelming majority of Ossets and half the Ingush is actually Russian. However, practically all Ingush are bilingual: deportation forced them to learn Russian and sometimes deliberately kept them from speaking their native language.

There was a need for special measures to ensure the rights and cultural aspirations of the Ingush in North Ossetia – not only in the Prigorodny *raion*, but also at the level of the republic's Center. Prevailing opinion among the North Ossetian leadership, including members of the Presidium of the Supreme Soviet, was that it was impossible to grant any kind of preferences for the Ingush minority in the cultural-language sphere unless accompanied by parallel preferences for Ossets. Programs in support of Ingush language and culture in the republic were totally lacking. Distance and alienation between the two communities were ensured by restricting certain social rights of the Ingush population. Here we may mention the policy of limiting Ingush residency in the Prigorodny *raion*, hindering access to plots of land, and numerous cases of prejudiced treatment of the Ingush minority by the internal police and local courts where Ossets dominated, especially in the period of state of emergency imposed in Prigorodny in April 1992. The latter circumstance was extremely demoralizing to local Ingush because the emergency measures often took forms which insulted personal and collective worth.

The influx of large numbers of Osset refugees from Georgia after the Georgian–South Ossetian conflict was to pose an additional threat to the Ingush minority status in North Ossetia. This became a serious social and political problem for the republic in 1991 and 1992. The overall number of refugees reached 60,000–70,000, concentrated mainly in Vladikavkaz. Social tensions increased, also in the sphere of inter-ethnic relations. Many of the South Ossets moved to the Prigorodny *raion* and behaved hostilely towards Ingush settlers, many of whom had a semi-legal status (without official registration).

It is not easy to determine whether the considerable number of refugees who found themselves in Prigorodny, which could boast the most fertile agricultural land of the republic, landed there by choice or through special measures. On 15 January 1992 there were 15,563 refugees from Georgia, and 11,916 at the beginning of July. These are official figures from the Committee on Inter-ethnic Relations of North Ossetia, but they did not reflect the real situation after the summer of 1992. Refugees simply stopped registering with the Committee because of a rumor that all of them would be returned to South Ossetia. After 1 September, a new influx of refugees came, hoping to receive Russia's privatization vouchers.

South Ossets, formally citizens of another state (Georgia), used their cultural kinship with the main population to lay a specific claim to rights in the Prigorodny *raion* and to provoke further anxiety within the Ingush community regarding the possible increase of ethnic 'aliens'. These concerns proved quite justified, as subsequent events were to demonstrate. During open clashes, South Ossets played the most brutal role in the expulsion of the Ingush. Representatives of authority, including the federal government, opted to support 'blood ties' instead of civic solidarity and protection. They distributed weapons to foreign citizens to enable them to repel 'aggression' on the part of their own citizens. Alan Chochiev, Vice-Chairman of the South Ossetian Supreme Soviet, later issued a statement that can be read as a triumph of the ideologies and practices of ethnic nationalism over the principles of civic society and governance. Chochiev wrote in *Nezavisimaya gazeta*: 'the Ossetian people acted as one for the first time in the course of armed conflict in the Prigorodny district', and that the events in Prigorodny were the 'first mutual military–national display of the Ossets within human memory'(5 January, 1993).

Thus, the sociopolitical and cultural status of the Ingush minority in both republics was a sufficient foundation for dissatisfaction, complaints and aspirations to change the status quo. But was it sufficient grounds for the representatives of the discriminated group to take such strong actions, culminating in open confrontation? Similar situations exist all over the world; however, it is particularly in the post-Soviet societies that they assume violent form. Why is this so? We must search for the answer in the social structure of the former Soviet nationalities and the doctrines inherited from the totalitarian regime. Social structure is the key to understanding the exceptional 'vocality' of Soviet nationalities under liberalization and the deep societal transformations that started in the late 1980s. By 'vocality' I mean the capability of an ethnic group, or rather their symbolic elite, to give voice to complaints and needs, as well as mobilizing members around them.

Despite all the malfunctions of the Soviet system, its ability to provide broad access to education and to create numerous prestigious elites among the non-Russian nationalities, thereby demonstrating the successful 'solution of the national question in the USSR', was undoubtedly a notable achievement. Higher education – and scholarly degrees and honorary titles in particular – became the most important form of social mobility for representatives of the peripheral elite. Receiving a higher education and acquiring an academic degree from the leading universities in Moscow and Leningrad held exceptional significance. The race for education was especially intense in the 1960s–1980s, particularly for the younger generation of so-called 'punished peoples', like the Chechens and Ingush, who had been restricted from higher education for almost two decades. Ruslan Khasbulatov, for example, considered his admission to the Moscow State University a rare stroke of luck, since he came from a repressed Chechen family and spent his childhood in Kazakhstan.[3]

The dramatic changes in education are demonstrated clearly in the data from the last two Soviet censuses (see Table 8.1). In the 1970s, the general educational level among the Chechens, Ingush, and Ossets was already equal to or higher than that among Russians; by the end of the 1980s it had risen considerably higher, especially among Ingush and Chechens.

The existence of a large number of highly educated people leads to at least two very important results: the creation of a powerful reservoir of excessive social expectations, and the invasion of sociopolitical discourse by an intellectual elite seeking to apply their

Table 8.1 *Educational Level of Soviet Citizens by Ethnic Group, 1979 and 1989 (per one thousand persons over 15 years of age)*

Ethnic group	Completed secondary school	2-year special degree	Incomplete higher education	Higher education degree
Chechen				
1979	196	51	11	22
1989	346	111	16	45
Ingush				
1979	226	63	16	35
1989	345	123	24	60
Osset				
1979	241	135	30	110
1989	294	202	32	153
Russian				
1979	203	131	17	77
1989	257	197	17	115
All USSR population				
1979	205	127	17	77
1989	274	192	17	113

Source: Compiled from USSR census data

knowledge to achieve specific rewards. In addition, in such a highly literate or 'overeducated' society, elite-produced perceptions and mythological constructions easily translate to the mass level. And vice versa – grass-roots perceptions and myths can rise to the level of official statements and formulated demands.

In the Ingush–Osset case, the conflicting parties more than succeeded in amassing mutually exclusive myths and interpretations based on historical and political-legal arguments in particular. On the Ossetian side came a massive flux of academic, literary, and journalistic texts positing the 'noble' history of the Ossetian nation. According to this self-assertive literature, the Ossets had produced more heroes of the Soviet Union than any other nationality – which was a clear testimony to the superior bravery and strength of the Ossets. On the Ingush side, the initiatives stemmed from the urban intelligentsia residing for the most part in Grozny, the capital of the Checheno-Ingush Republic. The first People's Deputies to the Russian Parliament of Ingush nationality came from this area; Bembulat Bogatyrev and Ibragim Kostoev, both Ingush, played important roles in lobbying for the Law on Rehabilitation of Repressed Peoples, and then the Law on the Formation of the Ingush Republic. Both men headed two of the most active political organizations: Bogatyrev led the Ingush People's Council, and Kostoev headed the *Neeskho* Party. Other leaders and activists included: Professor Beksultan Seinaroev, a judge from Grozny; Tamerlan Mutaliev, professor of history and the Provost of the Grozny Institute of Education; and assistant professor Fedor Bokov of the Checheno-Ingush University. Almazev, Tumgoev, and Mashtagov, the administrative heads of three Ingush *raions*, also played an active role in Ingush public activities.

The Ingush nationalist movement built its strategy on demands for the reinstatement of Ingush autonomy and return of the Prigorodny district to the Ingush people. This was the only goal of rehabilitation. 'We will not ask for material compensation for our people as specified in the law, nor any rehabilitation measures on the part of the state toward the Ingush. Just return our land to our people,' Bembulat Bogatyrev told me when I met a group of Ingush leaders in my ministerial office in May 1992.[4] For the Ingush, rehabilitation occupied a major place in the pre-history to the conflict, and this topic requires special analysis.

8.3   The 'Outcast People' Complex

The legacy of the Stalinist regime imparted an extremely complicated profile to the conflict situation. It would, however, be an over-simplification to reduce an analysis of the conflict's causes to a reaction to past injustices and offenses. In situations of ethnic conflict, history is usually mobilized for the achievement of present-day goals. Demands for the reinstatement of a past 'norm' most often come down to the search for that exact moment in history which can best serve the achievement of these goals. With Stalinist deportations, the matter becomes far more complicated. First, these deportations were executed solely on the basis of ethnic discrimination. They affected an entire group without exception, even members who resided elsewhere in the country or had served at the front during the war. Moreover, deportations and the subsequent limitations connected with them do not belong to the annals of 'dead' history: many people still living today were victims of deportation and retain the painful memories of absolute coercion. And finally, until recent times, no actions to define these crimes were taken on the part of the government or society. The law of 1991 was an exception, it is precisely for these reasons that the problem of repressed peoples developed into the most acute and troublesome of all aspects of inter-ethnic relations in recent years.

The deportation of peoples, including Chechens and Ingush, had a dual influence on the fate of ethnic communities. Of course, there was the enormous trauma (in terms of physical scope, and socio-cultural and moral dimensions) for hundreds of thousands of people on both the collective and personal levels. Cruel and aggressive actions aroused the desire for vengeance among the victims; first as a curse, then as a means of collective survival, and finally, at the present stage, as a form of therapy (catharsis) from the unspeakable trauma – a means to reinstate and mend collective and individual dignity. Deportation never managed to annihilate the collective identity; indeed, it further strengthened ethnic sentiment by drawing rigid borders around ethnic groups, in many cases borders which had not existed in the past. Deportations provoked feelings of ethnicity, just as the Karabakh conflict stirred thousands of Armenians and Azerbaijanis to action, especially among those with 'acquiescent' or 'latent' ethnicity in the peripheral diaspora of these groups.

A short history of the Ingush can help us to better understand the nature of the conflict and the complicated issues connected with the territorial argument. Here, 'history' will not be presented as the definitive 'objective' account or 'correct' interpretation – over this, historians and ethnographers still argue vehemently. In contemporary historiography and social-cultural anthropology it has already been shown how interpretations of the past are primarily a present-day resource, a means for attaining certain group and individual goals. Through archeological and historical reconstruction and ethnographic descriptions, people seek arguments that not only favor their personal and collective integrity, but also advance emotional and political-legal reasons that support their programs and positions. Representatives of any ethnic group will generally strive to embellish their history, enriching it with cultural heroes and achievements as much as possible to invent 'tradition'. These efforts – above all by accomplished historians, anthropologists, writers, and journalists – are employed to substantiate group legitimacy, strengthen group integrity, and frequently to justify arguments for status, territorial, cultural, or other demands.

The cultural landscape of the North Caucasus region is notable for its complexity and dramatic quality: the ethnic mosaic of the population of the foothills and mountain ravines is based on aboriginal tribal groups, and their migrant displacement under the powerful influence of Russian colonization even from the 18th century (see Novoseltzev, 1987; Volkova, 1974). During the Bolshevik Revolution and the Civil War in the 20th century, the North Caucasus became a testing ground for 'nationhoods construction', and the object of especially cruel collective repression. The territorial settlement of various ethnic groups, their political status, administrative borders and even the nomenclature of nationalities have changed repeatedly within living memory.

Two historical circumstances are particularly relevant to the pre-history of today's conflict. The one is connected with the Bolshevik experiment in territorializing ethnicities, or rather in creating inner-state administrative formations along ethnic lines. Historically this issue has a vital aspect which many political figures and experts have failed to recognize, and which social engineers of the Lenin–Stalin era never considered. Government-administrative boundaries are usually drawn around specific ethno-cultural areas, or at least this is the goal: it facilitates administration, while also reflecting the aspirations of the cultural community to defend their interests and integrity within the framework of a state system at various levels. Thus, the formation of the Autonomous Highlands Soviet Republic as part of the RSFSR in January 1921 was quite justified; it included lands occupied by Chechens, Ossets, Ingush, Kabardins, Balkars, and Karachais, as well as Cossacks. In order to avoid exclusive claims to power on the part of any one group of the population, the administrative center Vladikavkaz and the industrial center Grozny were chosen as independent administrative units, while Cossack areas with a predominantly Russian population were made directly subordinate to the central government. In 1921–24, however, the 'will of the peoples settling in the Autonomous Highlands Soviet Socialist Republic' and 'the goals of wider involvement of the working masses of this republic in the affairs of Soviet government administration' (*Izvestia*, 26 January 1921) led to a division of this multi-ethnic formation into the following autonomous *oblast*s: Kabardino-Balkar, Karachai-Cherkess, Chechen, Ingush, North Ossetia, as well as the autonomous territorial district of Sunzhenskii with the rights of a provincial administration.

The Ingush and Ossets were granted separate autonomy in 1924, but the city of Vladikavkaz was earmarked as an independent administrative unit of the RSFSR and the administrative center of both the autonomous *oblast*s and the Sunzhenskii district. In 1934, the Ingush Autonomous Oblast was merged with the Chechen Autonomous Oblast into a single Checheno-Ingush Oblast; this became an autonomous republic with its center in Grozny in 1936. All these actions were more or less dictated from above, but we should not ignore the powerful pressure exerted by local leaders lobbying in the center, as well as other contributing circumstances. One of the underlying ideas was to merge two groups into one people in a short-term perspective (Martirosyan, 1933, pp. 311–314). Putting the city of Vladikavkaz under the total control of the North Ossetia administration in 1933 proved most painful for the Ingush. This deprived the main area of Ingush settlement of a large urban center, and of the many industrial and cultural opportunities such a center provides.

The issue of administrative centers of ethnonational formation during the Soviet period has remained a topical question in the post-Soviet space. Once such a formation is constituted, the accompanying bureaucratic and symbolic institutions will also appear; they prefer to locate their offices in a single place called the capital. Major population centers with a developed economic and cultural infrastructure, which can ensure the bureaucracy the conveniences of life and administrative work, usually serve as these capitals. For many Soviet nationalities who received their 'own' government during the period of USSR formation, only cities with a predominantly ethnic Russian population were available. The North Caucasus region was no exception. In Vladikavkaz, in whose environs both Ossets and Ingush settled, these groups comprised only 10% and 2% of the population respectively, and Russians made up the majority. Chechens likewise were a minority in Grozny. As a rule, subsequent demographical developments favor the titular group, whereas the capital cities almost everywhere preserve the complex composition of the population (see Guboglo, 1992a, 1992b), although the 'indigenous nations' already see the city as their exclusive national property. In Vladikavkaz, the proportion of Ossets increased from 23.6% in 1959 to 40% in 1979. By 1989, Ossets made up about half of the population (147,400 people), and Russians had lost their majority status (114,000). Compared to the pre-deportation period, Ingush increased their numbers in this city seven-fold: 14,400 setted in Vladikavkaz between 1957 and 1989. But it was never 'their' capital; and as Russians have lost their dominant status to Ossets over the past two decades, it has become even more difficult for the Ingush minority to have to face Ossetian domination in the administrative center.

Neither did those who lived in Checheno-Ingushetia have a capital in Grozny, where Chechens became 'masters' of the city after 1991. Because of Chechen infringements of the rights of other peoples, a powerful complex arose, especially among the Ingush intelligentsia and executive elite. Throughout the period of industrialization, no new city that . could assume the role of a national center emerged on Ingush territory, and the subsequent tragic history of the Ingush never even gave them a chance. This is why transferring part of Vladikavkaz so as to situate the administrative capital of the reconstituted republic there became a major point for the radical wing in the Ingush ethnic movement.

The indelible effect of mass deportation in 1944 on the mentality and behavior of this group has acted as a second important factor in contemporary Ingush history. The Checheno-Ingush Republic was obliterated by the 7 March 1944 decree of the Supreme Soviet Presidium. All Chechens and Ingush were deported, mostly to Kazakhstan and Kirgizia. The Groznenskaya *oblast* was formed on part of the territory of the republic, with the remainder divided among North Ossetia, Daghestan, and Georgia. Deportees faced physical deprivation, limitation of civil rights, disintegration of social ties, and suppression of their religion, language, and culture. They were even deprived of the hope of returning to their homeland because their resettlement had a 'permanent' quality. A deep-rooted psychological complex of outcast people developed among members of this nationality.

8.4 The Territorial Argument

After Stalin's death, the rehabilitation of the Ingush, like that of other repressed peoples, was to be leisurely and incomplete. The 1956 decree on lifting the restrictions on special deportees retained the prohibition against returning to places from which they had been deported. The restoration of the Checheno-Ingush Republic in 1957 took on a different configuration; the Prigorodny *raion* remained a part of North Ossetia, but Checheno-Ingushetia was handed over to three districts of Stavropol *krai*: Kargalinskii, Shchelkovskii, and Naurskii. Since no organized program of resettlement existed, the streams of returning Ingush were directed primarily to places of their former settlement, including the Prigorodny *raion*. Local authorities hindered Ingush settlement in every way possible, and on their initiative the USSR Council of Ministers adopted a resolution in March 1982 on the restriction of *propiska* (residence permits) for citizens living in the Prigorodny *raion*. This was actually a continuation of hidden repression, a renunciation of rehabilitation.

The Ingush persevered in returning to their native origins despite the rigid restrictions. Many families moved and settled in villages in the Prigorodny *raion* without authorization, so the real number of citizens of this nationality considerably exceeded the official census figures. Many built permanent homes, owned plots of land, and worked on local state farms or in industry.

A rather tense demographical situation took shape in Prigorodny toward the 1990s. The area became the most densely populated in the whole republic – which had one of the highest population densities in the USSR even without this *raion*. By 1990, more than 75,500 people were living on the 1,440 km^2 of this *raion*. Within the boundaries of the Prigorodny *raion* population density reached 186 persons per km^2, as compared to the average for the republic of 80 persons per km^2. At the time of my visits to Prigorodny in the summer of 1992, there was not a single vacant plot of land. The restrictions on residence permits had been preserved, and from 1982 to 1992 only around 1,000 persons of Ingush nationality were registered.

Serious concern about the fate of Prigorodny existed among the Ossetian population. They had what seemed to be a weighty argument, reflected not only in official statements, but also in documents of local public organizations. Two weeks after the Supreme Soviet of the RSFSR adopted a Law on Rehabilitation of Repressed Peoples in April 1991, a letter was sent by the Ossetian nationalist organization *Adashon Tsagis* (The People's Union) to Gorbachev, Lukyanov, Yeltsin, and the People's Deputies of the USSR and the RSFSR. The letter pointed out that

> implementation of this law leads to new repression with regard to the Ossetian population of the Prigorodny *raion* of the North Ossetia S.S.R. The Ossetian people will again be driven to the abyss of calamity and misery. The point is that a significant portion of the Ossetian population of Georgia was forcibly settled in the Prigorodny *raion* in 1944 to please Beria and the Georgian authorities. Since 1944, people have established themselves in places of new residence, and built industries and agricultural enterprises; the region has become a new homeland, a small fatherland, and an inseparable part of North Ossetia for thousands of Ossets, Russians, and representatives of other peoples. Suffice it to say that in the villages of Prigorodny, 99% of the houses were built by settlers after 1944. We still have not spoken about the fact that the lands of the Prigorodny *raion* never belonged to the Ingush (who lived here from 1921, after the expulsion of the Cossacks, until 1944). Thousands of Ossets and Russians, participants in World War II, and veteran workers found peace on this land for 50 years. It is not just the length of our settlement, but also the remains of our predecessors, that give us greater right to these lands than the Ingush (Author's files).

If the land issue was an important social problem, then its projection into the sphere of political and mass psychology became a question of territorial affiliation, or rather, administrative subordination. Land as a resource, not as a territory, became the subject of rivalry for the two communities. On both sides political figures and public activists argued vehemently about their right to possess the most valuable resources. For North Ossetia, the withdrawal of part of the Prigorodny *raion* from their control meant the loss of the most important portion of the agrarian complex. For the Ingush, it was quite impossible to create a republic with a sustainable economy without this territory. A factor of historical significance increased the appeal: most ancient Ingush settlements were found here, including the village of Angusht, from which the name 'Ingush' itself is derived. At least this is the version presented by Checheno-Ingush historiographers and other writings by Caucasus experts which in recent decades have been translated to mass consciousness on the level of established myth.

The outside observer cannot fail to be struck by the level of emotional involvement of the Ingush in the territorial issue. Practically all my meetings and conversations with local activists started and ended with this topic. On 9 September 1992, I had a meeting with Ingush elders and religious leaders of Prigorodny at the hotel 'Vladikavkaz'. I was asked questions with built-in answers: 'Don't you, Mr Minister, have your own motherland? But we, the Ingush, do not'; 'Is it possible to build a house without a foundation? This is why we cannot build our statehood without its basis – our people's historical land.'[5] The elders seemed deeply convinced of the wisdom and righteousness of their position, and were quite unaware that they were in fact parroting the same statements of the very activists who had called them for this meeting.

The collectively experienced trauma gave rise to a special sensitivity toward the territorial issue among repressed groups, and put a special halo around the idea of a 'homeland'. The following is a good example from contemporary writing by Ingush authors:

> Land onto which sweat and blood is abundantly poured, not only of ourselves, but also of our ancestors, is not abandoned under any circumstances. For generations this feeling only grows and strengthens – as is known to everyone, but not everyone naturally admits this to themselves at all times. And for others the sacred feeling of the inseparability of personal fate from a plot of land, which although not large, is the cradle of your forefathers and preserves your roots, means it is also your Motherland. For a person separated from this land, the thirst for justice subordinates all remaining feelings and sweeps aside other concerns; personal fate scarcely concerns him, but the desire to share his fate with the fate of his people becomes overwhelming, no matter how bitter it proves to be (Mutaliev et al., 1992, p. 13).

Beginning in the spring of 1992, the movement for an Ingush statehood took on a mass character and organized form. On 17 March that year, a group of local administrative leaders in Ingushetia and Prigorodny sent to the President of the Russian Federation, the Chairman of the Supreme Soviet, and the People's Deputies of the Russian Federation a collective letter with the following complaints:

1933 – 'they seized the administrative and cultural center of Vladikavkaz and turned it over to the Ossets';
1934 – 'they deprived us of statehood;
1944 – 'they took away our homeland and gave it to North Ossetia';
1957 – 'they didn't return half of our homeland and they left it to a particularly privileged Ossetia as a present, which has two statehoods: North Ossetia and South Ossetia, and Ingushetia does not have a single one.'

The document bristles with highly emotional remarks to inflame the popular consciousness: 'they will lead us to national degradation', 'the Ingush people are outside the law, outside the constitution; it is permissible to crush, rob and hack up their homeland', 'poverty and tyranny oppress Ingushetia'. The demand was 'to restore the historical homeland of the Ingush people with Ingush Republic status, with the administrative and cultural center in the city of Vladikavkaz' (Author's files).

Nazran, the largest population center of Ingushetia, became the hub of the national movement. Meetings and public gatherings of the Ingush, at which the most radical sentiments and suggestions were expressed, began here. Let me cite the record of proceedings of the 'national Ingush meeting' of 21 May 1992, at which several new motives were heard that had not been reflected in the official statements of Ingush leaders. One of these factors concerned relations with Chechnya, which continually lurked behind the scenes in the evolution of the Ingush–Ossetian conflict. At the meeting, the prevailing position of those who spoke was as follows: 'I am for a union with Chechnya, but an equal union' (Tamerlan Mutaliev, from Grozny); 'We are inseparable from Chechnya' (Magomet Dolgiev, from the village of Surhali); 'I am for a union with Chechnya one hundred percent' (Magomet-Khadzhi Barahkoev); 'I said that the people themselves headed by Dudayev will decide the Ingush issue' (Beslan Habriev, from the village of Troitskaya) (Author's files).

Also noteworthy were the calls for concrete, direct action to resolve the territorial issue. 'I am waiting for the Ingush people to understand that not only their enemies, but their own leaders, are leading them by the nose' (Issa Ozdoev, from Nazran); 'I propose the creation of detachments for self-defense in every village' (Hasan Ozdoev, from Nazran); 'There is a very good base for maintaining a national guard in the Sunzhenskii region. It is necessary to collect the means for forming them from the people' (Akhmet Tochev, from Troitskaya); 'We need to strengthen our position, create squads and arm them in order to protect law and order' (Mukhamed Gazdiev, from Grozny); 'The Prigorodny *raion* should be settled by its original inhabitants. We should not fear the Ossets. There were never men among them and there never will be' (Akhmet Malsagov, from the village of Maiskoe); 'As long as one Ingush lives, the Prigorodny *raion* won't belong to the Ossets' (Beslan Habriev, from Troitskaya) (Author's files).

From the above we could conclude that although the leaders had initiated the mobilization of group members, it might well develop independently of the control of these same initiators. Beginning in the summer of 1991, it was as though two parallel processes were at work: high-level progress was made in resolving the issue of creating a new republic; at the same time, another legitimacy was established on the grounds of directly delegated powers or usurpation of authority. Pressure from below exerted a powerful influence on the behavior of the leadership. Thus, the resolutions proclaiming an Ingush Republic at the Ingush Popular Congress on 27 March 1991, and at the Meeting of People's Deputies of all levels in Nazran on 20 June 1991, became decisive arguments for the adoption of the Law on the Formation of the Ingush Republic. Finally, on 30 November 1991, a referendum was conducted among the Ingush population, in the course of which 92.5% of those who voted (around 100,000 people) favored the formation of a sovereign Ingush republic within the RSFSR and the return of the Prigorodny *raion* and the part of Vladikavkaz on the right bank of the Terek River. In the referendum, the question was formulated as follows: 'Do you favor the creation of an Ingush Republic in the RSFSR along with the return of the illegally seized Ingush land and with a capital in the city of Vladikavkaz?' Conducting the referendum in this format undoubtedly exacerbated Ingush–Ossetian tensions and added a new incentive to the most radical demands of the Ingush.

On 5 February 1992, President Yeltsin introduced a draft law to the Supreme Soviet on transforming the Checheno–Ingush Republic into the Ingush Republic and the Chechen Republic of the Russian Federation. At the same time, a draft law was promulgated on the division of yet another autonomous formation – Karachai–Cherkessia – in two: the Karachai and the Cherkess Autonomous Oblasts. This draft law, initiated by a few radical activists together with Presidential adviser Galina Starovoitova, was likewise motivated by 'taking into account the will of the Karachai and Cherkess peoples'. However, it was not adopted, due to strong opposition on the part of the Karachai-Cherkess authorities, and the many possible complications involved in implementing such a division. Why then was the law on Ingushetia adopted, and what did it represent?

That the introduction of the draft law came from the President himself was a powerful argument in favor of its adoption by the Supreme Soviet. Substantiation of the law was based on a singular argument – reinstatement of the abolished autonomy of Ingushetia and creation of an Ingush statehood, of which they had been deprived in 1944. There were no calculations of the resource base, nor proposals regarding territorial borders of the new formation, although both these issues were critical. The following statements were found in the notes affixed to the draft law:

> The territorial issues are the most complicated. The Ingush demand the borders of the Ingush Republic be settled so as to include part of the Prigorodny *raion* (the 1944 borders), part of the Mozdokskii *raion* (which had been part of the Checheno-Ingush ASSR before 1944) of the North Ossetia Republic, and also Nazranovskii, Malgobekskii, and Sunzhenskii *raion*s (minus the territory of the Sernovodskaya Village Council) of the Checheno-Ingush Republic. Taking this into consideration, in our view, one would need a 3-year period to study the legal and organizational measures on national-territorial demarcation and to consider other problems, as well as to form a government commission, with the participation of all interested parties, for these purposes (Author's files).

On 4 June 1992, the Supreme Soviet passed the law almost unanimously and without discussion. As Anatoly Anikeev, Chairman of the Parliamentary Committee on Repressed Peoples, told me enthusiastically just before the session started: 'So, let's make a republic for the Ingush today. They have been asking for it for a long time. You as a Minister should speak in support of this law.'[6] This decision created a republic without borders, and permanently sealed the controversy over the text of the Federal Treaty on the impossibility of altering republic borders without consent. On the other hand, restoring autonomy to people repressed in the past was a positive move that was met with great enthusiasm by the Ingush. After the law was passed, a large group of Ingush present in this session went out of the Parliament building to take a group photo. Standing beside me, Khazbikar Bokov watched his joyful compatriots and gloomily remarked, 'They do not suspect that probably half of them have donned their shrouds today.'[7] He was right and wrong at the same time: in the next few months there were to be many deaths among the Ingush – but not from the group posing for the photo. Hope still remained that the recommendation to government authorities, parties and other public associations contained in the text of the law 'to abstain from unconstitutional methods of resolving disputed issues' would exert an influence on parties to the conflict.

8.5   The Politics of the Center in Ingushetia

Now that the law had been adopted, several steps had to be taken by the federal authorities to bring about its implementation. First of all, a temporary administration had to be established to begin constructing Ingush statehood. Vladimir Ermakov, People's Deputy of the Russian Federation, and General of the Army who retired after the events of August 1991, was appointed as the representative of the Supreme Soviet of the Russian Federation in Ingushetia. Isa Kostoev, an investigator of the Procurator-General of the Russian Federation, legal advisor (with the rank of a general), and an

Ingush by nationality, was appointed as the representative of the President of the Russian Federation in Ingushetia. Both of these 'Moscow men' were energetic, intelligent, and responsible individuals ready to work under difficult conditions. Their efforts to organize public life in the newly created republic were valuable, but various circumstances were to limit their work and prevent them from fulfilling their mission as representatives of federal authorities.

First of all, Ermakov and Kostoev received no effective support or provisions for their activities from the Center. There were no real financial resources or assistance on the part of the federal ministries or any public institutions. The ministerial representatives sent to Nazran to investigate the situation and prepare suggestions became bogged down in bureaucratic procedures of financial 'estimates and calculations'. The lack of routine lobbying in the federal governmental structures in favor of implementing economic and social-cultural programs for the new republic was keenly felt. The interministerial commission for implementing rehabilitation measures for Chechen and Ingush (one of the governmental commissions established for all repressed peoples in 1991, headed by Viktor Barannikov, Minister of Security until this became my responsibility in May 1992) acted only sporadically, especially after representatives of North Ossetia stopped participating in its activities. It lacked an organizational core and barely managed to conduct its day-to-day business. With hindsight, I can see that the coordinating role of this structure should have been strengthened. Perhaps I failed in my responsibility to ensure that this was so.

As far as the Ingush leaders were concerned, their efforts were limited by political fighting. After the adoption of the Law on the Formation of the Ingush Republic, this fighting became more focused around questions of authority. The Center appointed candidates to two positions, but the main job – provisional head of the administration – remained vacant. The arrival of Ermakov was first met with sharp negative reactions and threats on the part of local paramilitary fighters. Kostoev was accepted more quietly. Nevertheless, both were regarded as 'aliens' by the local leaders. Almost up to the very beginning of the open conflict, the representatives of the Center remained isolated in their efforts to do anything in this complex and agitated situation. Ingush activists extended the rivalry to the office of the provisional head of the administration; more specifically, the Ingush People's Soviet began to press to get Bogatyrev appointed to the still-vacant post. This situation also hindered the work of creating a government for the new republic, since the issue of who was to head the administration remained unresolved for so long.

Letters and petitions from regional groups and public meetings were delivered to Moscow in support of Bogatyrev. On 26 June, a joint session of Ingushetia's Soviets held in Nazran decided to: 'Request the President of the Russian Federation, Boris Yeltsin, to appoint People's Deputy of the Russian Federation Bembulat Bogatyrev as chief of the provisional administration of the Ingush Republic.' Heavy pressure was exerted on Yury Boldyrev, the head of the Control Department of the Presidential administration, who immediately prepared a proposal for Yeltsin to appoint Bogatyrev to this position. As Boldyrev explained to me, 'it is the explicit will of the Ingush people to have Bogatyrev; any other choice may cause an explosion'. I had very serious reservations about Bogatyrev, a man with little education, a tragic personal history (he had recently lost his son in an accident) and an emotionally unstable personality who constantly carried in his briefcase old maps of Ingushetia and assured me personally that 'after we get our lands back we will allow Ossets, Russians and others to live there'.[8] But I nevertheless wrote a formal letter to the President suggesting Bogatyrev for the position. At that time, the most important thing was to overcome the power vacuum and to get influential leaders engaged in constructive activity. However, the draft presidential decree on Bogatyrev was not signed: several influential people spoke out against it, possibly including Khasbulatov; it is also conceivable that Yeltsin could have known Bogatyrev from his work in the Supreme Soviet. Only toward the beginning of September did another candidate appear (at the sugggestion of Ermakov and Kostoev and supported by myself). This was Tamerlan Didigov, the Chairman of the State Committee on Building Construction of the former Checheno–Ingushetia.

Leaders of the People's Soviet of Ingushetia, headed by Seinaroev, tenaciously pressed for a meeting with Gennadi Burbulis and presidential assistants in order to push through the candidacy of Bogatyrev. An inconceivable event, in terms of normal government practice, took place: after Yeltsin's decree on the appointment of Didigov had been signed, a group of Ingush activists marched into the office of Korabelshikov, an assistant to the President, and under their influence Korabelshikov stopped the release of the decree – which was already signed! Thus, up to the beginning of the open skirmishes, this important post had not been filled.

Virtual anarchy was the result of these conditions of political upheaval and social crisis in Ingushetia. Financial and economic activity in Ingush regions was paralyzed after the separation of Chechnya. Here is the evaluation given by the local newspaper *Yedinstvo* (which ironically means 'unity'):

> The social-political situation in Ingushetia is strained to the limit. Social tension has sharply intensified. Plundering, robbery, murders, weapons trading, unrestrained speculation, car theft, stealing of personal and government property have become the norm. There is no one who can be entrusted with our personal safety (*Yedinstvo*, no. 7, September 1992).

The redistribution of land became a main issue. In the Sunzhenskii *raion*, for example, collective farm lands were distributed among residents of this and other regions as peasant (rural) farms ranging from 8 to 100 hectares in size.

> These lands are not cultivated for the most part, they are overgrown with weeds. At the same time, those who received these lands don't allow the cutting of hay on the territory adjacent to their possession (in ditches and on hill-sides), defending it with guns in their hands. As a result, arguments and fights occur which threaten to develop into full-scale conflicts (*Yedinstvo*, no. 7, September 1992).

Traditional structures, in the form of elders and leaders of family clans (*taips*) attempted to restore social control. A most alarming development was the revival of the custom of blood vengeance, further complicated by the fact that the traditional peace-making institutions which facilitated the reconciliation of those who had shed blood were forgotten. At this point, the gathering of elders, together with Hadji pilgrims, in the central mosque of Ordzhonikidzevskaya village reached a decision (*vaad*) to fight the transgressors of law and order and to stabilize the situation in the Sunzhenskii *raion*. To what extent the traditional social structure of the elders could replace the militia and courts is rather difficult to imagine and this issue has not been studied. It does seem reasonable to assume, however, that resurrecting the role of traditional social control, even in a partially modernized society, is extremely complicated if at all possible. Young Ingush men who traded weapons at the 'Kalashnikov stalls' of Nazran market in the summer of 1992 could scarcely be subordinated to *vaad*.

To the same extent, the *taip* (clan) structure also found a contemporary form, frequently shielding internal discord amidst Ingush politics and social rivalry. On 5 September, about 600 representatives of the *taip*s of Bogatyrev, Vedzizhev, and Dahkilgov, who profess to have a common ancestor by the name of Bohktar, gathered in Muzhich village. According to my information, this meeting of clan representatives resembled a kind of a micro- or proto-party. Deliberations on the higher interests of all the Ingush peoples and not just those of the *taip*s were accompanied by expressions of indignation against the 'Kostoev clan', whose representatives were preoccupied with denouncing the Bogatyrev *taip*s to the leadership of Russia. Those who stepped forward were united in not tolerating slanderous attacks on representatives of their *taip*s and in demanding that the culprits be made answerable. The gathering appointed a special delegation to 'record *taip*s' assaults of slander and denunciations which they will have to be called to account for' (Author's files).

The session of the People's Soviet of Ingushetia, that took place on 12 September in the village of Ordzhonikidzevskaya reflected the complicated situation facing the Ingush movement. The main political priority was formulated by Beksultan Sainaroyev, Chairman of the Ingush People's Soviet:

> The elections must be conducted only after the return of all Ingush territory. The main task is the return of the Prigorodny *raion*. When there will be a territory - there will also be a state. The capital of Ingushetia should be in Vladikavkaz, not Nazran. The will of the Ingush peoples is conveyed by all social movements: Bembulat Bogatyrev must be the chief of the administration. If Yeltsin doesn't confirm our candidate, we must elect him at the Congress (Author's files).

The loyalty to authorities in Moscow was combined with feelings of distrust and alienation toward the center, personified by the concept of 'Russia'. The language of the address reflected the persistent stereotype about machinations and anti-Ingush plans of the Russian authorities. The Ingush People's Council clearly aspired to acting as the exclusive representative; the Council was especially dissatisfied that inclusion of representatives of the 'Neeskho' party, whose leading activists were apparently from the Kostoev and Aushev clans, were included in the Coordination Committee. They were reminded of old injuries, including non-support for the demand of the return of the Prigorodny *raion* in the past, and a statement opposing the referendum. Finally, all efforts of the representatives of the federal authorities in Ingushetia were called into question: 'The presence of Russia's representatives here is illegal by itself. For whom have they come? We have no administration.' There were most likely people who were also critical of my own position, because a report of the meeting contains the following remark by Isa Khamatkanov: 'The People's Council does not work and has lost touch with the masses. Concerning Tishkov, it is Seinaroev who is more guilty than Tishkov' (Author's files).

A more radical and provocative variant of republic formation was formulated by the Ingush People's Council. In my personal files there is a draft plan on measures for realizing laws on 'Formation of the Ingush Republic' and on 'Rehabilitation of Repressed Peoples', given to me by one of the Ingush leaders. According to this draft plan, 'All homes and other private property, belonging to them by right of personal property at the moment of resettlement on February 23, 1944, are subject to return to their owners and settlements should change their titles'.[9] A paragraph on working out a plan for socio-economic development for the Ingush Republic appears only at the end of the list.

8.6   The North Ossetian Position

In North Ossetia, activities of the Ingush were carefully monitored. The strategy of rejecting compromise and of building a strong position accompanied by anti-Ingush propaganda was adopted. During my numerous conversations with Ossets, both with representatives of local authorities and with many residents, strongly negative stereotypes concerning the Ingush were heard: lazy, insidious, dishonest, trespassers and so forth. North Osset leaders felt quite sure of themselves, having closer contact with the Center, and a constitutional position on the inviolability of borders – including the decision made by Russia's Congress of People's Deputies on a moratorium against border changes for a period of up to three years.

There is evidence that a plan for ethnic cleansing – that is, Ingush expulsion from North Ossetia – was formulated within the republican leadership in the late summer of 1992. Such views were not expressed openly. However, Mark Deich, a correspondent of *Radio Svoboda* (Radio Liberty), broadcast a statement made by Militia Captain Vladimir Valiev, of the Chermensky village militia division, in his report from the conflict zone on 30 October:

> . . . closed meetings about the preparations for military action took place on Mondays for the past three months, usually in the office of Dzikaev, Chief of the Regional Department of Internal Affairs (ROVD). Either Minister Kantemirov or one of his deputies was usually present at these meetings. At the beginning of August, at a conference of officials of the Prigorodny *raion*'s ROVD, at which Minister Kantemirov was present, there was the following agenda: 'Concerning the commencement of intensified preparations for military action and tasks stemming from these.' The Minister claimed that the idea came from Moscow, and more specifically from Minister of Internal Affairs Erin. According to Minister Kantemirov, Moscow had promised the ministry higher salaries and all kinds of support in equipment and weapons in the case of successful implementation of these actions. The first results were already apparent by the next conference; in particular, they had increased the OMON staff [special-purpose militia detachments] from 200 to 1,000 people (*Ingushkaya tragediia*, 1993, p. 15).

According to the same source, the Ossetian police received the implicit order to find the smallest excuse to stir things up further with the subsequent involvement of Russian forces. Even the approximate date of armed provocations was worked out at the meeting on the last Monday of August, and it was agreed that a conflict should be provoked at the end of October, when the field-work was basically finished. In the first half of October, additional means were allotted even for an unconstitutional 'people's militia', and, in particular, armored personnel carriers (BTRs) were earmarked for Tarskoie and Chermen villages. Automatic weapons were also provided and a decision was made to hide the BTRs in the village of Olginskii for the time being. As Mark Deich reported, the coordinator of all these actions was Galazov himself and Kantemirov was his deputy (*Ingushkaya tragediia*, 1993, p. 16).

It is difficult to judge to what extent this account by Mark Deich is accurate; however, from personal observation I can confirm as a fact the organization and arming of a so-called national guard in North Ossetia. Galazov's car was escorted by 'national guards' while the two of us drove from Pyatigorsk to Vladidavkaz on 9 October 1992. Ingush activists from the Prigorodny *raion* informed me about the BTRs which appeared 'for defense purposes' in North Ossetian villages. In summer 1992 arms were seized and stolen from arsenals of the Russian army. By the time violent conflict broke out the

North Ossetian police had acquired 1,085 machine-guns, 113 anti-tank grenades, 11 artillery pieces, 36 war-armed vehicles and more (*Izvestia*, 25 January 1994). It is enough to recall the lack of response from Minister Victor Erin when, after returning to Moscow from Vladikavkaz on 10 October, I told him of my concern about the necessity of disarming the civilian population in a zone of potential conflict: 'What can I do if they do not carry out my orders there?' On the other hand, this does not necessarily lead to any conclusions about Moscow's initiative in the preparation of 'armed action'. I am well enough aware of the government's concerns with preserving the civil peace and preventing conflicts at that time. Most likely, what ensued was what had become normal for post-Soviet space: the demonstration of the arrogance of force in addressing conflict issues.

Among North Ossetian leaders it was the representatives of local power structures, with experience gained in the Georgia–South Ossetian conflict and now prepared for forceful operations, who particularly demonstrated the presumption of armed response to provocative Ingush claims. Having been involved in peace-keeping measures in South Ossetia, North Ossetia had become noticeably militarized and had established close contact with the federal power structures. Special residences of local leaders became the usual place for visiting representatives of the Russian authorities to stop over. Such hospitality made it more difficult for representatives of the Center to present a critical appraisal of the situation relating to the Ingush problem. The problems of refugees from Georgia displaced from the foreground the trouble growing inside the republic with the Ingush segment of the population, even though serious alarm signals began to ring out already in the spring of 1992. For example, five deputies of Ingush nationality of the Supreme Soviet of North Ossetia directed a letter to Yeltsin and Khasbulatov and to the Sixth Congress of People's Deputies of the Russian Federation in which it was said:

> The behavior of the Ossetian generals, who do not miss an opportunity to rattle their weapons once again, is particularly scandalous. Not a day passes without threats directed against the Ingush from the television screen, and those of them who live in North Ossetia are declared outright hostages (Author's files).

My last pre-conflict visit to the republic, and the meeting which took place on 9 October with members of the Presidium of the Supreme Soviet, confirmed the extremely negative attitude of local legislators to any kind of compromising policy with respect to the Ingush minority: these citizens were considered, unreservedly and exclusively, as 'aggressors' who were laying claims to Ossetian territory. The evening of the same day of my visit to Nazran, I arrived with three leading Ingush activists – Ibragim Kostoev (a member of the Supreme Soviet of the Russian Federation), Salim Akhilgov (an official of the Ministry of Nationalities) and Mogushkov (Chairman of the Nazran Regional Soviet) – at the dacha of the North Ossetian leader, Akhsarbek Galazov, and we all stayed for dinner with the top leaders of the republic. No serious conversation along compromise lines was to take place, however, especially since Galazov walked away from the dinner table, angered by arguments put at the table by Ingush visitors. This was probably the last missed opportunity to build a dialogue between the two parties.

8.7   The Violent Stage

The escalation of violence in the Ingush–Ossetian conflict has been well documented. On 20 October, in the village of Sholki in the Prigorodny *raion*, an Ingush schoolgirl was crushed by an armored troop-carrier of the North Osset OMON of the Ministry of

Internal Affairs. This outraged the village residents. On the night of 21 October, two Ingush were killed in the village of Yuzhny, also in the Prigorodny *raion*. That same day, a skirmish broke out between residents of this village and Ossetian police, in the course of which another seven people were killed and wounded on both sides. In Nazran, on 24 October, a joint session of three *raion* councils of Ingushetia and of a group of deputies from Prigorodny *raion* 'expressing the will of the Ingush people' passed a provocative resolution 'to organize volunteers into self-defense detachments and to monitor the situation in all Ingush settlements of the Prigorodny *raion* so it would be placed under the jurisdiction of the Ingush republic' (Orlov, 1994, p. 18). In response, the Supreme Soviet of North Ossetia proclaimed an ultimatum requiring the Ingush to surrender all weapons and to stop all militant activities; otherwise a military operation of the republican guard and militia would be mounted against 'intruders'. In this extremely tense situation, all Moscow did was to send a proposal for establishing a joint Ingush–Ossetian committee and for working out proposals relating to the disputed issues. Russian internal forces assumed the position of observers rather than enforcers of civic order.

During the few days prior to 30 October, villages with dense Ingush settlement saw sporadic skirmishes, which escalated into a mass armed conflict in Prigorodny *raion* settlements on 31 October. Groups of youths armed with rifles came forward in the fighting on the Ingush side, and there was no indication that this action was organized from a single center under the guidance of trained commanders. It was a spontaneous action, provoked rather than prepared in advance. Later on, in his public appearance before Russia's Supreme Soviet, Bogatyrev provided the following version of events:

> On the morning of October 30, Ingush boys armed with automatic rifles and hand grenades approached Ossetian armored personnel carriers. Their path was blocked by shelling from Russian armored personnel carriers. In this incident, two Ingush were killed and four were wounded. In the skirmish that ensued, the Ingush seized nine personnel carriers, disarmed their detachments and then occupied Ossetian posts that were bombing Ingush population centers daily.[10]

On 31 October, Vice Prime Minister of the Russian Government Georgii Khizha, Minister for Emergency Situations Sergei Shoigu, and the commander of the internal troops of the Ministry of Internal Affairs, General Eugeni Savin, arrived in Vladikavkaz. Khizha flew in from Moscow together with Sergei Khetagurov, the North Ossetian head of government, and on arrival was housed at Galazov's residence. He was briefed by local hosts, and his vision of the conflict proved to be strikingly one-sided: 'There are two peoples who have lived together for a long time and one of them is trying to solve its problem through military means', stated the Vice Prime Minister (*Severnnaya Ossetia*, 3 November 1992). The atmosphere was already extremely tense in the capital of the republic: demonstrators in the central square demanded that weapons be distributed to them, and on local television Galazov's address on 'Ingush aggression' was broadcast nonstop. Khetagurov demanded of the Vice Prime Minister that 15,000 machine guns be distributed among civilians. Perhaps it was Khizha's fatal mistake to give permission for the distribution of 600 machine guns to the Ossetian volunteers, a move that virtually sanctioned the most barbarous murders and arsons. According to some, Khizha coordinated this decision with Yegor Gaidar and Pavel Grachev. Sergei Shoigu, who had been cultivating friendly relations with Galazov since the spring of 1992, issued an order for the transfer of 57 T-72 heavy tanks to the command of the North Ossetian police. From that point on, the federal Center fully supported the one (Ossetian) side in the conflict, and began providing all the material and political conditions for executing mass violence against the Ingush minority. The large military units deployed to the conflict region failed to accomplish their main mission – separation of the conflicting parties. Instead they blocked off the border between Ingushetia and North Ossetia and even marched through Ingush territory toward the border with Chechnya. The Prigorodny *raion* fell under total control of the Ossetian paramilitary formations, including South Ossetian detachments. Journalist Irina Dementieva has analyzed President Yeltsin's message to Russian troops acting in the region and has come to the solid conclusion that the real target of the army was Chechnya (*Izvestia*, 27 January 1993). Later on, Yegor Gaidar also acknowledged this (see Chapter 10).

The representatives of Russian authority were unable to organize negotiations under these difficult circumstances or apply firm measures in defense of the civilian population. On 2 November an action was executed under the aegis of the regular army against those Ingush settlements which were defended by local residents. For several days there were mass killings, seizing of hostages, pillaging and arson of homes, and expulsion of the Ingush from Prigorodny territory and from Vladikavkaz. The state of emergency introduced in the territories of North Ossetia and Ingushetia by presidential decree of 2 November in no way limited the activity of the North Ossetian authorities. Ethnic cleansing was soon completed, with more than 40,000 citizens of Ingush nationality driven from the republic. Approximately 3,400 houses had been burned or destroyed; the number of casualties between 31 October and 5 November reached 350 Ingush and 192 Ossets, as well as 457 Ingush and 379 Ossets wounded, and 208 Ingush and 37 Ossets missing. About one thousand people were taken hostage by both sides.

The violence was particularly brutal. The main targets were male adults and young people but there were also women and children among the casualties. Both sides provided quite careful documentation, by photographing dismembered bodies and other atrocities committed during the fighting. Compared to the Central Asian experience in the Osh conflict where the main instruments of killing were knives, sticks, and stones, this conflict was characterized by the use of mechanical weapons, especially machine guns and hand grenades. A number of people were killed by federal and Ossetian troop shelling, with tanks and armored vehicles targeting Ingush homes. The dominant feature of the violence was the forceful expulsion of all Ingush from the territory of North Ossetia. Atrocities were committed not only in and around Ingush villages where armed Ingush fighters were concentrated, but in other areas of mixed settlements and in the capital city of Vladikavkaz where there were no signs of armed clashes. Ingush families were expelled from their apartments in Vladikavkaz and from their homes in rural areas.

During the week of open fighting and military activities the number of homes destroyed was actually rather small. Only afterwards did the Ossetian armed militia and 'national guard' implement systematic destruction of abandoned houses, seizing personal belongings. Sergei Khetagurov told me later how 'inventively' Ingush homes had been destroyed: 'Our men just opened the domestic gas system and then fired bullets inside from a distance, and the house blew up immediately.'[11] In some places, like the village of Tarskoie, there had been no clashes at all, but during the following weeks in November the Ingush section of the village was completely destroyed. Some evidence indicates that this destruction was carried out by an armed group from South Ossetia (Orlov, 1994, p. 23). Vandalism of property was meant to carry an explicit message to the Ingush: never to return to their former places of residence. Even after a state of emergency had been introduced and this area had been put under the control of the federal Provisional Administration, the destruction of homes continued. And the Ingush retaliated: in the first half of 1993 alone there were 143 Ingush and 88 Ossetian homes destroyed, testifying to the failure of federal control of the conflict area. Incidences of vandalism increased after President Yeltsin signed a decree to return refugees to their former places in December 1993/early 1994.

While individual houses were destroyed, apartments formerly belonging to Ingush residents were occupied by Ossets, many of whom had had to leave South Ossetia and did not want to or could not return. Thus, according to the human rights organization 'Memorial', which monitored the situation after the conflict, three apartment buildings in the village of Dachnoie had been occupied by Southern Ossets. But what is most striking is that some 800 apartments of Ingush who had been expelled from Vladikavkaz were occupied by Ossets working in the republican police: that is, by those directly involved in ethnic cleansing (Orlov, 1994, p. 24). This indicates that the inducement factor can be highly relevant in the ethnic cleansing phenomenon. Expected rewards in the form of valuable property could be a driving force behind the perpetuation of ethnic hatred and violence.

8.8   Winners and Losers

A major outcome of the Ingush–Ossetian conflict was the huge influx of refugees from the Prigorodny *raion* to the territory of the Ingush Republic. This conflict is still not resolved, so the possibility of another cycle of violence in the future remains open. Between 46,000 and 64,000 refugees have come to the small and economically deprived territory of Ingushetia, and about 70% of them are living with relatives. In February 1995 I observed in some houses in Nazran about 20–30 people (three or four families) living together without any permanent jobs and with children not attending school. Thanks to traditions of close kinship relations and of reciprocality, these people can perform all kinds of work and services to survive without starvation or strong social tensions. Displaced people have no wish to settle in the temporary shelters (*vagonchiki*) delivered and installed by the Federal Migration Service and by the Ministry for Emergency Situations because they are afraid that this may be interpreted as consent not to return home. After the first winter of hardships, some refugees moved to several temporary centers where they received humanitarian aid and small allowances from the authorities. During my latest visit to Nazran in February 1995 I could not obtain any statistics on the refugee problem from the government of Ingushetia, but President Ruslan Aushev complained that there was no way to manage the situation due 'to lack of resources and the prevailing feeling of despair and apathy among the new settlers'.[12]

By some estimates, 90% of the population still believe that the problem can be solved only by the President of Russia; 6% named the government of Ingushetia, 7% indicated the government of North Ossetia and no one suggested the refugees themselves (*Problemy Bezhentsev*, 1994, p. 21). In the meantime the 'Memorial' report points to how the local population are increasingly distrustful of the capability of the state to resolve their problem: 'If Russia cannot return us, let it withdraw its troops from here and we shall work things out with the Ossets with whom we have to live here' (Orlov, 1994, p. 29).

All attempts to solve the problem of expelled people immediately after the tragic events proved fruitless. Akhsarbek Galazov made a statement in November 1992 on the 'impossible co-habitation' of both groups in the territory of one republic. This formula was accepted by the local public, nor were there any protests or criticism on the part of Ossetian intellectuals. Likewise, the federal authorities showed no reaction to this speech of ethnic hatred. Political and criminal investigations undertaken by the Russian Security Council and the Prosecutor-General failed to generate any political conclusions or court cases. This was a whitewashing procedure to cover up irresponsible activities of the Center and the criminal behavior of local perpetrators of violence. Investigations failed mainly because the Ossetian authorities demonstratively blocked the work of prosecutors sent from Moscow. Local prosecution personnel were completely corrupt and strictly controlled by the top leadership. A similar situation was observed in the Ingush Republic, where all prosecutors were dismissed by the Prosecutor-General in June 1994.

It was not until December 1993 that Yeltsin summoned a meeting of all leaders of the North Caucasus and afterwards issued a decision to return refugees to four villages of the Prigorodny *raion* and to disarm all illegal formations in North Ossetia and Ingushetia. It was agreed at this meeting that the Ingush would retract any territorial claims, and that the Ossets would change their stand on the impossibility of Ingush and Ossets living together in North Ossetia. Agreement was reached to return refugees to the villages of Chermen, Kurtat, Dongaron, and Dachnoie before spring 1994. The emergency status for the region was prolonged several times and the acting Provisional Administration was assigned by President Yeltsin to implement this agreement in cooperation with the authorities of both republics. However, such cooperation was not forthcoming. This time North Ossetia demanded to undertake reconstruction work and peace-making procedures among citizens before allowing the expelled people to return to their villages. Viktor Polyanichko, Head of the Provisional Administration, was adamant in his insistence that the agreement and the Presidential decree be enforced. This was to lead to his assassination under unclear circumstances.

A new agreement on the return of refugees was reached between Galazov, Aushev, and Vladimir Lozovoi (new head of the Provisional Administration) in June 1994, but again it failed because of the obstructionism of the North Ossetian authorities. The latter mobilized the nationalist organization *Styr Nykhas* (People's Council) to call for public meetings to protest against the return of Ingush and demand they be allowed to live in only the one village – Maiskoie – from which Ingush had not been expelled during the conflict. The local press continued to disseminate anti-Ingush materials, and non-disarmed militants committed terrorist acts against those who dared to return to their native places. All efforts of the Provisional Administration to organize resettlement to four villages yielded only meager results.

About 3,000 Ingush still live in the village of Maiskoie along with about 1,000 Ossets. The village of Karza, where about 12,000 mainly Ingush lived prior to the conflict, is now populated by 900 Ingush, while about 350 houses stand empty because the authorities do not allow their owners to return. By August 1994, in Chermen – where prior to the conflict about 3,000 Ossets and 4,000 Ingush had lived – some 1,600 Ossets and 2,260 Ingush remained. Most of the Ingush returned immediately after the violent clashes of November. This indicates how the full-scale operation of ethnic cleansing was executed only some time after the end of open clashes, when the border between the two republics was blocked by Ossetian and federal authorities and Ingush could no longer return to their homes. There is another small village called Ezmi, near Vladikavkaz, where 300 Ingush live. In other villages, however, the Ingush were not allowed to return.

Who were the 'winners' of ethnic cleansing – winners, that is, besides those who seized property, or who rose to power positions, or acquired the reputation of defenders of national interests of the Ossets? Because a large-scale conflict generates huge problems for the state, the state reacts by producing bureaucracies to resolve these problems. The conflict stops being the property of the warring parties, and state interference becomes far more extensive than when there was actually a greater need for it. The Provisional Administration with a status of federal ministry established for resolution of the conflict was located in Vladikavkaz, staffed by a few hundred people recruited from Moscow and the local citizenry. With double salaries because of the state of emergency and with huge administrative expenditures, the staff soon began to view their mission as a kind of sinecure which is best prolonged. They operated in close contact with one side to the conflict and were considerably influenced by the Ossetian government and the public. During the three years it was active, the administration expended resources more than sufficient to build two houses for every expelled family and to rebuild destroyed communal properties and facilities. What a striking irony of ethnic conflicts – when a tragedy produces a response in the form of bureaucratic structures that may have played a greater role in exacerbating the conflict than in resolving it.

Notes

1   For a discussion on the use of the logic of collective action theory in Soviet-type societies, see Jerry Hough's article and others in *Journal of Soviet Nationalities*, Summer 1990, vol. 1, no. 2, pp. 1–65.

2   Personal communication with Khazbikar Bokov, 12 May 1992, Moscow.

3   Personal communication with Ruslan Khasbulatov, 20 February 1995, Moscow.

4   Personal notes, 19 May 1992, Moscow.

5   Personal notes, 9 September 1992, Vladikavkaz.

6   Personal notes, 4 June 1992, Moscow.

7   Ibid.

8   Conversation with Bembulat Bogatyrev, 27 June 1992, Moscow.

9   Author's files. (A list contained 12 settlements, among which Tarskoie was to be renamed 'Angusht'.)

10   Bembulat Bogatyrev's speech in the Supreme Soviet of Russia session, 6 November 1992. Author's files.

11   Conversation with Sergei Khetagurov, December 1992, Moscow. Khetagurov was subsequently appointed federal Deputy-Minister for Emergency Situations in Moscow after he lost the presidential campaign to Akhsarbek Galazov.

12   Conversation with Ruslan Aushev, 22 February 1995, Nazran, Ingushetia.

9

Ambition and the Arrogance of Power: the Chechen War (Part I)

9.1 Explanatory Models

How can we categorize and explain the Chechen crisis? One widely used approach involves conspiracy theory, where the presence of some powerful internal subtext or 'true causes' – most often oil and money – is cited to explain the development of the crisis. Eduard Ozhiganov, an expert at the Analytical Center in the State Duma, reasons:

> Today there exist only two lines for hauling strategic goods out of Russia – the Baltic route and the Caucasian one, which passes primarily through Chechnya. The entire struggle is for control over these two lines, or more exactly over the hauling itself. And therefore, any changes in leadership, personnel shifts, and conflict situations are nothing more than an expression of this struggle. . . . The roots of the conflict are not in Grozny but in Moscow. In the Baltic direction, the Russian state mafia has already felt out channels for carting out goods and raw materials, and big problems do not arise there. In Chechnya, however, the situation is fundamentally different. The Dudayev regime has not agreed to the role of 'client': it fancies the role of patron – the more so since the money involved is truly fantastic. 'Business' developed in three directions: trade in weapons, in petroleum products, and in stolen automobiles. In addition, there was the opportunity for uncontrolled export of hard currency from the republic and its subsequent distribution to accounts in foreign banks. Therefore, at a certain moment Dudayev's crew simply declared its exclusive right to all this income and blocked the 'Chechen channel' to Russia. This caused the crisis (*Obshchaya gazeta*, 9–15 February 1995, p. 5).

Undoubtedly, the economic factor, including its criminal aspect, did play an important role in the evolution of the Chechen conflict. The remark made by Sergei Shakhrai, Deputy Premier of the Government of the Russian Federation, regarding Chechnya as a 'free criminal zone' became well known. Comparisons of Chechnya and the Dudayev regime to the Medellin cartel in Colombia and to the regime of General Noriega in Panama set forth by Emil Pain and Arkadii Popov came from the President's Analytical Center (1995). In the annual Presidential message to the Federal Council, the 'criminal' nature of events in Chechnya had already become the official version of the federal authorities, or more correctly, of the President and his circle. In his speech to the Federal Council, Boris Yeltsin said:

> On the territory of the Chechen Republic as the result of an armed coup, there was established the most dictatorial kind of regime. The fusion of the criminal world and the regime – about which politicians and journalists spoke incessantly as the main danger for Russia – became a reality in Chechnya. This was the testing ground for the preparation and dissemination of criminal power to other Russian regions (*Nezavisimaya gazeta*, 17 February 1995, p. 1).

An analogous evaluation has been given by representatives of far-right nationalist forces in Russia. On 14 December 1994, the Central Council of Russian National Unity (Barkashkov's Party) adopted a declaration on the events in Chechnya which contains the following characterization:

> It is no secret that as a result of the activity of the Dudayev regime, almost all macro- and micro-economic activity in Chechnya practically ceased. The expansion of Chechen criminal groups throughout the territory of Russia was a consequence of this, which encouraged the present Chechen administration as practically the only economic activity bringing in income. The present Chechen administration has turned Chechnya into a parasitic, thieving conglomerate, and thereby lowered its people to the level of the early Middle Ages (*Russkii poryadok*, 1995, no. 1–2, p. 8).

Being rather sceptical about the 'criminal version', I cannot ignore some very recent journalistic investigations in this direction. Alexei Tarasov, in his article on the 'aluminium mafia' in Russia acting partly through a 'Chechen channel', formulated some reasonable questions: why did the chief curator of Russia's metallurgy industry, Deputy Prime Minister Oleg Soskovets, become unexpectedly in December 1994 a coordinator of military operations in Chechnya and why did the Russian army bomb first the National Bank and Ministry of Finance as well as Grozny's offices of Moscow's commercial banks, but not the 'gatherings of bandit gangs' (*Izvestia*, 12 July 1996, p. 4).

A second approach explains the conflict as an unsuccessful variant of a blitzkrieg against a self-proclaimed independent Chechnya. According to this interpretation, the war was staged by the Center, primarily by the Russian President and his circle, in order to carry out political tasks connected with strengthening and preserving power in conditions of deepening economic and political crisis in the country. This view of the Chechen crisis developed mainly among the political and intellectual opposition, notably on the liberal political side.

To politicians and experts of a more radical-democratic cast, Chechnya is a conspiracy of the 'enforcers', the closest aides and even the 'bodyguards' of the President, with the aim of ending the democratic transformations and establishing an authoritarian regime, based on 'Great Power politics' and national-patriotic ideology. As Yegor Gaidar declared, the forceful solution to the Chechen problem is a practical step toward the formation of a police state in Russia (*Moskovskie novosti*, 25 December 1995).'Hands off Chechnya!' remains the slogan of radical democracy, although the arguments of the latter have altered somewhat: at first sympathy in favor of 'national self-determination' for the Chechens predominated; then – after the beginning of the war – concern for mass violations of human rights, primarily by the Russian army.

Seeing the Chechen crisis as a manifestation of the national-liberation movement of the Chechen people which imperialist forces have attempted to suppress has been and remains highly popular among Russian and the overwhelming majority of foreign experts. The most substantial analysis of the history of the 'Chechen revolution' on the basis of such general categories as 'the people', 'freedom', 'sovereignty', 'the state', 'religion' has been given by specialists such as Lev Perepelkin. He concludes that the peculiar course of the recent political development of the Chechen Republic was predetermined by a 'unique combination of historical socio-economic, ethnic, demographic, psychological and other factors, by virtue of historical chance concentrated on precisely this small republic' (Perepelkin, 1994, p. 5). Nikolai Petrov, who has also analyzed the course of the war in Chechnya in terms of deeply geopolitical categories, expresses the unreserved opinion that 'the exit of Chechnya from Russia is now unavoidable in any possible course of events', because 'the Chechen people have paid for their freedom with blood' (Petrov et al., 1995, p. 21) .

Emotional and political involvement in evaluating the events in Chechnya has been demonstrated by many foreign experts, among whom a pro-Chechen position has become linked up with an unexpectedly strong recidivist anti-Russian position. A favorable attitude toward separatism in Russia remains characteristic of many former 'cold warriors', who continue, by force of inertia, to battle the 'Evil Empire'. For example, as a summary of the fact-finding mission sent to Chechnya by the London-based NGO International Alert in the autumn of 1992 a report was prepared (*Chechnia: Report . . .*, 1992), the main author of which was a researcher at RAND Corporation (USA), Paul Henze. This report set out the history of the Chechen and in general the North Caucasian 'liberation movement against Russian colonization', demonstrating the radical distinctiveness of the Chechens and their exclusive internal solidarity on the question of achieving state independence. Much of this line of interpretation stems from the Western historiographic tradition of Islamic studies in Russia, which was founded by an emigre historian of Russian origin, Alexander Bennigsen (Bennigsen & Wimbush, 1985). The basic conclusion of the International Alert report contained admonitions against attempts to resolve the conflict through force, but the overall tone was unconditionally favorable to Chechen independence as an accomplished fact. For Western experts like Paul Henze there was no doubt that in 1991 there had occurred a popular and democratic revolution led by Dudayev against the imperial Center and the local *nomenklatura*. The war of 1994–95 was the response from neo-imperial Russia.

The summary conclusion of the document, which for Chechen radicals became a kind of moral blessing to secession, states:

> The Chechen republic has made impressive beginnings in creating a state and governmental structures. Chechen society is characterized by a remarkable degree of political openness and freedom of expression. All parties bear responsibility for maintaining this favorable situation. In some ways, not surprisingly given the short time during which it has been evolving, the political system does not seem to be working smoothly. Legitimate questions about the validity of elections, parliamentary processes, relations between the branches of government, governmental openness, and relations between Chechnya and neighbors are continually raised by responsible citizens. The leadership needs to find ways of addressing these concerns. Chechnya cannot solve the problem of its status and relations with Russia and other components of the former Soviet Union by force. Russia cannot 'settle' its Chechen problem, or any of the broader related problems of stabilization of the Caucasus and any facilitation of constructive political evolution in the region by political intrigue or subversion, by armed intervention or by economic sanctions. The Russian government has a responsibility for keeping its own people informed of the true dimensions of Caucasian problems and the realistic choices that it confronts in trying to deal with them. Patience and negotiation are the only avenue all parties concerned with the difficulties of the region can follow to avoid further deterioration of the situation and tragedies possibly in human life and hope for a better future (*Chechnia: Report . . .*, 1992, p. 56).

Western analyses produced after the major war has started vary in their interpretations of the conflict: from the open fury at mass human rights' violations by the Russian military, which demand a more energetic reaction from the international community (see Dragadze, 1995), to detailed observations of the complexity of the situation that evolved from Soviet structural legacies, failures of leadership in Moscow and Chechnya, and the inability to use negotiations to resolve political disputes (see Hill, 1995, pp. 74–94).

Examples of re-evaluative reflections on 'anti-imperial' interpretations are rare among liberal-minded authors. A clear example of this critical re-evaluation was demonstrated by Pain and Popov, who posed the question of why Moscow politicians had worked to see Dudayev established in Chechnya:

> It seems that we are dealing not with personality as such, but with the idea which the rebellious general embodied and in accordance with which his heroic image was molded. We are speaking here of the idea of 'national-liberation' (i.e. separatist) movements of non-Russian peoples as some sort of natural and unavoidable form of realization of their democratic strivings. From the moment of the origin of the first 'national fronts' in the republics of the USSR, this idea was so popular among Russian democrats that it seemed that they were commanded not to notice the large and small sins of the nationalists, and forgive them first quiet illegalities, and then open force . . . And one had to be very blind or quite politically engaged in order not to see, behind the calls for 'a struggle for self-determination of the native peoples', an elementary desire on the part of local leaders freed from Moscow's hand to 'saddle' a complex of nationally deprived ethnic minorities to their aims, far from the interests of both democracy and national rebirth. Examples of similar political blindness dot the entire history of post-Soviet liberalism (*Izvestia,* 7 February 1995, p. 4).

Yet another approach is civilizational-ethnographic romanticism. This can be seen as a variant practiced by some scholars and often borrowed by politicians. Its essence lies either in the 'clash of civilizations', Islamic and Christian, or in the basic incompatibility of ethnic systems combined with the lack of understanding on the part of Russian politicians of the profoundly specific nature of Chechen society. As Aleksei Malashenko, an Oriental specialist, explains the situation:

> the Chechens have their way of life, their thoughts, their ideas of norms of behavior, and their faith. There a specific system of social institutions developed, which is called by ethnologist Yan Chesnov 'Vainakh democracy' . . . In the scheme of historico-philosophical juxtapositions of two socio-cultural systems, their mutual and constant rejection is inevitable. There was never any peace in Chechnya under any of the political systems . . . Chechnya, it seems, will always be strikingly different from Smolensk Oblast or Primorskii Krai. And therefore she will someday acquire her independence and, God grant, there will be on Russia's borders one more friendly state (*Nezavisimaya gazeta*, 31 December 1994).

With respect to Yan Chesnov, his version of contemporary Chechen society as based on deeply traditional social structures is an example of a widespread practice in ethnography, whereby a cultural complex is constructed by an outsider-professional, for whom field research mainly means writing a text with an indoctrinated informant (Chesnov, 1994a; 1994b). Sergei Arutiunov, a leading specialist on problems of the Caucasus, also tends to focus almost exclusively on the Vainakh military democracy in explaining the high degree of mobilization of the Chechens in the conflict (Arutiunov, 1995). This being said, these authors have also undoubtedly made serious contributions to an explanation of the Chechen crisis.

What I call ethnographic romanticism has a far deeper nature and degree of influence than it might seem. The Chechen crisis gave birth to a rich pseudo-scientific mythology about the history and modern aspects of the people. This mythology was spread from academic, literary and public-affairs texts to the mass consciousness, including that of the Chechens themselves. One dominant myth extolls the exceptionally freedom-loving and noble nature of the people as demonstrated over the entire course of their history, especially during their 200-year resistance to Russian colonialism. The nature of this myth is

a purely literary one, and among its chief authors we find a leading light of world literature, Leo Tolstoy. For him, the tale of 'Hadji Murat' was a kind of personal expiatory act
and the realization of a creative theme – the unmasking of autocratic despotism. Having
created the 'image of the other' in a person full of valor and nobility – the Chechen Hadji
Murat – Tolstoy was in fact writing about the problems of Russian society and the constant search for the human ideal amidst 'the nastiness of everyday life'. But with his
mighty pen, Tolstoy also gave 'an image of a people' to the modern generation of reading Chechens, which over time became absorbed into the mass consciousness. This can be
seen in the repeated appearance in explanations by academic romantics of stereotypes like
'the impossibility of the highlander being without a weapon', 'the national Chechen culture of military action', the lack of a tradition of submission to authorities or to written
law, the decisive role of the elders, etc. These beliefs are so deeply rooted that in an opinion poll this novella by Tolstoy was recommended as primary material for those who take
decisions on Chechnya (*Moskovskie novosti*, 1 March 1995, p. 2).

Another firmly entrenched myth concerns the exceptional antiquity of the Chechen
people, which derives its arguments from the historico-linguistic research of scholars in
Moscow and St Petersburg (and following them, local scholars) about the kinship
between the Khurrito-Urartic languages disseminated during the Second and First
Millennia BC in the Transcaucasus, Eastern Asia Minor and Northern Mesopotamia,
and modern Vainakh languages. Citing this purely academic postulate, President
Dzhokhar Dudayev formulated the political slogan that the Chechens as 'the most
ancient people of the Caucasus' should by right play the role of leader for all the
Caucasus (see Dudayev's statement in *Ternistyi put' k svobode*, 1992, pp. 15–16).

Independent of the politico-ideological motivation underlying all these interpretations there is the limited nature of the objectivist methodology, which prefers to delve into
the social process (or into the course of events) until it can hit on some profound causes
and historical regularities. This approach ignores any explanation based on a modern personal strategy and individual motivation; or on the role of a constantly changing
disposition of participants in social space, including the sphere of power relationships; or
indeed, on the role of accidental, emotional-subjective, and moral impulses and actions.
A major societal event, and even more so a major military conflict, is considered too serious a phenomenon to have its origin explained by such 'superficial' circumstances as the
personal ambitions of leaders or the search for vengeance after a collective trauma.

Along with a powerful historico-cultural and sociopolitical dimension, the Chechen
conflict, in my opinion, contains decisive elements of individual, emotional, and moral
influence, elements which cannot be explained by the usual categories of positivistic
causality. One example of the highly personalized character of the conflict – especially at
a decisive moment – is seen in the personal relationship between President Yeltsin and
Dudayev. In a private conversation on 15 August 1996, the President of Tatarstan,
Mintimer Shaimiev, made an important remark: 'While visiting Tatarstan in March 1994,
Yeltsin told me that, in spite of not all at the Security Council agreeing with him, he was
ready for talks with Dudayev on the Tatarstan model. But then suddenly the press
reported (probably it was done deliberately) that Dudayev was speaking negatively of
him'. Apparently from that moment on, Yeltsin (undoubtedly under the influence of aides
and some members of the government who were nursing the presidential ego) crossed
Dudayev off the list of those with whom he could somehow communicate and placed him
in the ranks of the main enemy after the others were smashed or pacified. The best confirmation of this thesis is the testimony of yet another politician who had contact with the
Russian President. Valery Vyzhutovich, the *Izvestia* correspondent, asked the Director of
the Federal Security Service (FSK), Sergei Stepashin, what question the President

addressed to him most frequently in recent times. The answer was – 'most frequently the same one: "When will you catch Dudayev?" ' (*Izvestia*, 2 March 1995, p. 4).

I would like to pursue this aspect of conflict analysis as the dominant line in looking at the sequence of events and the socio-cultural context. We cannot understand the war in Chechnya, especially its internal logic, intensity, and dramatic nature, without looking at the factor of the influence of modern mass media on the conflict: this was the first 'television war' in the territory of the former Soviet Union. What interests me here is not so much the problem of the 'illumination' of the conflict in the mass media, as the problematic role of the mass media as participants in the conflict once the professional creators of electronic images and newspaper texts have created a version (or versions) of the conflict in dramatically marketable forms and then return these versions to the participants themselves – influencing not only their attitudes but also the behavior of the participants, at times more strongly than military orders. In my interview with the commander of the 'Afghan battalion' in Chechnya, Ballaudi Movsaev, the field commander repeatedly mentioned radio and television ('although we don't have it on the front lines'), implicitly confirming the role of the mass media as an active participant in the drama taking place. As an example of the complete trust people had in the mass media, Ballaudi declared: 'If the politicians say, announce on the radio . . . that they've stopped the war, that I have to give up my weapon, . . . I will go and give up the weapon.'[1]

In contemporary conflicts, electronic mass media constitute an enormous mobilizational and fighting force. This is just as much a military resource as tanks and artillery, for with the help of television and the press, crucial goals can be achieved – such as instilling a military spirit in rank-and-file soldiers, and recruiting public (including international) support. After unsuccessfully adopting the outdated practice of air-dropping leaflets, the head of the FSK Sergei Stepashin made a characteristic admission: 'Yes, the Russian regime has lost the information war. How brilliantly the Chechen Minister of Information Movladi Udugov works, how artfully and easily he releases to the press any lie, distortion, fact-juggling! . . . But we push away the journalists: We are not releasing anything anywhere, we are not giving anything! And I myself for a long time did not want to express myself' (*Izvestia*, 2 March 1995, p. 4).

The mass media play a special role in post-Soviet conflicts. Citizens have become accustomed to and continue to believe in that version of events and judgements which bears the mark of authority of the television screen or a newspaper page. Moreover, post-Soviet citizens are a literate population of avid readers. This means they subject themselves to the influence of external versions much more strongly than the inhabitants of, say, Somalia, Mexico, or India, where open conflicts and internal wars also take place. In this respect we can compare only other former socialist countries, including Yugoslavia, with the former USSR. Finally, in Russia the perestroika years gave birth to a new generation of young and ambitious journalists who sought to affirm themselves through the motif 'the conflict and me'. As yet, Russian journalism lacks any generally shared code of ethics applicable to its presentation of conflicts and wars.

9.2   Chechnya and the Chechens

It is important to understand the historico-cultural aspect of the conflict, although this by no means determined the essence and form of the current Chechen crisis. History is first of all a mobilized resource in the adopted stands and argumentation of contemporary actors in social space. References to history, including to the distant past, reappear in the arguments of opposing sides. This is especially the case with ethnic conflicts, because the national/ethnic consciousness is primarily the mobilized collective memory shaped by intellectuals as 'the history of the people'. The commonly shared version of the past serves as a necessary resource for consolidating an ethnic group, and is frequently one of the main arguments used in formulating modern demands or claims. Members of a group will usually hold a firm faith in the historical justice of their cause, even if each separate individual may recall only the history he himself has experienced, which may be far from heroic or tragic. 'Historical memory' (a term often used but devoid of scientific meaning), or more properly the mobilized past, becomes a powerful resource when dramatic collisions occur in contemporary lives, touching the fate of all members of the group. This is precisely what happened to the Chechens, who 50 years ago experienced the collective trauma of deportation, and among whom almost the entire older generation remembers the time of exile and humiliation.

The actual origin of the Chechens is rather obscure. Apparently, the indigenous communities, later called Chechens, arose on the basis of a group of autochthonous population which incorporated different North Caucasian cultural components. Some Chechen *taip*s trace their origin to the Cossacks who fled to Chechnya and joined the Shamil's army during the early 19th-century Caucasian War. The first inhabitants of these territories are mentioned in a 7th-century Armenian source under the name *Nakhchamat'ian*. The Kumyks called them *Michigish*, the Kabardins *Shashen*, the Ossets *Tsatsan*, the Avars *Burtiel*, and the Georgians *Kisty*. The Russians originally called the Chechens *Okochany*, *Akkintsy*, and finally their present name, which comes from the name of *Chechen-Aul*, a village at the foothills near Grozny. The historical territory of Chechnya can be divided into main parts. There is the southern, mountainous Bolshaya ('Great') Chechnya between the Argun River in the west and the Aksay River in the east, with its southeastern highland part (known as Ichkeria); and there is Malaya ('Little') Chechnya which lies to the west and north-west of the Argun river and includes both highland and lowland territories. It borders on Ingushetia in the west and includes Nadterechny *raion* – a territory between the Terek and Sunzha Rivers. Before the 15th–16th centuries, the Chechens lived basically in the mountains, forming separate territorial-political groups: *michikovtsy* lived on both banks of the river Michik; the *kachkalykovtsy* on the northeastern slopes of the range with the same name; the *aukhovtsy* in the upper reaches of the rivers Yaryks, Yamans, and Aktash; and *ichkerintsy* in the central section of the mountainous area. According to popular legends, the first settlements on the plains were founded by mountain people from the Akka Mountains at the end of the 16th century. By 1587, Russian ambassadors noted a significant number of settlers named Okot people (*akkintsy*) by the Sunzha River and near the Terek River. In 1760, the Chechen village of Stara-Yurt arose at the mouth of the Sunzha. A great many Chechen-Orstkhoy lived along the River Karabulak, which runs between Malaya Chechnya and Ingushetia.[2]

In the 17th and 18th centuries, the North Caucasus, including the territory of Chechnya and Ingushetia, was a sphere of military and political competition for the Russian and Ottoman Empires and Persia. On the left 'northern' bank of the Terek, there arose a system of Cossack settlements and fortresses, and then the so-called 'Caucasian military line' from the Caspian Sea to the Sea of Azov. Russian military penetration into the North Caucasus and the economic colonization of its territory damaged the interests of the mountain peoples. In 1785–91, in the territory of Chechnya and other regions of the North Caucasus, there was an armed struggle under the leadership of Ushurma (Sheikh Mansur), directed against the tsarist administration and the local mountain princes. Mansur, a proponent of 'pure' Sufi Islam, called for a *hazavat* – a holy war – against the mountain pagan 'unbelievers,' who held to the more traditional norms of *adat* (Muslim customary law), and, finally, against tsarism.

Calls for asceticism, moral purification, and unification of the mountain peoples received wide support among the poorest parts of the population who were tormented by constant inter-clan (*taip*) strife, the requisitions of local feudal lords, and the attacks of Russian colonists. A victory for the mountain peoples in their first battle with a detachment of the tsarist army gave Ushurma authority and a large number of supporters. From a spreader of Islam among the mountain peoples of the North Caucasus, he became a military and political leader. Over the next few years he led an armed struggle in the regions of Chechnya, Daghestan, Kabarda, and the Kuban. After several defeats, Mansur was taken prisoner and sentenced to life imprisonment in Schluesselburg Fortress, 'for raising the people of the mountains against Russia and causing great harm to the empire' (Akhmadov & Akaev, 1992, p. 5).

From the early 19th century, the Chechens attacked border settlements and military posts, despite having repeatedly sworn allegiance to the Russian tsar. Attacks increased, especially after the borderline was moved to the Sunzha River in 1817–21, which deprived the mountain people of part of their land. The year 1817 is considered the beginning of the Caucasian War, which the natives conducted under the leadership of the religious figures Kazi-Mohammed, Gamzat-bek, and Shamil (see also Bennigsen, 1992; Henze, 1958). One of the headquarters – the *aul* (non-Russian village) of Vedeno – was in Chechnya. Chechnya was also an important provider of weapons, powder, and grain for Shamil. After the Russians seized the *auls* of Akhul'ga and Dargo, Shamil moved from Daghestan to Chechnya. In 1846, Shamil managed to break through Russian positions and entered Kabarda. However, the very limited support, if not even hostility, he received there ruined his plans to expand the war and caused him several serious defeats. This march to Kabarda marked the beginning of the decline of Shamil's state and armed force.

By the end of the 19th century, there were about 200,000 Chechens. A staple economy for the Chechens living on the plains was plow agriculture. Chechnya was one of the leading grain-producers of the North Caucasus, growing corn, winter wheat, barley, and millet. Orchardry was developed, but little attention was paid to vegetable farming. In terms of livestock, cows, oxen, and buffalo predominated. Horses were bred during the years of the Caucasian War for the needs of Shamil's army, but horse-breeding began to decline after that. In the first half of the 19th century, there was free land tenure within the commune on the plains. In the mountains, the main activity was pastured sheep-herding (sheep being kept all year round on grass), and terraced agriculture. Any plowlands and hayfields there were privately owned, whereas the forests and pastures remained community property. Barley and millet were the leading mountain crops, and vegetables included onions and garlic. Throughout Chechnya there was bee-keeping.

Chechen crafts included inexpensive felt cloaks (in demand among the Cossacks), and felt carpets, cloth-making, and the working of skins. In the settlements of Staro-Yurt, Novo-Yurt, Shali, and elsewhere, pottery was developed. Weapons, copper bowls, platters and pitchers, and silver articles were made in Starye Atagi, Vedeno, and Shatoi. From the 1820s on, oil was extracted from the territory of Chechnya. By 1917, there were 386 wells in operation, but very few Chechens were working in the oil industry.

Social stratification was not pronounced among the Chechens. The plains-dwelling peasants were somewhat less independent, since in the 18th and 19th centuries a number of feudal lords mainly from Kabardin nobility were settled here. Although Shamil had declared the abolition of any dependence, his *naibs* oppressed and robbed ordinary mountain people. The Chechens had small numbers of slaves (*yasyri, lai*), who were outside Muslim customary law (*adat*). The Muslim clergy played a definite role in community life.

There existed among the Chechens (and still exist in part) large kinship groups – *taip* – and smaller groups (10-15 households) – *nek'e* or *gar*. Sometimes several *taip*s were united into a *tukhum*.

Before the 1917 Revolution, Chechnya formed part of Terskaya *oblast*, along with Khasaviurtovskii *okrug*, settled by Aukhov Chechens and Kumyks. The establishment of Soviet power in Chechnya was accompanied by fierce civil strife. In August 1917, a congress of Islamic religious figures held in the *aul* of Andi (in Daghestan) elected Sheikh Nadzhimuddin (Gotsinskii) as imam of Daghestan and Chechnya. Allied with Sheikh Uzun Hadji, he began to create a religious monarchy made up of Daghestan and Chechnya. They later collaborated with the Bolsheviks against the White Army of General Denikin. In the autumn of 1919, Sheikh Hadji proclaimed Chechnya and the northwestern part of Daghestan the 'North Caucasian Emirate.' His goal was to create a theocratic state similar to that of Shamil over half a century earlier. Hadji is said to have proclaimed, 'I am weaving a rope to hang engineers, students, in general all those who write from left to right' (Bennigsen & Wimbush, 1985, pp. 24–25). After the death of Hadji in May 1920, some Chechen leaders supported the Bolsheviks; by 1922, the organized movement against the Bolsheviks had ceased. In November 1920 at a congress of peoples of Terskaya *oblast* held in Vladikavkaz, the Gorskaya Autonomous Republic was formed, containing Chechnya and Ingushetia as Chechenskii and Nazranskii *okrug*s. The Chechen territorial autonomy was first created in 1922 as part of the RSFSR, and part of the land taken from Chechnya in the Caucasian War was returned. In 1924, the Gorskaya Republic was dissolved, and the Ingush Autonomous Oblast was formed on part of its territory.

The first years of Soviet power saw the introduction of clerical work and teaching in the local native languages. Other positive changes included the creation of written languages for the Chechens and Ingush, although the first primer for the Chechen language based on the Russian alphabet had been compiled in the previous century by the Chechen Kedi Dosov with the help of a Russian linguist and specialist on the Caucasus, P. K. Uslar (Uslar, 1869). Before 1920, fewer than 1% of the Chechens were literate. The policy of 'nativization' involved mass teaching of literacy to Chechens, who were promoted to many prestigious positions. In 1934, the Chechen and Ingush Autonomous Oblasts were united into the Checheno-Ingush Autonomous Oblast, which in 1936 was granted the status of an autonomous republic within the RSFSR.

Forced collectivization which began in the 1920s caused great damage in Chechnya, as it was accompanied by massive confiscation of livestock and agricultural tools. The mountain regions were also subjected to collectivization; raising livestock with alternating summer and winter pasturing was declared 'reactionary' because it required a semi-nomadic lifestyle. The Soviet regime began to persecute religion and repress those working at the mosques and Islamic schools.

The first large-scale 'pacification' of Chechnya was conducted by detachments of the Red Army in the summer of 1922. Three years later, between August and September, 16 settlements were bombed, and more than 100 subjected to artillery strikes; 119 homes were burned; 25,000 rifles and more than 4,000 revolvers were confiscated. In December 1929, the Red Army and the secret police again had to suppress a Chechen uprising with the help of armored cars and planes. The next big operation came in the spring of 1930. More than 3,500 soldiers of the North-Caucasian Military District took part; 1500 rifles and revolvers were confiscated; 19 people were killed, and 122 were arrested. To quote the report of the military district staff: 'The experience of the operation remains unstudied. The mistakes of the first campaigns were not only repeated, but intensified . . . Since we learned nothing from the past, we repeat the previous mistakes, and again have no decisive successes, allowing the bandits to get away unpunished, thereby undermining the authority of the Red Army' (Aptekar, 1995, pp. 1–2).

Up to the beginning of World War II, the local population engaged in various forms of resistance, including open demonstrations and desertions from the Red Army, particularly when the war with Germany began in 1941. We can find an evaluation of this resistance in the report of the Division of Special Settlement of the NKVD of the USSR dated 5 September 1944:

> . . . Concerning the Checheno-Ingushy. At the beginning of the 1930s, there was created in the region a real threat that significant masses would be drawn into a rebellion. A number of serious Chekist-military operations with the support of artillery and planes were conducted in March-April 1930 to liquidate this counter-revolutionary movement. In 1932 an armed uprising of more than 3,000 persons was organized, which embraced all the *auls* of Nogai-Yurt *raion* and a number of other *auls*. At the end of January 1941, in Khilda-Khara, Itumkala *raion*, an action against the Soviet regime was provoked, in which the local inhabitants took part. In this period desertions from the Red Army on the part of Chechens and Ingush acquired mass character. From July 1941 to April 1942 from among those called up into the Red Army and work battalions, more than 1,500 deserted, and more than 2,200 persons refused military service. From one native cavalry division, 850 persons deserted . . . (Bugai, ed., 1994, pp. 28–29).

At the beginning of World War II, the Chechens were the most numerous group among the North Caucasian nationalities (if we exclude the Russian population of this region). One of the demographic characteristics of this people can be seen in a rapid natural increase, especially in recent decades (Table 9.1). According to the first Soviet census in 1926, about 318,000 Chechens were living in the RSFSR, including 291,300 in the Chechen Autonomous Oblast, meaning that more than 90% of the Chechens were densely settled on the territory of this autonomous area. Another group of Chechens (*akkintsy*) were living in the neighboring region of the Daghestan ASSR (21,900) and a small number in the Ingush Autonomous Oblast (2,600). The 1937 census lists only the total number of 'Checheno-Ingush' (435,900) throughout the Russian Federation. In the Checheno-Ingush ASSR itself after the unification of the two autonomies in 1934, the percentage of Chechens and Ingush by this time had declined markedly (65.1%), partially because of the increase in the number of Russians, who numbered 189,100 (28.6%) in the republic in 1937. At the time of deportation in 1944, Chechens numbered approximately 400,000 persons.

Table 9.1   *Chechens on the Territory of the Russian Federation*

	1926	1937	1939	1959	1970	1979	1989
Total population	318,373	435,922	400,344	301,311	572,220	712,161	898,899
Urban (%)	–	1.0	7.9	14.3	20.2	24.2	26.9
Rural (%)	–	99.0	92.1	85.7	79.8	75.8	73.1

Source: Compiled from USSR census data

9.3   The Trauma of Deportation

The total deportation of Chechens and Ingush started on 23 February 1944 and was completed in only a few days. This is illustrated by Lavrentii Beria's telegram to Stalin dated 29 February 1944:

> I report the results of the operation of resettling Chechens and Ingushi. The resettlement was begun on February 23 in the majority of *raions*, with the exception of the high-mountain populated points. By 29 February, 478,479 persons were evicted and loaded onto special railway cars, including 91,250 Ingush. One hundred and eighty special trains were loaded, of which 159 were sent to the new designated place (Bugai, 1994, p. 51).

In July 1944, Beria reported to the Kremlin that 'in February–March 1944, 602,193 residents of the North Caucasus were moved to the Kazakh and Kirgiz SSRs, including 496,460 Chechens and Ingush, 68,327 Karachais, and 37,406 Balkars.' (Bugai, 1994, p. 85) The Chechens and Ingush were moved to Kazakhstan (400,600) and to Kirgizia (88,300), where they were scattered (Bugai, 1994, p. 59).

Deportation led to significant demographic losses. In addition to those who died from disease and other deprivations during resettlement, the decline in the number of 'special settlers' in the period of 1945–50 continued because of a significant excess of deaths over births. Among those deported from the North Caucasus during this period, 104,903 died but there were only 53,557 births (p. 63). According to the 1959 census, the number of Chechens in the USSR was 419,000. The indirect losses for the 15 years after deportation among the Chechens can be thus put at about 200,000 persons.

After the exiles returned to the territory of the restored Checheno–Ingush Republic, there was a sharp increase in population: 46.3% in 11 years! Some specialists explain this by the fact that during the period of deportation the oldest and weakest part of the population died, so that the majority of those who returned were young and of reproductive age (*Chechnia: Report . . .,* 1992, p. 26). In 1970, there were 612,674 Chechens in the USSR, in 1979 there were 755,782, and in 1989 the number was 958,309. The last census reports 898,899 Chechens living in the Russian Federation, including 734,500 in Checheno–Ingushetia, about 58,000 in Daghestan, 15,000 in Stavropol *krai*, 11,100 in Volgograd *oblast*, 8,300 in Kalmykia, 7,900 in Astrakhan, 6,000 in Saratov, 4,600 in Tiumen *oblast*, 2,600 in North Ossetia, and 2,100 in Moscow. The latter figure has risen significantly in recent years; the real number of permanent and temporary Chechen residents of Moscow is about 30,000 persons.

Some Chechens have continued to live in Kazakhstan (49,500) and in Kirgizia. These were generally people who had managed to adapt during the years of deportation, particularly professionals, and also residents of some relatively prosperous rural communities. Many of them live in ethnically mixed families.

According to the 'official' national myth, repeated in numerous scholarly texts and in political declarations, the dominant idea was the exceptional love of the Chechens and Ingush for their primordial homeland and the graves of the ancestors. This is often called a 'trait of national character', and so forth – although science recognizes neither the category of 'national character' as such, nor (especially) the above-mentioned traits as empirically established distinguishing attributes of any one ethnic group. In ordinary rhetoric, such traits of 'national character' are ascribed to, or more correctly, *self*-ascribed by every people. Yet for all this, despite the mythological quality of this thesis, we cannot deny the feelings of nostalgia and the strong urge to return to the place of age-old habitation which were shown by the deported peoples. Highly relevant here was the need to return to the accustomed natural and cultural milieu in which the basic daily activities of the Chechens were carried out. Resettlement from the mountains and foothills to steppe regions, the almost complete change of economic activities, the destruction of social ties and a new cultural setting – all of this, under conditions of a semi-prison-camp regime and continuing repression, could not but give rise to intense longings for the homeland.

The process of return took on a sacred character and a form of persuasive collective will. One example from a life history connected with 'late' return was told to me by an Ingush, Isa Buzurtanov, but can be applied in equal measure to Chechens. After the dissolution of the regime of special settlement in Kazakhstan, Isa, having graduated from a technical secondary school for construction workers, settled in Abakan (Khakassia) with his wife and four children. There he held a good position, got an apartment, built a dacha, and was satisfied with his life. At home they tried to speak only in their native language, although they all knew Russian well, and they also upheld some Muslim customs. The return to Nazran occurred for family reasons: a younger brother living with the parents in Ingushetia had almost completed the construction of a very spacious and comfortable house intended to accommodate his future family, but he was killed in an automobile accident. It was more an obligation to his parents and the inheritance of a solid piece of property than the pull of the homeland which probably made Isa leave southern Siberia.

> For the first years in Nazran it was hard for me to become accustomed to the local norms and conditions of life: almost every year I tried to go back to our former place. Here I have to submit to too many community demands and traditions, but there I was freer. But what is most important, our children do not receive a tenth of the education here they could get in Abakan schools. And now because of these conflicts, they are hardly studying at all.[3]

Isa is an enterprising, intelligent person. He has his own small business along with the post of chief of a construction department of the Ingush government and, even under the conditions of local economic collapse, he has managed to secure a good standard of living for his family. Two days spent as a guest with this family in their lavish house convinced me that the inflammatory political rhetoric about independence and territories, and especially the armed conflicts in the Prigorodny *raion* in 1992 and later in Chechnya, posed a threat to his personal well-being and working plans. Thus, he strongly opposed such polices and disliked 'agitators'. Similar motives were heard in almost all my private conversations with local residents. The exception was the hall where a conference took place, devoted to the 51st anniversary of the deportation of the Chechens and Ingush. Here I heard inflammatory speeches and accusations against 'imperial Russia,' mainly from the mouths of scholars and politicians arrived from Moscow.

9.4　Building Chechen Disloyalty

After their return from exile, many Chechens retained a mood of social and political dissatisfaction, as well as a relatively higher level of criminality, provoked primarily by the consequences of deportation and the socio-economic problems of re-establishing the republic. Chechnya and the Chechens, along with the Ingush, remained the object of special attention for Party organs, and also the KGB and MVD of the USSR, which continued to consider them insufficiently 'loyal' to the regime and prone to 'nationalistic prejudices'. For example, on 30 April 1966, the chairman of the KGB, Vladimir Semichastny, sent a document to the Central Committee of the CPSU about 'the revival of nationalistic and chauvinistic [!] manifestations' among the intelligentsia and young people of the Checheno-Ingush ASSR and the increase in cases of inter-ethnic dissent, which 'frequently grew into group incidents and excesses'. This document notes several examples of the 'dissemination of anti-Soviet slanders against the Communist Party and the nationalities policy of the Soviet Union'. In particular, the statement of A. Vedzizhev, a member of the CPSU and a management executive of the main oil pipeline station, is cited in conversation with Professor D. Mal'sagov: 'The whole world is waking up, everyone is talking about independence . . . there remains only the colonial East of Bolshevism, where there are no rights at all . . . I swear to you, there will come a time when we will have to cut out the Communists. People are dissatisfied with the current situation' (Author's files).

The KGB chairman reported that 'individual representatives of the creative intelligentsia in their works and private conversations insinuate politically harmful judgements'. As an example, he cited the well-known Ingush writer Idris Bazorkin (also a member of the CPSU) in conversation with a friend:

> Russia pretends that the national republics are independent. . . . Abroad it's correctly said that we have a system of state capitalism. This is thought to be a hidden form of colonialism. . . . I feel an urge to write down the whole list of calamities and misfortunes which Russia has brought to this people. . . . Let no one speak there of national independence and national sovereignty, but all native peoples feel the spiritual oppression from the Russians (Author's files).

Semichastny also wrote that among Chechens and Ingush there were 'hostile attitudes towards people of other nationalities living in the republic, especially the Russians, and attempts to crowd workers not from the local nationalities out of leadership positions'. He further noted the tendency of 'nationalistically inclined persons' to focus on young people, whom they see as a force capable of occupying leading positions in the republic and making it 'theirs'. Even at that time, one of the manifestations of local discontent was the question of returning Prigorody to the republic. Representatives of the intelligentsia and the Muslim clergy, 'using memories of the past, attempted to ignite hatred for the Ossetian people, inciting insufficiently aware citizens to harmful acts, declaring the necessity on the right occasion "to spill blood for one's homeland" and by force to push out the Ossets' (Author's files).

In the republic, inter-ethnic tension manifested itself in forms rare elsewhere in the country – such as group clashes, accompanied by killings. According to KGB data on the Checheno-Ingush Republic, in 1965 alone there occurred 16 group clashes and a significant number of flagrant crimes; furthermore, a total of 185 severe bodily injuries from gun and knife wounds, 19 of them fatal. In the course of 14 weeks in 1966, there were 26 murders and 60 severe physical injuries. 'Remarkable' analyses of the reasons for all these phenomena were given by the organs of state security. Among the reasons cited were the influence of 'anti-Soviet propaganda by foreign radio stations broadcasting in the Chechen and Ingush languages', and the harmful activity of 'people of the older generation, including part of the creative intelligentsia'. Finally, it was noted that 'nationalistic and other harmful phenomena arise from religious and clan memories': 'Individual authorities, taking advantage of the dogma of Islam, preach hatred of "unbelievers", prophesy the destruction of Soviet power, exert harmful influence on believers, incite fanaticism, and attempt to preserve and support obsolete traditions and morals' (Author's files).

The Ministry of Internal Affairs (MVD) of the USSR sent information to the Central Committee of the CPSU during the same years and on the same themes. On 7 May

1971, Minister N. M. Shchelokov reported that 'for a long time criminal gangs from among the Chechens and Ingushi have continued to operate in the territories of Checheno-Ingushetia, North Ossetia, Daghestan, Kazakhstan and Kirgizia. In a number of regions they have carried out robberies of banks, cash-boxes, and stores, as well as terrorizing the population and stealing livestock' (Author's files). In 1969–71, the MVD implemented various measures, including an 'army operation' in December 1969 for 'the full liquidation of the criminal gangs'. As Minister Shchelokov reported, in the past 18 months alone, 347 concealed criminals from among the Chechens and Ingushi were discovered. Information about the confiscation of firearms from the population in the republics of the North Caucasus, Kazakhstan, and Kirgizia was sensational for such seemingly 'stagnant' times of totalitarian control over society: in 1968, 6,704 firearms were confiscated or voluntarily surrendered; in 1969, the number was 7,039; and in 1970 the total reached 6,787, including four machine guns, 54 automatics, and 2,105 pistols and revolvers (Author's files).

Throughout those years, all such information was generally secret and designated for Party organs and special state services. Any analysis of problems was limited to ideological labels or criminal categories, and was not the subject of scientific study or public discussion. The deeper social and psychological reasons for 'Chechen criminality' or 'disloyalty' were never investigated. In the propaganda literature, platitudes about the Checheno-Ingush Republic successfully developing within 'the fraternal family of the peoples of the USSR' predominated. Such was the general situation for the whole country. Indeed, this was to become part of the reason for the 'unexpected' (i.e. not foreseen by the politicians and experts) ethnic explosion in the years of perestroika. On the other hand, the policy of denial and science of 'congratulatory toasts' (to use Gorbachev's expression) also contained a certain positive element: by its very silence, this policy prevented mass ethnic phobias, including anti-Chechen moods among Soviet citizens.

It would be misleading to judge the general situation in the republic and the social behavior of the Chechens solely on the basis of KGB and MVD documents. After 1957, the mass return of Chechens and Ingush to their native lands began: in 1957 alone, 48,000 families returned. This was a complicated process which was accompanied by inevitable social and psychological conflicts. After 1944, about 77,000 new settlers from various regions of Russia had settled on land vacated by Chechens and Ingush – most of them with special orders from the authorities. Some of these settlers came from regions devastated by the war, and some from Ossetia and Daghestan. When the return began and work on reconstituting the republic got under way, there were in the Groznenskay *oblast* 540,000 persons. Many were occupying houses and urban apartments once lived in by the deported individuals. This could not fail to create sharp collisions and social tensions which inevitably assumed an inter-ethnic form. In 1958, there were open clashes between Chechens and Russians in Grozny.

In rural areas there were constant disputes and squabbles because of land held by *kolkhozy* and state farms. Much of the former land was now inaccessible to the returnees: several mountain areas were closed to habitation and their former residents were forced to settle in lowland *auls* and Cossack *stanitsy* (settlements). The Akkintsy Chechens who returned to Daghestan could not live in their native villages, since these lands were settled by people from the mountain *auls* – the Laks. A new administrative district – Novolakskii *raion* – had already been created, and the national region for the Akkintsy which existed before deportation was not restored. Part of the territory (978 km²), mostly inhabited by Ingush, remained part of North Ossetia.

The central authorities tried to resolve the territorial problems of re-establishing the republic by granting Chechnya control of two *raions* of Stavropol *krai* – Naurskii and

Shelkovskoi (5,200 km²) – mostly inhabited by Russians, Kumyks, and Nogais. The literature relates that this was done in order to prevent the Chechens from predominating in the new republic (*Chechnia: Report* . . ., p. 16). This, however, is not confirmed by any documentation. Quite the contrary: the government implemented several measures to help those who had been deported: Chechens and Ingush received substantial credits and financial aid, including subsidies for building new homes and buying livestock, tax breaks, special supplies of agricultural equipment and seed, etc. Programs of social support for pensioners and the disabled, and speedy construction of schools, hospitals, and cultural institutions were implemented (Bugai, 1994, pp. 213–233).

The years 1960–80 were a period of intense socio-cultural development for the Chechens and Ingush, who had experienced clear setbacks from the years of deportation and political restrictions. Urbanization accelerated, and a significant part of the population acquired industrial skills, primarily in oil-extraction and processing, and in the lumber and textile industries. At the same time, growth rates among the urban population remained modest, and the percentage of urban residents was one of the lowest among the peoples of Russia. In 1989, in Grozny, the capital of the republic, where approximately 30% of the population of Checheno-Ingushetia was concentrated, Chechens themselves comprised 30.5% (121,350) and the Ingush made up 5.4% (21,346). Russians, together with Ukrainians and Belorussians, totaled 55.8% (222,086) – i.e. a significant majority.

After 1991, approximately one-third of the Russians left. In the capital, there followed intensive occupation of the vacant or seized housing by Chechens from other cities and villages. However, the basic division of society on a socio-ethnic principle remained. The 'Russian' sector was represented primarily by city-dwellers employed in the oil-extracting industry, machinery manufacture, transport, and administration; the 'Chechen' sector by the intellectual and administrative elite, and by country dwellers working in semi-subsistence agriculture, seasonal migrant crafts and small-scale private enterprise (Table 9.2).

Table 9.2   *Ethnic Differences in the Employment Structure of the Checheno-Ingush Republic, 1989 (employment indices for 1,000 persons as % of average index for Russia)*

Type of employment	Russian	Chechen	Ingush
Physical labor	99	122	112
machinery manufacturing	105	45	35
light industry	100	331	169
construction	93	244	190
agriculture	83	331	317
transportation	100	81	63
trade, public catering, communal housing, consumer services	99	94	104
Mental labor	102	77	59
administration of production	100	74	52
specialists in industry	106	50	32
specialists in agriculture	100	180	140
planning and accounting	104	74	58
medicine	100	78	59
science, the arts, education	100	100	84

Source: Tishkov et al., 1995, p. 15

Table 9.3   *Language Situation Among Chechens in Checheno-Ingushetia (%)*

	1979	1989
Native Chechen speaker	99.7	99.8
Russian as native language	0.3	0.2
Russian as second language	76.8	73.4

Source: Compiled from USSR census data

Until the early 1990s, there were many Chechens in agriculture, and relatively few in white collar occupations and having higher education (see Table 8.1). At the same time, the Chechens ranked very high on command of the native language and percentage of those who considered the language of their nationality as native to them. The knowledge of Russian was also extremely high, making the whole group bilingual (Table 9.3). In the 1940s, many rural Chechens knew no Russian, but deportation made them learn to speak the language. As Djabrail Gakkayev mentioned, his father, an uneducated rural Chechen, learned Russian in southern Kazakhstan where his family had been sent. 'The settlement was a virtual Tower of Babel with so many different peoples. My father became foreman of the *kolkhoz*. At first he used a Chechen boy to translate for him, but he soon managed to do it on his own.'[4] In the past two decades, bilingualism has been quite general. Inter-ethnic marriage has never been widespread, and has tended to be a matter of Chechen men marrying Russian women.

A veritable explosion has taken place in the sphere of social Chechen mobility – due to the rapid rise in the level of education, to the relatively new tradition of taking income-producing jobs on contract beyond the borders of the republic, and, most recently, to individual entrepreneurial activity. Many Chechens and Ingush have been engaged in highly profitable trading and middleman activity, allowing them to bring in private income with which to buy apartments in Moscow and elsewhere, or to build large, comfortable houses in their native places.

On the whole, at the end of the 1980s the situation in the republic was outwardly stable, which prompted local Party and government leaders to give optimistic reports at various all-Union fora. However, Chechen society and the situation in the republic were considerably more complicated than was represented in official reports. Thus, for example, the tradition of blood revenge was preserved: the local government even had a public commission for reconciling the feuding parties. Feelings of inter-ethnic tension and distrust persisted, on the level of the local population in the republic itself and in some border territories, especially among Chechens living in Daghestan and in North Ossetia. The employment situation was critical, as were the environmental and social problems in several areas, especially in oil-processing centers (see Tishkov et al., 1995, pp. 11–19).

9.5   Dzhokhar Dudayev's 'National Revolution'

The idea of self-determination for the Chechen nation arose under Gorbachev's perestroika. However, Checheno-Ingushetia was not a pioneer among republics in the political dialogue initiated by the Union republics. The old political elite, headed by Doka Zavgayev, preferred loyal caution to the more headlong behavior of such leaders of autonomous units as Ardzinba, Shaimiev, and Rakhimov. On the other hand, Chechnya was no laggard either. On 27 November 1990, the Supreme Soviet of the Checheno-Ingush ASSR adopted a declaration on sovereignty, and also established the conditions under which the republic would agree to sign a new Union Treaty: these were that the question of transfer of the territory of the Prigorodny *raion* and the right-bank section of Vladikavkaz 'back to the Ingush people' should be resolved.

In March 1991, Doka Zavgayev put a decision through the Supreme Soviet of the Republic, refusing to conduct the referendum on affiliation with the Russian Federation. This was later to serve as one of the arguments in favor of the legitimacy of declaring complete independence, although at the time for the leaders in Grozny this was nothing more than a political game to affirm more power. Within the republic itself and among influential Moscow Chechens, a more radical political scenario was maturing. The decisive moment was, first, the creation of the Vainakh Party, followed on 25 November 1990 by the convocation of a National Congress of the Chechen People (OKChN), the leadership of which was seized by Zelimkhan Yandarbiev, Beslan Gantemirov, and Yaragi Mamodayev. They proclaimed as their aim a struggle for democratic transformation in the republic and for the national rights of the Chechen people. One of the chief ideologues of this new movement was Yandarbiev, leader of the Bainakh Democratic Party. He had been a fairly mediocre and little-known writer – one of dozens or even hundreds in all the republics during the Soviet period. Mamodayev, head of the Checheno-Ingush construction department, belonged to the category of Soviet 'parochial professional man'; even at that time he possessed large sums of money which allowed him from April 1991 to pay Dudayev's salary and in June to provide a separate building for the OKChN.

According to Chairman Yusup Soslambekov, the Congress of the Chechen People was formed on the basis of 'local surveys', and 1,000 delegates attended, along with invited guests like Dzhokhar Dudayev. The resolution adopted by the Congress reflected a radical program for Chechen nationalism, which had not yet assumed a clearly separatist character. The key points were 'a whole range of specific national problems which have arisen before the Chechen people, and which must be resolved to secure Chechnya's further development as a nation'. The elimination of the Chechens' unequal position, 'discrimination against them even in their own country' was the main issue here. This discrimination was held to be manifested in the fact that Chechen representation in the organs of state power and administration of the economy as well as in culture and public life did not correspond to their share in the population of the republic. Also noted were 'delays by the central government in the resolution of the problem of the Aukhov Chechens and the question about the restoration of Ingushetia's autonomy, and the presence of more than 230,000 Chechens forced to live beyond the boundaries of their national state' (Resolution of the National Congress of the Chechen people, 25 November 1990. Author's files).

In complete accord with the Soviet doctrine of ethnic nationalism and the underlying academic theory, Chechen ethnic entrepreneurs saw the gathering of the Chechen nation (ethnos) into a single body on 'their own' territory so as to expand this territory, as well as the return of those 'forced' to live outside this territory, as some sort of natural norm and even a condition of development. (Not one national movement in post-Soviet space has ever suggested bringing ethnic and administrative boundaries into better accord by means of diminishing the territory of 'their' state!) This apparently obligatory postulate of aggressive nationalism will almost always find adherents, although it is unrealizable in practice. At least, we know of no cases where neighboring or foreign diasporas have returned to the territory of 'their own state' – be it among Chechens or Abkhazians, or Armenians or Estonians and Latvians. The exceptions here have been where single individuals have been tempted by offers of high state positions or prospects for easy money.

In the November 1990 resolution a program for resolving ethno-territorial questions was emphasized: the Chechen Republic was declared to be within the borders of the entire Checheno-Ingush ASSR, with the exception of two western *raions*. These were 'assigned' to the Ingush (the latter were to return to 1934 boundaries); in Daghestan, the Aukhov Chechens (*akkintsy*) were to have their former lands returned to them; in Chechnya itself, the influx of immigrants from outside was to be limited, 'with the exception of persons of Chechen nationality'. The Congress approved measures supporting the Chechen language and culture, the Muslim religion and restitution of losses from deportation.

Since any nationalism is based on a compatible version of national history, it is intolerant of any other interpretation of the past. In this case, the Congress resolved to deprive the local historian V. B. Vinogradov of all awards and titles as well as citizenship in the Republic, as his works did not reflect the generally accepted version of the deep-rooted autochthonous nature of the Chechen people. Moreover, the Congress resolved to introduce nation-wide censure of any and all representatives of the Chechen people who supported the 'propaganda of Vinogradov's pseudo-scientific conceptions'. Ethnic Chechens were to have exclusive power in the Republic – as expressed in the point about the ineligibility of 'persons of non-native nationality' for the posts of Chairman of the KGB, Minister of Internal Affairs, and Procurator of the Republic.

Like any nationalism, Chechen nationalism needed a 'leader of the nation' to express its will and interests. Thus, the emergence of Dzhokhar Dudayev marks a milestone in the history of the Chechen conflict. Dudayev was born in 1944, in the mountainous area of Chechnya, a few weeks before the deportation, and spent the first 13 years of his life in Kazakhstan. After graduating from night school, he enrolled in flying school, followed by Tambov Military College. He served as a military pilot in Siberia, in the Ukraine, in Afghanistan, and then in Estonia, where he occupied a high command position in the long-range strategic aviation forces. His life exemplified the successful military career of a Soviet officer. Married to a Russian woman and having almost never lived in Chechnya, Dudayev had little actual connection with the Republic, although he had maintained a working knowledge of the native language and a strong Chechen identity. He possessed an imposing appearance and a strong-willed character.

Here we should note that both for Chechen activists and for ordinary citizens, people promoted to Union-wide administrative positions always had a special significance: they were a kind of testimony to the merits and talents of Soviet society – and also offered hope of broader influence and possible protection. It is no accident that in Soviet times there was constant competition among non-Russian nationalities to have produced the greatest number of heroes of the Soviet Union, important politicians, well-known cultural figures, etc. Special significance was attached to instances of marriage of well-known Center figures to women of this or that nationality, which gave rise to the expression 'Georgian (or Osset, Azerbaijani, etc.) son-in-law', i.e., an influential Muscovite (Russian, Jew, Ukrainian, etc.) who had married a representative of the local nationality.

In the new situation, the non-Russian nationalities preserved this image of the 'big man', who had attained the rank of general or academician, or the position of Minister and high Party functionary, but it also began to play another role. In place of 'an agent of influence' in a Center which had now lost its draw, there was an attempt to invoke famous native sons who had been promoted from the ranks to the local administration. An analogous situation occurred with Dudayev, except that there was also a prelude: petitions from influential Chechens, including Doka Zavgayev, to the Russian leadership to make 'just one Chechen a Soviet general'. And this was in fact done: in 1990, Dudayev received the rank of general. That summer, Dudayev visited the Republic, where his relatives held a bountiful feast in honor of 'our own general'. At the same time, Yandarbiev, Mamodayev, Soslambekov and other activists hatched out the idea of inviting Dudayev into the leadership of the national movement.

At the second National Congress of the Chechen People (OKChN) held in July 1991, Dudayev was already acting as the leader of the movement. At that time a declaration was adopted, proclaiming that Chechnya was not part of the USSR or the RSFSR. The executive committee of OKChN, headed by Dudayev, was declared the only legal organ of power of this new republic, named Nokhchi-Cho. Democrats in Moscow were sympathetic, which strengthened the position of OKChN and exacerbated the political situation in the Republic. The leadership headed by Zavgayev (like many other leaders of autonomous regions), failed to take a strong stand against the August 1991 coup. This immediately deprived it of the support of the Russian leadership. In Grozny demonstrations were begun against the authorities. Dudayev acted as the main figure, although Yandarbiev's group constantly stood behind him.

In itself, the phenomenon of Chechen collective manifestations is interesting from an anthropological perspective. These were not political actions, but rather a demonstration of solidarity, free spirit or libertarianism, and militancy, mobilized and directed by local leaders. Participants in the demonstration in Sheik Mansur Square received up to 100 rubles per day (at that time a rather significant sum); livestock was specially slaughtered and meat was constantly being prepared in the Square. Men who were not otherwise employed (there were few women at the Chechen demonstrations) – basically the older generations – were the backbone of the demonstration and guaranteed its spirit by performing the traditional *zikr* warrior dance. Even on Russian television screens, in reports from Grozny the same faces of demonstrators kept reappearing.

According to the chief of the KGB of the Republic at that time, Igor Kochubei, the organs of state security constantly monitored the situation and even controlled it. In those days Yandarbiev was called in for a talk – 'for prevention' – with the local KGB, where he pledged that OKChN would not break the law.[5]

Zavgayev demanded that Moscow take stern measures to disperse the demonstrators, but it was not until 3 September that the Presidium of the Supreme Soviet of the Russian Federation adopted a resolution declaring a state of emergency. On the same day, Dudayev declared the deposition of the Supreme Soviet of the Republic; on the following day, Moscow's declaration of a state of emergency was revoked. A delegation of representatives of all nationalities in Checheno-Ingushetia arrived in Moscow but was not received by Khasbulatov, who then made an unambiguous choice in favor of Dudayev. This is confirmed by many witnesses and documents, including Kochubei's testimony before the Commission of the Security Council.

On 26 August, Chief Procurator Zemlyanushina arrived in Grozny. The curators in Moscow didn't give the local KGB anything to do. They demanded that the guard be taken from Zavgayev and that support of the Supreme Soviet be stopped. From 17 August until 6 September, when I was relieved of my position, not a single written instruction came from Moscow. We knew that Dudayev had telephone conversations with Khasbulatov and Aslakhanov [yet another important and influential Muscovite Chechen politician at the time, who headed the Committee of the Supreme Soviet of the Russian Federation on Legislation and Criminal Affairs – V. T.]. On 25 August, Yandarbiev spoke with Vakhidova, and she said that a conversation had taken place with Khasbulatov and Aslakhanov about removing Zavgayev from power. Then there appeared people with weapons among the demonstrators, but it was difficult to take them away and there were no instructions of any kind. Moreover, this was not a direct responsibility of the KGB.[6]

Dudayev's armed supporters forcibly seized the building of the Government of the Republic, the radio and television center, and on 6 September penetrated the building where the Supreme Soviet was in session and overpowered the resisting deputies. The chairman of the City Soviet of Grozny – a Russian by nationality, Vitalii Kutsenko – was killed by being thrown out of a window. The authorities in the republic, having lost the support of the Center, were demoralized. Khasbulatov and Aslakhanov demanded that the Supreme Soviet disband itself.

After Dudayev had seized the government building in Grozny, representatives of federal authorities Gennadi Burbulis and Mikhail Poltoranin, then Khasbulatov, arrived and formed a temporary Supreme Soviet of 32 deputies, headed by Lecha Magamadov. Moscow played a decisive role in the overthrow of the old regime and in the coming to power of national-radical elements. According to Kochubei, the KGB had 700 active operatives in Grozny and together with MVD forces was capable of 'neutralizing the radicals'. 'But they reproached us from the Center even for the fact that we had called Yandarbiev for a talk.'[7] Until mid-September there was still no mass theft of weapons, although some weapons began to reach Dudayev coming from Zviad Gamsakhurdia, then President of Georgia. They came through the Akhmetovskii border *raion*, where the head of administration was a Kistinian by ethnic origin (*Kisty* is a Georgian name for local Chechens). Some misgivings began to appear among the Muscovite initiators of 'decommunization' of Chechnya about the increasingly independent behavior shown by Dudayev. As Khasbulatov later admitted, he 'spoke with Yeltsin about adding one more star to Dudayev's shoulder-strap and returning him to the army'.[8]

On 8 October 1991, OKChN declared itself the only power in the Republic, and on 27 October held elections for President and Parliament. Before that, OKChN had declared the universal mobilization of all males between 15 and 55 years of age and the military readiness of its 'national guard', branding all opponents of an independent Chechnya as 'enemies of the nation'. In the elections, by some estimates, turnout was only 10–12% and voting took place in only 70 of 360 electoral districts. General Dudayev received more votes than the three other candidates and was declared President. By 1 November, Dudayev had published a decree on the declaration of sovereignty of the Chechen Republic. With this act there appeared a new state entity within the boundaries of the former Checheno-Ingush ASSR, excepting two of the 14 administrative regions, which were left for the Ingush state (Figure 9.1). It seemed to the Chechen leaders that the Ingush were too loyal to Russia, and that if the Ingush national movement wanted to create a republic within the RSFSR, it should do so, taking more territory from North Ossetia. Dudayev left part of the Sunzhenskii *raion*, where the majority of the population were Chechen, under the control of Chechnya, and a new Shatoiskii *raion* was constituted on this basis. 'The Ingush must travel their own path of hardships in the struggle for their statehood,' Dudayev declared in an interview for Russian television.

Only then did the still-existing Union and Russian authorities begin to admit that they had lost control of Chechnya, and that Dudayev was in no way inclined to take account of Moscow's wishes. However, the Yeltsin–Gorbachev rivalry, which was about to come to a head, paralyzed the activity of the Center and indirectly contributed to promoting Chechen separatism. On 2 November 1991, the Congress of People's Deputies of the RSFSR declared the elections in Chechnya illegal; five days later, the President of the RSFSR issued a decree declaring a state of emergency in Chechnya. But the Union authorities were not prepared to bring troops into Chechnya and the decree was set aside (i.e. not confirmed) by the Supreme Soviet on 11 November, to which Yeltsin agreed (more probably, this act was agreed upon between them). In Chechnya this was taken as a significant victory over Russia and de facto recognition of the republic's independence.

Figure 9.1 *Administrative division of Checheno–Ingushetia (raion)*

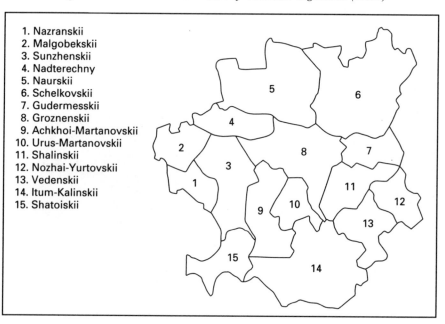

1. Nazranskii
2. Malgobekskii
3. Sunzhenskii
4. Nadterechny
5. Naurskii
6. Schelkovskii
7. Gudermesskii
8. Groznenskii
9. Achkhoi-Martanovskii
10. Urus-Martanovskii
11. Shalinskii
12. Nozhai-Yurtovskii
13. Vedenskii
14. Itum-Kalinskii
15. Shatoiskii

Figure 9.2 *Ethnic composition of Checheno–Ingushetia, 1989*

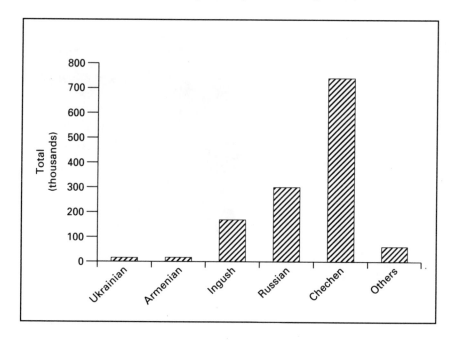

Figure 9.3   *Distribution of Chechens in Checheno–Ingushetia, 1989*

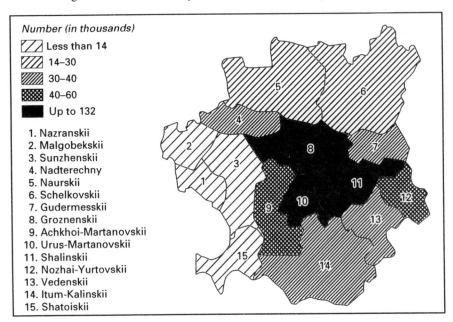

Figure 9.4   *Distribution of Russians in Checheno–Ingushetia, 1989*

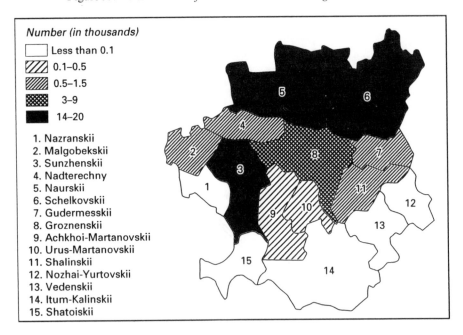

Figure 9.5   *Distribution of Ingush in Checheno–Ingushetia, 1989*

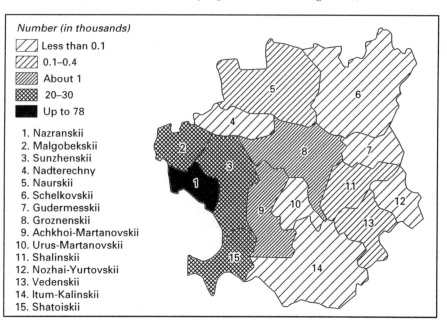

Number (in thousands)

- ▨ Less than 0.1
- ▨ 0.1–0.4
- ▨ About 1
- ▨ 20–30
- ■ Up to 78

1. Nazranskii
2. Malgobekskii
3. Sunzhenskii
4. Nadterechny
5. Naurskii
6. Schelkovskii
7. Gudermesskii
8. Groznenskii
9. Achkhoi-Martanovskii
10. Urus-Martanovskii
11. Shalinskii
12. Nozhai-Yurtovskii
13. Vedenskii
14. Itum-Kalinskii
15. Shatoiskii

However, the events of August–November 1991, later reconstructed into an official account of a national Chechen revolution, had a rather more complicated, and at the same time a rather common character. This was first and foremost a struggle among leaders and their ambitions, augmented by the dominant idea of affirming democracy and implementing decommunization after the August coup. Autonomous units within the Russian Federation became to some degree victims of the main political squabble between the still-existing Union and the Russian radical-democratic leadership. It is noteworthy that when the leaders who were losing power in Chechnya phoned Moscow after Dudayev's 3 September declaration on the deposition of the Supreme Soviet, Deputy Prime Minister Gennadi Burbulis's answer was the following: 'This has to be thought out conceptually' – in other words, within the context of the wider political constellation. Vice President Alexander Rutskoi reported at hearings in the State Duma commission on investigation of the events in Chechnya that, towards the end of August or beginning of September, he had raised the question of whether the activists of Democratic Russia were acting illegally in Chechnya, in reply to which President Yeltsin had told him not to interfere in these events. When attacks on the state authorities and seizure of weapons began, a proposal was worked out to blockade Chechnya with the internal troops of the USSR and if necessary to dispatch special forces. 'The appropriate draft of the decree was prepared, but the President then disappeared for five days and there was no contact with him whatsoever.'[9]

This was Rutskoi's version of the implementation of the 7 November decree, which had been discussed during the November holidays before being signed by Yeltsin. It turns out that on 7 November a reconnaissance group of the Soviet army was sent out to Grozny airport, and troops were already moving toward Mozdok. But in the end, force was not applied because, 'possibly, Gorbachev gave the command to break off the operation and the military hardware was sent to Mozdok, and the personnel to Vladikavkaz.'[10] Head of the Union KGB Vadim Bakatin and Minister of Internal Affairs Viktor Barannikov refused to undertake any measures involving force in Chechnya because orders were issued by Yeltsin, not by Gorbachev who still retained power in the as yet undissolved Soviet Union. For Gorbachev, Yeltsin was his own 'Dudayev'. The Union leadership remained interested in creating crisis situations for the rebellious authorities of the Russian federation. This was later confirmed by Khasbulatov in hearings in the State Duma in March 1995:

> We revoked the decree when it had already miscarried (for this we later removed Barannikov). None of the Union Ministers wanted to implement the decree of the President of the Russian Federation in order to thumb their noses at Yeltsin on Gorbachev's behalf, and as a result in a month they got the Belovezhskaya Preserve [referring to the place where the end of the Soviet Union was agreed upon].[11]

For Dudayev, on the other hand, the fact that the decree was not implemented provided a very powerful impetus for acquiring additional popularity. He and his supporters in fact now became masters of the situation in the republic.

Notes

1   Interview with Ballaudi Movsaev, 23 February 1995, between Nazran and Samashky, Ingushetia.

2   Now some Ingush political activists are trying to redefine the identity of the 'Orstkhoy *taip*' which includes both Chechens and Ingush (or, probably, there are two *taip*s with one name and a similar origin myth) into a separate group, culturally and linguistically closer to the Ingush. This would make Ingush claims for the south-central part of Sunzhenskii *raion* look more legitimate.

3   Interview with Isa Buzurtanov, 24 February 1995, Nazran, Ingushetia.

4   Conversation with Djabrail Gakkayev, 8 October 1995, Grozny.

5   Testimony of Igor Kochubei at the Security Council of the Russian Federation, 31 March 1995. Personal notes.

6   Ibid.

7   Ibid.

8   Testimony of Ruslan Khasbulatov at the Public Hearings of the State Duma's Commission on the Investigation of events in the Chechen Republic, 20 February 1995. The Commission's files, vol. 3, part 5, p. 71.

9   Testimony of Alexander Rutskoi, ibid., vol. 3, part 2, p. 21.

10   Ibid., p. 26

11   Testimony of Ruslan Khasbulatov, ibid., vol. 3, part 5, p. 79.

10

Ambition and the Arrogance of Power: the Chechen War (Part II)

10.1 Failures of Chechen Seccession

By the end of 1991, the 'Chechen revolution' was assuming its own active content and developmental logic largely independent of Moscow. Most important was arming the adherents of secession, a process not always controlled by Dudayev himself. According to some estimates, at that time the number of so-called national guards was only about 2,000, although Dudayev had announced the mobilization of the entire eligible male population. Various groupings of local residents began to carry out attacks on military installations of Russian troops, which increasingly had lost central command and control, discipline, and even soldiers. According to General P. A. Sokolov, commander of the 173rd Training Center of the North Caucasus Military District in Grozny, there were 653 officers, and only about 300 soldiers in his center. In February 1992, Dudayev's armed personnel were moved into the military settlements and began to control the activity of the Russian troops. 'Shamil Basaev was constantly sitting in my office, a real bandit who kept asking me to give him a machine gun which stood in my office,' said General Sokolov at a session of the commission of the Security Council on 31 March 1995.[1]

At the beginning of June 1992, Dudayev decided to expel Russian troops from Chechnya and sent a kind of ultimatum to the local Russian commander. On 6 June, the commander of the military district gave General Sokolov an order (by telephone from Vladikavkaz!) to leave the territory of Chechnya. At that time, only part of the enormous military arsenal was carried away (several echelons of artillery and about 100 tanks), while the rest was mined. Vigorous action on the Chechen side, including using the civilian population (women and children) as cover, allowed Dudayev to seize most of the weapons as the troops withdrew. This amounted to 40,000 automatic weapons and machine guns, 153 cannons and mortars, 42 tanks, 18 'Grad' vehicle-mounted rocket launchers, 55 armored personnel carriers, and 130,000 hand grenades. Dudayev also rounded up 240 training airplanes, 5 fighters and 2 military helicopters left at the local airfields.

However, there is another version of the arming of Chechnya. Rutskoi later said at hearings in the State Duma that 'weapons were sold to the Chechens by the local military. Even some of the weapons of the Trans-Baikal Military District were sold to Dudayev at clearance prices.'[2] There was a report in the press that General Sokolov himself was involved in the sale of weapons.

The possession of an enormous military arsenal radically changed the internal situation in the republic. Weapons fell into the hands of the civilian population, who were poorly controlled by the authorities. Local military groupings began to arise, headed by charismatic leaders, some of whom had a criminal past – like Ruslan Labazanov. In Chechnya an emotionally charged climate of 'insurgency,' of 'the people's war', was being formed, and individual warriors acquired Robin Hood fame among the people. The first 'military successes' came to the Chechens in Abkhazia, where their 'Abkhazian battalion' was one of the chief military units of the Abkhazian separatists. By an irony of fate, in summer and autumn 1992, the Chechens fought in Abkhazia against Georgian detachments with the support and full knowledge of the Russian military contingent deployed in this Georgia's autonomous district (see Chervonnaya, 1994).

The second important process in the self-proclaimed state occurred with the formation of new political structures and legal bases for public life. In this respect, Chechnya's downfall lay in the very weapons it had acquired. Local intellectuals prepared a constitution for the Chechen Republic (Ichkeria), imbued with the spirit of representative democracy of the presidential type and secular law. Islam and various traditional social institutions were relegated to a more ritual role: in the constitution there was no mention of Islam or Allah, and religious liberty for all citizens was recognized. Nor does this constitution place any restrictions on its citizenry on the basis of ethnicity or religion. But from the very beginning, the construction of the new state was faced with several insurmountable problems.

In the first place, the constitution provided for a tripartite division of state power – into the legislative, executive, and judicial branches. This was seriously violated because of the authoritarianism of President Dudayev, who continued to dominate the political arena completely. Initial euphoria after the presidential elections passed quickly and opposition to Dudayev and criticism of his policies began to grow in Chechnya. The parliament of the Chechen Republic set the date of 5 June 1992 for a referendum on the question of the form of power in the Republic, looking toward the dissolution of the presidential form of administration. In response, however, Dudayev simply dissolved Parliament and introduced direct presidential rule; then his armed soldiers took the Parliament building, killing several opposition deputies and arresting many. Opposition parties and newspapers were forbidden, and leaders of the opposition assumed an illegal position.

The 1992 fact-finding mission of International Alert summarized the existing dissatisfaction with Dudayev as follows:

1 Dudayev has done little to consolidate Chechen statehood and has been very slow to implement economic reform. His military background has not equipped him to develop a clear concept of political leadership or understanding of the complexities of forging a democratic government.
2 He has gathered a small clique of followers around him and governs arbitrarily and secretively. As a result he has fallen increasingly under the influence of corrupt 'mafia' types and political adventurers.
3 Dudayev's response to any form of opposition criticism has been to stir up fears of Russian intervention, which frustrates efforts to initiate a rational negotiation process with Russia. He thus plays into the hands of conservative party and military elements in Russia who advocate 'settling' all Caucasian problems by force (*Chechnia: Report . . .*, 1992, p. 50).

From the very beginning of the 'national revolution' in Chechen society, aggression and anarchistic behavior increased, as well as the activation of marginal social groups – primarily unemployed young men from the countryside. The aggression came to be clearly targeted at ethnic 'aliens', first and foremost Russians, most of whom lived in Grozny and in former Cossack *stanitsy*. There are a large number of reports of psychological and physical terror and serious crimes, including murder, which were carried out against the non-Chechen inhabitants of the Republic.[3] According to the data of the MVD of Russia, in 1992–93, up to 600 premeditated murders were committed in Chechnya yearly, which was seven times more than for 1990 (*Kriminal'nyi rezhim*, 1995).

Many well-known residents of Russian origin in Chechnya became victims of violence. As Djabrail Gakkayev explained, 'Chechen marginals were ready to rob everybody irrespective of their nationality, but Russians were an easier target because they could not defend themselves, like Chechens who have many relatives.'[4]

Political secession and Dudayev's actions generated a profound economic crisis in Chechnya. Never having been a particularly prosperous region, the republic was transformed in two years into one of the most crisis-ridden regions of Russia in the socio-economic sense. Overall production fell by about 60% a year in the course of 1992 and 1993. More than two-thirds of Chechnya's industrial production came from the oil and gas industry, which was heavily dependent on suppliers and consumers in various regions of the former USSR. Now all these economic ties were destroyed. In addition there was the mass exodus of the Russian population. A survey conducted by VTsIOM (All-Russia Center for the Study of Public Opinion) in early 1992 showed that the percentage of Russians wanting to leave Chechnya was higher (37% of all those surveyed) than in any other part of the former USSR. As a rule, these were the most qualified professionals on whom the republic's few enterprises (basically the oil and gas industry) depended. According to the Federal Migration Service of Russia, from 1991 to 1993 more than 90,000 people left the Republic.

However, the departure of the Russians did not improve the local employment situation. Unemployment had been running at around 33% even before Dudayev came to power; with the crisis in the economy came mass unemployment. The Chechen capital began to be filled with crowds of angry young people, also from the countryside. Participation in the revolution – behind which were hidden social disorder, moral disorientation, and an attempt to confirm one's status and to improve one's material position – by force of arms became the only accessible and 'worthy' occupation. It was this segment of the population that provided the social base of Dudayev's regime, guaranteeing recruits for the army and for the numerous armed groups involved in theft and racketeering.

Public health and education were in complete collapse. Many schools were closed, and most retired people stopped receiving pensions and social assistance. Characteristic of these years was the formation of small elite groups who used their position and especially political and military power for personal enrichment. No data are available on the capital assets held by Dudayev or anyone else, but tales of universal corruption and plundering of the republic, including income from the sale of oil, are convincing – the more so because these accounts are disseminated among the Chechens themselves. Dudayev himself even used the accusation of corruption to remove his former associate Mamodayev from power and to dissolve the Assembly of the republic. To my question as to why Dzhokhar Dudayev did not want to end the war, a field commander answered:

> Dzhokhar and others like Dzhokhar are bound together . . . With the pension and oil [money] that they, his circle, have gobbled up, you could make a republic like Kuwait! If even 5% of the sale of oil were given to the needs of the population, how we could live! . . . And the children would not starve, and our parents would not have to go to Ingushetia and Daghestan to receive pensions. . . . They've gobbled the oil identically: he gobbled it, Gantemirov gobbled, Mamodayev gobbled, and now they sit there as a government of popular trust.[5]

In the opinions of that Chechen fighter we can note one of the characteristic traits of the 'poetics' of self-proclaimed secession: the illusory hope of a more prosperous life. This notion is nourished by the firm idea that one or another region or ethnic group is the object of repression and theft on the part of the government or of the other people. Throughout the former USSR, this myth has remained one of the most stable among nationalist movements. In Chechnya, the thesis of oppression by Russia is especially firmly implanted by local propagandists. Members of International Alert's fact-finding mission reported:

> The highest official of the executive branch who received us was Arslanbek Akbulatov, chief of the presidential staff, who gave us a carefully articulated account of Chechen history, concluding with an account of ways in which Chechens continued to suffer discrimination in employment, education, and allocation of resources until 1987: 'we were treated like the Untermenschen of the Nazis!' he declared. He had at hand, and later provided us with copies of, a large quantity of statistical and other data on Chechnia's demographic, financial, and economic situation (*Chechnia: Report . . .*, 1992, p. 52).

But the attractiveness of secession is by no means always based on plans for improving the life of the entire population; indeed, it most often promises the contrary. However, for the initiators of independence and a certain part of the population, a 'free state' regime can bring quick rewards, including economic ones. The three-year-old Chechen independence did not cause the republic to bloom, nor could it promise such growth in the future. However, the open border and the access by higher-ups in Dudayev's regime to the sale of some resources and the possibility of criminal expropriation of funds from the poorly controlled Russian economy created powerful incentives for 'freedom from Russia' – or, more precisely, for freedom from some central procedures and deductions for use by the Center.

Beginning in 1992, Chechnya paid no taxes whatsoever to the federal budget. In that same year, the republic received more than four billion roubles in the form of various subsidies. According to Yegor Gaidar, economic and financial relations with the separatist regime were one of the most complicated problems for the federal government:

> The government continued to ship oil to the Grozny oil refinery, although in 1992 delivery was curtailed by one-third (from 14 to 9 million tons) and another cut of 5 million tons was planned for 1993. . . . On 10 May 1993, Dudayev asked me to set an export quota at 2.5 million tons. The Ministry of Fuel and Energy, which was the patron of the plant in Grozny, set an export quota of 230,000 tons. . . . Until March 1993, Chechnya received money from the federal pension fund, which was controlled by the Supreme Soviet.[6]

In fact, the Chechen government was able to evade the export rules. It sold oil, bypassing the Russian authorities.

In conflict analysis, it is vital to understand the motives, arguments and style of behavior of the leaders, and also to try to avoid automatically dehumanizing the initiators of the conflict. In this respect, the text of Dudayev's appeal to the First Vice Premier of the Government of the Russian Federation dated 10 May 1992 on the problem of 1992 export quotas for oil products from the Chechen Republic is noteworthy. Dudayev proposed drawing up an intergovernmental agreement on this question in order to lay down 'good-neighborly relations between the Chechen Republic and Russia' and to provide the 'necessary financial basis for resolving the most pressing socio-economic and ecological problems'.[7] However, Dudayev's formulation of the first task for the federal authorities was unacceptable because it presumed the indirect admission that Chechnya was no longer part of Russia.

In the course of talks with Tatarstan in 1992 on the preparation of a treaty, I personally, as a Federal Minister, also insisted that the word-pair 'Russia–Tatarstan' was politically incorrect because Tatarstan was still a part of Russia. Instead, I proposed as the title of the treaty 'On the Delimitation of Authority between Russia's Federal Organs of Power and the Organs of Power of the Republic of Tatarstan' (in the final version there was a compromise: both formulations were used). From a formal legal point of view, this position is completely understandable and for the official language of the federal authorities possibly the only permissible one. The point here is that both in the former Union republics and in the Russian autonomous areas there is the persistent image in the mass consciousness and in the political language, of 'Russia' as the Center. The inhabitants of the North Caucasian republics almost always use the concept 'Russia' to denote that which is beyond the boundaries of their republics. Today, as in Soviet times, the words 'Russia and the Caucasus', 'Russia and Chechnya' are not mutually exclusive categories but rather synonyms of the concept 'Center–Periphery'. Considering this historico-cultural context, the linguistic rigorism of the politicians is not always justified. It demonstrates not so much 'legal clarity' as a lack of awareness of the mentality current in the autonomous units of the country.

With respect to the second task formulated by Dudayev, the following text reveals his firm, and to some extent well-founded, idea that was the most important argument in the program of Chechen nationalism:

> Let us remember that in the Chechen Republic there developed a situation which was in clear contradiction with common sense: while possessing vast stores of the highest quality oil on the territory of the countries of the CIS, processing yearly up to 15 million tons of oil coming into the Republic from Russia, the Chechen Republic is the poorest region of the former USSR, ranks lowest in social security, has the highest indices for infant mortality, unemployment, pollution of the environment, cancer and tuberculosis. At the same time, the funds coming into the Republican budget from the activity of the oil-extracting and processing complexes is unsatisfactorily (not to say offensively) small, which does not allow putting on the agenda the solution of a single national problem.[8]

There can be no doubt whatsoever that maintaining the freedom to export petroleum products throughout Russia brought solid personal rewards to a certain circle of leaders, including Dudayev. But there were hundreds and possibly thousands of young male Chechens who exchanged the long-time practice of seasonal 'moonlighting' for trips to Turkey and other countries to sell goods, providing them with the means of subsistence and even relative success. Every month, 100–150 flights were made out of Grozny by planes of various Russian airlines to foreign destinations (with the knowledge of, and unhindered by, the Russian authorities). It was chiefly goods from Russia which were exported, in small batches, and goods in wide demand which were marketed both in the Chechen Republic and beyond its borders, including even Moscow. A small-scale but energetic barter trade stimulated economic activity, and even gave the appearance that the market was saturated with goods, chiefly on the level of street trade. This helped form the material base of many Chechens. Here is a typical portrait of one Chechen fighter given by a journalist from the time when Russia's military campaign started in December 1994:

> He is 25, wears a black leather jacket and blue jeans, and carries a Kalashnikov automatic. In peacetime he flies regularly to Iraq and buys clothes, shoes, kitchen appliances, TV stands, and other things. Thus, his so-called 'military profession' is just a middle-size wholesaler bringing in moderate revenues. Dudayev as President of an independent Chechnya is completely irrelevant for him. What is not irrelevant is his business, his wife and children, and his house, which he is ready to defend by force of arms (*Izvestia*, 6 January 1995, p. 2).

The lack of federal control in Chechnya made it possible to transform this territory into a base of operations for the Russia-wide criminal community and into a place of refuge for criminals. As early as 1992, Chechnya had become a center for counterfeiting and the production of false documents. In 1993 alone, about 4 billion counterfeit bills of Chechen manufacture were confiscated throughout Russia. Thefts from Russian banks to the tune of some four trillion roubles were made possible through forged letters of credit, with the active participation of Chechen criminal organizations. Narcotics were sent from Chechnya into various states of the former Soviet Union, and attempts were made to supply weapons to certain nationalist organizations in other republics of Russia. Chechnya was made into a military and political base for the North Caucasian nationalist organization, 'Confederation of the Peoples of the Caucasus' (KNK); one of its leaders, Yusup Soslambekov, was also Dudayev's closest advisor and a leader of OKChN. The leaders of military KNK detachments were always Chechens.

Although Chechen nationalism is to some degree historically and socially conditioned, we can only agree with the evaluation of the situation in Chechnya given in the 'Message of the President of the Russian Federation to the Federation Council':

> . . . in the course of a little more than three years on the territory of the Chechen Republic, an anti-constitutional regime has been active, set up and maintained by force of arms; illegal organs of power and illegal armed formations have functioned (*Poslanie Presidenta*, 1995, p. 35).

10.2   Response from the Center

The 'Chechen revolution' and its material security was largely a Muscovite initiative, even if in the Center politicians of Chechen origin or other emigrants from the North Caucasus were the most active. A self-proclaimed independent Chechnya eliciting Dudayev's political behavior and the swiftly developing crisis in the republic took the federal authorities and Russian society by surprise. None of the experts on Chechnya, at least before the summer of 1991, had expected secession. 'Independence' from Russia was seen as an extravagance of emotional Chechens, who sooner or later would realize the impractical nature of their project. That was the prevailing view among members of Gaidar's government in 1992 when economic reforms, growing rivalry among political forces in Moscow, and hard dialogue with Tatarstan were among the most important issues.

Moscow continued to maintain some necessary ties with Chechnya in the socio-economic and humanitarian spheres. Checheno-Ingushetia, and then the Chechen Republic (after June 1992, when the Ingush Republic was founded) featured in all basic state plans and programs. Even the privatization program of 1992 described in detail the enterprises to be privatized in Chechnya, and the time-frame for privatization, although in the republic, where corruption and nepotism had long flourished, real privatization was already a thing of the past. Only some factories and the oil pipelines remained under the control of the authorities, but even here private citizens had placed their own taps. 'If something is on your territory, that means it's yours, even if it's a pipeline,' remarked Ballaudi Movsaev.[9]

Peaceful attempts to normalize the situation in Chechnya and relations with Grozny were undertaken repeatedly. As Galina Starovoitova testified, during a discussion among members of the Russian Supreme Soviet who were involved in this issue and who tried to find a solution, she decided to call Grozny and talk to Dudayev. Dudayev agreed to start negotiations and suggested Estonia as a meeting ground. 'A few days later Khasbulatov called Dudayev a criminal and demanded that he be arrested . . . Our initiative failed'.[10] Sessions of the Government of the Russian Federation in the period from February to October 1992 did not specifically discuss Chechnya, but as Yegor Gaidar reported, 'at sessions of the Security Council the question of Chechnya was discussed many times and they tried to avoid the attempt to implement forceful measures. . . . The Ministry of Security spoke against the adoption of force.'[11] Moscow knew that although Chechnya possessed an enormous arsenal of weapons, there were no battle-ready units aside from the so-called presidential guard. What Moscow did not understand was that since the civilian population possessed weapons, they could easily be mobilized to armed action, especially under the slogan of repulsing 'external aggression'.

The first attempt to use the Russian army against Chechnya came in autumn 1992 during the Ingush–Ossetian conflict. In North Ossetia large army units, including tanks, were employed with no military justification. Under a cover of 'Ingush aggression', federal troops rushed straight to the borders of Chechnya. Yegor Gaidar indirectly acknowledged this scenario when he declared in his testimony: 'The question of using force arose in November 1992 when the continuation of the campaign in the zone of the Ingush–Ossetian conflict, including against Chechnya, was discussed.' Russian armed forces on the borders of Chechnya were met by an energetic demonstration of political will and military actions to affirm the seriousness of Chechen intentions. Gaidar arrived in Vladikavkaz, visited Nazran, met with the Russian military, and as he himself admitted, 'was convinced of the low moral and other preparedness of the troops'. He invited Yaragi Mamodayev to a meeting, and with him reached an agreement on the withdrawal of troops: 'I convinced Boris Nikolayevich Yeltsin to carry out this agreement.'[12] On 13 November 1992, the Head of the Provisional Administration of the territories of North Ossetia and Ingushetia, Sergei Shakhrai, met with representatives of Chechnya and agreed to the protocol, which was signed two days later by the Deputy Head of the Provisional Administration, Alexander Kotenkov, and the Deputy Chairman of the Cabinet of Ministers of the Chechen Republic, Yaragi Mamodayev.

January 1993 saw negotiations in Grozny between the Russian delegation headed by Sergei Shakhrai and Ramazan Abdulatipov, and representatives of the Parliament of the Chechen Republic, headed by the chairman of the Parliament, Khalil Akhmadov. It was agreed to prepare a treaty between the Russian Federation and the Chechen Republic on the delimitation and mutual delegation of powers. However, on the following day, Dudayev dismissed these talks by stating: 'no political agreements with Russia are possible'. This caused serious disagreement between the President and the Parliament, whereupon Dudayev dissolved Parliament by force and sent the head of the government, Mamodayev, into retirement. All that Dudayev would agree to was talks with Yeltsin personally, and then only on the question of Moscow's recognition of Chechen independence. On 30 March 1993, he sent to the President of the Russian Federation a letter phrased in a superficially courteous style and politically uncompromising :

> Dear Mr President! I express my deep respects, I wish health and good fortune to you and your family, peace and prosperity to the people of the Russian State. I appeal to you in the name of all the Chechen people on a question which has a fateful significance for mutual relations between our states. . . . I appeal to you with the proposal to discuss the question of recognition by the Russian Federation of the sovereign Chechen Republic. Resolution of this question would remove all barriers in the path of overcoming the many problems in the mutual relations of our states. The Russian Federation would acquire in the Chechen Republic a reliable partner and a guarantee of political stability in the entire Caucasus. I am sure that you, as President of a Great Power, will show the political wisdom characteristic of you and do everything possible

to resolve the question of recognition of the Chechen Republic by the Russian Federation. Our consciences will be clean both before history and before future generations if we can smooth out relations between our peoples and guarantee equality and mutually advantageous cooperation between our states.[13]

General Dudayev chose to adopt a style of personal appeal to Yeltsin, not so much to achieve resolution of the conflict and crisis situation, as to obtain a meeting with him and thereby strengthen his own position. Several days later he wrote yet another letter to the President of the Russian Federation of an even more 'personal character' (not even on official stationery!), which was more reminiscent of a report by an expert or an assistant to his boss. This letter contained Dudayev's thoughts about the political situation in Russia on the eve of the referendum of 25 April 1993, and was in fact highly pretentious:

Being in possession of vast and, believe me, highly reliable information about the activities of the opponents of the viability of the executive power in Russia and also of those historical reforms for which you so selflessly battle, I would like to protect you from the possibility of further growth of opposition in the Russian Federation, which could lead to unpredictable and irreparable consequences. I would like to direct your attention towards serious analysis of the prognosticated results of the referendum and the post-referendum strategy of action.[14]

Dudayev thus recommended that Yeltsin settle for the lesser of two evils – the dissolution of the Supreme Soviet and the calling of elections for a new Parliament and the adoption of a new constitution in September 1993.

In jurisprudence there is justification of a less severe crime which does not entail judicial consequences if it is committed with the aim of preventing a more serious crime. It's right the way they do it in the troops: as long as a decision has been made – even if it is incorrect – it is wiser and more expedient to carry it out to the end than to stop half way and adopt a new decision . . .[15]

This letter, which was written either by Dudayev himself or with his direct participation, reflects the arrogance and ambitiousness of post-Soviet politicians. However, it was not so much Dudayev's cunning perspicacity but rather Yeltsin's political morality and civic consciousness that led the latter to adopt a course of action that really seemed to follow the 'prescriptions' of the Grozny forecaster: he dissolved the Russian Parliament in October 1993, and then, 'as is done in the troops', took the position recommended by Dudayev for the course of the war in Chechnya.

Moscow did not awaken to the situation in the Chechen Republic until the spring of 1994. The catalyst was the signing of a treaty between Russia and Tatarstan in February. Peaceful resolution of one of the two most serious conflicts with the territorial autonomies created the opportunity for Russia to propose to Chechnya a similar treaty, which would divide the plenary power between Moscow and Grozny and would set the boundaries of Chechnya's sovereignty just before the point at which Chechnya's status as a state associated with Russia and as a 'subject of international law' was recognized. This was what had been done in the case of Tatarstan. This process was begun, and definite and serious activities were undertaken on both sides. The head of the Presidential Administration of the Russian Federation, Sergei Filatov, has confirmed this in defining 'four stages' in the evolution of the Chechen crisis:

The first stage was winter–spring of 1994 when the negotiations and the meeting of Boris Nikolayevich with Dudayev were being prepared. The second stage was in

June–July, when the internal settling of scores and mass annihilation of people by Dudayev began; by this he himself cancelled hopes for a meeting. Everyone understood that he thirsted for a meeting to support his authority which had been shaken and perhaps already destroyed. Therefore at this stage support was given to the Provisional Council, formed at the Congress of the Chechen People, which was in opposition to Dudayev . . . The third stage was in the summer and autumn, when Dudayev began to turn the conflict from political confrontation into a military channel. And it must be said that he succeeded in this (*Argumenty i fakty*, no. 9, March 1995, p. 3).

And the fourth stage? That was the war.

Here let us accept this periodization of the conflict, and attempt to analyze the internal dynamics of the situation in terms of the disposition of political forces in Russia and the role of personalities. For all the enormous powers which President Yeltsin received after the adoption of the new Constitution in December 1993, an elected Parliament – represented in the upper house (the Federation Council) by almost all regional leaders – was much more inclined to be uncompromising in relation to separatism in the republics, and the preservation of Russia's territorial integrity. As to ratification of the Tatarstan treaty, the Federation Council, in Emil Pain's opinion, would 'certainly reject it'(*Izvestia*, 9 February 1995, p. 2).

In March 1995, the State Duma adopted a resolution (proposed by inter alia Sergei Shakhrai) on the situation in the Chechen Republic which excluded the possibility of direct negotiations with Dudayev. The Duma advanced as a condition for concluding a treaty with Chechnya that new elections be held to organs of power in the Republic and to the Russian Parliament, and also recommended to the President and the government that they arrange political contacts with forces opposed to Dudayev in the process of preparing the Russian–Chechen treaty.

It would be correct, in an analysis on the level of 'forces' and 'tendencies', to explain this step by the State Duma as reflecting preservationist/patriotic tendencies growing in society and as a step to avoid the further 'decline of Russia'. However, the fact that Sergei Shakhrai stood behind this decision is of no small importance. This politician devoted special attention to the North Caucasus and, of course, the most painful question for the Russian leadership was the situation in Chechnya. The attempt at resolving the Ingush–Ossetian conflict in the autumn of 1992 by force may have been connected with him, to some degree. But significant activities were also connected with him on the peaceful resolution of the crisis, including negotiations in Grozny in January 1993. It is no coincidence that Dudayev repeatedly spoke of the undesirability of having Shakhrai as the chief representative of Russia in talks with Chechnya. What Dudayev needed was the President himself as a partner for the negotiations. This circumstance and a change in the situation in the republic prompted Shakhrai to take the opposite stand and go public with his views on 'the impossibility of an agreement with Dudayev'.

As Filatov acknowledged, a group was created within the Russian leadership for coordinating activity with the opposition: 'We carried out measures for normalization of life on the territory not ruled by Dudayev. Shakhrai in fact led the operative group. But unexpectedly in November he was removed from nationalities policy and coordination of the group was entrusted to other people' (*Argumenty i Fakty*, no. 9, March 1995, p. 3). Thus it was that one of the Center's key politicians who actually opposed the use of force could not manage to overcome his own ambitions for influence in resolving the crisis – preferring the exclusion of Dudayev, who did not recognize him, to being excluded himself from the dialogue between the conflicting sides. This personal aspect was to have great influence on the future course of events, as Shakhrai's place was taken over by

proponents of force, like a new Minister of Nationalities Nikolai Yegonov, who were prepared to use such tactics to resolve the impasse with Dudayev.

However, by 14 April, despite the Duma resolution, Yeltsin officially instructed his
government to hold consultations with Grozny and prepare a treaty with the Chechen
Republic on the basis of those consultations. But this wise and quite feasible approach,
which recognized Dudayev's legitimacy, immediately provoked a powerful response. Emil
Pain, for example, notes 'several obvious peculiarities', like the three-month delay in forming the delegation for the negotiations, and the appointment of Shakhrai, whom Dudayev
had called 'an enemy of the Chechen people', as its head. We can only agree with Pain's
conclusion that 'Russian political reality at that time was such that the President was
forced to create the appearance of negotiations' (*Izvestia*, 9 February 1995, p. 2).

Here we need to ask what is hidden behind the semblance of 'reality' – namely the personal motivations and dispositions of key political figures. There is insufficient evidence
as to whether the federal authorities had developed a plan for a forceful resolution to the
conflict. No such plan existed until early autumn; otherwise the government of the
Russian Federation would not have decided in September to construct the
Kizlyar–Karlan–Yurt railroad, which stretched 78 kilometers into Chechen territory and
was justified on the basis of the situation in Chechnya which no longer permitted the safe
passage of trains by the old route via Gudermes. Later, anti-Dudayev Chechen politicians
who were supported by the 'coordinating group' became influential in the Kremlin; these
politicians included Doka Zavgayev, then a ranking member of the President's administration. Undoubtedly, in the spring the course was set for both material and military
support for the opposition, headed by such politicians as Salamber Khadjiev, Umar
Avturkhanov, and Beslan Gantemirov.

10.3   The Khasbulatov Factor

In summer 1994, Ruslan Khasbulatov, who enjoyed high status and considerable support
in the republic, began to play an active role in Chechnya on the side opposed to Dudayev.
His evaluation of the situation was quite clear-cut: the whole population opposed
Dudayev's regime which was 'attempting to rule'; Dudayev had lost his grip on the levers
of administration and was unable to implement the declared universal mobilization;
Dudayev's sole source of support was a comparatively small, well-paid elite sub-unit of
the military – and it was this group that took part in all actions against the opposition.
Like other opposition leaders, Khasbulatov favored additional help from Russia in arming the opposition and in military training of 'the people's militia', but he opposed direct
Russian military interference. Moreover, in an interview he expressed fears that 'the popular struggle could deprive the Republic not only of Dzhokhar Dudayev but of the
population as well' (*Segodnya*, 21 September 1994, p. 1). Khasbulatov, by his own admission, spent seven months during the summer and autumn of 1994 in Chechnya ('more
than during my entire previous life'), acting energetically and not without success.

Operating in the village of Staryi-Yurt under the protection of his armed relatives and
followers, Khasbulatov formed a peace-making group composed of 'important spiritual
authorities for the people', who succeeded in holding mass meetings and demonstrations
in August and September in the towns and villages ouside Grozny. Khasbulatov asserted
that 'at these gatherings, mass meetings, and local assemblies, about one million citizens
participated [out of a total population of 1.2 million!]' and 'the will of the Republic's population was determined clearly and unambiguously: Dudayev should immediately leave
the position he occupied'.[16]

Khasbulatov's behavior, like that of other Chechen leaders, was a typical example of how political activists can use a collectivist strategy of nationalism to confirm themselves as 'leaders of the nation', expressers of 'the will of the people', and defenders of its interests. There existed an almost standard collection of arguments and methods, which made it possible to mobilize and manipulate rank-and-file participants in the drama. The Chechen crisis yields remarkable material for such analysis.

In the first place, the people create the figure of a hero-leader who fights (or is ready to do so) for the interests of the people against external and internal enemies (the more enemies there are and the more threatening they are, the greater the significance of the hero). Khasbulatov intentionally played on this image, enhancing his own reputation:

I did not change my views; they were formed long before I reached the heights of political power and became the head of the Russian Parliament. These views did not change even when I was insulted and illegally thrown into Lefortovo Prison after the criminal shelling of Parliament by tank weapons on 4 October 1993. . . . Dudayev sent a congratulatory telegram to Yeltsin in connection with this 'victory'. With my mother's milk I was nourished in the consciousness of the injustice of the existing system: I always stood to defend the oppressed and plundered and spoke for democracy and human rights . . .[17]

Next to be created is the image of the suffering hero – a figure with whom the people sympathize and whom they support completely. The leader of the peace-making group, who had been assaulted and thrown into Lefortovo appealed to citizens and the clergy to defend his good name and stop the slander against him: '. . . They want to take Honor from me which they themselves do not possess. But even people much stronger than rulers around here did not succeed in doing that. And you know this well.' Nor did Khasbulatov hesitate to voice his reprimand to 'the people': 'I have repeatedly said that I am here not for fame and homage but at the call of the people and at the dictates of my spirit and heart. In view of this I, apparently, should enjoy the protection of the people. But you allow my name to be held up to scorn from the television screen and me to be slandered . . .'[18]

Thirdly, the enemy has to be presented in dehumanized form, attributing to him the most negative associations and feelings:

It is apparent to everyone that Dudayev should depart . . . He has ruined everything. Everything that can be ruined. He has even ruined what is impossible to ruin. The only thing that he did not do was to tear down the mountains. Elementary decency demands of him that he depart as a leader who did not deal with his tasks. However with the help of tanks and machine guns and hired killers he attempts to preserve his power. What respect can the people feel for him? What can they respect him for? Who needs this 'little Hitler'? What threat does he hold over his compatriots? The threat of complete physical annihilation.[19]

Often the enemy is represented in mythological form – forces of darkness who tear at the body of the people. Khasbulatov uses this imagery in relation to Dudayev and his followers, but indirectly means the Russian authorities: 'We have only a little way to go until the triumph of justice if the forces of darkness don't interfere. Stand against these forces and they will submit to you.'

Fourthly, the leader formulates (again in morally tinged form) a prescription of action for 'the people'. Well aware of the major role played by blood and kinship ties and moral and literary rhetoric in the North Caucasian communities, he appeals to 'close relatives, fellow clansmen, and elders' to exert on 'all these heads of the general staff', 'the leaders of tank troops', 'field commanders' – 'various Geliskhanovs, Maskhadovs, Satuevs, Abubakarovs, Merzhuevs, Yandarbievs and others' – the necessary influence and to tell them that 'one must not make war on the people; the people will not forgive that'. 'Who will help them tomorrow when Dudayev sits at the controls of a plane and flies off somewhere into oblivion?' Khasbulatov's chief prescription is to create people's militias to defend the peaceful population from the attacks and provocations of Dudayev's armed groups. 'The population has an enormous quantity of weapons within reach, but many hide them like "a hoard of gold"; some do not want to be in the ranks of defenders of their own villages and towns. This is a shameful, cowardly position. Abandon it.'[20]

Indeed, the authoritarian strategy of nationalist leaders was almost guaranteed success in the semi-modernized 'little' communities. In a personal conversation with me on 31 February 1995, Khasbulatov said that by October 1994 almost all field commanders were on his side, including the commander of the Abkhazian battalion who sent him his brother as a hostage as a sign of loyalty to the treaty. With characteristic exaggeration, this Moscow politician could not restrain himself from making the grand gestures of 'the leader of the nation'. For example, he claimed that: 'My popularity in Chechnya is enormous. When I speak at demonstrations, 100, 200, 300,000 people gather. My opinion is law. If they want to put up a Prime Minister, they put up the person I recommend. And so on for all posts. I decide the fate of an entire people' (*Moskovskii komsmolez*, 9 December 1994). In the same interview, Khasbulatov declared: 'I could place 60,000 people under arms in the course of a week and advance on Grozny, but I am not a general, and shedding blood is not my passion.'

The behavior of the Chechen leaders during the autumn confrontation is extremely interesting from the perspective of socio-cultural analysis. In traditional and contemporary societies alike, threats are often used in warfare to force the enemy to capitulate. An alternative approach is the tactic of sudden attack. The demonstration of force and the resolve to fight which does not lead to open clashes can stem from various different motivations and goals. Such a demonstration safeguards against possible unacceptable mutual harm and the danger of bloody feuding and revenge. It can halt the conflict at a stage when the logic of war and vengeance are not yet active and the recognition of the danger of war still plays a restraining role. This was the climate present in Chechnya until the beginning of the war. The hostile Chechen-based groups and the behavior of Dudayev's regime were held in check by the fear of massive vendettas which threatened to destroy not only the leaders but the very population of the republic. The threat of war, and not war itself, was the preferred tactic in the small warring communities, where the mechanisms of self-preservation were stronger. However, this self-limitation weakens or disappears when one or more of the parties involved lack the custom of the vendetta and have weakened feelings of self-preservation. This transformation occurred in Chechnya with the entry of the Russian army.

The Khasbulatov factor played an important role in Yeltsin's decision to introduce armed forces into Chechnya, although the President's principal reason was to bolster his own declining popularity. Sergei Yushenkov, an advisor to Sergei Kovalev on the defense of human rights in the course of the Chechen War, said at a round-table session on 16 January 1995 at the Institute of Economic and Social Problems in the Transitional Period:

> Oleg Lobov [Secretary of the Security Council of the Russian Federation] cynically told me in a telephone conversation when I was for the first time upset by the President's decree on the measures undertaken in Chechnya: 'All that has no significance. We now need a small victorious war, as in Haiti. We must raise the President's rating.'[21]

The chronology of this 'victorious war' is fairly well known today. But what was the effect of the Chechen crisis on Russian society, and on international politics? To this question we now turn.

10.4   Chechnya and Russian Society

Prior to autumn 1994, the situation in Chechnya was on the periphery of Russian public opinion. Once the military campaign had begun, however, it dominated national interest. The Radical Democrats expressed the most alarmist views: Yuri Afanasiev, for example, claimed that after the Chechen War 'we can speak of any future democracy in Russia in principle only about 20 years from now'. The Moscow City Duma characterized the introduction of troops into Chechnya as an anti-constitutional act and as the beginning of the overthrow of democratic processes throughout Russia. Representative organs in a number of *krais* and *oblasts* (Stavropol, Krasnodar and Altai *krais*, Amur, Astrakhan, Kaliningrad, Kemerovo, Tambov, Tula, Tver, Sverdlovsk, and Chita *oblasts*) called for a peaceful political resolution to the conflict. As for the overwhelming majority of the heads of administration of the *krais* and *oblasts* who were appointed by the President of the Russian Federation, they found it preferable not to express any position on the Chechen question.

The leaders of the republics within the Russian state, for whom the 'new nationalities policy' meant a serious threat to republican sovereignty, took a more definite position. They could not help taking into account the reaction of the local population, especially those radical nationalistic groups who sympathized with the 'Chechen revolution'. Ruslan Aushev, the President of Ingushetia, was the first to express his disagreement with the military operations and the use of the territory of the Ingush Republic for the movement and deployment of troops. The government of Daghestan expressed its opposition to the use of armed forces and the introduction of troops throughout Daghestan's territory. In Makhachkala and Khasav-Iurt, there were protest demonstrations organized by local activists, particularly by Akkintsy Chechens.

At the beginning of December, during a military operation in the region of Khasav-Yurt, a column of Russian troops and a group of military personnel were captured and redirected to Dudayev. However, information about the participation of the Akkintsy Chechens from Daghestan on Dudayev's side is somewhat contradictory. For example, on 8 February, *Izvestia* ran an editorial entitled 'Daghestan's Territory Can Become a New Staging Ground for the War', in which the journalist Aleksei Chelnokov reported that 'people from Daghestan are fighting in the Aukhov battalion of Dudayev forces – the Chechen-Akkintsy, Avars, Dargins. Having fought for a week or two, they return home and soon once again reach for their weapons.' One day earlier, on 7 February, at an expert meeting in the State Duma, Magomed Gusayev, a minister of the government of Daghestan, declared that in the region inhabited by Chechens in Daghestan not one coffin had been brought in and there were no funerals; furthermore, that the Akkintsy did not participate in military actions, and that there were in fact no Akkintsy around Dudayev, as there were none in the government of Chechnya. At the same meeting, Yuri Kalmykov, the former Minister of Justice of the Russian Federation who had resigned immediately after the commencement of military activities, reported data on the participation of about 200 Kabardins on Dudayev's side. In Nalchik and in Karachaevsk, there were public demonstrations in support of Chechnya, although the authorities appealed to the people not to oppose the federal agencies in the implementation of measures against Chechnya. In Kabardino-Balkaria a decision was made prohibiting meetings and demonstrations while military operations were active in Chechnya.

The leaders of Krasnodar Krai and Rostov Oblast took a rather evasive position; the governor of Stavropol, however, where the population suffered primarily from criminal activities originating from the territory of Chechnya, completely supported President Yeltsin's position, as did the Cossack groups of the North Caucasus. The Don (ataman Ratiev) and the Kuban (ataman Gromov) Cossacks discussed the introduction of troops into Chechnya and spoke in favor of a peaceful solution to the conflict, but they also spoke from positions clearly representing the interests of the Russian state against the separation of Chechnya. Vladimir Gromov, for example, declared that:

> these effects are the direct consequence of the President's well-known position: 'Take sovereignty, as much as you can swallow.' And we are reaping the fruits. In addition, those measures which are now being taken should have been taken two or even three years ago. Now, however, the situation causes serious alarm. Will the President be able to be decisive to the end? Won't we have what we did before, when the fist was brandished but the blow was not delivered, and people thought that everything would sort itself out? (Lysenko, 1995, p. 115)

Repeating the usual slogans of Russian nationalist organizations about gaining a victory over anti-state forces that 'subscribe to the West's plans for the destruction of Russia', and about the 200,000 Russians who were hostages in Chechnya, the local Cossack movement was disturbed about the conflict 'spilling over into the North Caucasus'. Some local leaders of the Cossack movement began to arrange contacts with the Chechens: 'We understood that without looking at Moscow we had to search for a common language with them ourselves, in order to avoid war.' The Union of Cossacks of Russia (ataman Martynov) and the Caucasian Line Cossack troops supported forceful actions. The Tersk Cossacks in Daghestan even began to form a subsection for participation in 'the restoration of constitutional order' in Chechnya.

Elsewhere in Russia, the Presidents and Parliaments of Tatarstan, Bashkiria, Yakutia, Tuva, Chuvashia, Kalmykia, and Buryatia took a strong stand against the war in Chechnya. Mikhail Nikolaev, the President of Yakutia, feared that the use of force in Chechnya 'may lead to the further collapse of the entire administrative-territorial system of the Russian Federation'. The President of Tatarstan, Mintimer Shaimiev, proposed that the leaders of the republic should submit to mediation. The President of Karelia, Vladimir Stepanov, also declared that '50 years of negotiations are better than one year of war', and at a session of the Federation Council he proposed jointly drafting with the State Duma an amendment to the Constitution which would allow elections to be held for President of Russia in the summer of 1995. On 5 January, in Cheboksary, the capital of Chuvashia, there was a meeting of the leaders of the Volga republics in which Karelia also participated. Later the President of Ingushetia, Ruslan Aushev, joined in the decisions of this meeting. The summary communiqué contained the following points:

(a) Federalism, democracy and law should remain the main principles of the political leadership of Russia and its regions; only on the basis of these principles can the construction of a new Russian state which respects the rights of peoples and persons be secured.

(b) It is necessary to revive immediately the activity of the Council of Heads of Republics, in the work of which leaders of other regions of the Russian Federation and representatives of federal organs of power can participate.

(c) The fratricidal war in the Chechen Republic must stop without delay and all problems must be settled on the basis of law, justice and humanitarian concerns.

(d) Transformations in Russia were begun with the aim of securing a decent standard of living for its citizens and defending their rights and interests; in this connection, the question arises of holding leaders at all levels accountable for the fulfillment of their pre-election promises.

(e) One of the most important tasks is the organization of a Congress of the Peoples of Russia as a democratic means of working out and implementing decisions on the most complicated nationalities question.

The most serious actions have been undertaken by some leaders of the republics in relation to army service. The President of Chuvashia, Nikolai Fedorov, published a decree extending legal protection to military personnel who refuse to fight in Chechnya. This decree was set aside by President Yeltsin. However, on 23 January 1995, the President of Bashkiria, Murtaza Rakhimov, published an analogous decree, which says: 'Inform the Federal organs of state power that without a legal solution to the question of use of military personnel by the Russian Army and the military troops of the MVD on the territory of the Russian Federation, military personnel cannot bear the corresponding juridical obligations and responsibility' (*Rossiiskaia Federatsia*, 1994, no. 21, p. 5). This time reprisals from the Center followed in indirect form; the governmental newspaper ran the provocative article, 'Apanaged Prince, But With His Own Oil', which contains threatening remarks and parallels:

> In Bashkiria, as in Chechnya, nationalism and the usurpation of sovereignty include an entirely economic interest. First of all it is based on oil, . . . when we can see the not disinterested involvement of people from Rakhimov's inner circle' (*Rossiiskaia gazeta*, 11 February 1995).

The Chechen crisis provoked manifestations of Russian and peripheral nationalism. The demands of nationalist movements in the republics were radicalized: from condemnation of military activity they proceeded to demands for non-payment of taxes, the abolition of universal military service, and even secession from Russia. The Tatar party 'Ittifak' declared that it would not hinder the sending of volunteers to Chechnya, although there was no activity for the recruiting of mercenaries in Tatarstan. The Confederation of Peoples of the Caucasus made the sharpest declarations to the Russian leadership, while quietly aiding Dudayev's faction.

What of the Russian nationalist organizations? They in fact came out as full proponents of the use of force and supported President Yeltsin, at the same time propagandizing the idea of re-creating 'Greater Russia' as a Russian national state. Vladimir Zhirinovsky, the leader of the LDPR, suggested in the State Duma that the President of the Russian Federation publish a decree calling for a return to the administrative division of the country into *gubernias*: in other words, the dissolution of the republics.

When we turn to the question of public opinion throughout Russia on the Chechen war, one attitude in particular remains both the most stable and in a way the most surprising: the decidedly anti-war mood of the populace. Never did anti-Chechen sentiments grow and spread in Russia as a whole. Rather, there has been a feeling of guilt and compassion for the Chechen people who bore such heavy losses. Under the enormous influence of the mass media, which expressed solidarity with Chechen resistance and created a heroically romantic image for Chechen warriors, there was no activation of anti-Caucasian sentiment during the war. Nor have there been any known cases of clashes or violent acts at the grass-roots civilian level – with the exception of the activity of some criminal groups who decided to take advantage of Chechen entrepreneurs and criminals 'at the bottom', in order to squeeze out competitors, especially in cities like Moscow, where Chechens were rather visibly represented. The fears of the Russian authorities that Chechen terrorism could emerge in Russian cities were not justified (until events in Budennovsk of June 1995), and failed to yield the expected propagandistic opportunities to create an image of the 'evil Chechen' – the dehumanized enemy, a non-human monster.

In several places, local authorities sought to exploit the situation in order to resolve some problems of establishing public order and law enforcement. The Moscow militia seem to have conducted an almost universal 'door-to-door' search of all Muscovites of Chechen nationality registered in the city. A secret order to the militia in Moscow *oblast* called for the thorough verification and documentation of all persons of Chechen nationality in the region. One Moscow schoolboy of Ingush origin remarked, when I praised his excellent Russian, 'All the same, the militiamen stop me because of my accent.'[22] On 11 February, *Izvestia* published an article by the journalist Said-Emin Bitsoyev entitled 'I Am Guilty Only of Being a Chechen'. Here he describes the attitude toward Chechens on the part of Russian military and militia outside Chechnya and the feelings he experienced in this connection. Flying from Moscow to the resort area Mineralnye Vody in the Caucasus with the aim of going to Grozny to get his seriously ill mother, Bitsoyev was detained at the airport by the militia. A large sum of money was taken from him before they released him.

> As strange as it may seem, after all the humiliation I wanted to thank these guardians of the law. For not having detained me for a month – 'pending clarification'. To whom would I complain? You are a Chechen and are guilty because of that alone.

The cordon sanitaire placed around the republic so as to uncover possible 'terrorists', especially at airports, was in fact based on initial impressions of physical appearance, and only afterwards on verification of documents – a practice especially offensive to the many citizens whose appearance did not coincide with the 'Slavic type'. Describing the document checkpoint in Mineralnye Vody, where a group of children from Chechnya were gathered around the captain of the militia, Bitsoyev writes:

> Fortunately, my external appearance did not arouse the captain's suspicions, and Mamma and I were able to fly out without trouble. In Moscow the inferiority complex did not disappear. The following morning two militiamen from the local militia appeared at the apartment, and, apologizing, again wrote down the particulars of all adult members of the family. They also had Erin's orders to note in the fifth column of the passport if anyone had a 'disorder'. The oppression was intensified when one of the hospitals refused to admit my mother for treatment, citing the same difficulties. The presence of persons from Chechnya was undesirable. . . . In a word, there was a complete blockade . . . (*Izvestia*, 11 February 1995).

Here in a nutshell is almost the entire range of feelings and reactions of the Chechen citizen of Russia: humiliation, inferiority complex, oppression, a feeling of 'a complete blockade', etc. These feelings can only exacerbate negative feelings towards the Russian state and the desire to defend one's rights by any means available – if neither the law nor society seems capable of doing so.

The Chechen war generated an extremely negative attitude toward the political elite in Russia. This was the greatest loss of face for this elite in recent decades, and was expressed both in an upwelling of popular folklore about incompetent politicians and soldiers and their criminal actions and in more rigorous sociological surveys. The national survey conducted at the end of January 1995 by the Public Opinion Foundation (1,353 respondents) is relevant here. Among those surveyed only 16% had positive feelings towards the introduction of Russian troops into Chechnya's territory, whereas 71% were negative.

Responses to the question 'Will you consider the position of candidates on the war in Chechnya when voting in the future elections?' broke down into the following percentages:

No, I won't – 25%
Yes, I will vote for supporters of military actions in Chechnya – 8%
Yes, I will vote for opponents of military actions in Chechnya – 42%
I have difficulty answering – 25%

To the question 'Do you consider the events in Chechnya sufficient reason for the resignation of President Yeltsin?' answers were distributed as follows:

Yes – 38%
Probably yes – 20%
Probably no – 14%
No – 12%
I have difficulty answering – 16%

This survey revealed that the farther from the capital they lived, the more often Russian citizens, particularly city and town dwellers, were in favor of Yeltsin's resignation. In Moscow and St Petersburg 25% expressed this opinion; in the *oblast* centers, 39%; in towns, 43%; in villages, 34% (*Obshchaya gazeta*, 9–15 February 1995, p. 5).

10.5   The Diaspora and the International Community

The question of the role of the ethnic diasporas in the post-Soviet conflict situation has not received scholarly attention, although it is extremely significant. As a concept, 'diaspora' has a definite meaning here: it refers to that part of the population related ethno-culturally to groups who are drawn into the conflict, but who live outside the conflict zone or even in other states. Various historical reasons may result in the formation of ethnic diasporas, almost all of them connected with the direct or indirect effects of violence, which leads some people to emigrate from their original home areas. Purely economic reasons also lead to the formation of diasporas, and they most frequently lie at the base of mass migrations of population. In the Soviet context, force played the decisive role in the formation of diasporas, especially under the influence of the huge social upheavals of the 20th century. For the Caucasus, the formation of mass diasporas was largely connected with the earlier period of forced colonization of this region by tsarist Russia, mainly in the second half of the 19th century in the course of the so-called Mokhadjir movement. In any case, representatives of the diasporas, especially those living in wealthy countries who had achieved some social success, preserved and cultivated feelings of community with their native origins, and possessed the ability to influence the local situation under the more or less liberal regimes existing there.

Characteristic of representatives of a diaspora are feelings of sympathy and participation in the fate of their former compatriots, expressed as solidarity and aid when needed. In turn, the very existence of the diaspora, especially if it is numerous and influential, can be a powerful political and social resource for those peoples and their politicians. This is a resource which can be mobilized for various goals, including the fulfillment of such radical projects as political independence. As a rule, the diaspora – at least its active elements – will be politically and emotionally engaged in unambiguous support of 'its' people, even if its representatives have long since become loyal and equal citizens of other states and even assimilated to other cultures.

The Chechen diaspora is comparatively small (about 10,000). Its greatest concentration is in the countries of the Near East, especially Jordan, where the Circassians and the Chechens were resettled by the Ottoman government as military colonists after the end of the Russo-Turkish War of 1877–78. Some Chechens left the USSR during the Civil War and World War II. Among Chechens based abroad there are well-known politicians and public figures, as well as wealthy entrepreneurs, who from the beginning supported the 'Chechen revolution'. Some of them came to Chechnya to work with Dudayev – for example, his Minister of Foreign Affairs, Yusef Zhamsuddin, a citizen of Jordan known for his extreme anti-Russian bias and personal ignorance.

Several prominent Chechens created the 'Vainakh' Party and the North Caucasian Committee in America, which supported Chechnya's independence, although some of its leaders (e.g., Abdurakhman Avtorkhanov, the well-known historian and writer) did not support a complete break with Russia. Even during the active anti-Dudayev opposition in the summer of 1994, the North Caucasian Committee promulgated an appeal which expressed the fear that 'Russian special services have decided to smother independent Chechnya with the hands of the Chechens themselves':

> The Chechen Republic was the only one of the former Soviet republics which by means of peaceful revolution overthrew the regime of the Bolsheviks and declared itself an independent state in the autumn of 1991. In free democratic elections the Chechen people chose as their first President the Soviet general Dzhokhar Dudayev. The President understands perfectly that in a democratic state there should be a democratic opposition, armed with a constructive alternative program. But an opposition armed with bombs and submachine guns is called a gang in all states of the world. This Chechen gang has no chance whatever of seizing power over the Republic, but, unfortunately, it has a chance at provoking Russia to intervention. . . . We would like to close our letter with an appeal to the President of Russia, Boris Yeltsin. Reprisals against the Chechen people on the Stalinist model must not be permitted. There must be peaceful resolution of the extreme position that has been created (*Novoe Russkoe Slovo*, 19 August 1994).

As far as the reaction of the wider public is concerned, the decisive factor was the negative evaluation of the methods of conducting the war in Chechnya, which led to mass victims and widespread material destruction. The adoption on 3 February 1995 of a decision of the Permanent Council of OSCE on the Chechen question, based on the report of the personal representative of the Chairman for the Chechen Republic, was an important point. Affirming its positive attitude toward the problem of the territorial unity of Russia, the OSCE expressed 'deep anxiety with respect to the disproportionate use of force by the Russian armed forces' and 'regret about serious violations of human rights both before and after the beginning of the present crisis'. The OSCE urged an immediate ceasefire in Grozny, unhindered provision of humanitarian aid to all groups of the civilian population, and guaranteed free access to all regions of the republic for other international humanitarian organizations operating in Chechnya.

The Permanent Council of OSCE called for a speedy start to the political process for resolving the conflict.

10.6   Crisis into Tragedy: An Evaluation

The Chechen crisis can be described as an intra-state war, underlaid by the striving of one side to secede illegally – taking part of the territory of the state upon which to build a new state structure. Usually such a program of separatism is born and its supporters (both the leaders and the rank-and-file participants) are mobilized on the basis of the doctrine and political practice of ethnic nationalism. In essence, this holds that each people – understood not as a territorial association (demos) but as an ethnic community or ethnonation – has the right to self-determination, to 'its own' state. Even though this doctrine fails to correspond to international legal norms and contradicts the legislation of all the states in the world (except the text of the former Soviet Constitution), and despite the practical impossibility of achieving it, this is a doctrine with many supporters in today's world. Dan Smith, director of the International Peace Research Institute in Oslo, has calculated that, of the 82 armed conflicts of varying size which took place in 60 states from 1989 to 1992, 41 (possibly 45) had ethnonational characteristics (Smith, 1994a, pp. 224-225). In these conflicts, at least one side could be identified as belonging to a definite ethnic group. To this category belongs the Chechen crisis.

This evaluation is not changed by the fact that non-Chechen nationals were among the leaders and rank-and-file participants of the conflict on Chechnya's side (and even foreign mercenaries and volunteers), nor by the fact that on the opposite side there was a state with a multi-ethnic military personnel. This is the way things most often are in the world. Cases of ethnic conflicts in their 'pure form' – with one group acting against another because of some 'natural' hostility – are rarely encountered, although as violence escalates, ethnic affiliation can emerge as the sole elective principle in the choice of victims (for example, in Karabakh, Rwanda, North Ossetia).

Many representatives of the intellectual and political elite of Russia stimulated and supported the 'Chechen revolution' in the autumn of 1991. In a doctrinal and political sense, Chechnya's 'national independence' was prepared and legitimated precisely by Russian ideology and political practice of those years when it seemed to many that along with improving government there was a simpler, more natural way to realize democratic transformations: and that was to create sovereignty on an ethnic basis.

For many reasons, Chechnya became one of the first actors to implement such a radical scenario of sovereignty. First, the Chechens, as one of the largest peoples in the Russian state and the least assimilated to Russian culture, had experienced events in relatively recent history which generated feelings of injured collective dignity and need, and – especially among active social elements – for extreme forms of self-assertion. Neither the state nor Russian society managed to understand this. There was no place in the programs of liberalization and social transformations for even symbolic activity to heal such profound social trauma. The leaders of the state, including the President, could not find a compromise approach which would be acceptable to the politicians of the Periphery.

Second, Chechnya suffered from many social problems; these included surplus labor resources and unemployment, a relatively low standard of living, and a general lack of modernization. This provided the human material for mass political manipulation and the implementation of extra-legal anarchy and criminal activity, and later supplied a good number of recruits for the ranks of professional soldiers and armed militias. The ethnic factor in Chechnya was to act as a line of resistance: in the republic and even in the country as a whole, a situation developed in which the existing social, political, and cultural inequalities and injustices followed ethnic boundaries – or were perceived as doing so.

Third, from the 1960s and through the 1980s, some Chechens, especially the urban dwellers, traveled an accelerated path of modernization. They acquired higher education and became major administrators of the economy, or soldiers, politicians, and scholars. Under the collapse of the unitary Soviet system and weakening of the Party *nomenklatura*, this new elite began formulating claims in 'the name of the people' for the redistribution of power in their favor, and for priority access to resources. Independence from the federal Center and national (i.e. Chechen) sovereignty promised such rewards to the leaders – but not to the people, given the limited resources, the character of the economic ties, and even the geographical situation. However, the most bombastic leaders, with the direct and even decisive support of some politicians in the Center and representatives of neighboring and foreign diasporas, managed to mobilize part of the population around the slogan of struggle with Communism and the idea of independence and self-determination. Dudayev's accession to power began as a variant of the decommunization conducted by the Center, was invested with the form and rhetoric of popular revolution, and was completed in the form of political mutiny.

Fourth, decisive for the insurrectionary separatism implemented by the Chechen authorities was the transfer of weapons from the arsenals of the Russian army. This guaranteed Dudayev the opportunity to strengthen Chechnya's declaration of independence with threats of pure force, and then to organize impressive resistance to federal armed forces.

The Chechen crisis could have been resolved without using the army by various means and methods. Such possibilities continued to exist right up until December 1994. I find it impossible to agree with the opinion of the President of the Russian Federation that 'state coercion was used in Chechnya when the federal regime had exhausted all other means of influence' (*Poslanie Presidenta*, 1995, p. 30). As far back as the autumn of 1991, the federal regime left undone many of those things which it ought to have done.

First, throughout the entire crisis, not one of the government top leaders contacted President Dudayev to listen to his position and propose ways of resolving the collision. Emotional arrogance combined with lack of the tradition or skills in political compromise, as well as self-limitation in the two main leaders of the conflicting sides and in the other post-Soviet politicians, became a tragic and subjectively personal but vital feature in the escalation of the crisis.

Second, a whole complex of necessary measures were not adopted in the field of economics, control of the borders and of air space. These are measures that states will normally adopt with the appearance of rebellious regions, in order to demonstrate the impossibility of forcible separatism.

Third, Russia – and primarily the Ministry of Foreign Affairs – did not declare this internal crisis to the international community. Nor was any mention made that a process of regulating relations with one of the subjects of the Federation was taking place, and that any support – even indirect – or establishment of contacts with representatives of the rebellious regime would be viewed as hostile to relations with Russia.

Fourth, there was an impermissible political double standard: here I refer to the separatism on the part of (among others) the Russian armed forces during involvement in analogous events in Georgia, when participation of Russian citizens in the so-called 'Abkhazian battalion' on the side of the Ardzinba government was permitted.

All these major miscalculations and mistakes can partially be explained by the complexity of the general situation in Russia and also by the insufficient experience of the new generation of Russian politicians. This is not to say that the war in Chechnya was predetermined by the existing situation. This crisis could still have been played out on a much lower level of confrontation; indeed, with certain changes in the situation in Chechnya, it could even have been resolved within Chechnya itself.

No fatal threat to the territorial unity of Russia existed, except that which it allowed itself. This was the same myth as the myth about Chechen independence. Those who believed in these myths and allowed themselves to make decisions on that basis, it is they who should be labeled the chief culprits in the tragedy which has befallen the country.

The poorly managed ego of one man may have a high price for a society at large. After 18 months of war in Chechnya, some 40,000 lives had been lost. Dzhokhar Dudayev was killed, to be succeeded by the even more nationalistic leader Zelimkhan Yandarbiev, together with Aslan Maskhadov, a military mastermind who stays in command of Chechen guerrillas. In this situation Boris Yeltsin announced on 2 May 1996 his intention to visit Chechnya and to meet separatist leaders : 'I could not negotiate with Dudayev. Dudayev was a man the President could not meet.' Surely this was a painful disclosure of failed policies based on poor advice and personal arrogance.

Notes

1   Testimony of General Sokolov at the Security Council of the Russian Federation, 31 March 1995. Personal notes.

2   Testimony of Alexander Rutskoi at the State Duma's Commission on the Investigation of Events in the Chechen Republic, 20 February 1995. The Commission's files, vol. 3, part 2, p. 25.

3   See the testimony of Vasilii Zeloval'nikov, head of one of Grozny's territorial administrations, at the State Duma's Commission, the Commission's files, vol. 7, part 1, pp. 1-47.

4   Conversation with Djabrail Gakkayev, 8 October 1995, Grozny, Chechnya.

5   Interview with Ballaudi Movsaev, 23 February 1995, between Nazran and Samashky, Ingushetia.

6   Testimony of Yegor Gaidar at the public hearings at the State Duma's Commission on the Investigation of Events in the Chechen Republic, 20 February 1995.

7   Dzhokhar Dudayev to Yegor Gaidar, 10 May 1992, Grozny. Author's files

8   Ibid.

9   Interview with Ballaudi Movsaev, 23 February 1995, between Nazran and Samashky, Ingushetia.

10   Testimony of Galina Starovoitova, the Commission's files, vol. 8, part 2, p. 5.

11   Testimony of Yegor Gaidar, ibid. vol. 3, part 3, p. 16.

12   Testimony of Yegor Gaidar, ibid. vol. 3, part 3, p. 9.

13   Dzhokhar Dudayev to Boris Yeltsin, 30 March 1993, Grozny. Author's files.

14   Dzhokhar Dudayev to Boris Yeltsin, 11 April 1993, Grozny. Author's files.

15   Ibid.

16   Statement by Ruslan Khasbulatov, 11 September 1994, Staryi-Yurt, Chechnya. Author's files.

17   Ibid.

18   Ibid.

19   Ibid.

20   Ibid.

21   Transcript of the round-table 'The Chechen Crisis: Ethno-social and Cultural Aspects' at the Institute of Economic and Social Problems in the Transitional Period, 16 January 1995, Moscow, p. 32.

22   Conversation with Alber Aleev, 22 February 1995, on a plane from Moscow to Nazran. Personal notes.

PART THREE

GOVERNING CONFLICTING ETHNICITY

11

Post-Soviet Nationalism

11.1 Introduction

Ethnonationalism has played two very different roles in the cause of the deep societal transformations occurring in and after the Soviet Union. On the one hand, the rise of ethno-politics was a major factor in tearing apart the unitary Soviet state and undermining its Communist ideology. Nationalist movements fueled concerns about cultural integrity among ethnic groups and mobilized citizens demanding democratic reform and self-governance. And today, in its cultural and political forms, ethnonationalism is contributing to the process of state-building from the wreckage of the old Soviet system.

On the other hand, ethnonationalism has made the post-Soviet space an arena of destruction, ethnic cleansing, and uncontrolled violence. Thousands of people have been killed, and millions more displaced, in addition to the enormous material loss. All this has contributed to growing political instability. Ethnonationalism has served to legitimize the activities of ethnic warlords and justify widespread violations of human rights. It has stimulated irresponsible political behavior and increased the spread of xenophobia and intolerance. While helping to build the new post-Communist successor states, ethnonationalism has also been employed to challenge their sovereignty from within and call into question their ability to maintain social order and provide acceptable standards of living. Indeed, ethnic nationalism and the conflicts it has generated have become major obstacles to reform and modernization in the former Soviet Union, seriously challenging liberal transformations in Russia and other states.

Scholars and political experts have offered many interpretations for the 'furies of nationalism' in the former Soviet Union (see Armstrong, 1992; Bremmer and Taras, 1993; Drobizheva et al., 1996; Dunlop, 1993; Gleason, 1990; Kaiser, 1994; Lapidus, 1984, 1989; Lapidus & Zaslavsky, 1992; Motyl, 1990; Szporluk, 1989.) This is a part of the general search for better understanding of contemporary nationalism. As noted by Dan Smith, the major shift in research now should be away from the 'normative cosmopolitanism, functionalism and ... narrow historical focus' (1994a, p. 219) of the mainstream school of Anglophone theories of nationalism. But this search for political conclusions about the durability of nationalism is still often encumbered with the rather narrow visions and inertia of political battles. Some authors writing 'in defense of liberal nationalism' (Lind, 1994) include in their text a map of Europe anno 1600 as proof of a previously existing mosaic of small nations that, after a long period of suppression or dormancy, are now rising to assert their sovereignty. Catalan scholars Salvador Cardus and Joan Estruch have stated polemically that all big names in nationalism studies who express a critical view of nationalism as a failed political project are 'those who are in the comfortable position of belonging to a nation formally recognized by other states' (1995, p. 348). They read 'between the lines of theories of nationalism' a message for abolishing nations, at least in a 'post-national Europe', while they argue that 'we need a Europe with a positive definition, such as the Europe of peoples and nations' (p. 352).

Challenging the 'politically correct anti-nationalism', modern criticisms often repeat the old maxim, 'one nation – one state' which leaves the Catalan nation with no place to belong. Cardus and Estruch call this 'unrealized self-determinism'. But those whom they criticize and consider to be in a 'comfortable position' – such as John Keane, Eric Hobsbawm, Anthony Smith – are English and thus also belong (using the language of ethnonationalism) to 'non-recognized nations' along with the Scots, Welsh, and Irish of Great Britain, all of whom are considered members of the multi-ethnic political British nation. Thus, when we perceive 'nation' as a civic community, then the 'Spanish nation' or the 'British nation' are sovereign state entitites through which Catalans and Castilians or Scots and English realize their right for self-determination. When we take 'nation' to mean ethno-cultural community, then none of the above-mentioned groups meet these criteria: not the English nation, not the Castilian nation. There is no difference in principle between Cardus and Estruch as Catalans – and Hobsbawm and Smith as Englishmen. The only difference is in how these two situations are perceived. For example, in Spain, the Catalan and Basque nations strive to achieve 'normality' through 'their own' statehood and consider the existing Spanish nation-state an anomaly; in Great Britain, belonging to the British nation is perceived as quite comfortable for most Scots, Welsh, and Irish living in this country. Contemporary civic nations (British, Mexican, Indian, Australian, Indonesian, Italian, etc.) are fully accepted as a scholarly/political category and as an identity.

There are many reasons why nationalism became a crucial factor in dissolving the Soviet Union. Rather than an organic phenomenon that can be defined with textbook formulae, nationalism should be understood as a series of postulates and actions formulated and initiated by activists within a social space. Ethnonationalism thus becomes a set of simplistic but powerful myths arising from and reacting to Soviet political practices. Despite the incompatibility of the two philosophies (see Connor, 1984; Szporluk, 1988), nationalism and communism are close relations in real politics. As Zbigniew Brzezinski notes, 'although communism declared itself to be an international doctrine, in fact it fostered nationalist sentiments among the people' (1989–90, p. 2). Other authors have gone even further, concluding that,

> Soviet nationality policy was devised and carried out by nationalists. Lenin's acceptance of the reality of nations and 'national rights' was one of the most uncompromising positions he ever took. His theory of the good ('oppressed nations') nationalism of the Soviet Union and his NEP-era policy of compensatory 'nation-building' (*national'noe stroitel'stvo*) were spectacularly successful attempts at a state-sponsored conflation of language, 'culture', territory and quota-fed bureaucracy (Slezkine, 1994c, p. 414).

This interesting statement echoes the observations of those few authors who, after the breakup of the Soviet Union, were wary of the dangers involved in new doctrinal engagements in times of political turmoil. Now, with the wisdom of hindsight, it is possible to develop a more balanced interpretation of the phenomenon of nationalism in and after the Soviet Union. For me, it is clear that a 'Sleeping Beauty' theory of nationalism, 'one that would claim that nationalism is always present but can only express itself once a political opening is offered' (Suny, 1989, p. 505), is not workable here. That is why I want to look more carefully at how Soviet politicians and theoreticians have regarded nationalism in the

Soviet Union and how they view it today. I then draw attention to the role of elites and scholarly discourse, and how theory and doctrine are issued and abused in everyday practice.

11.2 Academic and Official Nationalism

Nationalism used to be – and still is in many respects – a dirty word in the Russian language, 'a bourgeois and petit-bourgeois ideology and policy' which should be demystified and discarded. Vague semantics and misreadings abound in Soviet and post-Soviet studies concerning nationalism. The most important factor in understanding the language and politics of nationalism in Russia is understanding the meaning of 'a nation'.

The point of departure for the traditional Soviet treatment of nationalism can be found in the *Great Soviet Encyclopedia*'s definition of 'nation': 'a historic entity of people with its territory, economic ties, literary language, and specific culture and character comprising the whole of a nation's features' (*Bol'shaya*, 1974, p. 375). This definition differs little from Stalin's (see Chapter 2). Subsequent Soviet scholarship added one more important element: a feeling of common identity or 'national self-consciousness'. As such, Soviet scholars defined nations basically in ethno-cultural terms, referring to a common history, culture, and language as well as a certain 'ethnic territory'. According to the Soviet theory of ethnos, the nation was the highest stage reached by an ethnos in its evolution to capitalism and socialism. In the past, there were never any attempts to introduce the notion of a political or civic nation in the Soviet Union, despite the use of terms like 'national' economy, health, education, army, etc. In other words, what is defined mainly as 'nationalism' in the Western context – civic, or state nationalism versus ethnic particularism or separatism – in a Soviet/Russian context would be defined as patriotism or chauvinism.

In Russia, nationalism is understood exclusively as ethnic nationalism – and that with a strongly negative connotation. Indeed, in the Russian language the specific term 'ethnonationalism' did not exist: there were simply no other forms of nationalism under discussion. In recent times, things have changed very little. When somebody writes or speaks about nationalism in Russia, the meaning still includes all forms of political propaganda and activities on behalf of and to the advantage of a certain ethnic group – 'a nation'. There are hardly any ethnic activists or leaders who do not define the group they speak for as a 'nation'.

Evdokiia Gaer, an indigenous ethnographer and member of the all-Union Congress of People's Deputies under Gorbachev, and former member of the Federal Assembly of Russia, once asked me a simple question: 'If the Russians are a nation, why can't I start calling my people, the Nanai [a group of about 12,000 people in the Far East – V.T.] a nation as well?'[1] I was also approached by Ilya Fuki, President of the National League of the Karaims (who number about 700 people in Russia, and 2,600 throughout the former Soviet Union) for support to include the 'Karaim nation among other small numbered people listed in the draft law on the Rights of Small Numbered People of Russia'.[2] Both cases demonstrate that lengthy debates about 'when is a nation?' (Armstrong, 1982; Connor, 1994) are fruitless in many respects when not used in a civic/political sense to imply actual statehood. 'Nation' is a word loaded with a vague but alluring political content. It is used by activists for specific purposes of mobilization and for establishing their own in-group and out-group statuses. When it is introduced to a larger audience and becomes a part of everyday discourse, a group may be called a 'nation' – without any specific outcome. Surely, it is no more than a recognition of what intellectuals and political activitists choose to call their group, or how people think of themselves on an aggregate level. All the same, I myself cannot recall a case when ordinary people, whether of Russian or of non-Russian background, demonstrated in their vocabulary any familiarity with the word 'nation', except when they had to respond to questionnaires written by Moscow sociologists or to shout it out at public meetings and demonstrations. Thus, my answers to both the Nanai and Karaim leader were the same: the Nanais and the Karaims are nations if people like you think they are. It is a question of self-labeling, not of scholarly definition. Thomas Hylland Eriksen put it succinctly:

> At the identity level, nationhood is a matter of belief. The nation, that is the *volk* imagined by nationalists, is a product of nationalist ideology; it is not the other way around. A nation exists from the moment a handful of influential people decide that it should be so, and it starts, in most cases, as an urban elite phenomenon. In order to be an efficient tool, it must nevertheless eventually achieve mass appeal (1993, p. 105).

Thus ethnonationalism is an idea and political practice based on the notion that only ethnonations comprise basic human collectivities and that only ethnonations can provide the most natural and legitimate basis for a state and its economy, social order, and cultural institutions. Ethnonational states are viewed as a historical and political inevitability which will be realized sooner or later on a global scale. Such an interpretation of ethnonationalism does not differ substantially from how it is understood by many contemporary scholars (Connor, 1994; Gellner, 1983; Greenfeld, 1992; Hobsbawm, 1990; A.D. Smith, 1991; D. Smith, 1994a; Stavenhagen, 1990). However, it places greater emphasis on the exclusively ethnic parameters of the phenomenon because civic nationalism, although related to ethnonationalism, does not appear in Soviet and post-Soviet programmatics – or at least not in so many words.

As discussed in Chapters 1 and 2, ethnonationalism has deep roots in the post-Soviet space. Also, before the Revolution of 1917 the Bolsheviks were involved in heated debates with their social democratic opponents in Eastern Europe about the 'national question'. Although World War I brought the issue into focus in Russia, it was the drive towards decentralization on the part of the regional and ethnic peripheries in the Russian Empire that truly moved it to the political and social forefront. A lively debate about federalism and autonomy had been under way in Russia for some time, but these new notions of governance were not automatically translated into demands for ethno-territorial autonomy. In their struggle for power, the Bolsheviks sought an appropriate (opportunist) and politically effective strategy – and they found it in the realm of 'nationalism'.

The new Soviet strategy neatly coincided with the core rationale of nationalism. As Ernest Gellner has pointed out, 'nationalism is primarily a political principle, which holds that the political and the national unit should be congruent' (Gellner, 1983, p. 1). In the Soviet context, then, ethnographers used ethnic territories as maps for Soviet state-building; ethnonations became political facts through territorialization and the assigning of an officially recognized administrative status. 'Far from having been fully formed at the time of the Revolution, the major Soviet nationalities emerged as coherent, articulate and conscious nations largely during the first 70 years of Soviet power' (Suny, 1989, p. 506).

Ethnicity also provided the basis for 'socialist federalism', which was promoted as radically different from 'bourgeois' (read: territorial) federalism. According to this theory, the federal government of 'nation-states' (read: ethno-states) granted a specific status to all major Soviet nationalities save the most numerous and dominant – the Russians. This dominant group, although it comprised a majority of the country's population, was never considered a potential candidate for titular territorial self-determination. Implicitly, however, the largest of the union republics – the Russian Soviet Federal Socialist Republic (RSFSR) – was viewed as a proper Russian national state. In comparison, the ethnic Russian situation was, and still is, quite similar to that of the English in the UK or of the Castilians in Spain.

Unlike other republics, the RSFSR had no special institutions or a cultural policy directly addressing the political or cultural rights and aspirations of ethnic Russians. The Russian Republic itself was a federal structure within a larger federal Soviet Union. About 60% of its territory was assigned to the ethno-territorial autonomies of many smaller groups, largely without external borders (which were considered a prerequisite for acquiring the highest status, of Union republic). Some of these autonomous republics actually had territories and populations larger than Union republics.

In today's Russia, of 27 million non-Russians, about 18 million are living in autonomous regions; but among them only 9.7 million live in what is called 'their own' national states. The titular nationality might comprise a decisive majority, as in Chuvashia, Tuva, and the republics of the North Caucasus, or a sizeable minority (Mordva, for instance, comprised only 27.1% of the population of the Mordovian Autonomous Republic, and Karels a mere 10% of the Karel Republic in 1989). Neither at the moment of constituting an autonomous polity, nor later, was a demographic majority of 'titulars' any requirement for 'national statehood'. There were about 26 million people living in all the territorial autonomies of Russia (republics, *oblast*, and *okrugs*) in 1989. The proportion of titular groups was 37.5%, with the 11.8 million Russians who live there making up 45.7% (Tishkov, ed., 1994, p. 33).

The autonomous polities were designated with administrative borders around so-called 'ethnic territories', irrespective of the presence of ethnic Russians on the territories in question. A problem arose only when two or three non-Russian minorities, considered to be holders of their own 'national statehood', were so intermingled that it was impossible to draw 'a just border' between them. In such cases, priority was granted to the rural population, or the decision was influenced by political/geopolitical factors. The Nagorno Karabakh and Nakhichevan areas in the Transcaucasus provide the best example here: the competing territories were assigned to Armenia in 1920; then the decision was reversed in 1921. Both regions were made part of Azerbaijan with the status of ethno-territorial autonomies. As Shireen Hunter has noted, 'again, regional power politics, notably the desire of the new Bolshevik government in Moscow to reach a modus vivendi with the nationalist forces of Mustafa Kemal, played a key role in this reversal' (1994, p. 98).

Soviet decision-makers frequently redrew the map of ethno-territorial formations, raising or abolishing some statuses, reorganizing administrative boundaries, and even reshaping territories. But once drawn, the map was never reconsidered because of facts of changing demography and ethnic composition. After all, no one could challenge the map from below. Only with the liberalization processes of glasnost and perestoika did it become possible to actualize new claims and projects. Local activists developed a deep belief that democratization, as announced by the Moscow leadership, meant first of all that previous 'historical injustices' would be corrected, and that each nation would be allowed to realize its right to free choice of status and political affiliation. The first rallies and mass demonstrations in Armenia and Karabakh in 1988 featured slogans such as: 'Long live Leninist nationalities policy!', 'Glory to Gorbachev!', etc. As an Armenian student told me: 'How I loved my nation during those rallies at the Theater Square! We were all united and we believed that Karabakh would be returned to Armenia: there was only 10% of Armenia's historic territory left for us.'[3]

As discussed in Chapter 1, another important element of Soviet-style ethnonationalism is viewing a nation as a homogeneous body, a kind of collective individual with common blood and soul, primordial rights, and a single will. Over the course of many decades, this vision of an ethnonation acquired deep emotional and political legitimacy. Only by belonging to a specific nation could an individual acquire proper status and rights, just as only membership in the Party could guarantee access to positions of power and prestige.

'National affiliation' (*natsional'naya prinadleznost*) thus became a tool for mass manipulation, political control, and repression as well as for individual strategy. For more than half a century, Soviet citizens lived through a culture of 'point five' (five was the number of the nationality line in a Soviet passport), filling out numerous forms where nationality had to be supplied (even for a library card). Through the dual procedures of census and passport, the whole country, each republic and administrative region, every factory or institution was well acquainted with its 'national composition', and would publicly announce propagandist clichés like 'there are 100 nations and *narodnost*s living in Ukraine!' (or in the Omsk region, or in Moscow, or wherever), or 'there are 53 nationalities working at our plant' (studying at this university, reading books at this library, etc.). Scant care was taken to use more precise language like 'individuals' or 'representatives of ... nationalities'. No, the main point was to demonstrate ideological slogans of 'flourishing nations' and of the 'successful solution of the national question' of the Soviet Union. But 'point five' could also carry negative implications: to those who had to use a special serial number for members of 'punished peoples', the passport was a constant reminder of deportation and humiliation. Thus for the millions of Soviet citizens, membership in an ethnonation could be either a blessing or a curse – but it was rarely irrelevant.

Imposed by academic and political prescriptions, the notion of nationality as something biologically determined is so strong that it is impossible to change or to dismantle briefly and easily. After long debates, the Presidential Committee on Citizenship Affairs announced in March 1995 that the draft of a new Russian passport had been approved and would have a space for declaring one's nationality. The only difference from the previous system is that this line in a passport may be left blank by the bearer. As explained to me by Committee Chairman Abdulakh Mikitaev, the main reason for this was a strong urge on the part of the leaders of Russia's many republics to preserve the existing 'point five' system so as to guarantee the avoidance of a 'disappearence of nations in Russia'.[4] Most likely, however, the real motives have more to do with facilitating political recruitment and mobilization based on ethnic membership. Titular non-Russian ethnonations – or rather, their leaders – need their 'constituents' to register their nationality to both solidify their ethnic boundaries and to give weight to the leader's claims of acting in the 'national interest'.

This ideology of 'national belonging' and of 'service to the nation' is the most authoritarian element of ethnonationalism because it presupposes an elite that can interpret the national interest. As Liah Greenfeld writes, 'the reification of a community introduces (or preserves) fundamental inequality between those of its few members who are qualified to interpret the collective will and the many who have no such qualifications; the select few dictate to the masses who must obey'(Greenfeld, 1992, p. 11). Throughout the Soviet Union, elites emerged among most ethnic groups as 'national' poets, writers, artists, film-makers, and academicians, all industriously engaged in constructing myths of the nation. Among these mobilizing myths the most popular and universal one is a myth of the ethnogenesis of a nation, from the late Paleolithic period through its glorious ancient history. The point of departure for all reference texts on 'Soviet nations and *narodnost*s' in the past, and now for 'new nations', remains archeological culture. The point of departure for all political debates is the argument as expressed by separatist leader Vladislav Ardzinba: 'We Abkhazians have a 2,000-year history of our 'own' state-hood, and are no doubt entitled to this right.'[5]

For decades, the doctrine of ethnonationalism – with its crucial right of nations to self-determination including secession – was preached in propaganda and was incorporated in the various Soviet constitutions. True, a strong unitary political regime strictly con-trolled this political process and sought to micromanage inter-ethnic relations. But despite many crimes committed by the Soviet government against ethnic groups, enor-mous resources also flowed into comprehensive programs to support 'national cultures'. No ethnic groups disappeared from the map of the Soviet Union during the 20th century; and the cultural mosaic was thoroughly documented, academically described, and staged in the repertoires of numerous central and peripheral theaters, operas, museums, and folk music and dance groups. Precisely this Soviet policy of nurturing local cultures, facilitated by the professional elite of intellectuals and managers, provided a powerful material and symbolic basis for the local nationalism that would ultimately challenge the overarching culture and common citizenship identities of the Soviet Union.

Local nationalism, benign in its cultural and anti-hegemonic aspects, soon began to demonstrate an uglier side. Asbjørn Eide, director of the Norwegian Institute for Human Rights, has written on the many dangers inherent in ethnonationalism: 'It can be expan-sionist, exclusivist, and/or secessionist. In all of these modes it generates conflicts, sometimes with grave consequences for peace and for human rights' (Eide, 1993, p. 5). Two varieties of conflict-generating nationalism – hegemonic and periphery – flourished before and after the demise of the Soviet Union. The interplay between these two phe-nomena has greatly affected the process of post-Soviet reform, thwarting the development of a less aggressive, inclusive type of nationalism based on civic identity.

11.3 Hegemonic Nationalism

The term 'hegemonic nationalism' is often used to refer to the expansionist or suppres-sive tendencies of dominant ethnic groups toward other ethnic states or internal ethnic minorities. One obvious example in the ex-Communist world is Serbian nationalism, fre-quently considered a manifestation of the ambition of a dominant ethnonation to maintain its privileged status at the expense of others. Because hegemonic nationalism is a nationalism of the majority – of titular groups – its elements can also readily be found among the dominant groups of the former Soviet republics, now independent states. Of all these hegemonic forces, perhaps the most commented upon is Russian nationalism.

The concept of the Russian nation in its ethnic sense (as people of the same blood, cul-ture, and spirit) was introduced into the public discourse rather recently as a logical ingredient of what official propaganda and academic language had labeled 'the building of Soviet nations'. Stalin had employed similar nationalist rhetoric – 'the glory of Russia', 'its deep historical roots', 'its mystical soul' – as part of popular mobilization during World War II. Until the late 1960s, the nationalist paradigm remained predominantly patriotic, self-glorifying, and paternalistic. Later it began to reflect social changes within the Soviet Union, especially in the demographic patterns and growing social mobility of non-Russian nationalities. The new Russian nationalists clothed their hegemonic motives with emotional rhetoric about the impending extinction of the Russian people and the degradation of their traditions and culture. Writers and social scientists, the true found-ing fathers of this new Russian ethnonationalism, provided arguments for these emotional appeals, and their texts served as the basis for all later political programs and statements (see Dunlop, 1985).

As a political movement, contemporary Russian ethnonationalism was born in the 1980s with the organization *Pamyat* (Memory) and its programs for cultural, historic, and ecological preservation. The ideology was a mixture of Orthodox monarchism, national Bolshevism, and anti-Semitism. Perestroika and the crisis of the Soviet state and Communist Party rule politicized *Pamyat*, especially under the charismatic leadership of Dmitrii Vasiliev. In 1989–90, the group publicly distributed its 'Manifesto', a non-official program of hegemonic nationalism devoted to the Soviet Union's dominant ethnicity – Russian.

According to *Pamyat* doctrine, the Russian Orthodox religion is the sole possible spiritual basis for Russia and the Russians; likewise, the tsarist monarchy, with its sacred base, is the best form of state power. The centralized state should be neither disintegrated nor weakened, and the Russian Empire must remain intact. As a great nation, Russia must continue as a trinity of Slavic peoples – Russians, Ukrainians, and Belorussians. All negative forces, such as disintegration and conflict, stem from the global Zionist–Masonic conspiracy directed against the Russian people and their state. All power in Russia must reside with ethnic Russians; other groups should be represented proportionally in the institutions of politics, culture, and science (Erunov & Solovei, 1991, pp. 73-75).

After a series of internal crises, *Pamyat* lost its leading place within the Russian nationalist movement. The political project of Russian ethnonationalism was seen as too important and potentially profitable to be undertaken by marginal activists without the proper prestige, abilities, or resources. Since the disintegration of the Soviet Union, a series of Russian nationalist movements and organizations have emerged with much stronger and more cautiously phrased appeals. Responding to new social and political conditions, these groups have managed to mobilize considerable mass support.

A major reason for the rise in Russia of this more 'respectable' hegemonic nationalism has been a rather simple geopolitical factor: with the collapse of the Soviet state, 25 million ethnic Russians suddenly found themselves part of a new and unforeseen Russian diaspora. These ethnic Russians were excluded from the political process in many newly independent states; in the case of Latvia and Estonia, they were excluded even from membership in the new civic communities. In several regions, such as Central Asia and the Transcaucasus, Russians found themselves in a turmoil of ethnic and clan disputes. In this highly stressful psychological climate, many Russians succumbed to fear and joined the exodus back to their 'historic homeland'. The democratic leaders of Russia – Boris Yeltsin, Yegor Gaidar, and Andrei Kozyrev – believed that their republican allies in the fight against the Party and Gorbachev's Center would remain in a united front of 15 independent states. But here they miscalculated: the ethnonationalism of the titular groups became the priority option for republican leaders and activists who had achieved their independence under a slogan of national self-determination.

This new Russian diaspora was not the only reason for heightened ethnonationalism. In Russia itself, the collapse of the central, full-employment economy and the redistributive state – however inefficient and impoverished these institutions may have been – caused massive social dislocation and growing disparities in individual fortunes. Hardest hit were the urban populations, especially the predominantly ethnic Russian employees of the military and heavy industries. The demobilization of Russian forces deployed abroad, along with the paring down of the work force of repressive institutions such as the KGB, produced a pool of ideologically engaged, well-trained, formerly privileged and energetic male officers who resented the passing of the 'good old days'. Many – particularly the older generation and war veterans indoctrinated in the verities of the 'great Soviet state' and the 'great Russian people' – suffered a crisis of identity, confronted with the traumatic loss of their former status.

All of these factors pushed nationalism into political debates at the highest levels. At the very top, President Yeltsin, Minister of Foreign Affairs Kozyrev, and Russian parliamentary leaders made the defense of ethnic Russians in the 'near-abroad' a political priority in the aftermath of the summer of 1992. The most striking example was Yeltsin's speech at the UN General Assembly in September 1994, which sent a message not only to neighboring countries and to the West, but also to an internal electorate concerned about the fate of its ethnic compatriots. The same message lay behind Yeltsin's pronouncements on the re-emergence of Russia as a great power in world politics and his support for the resurgent Cossacks, the primarily Russian nationalists so active in the southern region of the country. In this articulation of hegemonic nationalism, Yeltsin found an ally in the Russian Orthodox Church: the President took his oath of allegiance on the Bible and, though a professed atheist, announced his intention to attend church regularly.

Other high-ranking federal officials have articulated more openly extreme nationalist stands. In Yegor Gaidar's government, for instance, Minister of Information Mikhail Poltoranin was infamous for his nationalism and anti-Semitism, revealing his sentiments in a notorious remark about the contemporary Russian mass media, which he said often 'speaks a kind of prisoners' Hebrew' (*lagernii ivrit*). His protégé for the ministerial post in the subsequent government, Boris Mironov, became known as the 'iron nationalist' for statements such as 'if Russian nationalism is fascism, then I am a fascist' (*Moskovskie novosti*, 28 August–4 September 1994, p. 11). Mironov was dismissed from his position in September 1994, following an outcry from liberal journalists.

The December 1993 federal elections ushered into the State Duma a new phalanx of ultra-nationalists, the 40 parliamentary members of the Liberal-Democratic Party. The party's leader, Vladimir Zhirinovsky, is surely one of the most provocative and charismatic propagandists of Russian nationalism. Another influential party bloc, the Communists and the Agrarians, also appeal to the *russkii narod* (the Russian people). In his book *Derzhava* (State Power), the leader of the Communist Party of Russia, Gennadi Zuiganov, defines Russia's vital interests as 'gathering together under the protection of a unified and powerful state all Russian people, all who consider Russia as their Motherland, and all those peoples who agree to share with Russia their historical fate' (Zuiganov, 1994, p. 77).

Outside the power elite, there are numerous groups of intellectuals and activists who subscribe to extreme forms of Russian ethnonationalism. Vasiliev's *Pamyat* continues to organize small-scale meetings and demonstrations blocking other extremist groups. A similar organization, *Russkaya Partia* (Russian Party), has anti-Semitism at the core of its doctrine. Its leader, Nikolai Bondareek, identified the party's main priorities as the following:

> In Russia it is the Russians who should govern. . . . Russia must have a Russian government, a Russian parliament of ethnic Russians belonging to the Great Nation by blood and by spirit. . . . Everything is for the Nation and nothing against it – this motto must be in the brain and spirit, in the flesh and blood of every Russian, because we are all only cells of one great organism named the Nation (*Rech*, 1994, no. 1, p. 4).

In February 1992, a group of Russian nationalist leaders, including the writer Valentin Rasputin and Communist Party leader Gennadi Zuiganov, founded a new organization called *Russkii Natsionalnyi Sobor* (Russian National Assembly – RNS) as an umbrella coalition for the many groups operating in Russia, Ukraine, Belorussia, the Baltic states, Moldavia, and Georgia. Their first congress attracted 1,500 delegates from 117 towns, representing more than 70 Russian patriotic organizations. RNS has called for 'unifying Russian and other indigenous peoples of Russia for the sake of reviving a united Motherland, defending nation-state interests, and preserving the traditional moral and religious values of Russia's citizens'. Its Manifesto ends with the words: 'We are Russians. God is with us!' (*Russkii Sobor*, 1994, no. 10, p. 2).

In its extreme forms Russian nationalism resembles fascism – a word often bandied about by scholars and politicians. Even top-level officials, like Deputy Prime Minister Anatoli Chubais, and the leader of 'Choice of Russia' Yegor Gaidar, publicly branded as fascists Zhirinovsky and other members of the State Duma from his party. It is interesting to note that the Soviet lexicon listed the term 'fascism' as a synonym of 'total evil', and so it remains to this day. In contemporary political language the term is more often a label used to dehumanize political opponents than to reflect their actual political leanings. Comparing Russian pro-fascist groups with their Western counterparts illustrates this phenomenon. Zhirinovsky, who became a media sensation, can scarcely be considered a 'fascist' in the European sense of the word. Alexander Nevzorov, right-wing journalist and a member of the State Duma, made the following comment about Zhirinovsky: 'As a qualified extremist, I do not view Zhirinovsky as an extremist. To my mind, he is too soft and neutral to meet these requirements.'[6]

The real question is how fascism corresponds to Russian nationalism and how both extreme platforms interact on the contextual and organizational levels. There is no doubt that fascism *à la russe* has transformed itself from a marginal political tendency of the late 1980s into a real political phenomenon of today. The landmark for establishing organized fascist groups was September 1990, when *Russkoie Natsional'noe Edinstvo* (Russian National Unity – RNU) headed by Alexander Barkashov was constituted. From the very beginning this was an organization with strict discipline and a paramilitary avant-garde. Some representatives of the political establishment with nationalist orientations had made contact with RNU which allowed '*barkashovzy*' to show themselves in and around 'the White House' (the Russian Parliament building) during the troubled autumn months of 1993. In October 1994, RNU nominated its candidate Alexander Fedorov for election to the State Duma from a Moscow suburban electoral district (where the deputy had been assassinated by a mafia-style hit) but received the modest support of only 6%. For the 1995 national election, RNU could not manage to present 200,000 supporting signatures to be officially registered. *Barkashovzy*'s electoral platform stands on the explicit postulate that 'Russia can be saved only by nationally-thinking politicians, that is – by nationalists', as announced by Fedorov during his election campaign (*Moskovskie novosti*, no. 52, 30 October–6 November 1994, p. 6).

In January 1995, Alexander Barkashov published his paper 'The Crisis of World Civilization: The Role of Russia and the Goals of the Russian National Movement'. Barkashov repeats rhetoric on Russia as the only source of salvation for the dying Western and Eastern civilization, and formulates a kind of political proto-platform. The platform is created in a cautious, yet appealing way, and reflects the most recent trends in Russian ultra-rightists of acting within the limits of the law and acquiring an image of flexibility. He writes:

> The historical mission of Russia and the Russian people (*russkovo naroda*) is to break away from a dying materialistic civilization . . . That is why the Russian National Movement has three main tasks:
> 1   to prevent the disintegration of Russia;
> 2   to unite the Russian nation under one ideology built on historical realities;
> 3   to establish throughout Russia a rigidly disciplined organization comprising the strongest and most active Russian people.

The fulfillment of these three tasks will restore national power. And we will accomplish these tasks because there is no other appropriate way for a Russian. Glory to Russia! (Barkashov, 1995, p. 2)

Some experts are deeply skeptical of the possibility that ultra-nationalism may be transformed into a kind of Russian fascism. They cite two arguments: first, that as a legacy of World War II, Russians have a strong immunity to fascism. Second, sociological surveys have shown that no more than 1.5%–2% of the electorate is ready to vote for the fascists. In fact, however, these arguments are not very strong. The mentality and values of former Soviet citizens are shifting rapidly. It took only a few years for Soviet symbols and history to be de-mythicized. Moreover, anti-fascist values are practically absent among the younger generation: and the core pro-fascist groups in Russia are made up of people under the age of 35. Furthermore, even 1.5% of the electorate comprises over 1.5 million people – a large group for any political or paramilitary activities. By some estimates, there are no less than 200,000 people under the sphere of influence of the RNU. Most of these are not fully fledged members, but rather persons who occasionally support the party and its leader (see Solovei, 1995).

Why then do I address the subject of Russian fascism if it is not directly analogous to Russian nationalism? Both have much in common with respect to their programmatic contexts. Russian ultra-rightists use the Nazi racial doctrine as their theoretical basis, making the slight adjustment that ethnic Russians are the supreme embodiment of the Aryan race. From this, it follows that the Russian ethnonationals should enjoy all privileges in this state, and that various forms of racial and ethnic segregation are permissible. The RNU's doctrine includes strong barriers to mixed marriages, efforts to boost the fertility rate of Russians, ethnic proportional representation in all state and public institutions, and a struggle against 'parasitic' peoples (i.e. Jews and Gypsies). As in all other forms of Russian nationalism, the RNU has a very strong anti-Western, isolationist stance. The election platform of Duma candidate Alexander Fedorov included a separate point to 'clean' educational programs of 'pan-human values'. As Fedorov explained,

> these are values which the so-called 'world government' is trying to implant in our minds. For several centuries this government has sought to construct a kind of salad (*vinegret*) of peoples. One example is America where national traditions, culture, and national spirit are under siege by these 'pan-human values'. Who is in power in these international states? – The Free Masons. And they present their own 'values' as 'pan-human'. The two are synonymous (*Moskovskie novosti*, no. 52, 30 October–6 November 1994, p. 6).

Hegemonic nationalism in Russia has been undergoing a metamorphosis since the December 1993 elections, and especially since the war against the breakaway Chechen Republic began. As a leading expert on this issue, Valery Solovei, observed, 'since the beginning of 1994 the melody of Russian domestic and foreign policy has been changing evidently toward a nationalistic and "great power" repertoire. It reached its crescendo when the Russian president started the Chechen "expedition"' (Solovei, 1995, p. 3). A statement by the well-known Russian analyst, Andranik Migranyan, supports this observation. Migranyan predicted that 1995 would become a 'year of great change' in terms of strengthening Russian statehood, and that through their actions in Chechnya federal authorities would overcome the syndrome of the disintegrating state. To this syndrome belong feelings of guilt among the Russian people and authorities for the tsarist and Soviet empires; a paralysis of the political will to preserve and strengthen the state; and the 'Afghanistan syndrome', which has led to anti-military, pacifist attitudes. According to Migranyan, the future of Russia is at stake in Chechnya: this is not a fight between a party of war and a party of peace, but rather a clash between forces of order and chaos. 'For the President and for the supporters of the state (*gosudarstvennikov*) there is no other choice but to use all available force to overcome the defeatist (*porazhencheskii*) syndrome, for the sake of preserving and strengthening the Russian state' (Migranyan, 1995, pp. 1–2).

In fact, however, the Chechen War did not give rise to an immediate upsurge of chauvinist and nationalist feelings in the country. Off the battlefield, there were no growing anti-Chechen attitudes, nor were there serious activities by right-wing groups, including the Cossacks of the regions bordering on Chechnya. Unlike in Serbia, no ethnic Russian volunteers came forward to fight for the territorial integrity of their country; many more preferred to avoid military service. Human rights activists, the liberal mass media, and organizations of soldiers' mothers dominated the public discourse on the crisis. Sergei Kovalev and Yegor Gaidar were the major spokesmen against the 'war party' and the brutality of the Russian army in Chechnya. Their political opposite, ultra-nationalist Alexander Nevzorov, had no luck in getting a good broadcasting time to spread his flamboyant patriotic propaganda. The most visible fascist in Russia, Alexei Vedenkin, was arrested for the provocative statements – 'to finish with people like Kovalev' – he made during a television interview. Furthermore, Yeltsin signed a decree against extremist (primarily ultra-nationalist) propaganda, which demanded criminal prosecution for those who spread ethnic hatred and extremism. This, however, did not prevent him from delivering his annual State of the Nation address, full of rhetoric in favor of a highly centralized state with great power.

These ambivalences in Russian politics reflect deeper trends which strengthen positions of hegemonic nationalism. After the December 1993 national elections, popular sentiment shifted toward traditional Russian and imperial values. According to some sociological surveys, this is a trend that continues to grow. Most likely, communism and liberalism have now exhausted their potential and are gradually being replaced by the ideology of nationalism in its specifically Russian guise. This can evolve in two directions: exclusive ethnonationalism, or the more tolerant form of civic patriotism.

At certain times in Russian history, words like 'democracy' and 'liberalism' have provoked hostile feelings among the majority of the country's population. Despite the considerable power granted to the President by the new constitution, Yeltsin's political support has been eroding. This can explain why the President and many other politicians have rushed to appeal to other sources of legitimization, opting for a new vocabulary (*derzhava*, national pride, the greatness of Russia, etc.), as well as symbols and slogans of state nationalism.

In August 1994, Yeltsin distanced himself from the radical democrats who celebrated the third anniversary of Russian sovereignty. Instead, he preferred to meet with the head of the Russian Orthodox Church, Alexeii II, and with writer Alexander Solzhenitsyn, and to visit an exhibition of Ilya Glazunov, a Russian nationalist artist. He also made a series of statements in defense of ethnic Russians abroad. These actions most likely signify a change of political strategy and the beginnings of an internal evolution of the existing political regime in Russia.

There are serious obstacles and limitations to this scenario, however. The Chechen War has marginalized but not destroyed Zhirinovsky's party, which still enjoys support among urban intellectuals and a number of new financial groups. New powerful centrist forces which are more pragmatic and neutral with regard to nationalist/patriotic rhetoric are reassembling around Viktor Chernomyrdin, Alexander Lebed and other politicians. The mass media remain strongly opposed to any nationalistic stands and propaganda. The presidential campaign of 1996 was marked by the playing down of the Russian ethnonationalistic card and ended with a victory of the more liberal civic/democratic platform embodied by Boris Yeltsin. And finally, the West is monitoring the situation carefully, and its voice is a powerful factor against the 'nationalization' of the regime in Russia. Thus, all that can be said now is that the future of Russia is unclear. Its shape will depend also on other challenges – among them, yet another type of nationalism.

11.4 Periphery Nationalism

While Vasiliev and Zhirinovsky brought Russian nationalism to the front pages of Western newspapers, the topic of Periphery nationalism became widely known and discussed because of the separatist actions of several autonomous republics within the Russian Federation. This nationalism, sprouting up far from Moscow, has been perhaps the most significant ideological doctrine and political practice of the post-Soviet Union.

   Non-Russian nationalism has long flourished in the political landscape. Even during the tsarist period, ethnic elites formulated the idea of a nation for some groups – like the Finns, the Poles, the Tatars, and the Georgians – and several nationalist political movements arose before 1917. But Periphery nationalism is really rooted in the Soviet legacy; the emphasis was on acquiring one's 'own national state' within the limits of the USSR and on realizing the right of self-determination (see, e.g., Balzer, 1994; Nahaylo and Swoboda, 1990; Rorlich, 1986; Suny, 1988, 1993.) The institutionalization of periphery ethnicity was a key element in constructing a basis for Soviet ethnonationalism. Short-lived independent states, such as the Transcaucasus republics in 1918–21 and the Baltic states in 1918--40, or anti-tsarist resistance in the more remote past, provided a great impetus and a legitimate starting point for future secessionist projects. Autonomous administrative units based on the principle of ethnicity mushroomed during the first two decades after the 1917 revolution. Practically all groups capable of formulating their 'national aspiration' were granted varying kinds of statehood or local power embodiments. Thus, from its early years, the Communist state took charge of building nations and could be considered a principal creator of 'a multi-national Soviet people'.

   That this nationalism was state-sponsored did not detract from the fact that relations between the Center and the ethnonations were basically imperial. It was Moscow that made all major decisions, from economic strategy to key political appointments. And the beneficiaries of these decisions were very often ethnic non-Russians, or at least those bureaucratic elites enmeshed in Russian culture. As Suny observes:

> Non-Russian republics were treated as objects of central policy rather than as subjects capable of independent decision-making, and their national destinies were fundamentally altered as a result. A fundamental contradiction between empire and emerging nations grew like a cancer within the Soviet state. Much more than the tsarist empire, the USSR had become a 'prisonhouse of nations' – indeed, of nations that had grown up within the Soviet Union (1993, pp. 112–113).

It is probably more correct to say that the USSR was both a cradle and a cage for Soviet ethnonations, although this was not always the perception. Awareness of this contradiction emerged only when it was formulated by elites under conditions of liberalization and high political mobilization.

   It should come as no surprise, then, that the nationalism of titular non-Russian nationalities was essentially defensive – based on protecting locally dominant minorities against political centralism and Russian cultural hegemony, but also treating smaller minorities with intolerance in case they should be formulating their own dissent. The last issue is crucial for understanding ethnic conflicts, although it has never been properly analyzed by experts on this region. In the former Soviet Union, titular nationalism in the republics created 'double minorities' – minorities within minorities like Tajiks and Meskhetian Turks in Uzbekistan, or Abkhazians and Southern Ossets in Georgia – who were frequently deprived, or felt deprived, of the rights of free expression and decision-making on the republican as well as on the local level. After acquiring full control of the new independent states, ethnic titular elites started to exercise hegemonic power over their own stateless minorities. The goal of radical nationalists became to create 'normal' national states that were culturally and even demographically more homogeneous and that excluded 'non-natives' from access to resources, power, and even citizenship.

Trapped by the legacies of Soviet nationalism, the new leaders of the successor states, as well as leaders of the internal autonomies, have found themselves unprepared to transform ethnonationalism into civic nation-building. The enforcement of ethnically selective citizenship and official language laws in societies with sizeable and culturally distinct communities has caused massive discontent and inter-ethnic tensions in Estonia, Latvia, Moldavia, Georgia, Ukraine, and in Central Asia. Former 'double minorities', now simply minorities, are calling for their own national states. Or they have started irredentist movements, preferring to leave political systems where they have neither proper voice nor representation. The Armenian enclave in Nagorno Karabakh has fought to be reunited with its 'historic motherland' of Armenia. Abkhazian leaders responded to Georgian hegemony with a ferocious struggle for secession that resulted in the expulsion of ethnic Georgians from Abkhazia. In Moldavia, the Russian-Ukrainian minority has proclaimed their own state in the Trans-Dniestrian region, while the Gagauz minority has demanded greater territorial autonomy. And whereas the Russian majority in Crimea wants to be a part of Russia and not Ukraine, the Crimean Tatar minority dreams of making Crimea their own national state. The list of mutual dissatisfactions goes on and on, with many more potential candidates for future confrontations.

The Russian Federation inherited more complex ethno-politics than any other Soviet successor state. A large multi-ethnic entity very much like the Soviet Union, Russia today is a country where defensive titular nationalism has not exhausted its potential for dismantling a highly centralized state structure and pluralizing a political and cultural realm dominated by one ethnic group. In virtually every ethnic enclave of this vast country, micro-nationalism is incubating. Consider, for instance, the nationalist manifesto of an author representing the 'stateless' minority of Shorts (an Altaic group numbering 16,000 people in southern Siberia):

The time has come for Great Russians to concentrate themselves in their historical motherland . . . Conquered lands should be returned to their original owners, with whom they can establish equal relations . . . We must take all efforts to form a united state in Altai and Sayani under one name, a project that our predecessors unfortunately could not realize (Kashkachakov, 1992, p. 12).

In recent years, defensive nationalism in the periphery has moved from cultural revival to well-organized political movements that have vaulted their advocates into power positions in practically all autonomous ethnic regions of the Russian Federation. Ironically, radical nationalists have managed to bring to or to keep in power former Party officials who have skillfully exchanged their Communist ideologies for nationalist doctrines and used such nationalism as a counterbalance in negotiations with the Center for control of local resources.

The most striking example is the Republic of Tatarstan. Here, the ruling elite employed Tatar ethnonationalism, radically expressed by ultra-nationalist organizations and local intellectuals, to establish a firm and indisputable political order based on titular representation. About 85% of all key appointments at the republican and local levels have gone to ethnic Tatars, even though they comprise no more than half the population. Using the powerful slogans of national sovereignty and self-determination, the Tatarstan authorities have defined their republic as a fully sovereign state and 'a subject of international law'. This provocative assertion has been used effectively with other popular slogans ('associated state,' 'equal partnership with Russia') to defy both the federal constitution and the Russian authorities.

In March 1992, the local authorities held a referendum on the question, 'Do you want the Tatarstan republic to be a democratic and sovereign state building its relations with Russia on a partnership basis?' The President of Tatarstan's statement accompanying the referendum clarified for the public that voting 'yes' would not mean secession from Russia. Manipulated by local administrators and by the controlled mass media, the public passed the referendum by a very slim margin – 1%. Yet these results were immediately proclaimed as an expression of the people's will to an independent state. As a realization of this 'will,' the Tatarstan Supreme Soviet approved a new constitution in November 1992. Article 61 defines the republic as a sovereign state associated with the Russian Federation.

It seemed as though a confrontation was imminent. But after two years of intensive negotiations, Tatarstan and the federal authorities signed a treaty in February 1994. It grants more responsibilities and rights to the republic and also demonstrates symbolically the possibility of peacefully accommodating even the most radical nationalist scenarios. By concluding this treaty with Moscow, the government of Tatarstan achieved at least three goals: strengthening the republic's position and legitimacy, easing potentially dangerous tensions between the two major local ethnic groups, and minimizing the political role of Tatar extremists.

Other republics were carefully watching this dispute. Regional leaders soon learned that challenging the Center could be much more impressive and legitimate when framed in the language of ethnonational demands. In confronting this challenge of political nationalism, the federal authorities would have to negotiate more responsibly than in cases of mere regional separatism (as when Yeltsin simply dismissed the local governor of the self-proclaimed Urals Republic in the Sverdlovsk administrative region).

Moderate official ethnonationalism thus became an appealing model for other ethnoterritorial elites to emulate in the federal political arena. That is why republican leaders in Russia still strongly oppose any attempts to grant equal status to all units ('subjects') of the federation or to deprive the republics of their constitutional definition as 'national states'. They see in these moves a danger of losing a special status based not on economic or demographic resources but on ethnicity, a factor viewed in post-Soviet societies as indispensable for claiming political power.

Not all ethnonationalists on Russia's periphery are choosing negotiations rather than military confrontation. Separatist leaders in the Chechen Republic have opted for a coup d'etat style of political behavior since the autumn of 1991, when the former Soviet general Dzhokhar Dudayev proclaimed an independent Chechnya. Here, nationalism has proven quite literally to be 'ethnicity plus an army'.

Chechen militant nationalism has sent a clear message to its potential proponents. Its irresponsible strategy has had a sobering effect on other regions of the country where ethnonationalism is still strong. Ethnic leaders in Russia and other successor states are becoming more interested in avoiding conflict-generating confrontations, following the

Tatar and not the Chechen lead. On 14–15 January 1995, at the Peace Palace in The Hague, a meeting took place to provide an opportunity for the top leaders of breakaway regions to engage in discussion with senior officials from the central governments of Russia, Ukraine, Georgia, and Moldavia. The idea was to examine the factors that lead to successful avoidance of the use of force in dealing with regional conflicts in the former Soviet Union. By general agreement, the case of Tatarstan was presented as a model or method for resolving conflicts of separatist or irredentist nature. Tatarstan and Chechnya had both refused to sign the Russian Federation Treaty in March 1992, but each took a very different path.

The leadership of Tatarstan, especially President Mintimer Shaimiev, a former Party bureaucrat originally from the countryside, has kept a low profile, opting for a complex game of confrontation and compromise in a prolonged negotiation process. In 1992, a series of meetings took place with officials and experts from Tatarstan. At the very beginning of the meetings, two irreconcilable positions were presented by federal and regional representatives: the former insisted that Tatarstan was a subject of the federation, while the latter maintained that 'Tatarstan is not Russia and it is a subject of international law'. On 15 February 1994, however, Tatarstan signed a treaty and 12 agreements with Moscow, affirming the republic's constitution and presidency, republican citizenship, guaranteeing a significant degree of sovereignty over oil and other natural resources, granting special provisions for military service, as well as various other rights and powers. At the round-table in The Hague, Shaimiev provided the following explanation of his policy:

> In an effort to find non-violent ways to resolve the status of Tatarstan, we conducted negotiations for three years with President Yeltsin. . . . We managed to arrive at a compromise and we signed the Treaty on Mutual Delimitation and Delegation of Authority. As a basis for the Treaty, we agreed to acknowledge both constitutions although these constitutions still have some contentious issues. At this stage, however, it is a matter of finding a compromise. . . . We came to an agreement stating that Tatarstan is uniting with the Russian Federation on the basis of the constitutions of both Republics and on the basis of the signed Treaty. We agreed to delegate the strategic issues (defense, security and some other issues) to the Center and we think it is reasonable...The Treaty is a safeguard against a possible unitary development on the part of Russia. The imperial mentality, unfortunately, is still prevalent in Russia today. The main point now is to focus on building a democratic federation (*EAWARN*, 1995, February, p. 11).

Against the background of the failure of negotiation and compromise in Chechnya, this kind of persistent non-violent nationalism became an encouraging point of departure for many Periphery leaders trying to balance violent and peaceful times and political methods. Even the most aggressive Abkhazian separatist leader, Vladislav Ardzinba, had to change his position at that moment. As reported in the *Economist*, 'rebels in Abkhazia said they would give up their struggle for independence from Georgia, citing Chechnya as evidence that the West would do nothing to help separatist states' (18 February 1995).

Here we approach a crucial issue: what kind of sources are feeding extreme nationalist scenarios on the part of minority groups? Which arguments are used to legitimize challenging the status quo? As distinct from hegemonic (or majority) nationalism, which is more often characterized by preserving the system and by maintaining the dominant status of a group, defensive (or minority) nationalism usually challenges the order of things, or prefers to 'exit' from the system. This 'revolutionary' nature of defensive nationalism makes it no less conflict-generating, militant and aggressive than hegemonic nationalism. Trans-Dniestria in Moldavia, Abkhazia and South Ossetia in Georgia, Nagorno Karabakh in Azerbaijan, and Chechnya in Russia, all have had violent manifestations of ethnic dissent. Not one of these cases could be considered successful since the goals were not achieved, at least not in the short term. All of these manifestations have caused destructive conflicts and wars involving many casualties, refugees and huge material losses.

The main reason for the limited military and political success of extreme forms of minority nationalism is such groups' lack of resources in comparison with their more powerful opponents, who represent a larger and established state and a dominant society. These resources, which provide the motives and basis for the transformation of Periphery nationalism from cultural/political into militant/violent forms, are of various types and are very often far from being predetermined. All 'predictions' or 'mapping' of potential candidates for separatist scenarios tend to be superficial, usually involving a certain degree of prescription. Meanwhile, from analyzing existing cases, we may define a number of important factors (or resources) which allow the 'mild-to-wild' transformation of ethnonationalism.

First, a certain historical and socio-economic background is needed for the emotional mobilization of rank-and-file fighters and for the programmatic discourse of elite elements. Real or imagined 'historical injustices' and the sufferings of previous generations, transmitted through literary texts or oral tradition, are powerful resources for fighters. Second, charismatic leaders are needed (not dull and pragmatic figures like Shaimiev), mainly recruited from among articulate intellectuals or from the ranks of impressive-looking professional military officers ready to sacrifice their relative social comfort and the fate of 'their people' for the sake of political projects, and capable of formulating irrational appeals and inflammatory propaganda to rally people around the 'interests of a nation'. Third, there should be access to military arsenals or money for arms purchases to build paramilitary groups headed by field commanders (primarily from war professionals). A final crucial factor is the need for internal allies and outside support, and the search for that resource. Such internal supporters or sympathizers could be local non-titular or military garrisons of the Russian army, as was the case in Abkhazia and Trans-Dniestria.

Outside support may acquire varying dimensions, from involvement on the part of the international community and its structures, to soldiers of fortune traveling from one hot spot to another as professional killers. The most powerful outside resource is an ethnic diaspora or geopolitical actors who can provide decisive support for secessionists. Sometimes these two factors combine – as with the Russian army and local ethnic Russians in Trans-Dniestria and Abkhazia, and military and civic Armenians of the motherland and diaspora who initiated the conflict and fighting in Karabakh. Some separatist projects are lucky in one respect and unsuccessful in others. The Chechens were lucky (or unlucky!) to have a charismatic and militant leader imposed by the Center to carry out local 'decommunization' after the August 1991 coup. The Chechens stockpiled ammunition and heavy weapons from the corrupt Russian military – a dream of all separatists. However, the Chechens made a fatal mistake in expelling ethnic Russians from the republic, provoking in-group differences and rivalries as well as negative attitudes in the rest of the country among members of a major ethnic group – Russians. Because of a widespread mafia notoriety and a weak diaspora abroad, outside support for Chechnya was belated and more formalistic. Finally, what the Chechens were challenging was not a weak and disoriented new government of a successor state, such as the Georgian and Moldavian governments, but the authoritarian rule of the Kremlin and its massive military machine.

Today, the separatist projects in the territory of the former Soviet Union are in mid-stream: none has been accomplished successfully; none has fully failed. Too many factors are at work behind the rhetoric of national self-determination; various power dispositions and personal ambitions could influence future events. What is clear now is that the rewards promised by the extreme form of Periphery nationalism are proving inadequate: instead of acquiring a proper voice and improving governance, the Periphery separatists are now seeking to exit the system and build their 'own' states. The newly emergent post-Soviet states can scarcely afford further disintegration, and would do well to consider other options.

Notes

1   Personal notes, 29 November 1991, Moscow.
2   Iliya Fuki to Valery Tishkov, 26 June 1995, Moscow.
3   Interview with Knarik Kamalyan, 25 July 1995, Oslo.
4   Personal notes, 13 July 1995, Moscow.
5   Statement by Vladislav Ardzinba at The Hague Round-table, 15 January 1995.
6   Interview with Alexander Nevzorov in 'Rossia', no. 44, 16–22 November 1994, p. 3.

12

What Is Rossia? Identities in Transition

12.1 Debates on Legitimacy and Threshold

After the demise of the Soviet Union, Russia rather unexpectedly found itself a multi-ethnic country with an open agenda – as did the other Soviet successor states. Besides the necessary economic and political transformations, the most serious challenge was and remains how to legitimize and govern such a sprawling multi-ethnic entity. Even established democracies do not always have a good record in this field – what then of the sudden and poorly institutionalized emergence of the Russian Federation? There are perhaps still more questions than answers concerning this new Russia. Many of these questions are relevant also for the other successor states: Azerbaijan, Georgia, Moldavia, Tajikistan, and Ukraine all face serious internal and external challenges to their status and borders. In this chapter I analyze the status of such new states, primarily Russia, as a political, psychological, and cultural problem, but also as an internationally recognized historical *fait accompli*.

States are not given by some supranatural dispensation. They are the result of purposeful activities exercised through forced projects or political contracts. States are not eternal – especially not as to size and shape – and they are perceived differently by members of the society, designated by state borders as well as by the outside world. States are constituted not only by territories, by citizenship, and by a legal-constitutional framework. Assessing the situation of newly emergent or of radically transforming states, we should bear in mind that 'a state exists chiefly in the hearts and minds of its people; if they do not believe it is there, no logical exercise will bring it to life' (Strayer, 1970, p. 5). Only shared values, symbols, and a mutually accepted legal-political order can provide the necessary broad popular legitimization: top-level agreements and even international recognition are insufficient to build or uphold a state. Furthermore, in today's highly interdependent world, an increasingly important prerequisite for a state's existence involves international norms and attitudes on the part of powerful neighbors and geopolitical actors. What do the people and political entrepreneurs who live in the new Russia think of this state? What are the mutual perceptions now evolving within and among the successor states to the once-powerful Soviet Union?

Today it seems only reasonable to regard Russia as a legitimate nation-state, now that it has been accepted in the United Nations as a full member together with other multi-ethnic countries like China, India, Mexico, Spain, or Great Britain – all generally considered to be nation-states. This, of course, is dodging the question of what a 'nation-state' actually is. There exists no proper definition of what is 'a nation-state', or 'a national state'. Strictly speaking, no such definition is possible, because these labels represent no more than political and academic jargon, well established in lay writings and in propaganda since the French Revolution. The vulnerability of the term lies in the very fact that there are no states in the world which could be qualified in any opposing categories (e.g. 'non-nation state'). From Jamaica and the USA, with their 'out of many, one people' and *e pluribus unum,* to India with the country's formula 'unity in diversity', and even including South Africa with President Mandela's appeal for building a multi-cultural nation, all countries like to define themselves as 'nation-states'. There are no external criteria, except perhaps membership in the United Nations.

'Nation-state' is meaningless in scholarly terms, and non-applicable in legal terms. It is an example of how 'praxis' rhetoric has been elevated to the level of a nearly universal and heavily misused category. In this chapter, my position is that a state is just a state. Labeling it as 'national', or not, is like giving it a color adjective ('blue state', 'brown state', etc.): quite meaningless, like the lengthy academic discussions on counting how many states may be called 'national' or 'nation-states', and how many not (see Connor, 1972, 1994; A.D. Smith, 1991; Stavenhagen, 1996). A 'nation' is a powerful, emotionally and politically loaded word which two forms of social groupings – polities and ethno-cultural entities – claim as their exclusive property.

With these reservations, I still feel it appropriate to participate in these imagined but politically powerful realities. What are the prospects for nation-building in Russia? Indeed, some experts and policy-makers have branded the nation-state project in Russia as 'mission impossible'. As recently as in spring 1994, Zbigniew Brzezinski asked: 'Is Russia primarily a nation-state or is it a multi-national empire?' and called for the firm creation of 'a felicitous environment for Russia to define itself purely as Russia'. He went on to say: 'In not being an empire, Russia stands a chance of becoming, like France and Britain or earlier post-Ottoman Turkey, a normal state' (1994, pp. 72, 79). Another observer, arguing 'in defence of liberal nationalism', has listed the Russian Federation among states – like India, Pakistan, South Africa, Iraq – which could be ripped apart by a wave of disintegrative nationalism in the next few decades (Lind, 1994, p. 99).

'What is Russia?' is also asked by many inside the country. Great-Russia nationalists and Russian traditionalists want to restore the Soviet Union or the Russian Empire in various ways. For example, Alexander Solzhenitsyn has appealed for restructuring Russia as a Slavic state embracing Ukraine, Belarus, and at least half of Kazakhstan as well (*Pravda*, 1, 2 November 1994). Others again have concluded:

> Reintegration of the post-Soviet territory in its various areas and in various forms is inevitable. This makes it all the more important to prevent nationalism, the ideology of one's exceptional place and role, from gaining ground in [the] greater [part of] the former state, i.e. in the Russian Federation. Sustaining the old traditional state, cultural, non-ethnic identification in the minds of the inhabitants of the Russian Federation could pave the way for a voluntary and free unification of the parts of the decomposed state which economically and politically gravitate towards one another (Tsipko, 1994, pp. 454–455).

Some research institutes of the Russian Academy of Sciences have produced expert reports on 'myths and realities' of reforming Russia – predominantly to express political opposition to the ongoing transformations and to return the Academy to its former status of advising scholarly institution (see, e.g., Osipov, 1994). Political parties and groups, like the Communists or the former Communists, have established 'research corporations' and 'funds' in order to exercise their cognitive intentions in forms of pseudo-scholarly 'general theories' of everything: the Cosmos, civilization, society, Russia, or whatever. The RAU Corporation – an odd combination of former tutors of Marxism–Leninism, shamanistic-type 'experts' and analytical specialists working for the military and 'strategic studies' establishments, including the Security Council of the Russian Federation – has suggested 'general theories' of that kind (in fact, 'everyday theories') as conceptual frameworks that act to determine the political strategy and the place of Russia in the world (see, e.g., Zinoviev, 1995; Zuiganov, 1995).

The same holds true for writings and statements of non-Russian nationalists, arguing that 'Moscow should define what is Russia first and then start negotiating with those who have already defined their sovereign statehood'.[1] Here, doubts concerning Russia's legitimacy are based on assessments of its ethnic composition and on the demands made by most militant leaders of non-Russian nationalities for their 'own' states. But even those who support Russia as it emerged after December 1991 have been expressing confusing and vague ideas as to the future of the state. The current literary and public debates are overwhelmed with alarmist speculations of 'social chaos'. Serving rapidly changing political realignments, mythopoetic scholarship is quick to produce a raft of new holistic concepts on 'national idea', 'vision of Russia', 'back to millennium Russia', 'Russia ahead!' – enough to make an analyst feel at times that the major obstacle to Russia on its way to 'normal' statehood is not the ethnic mosaic per se or the various societal cleavages. Rather, it is this 'mind aflame', nurtured by elitist social engineers into the mentality and language concerning ethnicity and state-building perspectives. This is an inflamed and imagined picture far too often out of touch with reality. And yet, to de-construct it in an intelligent manner is probably no easier a task than to build a market economy or a democratic system of governance.

It is very often the case that no single scientific criterion can be applied to these theories, and that they are true to the extent that there are people who exercise or believe them. These theories are not a subject of scholarly critique, but a subject of scholarly (or clinical) research – as a fact of sociology (or of psychiatry) – research which describes, systematizes, and finally, explains them (Kordonsky, 1995). This 'big mess', with painful conflations of ideas and wars of positions, might be explained through the theoretical metaphor of the 'ideological hegemony threshold' suggested by Ian Lustick in his profound study *Unsettled States, Disputed Lands* (1993). Analyzing several historical cases of major changes in the shape and size of states (Britain and Ireland, France and Algeria, Israel and the West Bank/Gaza), Lustick concludes that in the building of states, as in the building of any institutions, the process by which positively valued and stable expectations are produced or destroyed includes both continuous and discontinuous elements, as well as both political and psychological aspects. There exist political as well as psychological mechanisms of state-building and state contraction. The transformation of states – including partition, territorial acquisition, secession – is more than the straightforward effect of acts of war. It results not so much from people's will as from 'activities and pressures of elites positioned to benefit from an enlargement of the state as against more parochial elements able to calculate that enlargement of the domain would disadvantage them' (1993, p. 445). This observation could be projected also on the opposite case, that of state disintegration – a process of profound political change which presupposes the overthrow (substitution) of an existing hegemonic conception of the state over and beyond a threshold; this procedure can be accomplished 'only when forces pushing in that direction [are] overwhelming' (Lustick, 1993, p. 175).

In the case of the former Soviet Union, some aspects fit this concept, and some probably do not. As Lustick writes,

> the suddenness of the Soviet Union's contraction into Russia, the disappearance of the socialist regime, and the virtual elimination of the Communist Party were due to an unsuccessful attempt by Mikhail Gorbachev to separate and preserve the territorial shape of the Soviet state, as a weakly institutionalized feature of its existence, from other features which he desired to deinstitutionalize, remove, and reinstitutionalize in substantially different form . . . But the forces for change that had accumulated beneath the decrepit hegemonic conceptions inherited from the Brezhnev era were overwhelming . . . Unprotected by hegemonic conceptions of its naturalness, the territorial shape

of the state ruled by Moscow as including all fifteen republics was thrown open to question. Territorially based solidarities and irredentist sentiments thereby became ordinary usable resources for competing politicians struggling to install new regimes within the husk of the Soviet Union and take power within them. The result was a proliferation of independent republics out to rationalize their boundaries according to some principles (usually nationalist) that could serve the interests of elites positioned to benefit from them. In part because he lacked a new hegemonic conception for a post-Soviet 'Russian' state for which he could stand as a credible exemplar, Gorbachev himself, along with his party, was rendered politically irrelevant, plunging Russia into regime crisis and a protracted war of maneuvers (Lustick, 1993, pp. 440–441).

Basically, I agree with this explanation, but with a few reservations. First, as we shall see, the territorial shape of the Soviet state as a hegemonic idea was not such a weak feature of its existence. Second, forces pushing disengagement from the existing state direction were not so overwhelming. They began to gain this dominant position only after the major act of state dismembering took place. This accomplished political act did not provide even the necessary time for announcing it among all participants in the process, for arranging the transfer of power and of nuclear weapons – not to speak of serious doctrinal efforts to define the nature of post-Soviet states. This process, with psychological readjustments and doctrinal rethinkings of new realities, is taking place only post factum, which makes the institutionalization of successor states a vital and extremely difficult task. The major difficulty here is to abandon the previous hegemonic concept, through a transition of Soviet identity into . . . into what? That is the question.

12.2 The Dynamics of Soviet Legacies

All post-Soviet states are now on the path to 'nation-building', but Russia is not at the forefront of this historical race. There are various reasons for this, beyond the general lack of political wisdom and will. From previous regimes, the Russian Federation has inherited various ambivalences concerning nation-building efforts. In pre-revolutionary Russia the tsarist monarchy and the Orthodox Church were the major institutions that provided legitimacy to the state, defined as the personal domain of the Tsar. A process of introducing civic nationalism into the public discourse under the concept of 'fatherland' (*otechestvo*) and 'people' (*narod*) started in the 18th century, under Peter I and Catherine II (see Greenfeld, 1992). Figures like the historian Nikolai Karamzin, the scholar and writer Mikhail Lomonosov, and the poet Alexander Pushkin were among the first intellectuals who tried to instill in Russian society an idea of the nation in its civic meaning. This they did by elevating one standard language, one history myth, and one 'glory' for a country where ethnic Russians actually comprised only about a half of the population. Up until the late 19th century, in liberal discourse about a 'Rossian' or 'Russian' nation, the two words 'Russian' and 'Rossian' (*russkaya* and *rossiiskaya*) were often used synonymously, without strong ethnic connotations. It was enough to be baptized as Russian Orthodox to be considered as a Russian. Russian literature abounds with references to this inclusive sense of belonging. In Chekhov's 'Lady with a Dog', Dmitrii Gurov asks Anna Sergeevna after he sees the name 'von Dideritz' at her entrance door, 'Is your husband a German?'. 'No, it seems that his grandfather was a German, but he is an Orthodox himself,' answers Anna Sergeevna. Thus those who participated in Russian Orthodoxy and language were perceived as being one people.

This means that before the Bolshevik Revolution, a process of Russian civic nation-building was already under way – to the extent that this was possible in a predominantly illiterate and agrarian country: i.e. basically on the level of elite discourse. It was challenged mainly by smaller-scale projects of Periphery nationalism – propagated also among elites – of the Finns, Poles, Ukrainians, Georgians, and Tatars. Liah Greenfeld concludes her study of this process in Russia by saying: 'Moved by the restless spirit born out of the agony of its elite, Russia would never give in to despair completely. It would never give up hope to becoming the superior Western state, to fulfill the promise of France, to be the truly new New World' (1992, p. 274).

The nation-building process in Imperial Russia was abruptly halted by the Bolshevik regime, and the whole vocabulary was changed in favor of Austro-Marxist ethnonational categories. Now the 'socialist nations' were proclaimed and constructed in the Soviet Union on the basis of existing or invented cultural differences. Soviet ideology and political practice, while pursuing declaratory internationalism, also enforced mutually exclusive ethnic loyalties on the principle of blood, and through the territorialization of ethnicity on the principle of 'socialist' (read: ethnic) federalism. The very process of civic nation-building lost its sense, replaced by the clumsy slogan of 'making the Soviet people' from many nations, instead of making one nation from many peoples.

The recent deep transformations have brought to an end the Soviet state and, we may assume, its hegemonic conception. Radical intellectuals and political entrepreneurs in the Center and in the Periphery alike have strongly repudiated the 'Soviet people' project as part of the Communist legacy. And yet, ironically enough, it is now becoming clear that in many respects the Soviet regime did succeed in constructing a 'new entity' and a certain 'hegemonic idea'. After the demise of the Soviet Union, this has manifested itself not only in a highly interdependent economy and in partly guarded external borders, but also in powerful cultural symbols and values, in extensive human and professional links on the individual and collective levels, even in the behavioral patterns and perceptions of the outside world.

This Soviet identity phenomenon can be analyzed on two intermingling levels – that of the elite, and the grass roots. As to the first, we should ask what kind of interests and benefits the elites pursue in their appeals to the former state and order. There is an odd alliance of politically opposed and ethnically different elements around the issue of state transformation. The most 'natural' protagonists of the 'restoration' project are post-Soviet Communists, who have exchanged their adherence to Party rule and class ideology for a nostalgic rhetoric about how 'safe' and 'happy' a place Soviet society was, with the 'friendship of the peoples' in full bloom. Not all of them formulate the explicit demand to re-establish the Soviet Union as such. What we can see is the reflection of some irreversible cumulative changes in the identities of most stubborn enemies of ongoing reforms and of geopolitical shifts. The Communist Party of the Russian Federation puts among its platform's priorities the promise to abolish the Belovezhsky Agreement of December 1991 and 'to provide conditions for a gradual restoration of a union-state on a voluntary basis'. In its December 1995 election platform Gennadi Zuiganov's party promised that, if they came to power, they would 'address the governments and the peoples of the republics of the illegally dismembered Soviet Union with a proposal to reconstruct one union-state voluntarily'. On 15 March 1996, the Communist-controlled State Duma passed a resolution proclaiming the Belovezhsky Agreement as an illegitimate act. This led to a serious political crisis in the country and strong protests on the part of other states within the CIS. Several smaller Communist groups are even more straightforward in their missionary projects. The Russian Communist Labor Party and the Russian Party of Communists formed an electoral bloc 'Communists – Labor Russia – for the Soviet Union' which managed to collect 200,000 signatures to be registered for participation in elections to the State Duma in December 1995, and they nearly managed to pass the 5%

barrier to be represented in the Parliament. Similar marginal political groups are operating in other successor states, as in Belorussia, Ukraine, and Moldavia.

As to the top leadership currently in power in Russia and other successor states, this claim is now off the official agenda, with one exception: Belorussian President Nikolai Lukashenko, who has openly condemned the decision to dissolve the Soviet state. But there are more personalities in key positions who feel strong sympathy for the 'restoration' project, although they do not express these feelings publicly. We find them not only among the members of the present Russian government, the Presidential administration, and the Parliament whom I know personally, but also among influential acting politicians of other states. As Boris Oleinik, Chairman of the Committee on Foreign Relations of the Ukrainian Parliament, told me privately, 'all three of them [he meant Yeltsin, Kravchuk, and Shushkevich] were too drunk and too excited at being able to find a rescue from Gorbachev's KGB in the dark bushes of Belorussia not to do something that promised to bring them into the annals of history'.[2]

Legal aspects of political behavior still rank low in arguments based on inherited mentalities. In many cases, the feeling of Soviet loyalty can be explained by personal displacements from the comfortable positions previously enjoyed by many of the older generation who have remained active in today's political process. For example, the same Boris Oleinik was a Deputy Chairman of Gorbachev's Supreme Soviet and a highly acclaimed Ukrainian national poet and writer. But the most powerful motive behind this stand would seem to be the rational calculations of political individuals and activist coalitions to build a base among the electorate through direct appeals to nostalgia and the disorientations caused by the rapid and chaotic discontinuities of recent times.

This game, played by elite activists in a slowly changing psychological climate, is evident not only in the political marketplace but in other public domains as well – the mass media, commercial art and show business, and even consumer production. Let me give just a couple of examples. The long-established Soviet newspaper *Komsomol'skaya pravda* has managed to keep its wide audience probably largely through not changing its title, which may have seemed embarrassing during the radical dismantling of Communist symbolism. The 'Red October' chocolate factory in Moscow, in competition with foreign 'Mars' and 'Snickers' bars, has regained its customers not only by keeping the firm's name, but by dint of the clever slogan: 'The taste you remember from childhood!' Retrospective exhibitions, TV, theater, and concert programs under the motto 'We lived in a great epoch' are among the most popular in Russia today.

What is the meaning and message underlying this phenomenon? A simplistic approach suggests a 'neo-imperial syndrome' deeply rooted in Russia's politics and in ethnic Russians as a people. However, such an explanation ignores the fact that among 'pro-Soviet' agitators we also find non-Russians and 'anti-Russians'. Let us listen to a few powerful voices in this connection. There is Amangel'dy Tuleev, the governor of Kemerovo *oblast*, who, together with Gennadi Zuiganov, headed the list of Communist Party candidates in the December 1995 elections. Tuleev motivated his call for the restoration of the Soviet Union by arguments that were far from doctrinal postulates. Telling the story of his ferocious struggle for a decentralized but united and indivisible Russia, he added a point which is very important, one many people may feel and do not pronounce openly.

Through my own life experience I have come to the conclusion that I cannot live like it is now. There is no place for me to live until I can reintegrate Russia, Kazakhstan, Ukraine, Belorussia. For me, as an individual, today's situation is the end of everything. And there are millions, about thirty millions, of people such as myself, who have mixed blood, mixed marriages, and mixed children' (*Zavtra*, no. 51(56), December 1994, p. 3).

Thus, it would seem that people like Amangel'dy Tuleev are pro-Soviet not because of any doctrinal Communist position: no, they opt for a Communist stance because of deeper individual choices motivated by ethnic, even racial factors. In a socio-cultural context, many non-Russians felt themselves more at home within the larger Soviet ethnic mosaic than in the increased homogeneity of Russia today

These regional, and often ethnically non-Russian, political entrepreneurs are most vocal protagonists of crossing 'backward through the regime threshold' (Lustick, 1993, p. 440). Even Chechnya's rebellious leaders saw (at least before their military victory in August 1996) a better future in restoring the former state. During the first round of Chechen–Russian negotiations in December 1994, the head of Dudayev's delegation, Teimaz Abubakarov, directed an angry remark to the Moscow delegation: 'Had you not destroyed the Soviet Union, there would not be such a brothel in the country now.'[3] One year later, Dzhokhar Dudayev, in a newspaper interview 'Return Gorbachev to power' said sarcastically to the Russian journalist:

Show me the passport you are carrying now. You are a citizen of the USSR, not Russia. Absurd! No citizenship means no state. I would strongly recommend a doctrinal programme for restoration of the legitimacy of your state and of your citizenship: that means to return Gorbachev to power and to regulate all relations between subjects of the USSR (*Moskovskie novosti*, no. 80, 19–26 November 1995, p. 4).

No less important for my analysis is to measure grass-roots attitudes toward dismembering the Soviet state in order to answer the question of to what extent this state's hegemonic conception was 'decrepit'. A representative sociological survey carried out by Timothy Colton, Jerry Hough, and Susan Lehmann in collaboration with Mikhail Guboglo in November–December 1993 in all regions of the Russian Federation showed that only 21% of the respondents thought the breakup of the USSR was 'good' or 'more good than bad', whereas 70% answered that they saw it as 'bad' or 'more bad than good'. Among residents in Russia's republics, attitudes were strikingly similar: only 19% responded positively and 71% negatively. The small 'pro-Soviet' difference could generally be attributed to local ethnic Russians – but not in Bashkiria, where members of two non-Russian groups, Bashkirs and Tatars, demonstrated more pro-Soviet loyalty than local Russians. The highest level of negative attitude was registered among small groups of Laks and Lezgins in Daghestan (Table 12.1). These vulnerable minorities, especially those divided by new interstate borders, like the Lezgin, feel most endangered by the partition of the USSR.

The same American–Russian sociological survey showed major generational and political orientation splits on the feeling about the deceased state. Those who voted in the December 1993 elections for 'Russia's Choice' (Yegor Gaidar's party) demonstrated strongest support for the breakup (33%), followed by respondents who voted for other parties of democratic orientation: 24% – PRESS (Sergei Shakhrai's party) and 21% – YABLOKO (Grigorii Yavlinsky's party). The strongest rejection of the breakup was demonstrated by those who voted for the Communists (87%), Zhirinovsky's party (77%), and the Agrarians (76%). After the December 1995 elections, when these parties gained a majority in the new State Duma, restoration rhetoric has also gained in strength in the political debate.

More optimistic expectations for recognizable patterns of accomplished changes can be observed from the generational parameters. The younger generation demonstrates a

Table 12.1   *Soviet Identity in the Republics of Rossia (%), 1993*

Republic	Ethnic group (*no. of resp.*)	Q.: How do you evaluate the breakup of the USSR?				
		1	2	3	4	5
Bashkiria	Bashkir *(211)*	6	10	22	47	15
	Russian *(401)*	8	12	25	40	15
	Tatar *(259)*	6	9	27	45	13
Buryatia	Buryat *(248)*	6	14	26	35	19
	Russian *(728)*	6	9	28	45	12
Checheno-	Chechen *(588)*	12	9	29	44	6
Ingushetia	Ingush *(104)*	7	8	36	47	2
	Russian *(211)*	3	6	26	61	4
Chuvashia	Chuvash *(688)*	5	6	19	54	16
	Russian *(203)*	4	7	24	48	17
Daghestan	Avar *(291)*	9	12	12	48	19
	Dargin *(140)*	6	3	14	44	33
	Kumyk *(162)*	4	5	16	36	39
	Lezgin *(107)*	2	2	12	68	16
	Laks *(83)*	7	–	17	58	18
	Russian *(103)*	4	6	26	51	13
Kabardino-	Kabardin *(468)*	7	8	23	54	8
Balkaria	Balkar *(112)*	5	4	20	62	9
	Russian *(316)*	4	6	24	61	5
Kalmykia	Kalmyk *(502)*	9	14	25	44	8
	Russian *(396)*	9	8	21	55	7
Karelia	Karel *(204)*	11	12	15	40	22
	Russian *(636)*	10	17	20	37	16
Komi	Komi *(273)*	7	7	22	44	20
	Russian *(593)*	6	13	26	41	14
Mari	Mari *(354)*	5	5	24	46	20
	Russian *(538)*	6	7	21	53	13
Mordovia	Mordva *(291)*	6	8	24	53	9
	Russian *(624)*	5	8	28	54	5
North Ossetia	Osset *(524)*	3	7	16	68	6
	Russian *(303)*	4	5	17	65	9
Tatarstan	Tatar *(478)*	15	15	22	26	22
	Russian *(446)*	9	8	28	40	15
Tuva	Tuvin *(653)*	10	18	30	26	16
	Russian *(307)*	8	14	34	39	5
Udmurtia	Udmurt *(315)*	8	7	26	44	15
	Russian *(612)*	8	15	28	39	10
Yakutia	Yakut *(307)*	15	25	21	19	20
	Russian *(463)*	8	18	32	32	10

1 – Good; 2 – More good than bad; 3 – More bad than good; 4 – Bad; 5 – No answer.

Source: Colton, Hough, Lehmann, and Guboglo's survey, November–December 1993

higher level of 'forgiveness' and readiness to accept the new geopolitical map that has been carved out of the former state. Measuring attitudes among three generational groups (born in 1964–75, in 1944–63, in 1900–43), the same survey established that 30% of the young people support the breakup and 60% not, as against 23% and 70% for the second cohort of middle-aged people and the old generation (16% and 75%). Only among one category – the group of young people who voted for Russia's Choice – did more respondents consider the breakup as being to the good rather than harmful (48.6% and 41.4%).

However, what the sociological survey does not show is the growing tendency among young post-Soviet people, especially students and entrepreneurs, to build non-political movements and 'informal' coalitions, or networks, across new interstate borders. Here, let me mention the extremely popular TV program 'KVN', which unites students of the top universities all over the former Soviet Union, demonstrating 'one community of people playing one game' (KVN is a competition show with humor and parodies). What kind of more serious 'game' these informal communities may play in the future, however, is something we can only speculate on. Tellingly perhaps, one remark – 'to correct the mistakes of our fathers' – was made in a program broadcast on 12 December 1995.

The most difficult aspect of any quick recognition of nonlinear transformations in the shape and borders of a state involves the symbolic meaning of geographic space (territories) which has been generally transmitted and implanted through history texts, visual images of maps, and through personal experiences. 'Are you in the Soviet Union for the first time?', the President of the Republic of Tatarstan greeted Professor Donald Horowitz during our visit to this republic in October 1993. One summer day in 1994 I was struck by a question asked by three villagers in a rural area where my family has a country house. After the first question, 'What the hell has this Yeltsin done to us?', the next question was 'Tell us, Valery, are we really going to give up the Kuril Islands to Japan?' None of these men had ever been to the Far East, and two of them had not even visited Moscow, some 250 kilometers away. They would not have been able to explain what their real concerns were about this issue. But the image of the Kurils as in some way their symbolic property – that was alive and well! Nor is this an isolated case. A question in the Colton, Hough, Leimann, and Guboglo survey asked about attitudes toward possible transfer of the South Kuril Islands to Japan. The result was the following: only 11% agreed, and a full 62% were opposed to such a transfer of territory.

It is an interesting psychological aspect of state transformation that minor territorial issues may be more touchy and meaningful than a global change of a state – especially when the issue concerns 'loss' of territory.

In the same survey, a question on the Crimea disclosed that 69% of respondents supported uniting this part of Ukraine with Russia, and only 5% definitely opposed. I do not analyze here how easily such attitudes can be used by political entrepreneurs in order to damage relations between two states, as was the case after the Supreme Soviet of Russia passed a resolution in 1992 questioning the contemporary status of the Crimea. It is important to understand how deeply rooted and symbolically strong territorial images may be in mass mentalities, and how these images do not correspond to what Ian Lustick defined as quick, chaotic but recognizable patterns in the translation of 'decrepit' hegemonic conception into 'non-linear transformations' (1993, p. 441). Those who delivered public lectures on the 'international situation' or 'Soviet foreign policy' in the pre-perestroika era (when people were more interested to hear about the outside world than about their own country) might have observed an interesting phenomenon: for decades a regular question, especially in rural areas, was: 'Did Russia sell Alaska to America forever, or only for 99 years?'

Some territorial images, or hegemonic conceptions of the shape of a state, may live on in the public mentality. I myself am inclined to view the situation in Russia as comparable to that in Great Britain, where a dominant view of Ireland as a part of a core state, not a distant colonial territory, has emerged on the national level – making contraction in the case of Northern Ireland extremely difficult. Canada with Quebec and Spain with the Catalan and the Basque countries present similar scenarios. Both could be considered as cases where prevailing ideological consensus views the situation as a problem of subordination within one society rather than as a problem of the subordination of one society by another. To be sure, the case of France and Algeria is less relevant for comparison with the situation in the former Soviet Union, especially as concerns Russia and Chechnya or Tatarstan. A more relevant comparison could be the USA and either Hawaii (in terms of this geographically and culturally distant territory regaining its lost independence) or Alaska (in case of its secession from the lower 48). It may look like a provocative and paradoxical statement, but in a cultural sense, the hegemonic concept of the USA as a state still stretches 'From California to the New York Island, From the redwood forest to the Gulf Stream waters'. It would be much easier for this society to go through a contraction threshold than for the society brought up on Leo Tolstoy's *Sebastopol Stories* to go through the same exercise of contracting Russia by losing Crimea. This last case, hypothetically, resembles the greater difficulties to be expected should the 'Navaho nation' enclave or the Spanish-speaking political entrepreneurs south of the state of Texas formulate demands for radical changes of the shape of the USA. In this situation, it would be unacceptable for a larger state to acquiesce in secession because of resources and geostrategic issues, as well as because of the time distance, demographic shifts, and cultural interactions that took place after the mid-19th century. This would represent a tremendous challenge for the hegemonic conception of the USA.

Thus, what is politically qualified as the Soviet Empire was and still remains a system of elite vested interests and mass-level symbolic assets that is extremely difficult to divide or vanquish. It will take time for these assets to be devalued or partly transformed and maintained, as can be seen with regard to such powerful means of modernization and communication as the Russian language. The world community, Western strategists, and new post-Soviet leaders alike should realize that imperial legacies cannot be abolished by decree; what is needed are new loyalties, symbols, and values. These symbolic feelings and institutions are necessary universal elements of a culture and important legitimizing elements of power and state. How in this context do I see prospects for the situation in Russia? In which directions should it move in order to be considered a 'normal state'?

12.3 The Changing Essence of the Ethnic Challenge

As shown in previous chapters, post-Soviet ethnic manifestations are not only a question of protest against the diminished status and discrimination suffered by members of non-dominant groups. These manifestations are also a result of political efforts, mainly on the part of the state, to construct prestigious institutions of internal ethnonational statehoods, and of the extensive training of ethnic elites. These elites are now acquiring access to resources from which they feel they had been alienated by the unitarian state. They are beginning to exercise political and, partly, cultural control in their 'own' republics. In most of the ethnonational autonomies of the Russian Federation, political power is the assured domain of local nationals, even when the group does not comprise a majority but enjoys the status of a titular nationality. Simplistic interpretations may view this process of rising Periphery powers in the context of the decolonization paradigm, this time applying to the so-called 'inner empire'. 'Why don't you let them go?' a leading British expert on Russia's nationalities issues, Marie Bennigsen Broxup, asked me after visiting Tatarstan and Chechnya in 1992. New 'anti-imperialism' has become especially strong after the brutalities of the Chechen War (see, e.g., Dragadze, 1995).

The essence of the ethnic challenge facing the new Russia is still viewed as it was for a 'larger Soviet empire' – an authoritarian, dominating ethnic Russian Center against a submissive, suffering non-Russian ethnic Periphery. This formula excludes several quite important aspects. One of them is a mystery of post-Soviet politics – how local leaders have learned so quickly to use mobilization tools, legal procedures, material incentives, and personal contacts to influence and direct the process of power control. In some cases, direct physical threats and elimination of opponents are used, as in Daghestan in 1993 when two candidates for the Federal Assembly of Russia were killed. But basically, it is the old system of *nomenklatura* manipulation and doctrinal arguments preserved and put into the service of ethnic coalitions. Let us consider two rather moderate cases in the Volga area – Tatarstan and Bashkiria. Both are states, as defined by the Constitution, considered to be pioneers of decentralization and even of democratization. Their Presidents – respectively, Mintimer Shaimiev and Murtaza Rakhimov – together with their Yakutian colleague Mikhail Nikolaev, sent on 3 July 1995 an appeal to the President Boris Yeltsin, 'For a Consistent Policy to Democratize and Federalize Russia' (*EAWARN*, June 1995, pp. 15–16). The Tatarstan model of Center–Periphery conflict resolution was widely acclaimed, making the image of Tatarstan leadership into an avant-garde political force opposing Moscow-centered domination (see Khakimov, 1996).

I, personally, have led a dialogue with the Tatarstan leaders on the question of power distribution since 1992. In my meetings with President Shaimiev and with Farid Mukhamedshin, Head of the Republic's Supreme Soviet, this question was raised several times. I have heard the same argument: that there were no special efforts to exclude non-Tatars from the governing structures; and political promotion is based solely on individual qualifications and abilities.[4] This is probably so because there is a very strong pool of political and industrial managers and intellectuals among ethnic Tatars, capable perhaps of counterbalancing a similar pool among ethnic Russians. But the problem lies not only in ethnic representation: there is also the broader issue of political representation at large as a crucial element of non-totalitarian governance. The 5 March 1995 elections to the State Council of the Republic (local Parliament) yielded quite disturbing results, even though the elections were described by the President as 'a victory of stability'. From 466 candidates competing for 124 seats, in the first round, 69 deputies were elected, 43 of whom were heads of *raion* administrations, the head and the members of the Tatarstan executive government, the Vice President, and members of the Presidium of the Supreme Soviet. There was not a single representative of any political party. Only after the run-offs did the Communists get four seats, Equality and Legality Party (pro-Russian) one seat and Ittifak (radical nationalist) one seat as well. As to ethnic composition of the candidates, Tatars comprised 66%, Russians 28%, and representatives of other nationalities about 6%. After two rounds, the final ethnic breakdown of the State Council was Tatars 91 (73.4%), Russians 31 (25%), and other nationalities 2 (1.6%) (*EAWARN*, June 1995, p. 53).

Surely, such a decisive usurpation of power in favor of one group should give serious grounds for questioning the real political stability of this multi-ethnic polity – above and beyond the questions of manipulation. 'Those who believe in elections in Tatarstan are naïve people. Shaimiev and his people have already decided who will be sitting in the State Duma and there are no means to influence it in another way,'[5] noted Vasilii Bukharaev, a political scientist from Kazan State University, at a seminar discussing prospects for the coming election of December 1995. Bukharaev mentioned several names to expect as deputies from this republic; he was proven strikingly right when the results were announced.

In Bashkiria, the results of the 5 March 1995 local parliamentary elections can be also summarized as a victory of the 'party of power', and as a further syndification of the executive and legislative branches of power in the republic. Members of the *nomenklatura* were rescued by a new electoral law allowing incumbent representatives of the executive branch to combine their current positions with positions in the legislative body of the Republic. President Murtaza Rakhimov privately ordered all the heads of local administrations to run as candidates in the elections to the Chamber of Representatives of the State Assembly of the Republic. A total of 351 candidates were registered for the elections – among them only 10 women, 6 workers, 14 doctors, 38 teachers and professors, and 15 agricultural specialists. For elections to the Legislative Chamber 132 candidates were registered, among them 19 women, 19 teachers and professors. One hundred and eighty deputies were elected to the bicameral Parliament: 146 to the Chamber of Representatives and 34 to the Legislative Chamber. The ethnic composition of the new parliament does not reflect the ethnic structure of the population, nor of major social groups. Ethnic Bashkirs (21% of the total population) received 41% of all seats in the lower chamber and 56% in the upper chamber, whereas Russians (about 40% of the total population) got only about 20% of seats in both chambers. Ethnic Tatars (28% of the total population) were more or less proportionally represented. All 78 heads of local administrations appointed by the President managed to be elected, because it was they who fully controlled the election campaign (*EAWARN,* June 1995, pp. 35–37). It is they who now make up a majority of the Chamber of Representatives. Professor Rail Kuzeev, the Vice President of the Bashkir Academy of Sciences and a professional colleague of mine, offered the following succinct comment: 'Rakhimov's people have tried so hard that now the President has been put in the awkward position of being blamed for enforcing ethnocracy in the republic.'[6]

A democratic election process and active political opposition are probably the most crucial issues of democratization in ethnic autonomies of Russia today. Two or three years ago local rulers experienced fairly hard political challenges on the part of radical nationalists and Russian-oriented political activists. In Tatarstan, there was a growing political coalition 'Equality and Legality' headed by Ivan Grachev, who had enjoyed good support from the local electorate, especially in the capital city of Kazan. After he and two other local leaders were elected to the Russian State Duma on national democratic party lists (the Tatarstan authorities did not organize elections of December 1993 in the Republic) and the radical nationalists lost their support from below and manipulative incentive from above, Shaimiev could establish his leadership in an unchallenged position.[7] A similar situation has developed in Bashkiria, where the leader of the pro-federalist and pro-Russian party, Alexander Arinin, was elected to the State Duma in 1993, marking a turning point in political organization of these forces, which have not managed to regain their positions since. At a presentation at the Institute of Ethnology and Anthropology on 11 April 1996, Alexander Arinin, who had ensured his membership in the State Duma in December 1995, was reduced to expressing his complaints on the growing political autocracy in his native republic.

More serious conflict-generating political tendencies have emerged in some ethnically based republics with several competing non-Russian ethnic communities when those who control the top positions strive to exclude all others – not only Russians – from power. Weakened central control and the emerging market of democracy have brought serious disbalances into the functioning systems of unwritten consensus on more or less proportional representation of major ethnic groups living in one republic. This has most seriously affected the republics of Daghestan, Karachai-Cherkessia, and Kabardino-Balkaria, where no one group is strong enough to claim exclusive control of the institutions of power. A new system of negotiations and procedures for proper representation of minority groups is still only under discussion. The constitution and legislation – at the national and the republic level – do not provide adequate responses for local specificity. Some republics, like Daghestan and Karachai-Cherkessia, cannot yet finalize their legal structures because of these contradictions and complexities. On the other hand, in Daghestan consensus has been reached that it would be better not to follow general patterns and to introduce a presidential system of rule which could be interpreted as establishing imminent privileges for one group. As Ramazan Abdulatipov remarked wittily, 'everybody sees himself as a president in Daghestan, and that is why it is better not to have one at all in our republic'.[8] As a result, the political innovation of 'collective presidency' was introduced with two-year rotation of members of the State Council representing all major groups of this republic. Unfortunately, this promising policy of power-sharing in a multi-ethnic milieu was seriously damaged when, after the first two-year term had expired for representation of the Dargins, Magomed-Ali Magomedov extended his stay in power with the consent of the Constitutional Court of Russia.

Kabardino-Balkaria has chosen a presidential form of government. When an ethnic Kabardin, Valery Kokov, was elected President in 1992, this caused a serious political crisis. In September 1992, the local opposition organized a mass militant demonstration in front of the government building, which was taken under protection by the Russian militia forces. The situation in the capital city of Nal'chik was so serious that I, as Minister of Nationalities, had to fly there to assist in managing the crisis on behalf of the Federal Government. The situation was brought under control after an agreement was signed between the conflicting parties and certain measures were undertaken to broaden the representation of Balkar politicians and the opposition groups of radical nationalists.[9]

Probably the most difficult situation is that existing in Karachai-Cherkessia. Here political old-timers have controlled power ever since this autonomy got the status of republic in 1990. The government was headed by an ethnic Karachai, Vladimir Khubiev. Formerly deported to Central Asia, the Karachai comprise a little over 30% of the population of the republic now. The Karachai radical nationalist movement 'Dzhamagat' has formulated demands for resettling those 15,000 who still live in Central Asia for the formation of a separate national Karachai state. This has caused serious concern among Cherkess, Abazin, and Nogai minorities, as well as among the ethnic Russians (the latter comprising 40% of the population). The opposition responded with an alternative which in practice would mean breaking up the republic into three or four separate formations. Local activists were especially furious at the covert maneuvering of Khubiev to install his fellow Karachai in all key positions and to strengthen his power. One of the Cherkess activists provided me with a list of some 60 Karachais appointed by the Head of the Government to the most prestigious positions formerly occupied by Russians, Cherkess, and Abazins. It is only recently, in February 1995, that the joint session of the People's Deputies of the Republic of Karachai–Cherkessia elected a Coordinating Council composed of three persons from each of the five major ethnic groups. This step is just a small sign of what seems to be a promising strategy for ethnic accord, to which I return in the final chapter of this book.

Thus, there still exists a major dilemma for the state of Russia. The Center remains dominated by ethnic Russians and by those who had become integrated into the 'core' culture. Representative bodies like the State Duma lack proper representation of the regional enclaves of non-Russian nationalities. The Duma of 1993–95 was shamefully dominated by 'Garden Circle' (the downtown part of Moscow) politicians: 173 out of 450 deputies were Muscovites. The December 1995 State Duma elections cut the number of non-Russian deputies by one-third, depriving many small nationalities of the chance for political representation on the federal level. In addition come the executive governmental structures and other prestigious positions of the Center: high-ranking army officers, diplomatic servants, media barons, etc. These have never been an area for deliberate power redistribution. In reality, an opposite process of ethnic exclusion (or 'purification') could be observed recently, probably influenced in part by the Chechen War: in 1996, no more than three or four non-Russians remained among about 40 high-ranking administrators of the federal government's apparatus.

At the same time, local nationals (non-Russians residing in their 'own' territorial autonomies) are trying to grapple with the problem of keeping their culture and integrity vis-a-vis the larger society and culture. Still lacking a voice in the central system, they are unable to challenge its power. Until the time arrives when possible dramatic changes in the long-term demographic tendencies mean that Russians lose their majority status, it is unrealistic to expect that the existing ethnic system with one dominating group can allow a re-apportioning of power. The rational strategy chosen by many in the ethnic periphery is to lead a ferocious political struggle for the devolution of power, especially for control over the privatization of former state assets on the regional level, and in this way build their own father/motherlands. Regional ethnonationalism and group loyalties still play an important role in political mobilization, as a tool in negotiations with the Center, and in providing titular nationals with exclusive status in the republics. These elites have now begun opting for various scenarios – including extreme ones like 'exit' in the form of secession, or harsh repressions towards local 'double' minorities. What has become clear is that this competitive dialogue will remain a permanent factor in Russian society for the foreseeable future.

Russia today may not be falling apart, but it is faced with the serious challenge of barely manageable ethnicity. There are already exclusive ethnic political coalitions on the regional level, with the electorate split along ethnic lines. Ethnic intolerance, xenophobia, and violent manifestations in the form of territorial cleansing and communal clashes are found not only out in the republics but elsewhere as well, including large cities. State brutality, where force is used to counteract ethnically mobilized rebellions and to impose order, is bringing greater destabilization and ethnic alienation and hatred. What kind of 'creative symbolic action' might help Russia to meet the emerging ethnic challenge?

12.4   Towards a New State Doctrine

The quest for a new concept of nationalities policy and a formula for the new Russia has long been on the agenda of political and academic discourse – indeed, ever since it became clear that Gorbachev's major error lay in his nationalities policy and that Yeltsin could easily follow the same route. To date, the results of these debates and of political actions have been basically disheartening. The opinions expressed by influential experts and advisors and the position taken by President Yeltsin have often been mutually exclusive: from promising unlimited sovereignty for the regions, to bringing back unitarian rule and plans for abolishing ethnic autonomies. It has not been easy for them to recognize that any attempt to dismantle politically and emotionally legitimized realities – like the republics – would be yet another case of irresponsible social engineering. And it has been even harder to accept a formula for a multi-cultural nation based on dual non-exclusive loyalties (cultural/ethnic and state/civic) for the citizens. A formula like this would imply a strategy of gradual de-ethnicization of the state and of de-etatization of ethnicity, without questioning the existing system of ethno-territorial autonomies. A basic principle of nationalities policy is thus respect for individual rights, based on affiliation to a certain culture or an ethnic group. But such individual rights are not in themselves sufficient to provide a democratic system for governing a multi-ethnic Russia. Additional mechanisms must be implemented to define and provide collective rights, especially those of indigenous minorities.

Russia is not a 'national state' of ethnic Russians. Neither is any constituent part of it the exclusive property of any ethnic group. These fundamental points must be realized if Russia is to have a chance to move toward a civic society and a democratic state where human rights are respected and the cultural mosaic is preserved. I was glad to read in the text of the President's speech to the Federal Assembly these words, which I wrote at the request of Presidential political advisers Georgii Satarov and Emil Pain while they were drafting the annual 'State of the Nation' message: 'the sovereignty of the Russian Federation, as well as that of its constituent parts, is invested in its entire multi-ethnic population, not in ethnic groups. No single ethnic group can possess an exclusive right to control over territory, political institutions and resources. Equality of rights is conditioned by the need for mutually agreed decisions, taking into account the interests of various ethnic groups' (*Rossiiskaya gazeta*, 25 February 1994).

Together with a new Constitution which guarantees the integrity of Russia's republics and extends their rights (albeit it does not define the republics as 'national' states), this has marked the first serious step towards challenging the privileged status of titular groups in the republics. In it we can discern a new political tendency towards a civic principle of state-building and weakening disintegrationist projects – especially after all the top leaders of the republics and the administrative *oblasts* and *krais* managed to take control of the upper chamber of the federal Parliament – the Federation Council.

Since then, the federal authorities have taken serious steps to improve political dialogue and resource-sharing between Center and Periphery. In 1994–95, Tatarstan-style treaties were signed between Moscow and five new republics in the face of heavy criticism and alarmist warnings from 'strong state' advocates. In fact, these treaties and other concessions serve to strengthen the loyalty of republican leaders to Moscow. The latter became staunch supporters of the integrity of Russia; some of them now assist the federal government in dealing with militant separatism. Shaimiev's initiative to mediate negotiations with the Chechen rebels in spring 1996 was the most striking example of this changing political landscape. There is a prevailing mood among members of Russia's political club that disintegration is no longer on the country's agenda, especially in light of the reintegrationist agreements reached between Belorussia, Kazakhstan, Kirgizia and Russia in March–April 1996.

But a major project of civic nation-building still remains, and it needs to be introduced into public discourse within the context of competing approaches. Probably the best starting-point would be to define what it means for Russia to be a nation-state. The most important innovation in political symbolism could be the national idea of 'Rossia' (an accurate transliteration of the name of the country into the Latin alphabet) as a national state of 'Rossians' (*rossiyane* is a widely used word, quite distinct from the word '*russkie*', defining ethnic Russians) as citizens of the state. The idea of a 'Rossian' nation is not loaded with ethnic meaning as it is with 'Russian' (*russkaya*) nation. From a historical, political, and cultural perspective there are sufficient grounds for such a creative symbolic action. First, the Russian Federation is a member of the UN with other nation-states; and Russia (or better – Rossia) itself has a long tradition of using the term 'nation' in its international meaning. Previously, this was never properly legitimized because it contradicted the official Soviet doctrine of ethnic nationalism. Still, phrases like 'national anthem' or 'national coat of arms', 'national interests' or 'national security', or 'Yeltsin is the leader of the nation', 'the Kremlin is a symbol of the nation' and many others have become part of the permanent public discourse. Usually, the President starts his appeals to a national audience with the accustomed words, *'dorogie rossiyane!'* (Dear Rossians!) – as he did, for example, two days before the elections of December 1995.

Second, Rossia in its new borders is a historical fact, not the result of irresponsible political improvisation. It is a generally recognized geographical entity. Its economic, communication, and administrative infrastructures have been set and developed over the course of the 70 years when it existed as a constituent part of the Soviet Union. Even in the tsarist empire Rossia had its own administrative configurations bordering other regions of the country, like MaloRossia (Ukraine) or Turkestan (Central Asia). Despite huge and vital economic interdependencies within the borders of the former Soviet Union, the Russian Federation has its own economic and cultural profiles – and this makes the civic nation-building process not only possible, but indeed the sole realistic scenario.

Third, there is among the population a great degree of cultural cohesion and a sense of common identity. Just one example: with its 150 million people of different ethnic backgrounds (about one hundred ethnic groups, counting minorities from other successor states), Rossia is a large country where all the people can communicate in the same language. From that point of view, Rossia is more culturally homogeneous than many other large and even small countries considered to be nation-states.

Fourth, and most important despite all rhetoric, national identity and loyalty are real. To analyze accurately this important issue I included special questions in the programs of two major sociological surveys carried out in republics of Rossia to measure civic identity and its correlations with other identities. The results were interesting. Even in republics where independentist propaganda was at that time very strong, as in Tatarstan, only 24.4% defined themselves as 'only Tatarstani'; 12.8 % defined themselves as 'more Tatarstani than Rossiyane'; 35.8% as 'equally Tatarstani and Rossiyane; 12.3 % as 'more Rossiyane than Tatarstani'; 10.4 % as 'only Rossiyane'; while 4.3 % were unable to answer (see more, Tishkov, 1995d, p. 49). To be sure, a striking difference was found in another survey in the civic perceptions of Russians and Tatars living in this republic: 52% of Tatars, but only 15% of Russians evinced republican preferences. The lowest level of prevailing civic particularism was observed in the republics of Chuvashia, Karelia, Mari, Mordovia, Udmurtia; the highest levels were in Checheno-Ingushetia, Tuva, Daghestan, Yakutia (besides Tatarstan). In all republics except Checheno-Ingushetia, more respondents placed themselves in the category of citizens with two equally shared loyalties than in any other category (Table 12.2). Similar results were found in Leokadia Drobizheva's survey carried out in Tatarstan, North Ossetia, Yakutia, and Tuva, with an additional split between rural and urban citizens. The highest pro-republican identities were displayed among rural Tatars and Yakuts (86% and 80% respectively), and among urban Yakuts and Tuvins (72% and 66%) (Table 12.3).

Elsewhere in the country the level of multiple loyalties was even higher, and Rossian identity stronger. According to our observations a strong pan-Russian (or Rossian) identity exists among non-Russians living outside the territories of their 'own' states or autonomies. This part of the population comprises 18 million out of a total of 27 million non-Russians all over the country. For example, the 200,000-odd Tatars who have been living in Moscow for centuries find it extremely difficult to identify themselves with a 'Tatar nation' advocating self-determination on the territory of the Tatar republic. The same is true of the 4.5 million Ukrainians, 1.2 million Belorussians, as well as Germans, Kazakhs, and Armenians living in Rossia.

Table 12.2   *Civic Identities in the Republics of Rossia (%), 1993*

Republic	Ethnic Group (no. of resp.)	Q.: Of what polity do you consider yourself a representative?					
		1	2	3	4	5	6
Bashkiria	Bashkir *(211)*	25	18	48	4	1	4
	Russian *(401)*	5	6	51	23	12	3
	Tatar *(259)*	20	14	52	6	2	6
Buryatia	Buryat *(248)*	28	25	40	2	2	3
	Russian *(728)*	5	5	42	22	21	5
Checheno-	Chechen *(588)*	77	10	11	1	–	1
Ingushetia	Ingush *(104)*	14	41	45	–	–	–
	Russian *(211)*	8	11	51	18	6	6
Chuvashia	Chuvash *(377)*	14	9	57	7	5	8
	Russian *(230)*	2	2	35	32	26	3
Daghestan	Avar *(291)*	35	15	44	–	0	6
	Dargin *(140)*	29	26	31	–	–	14
	Kumyk *(162)*	40	15	37	6	1	1
	Lezgin *(107)*	31	8	44	3	5	9
	Laks *(83)*	25	14	51	-	-	10
	Russian *(103)*	23	17	50	3	2	5
Kabardino-	Kabardin *(268)*	22	25	47	1	0	5
Balkaria	Balkar *(112)*	15	21	52	2	–	10
	Russian *(316)*	4	4	58	18	8	8
Kalmykia	Kalmyk *(502)*	27	19	49	2	1	2
	Russian *(396)*	8	7	67	7	8	3
Karelia	Karel *(204)*	12	15	60	4	4	5
	Russian *(636)*	5	7	55	17	12	4
Komi	Komi *(273)*	22	15	48	4	3	8
	Russian *(593)*	5	6	43	22	17	7
Mari	Mari *(354)*	12	12	59	5	5	7
	Russian *(538)*	6	3	56	17	13	5
Mordovia	Mordva *(291)*	17	11	48	7	10	7
	Russian *(624)*	7	7	39	20	20	7
North Ossetia	Osset *(524)*	19	18	57	2	1	3
	Russian *(303)*	5	8	58	13	10	6
Tatarstan	Tatar *(478)*	33	19	34	2	1	11
	Russian *(446)*	8	7	49	18	10	8
Tuva	Tuvin *(653)*	42	22	33	1	1	1
	Russian *(307)*	3	4	52	27	13	1
Udmurtia	Udmurt *(315)*	17	12	60	4	2	5
	Russian *(612)*	5	6	43	22	18	6
Yakutia	Yakut *(377)*	38	21	39	1	–	1
	Russian *(463)*	8	9	56	14	8	5

1 – Only my republic; 2 – More my republic than Rossia; 3 – Equally my republic and Rossia; 4 – More Rossia than my republic; 5 – Only Rossia; 6 – No answer.

Source: Colton, Hough, Lehmann, and Guboglo's survey, November–December 1993

Table 12.3 *Civic Identities in Four Republics of Russia (%), 1994*

Q.: Of what polity do you consider yourself a representative?

	Tatarstan				North Ossetia				Yakutia				Tuva			
	Tatar		Rossian		Osset		Rossian		Yakut		Rossian		Tuvin		Rossian	
	U	R	U	R	U	R	U	R	U	R	U	R	U	R	U	R
Equally republican and Rossian	31	11	35	38	54	43	69	56	24	20	36	35	31	34	50	57
More republican than Rossian	59	86	19	30	43	55	13	7	72	80	34	48	66	64	13	13
More Rossian	3	1	36	20	2	1	17	29	1	0	23	13	1	1	31	27
No answer	6	2	10	13	1	2	2	8	3	0	6	4	2	1	6	3

U = urban; **R** = rural.

Source: Leokadia Drobizheva's survey, March–August 1994, IEA

Finally, the breakup of the USSR – which looked like a sudden and traumatic geopolitical change for Russians – was basically accepted by the citizens of Rossia, despite negative attitudes toward the event itself. A deep transformation of loyalty from one polity to another had already taken place among the majority of the population. Surveys were taken less than a year after December 1991, with questions parallel to those asked in 1987. In 1987 a majority in Moscow termed the Soviet Union their 'motherland' (68.6%) whereas the Russian Federation (at that time one of the Soviet republics) was called so by only 14.2% of the respondents. In 1992, 53.8% termed Rossia their 'motherland', while 27.1% mentioned the former Soviet Union. The most noticeable shift was found among young people (18–29 years of age): 62.8% regarded Rossia and 12.7% regarded the former USSR as their 'motherland'; among those over 50, the figures were 47% and 39%, respectively. No less interesting is the fact that the highest level of allegiance toward the former USSR was found among unskilled workers (35.6%) and at the directorship level (36%), whereas the strongest affiliation to Rossia was displayed by private entrepreneurs (66.5%) (Arutunyan, 1994, pp.138–139).

Probably most significant in the context of my idea of building a Russian nation is that a widespread feeling of being a Rossian ('*rossiyanin*') prevails over other identities in all national surveys carried out by professional sociologists. A survey from July 1993 in 10 regions of the Russian Federation (1,082 respondents) on the question of self-identification gave the following results: 5.8% considered themselves to be 'a Soviet man' ('*sovetskii chelovek*'); 47.9% as citizens of Rossia ('*rossiyanin*'); 14.2%, 'representative of their own nationality'; 31.4% , 'don't know/no answer'. Civic, not ethnic, identity is predominant among the majority and among all professional groups; it is highest among managerial personnel, qualified specialists, researchers and workers at commercial enterprises (51–58%); and lowest among workers and technical personnel at state enterprises (32–37%). Ethnic identity as a priority value was declared by a striking minority among all social groups (10–23%) (*Vestnik sodruzhestva sociologicheskikh assoziazii* [Newsletter of the Union of the Sociological Associations], no. 2, 1993, p. 10). These data present a picture very different from the everyday political rhetoric, mass media propaganda, and superficial academic exercises on the overarching role of ethnicity as a 'basic human need' for people in Rossia – and, I presume, also in other post-Soviet states.

12.5 The Power of Mentality Inertia

'Mentality inertia' is the major obstacle to the project of civic nation-building. By this I mean the inherited and tenacious dogmatic mentality induced through the long-cherished Soviet pseudo-theory of the 'national question'. This theory formed an integral part of Marxist–Leninist doctrine which produced its own political reality as well as hundreds of pseudo-academic practitioners, many of whom still occupy influential positions in the Establishment. It was thus no coincidence that the first negative reaction to Yeltsin's above-mentioned address came from Eduard Bagramov, formerly a leading Communist Party expert on the nationalities question and at the time Head of Department in the Ministry of Federation and Nationalities Affairs.

Bagramov cited several arguments against the new state doctrine. First, the Russians will not accept the notion of a Rossian nation because 'every Russian identifies himself as a representative of a great nation but not of an ethnic or tribal group'. Further, 'the Russians are a mature nation, not something like an amorphous ethnic group'. Bagramov went on to argue that such a new concept 'may deprive Rossian authorities of many arguments in defending the rights of ethnic Russians abroad'. His conclusion: 'Since it concerns an interpretation of basic theoretic and political categories in the most important official documents, there is an obvious need to discuss this question in order to correct the text of the Presidential address when it formulates a thesis about the nation' (Bagramov, 1994).

This resistance among older generation practitioners of the Russian nation (*russkaya natsiia*) metaphor means in reality an ideologically motivated elitist usurpation of grass-roots identity expressed in the notion of 'Russian people' (*russki narod*) and Russian culture. The term 'people' is still the basic category with which ethnic Russians – like other ethnic groups – identify themselves. There is nothing shameful or subversive if they remain attached to this basic category. The new concept does not deny the existence of Russian or other cultures – in the sense of feelings of belonging to certain ethno-cultural entities. As to ethnic Russians as a 'mature nation', Eduard Bagramov was far from the truth: like many other widely settled peoples Russians have in some aspects quite loose identities.

The cultural distances between geographical groups of Russians (those living in the northerly Pomor area and those living in the Caucasus, for example) may be greater than between Russians and the locals with whom they have had centuries of contact. In some areas, Russians participate in a phenomenon of border culture with mixed and specifically regional identities – as in the bilingual, bicultural belt between the Ukraine and Rossia, or between Belorussia and Rossia. For many of those Russians who recently found themselves in territories outside of Rossia, ethnic/cultural and civic identities may coexist peacefully. A recent survey carried out by Estonian sociologists shows that about 95% of the Russians living in northeastern Estonia wished to be Estonian citizens, or would like to see their children as citizens of Estonia. As Marika and Aksel Kirch wrote, 'Today, Estonians and Russians are forging a new national identity as members of the same state. The emerging new identity of Russians is more Estonian-centred and local-minded; already it is showing some features of desirable interaction and integration rather than confrontation' (Kirch & Kirch, 1995, p. 440).

If these Russians become loyal citizens of the new state and participate in its economy and culture, why could they not be members of the Estonian civic nation – as is the case in the United States or in France, where tens of thousands of Russians moved during this century and established themselves as members of these nations? Or, like hundreds of thousands of Rossians with Russian cultural identity and with long-time proto-German ethnic roots who moved to Germany in recent years to become members of this nation? This is a completely relevant question and comparison. If we exclude political statements and manipulative, imposed myths, there is no big difference between the two groups from the socio-cultural point of view. The difference lies in some accepted, or state-imposed political norms: in Estonia, this norm is exclusive for Russians, while in Germany, it is an inclusive one – but both are based not on a civic, but on an ethno-racial basis.

12.6 Responses of the Ethnic Periphery

Together with Russian nationalists, the most vocal opponents of building the state on the principle of civic and individual rights are non-Russian intellectual and political leaders in the republics of Rossia. Two processes are taking place in these republics. One can be seen as democratic: supported by the electorate, ethnic leaders carry on a resolute political struggle with the Center for a redistribution of powers in favor of the regions and for an effective federal system. Here they also enjoy support from leaders of the administrative regions. The second process is the imposition of narrow nationalistic and non-democratic norms and rules that imply an exclusive status for so-called 'indigenous nations', often at the expense of a Russian majority (or minority) and other local minorities. This generates new tensions and may lead to events like the ethnic cleansings in North Ossetia. In many respects the Rossian republics have become strongholds for the conservative opposition to democratic change, market reforms, and privatization. The elites in these republics have no wish to let the process of redistribution and power-sharing go too far, and they prefer to build their own 'mini-empires'.

A proposal to found the new political order on individual rights and to implant into the legal discourse a notion of civic Russian nation presents a serious challenge for these elites. It might undermine their status, which is based on the Soviet-style ethnonationalist doctrine. Keen resentment can be mobilized against a new doctrine, since it is not difficult to interpret it as a cover for Russian chauvinism or for the discredited slogan of 'merging Soviet nations'. These are serious obstacles to a civic state doctrine, but their importance should not be exaggerated.

First, the majority of non-Russians with territorial autonomies live outside their 'own' republic or *okrug* (see Table 12.4). I do not foresee any tendency towards a further 'gathering' of 'status' nationalities in ethnic enclaves, which does not exclude growing homogeneity because of differences in population growth and owing to the out-migration of Russians. About 9.5 million non-Russians, of 70 different ethnic affiliations, mainly of diaspora character (Armenians, Azerbaijanis, Georgians, Greeks, Gypsies, Kazakhs, Koreans, Moldavians, Poles, Ukrainians, Uzbeks, etc.) and of small indigenous cultures (Eskimo, Nanai, Nivkhy, Selkups, Ulchi, Veps, etc.) can be termed 'non-status' nationalities (see Table 12.5). There is among these peoples a very strong feeling of belonging to the Rossian civic entity – without thereby denying their own cultural identities and interests. The Rossian nation doctrine itself has already gained some support, providing as it does a basis for equal treatment with the rest of the population. At the same time it is impossible to deny that when the citizens of Rossia are asked about what they feel is their 'motherland' (*rodina*), most non-Russians, as well as many Russians, cite their republic, or where they are living. Striking examples here are Bashkiria (75% Bashkirs, 28% Russians, 60% Tatars), Daghestan, Tatarstan, Tuva, Yakutia – where the majority gave these republics as their 'motherland'. More than one-third of the resident Russian population showed strong attachment to the local motherland in Checheno-Ingushetia, Karelia, North Ossetia, Tatarstan, and Yakutia (Table 12.6). As Field Commander Ballaudi Movsaev told me, 'I am a Rossian (*rossiyanin*), like you, but above all I am a Chechen.'[10]

Second, there are various strategies and mechanisms that could be used to cope with ethnonationalism in the country and to build a multi-cultural polity: a polity with a referent Russian cultural component that would include the internal societies with the referent culture (or cultures) of the titulars. In all of this, a crucial issue is to invent and introduce new Russian symbols and values not associated exclusively with one culture and uncomfortably perceived by representatives of others. When it comes to civic symbols, the record of Yeltsin's government is quite poor: the double-headed eagle of the Russian Empire has been re-established as an official state emblem and the Russian Orthodox Church is seeking to become the state religion. Both elements receive short shrift from many non-Russians. Moreover, one of the newly emerged national symbols – *Belyi Dom* (the White House) of the Russian Parliament – was occupied by the executive bureaucrats after the October 1993 events. Despite this poor record, however, there are still many opportunities for imagination and effort to establish multi-cultural symbolism and a hegemonic concept for a new nation.

Table 12.4 *'Status' Nationalities in Rossia and Territory of Residence, 1989*

	Rossian Federation (No.)	Autonomy (No.)	In their own autonomy (%)	Outside of autonomy Within Rossia (%)	Outside Rossia (%)
Tatar	5,522,096	1,765,404	26.6	56.5	16.9
Chuvash	1,773,645	906,922	49.2	47.1	3.3
Bashkir	1,345,273	863,808	59.6	33.2	7.2
Mordva	1,072,939	313,420	27.2	65.8	7.0
Chechen	898,999	734,501	76.8	17.2	6.0
Udmurt	714,833	496,522	66.5	29.2	4.3
Mari	643,698	324,349	48.3	47.7	4.0
Avar	544,016	496,077	82.5	8.0	9.5
Jew	536,848	8,887	0.6	38.3	61.1
Buryat	417,425	341,185	68.2	15.3	16.5
Osset	402,275	334,876	56.0	11.3	32.7
Kabardin	386,055	363,492	93.0	5.8	1.2
Yakut	380,242	365,236	95.6	4.0	0.4
Dargin	353,348	280,431	76.8	19.9	3.3
Komi	336,309	291,542	84.6	13.0	2.4
Kumyk	277,163	231,805	82.2	16.1	1.7
Lezgin	257,270	204,370	43.9	11.3	44.8
Ingush	215,068	163,762	69.0	21.6	9.4
Tuvin	206,160	198,448	96.0	3.8	0.2
Kalmyk	165,821	146,316	84.2	11.2	4.6
Karachai	150,332	129,449	83.0	13.4	3.6
Komi-Permyak	147,269	95,415	62.7	34.1	3.2
Karel	124,921	78,928	60.3	35.1	4.6
Adygei	122,908	95,439	76.5	12.0	15.5
Laks	106,245	91,682	77.6	12.4	10.0
Tabasaran	93,587	78,196	80.2	15.8	4.0
Khakass	78,500	62,859	78.3	19.4	2.3
Balkar	78,341	70,793	83.2	8.8	8.0
Nogai	73,703	28,294	37.6	60.4	2.0
Altai	69,409	59,130	83.5	14.6	1.9
Cherkess	50,764	40,241	76.9	20.0	3.1
Nenets	34,190	29,786	85.9	12.7	1.4
Evenki	29,901	3,480	11.5	87.6	0.9
Khanty	22,283	11,892	52.8	46.1	1.1
Rutul	19,503	14,955	73.4	22.3	4.3
Agul	17,728	13,791	73.6	21.0	5.4
Chukchi	15,107	11,914	78.5	21.0	0.5
Koryak	8,942	6,572	71.1	25.7	3.2
Mansi	8,279	6,562	77.6	20.1	2.3
Dolgan	6,584	4,939	71.2	23.6	5.2
Tsakhur	6,492	5,194	26.0	6.5	67.5
TOTAL	17,714,471	9,770,864	47.3	38.7	14.0

Source: Compiled from Tishkov, ed., 1994

Table 12.5   *'Non-Status' Nationalities in Rossia, 1989*

Ukrainian	4,362,872
Belorussian	1,206,222
German	842,295
Kazakh	635,865
Armenian	532,390
Azerbaijani	335,889
Moldavian	172,671
Gypsy	152,939
Georgian	130,688
Uzbek	126,899
Korean	107,051
Pole	94,594
Greek	91,699
Lithuanian	70,427
Finn*	47,102
Latvian	46,829
Estonian	46,390
Kirgiz	41,734
Turkmen	39,739
Tajik	38,208
Abazin	32,983
Bulgarian	32,785
Crimean Tatar	21,275
Tat	19,420
Shorts	15,745
Veps	12,142
Nanai	11,883
Jew-Mountain	11,282
Gagauz	10,051
Meskhetian Turk	9,890
Assyrian	9,622
Abkhazian	7,239
Karakalpak	6,155
Romanian	5,996
Hungarian	5,742
Chinese	5,197
Kurd	4,724
Nivkhi	4,631
Czech	4,375
Selkup	3,564
Ulchi	3,173
Arab	2,704
Uigur	2,577
Persian (Irani)	2,572
Itelmen	2,429
Vietnamese	2,142
Khalka-Mongol	2,117
Udegei	1,902
Saami	1,835
Eskimo	1,704
Jew-Sephardic (Central Asian)	1,407
Chuvan	1,384
Nganasan	1,262

Table 12.5 *(cont.)*

Jew-Georgian	1,172
Yukagir	1,112
Udin	1,102
Ket	1,084
Orochi	883
Tofalar	722
Karaim	680
Aleut	644
Dungan	635
Negidal	587
Izhor	449
Crimchak	338
Beludzh	297
Talysh	202
Ents	198
Orok	179
Liv	64
Other nationalities	3,319
No nationality indicated	15,513
Total	9,413,592
% of population of Rossia	*6.4%*

*Includes Ingria (or Ingermanland) Finn.

Source: Compiled from Tishkov, ed., 1994

Third, there is no need to enforce mutually exclusive loyalties in the process of nation-building. All over the world, people are considered legally – and regard themselves – as, for example, members of both the Norwegian nation and the Saami people; members of the Spanish nation and of the Catalan, Castile or Basque groups; as being Mexican and at the same time Nahua or one of many Maya groups. In introducing a new definition of civic nation as an official and probably legal category, there is no need to exclude or forbid the old vocabulary. In Rossia, as in many other areas, the word 'nation' is used by minority leaders for political purposes. It may perform a consolidating role, and has even been implicitly recognized on the level of NGO structures. In Norway indigenous leaders may use the term 'the Saami nation', in the USA, 'the Hawaiian' or 'the Navaho nation', in Spain, 'the Basque nation', etc. There is no sense in opposing the use of this term among Rossian nationalities – although 'nationality' seems more appropriate, being less politically loaded as well as being widely recognized among experts in and outside Rossia. Political language innovations are important, but an exaggerated linguistic rigorism in politics is perilous. In any case, a constructive search for a new state identity is surely more fruitful than the appeal for 'a firm creation of a felicitous environment' formulated by Zbigniew Brzezinski (1994, p. 72)

It is potentially dangerous for the ex-Communist world to continue with the old Leninist/Stalinist project of drawing up two different maps: one for states, another for ethnonations, and then to try to arbitrarily reconcile the borders of these two entities. History has seen two states with constitutions and doctrines that reflected this political utopia: Yugoslavia and the Soviet Union. The fate of both shows why it is so important for the West to assist in overcoming the burdens of the Communist legacy – not only in restructuring the economy and political order but also with ideology and the practice of

Table 12.6   *Perceptions of Motherland in Republics of Rossia (%)*

Republic	Ethnic Group (*no. of resp.*)	Soviet Union	Considers self a citizen of Rossia	Republic of residence	No answer
Bashkiria	Bashkir (*211*)	11	12	75	2
	Russian (*401*)	26	43	28	3
	Tatar (*259*)	22	17	60	1
Buryatia	Buryat (*248*)	13	17	67	3
	Russian (*728*)	20	50	25	5
Checheno-	Chechen (*588*)	8	1	90	1
Ingushetia	Ingush (*104*)	9	1	88	2
	Russian (*211*)	40	20	37	3
Chuvashia	Chuvash (*688*)	42	20	35	3
	Russian (*230*)	26	52	19	3
Daghestan	Avar (*291*)	21	11	63	5
	Dargin (*140*)	16	4	64	16
	Kumyk (*162*)	14	5	72	10
	Lezgin (*107*)	41	2	50	7
	Laks (*83*)	34	7	43	16
	Russian (*103*)	47	25	21	7
Kabardino-	Kabardin (*468*)	9	4	85	2
Balkaria	Balkar (*112*)	28	4	65	3
	Russian (*316*)	33	36	27	4
Kalmykia	Kalmyk (*502*)	21	9	68	2
	Russian (*396*)	34	32	30	4
Karelia	Karel (*204*)	11	17	69	3
	Russian (*636*)	17	44	36	3
Komi	Komi (*273*)	17	14	65	4
	Russian (*593*)	24	46	24	6
Mari	Mari (*204*)	16	17	64	3
	Russian (*636*)	27	41	29	3
Mordovia	Mordva (*291*)	33	29	35	3
	Russian (*624*)	32	40	26	2
North Ossetia	Osset (*524*)	22	7	69	2
	Russian (*303*)	27	32	37	4
Tatarstan	Tatar (*478*)	18	4	74	4
	Russian (*446*)	29	31	36	4
Tuva	Tuvin (*653*)	2	2	95	1
	Russian (*307*)	16	59	24	1
Udmurtia	Udmurt (*315*)	18	18	60	4
	Russian (*612*)	25	44	28	3
Yakutia	Yakut (*377*)	9	3	87	1
	Russian (*463*)	18	38	39	5

Source: Colton, Hough, Lehmann, and Guboglo's survey, November–December 1993

ethnic nationalism. This does not mean financial aid. All that is required is the firm pursuit of the political principles and legal norms which Western societies and the international community at large generally apply. As a goodwill message, this process could start with linguistic changes, such as introducing into the international vocabulary two new words – Rossia and Rossians – as more proper translations of the Russian name of the state and of its people. A minor point? No: ambiguous language produces ambiguous politics.

Notes

1   A quote from Raphael Khakimov, Advisor to Tatarstan's President during negotiations on the Russia–Tatarstan Treaty, summer 1992, Moscow. Personal notes.

2   Conversation with Boris Oleinik, 15 January 1994, The Hague.

3   Personal notes, 14 December 1994, Vladikavkaz, North Ossetia.

4   Conversation with Farit Mukhamedshin, 11 September 1994, Kazan, Tatarstan.

5   Personal notes, 27 September 1995, Moscow.

6   Conversation with Rail Kuzeev, 19 May 1995, Moscow.

7   In March 1996, Mintimer Shaimiev was overwhelmingly re-elected President with 97% of the vote. I was talking to him onboard his jet flying to The Hague just four days after election day. He expressed his deep satisfaction with two things: 97% meant that a majority of Russians also voted in his favor, and that in the text of Chernomyrdin's congratulatory telegram there were words about 'strengthening *neighboring* relations between Russia and Tatarstan' [my italics].

8   Conversation with Ramazan Abdulatipov, 9 September 1994, Orenburg.

9   This was one of few cases when an extremely tense conflict situation was resolved through negotiations. It was also the only case when I as a Minister used a special plane to fly to a conflict area – for which I received a reprimand from Boris Yeltsin for wasting state money.

10   Interview with Ballaudi Movsaev, 23 February 1995, between Nazran and Samashky, Ingushetia.

13

Strategies for Ethnic Accord in Post-Soviet States

13.1 Introduction

Conflicts and intolerance in Rossia and in the other Soviet successor states have given rise to skepticism as to the ability of these states to undertake the process of democratic transformation. Most serious doubts were expressed after the territory of Rossia became an arena of ethnic cleansing and warfare. There is a noticeable apathy, and even resistance, to searching for constructive and peaceful approaches to manage conflicting ethnicity inside the country. Simplistic responses based on the politics of denial and force are finding a growing number of proponents, which promises to make the ethnic factor even more unmanageable. Outside Rossia, we may see the return of deeply entrenched clichés and long-cherished concepts concerning its society and politics. Global debates expressed in 'mysterious' and 'satanical' categories about Rossia make it difficult to view this society as one which is really not so fundamentally distinct from any other modern society, and to provide non-politicized expertise and assistance.

This politically overloaded, holistic discourse in and around Rossia often prevents the discussion of such 'low-level' factors as, for example, the quality of leadership, the lack of professional decision-making in politics, and the poor performances of experts and politicians in testing comprehensive and innovative approaches to govern a complex society. Under the shadow of ideological holism, it is also difficult to consider 'natural things' in the play of human relations, like morality and behavioral patterns among members of political clubs, when major things in a state may happen due to personal drive to crush political opponents or under the liberating influence of alcoholic inebriation. This politicized vision, when words like 'Russia' and 'Russians' re-acquire dehumanized images, excludes from consideration such fundamental aspects as individual choices and strategies – not to mention possible good intentions on the part of the leadership.

In this chapter I seek to formulate recommendations for managing conflicts in multi-ethnic states despite the growing number of publications on this issue (see, e.g., Burton, 1987; Coakley, 1992; Diamond & Plattner, 1994; Galtung, 1996; Gottlieb, 1993; Gurr & Harff, 1994; Horowitz, 1991; Montville, 1990; Rupesinghe, 1996; Sisk, 1996; Stavenhagen, 1996; Väyrynen, 1994; Young, 1993, 1994.) These policy-oriented recommendations are based on my understanding of post-Soviet experiences as well as on broader comparisons. Placing this experience into a wider context is an important analytical exercise because I share with some anthropologists the conclusion that 'the similarities between basic organizational characteristics of socialist Eurasia and modern conditions in the so-called First and Third Worlds may come to seem much more compelling than the differences' (Hann, 1993, p. 19; see also Verdery, 1995). Recognizing a significance of cultural and political tradition, I do not accept a cliché like a specific 'Russian Way' of acting and behaving. Again, as Chris Hann mentioned, 'the chances of anything radically different emerging in post-socialist Eurasia must be considered rather slim' (1993, p. 19).

13.2 Why Conflicts?

Human societies are a part of living nature. They share such basic characteristics as cultural differences, social disparities, competition, and domination. It is a grandiose utopia to seek to build a society with full social equality, just as it is to build a state with a culturally homogeneous population or with total inter-ethnic harmony. It is a part of human nature also, especially in modernized societies, to resist subordination and inequalities on the individual and group levels and to use group solidarity for achieving a more privileged status. In multi-ethnic societies, social and political disparities and cleavages often go along cultural (ethnic, racial, or religious) lines. When a society is not individual-centered and lacks civic forms of coalitions, people use their ethnic affiliation as one of the most accessible and understandable forms of group solidarity and as a tool to achieve various goals. That is why, as noted by Manning Nash, 'ethnicity is a reservoir for unrest in a World where power, prosperity and rank are distributed in an unequal and illegal way between and within nations' (Nash, 1989, p. 127).

The post-Soviet polities are brimming with conflict-generating disparities. Members of certain ethnic groups (or nationalities) enjoy a dominant status in the spheres of politics and culture. Because of historical, demographic, and even doctrinal factors, they may have better access to the resources of the state and better opportunities for social mobility. Among such groups we find the ethnic Russians in the Rossian Federation, Kazakhs in Kazakhstan, Ukrainians in Ukraine, and other titular ethnic groups in successor states. Recent additions to this list are the titular nationalities in a number of republics of Rossia, especially where they possess a demographic majority and have been able to organize themselves politically. Excessive centralization and the direct or implicit linking of political centers with one ethnic group and culture have caused major dissatisfaction on the part of 'periphery' groups, unleashing processes of disintegration.

The situation has not changed much with the appearance of new states. Previously repressed nationalities, or nationalities that perceive themselves as such, have become dominant majorities in states that are equally multi-ethnic, with a large number of minorities and millions of ethnically kindred people divided by new borders. These new dominant groups and their elites have been claiming the control of power and cultural institutions, and priority status in economic and social services. In turn, the former 'double' minorities (like Armenians in Nagorno Karabakh, Ossets and Abkhazians in Georgia, Gagauz in Moldavia) and those who became 'new minorities' have started to challenge their reduced status and the discriminatory attitudes they are now facing.

Decentralization of power and emerging regional self-government in Rossia and other states has been accompanied by a growth in ultra-nationalist rhetoric and actions, as well as explicit attempts to make government institutions and resources the exclusive property of one group. Old and newly emerged social inequalities and discriminatory attitudes toward dispersed or compact, but 'non-status', communities and a lack of institutionalized support for them on the part of the state in many regions of the former Soviet Union aroused expectations and political articulations on behalf of these groups, to improve their situation through the process of liberalization. This appeal for cultural or territorial autonomy and even for establishing their 'own' state has been met in many cases by repressive measures and by outbreaks of mutual intolerance. Weak minorities became an easy prey for those wishing to initiate ethnic cleansing and pogroms.

Socio-economic and political differences are important factors for understanding the nature of conflicting ethnicity, but they cannot suffice to explain why conflicts happen. Ethnicity has a powerful emotional and psychological function, a symbolic capital shared by a group and its members, one that provides a feeling of comfort and security in the face of outside challenges and competition. Ethnic groups through their leaders strive to build coalitions and to make state territory, government, language, and other cultural institutions into major proofs for legitimizing their existence, their integrity, and status. In the post-Soviet world there exist no other more powerful symbols and features for social groupings and coalitions. The dearth of a civic culture and of societies structured by other interests and ideologies makes this area particularly vulnerable to ethnonationalist ideology and practice. In recent years, many major political careers and achievements as well as state politics have taken shape thanks to ethnic or nationalist appeals and manipulations.

These appeals have found an enthusiastic response because there exist numerous intellectual, managerial, and military elites among the various ethnic groups and a well-educated populace already indoctrinated by nationalist propaganda and academic writings. It has mainly been the intellectuals and former *nomenklatura* bureaucrats, who, after coming to power under ethnonationalist slogans, have taken up the most radical and irresponsible political stands, not hesitating to use force – just as their Communist predecessors did. It has been the intellectuals and political activists, based partly in Moscow, Los Angeles, and Ankara, who have provided arguments and emotional legitimization for the Karabakh movement among Armenians, for Abkhazian and Chechen independence scenarios, as well as for many other violent ethnic manifestations. It has been the heads of local state industry and the top military officers, with their wives, who have played the most active role in provoking conflict situations in areas like Trans-Dniestria, Abkhazia, and Crimea, when the radical drive to political independence challenged their accustomed mentality and when prospects of dislocation endangered their comfortable social status.

But how, if these conflicts have been articulated and generated by elite entrepreneurs, do they find rank-and-file followers and evolve into violent forms? The reason is that power elites, including those who challenge the status quo, have acquired an opportunity to wage battle in a society where values like individual lives and human rights are of low priority, and where the power hierarchy is still built on inarticulate submissiveness. Post-Communist societies are only at the starting-point of transition from corporate-centered to individual-centered statehood. Post-Communist politicians have inherited the same low level of responsibility before public opinion and the law. To a considerable extent, they still share the same party (or corporate) discipline mentality. Ever since the very beginning of ethnic violence in this area, not one politician or activist has suffered any punishment or reprisal. The escalation of conflicts into organized wars would seem to exonerate initiators and executors from legal sanctions.

Violent conflicts have now become a routine reality because a highly militarized society, with low civic morality among its members, was confronted with the sudden collapse of strict state control in many areas, from military arsenals to air traffic – permitting a large number of ambitious, unbalanced, corrupt persons and groups to exercise their activities in a social space which had lost its many identity parameters and legal restraints. Rossian army officers and soldiers have sold weapons and ammunition to Chechen warriors, who are fighting that same army. Money for buying weapons has been procured from illegal operations, realized with the assistance of corrupt bureaucrats of the same country and of Estonia or countries of diaspora – where a revenge psychology of fighting the former 'big brother' has become tempting.

Open conflicts and destructive wars have become imminent because the existing political culture, inherited from former totalitarian societies, does not recognize self-restraint, negotiation, concession, or consent as priority values and principles in dealing with oppositions. Decision-making in crisis situations discloses a low level of competence and limited techniques. Too often, the only option seems to be to send in troops or organize armed resistance. Tolerance, peaceful attitudes, non-violent political behavior – these are viewed as signs of weakness and of malfunctioning.

There is also an important external factor that facilitates ethnic and interstate conflicts in this area of the world. At a certain historical moment, one of collapsing Communist regimes, the whole of this area started to be viewed in the West as *territorium nullis* for ambitious geopolitical designs and prescriptive ideological projects. The inertia of super-power rivalries and of bloc mentality made it easy for the international community to abandon the principle of territorial integrity and respect for existing borders. For the first time in postwar history, separatist scenarios as a solution for cultural, political, and gov-ernance issues found quite explicit support among many powerful politicians and representatives of ethnic diasporas. For the same reason, basically, Western states recog-nized the breakup of the USSR and Yugoslavia with remarkable speed. The tempo of such non-negotiated changes, not the very nature of these changes, became one of the rea-sons for violent conflicts. Alongside serious and sincere efforts in conflict resolution on the part of many national governments and international structures, there have also been many outside actors that provoke the growth of tensions and escalation of conflicts through one-sided image-making and direct involvement.

13.3   Governing Ethnicity at the Non-violent Stage

The territory of the former Soviet Union has been and will be made up of multi-ethnic polities, despite all efforts to realize the principle 'one ethnic group – one state'. With a long list of ongoing conflicts, there are still many potential situations and clients capable of escalating inter-ethnic tension and violence in this part of the world. Responsible pol-itics, including preventive steps and early interventions, have more chances for success, as well as costing much less than repairing human and material damage after an open con-flict has erupted. I am deeply convinced that ethnic management strategies in a peaceful form are possible, even in a situation of painful transitions from totalitarianism and of dramatic socio-economic and geopolitical changes.

Dismantling old doctrine and a search for new formulas

Soviet political and intellectual tradition had embedded both the language and the prac-tice of institutionalized ethnicity together with contradictory attempts to construct states and their internal structures on ethnic principles. After the demise of the USSR, citizen-ship and basic rights have remained a subject of 'blood calculations'. As a result, millions of people born in the territories of new states have found themselves with a diminished status, or even as stateless persons. New state ideologies, symbols, and constitutional and legal provisions reflect the dominant group's perceptions of itself as being of single com-mon descent and the sole 'holder' of a state, thus excluding from nationhood all those of other ancestral origins.

These conflict-generating doctrinal priorities based on historical, cultural, and even biological arguments need to be subjected to serious revisions and open criticism, show-ing how they may result in discrimination, persecutions, and, finally, in destroying emergent democracies. This is a difficult task for all segments of societies, especially for politicians and intellectuals: to start the process of unloading the basic definition of a 'nation' of its ethnic exclusiveness and moving towards a culturally pluralistic under-standing of political nation as co-citizenship. It is a long-term strategy demanding purposeful efforts which may not promise quick positive results. Many leaders, activists, and experts who used to speak on behalf of or for the groups labeled as 'nations' or which claim to be a 'nation' will not easily abandon this symbolic value and pragmatic project. However, this process of major doctrinal change has already started in Russia and other states, like Ukraine, Kazakhstan, Lithuania, Latvia, and these important efforts should be encouraged.

In spite of ideological and political legacies, social scientists will have to formulate and introduce into public discourse a conception of civic (or political) nation as a multi-cultural entity. Nations are not culture-neutral; they have certain cultural (or multi-cultural) profiles defined by referent cultures (usually of demographically and politically dominant groups) – but they are not a type of ethnic entity. To provide basic cohesion in a multi-ethnic state, steps should be taken – through legal provisions, mass media dissemination, and academic projects – to enforce the criterion that no nation can be equated with a primordial 'ethnos' claiming descent from a common ancestor. Such culturally constructed myths and biologically based beliefs are a breeding ground for conflicts. State institutions should abolish their practice of officially registering the ethnic affiliations of their citizens, especially through the passport system. It needs to be made clear that what international charters and declarations have in mind is 'demos', not 'ethnos', as the subject of state-hood and of self-determination.

Emerging symbols of successor states as well as existing ones should not reflect values and historical memories that are meaningful for only one group and alienating for others. The purpose of the state and of policy-makers in a multi-ethnic setting is to invent and to introduce a unifying ideology and symbols that can make ethnic pluralism work, rather than to seek the facile strategy of subdivision into ever smaller, apparently self-governing entities. I hold that a good guiding principle is to accept the continued existence of multi-ethnic states in the post-Communist world, and to recognize the inadvisability of excessive subdivision into mono-ethnic, exclusive statelets that are often neither economically viable nor democratically governable. Russia and other successor states will be able to evolve into viable civic nations only on the basis of doctrines and values that give priority to common civic and human rights, that actively discourage ethnic particularism and exclusivity, and respect cultural diversity and pluralism.

Dissolution of power through federalism

Strictly speaking, the structure of a state – be it a federal or unitarian one – does not pre-determine the democratic nature of its political regime. However, it is true that large and culturally diverse states can be better organized on federal principles. Federalism is a means to ensure that the institutions and services of the state will be able to address the needs and interests of culturally diverse groups living in one state. It is a means to provide self-government for lower-level authorities and for less spacious formations, which as a rule are ethnically more homogeneous.

For several of the post-Soviet states a promising strategy for reducing conflicting eth-nicity is, as David Horowitz says, to 'proliferate the points of power so as to take the heat off a single focal point' (1985, p. 348). This could be done by decentralizing state power through ethno-territorial federalism, which is a deep-rooted political reality in the Russian Federation and non-recognized but de facto also in Ukraine, Georgia, Uzbekistan, Moldavia, and Tajikistan. This specific state structure means 'an application of federalism to accommodate ethnic groups in a political system – to improve their position in the polity, via their autonomy and participation in power-sharing through a constitution which allocates power to different bodies with territorial jurisdiction in the framework of an established rule of law' (Stanovcic, 1992, p. 365). In Rossia, practically all sizeable and not too sparsely dispersed ethnic groups have this kind of territorial autonomy.

There are options for federalization (or for ethno-territorial autonomies) in Kazakhstan, Kirgizia, Azerbaijan, and Estonia as well. But there are important factors to be considered in the process of shifting power from a single center to federal units: what are the extent and limitations of shared power and what kind of political ideology lies behind these structures? In cases when internal units are proclaimed as 'sovereign' or 'national' states, there are two possibilities. One is to overstate a right to exercise unlimited control over the subject's territory; another is to view such governance as the exclusive 'property' of an eponymous group. To avoid these possible trends and to minimize central government's fears of uncontrolled disintegration, the practice of negotiations and agreements (vertical, between center and units, and horizontal, between units) should be introduced, besides constitutional principles and special legislation on mechanisms of power delimitation between central and regional governments.

Another important step towards a renewed formula for post-Soviet federalism would be to grant special status for ethno-territorial autonomies (republics) among other 'non-ethnic' members of a federation. This kind of asymmetric federalism assigns higher state symbolism, economic and political authority to the republics. At this moment in history, the problem of asymmetry and even of a special (associated) status features on the agenda of Rossia and, perhaps, of Georgia. In future, it may prove relevant for Ukraine, where the western and eastern parts of the country may initiate federalization, and for the existing Crimean autonomy, which may come to demand such status.

Being territorial units, republics and other possible forms of ethno-territorial autonomy cannot be treated solely as administrative provinces. They need to retain their ethno-linguistic and specific cultural profiles, as partly reflected in territorial configurations and in state and public institutions. What is more questionable, at least for Rossia, is any 'correction' or redrawing of administrative borders because of changing ethnic demography or mutual territorial claims. It may appear natural and desirable to procure conformity between administrative borders and ethnic frontiers, to have administrative lines congruent with ethnic territories. But this underestimates the power of bureaucracy, which tends to be a proponent of territorial enlargements but be against any territorial contractions which may arise as a result of such corrections. Besides, such administrative changes may provoke new fears among local communities. Thus it is better to preserve the territorial status quo, at least till there is a more favorable time for negotiation and mutual consent, reflecting democratically expressed public opinion.

While a proponent of asymmetric federalism, I also share the reservations expressed by Vojislav Stanovcic in his overview of approaches to governing ethnically divided societies:

> Although it brings about a dispersion of power, ethnic federalism does not necessarily promote democratization. It does not guarantee polyarchy, except perhaps an ethnic polyarchy of a kind that can threaten citizens in general, including even those who belong to the dominant ethnic group. Ethnic federalism presupposes and gives priority to corporate structures, but the ethnocentric political cultural values associated with it are parochial even when very large groups share them, and are not conducive to the establishment of civil society (1992, p. 367).

Cultural profiles and symbolism

After providing equal rights for all citizens of ethnic-based autonomies, the titular groups could go on to establish their languages and cultural institutions as referent cultures, together with a larger state referent culture. In Rossia, this would be the Russian language and culture; in Georgia, the Georgian language and culture. Such a practice of official bilingualism and biculturalism would be the most acceptable formula, allowing cultural distinctivness to coexist with social mobility and modernization in a larger state. In practice, however, it is not easy to achieve equal partnership between Rossian and local cultural systems. Long-term efforts may be needed, including further development of local languages, to introduce them into administration, management, and education on a major scale. Even in this case, the Russian language may well remain a preferential choice for a majority of non-Russians, and learning local languages for ethnic Russians may remain a question of adequate incentives. On the functional, 'non-official' level, bilingualism in Rossia will keep its 'unequal' character. What is wrong in this situation would be to view monolingual ethnic Russians as 'gainers', and bilingual or multilingual non-Russians as 'losers'. In today's competitive environment, especially on the territory of ethnic-based republics, surely the reverse applies.

Not all republics in Rossia can choose a policy of official bilingualism. Trilingualism (Russian and two local languages) should be introduced and encouraged officially in Kabardino-Balkaria, Karachai-Cherkessia, and in Bashkiria, where Tatars should have the same rights for official status of their language as Bashkirs and Russians. Official trilingualism would seem desirable in North Ossetia if the expelled Ingush minority is to be returned to this republic and peace is to be built between the two communities. Rising assertions of local language distinctions among different groups of Mordva, Mari, and Ossets may bring official status for languages formerly considered as 'dialects', if the titular populations increase their command of these local tongues. On the other hand, in several republics, like Karelia and Komi, official bilingualism is an unrealistic formula, because of the overall shift to the Russian language among the titular population. Daghestan may choose among several options: to proclaim all local languages or only one – Russian – as official, or not to give this issue any political articulation at all, in order not to cause internal tensions and rivalries.

As to other successor states, the desire of titular groups to retain exclusive official status for their languages as a symbol of newly consolidated integrity and as a proof of their higher legitimacy compared with other members of polities may remain very strong. However, it will probably not be as politically crucial as it was at the time of establishing independence. For purposes of internal consolidation as well as of respect for human rights, it is important to ease the burden of politicized linguicism in countries where the presidents and millions of their compatriots speak one language in offices and at home but feel obliged to accept another language as the official one. I would recommend that consideration be given to granting official status for other than titular languages as well: for Russian, in Ukraine, Kazakhstan, Latvia, and, probably, in Estonia; for Russian and Ukrainian, in Moldavia; for Tajik and Russian, in Uzbekistan; for Uzbek, in Tajikistan. The introduction of official titular/Russian bilingualism in Belorussia and Kirgizia has proved this strategy to be both possible and effective.

Making a multi-ethnic center

Another strategy concerns the changing character of power and culture: I mean, thus having a more culturally plural center. Much remains to be done in Rossia for the federal center to respond to the multiple aspirations and interests of numerous recruits from non-Russian groups, allowing them to participate in the governing structures of the state and to bring their culture, language, and other values into the national cultural and informational space. The USSR was, and the Rossian Federation still is, ruled by the representatives of the dominant group, whom I choose to label 'cultural Russians'. How to make the federal center multi-ethnic and raise the aspirations of non-Russians in the center – this is a new challenge for democratic reforms. If this challenge can be met, it may minimize ethnic conflicts based on alienation or on rejection of the center.

Most of the Soviet successor states have now made remarkable moves toward democratic governance. Free elections and representative institutions have become the basis of these new democracies. But representative democracy based on the principle 'one person – one vote' is not enough to ensure peace and justice in this part of the world. In addition, consociational democracy based on proportionality, political compromise, and other mechanisms of special inducements should be seen as key elements. (See further, Horowitz, 1991; Lijphart, 1977; Sisk, 1996.) Members of governments, those in high positions in the ministries, in educational and cultural institutions, the diplomatic and army officer corps, as well as influential persons in the information and mass media agencies – for all these groups, ethnic as well as professional criteria are important. Today there are very few representative and executive bodies of power in post-Communist countries that adequately reflect the ethnic mosaic of those societies on the national and regional levels. How to solve this political dilemma is perhaps one of the most crucial and difficult questions.

The process of political liberalization and of replacing the *nomenklatura* system has created a situation of real competition for access to power positions and privileges. It has brought to power not only former political dissidents and other democratic figures but also politicians who subscribe to nationalist ideologies and address an ethnically defined electorate. The leaders of successor states as well as of many republics in Russia have effectively used these opportunities, and 'national cadres' have managed to capture a majority in representative institutions and administrative positions. In such a situation, it is even more important to develop and introduce special measures and programs, including quotas and affirmative action, to increase minority representation in the power structures, the economic and cultural institutions of the state. Prestigious services, managerial positions, educational institutions, mass media and the many state bodies will all need to reflect and represent the ethnic mosaic of society, if they are to provide the desired 'unity in diversity'.

The cross-cutting coalitions

A striking feature of post-Communist politics has been the primary role of ethnicity in forming political coalitions. To dismantle or replace this legacy is no easy task. Attempts should be made to introduce the practice of inter-ethnic electoral and political coalitions, and to limit the promotion of politicians who are elected to positions of power on behalf of an ethnically defined group. This is no less important for consociational democracy than is the group proportionality principle (see Elazar, 1991; Horowitz, 1991). This is a delicate design in power-sharing – to procure cross-cutting coalitions and functional intergroup cooperation when, under ethnic federalism, elites will tend to support heterogeneity in the larger society while imposing homogeneity inside the groups which they themselves control. Nevertheless, it is possible, especially through the experience gained in election procedure whereby 50% of Russia's State Duma deputies may come from the lists of national political parties.

Multi-ethnic countries, as well as federal units of the Russian Federation, should explore election procedures that guarantee a candidate's nomination and election on the condition of representing a multi-ethnic electorate. For example, a candidate cannot be elected president of Rossia if he/she, besides getting a majority of the votes, has failed to get a mandate from a majority of the republics. The same practice may be extended to multi-ethnic republics and administrative units. Interest-group coalitions, including business, professional, and territorial associations, should be stimulated in multi-ethnic societies. Cross-cutting cleavages like these help to reduce the intensity of inter-ethnic rivalries.

Reducing ethnic disparities

The most profound issue of peaceful inter-ethnic relations is the question of reducing inequality and ethno-social disparity. Multiple historical, territorial, demographic, and cultural factors influence the opportunities and positions of individuals and social groupings – including ethnic ones. This is a permanent challenge, a perennial conflict-generating characteristic of complex modern societies. Most ethnic inequalities originate either from urban-rural and regional economic differences or from forceful actions of the state towards certain groups and their cultural practices. Other ethnic communities may suffer losses by coming into contact with more powerful cultural systems, or by simply being a minority amongst more numerous groups. This widespread phenomenon is quite often a voluntary choice, mainly on the individual level.

However, on the political level the issue of inequality often reflects not 'objective' but perceived, 'explained' situations. By their very nature, these explanations may be simply bargaining tools, as can be observed in the Rossian Federation during debates between leaders of constituent units on the issue 'who feeds whom' – a question that unavoidably acquires ethnic projections. In reality, it is a struggle for that still-sizeable share of national resources allocated by the federal government. One problem which ethnic federalism may give rise to, especially for the federal government, is how to deal with the feeling of 'unjust' redistribution of the national income. Even if it is not a fact, a claim for political sovereignty in the constituent units is highly possible. Another problem is how to avoid the emergence of a conservative alliance of central bureaucracy with ethnic elites which will serve exclusively the interests of power holders. In Russia, the central and regional bureaucracy is already growing at an unprecedented rate – at the taxpayers' expense.

Pointing to what may be 'imagined' disparities as well as the fact that not only 'losers' but also 'gainers' may initiate a conflict, I nevertheless regard as important the task of correcting striking inequalities and making this issue a major priority so as to reduce ethnic conflict and avoid open inter-ethnic unrest. First, this should involve economy and resource management, especially in the situation of privatization and the emerging market economy. It is common for members of certain groups to play leading roles in industrialization, land exploration, and resource development, and thereby enjoy better social status. Examples include the ethnic Russians and Ukrainians in the gas and oil industries in Siberia, in gold and diamonds in Yakutia, in electronics and the textile industries in the Baltics and Central Asia, and in military installations in the republics of Chuvash and Tatarstan.

The paradox of the present situation is that those industries with predominantly Russian-speaking personnel provide major sources of the GNP (for example, 80% in Tatarstan and Yakutia, 70% in Latvia and Estonia) to territories in which political power is in the hands of non-Russians. So, along with the process of devolution and redistribution of political power, measures could be undertaken in the field of economics: training of personnel and expanding participation in highly skilled occupations for underrepresented groups, provisions for balanced inter-ethnic participation in distributing shares in privatized enterprises, equal access to land sales, etc. Transformations in property ownership and market reforms need to be accompanied by appropriate measures that can prevent the development of mass marginalization and sharp contrasts between rich and poor, and inhibit obvious discrepancies in the relative status of regions, territorial and ethnic groups, and communities.

Programs for ethnic revival initiated by the intelligentsia and politicians should be aimed not only at restoring and preserving traditions, but also at improving social conditions, developing healthy cities, villages, and small communities, giving people access to modernization (and not 'archaization') of lifestyle by introducing more equitable standards of modern civilization. At the same time, however, existing traditional ways of life, especially among the indigenous peoples of Siberia, should be preserved, and not wantonly sacrificed for the sake of resource development projects. Equally, it is important to expand the representation of Russian-speaking minorities in the power structures of successor states, apart from Rossia. In the republics of Rossia, it is important that less urbanized titular groups do not get excluded from market reforms in industry. There are rural enclaves with minorities who are suffering economic deprivation, and where special assistance programs need to be implemented.

Strengthening local self-government

A key step would be to strengthen local self-government and community activities in governing grass-roots interests based on cultural distinctiveness. The role of the community as a basic institution of social control and regulation in civic societies was drastically reduced under the Soviet regime. The Local Self-Government Act passed by the Rossian Parliament in 1991 was a product of haste and reflected centralized political thinking and practice. It is evident that most of the disputed problems are local problems which are best resolved by local authorities. When conflict acquires the form of open violence, it is often not the federal or republican authorities, but the local ones, including traditional social institutions and grass-roots organizations, that are able to play a pacifying role.

Recent years have seen many cases in which potential conflicts or eruptions of violence were stopped by local forces – such as the Committees for Self-Defense in Dushanbe, community leaders negotiating in the North Caucasus, local government interventions to stop unlawful anti-alien decisions of community meetings, etc.. That is why local governments should be provided with the authority and financial resources to implement their own initiatives and policies with respect to ethnic issues. They must have the right to make decisions on their own educational systems, including questions of language of instruction and teaching, local broadcasting networks and press, local official festivities, cultural symbols, etc. An important issue for local politics is to institute proper respect for the local traditions and values through which small groups and individuals of different ethnic origins and religious beliefs realize their own identities. The variety and content of these activities are still limited and poor in the territory of the former USSR.

A special kind of local (community) self-government is needed for small indigenous groups with traditional subsistence economies (reindeer and cattle breeding, hunting and fishing, crafts). Indigenous governments should be granted the right to define community memberships, territory and resource management, local observances and police arrangements. Special state-sponsored programs are needed in health care, education, and training community leaders among indigenous peoples. Unless this is done, there may be another circle of conflicts in Rossia.

An important innovation for managing pluralist post-Communist societies is the rehabilitation – after decades of being harshly criticized as 'a bourgeois invention' – of the institution of non-territorial cultural autonomy. Self-determination today means that individuals and groups can determine their own identity and safeguard their rights and interests based on this identity, irrespective of territorial status and political-administrative borders. Self-determination means the right to participate in a wider political and cultural process.

For all countries in the area, it is healthy to support and to provide an appropriate legal basis for the activities of ethnic communities, including those directed toward legal pluralism ('indigenous law') and power representation, entrepreneurial and international activities. Ethnic communities and associations may have rights involving different forms of property, business and educational programs at various levels, mass communication networks, and direct links with cultural compatriots in other countries.

13.4   From Tension to Violence

Not all ethnic tensions evolve a stage of unrest and violence, but all open conflicts are preceded by tension and a period of escalation. The ethnic conflicts and wars which have erupted in the post-Communist world can be divided into two categories, according to how the violence has been expressed. One type concerns riots and pogroms directed against ethnic enemies – a short-term, grass-roots expression of manipulative hatred and explosion of violence, with a minimum of organized and structured activities. Another type is an open conflict or war with organized military or paramilitary forces on both sides and with a divided frontline and explicitly expressed positions and programs. Quite often riots evolve into protracted conflicts, which may then escalate into internal or interstate wars. Sometimes wars may stagnate into sporadic guerrilla activities and terrorist acts.

There have been pogrom-type conflicts in Uzbekistan (against Meskhetian Turks), in Azerbaijan (against Armenians in Sumgait), in Kirgizia (between Kirgiz and Uzbeks), in Rossia (against Ingush), and in many other places, including occasional violence in large cities, as in Moscow against traders from the Caucasus region. At the moment there are several ongoing ethnic wars and open conflicts in the area of the former Soviet Union: Chechnya, Nagorno Karabakh, Abkhazia, Tajikistan and some other places of lower-scale violence. What kind of symptoms and actions tend to precede the violent stage and allow tension and disputes to be transformed into unrest and clashes? Identifying these symptoms can enable us to formulate a list of suggestions to put a stop to open conflict at the pre-violent stage.

Population-shift factor

People may react explosively not to the plain fact of ethnically mixed population, but rather to the rapid changes caused by resettlement policies, spontaneous migrations, influxes of refugees, etc. Population movements, especially when they are mass and unorganized, can bring about serious social problems (job competition, housing shortages, criminal activities) that violate the accustomed order and way of life. Local groups and authorities start to express fear and anxiety – blaming the newcomers, usually ethnic aliens, for both old and new problems. Sometimes refugees and resettlers may be of the same ethnic stock (like Osset refugees from Georgia to North Ossetia or Russians moving from Central Asia and Transcaucasus to central and southern parts of Rossia) but they bring different cultural values and modes of behavior as well as negative feelings and hatred towards those who had caused their suffering. Quite often, newly emerging states enforce a climate and policy of pushing out any 'non-native' populations. Such attempts, like the settling of Kazakh emigrés from China among Russians in North Kazakhstan, can seriously aggravate the existing status quo in the ethnic situation.

In a new geopolitical situation it makes sense to counteract the policy of forced change of the demographic situation, to 'correct' it according to new interstate borders. All tools of influence, including international ones, must be used to ensure legal equality for all those living in the new states, beginning with the acceptance of the 'zero' variant of citizenship (all who were living in the territories of successor states at the moment of dissolution are eligible for citizenship). Migration policy must make it a priority to limit migration and to assist 'new minorities' in their integration into the recently changed political environment of the countries in which they reside. In its turn, Rossia should reconsider the policy of 'dual citizenship', which makes millions of new citizens outside its borders. This policy can give rise to false expectations among many residents of the new states, even leading to provocative behavior.

Dealing with xenophobia and intolerance

As a backlash reaction to official propaganda and the Russo-centric version of education and information, an opposite version of history and culture has now been invented in the public discourse of the new political nations and non-Russian republics of Rossia. While introducing enriching interpretations of history and culture, this new version still embodies ethnocentric myths and stereotypes capable of sowing new intolerance and hatred. The repudiation of 'Soviet culture' and 'friendship of the peoples' models leaves an intellectual space filled with revisionism for old grievances, and new culprits. Former time-distanced and ideologically abstract enemies, like 'tsarism' and 'world imperialism', are now replaced by recent targets closer to home – like 'Communists', 'colonizers', 'Russian fascists', 'faces of Caucasian nationalities', etc. This post-Soviet xenophobia and intolerance produces a climate favorable for group alienation and inter-ethnic tension.

The use of violence requires a certain psychological preparedness, especially for the direct participants and executors of violent acts. Verbalization and propaganda of negative ethnic attitudes on a large-scale usually play this role, signaling the probability for unrest and physical violence. For months preceding actual pogroms and riots, the press, politicians and local activists spread negative images of 'others' – with accusations of high criminality, unfairly high living standards, dishonest behavior, uncivilized lifestyles, etc. This pattern has occurred throughout conflict areas of the former Soviet Union.

Many countries have anti-racist legislation that forbids public expressions of racial and ethnic hate, especially when they potentially or directly cause violent actions and crimes. Similar laws exist in some post-Communist countries. Despite the large number of people potentially subject to legal prosecution pursuant to this law, it seldom functions in practice. Rare attempts to organize a court case exacerbate tensions, as well as mobilizing paranoic elements who thereby get undeserved publicity. In this context, state and public support as well as international judicial assistance need to be provided to implement urgent measures against the spread of ethnic hatred and prejudice, especially in areas of potential violence. To identify these places and to monitor the situation, special national and regional networks and services should be established for ethnological monitoring and early warning. The public and mass media should learn how to react to paranoid propaganda – not only through legal measures, but by denying access to publicity and creating moral isolation.

Schools in Rossia and elsewhere need educational approaches and curricula which can generate knowledge and understanding of the culture and history of other nations and ethnic groups, as well as understanding of the common threads linking all human communities. Academics and educators should learn how to identify signs of intolerance in their early stages and how to discourage it. The pedagogy of tolerance implies training and teaching skills for analyzing the atmosphere in one's school, association, or community, and being capable of adequate reaction. Historical re-evaluation and critical discussions of hostility, discrimination, and intolerance should be included in the curriculum. Students need to learn the history and geography of genocide, social segregation, religious persecutions, and ethnic conflicts, as well as mutual cultural interactions and enrichment. Rigid and closed interpretations of one's own nation or group as a victim or a sufferer as a result of the actions of other nations are, however, pedagogically unacceptable.

It is the task of the media and role of professional journalistic ethics to ensure that more comprehensive and accurate information is spread about the ethnic traditions and cultures which constitute the state. Specific inducements and rules should make the media committed to reporting on the positive experiences of ethnic cooperation and dialogue. In the content and way they present the news, the mass media should reflect the cultural mosaic, the ethnic and regional diversity of society, and the interests and needs of its constitutive groups.

Strengthening order and arms control

Executing a group violent act requires certain material preparations. Central here is to establish illegal structures in the form of paramilitary recruits ('guards', 'popular armies', 'volunteers', 'security forces', etc.). Sometimes these formations have come about on the initiative of regional or local authorities who provide (in breach of constitutional requirements) legal protection and a material basis for militant groups. This was the case in Abkhazia, Trans-Dniestria, Nagorno Karabakh, North Ossetia, and Chechnya before the outbreak of violence and organized warfare. Sometimes structures and recruits for violence are organized or initiated by public associations and political parties of a nationalist character, as was the case with the Confederation of Mountain Peoples of the North Caucasus.

This process has two significant components: acquiring arms and ammunition, and hiring and training 'field commanders' and rank-and-file warriors. A situation of weakened central authorities and paralyzed judicial, police, and state security institutions makes both possible. In the Soviet successor states we find some additional factors: the extremely powerful role of regular army personnel and the huge arsenal of weapons facilitating material preparation of ethnic violence. The Afghanistan War has also provided a reservoir of war professionals, many of whom are psychologically damaged and socially disoriented. Many more have to appear after the Chechen War.

In circumstances of growing ethnic tensions and group alienation, it is necessary to implement measures that can strengthen the public order and enforce strict limitations on illegal acquisition and bearing of weapons, as well as on the establishment of non-institutional military structures. The control over army arsenals should be tightened up, and any illegal arms sales and sponsoring or organizing military training for potential fighters among civilians should be prosecuted. Special rehabilitation and support programs should be provided for young war veterans and people leaving the reorganized security and military structures.

Educating ethnic leaders and militant activists

Obvious symptoms of a coming outbreak of violence are rising intolerance and provocative activities on the part of ethnic entrepreneurs who subscribe to non-negotiable options for resolving conflicting issues. Sometimes they may succeed in raising their demands to the level of official declarations and legal documents. Lacking experience and knowledge, they are inclined to read their concrete situation as a unique and abnormal one unprecedented in the world. The transitional stage toward violence is marked by psychologically and emotionally overloaded political rhetoric, insulting political language, and the refusal to listen to any other arguments. Such verbal warfare limits political contacts, pushing politicians and activists to extreme actions.

Another tactic is for leaders to pursue covert activities through intermediate forces. Sooner or later, these activities are usually discovered, as is information about leaders and activists who have chosen a path of confrontation. Some of them make no attempt to hide their pro-violent stance, and it is not difficult to draw up a list of active instigators and proponents of violence. What is much more difficult is to find measures that can neutralize or change the behavior of those actors, or call them to legal responsibility.

Sometimes at the pre-violent stage we can note a paralyzing and disoriented mode of behavior on the part of the central authorities, who may wish to avoid a dispute, but lack the experience and resources. The Chechen War has also demonstrated that a few top politicians, isolated by a tiny circle of close associates, can make major decisions without any proper analysis and preparations – with devastating, tragic results. The danger of one man's ego needs to be perceived and properly managed by various tools of public/legal control. That is why it is essential to make radical improvements in decision-making procedures, and to train and educate leaders and local actors in conflict resolution approaches, as well as sharing information on similar situations in other regions of the world and lessons learned from past mistakes. Nor would I exclude the use of a psychologist's assistance for those individuals who have become emotionally obsessed with certain issues which they see as their life destiny or chosen political mission.

Managing tension and sporadic clashes

Violent clashes – whether spontaneous or organized – are usually but a prelude to serious fighting. Street violence in urban settings or youth group assaults in suburban and rural communities are events that tend to escalate dangerously. A weak reaction on behalf of the authorities and the public to sporadic clashes can then be interpreted as a green light for proceeding to large-scale violence. Here at least two main strategies are possible: one is to mobilize local communities and public opinion against actions that disturb the peace, including establishing committees on the grass-roots level and watch-groups to monitor the situation in potentially dangerous areas; another approach is for the police and legal institutions to make energetic and concerted efforts to halt the outbreaks of violence.

Under conditions of tension and conflict, the mass media should adopt a calming stance, and help identify and condemn the causes and initiators of violence. What they should not do is promote an atmosphere which idealizes war or makes heroes of guerrilla leaders. The media have a responsibility to show the tragic consequences and pointlessness of doctrines and policies based on intolerance and violence. There is a need for a clear code of ethics for journalists working in areas of conflict and social tension, as well as for measures to support and encourage journalists to understand and report on the complexities of peace-making activities. In reporting on the Chechen War and other conflicts, Rossia's mass media have demonstrated a growing professionalism and liberal values, but have failed to play a constructive role in easing tension and promoting approaches towards peace.

This is a stage when international expertise is highly advisable and may provide most timely interventions. As mentioned earlier, third-party participation is often to be recommended here.

13.5   Out of Conflict

Never have there been conflicts that were programmed by history and ethnicity itself and that have lasted indefinitely. In recent times, even the most severe cases in the territory of the former Soviet Union, as in Moldavia, and Central Asia, have been de-escalated or resolved in some way or another. Likewise, there are prospects for managing the situations in Azerbaijan and Georgia, as well as in Chechnya. Modest though it may be, some experience in transforming situations of open violence into peaceful ones has already been accumulated for this area of the world. Enormous human and material resources have been involved in the effort to make peace without becoming hostages of ambitious leaders and fighters.

Stopping fire and destruction

In cases of ethnic riots with pogroms and mass killing, the situation is characterized by a lack of specially trained and effective military or legal forces. Here the violence could be stopped in different ways – including through self-exhaustion due to fear of reprisal and lack of recruits. But in most cases it does not stop without intervention of one of two kinds: forceful measures on behalf of the state, or public intervention on the part of the local community and other sectors. Energetic steps are crucial, even when a violent case burns itself out, because there must be a message against repeated violence and its further proliferation.

When mob violence breaks out, an immediate reaction is needed – strong public statements from the authorities and energetic measures empowering the police and other state forces to take control – which may mean martial law or a state of emergency. Bringing in non-local police forces may be the answer because of possible biases and sentiments on the part of local police. Providing proper equipment to strengthen communicative and mobility capacities for police as well as for documenting events can prove very useful as well. Detention, arrest, and removing the ringleaders from the scenes of the fighting are important elements for enforcing order.

When the conflicting sides cannot reach mutual agreement through their own accord or win the war by force, protracted and structured violent events which may become transformed into organized war-type activities could be stopped by two kinds of intervention. One involves the implementation of political measures to facilitate negotiations to reach ceasefire and peace agreements. For these purposes, urgent expertise and carefully designed measures are needed in order to structure a dialogue and negotiations that can define legitimate forces and individuals among conflicting parties or communities. There must be skillful mediators on both sides, as well as an acceptable negotiating site that can provide security and confidentiality to the process of peace talks.

Reaching ceasefire or peace agreements is relatively easy, in comparison to establishing mechanisms that can ensure that the peace will be lasting. Many agreements were reached during the war around Nagorno Karabakh and in Abkhazia, but most were short-lived and often used merely to win time to gather new resources before resuming military operations. A similar situation could be observed in Chechnya after an agreement on military aspects of the conflict had been reached between federal authorities and Dudayev's forces. Attention must also be focused on the conditions of ceasefire as well as the mechanisms and resources for implementing these conditions. The exact responsibilities of signatories, the repositories, sanctions in case of violation of the agreement, observatory forces and their obligations and authority – all these need to be dealt with in the negotiation process.

A second form of intervention to encourage a ceasefire and enforce peace is third-party intervention. Frequently this is perceived as a last resort. Indeed, it may have many unpredictable consequences, despite its growing popularity in the international arena, including UN structures. Third-party intervention has proven successful when carried out with the consent and participation of conflicting sides – such as the May 1992 mediation in South Ossetia. Here, the introduction of tripartite military forces with Russian army participation helped stop three years of armed conflict and reduce the level of tension. The main difficulty in dealing with a third party is ensuring this party's neutrality. For example, a bias occurred when the Russian army in Abkhazia sided, for all practical purposes and ideological emotions, with the local separatists and played a role in transforming a conflict into protracted war.

Forceful intervention from the outside, including joint efforts in the international arena, can be applied successfully only when political peace-keeping techniques have been exhausted or when the confronting parties request or agree to such intervention. The introduction of external force could be arranged as a joint action, with the participating fighting forces agreeing to monitor a ceasefire and establish peace. Win-war and large-scale operations on the part of outsiders should not be practiced in areas of ethnic conflicts and internal wars, because the situation may easily evolve into guerrilla-style war; or local rivalries may be overcome in order to mobilize against the 'outsiders'.

Security measures and widening peace-zones

Once riot-type violence is stopped, security measures should include steps designed to prevent the violence from reappearing or spreading to other places. Urgent measures are needed to prevent continuing violence in covert forms and remote areas as well as releasing all hostages on an 'all to all' basis. Police and troops, in cases where Emergency Law has been proclaimed or a provisional administration imposed by higher-level authorities, usually find themselves in the difficult situation of being 'newcomers', and quite often demonstrate incompetence and unpreparedness for actions of insubordination. Or, they may get involved in 'local diplomacy' and false forms of solidarity. This is what happened to representatives of the Russian federal government and the military commanders when they arrived at the zone of Ingush–Ossetian conflict in November 1992, and sided with one of the warring parties.

Once the confronting sides stop shooting and killing each other, peace is very fragile. Immediate measures should be undertaken to strengthen resources for peaceful conflict transformation. Such measures may include the withdrawal of troops from frontline positions, especially of heavy weapons like artillery, and establishing peace-zones or zones of special protection where the most severe fighting took place. Areas where the civilian population is concentrated should be a priority for security measures.

In open conflict there are usually two sides, but there may be many actors involved, each claiming its own power, position, and participation. The tragedy of internal feuds based on ethnic and clan loyalties in Tajikistan lies in the incapability of state forces, including Russia's military and diplomatic forces, to contact and negotiate with local field commanders. The non-obedience of separate paramilitary groups has been a disturbing factor in all violent conflicts in the former Soviet Union. At this stage of conflict transformation it is important to establish contacts with potential intruders into the peace process who are not at the top of the negotiation list but who possess arms and recruits capable of destroying an armistice and challenging agreements. This observation is fully relevant for the Chechen situation.

Fighting brings a lot of arms into a conflict area. Depending on the scale of violence and the sources of supply, these may be any conventional weapons, including tanks, aircraft, and artillery, although the most widely used weapons are guns and explosive devices. During the stage of mob and street violence, such weapons are usually not present; the means of violence in riots tend to be knives, sticks, stones, and incendiary materials as well as hunting guns. The latter should be confiscated by the authorities from all civilians in the area of conflict: this is a better protective and preventive measure than allowing people to keep and acquire new weapons, ostensibly for personal protection. Unarmed civilians behave less aggressively in a situation of tension and give less scope for separate tragic events which can cause major clashes.

Disarming in active war zones is a much more difficult issue, due to a number of factors – these may be technical (more time and resources), political (arms become a part of political capital and legitimacy), and psychological (people become used to weaponry and it becomes an element of hero-creation). Arms also represent a personal investment, and people will never want to lose what they have paid for. There have been different strategies employed to disarm civilians, and in most cases these have proven unsuccessful: practically all weaponry arsenals were kept by the local populations in the conflict zones in South Ossetia, Abkhazia, and Trans-Dniestria. The process of disarming failed in Chechnya as well. All the same, no firm measures were taken to address the problem. The widely recommended method of buying up guns and other deadly weapons while also setting deadlines and sanctions was discredited in Chechnya because of poorly organized procedures and the distrust of the continued massive presence of the federal military in the conflict zone.

New leaders and new responsibilities

Most ethnic conflicts do not result in the achievement of the goals pursued by ethnic warlords: refugees return home, territorial and political status changes are not accepted by more powerful actors. Restoring the status quo may be unsatisfactory for fighters but is often the only acceptable and realistic solution for stopping the violence. But status quo includes such basic things as personal and job security, return to places of residence and the return of seized property, as well as restoration of state and civic institutions. Conflict resolution involves deep structural changes that can result in a better system of governing a conflicting society or community. It is a process whereby a society can recover from previous losses and destruction as well as build mechanisms to prevent possible conflicts in future.

A change in the political leadership should be stimulated, allowing the power positions to be occupied by those who were not heavily involved in the violence or directly responsible for political fallacies and war crimes. This recommendation goes against the usual practice, where militant activists and politicians receive wider support than they would have had before the eruption of conflict. Violence tends to legitimize political leaders and often makes them heroes. But unless the major actors are changed, it is hard to start a new play. One reason for the difficulties in resolving the conflicts in Nagorno Karabakh, Abkhazia, North Ossetia, and Chechnya is that practically all major proponents of violent scenarios are still in power and do not want to leave their positions, partly because of a fear of being held responsible. As long as those who initiated and blessed the use of force in resolving conflicts stay in power, there will be a decisive lack of political will to recognize wrong goals and doings and to suggest radically new platforms for reaching accord. Those who got their people involved in conflicts and wars want to emerge from the acclaimed conflict as winners or peace-makers.

At times this may occur – as with Israel's Yitzhak Rabin, who paid for success with his life – but most often it is not so. Suffering people should not have to wait for decades because of the vested interests and career prospects of those who led warring parties or made wrong decisions which unleashed violence.

Serious political discussions, public debates, and legal measures should follow the post-violent stage, so as to give people a belief in mutually positive changes. Most of what has been recommended above for the conflict-preventive stage could be tested here as well. A new and vital element concerns legal investigations and punishment of criminals. The fact that – except after the Osh conflict – there have been no serious trials for crimes committed during ethnic violence in the former Soviet Union does not rule out the possibility of this becoming common practice in future. The inevitability of punishment for criminal actions – this should be a basic attitude. Failing to punish criminals is an invitation to renewed violence and other forms of irresponsible behavior.

Overall amnesty is an alternative approach. And indeed, it has been tested, especially in Chechnya, to stop the fighting – but without success. It is obvious that all rank-and-file participants of organized war activities cannot be brought to court. Amnesty is possible in this case – but not for those who organized the war or committed mass atrocities. Those who issued the order to move federal troops on Grozny in the night of the New Year 1994/95, and those who organized the terrorist act in Budennovsk in June 1995, must answer in court for their deeds, sooner or later.

Replacing current leaders with peace-oriented, responsible, and qualified persons is no easy task, not least because of the immense problems facing conflict zones and poor promises of rewards for those ready to take on these responsibilities. Many leaders and qualified managers simply opt out – leaving destruction and suffering behind them. Moving to other parts of the country or emigrating abroad, these people seek a new life and better opportunities. Appeals to feelings of patriotism or service to their own people are rarely enough to outweigh personal and family interests. In some drastic conflicts, as in South Ossetia, Abkhazia and Chechnya, the local communities have lost their most valuable human resources, which will be indispensable for the restoration of a fully functioning society. Special measures need to be considered, including international assistance, to induce influential and highly competent local people to return.

Dealing with human losses and traumas

Any conflict is an immense trauma on the collective and the individual levels, even for the victors – if indeed there are any true 'victors'. First, there will be the tragedies of those who have lost family members and friends and suffered other kinds of personal loss. For riot conflicts which are intense and short-lived, with a large and immediate number of deaths, a major problem is to provide a decent period of burial ceremonies and mourning procedures, with the proper conditions and a receptive public climate. Those who were not buried in cemeteries during the fighting, because of blockade, sieges or other reasons, should be reburied, to avoid a future sacralization of trauma, as well as to give an everyday message about past hatreds and sufferings. Local people need to realize that keeping a cemetery placed in a local schoolyard, as was done in Zkhinvali, the capital of South Ossetia, is merely lip service towards a real peace-building process.

Urgent measures for freeing hostages, finding missing persons, and returning those who fled their homes are needed to avoid a potential situation of 'cleansing' and the exaggeration of the number of casualties. In most cases in the former Soviet Union it has been impossible to return refugees and expelled people to their former residences. Reasons include fear and loss of property, but more often what is involved is illegal usurpation of land, houses, and apartments. There is a need to pass national laws or decrees as well as international declarations on the illegality and criminal character of seizing individual properties in situations of mass unrest and armed internal conflicts. This could help to build a proper basis for assisting suffering people and to outlaw the desire to profit from a conflict.

Medical treatment should be provided through local, national, and international resources and structures. Additionally, there needs to be medical help for displaced persons, with properly protected personnel and places for treatment. It was absolutely unjustified for the federal authorities of Rossia to refuse medical assistance to those citizens who fought among Dudayev's forces.

Two kinds of victims need special care and treatment: orphans and rape victims. For charities and child-protection organizations and activists, it should be a priority to assist in local and state efforts to provide remedies for these victims. Raped women, especially in less-modernized societies, often face dual 'punishment' – aside from the original trauma of the rape itself, they are subsequently shunned by their families and communities. Here I would recommend a combination of psychiatric help for victimized persons along with specialist educational efforts towards family members and local communities.

It is crucial at this stage to develop mass media programs on dismantling widespread hatred and negative stereotypes among conflicting communities and on mobilizing people for constructive behavior and projects. As has been observed in many post-conflict situations, people cannot return to a normal life or resume work without external assistance. A proper social environment connected with feelings of safety, hope, and support must be provided. But the main strategy for healing trauma is self-organization, empowering local communities and leaders to take on major responsibilities.

Restoring life-sustaining systems

Ethnic riots and wars severely damage the civic economy and its subsistence mechanisms. Small factions of society acquire vested interests in the militarized economy; individuals and groups may profit from riots and unrest by doing black-market business in a situation of disorder. Major infrastructures could be destroyed or paralyzed. The conflict area has usually been deserted by successful entrepreneurs and is not seen as a desirable place for new investments. That is why it is so hard to restore what was destroyed. Certain measures need to be undertaken to provide for basic human requirements and to avoid epidemics or a new exodus. For one thing, popular estimates tend to exaggerate the scale of damage. In towns and cities, it is usually glass, roofing, water, and heating that are most sorely needed to permit everyday life to be resumed in abandoned or severely damaged places. Next come energy and communication systems and basic food supplies. Grozny and Gudermes in Chechnya are exceptional cases of mass destruction – and here more serious long-term restoration measures will be needed.

All interested actors can – and should – use a situation of crisis to implement important development projects in areas of conflict. These areas will often be less privileged zones and regions sorely in need of development and improvements. Openly discussed, widely acclaimed and properly supported development programs could bring enthusiasm and a cooperative spirit among former enemies and rivals, and may produce results which people will come to cherish. A further point can be the additional responsibilities and employment generated. Local initiatives and involvement are crucial for development activities. Any attempts at restoration by sending in outside personnel, as in Chechnya, have limited potentials. Indeed, they may even be considered as a 'new occupation', or as a resource for taking hostages and demanding ransom. Several hundred energy and construction workers from other regions of the country shared this fate in Chechnya.

13.6 International Aspects for Ethnic Accord

A favorable outside climate and international support for the difficult transformations that totalitarian societies must undergo to become democratic are necessary preconditions for actions by those who believe in openness and tolerance in Rossia and throughout the former USSR. New forms of isolation or charges of 'neo-imperialism' merely give opportunities to the domestic opponents of democratization and to propagandists of hypothetical 'conspiracies against Rossia' to arouse hostility towards the external world and towards 'internal enemies'.

Restraint and peace-oriented politics among post-Soviet states can be established only in a wider context of external openness. The development of all kinds of international contacts and a broad exchange of information must be fostered – especially concerning experiences in governing complex societies and in conflict management. Qualified legal aid, all forms of expertise for conflict-prone areas and war-torn societies, educational programs, rehabilitation measures, humanitarian aid for victims of conflicts – these are necessary and will be welcomed by the people. This environment of outside monitoring and of constructive participation may have a major influence on local actors, helping the situation to change for the better. Since 1991, serious efforts have already been made by some international structures and NGOs, like the OSCE, the UN High Commissioner for Refugees, the International Organization of Migration, the International Committee of the Red Cross, Physicians Without Borders, the World Council of Churches, and several others.

However, even impartial, international participation may produce a double-edged effect. For those who seek a voice for and recognition of their political stands, the search for outside allies and sympathy moves them to exaggerate their complaints and demands. Conflicting parties learn how not only to appeal, but how to manipulate world public opinion and international structures. For example, Latvian and Estonian officials successfully presented their internal politics as meeting international standards, and a reference to positive 'international expertise' was the main argument for passing and implementing discriminating legislation in these countries. Dudayev's propaganda became the main source for judging the situation in Chechnya during the 1992 fact-finding mission of the NGO International Alert and for mass media reporting from the area for several years, including during the time of major war. A turning point in crushing the opposition and in strengthening power for Dudayev came when a local TV station broadcast Dudayev's visit to Yemen in 1992, where he was received in the manner normally reserved for heads of state. Ordinary Chechens read this message as a sign of accomplished independence from Rossia.

As soon as local activists succeed in breaking through the isolation of challenged political space, they become inclined to ignore the primacy of face-to-face dialogue and of nation-wide rules. There have been many cases when international participation, especially of minority-rights activists and conflict-resolution NGOs, has not improved but rather intensified tension and conflict escalation. Fragile local balances between political forces and communities may easily be upset by outside intruders, even if the latter are motivated by the most sincere and positive of intentions. One example is the Hague-based Unrepresented Nations and Peoples Organization, with a coordinating office in Tartu (Estonia) for the areas of the former Soviet Union. Its activists canvass for potential members to provide them with support, basically in the form of symbolic recognition as independent (sovereign) political entities. For separatist leaders like Vladislav Ardzinba and Dzhokhar Dudayev, references to this membership became a major argument as to international recognition for their militant stands. In Dudayev's public statements one could read:

On 5 August 1991 the State flag of the Chechen Republic was raised solemnly at the Headquarters of the Unrepresented Nations and Peoples Organization in The Hague. This day the Chechen Republic became officially a full-fledged member of the ONN [Russian abbreviation highly reminiscent of the UN - V.T.] (*Ternistyi put'*, 1992, p. 20).

We have already become a subject of international law as a full-fledged member of the Unrepresented Nations and Peoples Organization, and we are sure that this international organization will be the most effective mechanism in the global arena (1992, p. 13).

I possess much evidence that people in Chechnya, especially participants of political rallies and militant activities, read that kind of message as meaning that their republic had become an independent state and a member of the UN.

Another crucial issue is not to allow conflict zones to become a concentration of professional fighters, all kinds of adventurists and psychopathic personalities who rush across national borders in search of emotional and material rewards. A special poetics of war and killing has started to be preached in this part of the world. The Russian writer Eduard Limonov, a returnee from US emigration notorious for his pro-fascist views, stated in an interview to Radio Liberty on 3 June 1994 that 'war is a remarkable freedom, and many people, especially young ones, enjoy war'. These 'war lovers' commute between ex-Yugoslavia, Trans-Dniestria, Abkhazia, and Chechnya, quite often making a conflict their exclusive property. Some of them go about actively raising money and supplying ammunition, as was the case with the Chechen diaspora in Turkey (see Hill, 1995, p. 90, ref. 28) and other countries.

If ethnic conflicts in and around Rossia are to be managed, and tolerance and accord promoted in this part of the world, it will require tolerance with respect to Rossia itself and, above all, an understanding of the complexity of the internal situation and the sentiments of the people. The road to the creation of a new society and to stability in this area is difficult. We always face the risk of backlash and revenge provoked by former Cold War warriors, political orthodoxies, or by those representatives of the Russian and other ethnic diasporas who cannot face the non-confrontational reality of today. As for the international community, it needs to recognize that lack of outside understanding and respect towards the countries that have arisen in the post-Soviet space may hinder progress in establishing internal accord and self-respect within these countries themselves.

Among other things, respect for Rossia should include respect for its territorial borders. Following the defeat of federal troops in Chechnya this is especially relevant because of the growing number of actors who want to start another circle of state contraction instead of improving the governance and negotiating political differences. There is a move towards replaying the past and responding with action towards, in newly emerged academic jargon, the 'Russian Mini-Empire' (Balzer, 1994), or that is expressed as an explicit appeal to resurrect a 'proper Russia' (Brzezinski, 1994), meaning Rossia without the ethnic autonomies that comprise 53.2% of the state's territory. Proponents of this scenario can be found not only among the most influential statesmen, and governmental and international bureaucracies, including the European Union and the Council of Europe.[1] Just indignation at mass human rights violations committed by the Rossian government in this part of the country hinders the view of one far-reaching and important projection: that is, that non-negotiable rewards for Chechen rebels will be unacceptable to the country's leaders and the public, who have not yet had enough time to digest the first break-up of historic Rossia. These rewards mean decisive encouragement for separatists in

Azerbaijan, Georgia, Moldavia and Ukraine who are often in the same position of being military winners but without reaching political goals. Supporting these goals may bring another circle of disintegration among post-Soviet states – this time, for sure, with globally devastating results. An intriguing perspective at the end of the millennium!

Notes

1. I do not place into this category the President of the United States of America, William Clinton, but, in the meantime I am still expecting a response to my letter forwarded through US senator Sam Nunn on the eve of Clinton's visit to Rossia and at the moment when negotiations between the Rossian and Tatarstan authorities were approaching their conclusive stage. The unedited text of this letter, dated 5 January 1994, follows:

Dear Mr. President

As a Director of the Institute of Ethnology and Anthropology, Russian Academy of Sciences and former Minister of Nationalities in Yeltsin's Government, I am deeply involved in the issues of ethnic nationalism and conflicts in a post-Soviet space. Among them, the most serious one is the challenge of further disintegration of successor states (including Russia) under the pressure of internal separatist forces. There is no need to argue that 'Yugoslavization' of this part of the world will bring a lot of suffering and global destabilization.

One of the arguments used most often by proponents of secession is an argument of international support and of sympathy allegedly existing among Western leaders towards 'a struggle for national self-determination' (in the post-Soviet context it means ethnic self-determination), including those taking place in republics of the Russian Federation (Chechen, Tatarstan, Tuva) and in Georgia, Moldavia, and Azerbaijan. For example, after the recent visit to the USA by the Vice President of Tatarstan, Vasilii Likhachev, this event was widely publicized by local officials as a state visit and as a sign of implicit recognition of Tatarstan's full sovereignty. The interpretation was based on the very fact that all whom Likhachev has met in the USA preferred to follow the same political language used by Tatarian politicians: no mentioning of Russia as a state with territorial autonomies, including the Tatarstan.

In this situation I think it may be a very important gesture if you consider an opportunity to make any statement in favour of territorial integrity for all successor states and condemning narrow ethnonationalism. It will provide President Yeltsin with great political and moral support in dealing with one of the most serious issues. No doubt it will be positively met by other state leaders and by the public in this area of the world.

With deep respect,

Prof. Valery Tishkov, Director

CONCLUSION

DESTROYING REALITY THROUGH THEORY (OR 'BACK TO THE IVORY TOWERS')

It was a few nights before Christmas 1995. I lay sleepless in the home of my PRIO colleague Robert Bathurst, on the tiny island of Ormøya in the Oslo fjord. My mind was full of thoughts – about writing this conclusion and preparing to leave for Moscow to meet the New Year 1996.

During that long, cold northern night I recalled again the beauty of Dubrovnik in summer 1991 and the horrors of the landscape I had witnessed in Grozny in October 1995. Before, I had known that city as pleasant and peaceful. Now, after one year of war, it lay in shambles. Chechen men in black leather jackets rushing around with guns or with bureaucratic papers in their hands. Russian and Chechen women laying bricks and painting, trying to restore living spaces. Federal military and local militiamen with tense faces a few days after Commander General Anatolii Romanov had been blown up in his vehicle. Salamber Khadjiev, then head of the provisional government in Grozny, squeezed by a multitude of problems and rivalries, addressing the participants at the round-table 'Rossia and Chechnya: a test of statehood' with a plea for 'constructive ideas and concrete recommendations to overcome the crisis'. The sign on his cabinet door proclaimed 'Academician Khadjiev', as if to remind everyone that this was a wise man indeed. In a corridor of the governmental building I met Beslan Gantemirov, mayor of Grozny, who had introduced himself as 'a fighter' (*boevik*) in December 1994 during our first encounter in Vladikavkaz. Now he was surrounded by bodyguards watching him even in front of the toilet door. I met another carefully guarded personality, Vladimir Rubanov, Deputy Secretary of the Security Council, in the courtyard of the federal administration building, where he offered the profound and gloomy observation, 'Scholarly analysis is a good thing but some major decisions may be taken because of an extra drink the night before or the lack of *rassol* [the Russian Alka-Seltzer – V.T.] in the morning.' Vakhit Akaev, Director of the Chechen Social Science Research Institute, showed me the bombed building of his institute and asked me to forward to the Moscow-based Fund for the Support of Humanities Research an application for a new research project on 'national liberation movements in Chechnya in the 19th century'.

Something is definitely wrong with politics and scholarship in conflict-rent societies. Both appear as fundamentally stupid and immoral in many respects, and both as yet unready to admit 'We were wrong', as has been done by Robert McNamara about the Vietnam War that ended 20 years ago. Are unbiased and self-reflective analyses possible with so many things at stake – including tens of thousands dead – or are we destined to wait for another 20 years to learn all political lessons and to fulfill a mission of research intentions? Does this 'mind aflame' prevent us from drawing conclusions before society finally cools down? I believe that some conclusions are possible and indeed crucially needed, even if they may not be any more penetrating than the remark offered in 1992 by the Georgian intellectual/politician who was escorting me to Shevardnadze's office through the ruined streets of Tbilisi: 'Look, how all Georgians may become suddenly all insane!'

The problem lies not only in decrepit methodology or the limited visions I wrote of in the beginning of this book. The real problem is the tradition of servility and the distorted craft of social science scholarship throughout post-Soviet space. It shows itself in a lack of distance between politics and research, in the widespread practice of using scientific titles for greater prestige and personal significance. In times of weakened state support, scholarship in Russia and other new states is becoming increasingly willing to sell itself to state or business institutions. In turn, more and more political entrepreneurs want to acquire the status of scholars – without, however, practicing science as a profession. Ruslan Khasbulatov, former Speaker of the dissolved Supreme Soviet, has now become a member of the Russian Academy of Sciences. Both the Federation Council's speakers, Ivan Rybkin and Vladimir Shumeyko, together with party leaders Gennadi Zuiganov, Vladimir Lysenko and many other members of the State Duma, have been granted doctoral degrees from Moscow academic institutes for their publicist writings. Many ministers, senior staff of the Security Council and other public figures can today title themselves 'academicians' so as to display the strength of their personality in the 'scientific management of society'.

There is a difference from the Communist era: bureaucrats and top officials no longer need to ask permission from the party boss to use their position in the scramble for scholarly degrees; and the Russian Academy of Sciences, challenged by mushrooming 'non-official' academies and by budget cuts, does not feel ashamed at insisting on and indeed gaining the status of a ministry, with its President among the members of Rossia's government.

Post-Soviet ethnic and conflict studies have learned little from recent experiences. These studies not only reflect or construct, but can destroy realities with their manipulative power. If Russian and other Soviet successor societies cannot find a way to discipline this part of the public sector into restrained and professional behavior, they can expect even more trouble in future. If Russian scholars and other intellectuals do not take an anti-messianic stand and restrain the arrogance of prescriptions, they will suffer disillusionments and vulnerable status.

This, my position of intellectual anti-intellectualism, is not an extravagance of hypercriticism, but the result of serious considerations. In many respects it concerns also the rich research literature published in the West in my field of interest. After reading much of it, I have come to the conclusion that Rossia is unlucky with its 'outside' expertise because of the simple fact that Soviet and post-Soviet studies have been a product of the Cold War and of highly ideological engagement. Past legacies have not been swept away. Already, there are many who are ready to proclaim that 'the end of the Cold War is also over', as was done by the director of the Prague-based Open Media Research Institute, Jack Maresca (1995).

The clearest proof of ideologically motivated positions can be found in the willingness to use the destructive language of Soviet times on the 'national question' and on 'international relations' in countries like the former Soviet Union and today's Russia: the very same realities elsewhere in the world are seen in 'ethnic' or 'minorities' categories, with the term 'international relations' reserved for the study of interstate relations. The logic is obvious: why speak of 'ethnic problems' in Russia if domestic scholars prefer a language that implicitly calls into question their own state? When the editors and authors of the most comprehensive study of nationalism and ethnicity in the Soviet successor states (Bremmer & Taras, 1993) consider Middle Volga, North Caucasus, and Siberia as regions of Russia with 'nations without a state', they are doing more than simply parroting the naïve but provocative political rhetoric of 'non-represented peoples'. They are sending the clear message that citizens of Rossia with Tatar, Bashkir, Ossetian, Yakut, Chukchi, and other ethnic backgrounds do not have a state – that they are, in effect, stateless persons. What then are the 'nations with a state' in this country? Logically, there can be only one: the Russian ethnonation. And yet it is precisely Russian ethnonationalists who argue that only Russians do not 'self-determine' themselves as a separate 'national state (republic)'. Why not simply overcome the barrier of political correctness, and share this political speculation as well?

Symptomatically, members of the same national school of social sciences never pause to question a fully fledged US-type state consisting of members of more than a hundred indigenous peoples, they agree with official non-recognition of passports issued on behalf of the 'Odjibwee nation' or 'Hawaiian nation' in North America – while at the same time they can say that 'fully half or more of the Soviet Union's national groups had no political recognition as nations', to quote Ian Bremmer (Bremmer & Taras, 1993, p. 6). Surely this is no scholarly statement: it is a political one.

Despite the serious fallacies, important questions are raised by scholars and there is still room for fruitful research and policy-oriented recommendations. Among the most fundamental questions is one asked by Liah Greenfeld (1994): why is it that in some societies existing cultural differences are not perceived as important and not actualized in dramatic forms, whereas in others they represent basic identities and are seen to lie at the core of human and political interactions? Another is a research task formulated by David Laitin: how to build a theoretical model that can explain why in multi-ethnic regions of the former Soviet Union 'there is civil war in some places but ethnic peace in others' (in Guboglo, 1994a, p. 11). Indeed, there are thousands of places in the world where Ted Gurr's (1993) model of 'minorities at risk' is an apt description. The problem with this model is that most of the selectively included ones on his list of 233 groups and many more 'unnoticed' ones do not fight, choosing instead to live peaceful and cooperative lives.

'Objective' variables and sophisticated models are not enough to explain ethno-political conflicts and wars, including those in ex-Yugoslavia or in the former Soviet Union. Shortly before the bloody events in the Balkans, Asbjørn Eide, Director of the Norwegian Human Rights Institute, collected questionnaires on minorities' status, and the data provided from Yugoslavia showed rather good standards and accomplishments in this field of international concerns in preparing the UN declaration on minority rights. These were not faked data; my own observations in Beograd, Zagreb, and Sarajevo in 1988 as well as extensive research literature do not prove a post-factum 'cultural fatalism' where murder runs in the blood of the Balkan peoples, or that the Yugoslav empire was doomed to break up under the inevitable striving of the peoples to self-determination. This myth of 'cultural fatalism', whereby something about Serbs, Croats, and Bosnians condemns them to war, was strongly dispelled by the editorial columnist William Pfaff of the *International Herald Tribune*:

> But nature did not make them do it, nor did their national cultures or histories . . . The war was deliberately created in the struggle for personal power that followed Tito's death in 1980. This was no spontaneous rising of the Serbian, Croatian and Muslim peoples to slaughter one another. They had to be propagandized and provoked for more than a decade before the crisis was exploded by Slovenia's and Croatia's 'dissociation' of themselves from Yugoslavia in June 1991 (4–5 November, 1995).

Clear similarities exist between the Balkans and the former Soviet areas with regard to the nature of ethnic manifestations. For centuries, cultural differences were no reason for group hatred or fighting between major peoples – including Russians, Ukrainians, Tatars, Georgians, Abkhazians, Tajiks, Kirgiz, and many others – just as the case with Croats, Serbs, and Bosnians. Most of those who are now alive – especially political activists, intellectual writers, battlefield warriors – never experienced Stalin's deportations and political persecutions personally. Real group differences are much less pronounced than they are made to sound in the context of 'hostilities', 'injustices', 'violated rights', endangered 'basic needs', etc. These are intentional efforts to realize specific political choices – in this case to contract one state to several, to make more states within these new ones, to reshape territorial boundaries, or to redistribute power and the control of resources.

It is too naïve to interpret these choices as emanating from the groups in question. These are the choices – or the results – from a range of competing strategies professed by key actors within and outside the groups. Concerning the role of 'inside' actors, I am most struck by the result of the IEA 1994 sociological survey that measured political sympathies and orientations among the citizens of Rossia (it is only sympathies, not even direct involvement!). The proportion of people who could not provide any answer to this question, or who did not support any political party and public movement, comprised in Tatarstan among Tatars and Russians 84% and 72% respectively; in North Ossetia among Ossets and Russians, 62% and 68%; in Yakutia among Yakuts and Russians, 76% and 78%. Even more noteworthy was the absence of any interest and support for local parties and movements: 85% and 99% in Tatarstan, 62% and 81% in North Ossetia, and 81% and 89% in Yakutia. The picture for the rest of the country would be not very different, except in Moscow and St Petersburg, with their slightly higher level of political articulation. For me, these data serve to point up not only the emptiness of all sociological surveys and polls on what is called 'public opinion', but the very notion of society itself. What is viewed and studied as 'society' is, probably, made up of no more then 5% elite elements (especially when these 5% are in agreement) who can produce and impose any myth and project for the rest of populace. They are the ones who play the game and make history! A society and its political institutions find themselves in a state of disarray as soon as elite elements are lacking political and moral cohesion. The collapse of the USSR was a consequence of a fragmented and highly divided political elite (see Lane, 1996).

The 'outside' actors on the territory of the former Soviet Union were no less powerful, because important things are at stake and the game is much more thrilling and exciting. Rossia, with its great cultural influences, contradictory magnitudes, inherited worldwide images, geopolitical potentials, and international pool of practicing experts is and will continue to be an appealing scene for intellectual provocations and for political improvisation. The rank and file will remain the hostages of professional ideological and military fighters until the day when many more individual 'voices' have broken their silence and acquired more tools to determine their own private strategies.

It is wrong to view accomplished events as 'historical' or 'ahistorical', as done to 'the good' or to 'the bad'. History is wise and stupid at the same time with, probably, only one guiding Law – that of uncertainty. What has happened has happened: no one can replay the past. The USSR, like Yugoslavia, will never be put together again, even though there might have been other options available before the major shifts. As to the future, what is possible is more conflicts and more social disorders. Even a major war between states, like Rossia and Ukraine, may result if ethnic and political entrepreneurs can twist keywords like 'interests', 'rights', 'enemies' so as to mobilize fighters from people with a complex of 'small cultural differences', and if outside actors find it a thrilling scenario. No doubt, intellectuals will be happy to supply historical and other arguments for emotional preparations and for post-factum explanations. I myself was intrigued to listen to the impressive presentation and its enthusiastic reception by the audience when in April 1995 at the Berkeley, California conference on 'Identities in Transition' the young and gifted ethno-historian Veljko Vujacic, read from the diary of a 19th-century Sarajevo emigré, who seems to have heard deeply hidden inter-ethnic hatreds sounded in everyday Christian bells, Muslim mullahs' calls to prayer, and the appearance of Jewish rabbis in this city. This was cited to explain the bloodshed in Bosnia today. To me, however, it seemed more relevant to speculate on the psychological state of this diarist, and look into the undeclared social motives that might have made him leave Sarajevo – well known throughout the centuries as a peaceful meeting-place of many cultures – as well as to analyze how an ambitious modern scholar may use convenient historical 'evidence' for the purpose of establishing his authority within the prestigious academic community.

Local and global disparities, competitions, and rivalries – these are probably unalienated features of social evolution as well as their cultural projections and collectively exercised forms. The way to prevent these from manifesting themselves in violent guise lies not only in a strategy of active position and intervention: we need a strategy of restraint, non-participation, and critical self-reflection as well. And for intellectuals, the call 'back to the ivory towers!' may be a relevant warning in times of turbulent societal transformation.

Such an exercise in disengagement and self-reflection is necessary for students of Soviet/post-Soviet societies. Western social scientists may start to feel better once they have recovered from the wounds inflicted by wrongly formulated questions about their failed power of prediction. Moreover, they will get a chance to avoid a too-hasty response to the growing demand to replace the once-current 'evil empire' concept by another facile label, like the 'criminal state'. And in Rossia, scholars need to define better their professional boundaries, methods, and language, so as not to be drowned in a flux of superficial, inflammatory writings full of old arrogances on the 'scientific management of society' and a Russian-style 'manifest destiny'.

Bibliography

Abashin, Sergei N. & Valentin I. Bushkov, 1991. *Sotsial'naya napryazhennost i mezhnat-sional'nye konflikty v severnykh raionah Tadjikistana* [Social Tension and Interethnic Conflicts in the Northern Regions of Tajikistan. Studies in Applied and Urgent Ethnology]. Doc. no. 24. Moscow: IEA.

Abdulatipov, Ramazan, 1995. *O federativnoi i natsional'noi politike Rossiiskogo gosu-darstva* [On the Federal and Nationality Policy of the Russian State]. Moscow: Slavyanski Dialog.

Abdulatipov, Ramazan G.; Lubov F. Boltenkova & Yuri F. Yarov, 1993. *Federalizm v istorii Rossii.* [Federalism in the History of Russia]. Book 3, part 2. Moscow: Izdatel'stvo Respublika.

Abramyan, Levon A. & Anna A. Borodatova, 1992. 'August 1991: prazdnik ne uspevshii razvernutsa' [August 1991: Uncompleted Festivity], *Etnograficheskoe obozrenie*, no. 3, May–June, pp. 47–57.

Abramyan, Levon A. & Arthur T. Marutyan, 1991. *'Bor'ba za natsional'nuiu nezavisimost v Pribaltike i Zakavkazie'* [The Struggle for National Independence in the Baltics and Transcaucasus], pp. 36–37 in Asankanov & Drobizheva, 1991.

Adekanye, Bayo J., 1995. 'Structural Adjustment, Democratization, and Rising Ethnic Tensions in Africa', *Development and Change*, vol. 26, April, pp. 355–374.

Afanasyev, Yuri, 1990. 'Why the Empire Should Crumble', *Time*, 12 March, p. 35.

Agadzhanyan, Victor S., 1991. 'Armyano-azerbaijanskii konflikt' [The Armenian–Azerbaijan Conflict], pp. 4–14 in A.G. Osipov, ed., *Etnicheskie konflikty v SSSR: prichiny, osobennosti, problemy izucheniia* [Ethnic Conflicts in the USSR: Causes, Specificity and Problems of Study]. Moscow: IEA.

Akhmadov, Sharputdin V. & Vakhid Kh. Akaev, 1992. *Sheikh Mansur i osvoboditel'naya bor'ba narodov Severnogo Kavkaza v poslednei treti XVIII veka* [Sheikh Mansur and the Liberation Struggle of the Peoples of the Northern Caucasus in the Latter Third of the 18th Century. Summaries of Papers and Reports of an International Conference]. Grozny: Chechen Research Institute.

Akiner, Shirin, ed., 1991. *Cultural Change and Continuity in Central Asia.* London: Kegan Paul.

Alexeev, Valery P., 1974. *Proiskhozhdenie narodov Kavkaza* [Origins of the Peoples of the Caucasus]. Moscow: Nauka.

Amelin, Venalii V., 1993. *Mezhnatsional'nye konflikty v respublikakh Srednei Azij* [Ethnic Conflicts in the Republics of Central Asia]. Moscow: Ross.

Anderson, Benedict, 1983. *Imagined Communities: Reflections on the Origin and Spread of Nationalism.* London: Verso.

Aptekar, P., 1995. 'Chechniu pytalis' razhoruzhit' i ran'she [They Tried to Disarm Chechnya Earlier as Well]. *Argumenty i fakty*, No. 3, January.

Armstrong, John A., 1982. *Nations Before Nationalism.* Chapel Hill, NC: University of North Carolina Press.

Armstrong, John A.,1992. 'Nationalism in the Former Soviet Empire', *Problems of Communism*, vol. 41, no. 1–2, January–April, pp. 121–133.

Arutiunov, Sergei A., 1989. *Narody i kul'tury: Razvitie i vzaimodeistvie* [Peoples and Cultures: Development and Interaction]. Moscow: Nauka.

Arutiunov, Sergei A., 1990. 'Ob etnokul'turnom vosproizvodstve v respublikakh' [On Ethno-cultural Reproduction in the Republics], *Sovetskaya etnografiia*, no. 5, September– October, pp. 20–28.

Arutiunov, Sergei A. et al., 1994. *The Ethnopolitical Situation in the Northern Caucasus.* Paper 1 in the Project on Ethnicity and Nationalism Publication Series. Washington, DC: International Research and Exchange Board.

Arutiunov, Sergei A. 1995. 'Ethnicity and Conflict in the Caucasus', pp. 15–18, in *Ethnic Conflict and Russian Intervention in the Caucasus*. Policy Paper, No. 16, August. University of California, Irvine.

Arutunyan, Yuri V., ed., 1992. *Russkie. Etno-sotsiologicheskie ocherki* [The Russians. Ethno-Sociological Essays]. Moscow: Nauka.

Arutunyan, Yuri V., ed., 1994. *Rossiyane: stolichnye zhiteli* [The Rossians: Profile of the Capital]. Moscow: IEA.

Arutunyan, Yuri V., ed., 1995. *Rossiyane: Zhiteli goroda i derevni* [The Rossians: Urban and Rural Citizens]. Moscow: IEA.

Arutunyan, Yuri V. & Yulian V. Bromley, eds, 1986. *Social'no-kulturni oblik sovetskikh natzii* [Socio-cultural Profile of Soviet Nations]. Moscow: Nauka.

Asankanov, Abilabek, 1996. 'Ethnic Conflict in the Osh Region in Summer 1990: Reasons and Lessons', pp. 116–124 in Rupesinghe & Tishkov, 1996.

Asankanov, Abilabek & Leokadia Drobizheva, eds, 1991. *Mezhnatsional'nye problemy i konflikty: poiski putei ikh resheniia* [Nationality Problems and Conflicts: A Search for Resolution]. Part 1. Bishkek: Kirgiz State University.

Averyanov, Yuri, ed., 1993. *Kazaki Rossii. Donskoe Kazachestvo v Grazhdanskoi voine (Sbornik Dokumentov, 1918–1919)* [The Don Cossacks in the Civil War. Collection of Documents, 1918–1919]. Part 1. Moscow: IEA.

Azar, Edward E., 1990. *The Management of Protracted Social Conflict.* Brookfield, VT: Gower.

Bagramov, Eduard, 1994. 'Natsia kak sograzhdanstvo?' [Nation as Co-citizenship?]. *Nezavisimaya gazeta*, 15 March.

Bagramov, Eduard A. et al., eds, 1993. *Razdelit li Rossia uchast' Souza SSR?* [Will Russia Share the Fate of the USSR?]. Moscow: Russian Institute of Social and National Problems.

Balzer, Marjorie Mandelstam, 1993. 'Dilemmas of the Spirit: Religion and Atheism in the Yakut–Sakha Republic', pp. 231–251 in Sabrina Petra Ramet, ed., *Religious Policy in the Soviet Union*. Cambridge, MA: Cambridge University Press.

Balzer, Marjorie Mandelstam, 1994. 'From Ethnicity to Nationalism: Turmoil in the Russian Mini-Empire', pp. 56–88 in James R. Millar & Sharon L. Wolchik, eds, *The Social Legacy of Communism*. Cambridge, MA: Cambridge University Press.

Balzer, Marjorie Mandelstam, 1995. 'Introduction', *Anthropology and Archeology of Eurasia. A Journal of Translations*, Winter 1994–95, vol. 33, no. 3, pp. 4–13.

Barkashov, Alexander, 1995. 'Krizis mirovoi tsivilizatsii, rol' Rossii i zadachi russkogo natsional'nogo dvizhenia' [The Crisis of World Civilization, the Role of Russia, and the Goals of the Russian National Movement], *Russkii poryadok*, no. 1–2, pp. 1–2.

Barth, Fredrik, ed., 1969. *Ethnic Groups and Boundaries: The Social Organization of Cultural Difference.* Boston, MA: Little, Brown.

Baturin, Yuri, 1994. 'Chess-Like Diplomacy at Novo-Ogarevo. An Eyewitness Account to the Drafting of the USSR Union Treaty of 1991', *Democratizatsiya. The Journal of Post-Soviet Democratization*, vol. 11, no. 2, Spring, pp. 212–221.

Beissinger, Mark & Lubomyr Hajda, eds, 1990. *The Nationalities Factor in Soviet Politics and Society.* Boulder, CO: Westview Press.

Bennigsen, Alexander & S. Enders Wimbush, 1985. *Mystics and Commissars, Sufism in the Soviet Union.* London: Hurst.

Bennigsen Broxup, Marie, ed., 1992. *The North Caucasus Barrier: the Russian Advance Towards the Muslim World.* London: Hurst.

Bjørgo, Tore & Rob Witte, eds, 1993. *Racist Violence in Europe.* New York: St Martin's Press.

Bogoraz, Tan, 1934–39. *Chukchi* [The Chukchi]. 2 vols. Leningrad: Glavsevmorput.

Bogoraz, Tan, 1991. *Material'naya kul'tura chukchei* [The Material Culture of the Chukchi]. Moscow: Nauka.

Bogush, Tatiyana A., 1991. 'Mezhnatsional'nye otnosheniia v polietnichnom regione: Problemy i perspektivy razvitiia' [Nationality Relations in Polyethnic Regions: Problems and Prospects for Development], pp. 28–30 in Asankanov & Drobizheva, 1991.

Bol'shaya Sovetskaya entsiklopediia [The Great Soviet Encyclopedia]. Vol. 17, 1974. Moscow: Soviet Encyclopedia Publishing House.

Bourdieu, Pierre, 1984. 'Espace social et genèse des classes', *Actes de la recherche en sciences sociales.* No. 52–53, June, pp. 3–14.

Bourdieu, Pierre, 1990. *In Other Words. Essays Towards a Reflexive Sociology.* Stanford, CA: Stanford University Press.

Bremmer, Ian & Ray Taras, eds, 1993. *Nations and Politics in the Soviet Successor States.* Cambridge, MA: Cambridge University Press.

Bromley, Yulian V., 1973. *Etnos i etnografia* [Ethnos and Ethnography]. Moscow: Nauka.

Bromley, Yulian V., 1981. *Sovremennie problemy etnografii* [Contemporary Problems of Ethnography]. Moscow: Nauka.

Bromley, Yulian V., 1983. *Ocherki teorii etnosa* [Essays on the Theory of Ethnos]. Moscow: Nauka.

Bromley, Yulian V., 1987. *Etnosotsial'nie protsessy: teoria, istoria, sovremennost* [Ethnosocial Processes: Theory, History, Today]. Moscow: Nauka.

Bromley, Yulian V., 1989. 'Krazrabotke poniatiino-terminologicheskikh aspektov natsional'noi problematiki' [On Working Out Terminological Aspects of Nationality Problems], *Sovetskaya etnografiia*, no. 6, November–December, pp. 3–17.

Bromley, Yulian V., ed., 1977. *Sovremennie etnicheskie protsessy v SSSR* [Contemporary Ethnic Processes in the USSR]. Moscow: Nauka.

Bromley, Yulian & Viktor Kozlov, 1989. 'The Theory of Ethnos and Ethnic Processes in Soviet Social Sciences', *Comparative Studies in Society and History*, vol. 31, no. 3, July, pp. 425–438.

Brooks, Jeffrey, 1985. *When Russia Learned to Read.* Princeton, NJ: Princeton University Press.

Brubaker, Rogers, 1994. 'Nationhood and the National Question in the Soviet Union and Post-Soviet Eurasia: An Institutionalist Account', *Theory and Society,* vol. 23, no. 1, pp. 47–78.

Brusina, Olga I., 1990. *O nekotorykh prichinah mezhetnicheskogo konflikta v Oshskoi oblasti* [On the Causes of Interethnic Conflict in the Osh Oblast. Studies in Applied and Urgent Ethnology]. Doc. 10. Moscow: IEA.

Brusina, Olga I., 1992. 'Vostochno-slavyanskoe naselenie v sel'skikh raionakh Uzbekistana. Problemy adaptatsii i mezhetnicheskikh vzaimodeistvii' [East-Slavic Population in Rural Areas of Uzbekistan. Problems of Adaptation and Ethnic Interaction], pp. 79–88 in Alina Zhilina & Sergei Cheshko, eds, 1992, *Sovremennoe razvitie etnicheskikh grupp Srednei Azii i Kazakhstana* [Contemporary Status of Ethnic Groups in Central Asia and Kazakhstan]. Part 2. Moscow: IEA.

Brzezinski, Zbigniew, 1989–90. 'Post Communist Nationalism', *Foreign Affairs*, vol. 68, no. 5, Winter, pp. 1–25.

Brzezinski, Zbigniew, 1994. 'The Premature Partnership', *Foreign Affairs*, vol. 73, no. 2, March/April, pp. 67–82.

Bugai, Nikolai F., 1989. 'K voprosu o deportatsii narodov SSSR v 30-40h godah' [On the Deportations of the Peoples of the USSR in the 1930s and 1940s], *Istoria SSSR*, no. 6, November–December, pp.135–144.

Bugai, Nikolai F., ed., 1994. *Repressirovannie narody Rossii: Chechentsy i Ingushy. Dokumenty, fakty, komentarii* [Repressed Peoples of Russia: Chechens and Ingush. Documents, Facts, Commentary]. Moscow: TOO Kap.

Burton, John W., 1987. *Resolving Deep-Rooted Conflict. A Handbook*. Lanham, MD: University Press of America.

Burton, John & Frank Dukes, eds, 1990. *Conflict: Readings in Management and Resolution*. New York: St Martin's Press/London: Macmillan.

Bushkov, Valentin, 1990. *O nekotorykh aspektah mezhnatsional'nikh otnoshenii v Tajiksoi SSR* [Some Aspects of Inter-Ethnic Relations in the Tajik SSR. Studies in Applied and Urgent Ethnology]. Doc. 11. Moscow: IEA.

Cardus, Salvador & Joan Estruch, 1995. 'Politically Correct Anti-Nationalism', *International Social Science Journal*, no. 144, June, pp. 347–355.

Carrère d'Encausse, Hélène, 1978. *L'empire éclaté*. Paris: Flammarion. Published in English in 1979 as *Decline of an Empire*. New York: Newsweek Books.

Carrère d'Encausse, Hélène, 1991. *The Great Challenge: Nationalities and the Bolshevik State, 1917–1930*. New York and London: Holmes & Meier.

Carrère d'Encausse, Hélène, 1993. *The End of Soviet Empire – The Triumph of Nations*. New York: New Republic.

Carrère d'Encausse, Hélène, 1995. *The Nationality Question in the Soviet Union and Russia*. Norwegian Nobel Institute Lecture Series. Oslo: Scandinavian University Press.

Chechnia: Report of an International Alert fact-finding mission, September 24–October 3, 1992. London: International Alert.

Chelekhsaty, Kazbek, ed. 1994. *Ossetia i Ossetiny* [Ossetia and Ossetians]. Vladikavkaz: Ir.

Chervonnaya, Svetlana, 1994. *Conflict in the Caucasus. Georgia, Abkhazia and the Russian Shadow*. London: Gothic Image Publications.

Cheshko, Sergey. V., 1993. *Ideologiya raspada* [The Ideology of the Breakup]. Moscow: IEA.

Chesnov, Yan V., 1994a. 'Chechentsem bit' trudno. Taipy, ikh proshloe i rol' v nastoy-achem' [It is Hard to Be a Chechen. Taips, Their Role in the Past and Present], *Nezavisimaya gazeta*, 22 September, p. 5.

Chesnov, Yan, 1994b. Kto oni, chechentsy? [Who are they, the Chechens?], *Abkhazia*, no. 2(80), p. 23.

Chichlo, Boris, 1990. 'L' anthropologie soviétique à l'heure de la perestroi'ka', *Cahier du Monde Russe et Soviétique*, vol. 31, pp. 223–237.

Chizhikova, Ludmila N., 1988. *Russko-Ukrainskoe pogranichie* [The Russian-Ukrainian Borderland]. Moscow: Nauka.

Chochiev, Alan, 1994. *Uroki igry na boine* [Lessons from the Butcher's Game]. Vladikavkaz: No publisher.

Chugaev, Dmitrii, ed., 1968–1970. *Istoria Natsionalno-gosudarstvennogo stroitel'stva v SSSR* [History of National State Building in the USSR]. 2 vols. Moscow: Mysl.

Coakley, John, 1992. 'The Resolution of Ethnic Conflict: Towards a Typology', *International Political Science Review*, vol. 13, no. 4, pp. 343–358.

Comaroff, John, 1991. 'Humanity, Ethnicity, Nationality: Conceptual and Comparative Perspectives on the USSR', *Theory and Society*, vol. 20, no. 5, October, pp. 661–687.

Connor, Walker, 1972. 'Nation-Building or Nation-Destroying?', *World Politics*, vol. 24, no. 3, pp. 319–355.

Connor, Walker, 1978. 'A Nation is a Nation, is a State, is an Ethnic Group, is . . .', *Ethnic and Racial Studies*, vol. 1, no. 4, October, pp. 377–400.

Connor, Walker, 1984. *The National Question in Marxist-Leninist Theory and Strategy.* Princeton, NJ: Princeton University Press.

Connor, Walker, 1994. *Ethnonationalism. The Quest for Understanding.* Princeton, NJ: Princeton University Press.

Conquest, Robert, 1960. *The Nation Killers: The Soviet Deportations of Nationalities.* London: Macmillan.

Conquest, Robert, 1986. *The Harvest of Sorrow. Soviet Collectivization and the Terror of Famine.* London: Hutchinson.

Critchlov, James, 1991. *Punished Peoples of the Soviet Union: The Continuing Legacy of Stalin's Deportations.* New York: Helsinki Watch.

Critchlov, James, 1992. *Nationalism in Uzbekistan: A Soviet Republic's Road to Sovereignty.* Boulder, CO: Westview Press.

Dahshleiger, Grigorii, 1965. *Social'no-ekonomicheskie preobrazovaniia v aule i derevne Kazakhstana, 1921–1929* [Socio-Economic Transformation in Auls and Villages of Kazakhstan, 1921–1929]. Alma-Ata: No publisher.

Dambinova, Valentina D. & Alexander D. Korostelev, 1993. 'Etnoyazikovie protsessy u kalmykov' [Ethnolinguistic Processes among the Kalmyks], pp. 84–117 in Guzenkova, 1993.

Davies, James, 1973. 'Aggression, Violence, and War', pp. 234–260 in J.N. Knudson, ed., *Handbook of Political Psychology.* San Francisco, CA, and London: Jossey-Bass.

Dekrety Sovetskoi vlasti [The Decrees of the Soviet Power], 1957. Vol.1, Moscow: Politizdat.

Dementieva, Irina A., 1993. 'Voina i mir v Prigorodnom raione' [War and Peace in the Prigorodny *raion*], *Izvestia*, nos 14–18, 25– 29 January.

Demograficheskii ezhegodnik SSSR, 1990 [USSR Demographic Annual, 1990], Moscow: Finansy i Statistika.

Deportatsii narodov SSSR, 1930–1950 [Deportations of the Peoples of the USSR, 1930–1950]. Part 1. Moscow: IEA, 1992.

Diamond, Larry & Marc F. Plattner, eds, 1994. *Nationalism, Ethnic Conflict, and Democracy.* Baltimore, MD, and London: Johns Hopkins University Press.

Dobrovich, E., 1991. 'Paranoia as a Social Medium', *Twenty Two*, no. 74, pp. 15–27 (Jerusalem).

Dolgikh, Boris O., 1960. *Rodovoi i plemennoi sostav narodov Sibiri v XVII veke* [Clan and Tribal Structure of the Peoples of Siberia in the 17th Century]. Moscow: Izdatel'stvo AN SSSR.

Dollard, John; L.W. Doob, N.E. Miller, O.H. Mowrer & R.R. Sears, 1939. *Frustration and Aggression.* New Haven, CT, and London: Yale University Press.

Dragadze, Tamara, 1988. *Rural Families in Soviet Georgia: A Case Study in Ratcha Province.* London & New York: Routledge.

Dragadze, Tamara, 1995. 'Report on Chechnya', *Central Asian Survey,* vol. 4, no. 3, pp. 463–471.

Drobizheva, Leokadia M., 1981. *Dukhovnaya obchnost narodov SSSR* [The Spiritual Commonality of the Peoples of the USSR]. Moscow: Nauka.

Drobizheva, Leokadia M., 1993. 'Russkiye v novykh gosudarstvakh: izmenenie sotsial'nykh roleii [Russians in New States: Changing Social Roles], pp. 203–227 in Lidia Shevtsova & Vladimir Kiselev, eds, *Rossia segodnya: Trudnyi poisk svobody* [Russia Today: Hard Search for Freedom]. Moscow: IMEPI.

Drobizheva, L. M.; A. R. Aklayev; V. V. Koroteeva & G. U. Soldatova, 1996. *Demokratizatsia i abrazy Nationalisma v Rossiiskoi Federatsii 90-Kh godov* [Democratization and Profiles of Nationalism in the Russian Federation of 1990s]. Moscow: MYSL.

Drobizheva, Leokadia M., ed., 1994a. *Natsional'noe samosoznanie i natsionalizm v Rossiiskoi Federatsii nachala 1990-h godov* [National Self-Awareness and Nationalism in the Russian Federation in the Early 1990s]. Moscow: IEA.

Drobizheva, Leokadia M., ed., 1994b. *Konfliktnaya etnichnost' i etnicheskie konflikty* [Conflicting Ethnicity and Ethnic Conflicts]. Moscow: IEA.

Dudayev, Dzhokhar, 1995. 'Vernite k rukovodstvu Gorbacheva' [Return Gorbachev to Power]. *Moskovskie novosti,* No. 80, 19-26 November 1995.

Dunlop, John, 1985. *The New Russian Nationalism.* New York: Praeger.

Dunlop, John, 1993. *The Faces of Contemporary Russian Nationalism.* Princeton, NJ: Princeton University Press.

EAWARN, 1995. *Bulletin of Network of Ethnological Monitoring and Early Warning (EAWARN)* February, June, 1995. Cambridge, MA: Conflict Management Group.

Eide, Asbjørn, 1993. *In Search of Constructive Alternatives to Secession.* Prepared for the United Nations Sub-Commission on Prevention of Discrimination and Protection of Minorities.

Elazar, Daniel J, ed., 1991. *Constitutional Design and Power-Sharing in the Post-Modern Epoch.* Lanham, MD: University Press of America.

Elebaeva, Inura; A. Dzhusurbekov & Nurbek Omuraliev, 1991. *Oshski mezhnatsional'ni konflikt: sotsiologicheskii analiz* [The Osh Inter-Ethnic Conflict: Sociological Analysis]. Bishkek: AN Kirgizii.

Eller, Jack David & Reed M. Coughlan, 1993. 'The Poverty of Primordialism: the Demystification of Ethnic Attachments', *Ethnic and Racial Studies,* vol. 16, no. 2, April, pp. 183–202.

Eriksen, Thomas Hylland, 1993. *Ethnicity and Nationalism. Anthropological Perspectives.* London & Boulder, CO: Pluto Press.

Erunov, Igor & Valery Solovei, eds, 1991. *Russkoe delo segodnya* [The Russian Cause Today] Vol. 1. Moscow: IEA.

Eurasiiskii soiuz: Novye rubezhy, problemy i perspektivy. Materialy nauchnoi sessii 18 yanvarya 1996 goda [Eurasian Union: New Frontiers, Problems and Perspectives]. Proceedings of Scientific Session, 18 January 1996]. Moscow: ISPI RAS.

Feshbach, Murray, 1995. *Ecological Disaster: Cleaning Up the Hidden Legacy of the Soviet Union.* New York: Twentieth Century Fund Press.

Feshbach, Murray & Alfred Friendly, Jr, 1992. *Ecocide in the USSR: Health and Nature Under Siege.* New York: Basic Books.

Fierman, William, ed., 1991. *Soviet Central Asia: The Failed Transformation.* Boulder, CO: Westview Press.

Fierman, William, 1995. 'Independence and the Declining Priority of Language Law Implementation in Uzbekistan', pp. 205–230 in Ro'i, 1995.

Filippov, Alexander F., 1992. 'Nabliudatel' imperii' [Observer of an Empire], *Voprosy sotsiologii*, vol. 1, no. 1, pp. 89–120.

Foucault, Michel, 1980. *Power and Knowledge: Selected Interviews and Other Writings, 1972–1977*. New York: Pantheon Books.

Foucault, Michel, 1993. 'Space, Power and Knowledge', pp. 161–169 in Simon During, ed., *The Cultural Studies Reader*. London & New York: Routledge.

Galtung, Johan, 1969. 'Violence, Peace and Peace Research', *Journal of Peace Research*, vol. 6, no. 3, pp. 167–191.

Galtung, Johan, 1996. *Peace by Peaceful Means: Peace and Conflict, Development and Civilization.* London: Sage.

Gammer, Moshe, 1991. 'Shamil and the Murid Movement, 1830–1859: An Attempt at a Comprehensive Bibliography', *Central Asia Survey*, vol. 10, no. 1–2, pp. 189–247.

Garthoff, Raymond, 1994. *The Great Transition. American-Soviet Relations and the End of the Cold War*. Washington, DC: The Brookings Institution.

Geertz, Clifford, 1973. *The Interpretation of Cultures.* New York: Basic Books.

Gellner, Ernest, 1983. *Nations and Nationalism*. Oxford: Oxford University Press.

Gellner, Ernest, 1988. *State and Society in Soviet Thought*. Oxford: Basil Blackwell.

Gellner, Ernest, ed., 1980. *Soviet and Western Anthropology*. New York: Columbia University Press.

Gerasimova, Marina M., 1994. 'Paleoantropologiya Severnoi Ossetii v svyazi s problemoi proiskhozhdeniia Osetin' [Paleoanthropology of North Ossetia in Connection with the Problem of the Origin of the Ossets], *Etnograficheskoe obozrenie*, no. 3, May–June, pp. 51–68.

Ginzburg, Alla I., ed., 1995. *Russkie v novom zarubezhie: Kirgiziia* [Russians in the New Abroad: Kirgizia]. Moscow: IEA.

Gleason, Gregory, 1990. *Federalism and Nationalism: The Struggle for Republican Rights in the USSR.* Boulder, CO: Westview Press.

Gleason, Gregory,1992. 'The Federal Formula and the Collapse of the USSR', *Publius*, vol. 22, no. 3, Summer, pp.141–163.

Glebov, Oleg & John Crowfoot, eds, 1989. *The Soviet Empire: Its Nations Speak Out*. Chur, Switzerland, London, etc: Harvard Academic Publishers.

Goble, Paul, 1989. 'Ethnic Politics in the USSR', *Problems of Communism*, vol. 38, no. 4, July–August, pp. 4–14.

Goldenberg, Suzanne, 1994. *Pride of Small Nations: the Caucasus and Post-Soviet Disorder*. London: Zed Books.

Gottlieb, Gideon, 1993. *Nations against State. A New Approach to Ethnic Conflicts and the Decline of Sovereignty*. New York: Council on Foreign Relations Press.

Greenfeld, Liah, 1992. *Nationalism. Five Roads to Modernity*. Cambridge, MA: Harvard University Press.

Greenfeld, Liah, 1994. *Ethnically Based Conflicts: Their History and Dynamics.* Paper presented to International Seminar on Ethnic Diversity and Public Policies, New York, 17 August.

Guboglo, Mikhail N., 1984. *Etno-yazykovye processy v SSSR: Faktory razvitiia natsional'no-russkogo dvuyazychiia* [Ethno-Linguistic Processes in the USSR: Factors for Development of National-Russian Bilingualism]. Moscow: Nauka.

Guboglo, Mikhail N., 1992a. *Razvitiye etnodemograficheskoi situatsii v stolitsakh avtonomnykh respublik v 1959–1989* [Evolution of the Ethnodemographic Situation in the Capitals of Autonomous Republics in 1959–1989. Studies in Applied and Urgent Ethnology]. Doc. 33. Moscow: IEA.

Guboglo, Mikhail N., 1992b. *Izmenenie etnodemograficheskoi situatsii v stolitsakh soiuznykh respublik v 1959–1989* [Changes of Ethnodemographic Situation in the Capitals of Union Republics in 1959–1989. Studies in Applied and Urgent Ethnology]. Doc. 32, Moscow: IEA.

Guboglo, Mikhail N., 1993. *Mobilizovannii lingvicizm* [Mobilized Linguicism]. Moscow: IEA.

Guboglo, Mikhail N., ed., 1994a. *Yazyk i natsionalizm v postsovetskih respublikah* [Language and Nationalism in Post-Soviet Republics]. Moscow: IEA.

Guboglo, Mikhail N., ed., 1994b. *Bashkortostan. Shtrikhi k etnopoliticheskomu portretu. Yazyk i natsionalizm v postsovetskih respublikah* [The Ethnopolitical Profile of Bashkortostan. Language and Nationalism in Post-Soviet Republics]. Moscow: IEA.

Guboglo, Mikhail N., 1995. *'Etnopoliticheskaya situatsia v Kazakhstane'* [The Ethnopolitical Situation in Kazakhstan], pp. 235–293 in E. M. Kozhokin, ed., *Kazakhstan: realii i perspektivy nezavisimogo razvitiia* [Kazakhstan: Realities and Perspectives for Independent Development]. Moscow: Russian Institute of Strategic Studies.

Guchinova, Elza M. & Svetlana D. Tavanez, 1994. *Ethnopoliticheskaya situatsia v Kalmykii* [Ethnopolitical Situation in Kalmykia. Studies in Applied and Urgent Ethnology]. Doc. 65. Moscow: IEA.

Guenther, Hans, ed., 1990. *The Culture of the Stalin Period.* New York: St Martin's Press.

Gumilev, Lev N., 1989. *Etnogenez i biosfera Zemli* [Ethnogenesis and Biosphere of the Earth]. Leningrad: Leningrad State University Publishing House.

Gumilev, Lev N., 1990. *Geografia etnosa v istoricheskii period* [Geography of Ethnos in a Historical Period]. Leningrad: Nauka.

Gurr, Ted Robert, 1993. *Minorities at Risk. A Global View of Ethnopolitical Conflicts.* Washington, DC: United States Institute of Peace Press.

Gurr, Ted Robert & Barbara Harff, 1994. *Ethnic Conflict in World Politics.* Boulder, CO: Westview Press.

Guzenkova, Tamara S., ed., 1993. *Kalmyki. Pereputie 1980h. Problemy etnokul'turnogo razvitiia* [Kalmykia at the Crossroads of 1980s. Problems of Ethnocultural Development]. Moscow: IEA.

Haaland, Gunnar, 1969. 'Economic Determinants in Ethnic Processes', pp. 58–74 in Fredrik Barth, ed., *Ethnic Cultural Differences.* Boston, MA: Little, Brown.

Handelman, Don, 1977. 'The Organization of Ethnicity', *Ethnic Groups,* vol. 1, pp. 187–200.

Handler, Richard, 1988. *Nationalism and the Politics of Culture in Quebec.* Madison, WI: University of Wisconsin Press.

Hann, Chris M., ed., 1993. *Socialism: Ideals, Ideologies, and Local Practice.* London: Routledge.

Hannum, Hurst, 1993. 'Rethinking Self-Determination', *Virginia Journal of International Law*, vol. 34, no. 1, Fall, pp. 1–69.

Hannum, Hurst, 1996. 'The Right to Autonomy: Chimera or Solution?', pp. 287–295 in Rupesinghe & Tishkov, 1996.

Heiberg, Marianne, 1989. *The Making of the Basque Nation.* Cambridge, MA: Cambridge University Press.

Henze, Paul B.,1958. 'The Shamil Problem', pp. 415–433 in Walter Z. Laqueur, ed., *The Middle East in Transition.* London: Routledge & Kegan Paul.

Hill, Fiona, 1995. *'Russia's Tinderbox'. Conflict in the North Caucasus and its Implications for the Future of the Russian Federation.* Report of the Strengthening Democratic Institutions Project, Harvard University, Boston, MA.

Hint, M., 1988. 'Dvuyazichye i internatsionalism' [Bilingualism and Internationalism], *Druzhba Narodov*, no. 5, September–October, pp. 94–112.

Hirschman, Albert O., 1970. *Exit, Voice and Loyalty*. Cambridge, MA: Harvard University Press.

Hobsbawm, Eric J., 1990. *Nations and Nationalism since 1780. Programme, Myth, Reality.* Cambridge, MA: Cambridge University Press.

Hobsbawm, Eric J., 1994. 'Ethnicity and Nationalism in Europe Today', *Anthropology Today*, vol. 8, no. 1, February, pp. 3–14.

Hollinger, David A., 1993. 'How Wide the Circle of the "We"? American Intellectuals and the Problem of the Ethnos since World War II', *The American Historical Review*, vol. 98, no. 2, April, pp. 317–337.

Horowitz, Donald L., 1985. *Ethnic Groups in Conflict*. Berkeley, CA: University of California Press.

Horowitz, Donald L., 1991. *A Democratic South Africa? Constitutional Engineering in a Divided Society*. Berkeley, CA: University of California Press.

Hough, Jerry, 1969. *The Soviet Prefects: The Local Party Organs in Industrial Decision-making.* Cambridge, MA: Harvard University Press.

Hroch, Miroslav, 1985. *Social Preconditions of National Revival in Europe.* Cambridge, MA: Cambridge University Press.

Humphrey, Caroline, 1983. *Karl Marx Collective: Economic Society and Religion in a Siberian Collective Farm*. Cambridge, MA: Cambridge University Press.

Hunter, Shireen T., 1994. *The Transcaucasus in Transition. Nation-Building and Conflict.* Washington, DC: Center for Strategic and International Studies.

Huntington, Samuel, 1993. 'The Clash of Civilizations', *Foreign Affairs*, vol. 72, no. 3, Summer, pp. 22–49.

Ingushkaya tragediia [The Ingush Tragedy], 1993. Moscow: No publisher.

Iskandaryan, Alexander, 1995. *Chechenski krizis: Proval rossiiskoi politiki na Kavkaze* [The Chechen Crisis: a Failure of Russian Policy in the Caucasus]. Moscow: Moscow Carnegie Center.

Ivanov, Vilen N. & Vladimir G. Smolaynsky, 1994. *Konflikty i konfliktologia* [Conflict and Conflictology]. Moscow: Nauka.

Janis, Irvin, 1972. *Victims of Groupthink: A Psychological Study of Foreign-Policy Decisions and Fiascoes*. Boston, MA: Houghton Mifflin.

Kaapcke, Gretchen, 1994. 'Indigenous Identity Transition in Russia', *Cultural Survival Quarterly*, vol. 18, no. 2–3, Summer/Fall, pp. 62–68.

Kadyrov, Sharif, 1992. 'Dictatorship and Violations of Human Rights in Turkmenistan', paper presented at the international conference, 'Russia and the East: Problems of Interactions', Moscow, December.

Kaiser, Robert J., 1994. *The Geography of Nationalism in Russia and the USSR.* Princeton, N.J.: Princeton University Press.

Kalinovskaya, Klara P. & Gennadi E.Markov, 1990. *Natsional'naya i mezhetnicheskaya situatsiia v oblasti rasseleniia Nogaitsev* [National and Inter-Ethnic Situation in the Area of Nogai Settlement. Studies in Applied and Urgent Ethnology]. No. 3. Moscow: IEA.

Kaloev, Boris A. 1989. 'Osetino-Vaynakhskie etnokul'turnie svyazi' [Ossets-Vaynakhs Ethno-cultural Contacts], pp.137–158, in *Kavkazskii etnograficheskii sbornik*, vol. 9. Moscow: Nauka.

Karklins, Rasma, 1986. *Ethnic Relations in the USSR. The Perspective from Below.* Boston, MA: Allen & Unwin.

Karpov, Yuri Yu, 1990. *'K probleme Ingushskoi avtonomii'* [On the Problem of Ingush Autonomy], *Sovetskaya etnografiia*, no. 5, pp. 29–33.

Kashkachakov, A.P., 1992. 'Shoriyu – Shortsam!' [Shoria is for the Shorts!], *Zemlya Sibirskaya, Dal'nevostochnaya*, no. 11–12, November–December, pp. 3–12.

Khakimov, Raphael, 1993. *Sumerki Imperii. K voprosu o natsii i gosudarstve* [The Twilight of Empire. About a Nation and a State]. Kazan: Tatar Publishing House.

Khakimov, Raphael, 1996. 'Prospects of Federalism in Russia: A View from Tatarstan', *Security Dialogue*, vol. 27, no. 1, pp. 69–80.

Khalim, Aidar, 1993. 'Sovremennie smeshannie braki, ili kol'tso bezotvetstvennosti' [Contemporary Mixed Marriages, or a Ring of Irresponsibility], *Argamak,* no. 2, pp. 3–16.

Khamitsev, Valery & Alexander Ch. Balayev, 1992. *David Soslan, Fridrikh Barbarossa . . . Alania ot Palestiny do Britanii* [David Soslan, Frederick Barbarossa . . . Alania from Palestine to Britannia]. Vladikavkaz: Arian.

Khasbulatov, Ruslan, 1995. *Chechnya: Mne ne dali ostanovit' voinu* [Chechnya: I Was Not Allowed to Stop a War]. Moscow: Palea.

Khazanov, Anatoly M. 1990. 'The Ethnic Situation in the Soviet Union as Reflected in Soviet Anthropology', *Regards sur l'anthropologie soviétique*, pp. 213–222. Paris: EHRSS.

Kirch, Marika & Aksel Kirch, 1995. 'Search for Security in Estonia: New Identity Architecture', *Security Dialogue*, vol. 26, no. 4, December, pp. 439–448.

Kolstoe, Paul, 1995. *Russians in the Former Soviet Republics.* London: Hurst.

Kon, Igor, 1993. 'Nesvoevremennye razmyshleniia na aktual'nye temy' [Untimely Thoughts on Important Topics], pp. 3–8, *Etnograficheskoe obozrenie*, no. 1.

Kordonsky, Sergei G., 1995. 'Rossiiskaya intelligentsiia. Genezis, ontologiia, etika i estetika' [Russia's Intellectuals: Genesis, Ontology, Ethics and Esthetics]. pp. 496–508 in Tatyana J. Zaslavskaya, ed., *Where Russia Goes? Alternatives of Societal Development.* Moscow: Aspekt Press.

Kozlov, Viktor, 1988. *The Peoples of the Soviet Union.* London: Hutchinson/ Bloomington, IN: Indiana University Press.

Kozlov, Viktor I., 1990. 'Puti okoloetnicheskoi passionarnosti (o kontsepzii etnosa i etnogeneza, predlozhennoi L.N. Gumilevim)' [On Para-Ethnic Passionarism. On the Concept of Ethnos and Ethnogenesis suggested by L.N. Gumilev], *Sovetskaya etnografiia*, no. 4, July–August, pp. 94–110.

Kozlov, Viktor I., 1995. *Russkii' vopros. Istoriia tragedii velikogo naroda* [The Russian Question. A History of the Tragedy of a Great People]. No publishing data.

Kremenyuk, Victor A., 1994. *Conflicts In and Around Russia: Nation-building in Difficult Times.* Westport, CT: Greenwood Press.

Kriminal'nyi rezhim. Chechnya, 1991–1995. Fakty, dokumenty, svidetel'stva [A Criminal Regime. Chechnya, 1991–1995. Facts, Documents, Testimonies], 1995. Moscow: Ministry of Internal Affairs.

Krupnik, Igor I., 1990. 'Natsional'nyi vopros v SSSR: poiski ob'iasnenii' [The National Question in the USSR: A Search for Explanations], *Sovetskaya etnografiia*, no. 4, July–August, pp. 3–15.

Kryukov, Mikhail V., 1989. 'Etnicheskie Protsessy v SSSR i nekotorye aspekty vsesoiuznikh perepisei naseleniia' [Ethnic Processes in the USSR and Some Aspects of the All-Union Censuses of Population], *Sovetskaya etnografiia*, no. 2, March–April, pp. 24–35.

Kuanyshev, Zh. N., 1991. 'Natsional'naya politika i politicheskaya zhizn' Kazakhstana v seredine 50–80e: novie podkhody' [Nationality Policy and Political Life in Kazakhstan from the 1950s to the 1980s. New Approaches], pp. 39–41 in Asankanov & Drobizheva, 1991.

Kul'chik, Yuri & Sergei Rumyantsev, 1991. *O razvitii obchestvenno-politicheskoi situatsii v SSR Moldova.* [On the Evolution of the Political and Public Situation in Moldova SSR. Studies in Applied and Urgent Ethnology]. No. 14. Moscow: IEA.

Kulumbegov, Tores, 1991. 'Vina lish v tom chto rodilis' osetinami' [The Guilt of Being Born an Osset], *Literaturnaya Rossia*, 20 March, pp. 3–4.

Kuznetzov, Vladimir A., 1984. *Ocherki istorii Alan* [Essays on the History of the Alans]. Ordzhonikidze: Ir.

Laitin, David, 1991. 'The National Uprisings in the Soviet Union', *World Politics*, vol. 44, no. 1, October, pp. 139–178.

Laitin, David; Roger Petersen & John Slocum, 1992. 'Language and the State: Russia and the Soviet Union in Comparative Perspective', pp. 129–168 in Motyl, 1992.

Lane, David, 1996. 'The Gorbachev Revolution: the Role of the Political Elite in Regime Disintegration', *Political Studies*, vol. XLIV, no. 4, pp. 4–23.

Lapidus, Gail, 1984. 'Ethnonationalism and Political Stability: The Soviet Case', *World Politics*, vol. 36, no. 4, July, pp. 555–580.

Lapidus, Gail, 1989. 'Gorbachev's Nationality Problem', *Foreign Affairs*, vol. 68, no. 4, Fall, pp. 92–108.

Lapidus, Gail, ed., 1995. T*he New Russia: Troubled Transformations.* Boulder, CO: Westview Press.

Lapidus, Gail & Victor Zaslavsky, eds, 1992. *From Union to Commonwealth. Nationalism and Separatism in the Soviet Republics.* Cambridge: Cambridge University Press.

Larsen, Knud S., ed., 1993. *Conflict and Social Psychology.* London: Sage Publications.

Lazarev, Alexander V., 1995. *Donskie kazaki v grazhdanskoi voine 1917–1920. Istoriographiya problemy* [The Don Cossacks in the Civil War: Historiography of the Problem]. Moscow: IEA.

Lebedeva, Nadezhda M., 1996. *Novaya russkaya diaspora* [The New Russian Diaspora]. Moscow: IEA.

Lenin, V.I., 1962. *Polnoie sobranie sochineni* [The Complete Works]. Vols 34, 35. Moscow: Politizdat.

Levin, Maksim G. & Leonid P. Potapov, eds, 1956. *Narody Sibiri* [The Peoples of Siberia]. Moscow: AN SSSR.

Levin, Maksim G. & Leonid P. Potapov, eds. 1961. *Istoriko-etnograficheskii atlas Sibiri* [Historical-Ethnographic Atlas of Siberia]. Moscow-Leningrad: AN SSSR.

Lieber, George, 1992. *Soviet Nationality Policy, Urban Growth, and Identity Change in the Ukrainian SSR, 1923–1934.* Cambridge, MA: Cambridge University Press.

Lijphart, Arend, 1977. *Democracy in Plural Societies.* New Haven, CT: Yale University Press.

Lind, Michael, 1994. 'In Defence of Liberal Nationalism', *Foreign Affairs*, vol. 73, no. 3, May/June, pp. 87–99.

Lordkipanidze, Mariam, 1990. *Abkhazians and Abkhazia.* Tbilisi: Ganatleba.

Lubin, Nancy, 1984. *Labor and Nationality in Soviet Central Asia.* Princeton, NJ: Princeton University Press.

Lustick, Ian, 1993. *Unsettled States, Disputed Lands: Britain and Ireland, France and Algeria, Israel and the West Bank-Gaza.* Ithaca, NY, and London: Cornell University Press.

Lysenko, Vladimir N., 1995. *Ot Tatarstana do Chechni (Stanovlenie novogo rossiiskogo federalisma* [From Tatarstan to Chechnya. The Emergence of New Federalism]. Moscow: Institute of Contemporary Politics.

Maksakova, Lubov, 1986. *Migratsii naseleniia Uzbekistana* [Migration of Population in Uzbekistan]. Tashkent: Uzbekiston.

Maksimov, Pavel, 1991. 'Ekologia i mezhnatsional'nye dvizhenia' [Ecology and Inter-Ethnic Movements], pp. 92–93 in Asankanov & Drobizheva, 1991.

Maresca, John J., 1995. *The End of the Cold War is Also Over.* Working Paper of Center for International Security and Arms Control, Stanford University, California, April.

Markov, Gennadi E. & Vladimir V. Pimenov, eds, 1994. *Etnologia* [Ethnology]. Moscow: Nauka.

Martirosyan, Georgii K., 1933. *Istoriia Ingushii* [History of Ingushetia]. Ordzhonikidze:Ir.

Masov, Rakhim M., 1991. Istoriia topornogo razdeleniia [History of Dividing with an Axe]. Dushanbe: Irfon.

Materialy 27 s'ezda KPSS [Documents of the 27th Congress of the CPSU], 1986. Moscow: Politizdat.

McAuley, Alastair, ed., 1991. *Soviet Federalism, Nationalism and Economic Decentralization.* Leicester: University of Leicester Press.

Migranyan, Andranik, 1995. '1995: God velikogo pereloma ili okonchatel'nogo krakha rossiiskoi gosudarstvennosti?' [1995: A Year of Great Transition or of the Final Crash of the Russian State?], *Nezavisimaya gazeta,* 17 January.

Montville, Joseph V., ed., 1990. *Conflict and Peacemaking in Multiethnic Societies.* Toronto: Lexington Books.

Motyl, Alexander J., 1987. *Will the Non-Russians Rebel? State, Ethnicity and Stability in the USSR.* Ithaca, NY: Cornell University Press.

Motyl, Alexander J., 1990. *Sovietology, Rationality, Nationality: Coming to Grips with Nationalism in the USSR.* New York: Columbia University Press.

Motyl, Alexander J., ed., 1992. *Thinking Theoretically About Soviet Nationalities. History and Comparison in the Study of the USSR.* New York: Columbia University Press.

Murashko, Olga, 1991. 'Prava korennykh narodov ili perspektivy etnicheskikh konfliktov v Sibiri'. [The Rights of Indigenous Peoples or Perspectives for Ethnic Conflicts in Siberia], in *Nezavisimaya gazeta,* 28 December, p. 5.

Mutaliev, Tamerlan X., X. A. Fargiev and A.A Pliev, 1992. *Ternistyi put' naroda* [Hard Road for the People]. Moscow: Znanie.

Nahaylo, Bohdan & Victor Swoboda. 1990. *Soviet Disunion. A History of the Nationalities Problems in the USSR.* New York: Free Press.

Narodnyi Kongress, 1989. [The People's Congress. Documents of the First Congress of the People's Front of Estonia, 1–2 October 1988]. Tallinn: Periodika.

Narody mira. Etnograficheskie ocherki [The Peoples of the World. Ethnographic Essays], 1954–1966. General Editor, Sergei P. Tolstov. 18 vols. Moscow: AN SSSR Press.

Narzikulov, R.N., 1991, 'Respubliki Srednei Azii za 70 let' [70 Years of the Republics of Central Asia], *Vostok,* no. 5.

Nash, Manning, 1989. *The Cauldron of Ethnicity in the Modern World.* Chicago, IL: University of Chicago Press.

Natsional'naya doktrina Rossii (problemy i prioritety), 1994. [The National Doctrine of Russia (Problems and Priorities)]. Moscow: RAU Corporation.

Natsional'ny sostav naseleniia SSSR po dannym Vsesoiuznoi perepisi naseleniia 1989 goda [Ethnic Composition of the USSR's Population according to the All-Union Census of 1989], 1991. Moscow: Finansy i Statistika.

Nazarov, Alexander D. & Sergei I. Nikolaev, 1995. 'Russkie v Kirgizii: Est' li al'ternativa iskhodu?' [Russians in Kirgizia: Is There an Alternative to Exodus?], pp. 15–36 in Ginzburg, 1995.

Nekrich, Aleksander M., 1978. *The Punished Peoples: The Deportation and Tragic Fate of Soviet Minorities at the End of the Second World War.* New York: W.W. Norton.

Nenarokov, Albert P., 1991. *K'edinstvu ravnikh: Kul'turnie faktory ob'edinitel'nogo dvizheniia sovetskikh narodov, 1917–1924* [Toward the Unity of the Equals: Cultural Factors of Integration Movement of the Soviet Peoples, 1917–1924]. Moscow: Nauka.

Nenarokov, Albert P., 1995. 'Regionalizm – federalizm – separatizm. Istoricheskii opyt Rossii' [Regionalism, Federalism, Separatism: Russia's Historical Experience], pp. 132–143 in Gennadi Bordugov & Paul Goble, eds, *Mezhnatsional'nye otnoshenniia v Rossii i SNG* [Inter-Ethnic Relations in Russia and the CIS. Seminar of the Carnegie Moscow Center]. Vol. 2 [Papers for 1994–1995]. Moscow: AIRO-XX.

Neroznak, Vladimir, ed., 1994. *Krasnaya kniga yazykov narodov Rossii. Enciklopedicheskii slovar'-spravochnik* [The Red Book of Languages of the Peoples of Russia. Encyclopedic Guide]. Moscow: Academia.

Novoseltsev, Anatoly P., ed., 1987. *Istoriia Severo-Osetinskoi ASSR s drevneishikh vremen do nashikh dnei* [History of the North Ossetian ASSR from Ancient Times to Our Days]. 2 vols. Ordzhonikidze: Ir.

Ochirova, Tatyana N., 1990. 'Polemicheskie zametki' [Polemic Notes], *Slovo*, no. 2, February, pp. 17–21.

Olcott, Martha Brill, 1987. *The Kazakhs*. Stanford, CA: Hoover Institution Press.

Olcott, Martha Brill, 1995a. 'Islam and Fundamentalism in Independent Central Asia', pp. 21–35 in Ro'i, 1995.

Olcott, Martha Brill, 1995b. 'Soviet Nationality Studies between Past and Future', pp. 135–148 in Orlovsky, 1995.

Omuraliev, Nurbek A. & Inura B. Elebaeva, 1993. *Sovremennoe sostoiyane mezhnatsional'nikh otnoshenii v Kyrgyzstane* [The Contemporary Status of Inter-Ethnic Relations in Kyrgyzstan]. Bishkek: Institute of Philosophy.

Opler, Marvin K., 1964. 'Socio-Cultural Roots of Emotional Illness', *Psychosomatics*, January–February, pp. 55–58.

Orlov, Oleg P., ed., 1994. *Cherez dva goda posle voiny. Problema vynuzhdennih pereselentsev v zone osetino–ingushskogo konflikta* [Two Years After the War: Problems of Forced Resettlers in the Area of the Ingush-Ossetian Conflict]. Moscow: Memorial.

Orlovsky, Daniel ed., 1995. *Beyond Soviet Studies*. Washington, DC: Woodrow Wilson Center Press.

Osipov, Gennadi V., ed., 1994. *Reformirovanie Rossii: mify i real'nost' (1989-1994)* [The Reforming of Russia: Myths and Realities, 1989-1994]. Moscow: Academia.

Pain, Emil, 1996. 'Settlement of Ethnic Conflicts in Post-Soviet Society', pp. 69-82 in Rupesinghe & Tishkov, 1996.

Pain, Emil & Arkadii Popov, 1990. 'Mezhnatsional'nye konflikty v SSSR [nekotorye podkhody k izucheniyu i prakticheskomu resheniyu] [Inter-Ethnic Conflicts in the USSR: Some Approaches to their Study and Practical Resolution], *Sovetskaya etnografiia*, no. 1, January–February, pp. 3–15.

Pain, Emil & Arkadii Popov, 1995. 'Chechenskaya tragediia' [The Chechen Tragedy], *Izvestia*, nos 23–26; 7, 8, 9, 10, February.

Patkanov, Semen K., 1923. *Spisok narodnostei Sibiri* [A List of the Peoples of Siberia]. Moscow: Academia.

Perepelkin, Lev S., 1994. 'Chechenskaya respublika: sovremennaya social'no-politicheskaya situatsiia' [The Chechen Republic: Contemporary Socio-Political Situation], *Etnograficheskoe obozrenie*, no. 1, January–February, pp. 3–15.

Perepelkin, Lev S. & Ovsei I. Shkaratan, 1989.'Ekonomicheskii suverenitet respublik i puti razvitiia narodov' [Economic Sovereignty of Republics and Ways for Development of the Peoples], *Sovetskaya etnografiia*, no. 4, pp. 32–48.

Perevedentsev, Viktor I., 1993. 'Raspad SSSR i problemy repatriatsii v Rossiiu' [The Breakup of the USSR and the Problems of Repatriation in Russia], pp. 142-159 in Sergei G. Zdravomyslov, ed., *Bezhentsy* [The Refugees]. Moscow: Russian Institute of Social and National Problems.

Petrov, Nikolai V. et al., 1995. Chechenski konflikt v etno- i politiko-geograficheskom izmerenii [The Chechen Conflict in Ethno- and Politico-Geographical Dimensions]. Second Edition, revised and expanded. *Politicheskii Landshaft Rossii* [Political Landscape of Russia]. *Bulletin*, January.

Pfaff, William ,1993. *The Wrath of Nations. Civilization and the Furies of Nationalism.* New York: Simon and Schuster.

Pincus, Fred & Howard Ehrlich, eds, 1994. *Race and Ethnic Conflict. Contending Views on Prejudice, Discrimination and Ethnoviolence.* Boulder, CO: Westview Press.

Pipes, Richard, 1954. *The Formation of the Soviet Union: Communism and Nationalism, 1917–1923.* Cambridge, MA: Harvard University Press.

Plotkin, Vladimir, 1990. 'Dual Models: Totalizing Ideology and Soviet Ethnography', *Regards sur l'ethnographie soviétique*, vol. 31, pp. 2–8.

Polovetskaya Luna [The Polovets' Moon], 1991. Cherkessk. No publisher.

Polyakov, Sergei P., 1992. *Everyday Islam: Religion and Tradition in Rural Central Asia.* Armonk, NY: M.E. Sharpe.

Popov, Gavriil Kh., 1993. 'O khode konstitutsionnogo protsessa v Rossii' [On the Constitutional Process in Russia], *Nezavisimaya gazeta*, 26 January.

Poslanie Prezidenta Rossiiskoi Federatsii Federal'nomu Sobraniyu, 1995 [Message of the President of the Russian Federation to the Council of the Federation]. Moscow.

Prazauskas, Algis, 1991, 'Ethnic Conflicts in the Context of Democratizing Political Systems', *Theory and Society*, vol. 20, no. 5, October, pp. 581–602.

Problemy Bezhentsev v Ingushetii [Problems of Refugees in Ingushetia], 1994. Moscow: ISPI RAS.

'Punished Peoples, 1993. An Update on the Situation in the North Caucasus and Kalmykia', Special Issue of *Anthropology and Archeology of Eurasia. A Journal of Translations*, vol. 31, no. 4 , Spring.

Pypin, Alexander N., 1994–95. 'How Should Ethnography Be Understood', Special Issue of *Anthropology and Archeology of Eurasia. A Journal of Translations*, vol. 33, no. 3 ,Winter 1994–95, pp. 73–86.

Riches, David, ed., 1986. *The Anthropology of Violence.* Oxford: Basil Blackwell.

Roeder, Philip G., 1991. 'Soviet Federalism and Ethnic Mobilization', *World Politics,* vol. 43, no. 2, January, pp. 196–232.

Roeder, Philip G., 1993. *Red Sunset: The Failure of Soviet Politics.* Princeton, NJ: Princeton University Press.

Ro'i, Yaacov, ed., 1995. *Muslim Eurasia: Conflicting Legacies.* London: Frank Cass.

Rorlich, Azade-Ayse, 1986. *The Volga Tatars: A Profile in National Resilience.* Stanford, CA: Hoover Institution Press.

Ruban, Larissa S., 1994. *Development of Conflict in a Multiethnic Region.* Moscow: Institute for Socio-Political Research, RAS, unpublished manuscript.

Rupesinghe, Kumar, 1996. 'Governance and Conflict Resolution in Multi-Ethnic Societies', pp.10-31 in Rupesinghe & Tishkov, 1996.

Rupesinghe, Kumar; Peter King & Olga Vorkunova, eds, 1992. *Ethnicity and Conflict in a Post-Communist World: The Soviet Union, Eastern Europe and China.* New York: St Martin's Press.

Rupesinghe, Kumar & Valery Tishkov, eds, 1996. *Ethnicity and Power in the Contemporary World.* Tokyo etc.: United Nations University Press.

Rywkin, Michael, 1982. *Moscow's Muslim Challenge.* Armonk, NY: M.E. Sharpe.

Sakharov, Andrei N., 1995. 'Tyazhskii put' rossiiskogo reformatorstva' [The Hard Road of Russia's Reforms], *Svobodnaya mysl,* no. 7, pp. 66–84.

Sakwa, Richard, 1993. *Russian Politics and Society.* London and New York: Routledge.

Samarisinghe, S.W.R. de A. & Reed Coughlan, eds, 1991. *Economic Dimensions of Ethnic Conflict*. New York: St Martin's Press.

Sandole, Dennis, 1992. *Conflict Resolution in the Post-Cold War Era: Dealing with Ethnic Violence in the New Europe*. Working Paper No. 6. Institute for Conflict Analysis and Resolution: George Mason University, Fairfax, VA.

Savoskul, Sergei S., ed., 1993. *Russkie v novom zarubezhie. Sredniia Aziia*. [Russians in the New Abroad. Central Asia]. Moscow: IEA.

Semenov, Vadim M.; Mikhail V. Iordan, Vladimir G. Babakov & Vladimir A. Sagamonov, 1991. *Mezhnatsional'nye protivorechiia i konflikty v SSSR. Opyt sotsial'no-filosofskogo analiza* [Inter-Ethnic Tensions and Conflicts in the USSR: an Attempt at Socio-philosophical Analysis] Moscow: Institute of Philosophy, RAS.

Semenov, Yuri I., 1993. 'E'tnologia i gnoseologia' [Ethnology and Gnoseology], *Etnograficheskoe obozrenie*, no. 6, November–December, pp. 3–20.

Semenov, Yuri I., 1995. *Rossiia: chto s nei bylo, chto s nei proiskhodit i chto eiue ozhidaet v buduchem* [Russia: What Happened, What is Happening, and What to Expect in Future]. Moscow: No publisher.

Seton-Watson, Hugh, 1967. *The Russian Empire 1801–1917*. Oxford: Oxford University Press.

Shaw, Paul & Yuwa Wong, 1989. *Genetic Seeds of Warfare. Evolution, Nationalism and Patriotism*. London: Unwin Hyman.

Shils, Edward A., 1957. 'Primordial, Personal, Sacred and Civil Ties', *British Journal of Sociology*, vol. 8, no. 2, pp. 130–145.

Shirokogorov, Sergei M., 1922. *Mesto etnografii sredi nauk i klassifikatsiia etnosov* [Place of Ethnography Among Other Sciences and Classification of Ethnoses]. Vladivostok: No publisher.

Shirokogorov, Sergei M., 1923. *Etnos. Issledovaniie osnovnikh printsipov izmeneniia etnicheskikh i etnograficheskikh yavlenii* [Ethnos. A Study of Main Principles of Changing Ethnic and Ethnographic Phenomena]. Shanghai.

Shishkin, Igor, 1995. 'Simbiosis, Xenia i Khimera: Lev Gumilev ob etnosakh Rossii' [Symbiosis, Xenia and Chimera: Lev Gumilev about the Ethnoses of Russia], *Zavtra*, no. 4 (60), January.

Shnirelman, Viktor, 1993. *Struggle for the Past: Ethnogenetic studies and politics in the USSR*. Paper presented to the 13th International Congress of Anthropological and Ethnological Sciences, Mexico, 29 July–4 August.

Shnirelman, Viktor, 1996. *Who Gets the Past. Competition for Ancestors Among Non-Russian Intellectuals in Russia*, Washington, DC: The Woodrow Wilson Center Press.

Simes, Dimitri, 1994. 'The Return of Russian History', *Foreign Affairs*, vol. 73, no. 1, January/February, pp. 67–82.

Simon, Gerhard, 1991. *Nationalism and Policy Toward the Nationalities in the Soviet Union: From Totalitarian Dictatorship to Post-Stalinist Society*. Boulder, CO: Westview Press.

Simon, Gerhard, 1995. 'The Fall of Empires in Comparative Perspective: The Case of the Soviet Union', pp. 307–308 in *18th International Congress of Historical Sciences, 27 August–3 September 1995. Proceedings*. Montreal.

Sisk, Timothy D., 1996. *Power Sharing and International Mediation in Ethnic Conflicts*. Washington, DC: United States Institute of Peace.

Skalnik, Petr, 1988. 'Union soviétique – Afrique du Sud: les "théories" de l'ethnos', *Cahiers d'Etudes africaines*, vol. 28, no. 2, pp. 157–176.

Slezkine, Yuri, 1994a. *Arctic Mirrors: Russia and the Small Peoples of the North*. Ithaca, NY: Cornell University Press.

Slezkine, Yuri, 1994b. 'Naturalists versus Nations: Eighteenth-Century Russian Scholars Confront Ethnic Diversity,' *Representations*, vol. 47, Summer, pp. 170–195.

Slezkine, Yuri, 1994c. 'The USSR as a Communal Apartment, or How a Socialist State Promoted Ethnic Particularism', *Slavic Review*, vol. 53, no. 2, Summer, pp. 414–452.

Smith, Anthony D., 1983. *Theories of Nationalism*, 2nd edn. New York: Holmes and Meier.

Smith, Anthony D., 1991. *National Identity*. Harmondsworth: Penguin.

Smith, Dan ,1994a. 'Nationalism and Peace: Theoretical Notes for Research and Political Agendas', *Innovation*, vol. 7, no. 3, pp. 219–236.

Smith, Dan, 1994b. *War, Peace and Third World Development*. Human Development Report Office Occasional Papers, no. 16. New York.

Smith, Martin Cruz, 1990. *Polar Star*. London:Fontana/Collins Harvill.

Smith, M.P., 1992. 'Postmodernism, Urban Ethnography, and the New Social Space of Ethnic Identity', *Theory and Society,* vol. 21, pp. 493–531.

Soiuz mozhno bilo sokhranit, 1995. Dokumenti i fakti o politike M.S.Gorbacheva po reformirovaniyu i sokhraneniyu mnogonatsional'nogo gosudarstva [The Union Could be Preserved. Documents and Facts about M.S.Gorbachev's Policy Towards Reforming and Preserving the Multinational State]. Moscow: Aprel-85.

Sokolovsky, Sergei V., 1994, 'Etnichnost kak pamyat' [Ethnicity as a Memory], pp. 9-31 in Sergei Sokolovsky, ed., *Etnokognitologia. Podkhody k izucheniiu etnicheskoi identifikatsii* [Ethnocognitology. Approaches to the Study of Ethnic Identification]. Moscow: Russian Ministry of Culture.

Soldatova, Galina U., 1994. 'Ingushetia i Severnaya Ossetia: social'no-psikhologicheskie determinanty mezhetnicheskoi napryazhennosti' [Ingushetia and North Ossetia: Socio-Psychological Determinants of Inter-Ethnic Tension], pp. 153–180 in Drobizheva, 1994a.

Solovei, Valery 1995. ' "Natsionalizatsia" rezhima budet prodolzhatsya' ['Nationalization' of the Regime Will Go On], *Nezavisimaya gazeta*, 15 March.

Sovremennaya obchestvenno-policheskaya situatsiia v Srednei Azii i Kazakhstane [The Contemporary Public and Political Situation in Central Asia and Kazakhstan. Studies in Applied and Urgent Ethnology], 1993. Doc. 50. Moscow: IEA.

Sredniia Aziia. Spravochnye materialy. Istoriia, politika, ekonomika [Central Asia. Background Materials. History, Politics, Economy]. 1992. Moscow: EPI Center.

Stalin, Joseph V., 1947. *Voprosy Leninizma* [Problems of Leninism]. Moscow: Politizdat.

Stalin, Joseph V., 1947. *Sochinenia* [Works]. Vol. 4. Moscow: Politizdat.

Stalin, Joseph V., 1951-1952. *Sochinenia* [Works]. Vol. 2. Moscow: Politizdat.

Stanovcic, Vojislav, 1992. 'Problems and Options in Institutionalizing Ethnic Relations', *International Political Science Review,* vol. 13, no. 4, pp. 359–379.

Starovoitova, Galina, 1992. 'Nationality Policies in the Period of Perestroika: Some Comments from a Political Actor', pp. 114–121 in Lapidus & Zaslavsky, 1992.

Starovoitova, Galina, 1994. 'Tavridskie trevogi. Kak natchinaiutsya voiny za samoopredelenie' [The Tavria's Troubles. How Wars of Self-Determination Start], *Nezavisimaya gazeta*, 19 July.

Starovoitova, Galina V. & Konstantin Kedrov, 1992. Deklaratsia prav cheloveka dolzhna poluchit' garantii ot vsekh stran' [Declaration on Human Rights Must Get Guarantees from All Countries], *Izvestia*, 10 August.

Starr, Frederick, 1983. *Red and Hot: The Fate of Jazz in the Soviet Union*. New York: Oxford University Press.

Stavenhagen, Rodolfo, 1990. *The Ethnic Question: Conflicts, Development, and Human Rights*. Tokyo: United Nations University Press.

Stavenhagen, Rodolfo, 1996. *Ethnic Conflict and the Nation State.* London: Macmillan.

Stites, Richard, 1992. *Russian Popular Culture: Entertainment and Society since 1900.* Cambridge, MA: Cambridge University Press.

Stokes, Gale, 1995. 'Framing Post-Soviet Nationality Studies', pp. 149–155 in Orlovsky, 1995.

Strayer, Joseph R., 1970. *On the Medieval Origins of the Modern State.* Princeton, NJ: Princeton University Press.

Struve, Pyotr, 1990. *Iz glubiny. Sbornik statei o russkoi revolutsii* [From the Depths. A Collection of Articles on the Russian Revolution]. Moscow: Mysl.

Suny, Ronald Grigor, 1988. *The Making of the Georgian Nation.* Bloomington, IN: Indiana University Press.

Suny, Ronald Grigor, 1989. 'Nationalism and Ethnic Unrest in the Soviet Union', *World Policy Journal,* vol. 6, no. 3, Summer, pp. 503-528.

Suny, Ronald Grigor, 1993. *The Revenge of the Past. Nationalism, Revolution, and the Collapse of the Soviet Union.* Stanford, CA: Stanford University Press.

Susokolov, Alexander A., 1987. *Mezhnatsional'nye braki v SSSR* [Interethnic Marriages in the USSR]. Moscow: Mysl.

Szporluk, Roman, 1988. *Communism and Nationalism: Karl Marx versus Friedrich List.* New York: Oxford University Press.

Szporluk, Roman, 1989. 'Dilemmas of Russian Nationalism', *Problems of Communism,* vol. 38, no. 4, July–August, pp. 15–35.

Tabolina, Tatyana V., ed., 1994. *Vozrozhdenie Kazachestva: istoki, khronika, perspektivy, 1989-1994* [The Rebirth of the Cossacks: Sources, Chronicle, and Perspectives, 1989-1994]. Vol. 1. Moscow: IEA.

Tainy natsional'noi politiki ZK RKP [The Secrets of Nationality Policy of the CC RCP], 1992. Moscow: Insan.

Tenishev, Edham R. & L.G. Bystrov, 1989. 'Kul'tura nachinaetsya s perepisi' [Culture Starts with a Census], *Moskovskii Literator,* no. 3–4, January.

Tereshkovich, Pavel V., 1991. 'Sovremennaya etnopoliticheskaya situatsiia v Belorussii' [The Contemporary Ethnopolitical Situation in Belorussia], pp. 150-164 in Mikail Guboglo, ed. *Natsional'nye protsessy v SSSR.* [National Processes in the USSR]. Moscow: Nauka.

Ternistyi put' k svobode [The Hard Road to Freedom], 1992. Grozny: Kniga.

Ter-Petrosyan, Levon, 1991. Interview, *Komsomol'skaya pravda,* June 6.

Thompson, Richard H., 1989. *Theories of Ethnicity. A Critical Appraisal.* Westport, CT: Greenwood Press.

Tishkov, Valery, 1990a. 'An Assembly of Nations or an All-Union Parliament?', *Journal of Soviet Nationalities,* vol.1, no. 1, Spring, pp. 101–127.

Tishkov, Valery, 1990b. 'Ethnicity and Power in the Republics of the USSR', *Journal of Soviet Nationalities,* vol. 1, no. 3, Fall, pp. 33–66.

Tishkov, Valery, 1991a. 'Natsional'nost' – Kommunist? Etnopoliticheskii analiz KPSS' [Nationality is a Communist? Ethno-Political Analysis of the CPSU], *Polis,* vol. 1, no. 2, February, pp. 32–43.

Tishkov, Valery, 1991b. 'The Soviet Empire Before and After Perestroika', *Theory and Society,* vol. 20, no. 5, October, pp. 603–629.

Tishkov, Valery, 1992a. 'The Crisis in Soviet Ethnography', *Current Anthropology,* vol. 33, no. 4, pp. 371–394.

Tishkov, Valery, 1992b. 'Inventions and Manifestations of Ethno-nationalism in and after the Soviet Union', pp. 41–64 in Rupesinghe et al., 1992.

Tishkov, Valery, 1992c. *Russkie kak men'shinestvo: primer Estonii* [Russians as Minority: The Case of Estonia]. Moscow: IEA.

Tishkov, Valery, 1994a. 'Perspectives on Ethnic Accord in Post-Soviet Space', *Cultural Survival Quarterly*, vol. 18, no. 2, 3, Summer/Fall, pp. 52–57.

Tishkov, Valery, 1994b. *Nationalities and Conflicting Ethnicity in Post-Communist Russia*, Discussion Paper no.50, United Nations Research Institute for Social Development, Geneva, March.

Tishkov, Valery, 1994–95. 'Post-Soviet Ethnography. Not a Crisis but Something More Serious', Special issue of *Anthropology and Archeology of Eurasia. A Journal of Translations*, vol. 33, no. 3, Winter, pp. 87–92.

Tishkov, Valery, 1995a. 'Ambitsii liderov i nadmennost sily: Zametki o Chechenskom krizise' [Ambitions of Leaders and Arrogance of Force. Notes on the Chechen Crisis], *Svobodnaya Mysl*, no. 1, January, pp. 19–28.

Tishkov, Valery, 1995b. '"Don't Kill Me, I'm a Kyrgyz!"': An Anthropological Analysis of Violence in the Osh Ethnic Conflict', *Journal of Peace Research*, vol. 32, no. 2, May, pp. 133–149.

Tishkov, Valery, 1995c. 'The Russians in Central Asia and Kazakhstan', pp. 289-310 in Ro'i, 1995.

Tishkov, Valery, 1995d. 'What is Rossia? Prospects for Nation-Building', *Security Dialogue*, vol. 26, no. 1, March, pp. 41–54.

Tishkov, Valery, 1996. 'Ethnic Conflicts in the Context of Social Science Theories', pp. 52–68 in Rupesinghe & Tishkov.

Tishkov, Valery, ed., 1993. *Nazional'naya politika v Rossiiskoi Federatsii* [Nationality Policy in the Russian Federation]. Moscow: Nauka.

Tishkov, Valery, ed., 1994 *Narody Rossii. Entsiklopedia* [The Peoples of Russia. Encyclopaedia]. Moscow: Rossiiskaya Entsiklopaedia.

Tishkov, Valery, ed., 1996. *Migratsii i novyie diaspory v postsovetskih gosudarstvakh* [Migrations and New Diasporas in the Post-Soviet States]. Moscow: IEA.

Tishkov, Valery; Yelena Belyaeva & Georgi Marchenko, 1995. *Chechenskii krizis* [The Chechen Crisis]. Moscow: Roundtable Business of Russia's Research Center.

Tishkov, Valery & Leonid Koshelev, 1982. *Istoriya Kanady* [History of Canada]. Moscow: Mysl.

Tkachev, G., 1911. *Ingushi i Chechentsy* [Ingush and Chechens]. Vladikavkaz.

Toschenko, Zhan A., 1994. 'Potentsial'no opasnye tochki' [Potentially Dangerous Places], *Nezavisimaya gazeta*, March 1.

Tsipko, Alexander, 1994. 'A New Russian Identity or Old Russia's Reintegration?', *Security Dialogue*, vol. 25, no. 4, December, pp. 443–455.

Ugresic, Dubravka, 1992. 'Parrots and Priests: "Before" and "After" in Yugoslavia', *Times Literary Supplement*, 15 May, p.12.

Uralov, A. (A. Avtorkhanov), 1952. *Narodoubiistvo v SSSR* [The Peoples' Killing in the USSR]. Munich: Posev.

Uslar, Petr K., 1869. *Etnografiia Kavkaza. Chechenskii yazyk* [The Ethnography of the Caucasus. The Chechen Language]. Tiflis.

Valeev, Damir Zh., 1994. *Natsional'nii suverenitet i natsional'noe vozrozhdenie. Iz istorii bor'by Bashkirskogo naroda za samoopredelenie* [National Sovereignty and National Revival. From the History of a Struggle of the Bashkir People for Self-Determination]. Ufa: Kitap.

Van den Berghe, Pierre, 1981. *The Ethnic Phenomenon*. Norwich, UK: Elsevier Press.

Vaneev, Zakharii A., 1950. *Srednevekovaya Alania* [The Middle-Aged Alania]. Staliniri: Gosizdat Yugo-Osetii.

Väyrynen, Raimo, 1994. *Towards a Theory of Ethnic Conflicts and Their Resolution*. Notre Dame, IN: Joan B. Kroc Institute for International Peace Studies, University of Notre Dame.

Väyrynen, Raimo, ed., 1991. *New Directions in Conflict Theory*. London: Sage.

Verdery, Katherine, 1991. *National Ideology Under Socialism: Identity and Cultural Politics in Ceauşescu's Romania*. Berkeley, CA: University of California Press.

Verdery, Katherine, 1995. 'What Was Socialism and Why Did It Fail?', pp. 27–46 in Orlovsky, 1995.

Vinokurova, Uliyana, 1994. *Skaz o narode Sakha* [A Tale About the Sakha People]. Yakutsk: Bichik.

Volkova, Natalia G., 1974. *Etnicheskii sostav naseleniia Severnogo Kavkaza v XVIII-nachale XX veka* [Ethnic Composition of the Population of North Caucasus from the 18th to the Early 20th Centuries]. Moscow: Nauka.

Volkova, Natalia G. & Leonid L. Lavrov, 1968. 'Sovremennye etnicheskie protsessyĭ' [Contemporary Ethnic Processes], pp. 329-346 in Vladimir K.Gardanov, ed., *Kul'tura i byt narodov Severnogo Kavkaza, 1917–1967* [Culture and Everyday Life of the Peoples of North Caucasus 1917–1967]. Moscow: Nauka.

Wilson, Andrew, 1995. 'The Donbas between Ukraine and Russia: The Use of History in Political Disputes', *Journal of Contemporary History*, vol. 30, no. 2, April, pp. 265-288.

Wixman, Ronald, 1980. *Language Aspects of Ethnic Patterns and Processes in the North Caucasus*. Chicago, IL: University of Chicago, Department of Geography, Research Paper no. 191.

Worsley, Peter, 1984. *The Three Worlds: Culture & World Development*. London: Weidenfeld & Nicolson.

Yakubovskaya, Svetlana, 1966. *Obrazovanie i razvitie Sovetskogo mnogonatsional'nogo gosudarstva* [Formation and Development of the Soviet Multinational State]. Moscow: Nauka.

Yamskov, Anatoly, 1986. 'Ekologicheskie faktory evolutsii form skotovodstva u turkoyazychnykh narodov Severnogo Kavkaza' [Ecological Factors for the Evolution of Livestock Economy among Turkic Peoples of North Caucasus], *Sovetskaya etnografiia*, no. 1, pp. 22–34.

Yamskov, Anatoly, 1991. 'Ethnic Conflict in the Transcaucasus. The Case of Nagorno Karabakh', *Theory and Society*, vol. 20, no. 5, October, pp. 631–660.

Yamskov, Anatoly, 1994. 'The "New Minorities" in Post-Soviet States. Linguistic Orientations and Political Conflict', *Cultural Survival Quarterly*, vol. 18, no. 2–3, Summer/Fall, pp. 58–61.

Yeltsin, Boris, 1994. 'Ob ukreplenii Rossiiskogo gosudarstva' [On Strengthening the Russian State], *Rossiiskaya gazeta*, 25 February, p. 4.

Young, Crawford, 1993. *The Rising Tide of Cultural Pluralism: The Nation-State at Bay?* Madison, WI: University of Wisconsin Press.

Young, Crawford, 1994. *Ethnic Diversity and Public Policy: an Overview*. Occasional paper no. 8, World Summit for Social Development. Geneva: United Nations Research Institute for Social Development.

'Zayavlenie rukovoditelei Uzbekskoi SSR, Kazakhskoi SSR ot 23 iunya 1990' [Statement of the Leaders of the Uzbek and Kazakh SSR from 23 June 1990], 1990, *Kommunist Uzbekistana*, no. 8, pp. 56–58.

Zhdanko, Tatyana A., 1972. 'Natsional'no-gosudarstvennoe razmezhevanie i prozessy etnicheskogo razvitiia u narodov Sredney Azii' [National-State Division and Processes of Ethnic Development Among the Peoples of Central Asia], *Sovetskaya etnografiia*, no. 5, September–October, pp. 13–29.

Zhornitskaya, Maria Ya., 1983. *Narodnoie horeograficheskoie iskusstvo korennogo naseleniia Severo-Vostoka Sibiri* [The Folk Choreography Art of the Indigenous People of North-East Siberia]. Moscow: Nauka.

Zinoviev, Alexander, 1995. *Russkii experiment* [The Russian Experiment]. Moscow: Nash Dom.

Zuiganov, Gennadi, 1994. *Derzhava* [Super-Power]. 2nd edn. Moscow: Informpechat.

Zuiganov, Gennadi, ed., 1995. *Sovremennaya russkaya ideia i gosudarstvo* [The Contemporary Russian Idea and the State]. Moscow: RAU Corporation.

Zuziev, Arthur A., 1994. 'Istoricheskie aspekty territorial'nogo konflikta mezhdu Ingushskoi respublikoi i Respublikoi Severnaya Ossetia' [Historical Aspects of Territorial Conflict Between the Ingush Republic and the Republic of North Ossetia], pp. 181–191 in Drobizheva, 1994b.

Index

Entries in *italic* indicate tables and maps.